The Death Penalty
in the United States

SECOND EDITION

ALSO BY LOUIS J. PALMER, JR.,
AND FROM McFARLAND

*Encyclopedia of Capital Punishment
in the United States,* 2d ed. (2008)

*Encyclopedia of DNA and the United States
Criminal Justice System* (2004, paperback 2013)

*Organ Transplants from Executed Prisoners:
An Argument for the Creation of Death Sentence
Organ Removal Statutes* (1999)

BY LOUIS J. PALMER, JR., AND
XUEYAN Z. PALMER

Encyclopedia of Abortion in the United States, 2d ed. (2009)

The Death Penalty in the United States

A Complete Guide to Federal and State Laws

Second Edition

Louis J. Palmer, Jr.

McFarland & Company, Inc., Publishers

Jefferson, North Carolina, and London

LIBRARY OF CONGRESS CATALOGUING-IN-PUBLICATION DATA

Palmer, Louis J., author.
[Death penalty]
The death penalty in the United States : a complete guide to federal
and state laws / Louis J. Palmer, Jr.—Second edition.
p.   cm.
Includes bibliographical references and index.

ISBN 978-0-7864-7660-2
softcover : acid free paper ∞

1. Capital punishment—United States.   I. Title.
KF9725.P35 2014   345.73'0773—dc23   2013037330

BRITISH LIBRARY CATALOGUING DATA ARE AVAILABLE

Front cover image: death row in old prison (iStockphoto/Thinkstock)

Manufactured in the United States of America

*McFarland & Company, Inc., Publishers
Box 611, Jefferson, North Carolina 28640
www.mcfarlandpub.com*

Table of Contents

List of Tables and Boxes

Introduction

The death penalty landscape has changed considerably since the first edition of this book was published in 1998. In the U.S. we no longer execute persons under age eighteen when they commit capital murder or those found to be mentally retarded; defendants have the right to a jury presiding over the penalty phase of a capital prosecution, and fewer states allow capital punishment. To address these and other substantive changes in death penalty law, the second edition of this book includes 13 new chapters.

Capital punishment is a complex and expensive form of retribution. It is also an emotionally charged punishment because of the risk of executing an innocent person, and the belief by some that it is a punishment with no purpose. This second edition, like the first edition, is not intended to speak for or against the death penalty. Book shelves and Internet websites are saturated with advocates on both sides of the issue. This volume aims only to provide an objective review of how capital punishment works in the United States.

There is one qualification to the general theme. While some discussion is devoted to death penalty issues that arise before a defendant is convicted of a capital offense, the primary focus of the book is upon issues that are resolved after a defendant has been convicted of a capital crime. That aspect of capital punishment is the least understood by the general public.

On a more fundamental note, the reader should keep in mind that the United States is comprised of 52 sovereign legal jurisdictions: the 50 states, the federal government and the District of Columbia. All of these autonomous legal jurisdictions, tempered by the federal Constitution, make the death penalty a complex subject. Each jurisdiction has the authority, within the bounds of federal constitutional constraints, to design its own unique death penalty statutes. As a result of the majority of jurisdictions exercising their independent authority to create death penalty systems, no two death penalty systems are exactly the same in all particulars.

This book provides a comprehensive examination of the differences in death penalty systems in the nation. Not only will this book enable the reader to see the various distinct aspects of each jurisdiction's death penalty system, but it will also aid the reader in understanding why these differences exist.

This book will also detail the factors common to each system. The reader will learn that many of these common factors exist because of decisions handed down by the United States Supreme Court.

In the final analysis, the one constant that the reader will find running throughout this book is the role of the Supreme Court. Through its interpretation of the Eighth Amendment of the Constitution, the Supreme Court has established many death penalty legal principles that are binding in all capital punishment jurisdictions.

The material in this book has been divided into six major parts. Part I, which contains five chapters, lays out important foundational information. Chapter 1 provides a basic working knowledge of the common law origin of capital punishment in Anglo-American law. Chapter 2 builds on the previous chapter by exploring the impact of the Eighth Amendment on various specific death penalty issues. Chapter 3 examines the impact of the Double Jeopardy Clause and Ex Post Facto Clause on specific capital punishment issues. Chapter 4 looks at the meaning of a capital felon's constitutional right to counsel and right to remain silent. Chapter 5 rounds out Part I by examining the American Bar Association's suggested defense team for a capital felon.

Part II examines specific issues involving the governmental office responsible for enforcing death penalty statutes — the office of the prosecutor. Chapter 6 explores the general discretionary authority prosecutors have in seeking the death penalty. Chapter 7 contains a discussion of the charging documents used by prosecutors in death penalty cases. Chapter 8 looks at the type of information prosecutors must initially provide to defendants when the death penalty is involved. Chapter 9 sets out a discussion of the laws related to a prosecutor's ability to invoke death penalty statutes against defendants who have not actually inflicted death upon a murdered victim. Chapter 10 culminates Part II with a discussion of specific death penalty notice issues involved when a capital suspect is a foreign national.

In Part III, the reader is taken inside the courtroom for an examination of substantive issues involving primarily the sentencing phase of death penalty prosecutions. Chapter 11 sets forth a straightforward discussion of criminal conduct that triggers death penalty prosecutions. Chapter 12 provides a brief overview of how a capital felon's guilt is determined. Chapter 13 sets out a detailed discussion of the structure and nature of the penalty phase of a capital punishment prosecution. In Chapter 14 an exhaustive treatment is given to the factors used to permit a defendant to be sentenced to death. Chapter 15 takes a look at factors which may prevent the death penalty from being imposed upon a defendant who was actually found guilty of a capital offense. Chapter 16 provides a discussion of how the factors brought out in Chapters 14 and 15 are joined to determine whether a defendant will be sentenced to death.

Part IV is concerned with post-conviction remedies that a capital felon will try to obtain after being convicted. Chapter 17 provides a presentation of the mechanics involved with the initial direct review of a death sentence by an appellate court. In Chapter 18 a discussion is devoted to collateral legal devices — e.g., habeas corpus petitions — that capital felons employ in an effort to attack their conviction and sentence. Chapter 19 examines the use of post-conviction DNA statutes that allow defendants to attempt to establish their innocence. Chapter 20 examines efforts that have been made to legislatively allow capital defendants to establish that prosecutors sought the death penalty against them only because of their race.

Part V outlines the laws involving execution of the death penalty. In Chapter 21 a discussion is devoted to several factors that may temporarily or permanently delay execution of a sentence of death. Chapter 22 provides an overview of conditions on death row. Chapter 23 examines laws that regulate who may be present to observe executions. Chapter 24 sets out a discussion of the methods of execution and laws that control disposition of an executed capital felon's corpse.

Part VI provides some discussion of diverse death penalty issues. Chapter 25 looks at how the death penalty is implemented by the military. In Chapter 26 a discussion of capital punishment in Native American country is set out. Chapter 27 examines capital punishment on inhabited United States territorial islands. Chapter 28 sets out a brief discussion of arguments raised against the death penalty. In Chapter 29, the book concludes with a discussion of the costs associated with capital punishment.

This book is designed to provide descriptive information pertaining to its subject matter. The publisher and author are not engaged in rendering legal or professional service through this book. If legal advice or other expert assistance is required, an attorney should be consulted.

1

The Common Law
and Capital Punishment

The American legal system is indebted to the English common law for its understanding and acceptance of capital punishment, i.e., the death penalty.[1] Consequently, some observations are in order regarding crimes and punishments tolerated under the common law, along with those rejected by the American legal system.

The Meaning of Common Law

The phrase *common law* is often used without any understanding of its origin or meaning. Common law and all of its implications stem from England. The actual use of the phrase has been traced back to the reign of Edward I in the thirteenth century.[2] During that period of time two types of legal systems existed in England. The island nation had a temporal legal system and an ecclesiastical or religious legal system.[3] The legal principles that fall under the phrase *common law* were developed in the temporal courts of England.

An explanation of the words *common* and *law* is also in order. As for the word *common*, it was indicated by an American court that "[i]n the context of English law, use of the word 'common' ... does not mean 'ordinary' or 'vulgar,' but rather 'uniform.'"[4] Legal principles that derived from temporal courts were thought of as customs or beliefs that were commonly or uniformly recognized and accepted by the people of England prior to being embraced by temporal courts.

The word *law* is generally associated with statutes and ordinances that are enacted by legislative bodies. For example, the United States Congress and the English Parliament are legislative bodies that enact laws. The creation of laws, however, is not restricted to legislative bodies. Courts, through judges, create what are referred to euphemistically as unenacted laws (for constitutional reasons it is taboo in the American legal system to refer to judicial pronouncements as laws). For example, in the case of *Miranda v. Arizona*, 384 U.S. 436 (1966), the United States Supreme Court developed a legal principle, i.e., a law, which required all law enforcement agents to inform apprehended criminal suspects of certain constitutional rights before attempting to interrogate them. Although the legal system in America does not permit calling the *Miranda* warning a law — in the final analysis its application and effect are identical to that of a legislatively enacted law.

In putting the words *common* and *law* together, the legal profession is merely referring to principles that have the force and effect of law, but were developed by judges in England's temporal courts.

As a final point in this area, it should be noted that the phrase *common law* is also traditionally used to refer to England's temporal courts. For example, in saying that burglary was a common law crime, what is actually being said is that burglary was a crime created by the temporal courts of England.

Criminal Offenses and Punishment Under the Common Law

The common law recognized two types of criminal offenses: misdemeanor and felony. While numerous factors distinguished the two types of offenses, the ultimate difference resided in the fact that a convicted misdemeanant was not called upon to relinquish his life, but a convicted felon could be punished with death. A brief review of common law nonfatal corporal methods of punishment will precede the discussion of capital offenses and methods of capital punishment under the common law.

Nonfatal Criminal Punishment

If one compared the nonfatal criminal punishments that are permitted by the American legal system today with the nonfatal criminal punishments under the common law, the two would appear as different as night and day. A proper perspective on this matter should be maintained, however, because the common law practices in question occurred between the Thirteenth and Eighteenth centuries. Attitudes have changed greatly since that period.

Milder forms of nonfatal criminal punishment under the common law included confinement, hard labor, banishment, the pillory, stocks and the dunking stool.[5] More drastic forms of punishment included plucking out eyes, castration,[6] and cutting off feet, hands, noses, ears, upper lips and scalping.[7] Sometimes convicted prisoners were mercilessly whipped or were branded with hot irons on their cheeks or hands.[8]

Capital Offenses

The common law created only a few felony offenses, which included murder, arson, larceny, robbery, burglary, rape, treason and petty treason. The limited numbers of felony offenses under the common law help explain why the common law adopted the rule that all felony offenses were to be punished with death. Unfortunately for English citizens, however, the number of felony offenses in England expanded beyond what the common law created. As a result of legislative or parliamentary statutes, the number of felony offenses in England grew to 263 by the year 1822. Moreover, the common law rule that all felony offenses were to be punished with death was made applicable to each of the 263 felonies that developed in England.[9]

The great English jurist William Blackstone commented sarcastically upon the tragedy of imposing the death penalty on all felony offenses. He pointed out that, as a result of misguided intentions by Parliament, it had become a capital offense (1) to tear down the mound of a fish pond and allow fish to escape; (2) to chop down a cherry tree that was in an orchard; or (3) to be publicly seen with a gypsy for one month.[10]

Methods of Capital Punishment

The different methods by which the common law carried out the death penalty represents a journey through hell. The naked terror and devilish pain caused by common law methods of capital punishment shock and sober today's consciousness.

Many of the capital offenses under the common law had their own special execution methods. A male defendant convicted of treason or the felony crime of falsifying had to be dragged by horse to the place of execution and hung. A conviction for sodomy carried a penalty of death by being buried alive. A convicted heretic had to be burned alive. A conviction for a routine crime like murder, rape, arson, robbery or burglary was punished by simple hanging. If any of the latter offenses was found to be especially vicious, however, the defendant was beheaded.[11]

The crime of treason by a female was punished initially under the common law by burning alive the defendant. However, in the year 1790 this method was halted and the punishment became strangulation and burning of the corpse.[12] For the crime of high treason (affecting the Crown directly) a defendant was punished by quartering, disemboweling and beheading. In certain egregious murder prosecutions a convicted defendant would be publicly dissected while alive.[13]

Pre-Furman Capital Punishment in the United States

The decision of the Supreme Court in *Furman v. Georgia*, 408 U.S. 238 (1972), placed a moratorium on a form of punishment that had its origins in the American colonies. The death penalty was commonly authorized for a wide variety of crimes in the American colonies prior to the Revolution.[14]

The American colonies developed as an outgrowth of people migrating from England and other European nations. Virginia became the first colony when the first permanent English settlers arrived there in 1607. English settlers arrived to start the second colony in Massachusetts in 1620. By 1623 permanent settlements were made in New Hampshire. A year later New York was founded by Dutch families. The fifth colony, Maryland, was settled in 1634. Connecticut followed in 1635 and Rhode Island in 1636. Swedes settled Delaware in 1638. New Jersey was established in 1664. Pennsylvania was settled by Quakers in 1681. North Carolina was settled in 1653, and South Carolina was carved out of it in 1670. (The Carolinas actually formed a single colony until 1730.) Georgia, the last of the thirteen colonies, was settled in 1733.[15]

The colonies had from ten to eighteen capital offenses. In 1636 the Massachusetts Bay Colony listed thirteen crimes punishable by death. Most of the New England colonies made twelve offenses capital crimes. Rhode Island, with ten capital crimes, had the least number of all of the colonies. Offenses punishable by death typically included murder, treason, piracy, arson, rape, robbery, burglary, and sodomy. Execution of criminals was carried out by such methods as drowning, stoning, hanging, and beheading.[16]

In 1682, Pennsylvania, under William Penn, limited capital punishment to murder. Following Penn's death in 1718, however, Pennsylvania greatly expanded the number of capital offenses.[17]

After the American Revolution, which was ended by the Treaty of Paris in 1783, the states uniformly followed the common law practice of making death the exclusive and mandatory sentence for certain specified offenses. Almost from the outset, juries in the new nation reacted unfavorably to the harshness of mandatory death sentences. The states initially responded to public dissatisfaction with mandatory death statutes by limiting the classes of capital offenses. This mild effort at reform did not prevent juries from refusing to convict defendants rather than subject them to automatic death sentences.[18]

In 1794, Pennsylvania addressed the problem by confining the mandatory death penalty to murder of the first degree. Other jurisdictions followed and, within a generation, the practice spread to most of the states. Ultimately, however, the division of murder into degrees was not a satisfactory means of identifying defendants appropriately punishable with death.[19]

The next step taken, first by Tennessee in 1838, was to grant juries sentencing discretion in capital cases. Tennessee's decision to abandon mandatory death sentences was followed by Alabama in 1841 and Louisiana in 1846. By the turn of the century, the federal government and twenty-three states had made death sentences discretionary for first-degree murder and other capital offenses. Fourteen additional states followed the trend by 1920. (In 1907 Kansas took the ultimate step and abolished capital punishment. Eight more states followed suit over the next ten years.) By 1963 all automatic death penalty statutes were replaced with discretionary jury sentencing.[20]

Providing jury discretion in the imposition of capital punishment did not resolve dissatisfaction with capital punishment. In the early years of the 1960s, death penalty opponents

TABLE 1.0 EXECUTIONS IN THE U.S. 1930–1969

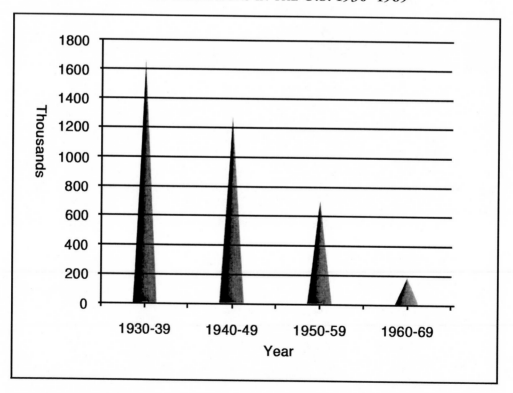

litigated in courts throughout the nation in an effort to halt capital punishment. The activities of death penalty opponents during that period led to an unofficial moratorium on executions, after Luis Jose Monge was executed in the gas chamber at Colorado State Penitentiary on June 2, 1967.[21]

The focus of discontent with capital punishment was threefold. Some people opposed the punishment because a disproportionate number of minorities were subjected to it. Other opponents found it unworkable because it was the poor in general who were subjected to it. Finally, others were opposed purely on the basis that it was a primitive and outmoded method of punishment.[22]

The unofficial moratorium that was generated in 1967 became official on June 29, 1972, when the United States Supreme Court handed down its decision in *Furman*, which held that the procedures used to impose capital punishment violated the Cruel and Unusual Punishment Clause of the Eighth Amendment of the federal Constitution.

2

The Eighth Amendment
and *Furman v. Georgia*

Under the common law, capital punishment was carried out in a variety of painful ways. This fact, while important, is not the central issue here. The critical point is that 263 forms of human conduct could be punished with death under the common law. Additionally, 99 percent of the offenses punished with death under the common law did not involve the taking of a human life.

The Eighth Amendment of the federal Constitution provides that "Excessive bail shall not be required, nor excessive fines imposed, nor *cruel and unusual punishments* inflicted" (emphasis added). To what extent does the Eighth Amendment's Cruel and Unusual Punishment Clause affect capital punishment in the United States? Would the Cruel and Unusual Punishment Clause permit the death penalty to be imposed for the 263 capital punishment offenses recognized by the common law? What, if any, limitation does the Cruel and Unusual Punishment Clause place on the ability of state and federal legislatures to enact offenses that carry the death penalty?

The intent of this chapter is to address the above questions, as well as bring out other aspects of the Supreme Court's interpretation of the Cruel and Unusual Punishment Clause. In carrying out the task of this chapter, the material has been placed under three broad headings: (1) origin of the Eighth Amendment, (2) limitations imposed by the Cruel and Unusual Punishment Clause, and (3) *Furman v. Georgia*.

Origin of the Eighth Amendment

The Eighth Amendment became a part of the Constitution in 1791.[1] The history of this amendment, however, does not begin with its insertion into the Constitution. The birth of the Eighth Amendment reaches back to the shores of England and the English Bill of Rights of 1689.

The tenth clause of the English Bill of Rights provided the following: "Excessive bail ought not to be required, nor excessive fines imposed; nor cruel and unusual punishments inflicted."[2] It was pointed out by Supreme Court Justice Thurgood Marshall that scholars are in debate over "[w]hether, the English Bill of Rights prohibition against cruel and unusual punishments is properly read as a response to excessive or illegal punishments, as a reaction to barbaric and objectionable modes of punishment, or both[.]"[3] While there is no consensus why the English Bill of Rights included a clause prohibiting cruel and unusual punishments, there is no dissent to the fact that the Eighth Amendment owes its existence to the English Bill of Rights.

The Eighth Amendment did not leap directly from the English Bill of Rights into the Constitution. "The precise language used in the [Eighth Amendment] first appeared in America on June 12, 1776, in Virginia's Declaration of Rights[.]"[4] A Virginia delegate named George Mason was responsible for taking the tenth clause of the English Bill of Rights and placing it into Virginia's Declaration of Rights. Delegate Mason was also a strong advocate, at the Constitutional Convention, for placing the tenth clause into the Constitution as the Eighth Amendment.[5] His foresight eventually paid off, and in 1791 the tenth clause, with slight modifications, became the Constitution's Eighth Amendment.

Limitations Imposed by the Cruel and Unusual Punishment Clause

In the case of *Trop v. Dulles*, 356 U.S. 86 (1958), the Supreme Court expounded upon the framework in which it viewed the Cruel and Unusual Punishment Clause. In succinct fashion the Supreme Court stated in *Trop*: "The basic concept underlying the [clause] is nothing less than the dignity of man. While the State has the power to punish, the [clause] stands to assure that this power be exercised within the limits of civilized standards. Fines, imprisonment and even execution may be imposed depending upon the enormity of the crime, but any technique outside the bounds of these traditional penalties is constitutionally suspect."

With the sweeping constitutional framework of *Trop* in view, this section of the chapter sets out to accomplish two things. First, to introduce specific principles that are used in interpreting the Cruel and Unusual Punishment Clause. Second, this section will provide a discussion of specific applications of the Cruel and Unusual Punishment Clause to death penalty issues.

The Brennan Principles

The decision in *Trop* sets out the general framework in which the Supreme Court views the Cruel and Unusual Punishment Clause. However, this framework is a nullity without active principles to give it life. In his concurring opinion in *Furman v. Georgia*, 408 U.S. 238 (1972), Justice Brennan reviewed prior Supreme Court cases which had addressed the issue of cruel and unusual punishment. This examination was done for the purpose of discovering which principles of law the Supreme Court historically relied upon to decide whether or not a particular punishment was cruel and unusual. It was determined by Justice Brennan that four basic principles were historically relied upon by the Supreme Court to make cruel and unusual punishment determinations.

The four principles that Justice Brennan found were as follows:

(1) The punishment must not be so severe as to be degrading to the dignity of human beings.[6]

(2) A government cannot arbitrarily inflict a severe punishment.[7]

(3) A severe punishment must not be unacceptable to contemporary society.[8]

(4) A severe punishment must not be excessive.[9]

Although it is not explicitly brought out in the material that follows, the Brennan principles were at play in the issues that are discussed.

The Death Penalty Is Not Cruel and Unusual Punishment

The Supreme Court did not squarely address the issue of whether capital punishment, per se, was a cruel and unusual form of punishment until it heard the case of *Gregg v. Georgia*, 428 U.S. 153 (1976).[10]

The Gregg ruling. The defendant in *Gregg* was prosecuted for committing two murders.[11] A jury found him guilty of both murders and he was sentenced to die for both offenses. One of the primary arguments the defendant made to the Supreme Court was that the Cruel and Unusual Punishment Clause prohibited, under any and all circumstances, the imposition of death as a punishment for a criminal offense. In rendering its decision on this argument the Supreme Court made the following observations:

> The death penalty is said to serve two principal social purposes: retribution and deterrence of capital crimes by prospective offenders.
>
> In part, capital punishment is an expression of society's moral outrage at particularly offensive conduct. This function may be unappealing to many, but it is essential in an ordered society that asks its citizens to rely on legal processes rather than self-help to vindicate their wrongs.... Retribution is no longer the dominant objective of the criminal law, but neither is it a forbidden objective nor one inconsistent with our respect for the dignity of men. Indeed, the decision that capital punishment may be the appropriate sanction in extreme cases is an expression of the community's belief that certain crimes are themselves so grievous an affront to humanity that the only adequate response may be the penalty of death.
>
> Statistical attempts to evaluate the worth of the death penalty as a deterrent to crimes by potential offenders have occasioned a great deal of debate. The results have been inconclusive....
>
> Although some of the studies suggest that the death penalty may not function as a significantly greater deterrent than lesser penalties, there is no convincing empirical evidence either supporting or refuting this view. We may nevertheless assume safely that there are murderers, such as those who act in passion, for whom the threat of death has little or no deterrent effect. But for many others, the death penalty undoubtedly is a significant deterrent....
>
> The value of capital punishment as a deterrent of crime is a complex factual issue the resolution of which properly rests with the legislatures....

While the Supreme Court vacillated in *Gregg* on the issue of whether the death penalty was a deterrent, it pressed forward nonetheless, and held "that the infliction of death as a punishment for murder is not without justification and thus is not unconstitutionally severe."

The Supreme Court's decision in *Gregg* must be held in its proper context. The decision did not address such issues as what method of execution is constitutional or under what circumstances imposition of the death penalty would be unconstitutional. *Gregg* merely held that, as a form of punishment, the death penalty does not violate the Cruel and Unusual Punishment Clause.

Mandatory Death Penalty Statutes Are Unconstitutional

It is a common practice for legislatures to enact criminal offenses that carry mandatory penalties, that is, if a defendant is convicted of the offense he or she must be sentenced according to the requirements of the statute. Mandatory sentencing statutes remove the discretion of trial judges to determine the appropriate punishment for defendants on an individualized basis.[12]

Mandatory death penalty statutes existed in all of the original thirteen colonies prior to the Revolutionary War. Offenses that carried mandatory death sentences included crimes such as murder, arson, rape, robbery, and burglary. However, after the Revolutionary War ended many states repealed all mandatory death penalty statutes, while others limited the number of offenses that were subject to mandatory death sentences. The Supreme Court did not squarely address this issue until it heard the case of *Woodson v. North Carolina*, 428 U.S. 280 (1976), where it noted: "The history of mandatory death penalty statutes in the United States ... reveals that the practice ... has been rejected as unduly harsh and unworkably rigid."

The Woodson ruling. The fact that individual states rejected mandatory death penalty offenses, while others limited such offenses, does not address the issue of the constitutional legitimacy of mandatory death penalty statutes. This issue was put to rest with the Supreme Court's ruling in *Woodson*.

Woodson involved the prosecution of two defendants for the crime of first-degree murder. At the time of the defendants' prosecution, the state of North Carolina imposed a mandatory death penalty on anyone convicted of first-degree murder. After all the evidence in the case had been presented to the jury, it returned first-degree murder verdicts for both defendants.[13] As required by statute, the trial judge imposed a sentence of death on both.

The issue presented to the Supreme Court by the *Woodson* defendants was whether North Carolina's mandatory death penalty statute violated the Cruel and Unusual Punishment Clause. The Supreme Court resolved the issue in the following manner:

> A process that accords no significance to relevant facets of the character and record of the individual offender or the circumstances of the particular offense excludes from consideration, in fixing the ultimate punishment of death, the possibility of compassionate or mitigating factors stemming from the diverse frailties of humankind. It treats all persons convicted of a designated offense not as uniquely individual human beings, but as members of a faceless, undifferentiated mass to be subjected to the blind infliction of the penalty of death.
>
> This Court has previously recognized that for the determination of sentences, justice generally requires consideration of more than the particular acts by which the crime was committed and that there be taken into account the circumstances of the offense together with the character and propensities of the offender. Consideration of both the offender and the offense in order to arrive at a just and appropriate sentence has been viewed as a progressive and humanizing development. While the prevailing practice of individualizing sentencing determinations generally reflects simply enlightened policy rather than a constitutional imperative, we believe that in capital cases the fundamental respect for humanity underlying the Eighth Amendment, requires consideration of the character and record of the individual offender and the circumstances of the particular offense as a constitutionally indispensable part of the process of inflicting the penalty of death.
>
> This conclusion rests squarely on the predicate that the penalty of death is qualitatively different from a sentence of imprisonment, however long.... Because of that qualitative difference, there is a corresponding difference in the need for reliability in the determination that death is the appropriate punishment in a specific case.
>
> For the reasons stated, we conclude that the death sentences imposed upon the [defendants] under North Carolina's mandatory death sentence statute violated the Eighth [Amendment] and therefore must be set aside.

It should be clearly understood that *Woodson* did not find mandatory sentencing per se unconstitutional. The decision narrowly held that mandatory death sentencing statutes are unconstitutional.[14]

On the same day that *Woodson* was decided, the Supreme Court also found Louisiana's mandatory death penalty statute unconstitutional in the case of *Roberts v. Louisiana (I)*, 428 U.S. 325 (1976). At the same time that the decisions in *Woodson* and *Roberts (I)* were rendered, the Supreme Court issued memorandum decisions in 43 capital murder cases, which invalidated death sentences because they were imposed under mandatory death penalty statutes. The states and number of cases involved in the memorandum decisions were: North Carolina (34 cases); Oklahoma (6 cases); and Louisiana (3 cases).

Additionally, in *Roberts v. Louisiana (II)*, 431 U.S. 633 (1977), it was held that a mandatory death sentence imposed for killing a law enforcement officer in the line of duty violated the Constitution. Further, Nevada's mandatory capital punishment statute, for inmates convicted of murder while serving life imprisonment without parole, was found unconstitutional in *Sumner v. Shuman*, 483 U.S. 66 (1987).

Imposing Death Under a Felony-Murder Rule Conviction

The felony-murder rule is a common law doctrine that makes it easier for a prosecutor to obtain a murder conviction when the victim is killed during the commission of a felony offense. "Under the felony-murder doctrine, a person who commits a felony is liable for any murder that occurs during the commission of that felony, regardless of whether he or she commits, attempts to commit, or intended to commit that murder. The doctrine thus imposes liability on capital felons for killings committed by co-felons during a felony."[15] In *Presnell v. Georgia*, 439 U.S. 14 (1978), it was held that the Due Process Clause prohibits imposition of a death sentence under a felony-murder theory, when the underlying non-capital offense conviction is invalid.

The common law did not make a distinction in punishment for co-defendants convicted of felony-murder. That is, even though a victim's death may have actually been caused by a single defendant, under the common law all defendants involved in the underlying felony (e.g., robbery) were subjected to the same punishment that was provided for the defendant who actually killed the victim.

The compact and simplistic punishment interpretation given to the felony-murder rule was fragmented and complicated, as a result of decisions reached by the Supreme Court in two separate cases. Both cases involved the issue of whether the Cruel and Unusual Punishment Clause prohibited imposition of capital punishment for felony-murder convictions. In addressing this issue, the Supreme Court dissected the felony-murder rule into three distinct new doctrines: (1) felony-murder simpliciter, (2) felony-murder aggravatus, and (3) felony-murder supremus. All three doctrines are discussed in the context of the two cases that immediately follow.

The Enmund ruling. The first case to begin the dissection of the felony-murder rule was *Enmund v. Florida*, 458 U.S. 782 (1982). Under the traditional felony-murder rule, the defendant and a confederate in *Enmund* were convicted of committing two murders during the course of a robbery. The defendant was convicted of the two murders in spite of the fact that he did not actually kill the victims, and was not present in the home at the time of the killings.[16]

In its analysis of the facts of *Enmund*, the Supreme Court was not disturbed by the fact that the defendant's convictions were based upon the application of the felony-murder rule. The Supreme Court viewed the defendant's role in the crime, driver of the get-away car, as sufficient to convict him for homicides committed during the course of the robbery.

The Supreme Court was disturbed, however, by the punishment the defendant received. In order to rescue the defendant from the death penalty, the Supreme Court created an exception to the punishment component of the common law felony-murder rule. The Court held in *Enmund* that the Cruel and Unusual Punishment Clause prohibits imposition of the death penalty upon a defendant "who aids and abets a felony in the course of which a murder is committed by others[,] but who does not himself kill, attempt to kill, or intend that a killing take place or that lethal force will be employed." This exception to the felony-murder rule is known as the felony-murder simpliciter doctrine. In *Cabana v. Bullock*, 474 U.S. 376 (1986), it was held that a violation of *Enmund* does not require a new sentencing hearing before a jury, because a trial judge or appellate court may determine the issue from the record in a case.

The Tison ruling. Several years after the *Enmund* decision, the Supreme Court was asked to apply the felony-murder simpliciter doctrine to invalidate the death sentences imposed upon two brothers in *Tison v. Arizona*, 481 U.S. 137 (1987).[17] The defendants in *Tison* took part in killing four people while helping their father escape from prison.

The defendants in *Tison* asked the Supreme Court to overturn their death sentences, on the grounds that the sentences were an unconstitutional imposition of capital punishment for felony-murder simpliciter. The Supreme Court analyzed the conduct of the brothers under the elements of felony-murder simpliciter and concluded that their conduct fell outside of the felony-murder simpliciter doctrine.

The Supreme Court next analyzed the conduct of the defendants under the elements of felony-murder supremus, which it described as "[a] category of felony murderers for which *Enmund* explicitly finds the death penalty permissible under the Eighth Amendment." The elements of felony-murder supremus are: (1) the felony-murderer actually killed, (2) attempted to kill, or (3) intended to kill. It was concluded by the Supreme Court that the conduct of the brothers in *Tison* did not fall within the elements of felony-murder supremus.

The Supreme Court then reduced the conduct of the brothers down to two factors: (1) their participation in the felonies was major and (2) their mental state was one of reckless indifference to the value of human life. Even though this conduct did not satisfy the elements of felony-murder simpliciter or felony-murder supremus, the Supreme Court determined that it was nevertheless a midrange level of felony-murder. This midrange felony-murder is the felony-murder aggravatus doctrine.

After reducing the conduct of the brothers to felony-murder aggravatus, the Supreme Court then concluded that the Cruel and Unusual Punishment Clause did not prohibit imposition of the death penalty for felony-murder aggravatus. However, since the defendants did not have a sentencing hearing based upon the elements of felony-murder aggravatus, the Supreme Court set aside their death sentences and remanded their cases for a sentencing hearing based upon felony-murder aggravatus.

Transferred Intent Doctrine

The transferred intent doctrine is a common law rule that is similar to the traditional felony-murder rule. Under the transferred intent doctrine, if a defendant attempts to injure a specific person, but an unintended bystander is injured instead, the defendant's "intent" to injure the specific person is transferred to the injured bystander. This doctrine is a powerful tool for obtaining convictions for crimes that require showing a defendant intended to harm a person. The doctrine has been used to obtain capital murder convictions where an innocent bystander is killed, instead of the person the defendant intended to kill. For example, in *Bradshaw v. Richey*, 546 U.S. 74 (2005), the state of Ohio charged the defendant with the capital murder of a child. The child was killed as a result of the defendant setting fire to the building where the child lived. The defendant set the fire in a failed attempt to kill his ex-girlfriend and her new boyfriend. In order to obtain a conviction for capital murder the prosecutor relied on the theory of transferred intent. One of the issues addressed by the Supreme Court in *Bradshaw* was whether or not Ohio could obtain a capital conviction under the transferred intent doctrine. It was said in *Bradshaw* that Ohio was constitutionally free to incorporate the doctrine into the state's jurisprudence.

Capital Punishment and Crimes Not Involving Death

Traditional popular thinking associates the death penalty with a number of nonfatal crimes. Popular thought may or may not be an accurate barometer of what is constitutionally permissible.

It was pointed out earlier that under the common law all felonies were punishable by the infliction of death. The American colonies incorporated the common law's position in their criminal statutes. The first codified capital punishment offenses in the American colonies were drawn up in 1636, by the Massachusetts Bay colony. The *Capital Laws of New England,* as they were called, provided the death penalty for rebellion, perjury, manstealing, rape, statutory rape, adultery, buggery, sodomy, murder, blasphemy, idolatry, witchcraft, and assault in sudden anger.[18]

All jurisdictions at some point in the past provided the death penalty for offenses that did not involve the death of a human being. For example, during the period 1930–1968, a total of 3,859 defendants were executed for criminal offenses: 3,334 executions were for murder, 455 executions were for the crime of rape, and 70 executions were for crimes other than murder or rape.[19] The constitutional issue of whether the death penalty could be inflicted for nonhomicide offenses was not addressed by the Supreme Court until it heard the case of *Coker v. Georgia*, 433 U.S. 584 (1977). Subsequent to *Coker* the issue was addressed in *Kennedy v. Louisiana*, 554 U.S. 407 (2008).

The Coker ruling. The narrow issue presented to the Supreme Court in *Coker v. Georgia*, 433 U.S. 584 (1977), was whether the Cruel and Unusual Punishment Clause prohibited imposition of the death penalty for the crime of rape of an adult woman. In addressing this issue, the Court observed "that Georgia is the sole jurisdiction in the United States at the present time that authorizes a sentence of death when the rape victim is an adult woman, and only two other jurisdictions provide capital punishment when the victim is a child." With this observation in sight, the Supreme Court concluded:

> Rape is without doubt deserving of serious punishment; but in terms of moral depravity and of the injury to the person and to the public, it does not compare with murder, which does

involve the unjustified taking of human life. Although it may be accompanied by another crime, rape by definition does not include the death of or even the serious injury to another person. The murderer kills; the rapist, if no more than that, does not. Life is over for the victim of the murderer; for the rape victim, life may not be nearly so happy as it was, but it is not over and normally is not beyond repair. We have the abiding conviction that the death penalty, which "is unique in its severity and irrevocability," is an excessive penalty for the rapist who, as such, does not take human life.

Coker stands for the proposition that it is unconstitutional to impose capital punishment for the offense of rape of an adult, without more. The issue of whether capital punishment may constitutionally be imposed for rape of a child was not directly addressed in *Coker*. This issue was confronted in *Kennedy*.

The Kennedy Ruling. The narrow issue presented to the Supreme Court in *Kennedy v. Louisiana*, 554 U.S. 407 (2008), was whether the Cruel and Unusual Punishment Clause prohibited imposition of the death penalty for the crime of rape of a child, without more. The defendant in *Kennedy* was charged by the state of Louisiana with the aggravated rape of his 8-year-old stepdaughter. After a jury trial the defendant was convicted and sentenced to death under a state statute authorizing capital punishment for the rape of a child less than 12 years of age. The Supreme Court was called upon to decide whether the Constitution permitted such punishment. The Court held that the Constitution prohibited such punishment when the victim was not killed.

> The constitutional prohibition against excessive or cruel and unusual punishments mandates that the state's power to punish "be exercised within the limits of civilized standards." Evolving standards of decency that mark the progress of a maturing society counsel us to be most hesitant before interpreting the Eighth Amendment to allow the extension of the death penalty, a hesitation that has special force where no life was taken in the commission of the crime. It is an established principle that decency, in its essence, presumes respect for the individual and thus moderation or restraint in the application of capital punishment....
>
> Consistent with evolving standards of decency and the teachings of our precedents we conclude that, in determining whether the death penalty is excessive, there is a distinction between intentional first-degree murder on the one hand and nonhomicide crimes against individual persons, even including child rape, on the other. The latter crimes may be devastating in their harm, as here, but "in terms of moral depravity and of the injury to the person and to the public," they cannot be compared to murder in their severity and irrevocability....
>
> As in *Coker*, here it cannot be said with any certainty that the death penalty for child rape serves no deterrent or retributive function. This argument does not overcome other objections, however. The incongruity between the crime of child rape and the harshness of the death penalty poses risks of overpunishment and counsels against a constitutional ruling that the death penalty can be expanded to include this offense.

Interpretation of Coker and Kennedy. At this juncture in Anglo-American jurisprudence, it may be reasonably asserted that, with *Coker* and *Kennedy* as the barometer, capital punishment for any offense that does not involve the death of a victim would be found unconstitutional by the Supreme Court.[20] This proposition is aided by the decision in *Cook v. State*, 251 S.E.2d 230 (Ga. 1978), where the Georgia Supreme Court interpreted *Coker* as invalidating statutes in that jurisdiction which had imposed the death penalty for armed robbery and kidnapping with bodily injury.

There may be a limitation to the application of *Coker* and *Kennedy*. While both cases counseled against the general imposition of capital punishment for nonhomicide crimes,

Kennedy cautioned that "[w]e do not address, for example, crimes defining and punishing treason, espionage, terrorism, and drug kingpin activity, which are offenses against the State." In other words, the jury is still out on whether the Constitution will allow capital punishment to be imposed for crimes against the government that do not involve the loss of life.

Furman v. Georgia

The decision in *Furman v. Georgia*, 408 U.S. 238 (1972), involved three consolidated capital punishment cases. The defendant in case No. 69-5003, William Henry Furman, was convicted of murder in Georgia and was sentenced to death. The defendant in case No. 69–5030, Lucious Jackson, Jr., was convicted of rape in Georgia and was sentenced to death. The defendant in case No. 69-5031, Elmer Branch, was convicted of rape in Texas and was sentenced to death. The defendants presented the same argument: the method used to impose the death penalty was arbitrary and capricious. The United States Supreme Court granted certiorari to consider the matter.

In a terse one paragraph per curiam opinion the Supreme Court held in *Furman* "that the imposition and carrying out of the death penalty in these cases constitute cruel and unusual punishment in violation of the Eighth and Fourteenth Amendments." The effect of the decision in *Furman* was that of nullifying all non-executed death sentences in the nation and placement of a moratorium on capital punishment.

All nine justices in *Furman* issued separate opinions. Five separate opinions concurred in the judgments in each case and four separate opinions dissented. The material that follows sets out excerpts from each separate opinion.

Concurring Opinion by Justice Douglas

Justice Douglas was careful to restrict his concurrence to addressing the constitutionality of the method by which the death penalty was imposed upon the defendants. He did not address the constitutionality of the death penalty as punishment per se. The critical portions of Justice Douglas' concurrence are as follows:

In these three cases the death penalty was imposed, one of them for murder, and two for rape. In each the determination of whether the penalty should be death or a lighter punishment was left by the State to the discretion of the judge or of the jury. In each of the three cases the trial was to a jury. They are here on petitions for certiorari which we granted limited to the question whether the imposition and execution of the death penalty constitute "cruel and unusual punishment" within the meaning of the Eighth Amendment as applied to the States by the Fourteenth. I vote to vacate each judgment, believing that the exaction of the death penalty does violate the Eighth and Fourteenth Amendments.

That the requirements of due process ban cruel and unusual punishment is now settled. It is also settled that the proscription of cruel and unusual punishments forbids the judicial imposition of them as well their imposition by the legislature....

It has been assumed in our decisions that punishment by death is not cruel, unless the manner of execution can be said to be inhuman and barbarous....

It would seem to be incontestable that the death penalty inflicted on one defendant is "unusual" if it discriminates against him by reason of his race, religion, wealth, social position, or class, or if it is imposed under a procedure that gives room for the play of such prejudices.

There is evidence that the provision of the English Bill of Rights of 1689, from which the language of the Eighth Amendment was taken, was concerned primarily with selective or irregular application of harsh penalties and that its aim was to forbid arbitrary and discriminatory penalties of a severe nature....

The words "cruel and unusual" certainly include penalties that are barbaric. But the words, at least when read in light of the English proscription against selective and irregular use of penalties, suggest that it is "cruel and unusual" to apply the death penalty — or any other penalty — selectively to minorities whose numbers are few, who are outcasts of society, and who are unpopular, but whom society is willing to see suffer though it would not countenance general application of the same penalty across the board....

Juries (or judges, as the case may be) have practically untrammeled discretion to let an accused live or insist that he die....

Former Attorney General Ramsey Clark has said, "It is the poor, the sick, the ignorant, the powerless and the hated who are executed." One searches our chronicles in vain for the execution of any member of the affluent strata of this society. The Leopolds and Loebs are given prison terms, not sentenced to death....

[W]e deal with a system of law and of justice that leaves to the uncontrolled discretion of judges or juries the determination whether defendants ... should die or be imprisoned. Under [current] laws no standards govern the selection of the penalty. People live or die, dependent on the whim of one man or of 12....

Those who wrote the Eighth Amendment knew what price their forebears had paid for a system based, not on equal justice, but on discrimination. In those days the target was not the blacks or the poor, but the dissenters, those who opposed absolutism in government, who struggled for a parliamentary regime, and who opposed governments' recurring efforts to foist a particular religion on the people. But the tool of capital punishment was used with vengeance against the opposition and those unpopular with the regime. One cannot read this history without realizing that the desire for equality was reflected in the ban against "cruel and unusual punishments" contained in the Eighth Amendment.

In a Nation committed to equal protection of the laws there is no permissible "cast" aspect of law enforcement. Yet we know that the discretion of judges and juries in imposing the death penalty enables the penalty to be selectively applied, feeding prejudices against the accused if he is poor and despised, and lacking political clout, or if he is a member of a suspect or unpopular minority, and saving those who by social position may be in a more protected position. In ancient Hindu Law a Brahman was exempt from capital punishment, and under that law, "[g]enerally, in the law books, punishment increased in severity as social status diminished." We have, I fear, taken in practice the same position, partially as a result of making the death penalty discretionary and partially as a result of the ability of the rich to purchase the services of the most respected and most resourceful legal talent in the Nation.

The high service rendered by the "cruel and unusual" punishment clause of the Eighth Amendment is to require legislatures to write penal laws that are evenhanded, nonselective, and nonarbitrary, and to require judges to see to it that general laws are not applied sparsely, selectively, and spottily to unpopular groups....

Thus, these discretionary statutes are unconstitutional in their operation. They are pregnant with discrimination and discrimination is an ingredient not compatible with the idea of equal protection of the laws that is implicit in the ban on "cruel and unusual" punishments.

Concurring Opinion by Justice Brennan

Justice Brennan's concurrence went to the point of concluding that the Constitution barred imposition of capital punishment per se. The critical features of his concurrence are stated as follows:

We have very little evidence of the Framers' intent in including the Cruel and Unusual Punishments Clause among those restraints upon the new Government enumerated in the Bill of Rights....

Certainly they intended to ban torturous punishments, but the available evidence does not support the further conclusion that only torturous punishments were to be outlawed.... Nor did [the Framers] intend simply to forbid punishments considered cruel and unusual at the time. The "import" of the Clause is, indeed, indefinite, and for good reason. A constitutional provision is enacted, it is true, from an experience of evils, but its general language should not, therefore, be necessarily confined to the form that evil had theretofore taken. Time works changes, brings into existence new conditions and purposes. Therefore a principle to be vital must be capable of wider application than the mischief which gave it birth....

At bottom, then, the Cruel and Unusual Punishments Clause prohibits the infliction of uncivilized and inhuman punishments. The State, even as it punishes, must treat its members with respect for their intrinsic worth as human beings. A punishment is cruel and unusual, therefore, if it does not comport with human dignity....

Death is truly an awesome punishment. The calculated killing of a human being by the State involves, by its very nature, a denial of the executed person's humanity. The contrast with the plight of a person punished by imprisonment is evident. An individual in prison does not lose the right to have rights. A prisoner retains, for example, the constitutional rights to the free exercise of religion, to be free of cruel and unusual punishments, and to treatment as a "person" for purposes of due process of law and the equal protection of the laws. A prisoner remains a member of the human family. Moreover, he retains the right of access to the courts. His punishment is not irrevocable.... [T]he finality of death precludes relief. An executed person has indeed lost the right to have rights....

The outstanding characteristic of our present practice of punishing criminals by death is the infrequency with which we resort to it. The evidence is conclusive that death is not the ordinary punishment for any crime.

There has been a steady decline in the infliction of this punishment in every decade since the 1930s, the earliest period for which accurate statistics are available. In the 1930s, executions averaged 167 per year; in the 1940s, the average was 128; in the 1950s, it was 72; and in the years 1960–1962, it was 48. There have been a total of 46 executions since then, 36 of them in 1963–1964. Yet our population and the number of capital crimes committed have increased greatly over the past four decades. The contemporary rarity of the infliction of this punishment is thus the end result of a long-continued decline. That rarity is plainly revealed by an examination of the years 1961–1970, the last 10-year period for which statistics are available. During that time, an average of 106 death sentences was imposed each year. Not nearly that number, however, could be carried out, for many were precluded by [a number of reasons]. On January 1, 1961, the death row population was 219; on December 31, 1970, it was 608; during that span, there were 135 executions. Consequently, had the 389 additions to death row also been executed, the annual average would have been 52. In short, the country might, at most, have executed one criminal each week. In fact, of course, far fewer were executed....

When a country of over 200 million people inflicts an unusually severe punishment no more than 50 times a year, the inference is strong that the punishment is not being regularly and fairly applied. To dispel it would indeed require a clear showing of nonarbitrary infliction.

Although there are no exact figures available, we know that thousands of murders and rapes are committed annually in States where death is an authorized punishment for those crimes. However the rate of infliction is characterized — as "freakishly" or "spectacularly" rare, or simply as rare — it would take the purest sophistry to deny that death is inflicted in only a minute fraction of these cases. How much rarer, after all, could the infliction of death be?

When the punishment of death is inflicted in a trivial number of the cases in which it is legally available, the conclusion is virtually inescapable that it is being inflicted arbitrarily. Indeed, it smacks of little more than a lottery system.... Furthermore, our procedures in death cases ... actually sanction an arbitrary selection.... In other words, our procedures are not constructed to guard against the totally capricious selection of criminals for the punishment of death....

Today death is a uniquely and unusually severe punishment. When examined by the principles applicable under the Cruel and Unusual Punishments Clause, death stands condemned as fatally offensive to human dignity. The punishment of death is therefore cruel and unusual, and the States may no longer inflict it as a punishment for crimes. Rather than kill an arbitrary handful of criminals each year, the States will confine them in prison....

Concurring Opinion by Justice Stewart

Justice Stewart, like Justice Douglas, found that the method of imposition of the death penalty violated the Constitution, but was not prepared to find that the Constitution barred imposition of the death penalty per se. The central aspects of Justice Stewart's concurrence indicated the following:

The penalty of death differs from all other forms of criminal punishment, not in degree but in kind. It is unique in its total irrevocability. It is unique in its rejection of rehabilitation of the convict as a basic purpose of criminal justice. And it is unique, finally, in its absolute renunciation of all that is embodied in our concept of humanity....

Legislatures — state and federal — have sometimes specified that the penalty of death shall be the mandatory punishment for every person convicted of engaging in certain designated criminal conduct....

If we were reviewing death sentences imposed under these or similar laws, we would be faced with the need to decide whether capital punishment is unconstitutional for all crime and under all circumstances. We would need to decide whether a legislature — state or federal — could constitutionally determine that certain criminal conduct is so atrocious that society's interest in deterrence and retribution wholly outweighs any considerations of reform or rehabilitation of the perpetrator, and that, despite the inconclusive empirical evidence, only the automatic penalty will provide maximum deterrence.

On that score I would say only that I cannot agree that retribution is a constitutionally impermissible ingredient in the imposition of punishment. The instinct for retribution is part of the nature of man, and channeling that instinct in the administration of criminal justice serves an important purpose in promoting the stability of a society governed by law. When people begin to believe that organized society is unwilling or unable to impose upon criminal offenders the punishment they "deserve," then there are sown the seeds of anarchy — of self-help, vigilante justice, and lynch law.

The constitutionality of capital punishment in the abstract is not, however, before us in these cases. For the Georgia and Texas Legislatures have not provided that the death penalty shall be imposed upon all those who are found guilty of forcible rape. And the Georgia Legislature has not ordained that death shall be the automatic punishment for murder. In a word, neither State has made a legislative determination that forcible rape and murder can be deterred only by imposing the penalty of death upon all who perpetrate those offenses....

Instead, the death sentences now before us are the product of a legal system that brings them, I believe, within the very core of the Eighth Amendment's guarantee against cruel and unusual punishments, a guarantee applicable against the States through the Fourteenth Amendment. In the first place, it is clear that these sentences are "cruel" in the sense that they excessively go beyond, not in degree but in kind, the punishments that the state legislatures have determined to be necessary. In the second place, it is equally clear that these sentences are "unusual" in the sense that the penalty of death is infrequently imposed for murder, and that its imposition for rape is extraordinarily rare. But I do not rest my conclusion upon these two propositions alone.

These death sentences are cruel and unusual in the same way that being struck by lightning is cruel and unusual. For, of all the people convicted of rapes and murders in 1967 and 1968, many just as reprehensible as these, the petitioners are among a capriciously selected random handful upon whom the sentence of death has in fact been imposed.... [I] conclude that the Eighth and Fourteenth Amendments cannot tolerate the infliction of a sentence of death under legal systems that permit this unique penalty to be so wantonly and so freakishly imposed.

Concurring Opinion by Justice White

Justice White, while finding the method used to impose the death penalty was unconstitutional, did not go so far as to find that the death penalty was barred by the Constitution per se. The essence of Justice White's concurrence said the following:

In joining the Court's judgments ... I do not at all intimate that the death penalty is unconstitutional per se or that there is no system of capital punishment that would comport with the Eighth Amendment. That question, ably argued by several of my Brethren, is not presented by these cases and need not be decided.

The narrower question to which I address myself concerns the constitutionality of capital punishment statutes under which (1) the legislature authorizes the imposition of the death penalty for murder or rape; (2) the legislature does not itself mandate the penalty in any particular class or kind of case (that is, legislative will is not frustrated if the penalty is never imposed), but delegates to judges or juries the decisions as to those cases, if any, in which the penalty will be utilized; and (3) judges and juries have ordered the death penalty with such infrequency that the odds are now very much against imposition and execution of the penalty with respect to any convicted murderer or rapist. It is in this context that we must consider whether the execution of these [defendants] would violate the Eighth Amendment.

I begin with what I consider a near truism: that the death penalty could so seldom be imposed that it would cease to be a credible deterrent or measurably to contribute to any other end of punishment in the criminal justice system. It is perhaps true that no matter how infrequently those convicted of rape or murder are executed, the penalty so imposed is not disproportionate to the crime and those executed may deserve exactly what they received. It would also be clear that executed defendants are finally and completely incapacitated from again committing rape or murder or any other crime. But when imposition of the penalty reaches a certain degree of infrequency, it would be very doubtful that any existing general need for retribution would be measurably satisfied. Nor could it be said with confidence that society's need for specific deterrence justifies death for so few when for so many in like circumstances life imprisonment or shorter prison terms are judged sufficient, or that community values are measurably reinforced by authorizing a penalty so rarely invoked.

Most important, a major goal of the criminal law — to deter others by punishing the convicted criminal — would not be substantially served where the penalty is so seldom invoked that it ceases to be the credible threat essential to influence the conduct of others. For present purposes I accept the morality and utility of punishing one person to influence another. I accept also the effectiveness of punishment generally and need not reject the death penalty as a more effective deterrent than a lesser punishment. But common sense and experience tell us that seldom-enforced laws become ineffective measures for controlling human conduct and that the death penalty, unless imposed with sufficient frequency, will make little contribution to deterring those crimes for which it may be exacted.

The imposition and execution of the death penalty are obviously cruel in the dictionary sense. But the penalty has not been considered cruel and unusual punishment in the constitutional sense because it was thought justified by the social ends it was deemed to serve. At the moment that it ceases realistically to further these purposes, however, the emerging question is whether its imposition in such circumstances would violate the Eighth Amendment. It is my view that it would, for its imposition would then be the pointless and needless extinction of life with only marginal contributions to any discernible social or public purposes. A penalty with such negligible returns to the State would be patently excessive and cruel and unusual punishment violative of the Eighth Amendment.

It is also my judgment that this point has been reached with respect to capital punishment as it is presently administered under the statutes involved in these cases. Concededly, it is difficult to prove as a general proposition that capital punishment, however administered, more effectively serves the ends of the criminal law than does imprisonment. But however that may be, I cannot avoid the conclusion that as the statutes before us are now administered, the penalty is so infrequently imposed that the threat of execution is too attenuated to be of substantial service to criminal justice....

I can do no more than state a conclusion based on 10 years of almost daily exposure to the facts and circumstances of hundreds and hundreds of federal and state criminal cases involving crimes for which death is the authorized penalty. That conclusion, as I have said, is that the death penalty is exacted with great infrequency even for the most atrocious crimes and that there is no meaningful basis for distinguishing the few cases in which it is not. The short of it is that the policy of vesting sentencing authority primarily in juries — a decision largely motivated by the desire to mitigate the harshness of the law and to bring community judgment to bear on the sentence as well as guilt or innocence — has so effectively achieved its aims that capital punishment within the confines of the statutes now before us has for all practical purposes run its course....

I add [finally] that past and present legislative judgment with respect to the death penalty loses much of its force when viewed in light of the recurring practice of delegating sentencing authority to the jury and the fact that a jury, in its own discretion and without violating its trust or any statutory policy, may refuse to impose the death penalty no matter what the circumstances of the crime. Legislative policy is thus necessarily defined not by what is legislatively authorized but by what juries and judges do in exercising the discretion so regularly conferred upon them. In my judgment what was done in these cases violated the Eighth Amendment.

Concurring Opinion by Justice Marshall

Justice Marshall, like Justice Brennan, argued that the Constitution prohibited the imposition of the death penalty per se. The salient features of Justice Marshall's concurrence stated the following:

The criminal acts with which we are confronted are ugly, vicious, reprehensible acts. Their sheer brutality cannot and should not be minimized. But, we are not called upon to condone the penalized conduct; we are asked only to examine the penalty imposed on each of the [defendants] and to determine whether or not it violates the Eighth Amendment....

Perhaps the most important principle in analyzing cruel and unusual punishment questions is one that is reiterated again and again in the prior opinions of the Court: i.e., the cruel and unusual language must draw its meaning from the evolving standards of decency that mark the progress of a maturing society. Thus, a penalty that was permissible at one time in our Nation's history is not necessarily permissible today.

The fact, therefore, that the Court, or individual Justices, may have in the past expressed an opinion that the death penalty is constitutional is not now binding on us....

Capital punishment has been used to penalize various forms of conduct by members of society since the beginnings of civilization. Its precise origins are difficult to perceive, but there is some evidence that its roots lie in violent retaliation by members of a tribe or group, or by the tribe or group itself, against persons committing hostile acts toward group members. Thus, infliction of death as a penalty for objectionable conduct appears to have its beginnings in private vengeance.

As individuals gradually ceded their personal prerogatives to a sovereign power, the sovereign accepted the authority to punish wrongdoing as part of its "divine right" to rule. Individual vengeance gave way to the vengeance of the state, and capital punishment became a public function. Capital punishment worked its way into the laws of various countries, and was inflicted in a variety of macabre and horrific ways....

It has often been noted that American citizens know almost nothing about capital punishment.... [E].g., that the death penalty is no more effective a deterrent than life imprisonment, that convicted murderers are rarely executed, but are usually sentenced to a term in prison; that convicted murderers usually are model prisoners, and that they almost always become law-abiding citizens upon their release from prison; that the costs of executing a capital offender exceed the costs of imprisoning him for life...; and that the death penalty may actually stimulate criminal conduct....

Regarding discrimination, it has been said that [it] is usually the poor, the illiterate, the underprivileged, the member of the minority group — the man who, because he is without means, and is defended by a court-appointed attorney — who becomes society's sacrificial lamb....

It ... is evident that the burden of capital punishment falls upon the poor, the ignorant, and the underprivileged members of society. It is the poor, and the members of minority groups who are least able to voice their complaints against capital punishment. Their impotence leaves them victims of a sanction that the wealthier, better-represented, just-as-guilty person can escape. So long as the capital sanction is used only against the forlorn, easily forgotten members of society, legislators are content to maintain the status quo, because change would draw attention to the problem and concern might develop. Ignorance is perpetuated and apathy soon becomes its mate, and we have today's situation.

Just as Americans know little about who is executed and why, they are unaware of the potential dangers of executing an innocent man. Our "beyond a reasonable doubt" burden of proof in criminal cases is intended to protect the innocent, but we know it is not fool-proof. Various studies have shown that people whose innocence is later convincingly established are convicted and sentenced to death....

No matter how careful courts are, the possibility of perjured testimony, mistaken honest testimony, and human error remain all too real. We have no way of judging how many innocent persons have been executed but we can be certain that there are some.... Surely there will be more as long as capital punishment remains part of our penal law....

In striking down capital punishment, this Court does not malign our system of government. On the contrary, it pays homage to it. Only in a free society could right triumph in difficult times, and could civilization record its magnificent advancement. In recognizing the humanity of our fellow beings, we pay ourselves the highest tribute. We achieve a major milestone in the long road up from barbarism ... by shunning capital punishment.

Dissenting Opinion by Chief Justice Burger

The dissent by the Chief Justice presented the most comprehensive challenge to the judgment of the Court and the concurring opinions. The thrust of his arguments were presented as follows:

I conclude that the constitutional prohibition against "cruel and unusual punishments" cannot be construed to bar the imposition of the punishment of death....

If we were possessed of legislative power, I would either join with Mr. Justice Brennan and Mr. Justice Marshall or, at the very least, restrict the use of capital punishment to a small category of the most heinous crimes. Our constitutional inquiry, however, must be divorced from personal feelings as to the morality and efficacy of the death penalty, and be confined to the meaning and applicability of the uncertain language of the Eighth Amendment. There is no novelty in being called upon to interpret a constitutional provision that is less than self-defining, but, of all our fundamental guarantees, the ban on "cruel and unusual punishments" is one of the most difficult to translate into judicially manageable terms. The widely divergent views of the Amendment expressed in today's opinions reveal the haze that surrounds this constitutional command. Yet it is essential to our role as a court that we not seize upon the enigmatic character of the guarantee as an invitation to enact our personal predilections into law.

Although the Eighth Amendment literally reads as prohibiting only those punishments that are both "cruel" and "unusual," history compels the conclusion that the Constitution prohibits all punishments of extreme and barbarous cruelty, regardless of how frequently or infrequently imposed....

Counsel for petitioners properly concede that capital punishment was not impermissibly cruel at the time of the adoption of the Eighth Amendment. Not only do the records of the debates indicate that the Founding Fathers were limited in their concern to the prevention of torture, but it is also clear from the language of the Constitution itself that there was no thought whatever of the elimination of capital punishment. The opening sentence of the Fifth Amendment is a guarantee that the death penalty not be imposed "unless on a presentment or indictment of a Grand Jury." The Double Jeopardy Clause of the Fifth Amendment is a prohibition against being "twice put in jeopardy of life" for the same offense. Similarly, the Due Process Clause commands "due process of law" before an accused can be "deprived of life, liberty, or property." Thus, the explicit language of the Constitution affirmatively acknowledges the legal power to impose capital punishment; it does not expressly or by implication acknowledge the legal power to impose any of the various punishments that have been banned as cruel since 1791. Since the Eighth Amendment was adopted on the same day in 1791 as the Fifth Amendment, it hardly needs more to establish that the death penalty was not "cruel" in the constitutional sense at that time.

In the 181 years since the enactment of the Eighth Amendment, not a single decision of this Court has cast the slightest shadow of a doubt on the constitutionality of capital punishment. In rejecting Eighth Amendment attacks on particular modes of execution, the Court has more than once implicitly denied that capital punishment is impermissibly "cruel" in the constitutional sense....

Before recognizing such an instant evolution in the law, it seems fair to ask what factors have changed that capital punishment should now be "cruel" in the constitutional sense as it has not been in the past. It is apparent that there has been no change of constitutional significance in the nature of the punishment itself. Twentieth century modes of execution surely involve no greater physical suffering than the means employed at the time of the Eighth Amendment's adoption. And although a man awaiting execution must inevitably experience extraordinary mental anguish, no one suggests that this anguish is materially different from that experienced by condemned men in 1791, even though protracted appellate review processes have greatly increased the waiting time on "death row." To be sure, the ordeal of the condemned man may be thought cruel in the sense that all suffering is thought cruel. But if the Constitution proscribed every punishment producing severe emotional stress, then capital punishment would clearly have been impermissible in 1791.

However, the inquiry cannot end here. For reasons unrelated to any change in intrinsic cruelty, the Eighth Amendment prohibition cannot fairly be limited to those punishments thought excessively cruel and barbarous at the time of the adoption of the Eighth Amendment. A punishment is inordinately cruel, in the sense we must deal with it in these cases, chiefly as perceived by the society so characterizing it. The standard of extreme cruelty is not merely descriptive, but necessarily embodies a moral judgment. The standard itself remains the same, but its applicability must change as the basic mores of society change.... Nevertheless, the Court up to now has never actually held that a punishment has become impermissibly cruel due to a shift in the weight of accepted social values; nor has the Court suggested judicially manageable criteria for measuring such a shift in moral consensus.

The Court's quiescence in this area can be attributed to the fact that in a democratic society legislatures, not courts, are constituted to respond to the will and consequently the moral values of the people. For this reason, early commentators suggested that the "cruel and unusual punishments" clause was an unnecessary constitutional provision. As acknowledged in the principal brief for petitioners, "both in constitutional contemplation and in fact, it is the legislature, not the Court, which responds to public opinion and immediately reflects the society's standards of decency." Accordingly, punishments such as branding and the cutting off of ears, which were commonplace at the time of the adoption of the Constitution, passed from the penal scene without judicial intervention because they became basically offensive to the people and the legislatures responded to this sentiment....

The selectivity of juries in imposing the punishment of death is properly viewed as a refinement on, rather than a repudiation of, the statutory authorization for that penalty. Legislatures prescribe the categories of crimes for which the death penalty should be available, and, acting as "the conscience of the community," juries are entrusted to determine in individual cases that the ultimate punishment is warranted. Juries are undoubtedly influenced in this judgment by myriad factors. The motive or lack of motive of the perpetrator, the degree of injury or suffering of the victim or victims, and the degree of brutality in the commission of the crime would seem to be prominent among these factors. Given the general awareness that death is no longer a routine punishment for the crimes for which it is made available, it is hardly surprising that juries have been increasingly meticulous in their imposition of the penalty. But to assume from the mere fact of relative infrequency that only a random assortment of pariahs are sentenced to death, is to cast grave doubt on the basic integrity of our jury system.

It would, of course, be unrealistic to assume that juries have been perfectly consistent in choosing the cases where the death penalty is to be imposed, for no human institution performs with perfect consistency. There are doubtless prisoners on death row who would not be there had they been tried before a different jury or in a different State. In this sense their fate has been controlled by a fortuitous circumstance. However, this element of fortuity does not stand as an indictment either of the general functioning of juries in capital cases or of the integrity of jury decisions in individual cases. There is no empirical basis for concluding that juries have generally failed to discharge in good faith [their] responsibility ...— that of choosing between life and death in individual cases according to the dictates of community values....

Since there is no majority of the Court on the ultimate issue presented in these cases, the future of capital punishment in this country has been left in an uncertain limbo. Rather than providing a final and unambiguous answer on the basic constitutional question, the collective impact of the majority's ruling is to demand an undetermined measure of change from the various state legislatures and the Congress. While I cannot endorse the process of decisionmaking that has yielded today's result and the restraints that result imposes on legislative action, I am not altogether displeased that legislative bodies have been given the opportunity, and indeed unavoidable responsibility, to make a thorough re-evaluation of the entire subject of capital punishment. If today's opinions demonstrate nothing else, they starkly show that this is an area where legislatures can act far more effectively than courts.

The legislatures are free to eliminate capital punishment for specific crimes or to carve out limited exceptions to a general abolition of the penalty, without adherence to the conceptual strictures of the Eighth Amendment. The legislatures can and should make an assessment of the deterrent influence of capital punishment, both generally and as affecting the commission of specific types of crimes. If legislatures come to doubt the efficacy of capital punishment, they can abolish it, either completely or on a selective basis. If new evidence persuades them that they have acted unwisely, they can reverse their field and reinstate the penalty to the extent it is thought warranted. An Eighth Amendment ruling by judges cannot be made with such flexibility or discriminating precision.

Dissenting Opinion by Justice Blackmun

The dissent by Justice Blackmun was concerned with the lack of justification for the majority's decision to use the Constitution to invalidate the method by which the death penalty was imposed. He argued that no precedent for such a course was evident. The essence of Justice Blackmun's dissent stated the following:

The several concurring opinions acknowledge, as they must, that until today capital punishment was accepted and assumed as not unconstitutional per se under the Eighth Amendment or the Fourteenth Amendment....

Suddenly, however, the course of decision is now the opposite way, with the Court evidently persuaded that somehow the passage of time has taken us to a place of greater maturity and outlook. The argument, plausible and high-sounding as it may be, is not persuasive.... The Court has just decided that it is time to strike down the death penalty....

The Court has recognized, and I certainly subscribe to the proposition, that the Cruel and Unusual Punishments Clause may acquire meaning as public opinion becomes enlightened by a humane justice....

My problem, however, as I have indicated, is the suddenness of the Court's perception of progress in the human attitude since decisions of only a short while ago....

I do not sit on these cases, however, as a legislator, responsive, at least in part, to the will of constituents. Our task here, as must so frequently be emphasized and re-emphasized, is to pass upon the constitutionality of legislation that has been enacted and that is challenged. This is the sole task for judges. We should not allow our personal preferences as to the wisdom of legislative and congressional action, or our distaste for such action, to guide our judicial decision in cases such as these. The temptations to cross that policy line are very great. In fact, as today's decision reveals, they are almost irresistible.

I trust the Court fully appreciates what it is doing when it decides these cases the way it does today. Not only are the capital punishment laws of 39 States and the District of Columbia struck down, but also all those provisions of the federal statutory structure that permit the death penalty apparently are voided....

Although personally I may rejoice at the Court's result, I find it difficult to accept or to justify as a matter of history, of law, or of constitutional pronouncement. I fear the Court has overstepped. It has sought and has achieved an end.

Dissenting Opinion by Justice Powell

Justice Powell's dissent displayed concern for the lack of precedent in the judgment of the majority, and the possible consequences of the majority's decision. Justice Powell presented the heart of his dissent as follows:

It is the judgment of five Justices that the death penalty, as customarily prescribed and implemented in this country today, offends the constitutional prohibition against cruel and unusual punishments. The reasons for that judgment are stated in five separate opinions, expressing as many separate rationales. In my view, none of these opinions provides a constitutionally adequate foundation for the Court's decision....

Whatever uncertainties may hereafter surface, several of the consequences of today's decision are unmistakably clear. The decision is plainly one of the greatest importance. The Court's judgment removes the death sentences previously imposed on some 600 persons awaiting punishment in state and federal prisons throughout the country. At least for the present, it also bars the States and the Federal Government from seeking sentences of death for defendants awaiting trial on charges for which capital punishment was heretofore a potential alternative. The happy event for these countable few constitutes, however, only the most visible consequence of this decision. Less measurable, but certainly of no less significance, is the shattering effect this collection of views has on the root principles of stare decisis, federalism, judicial restraint and — most importantly — separation of powers....

In terms of the constitutional role of this Court, the impact of the majority's ruling is all the greater because the decision encroaches upon an area squarely within the historic prerogative of the legislative branch — both state and federal — to protect the citizenry through the designation of penalties for prohibitable conduct. It is the very sort of judgment that the legislative branch is competent to make and for which the judiciary is ill-equipped. Throughout our history, Justices of this Court have emphasized the gravity of decisions invalidating legislative judgments, admonishing the nine men who sit on this bench of the duty of self-restraint, especially when called upon to apply the expansive due process and cruel and unusual punishment rubrics. I can recall no case in which, in the name of deciding constitutional questions, this Court has subordinated national and local democratic processes to such an extent....

On virtually every occasion that any opinion has touched on the question of the constitutionality of the death penalty, it has been asserted affirmatively, or tacitly assumed, that the Constitution does not prohibit the penalty. No Justice of the Court, until today, has dissented from this consistent reading of the Constitution. The petitioners in these cases now before the Court cannot fairly avoid the weight of this substantial body of precedent merely by asserting that there is no prior decision precisely in point. Stare decisis, if it is a doctrine founded on principle, surely applies where there exists a long line of cases endorsing or necessarily assuming the validity of a particular matter of constitutional interpretation....

Members of this Court know, from the petitions and appeals that come before us regularly, that brutish and revolting murders continue to occur with disquieting frequency. Indeed, murders are so commonplace in our society that only the most sensational receive significant and sustained publicity. It could hardly be suggested that in any of these highly publicized murder cases — the several senseless assassinations or the too numerous shocking multiple murders that have stained this country's recent history — the public has exhibited any signs of "revulsion" at the thought of executing the convicted murderers. The public outcry, as we all know, has been quite to the contrary. Furthermore, there is little reason to suspect that the public's reaction would differ significantly in response to other less publicized murders. It is certainly arguable that many such murders, because of their senselessness or barbarousness, would evoke a public demand for the death penalty rather than a public rejection of that alternative. Nor is there any rational basis for arguing that the public reaction to any of these crimes would be muted if the murderer were "rich and powerful." The demand for the ultimate sanction might well be greater, as a wealthy killer is hardly a sympathetic figure. While there might be specific cases in which capital punishment would be regarded as excessive and shocking to the conscience of the community, it can hardly be argued that the public's dissatisfaction with the penalty in particular cases would translate into a demand for absolute abolition.

Dissenting Opinion by Justice Rehnquist

Justice Rehnquist expressed concern about the usurpation of power he believed was represented in the judgment of the majority. The critical points of his dissent stated the following:

The Court's judgments today strike down a penalty that our Nation's legislators have thought necessary since our country was founded. My Brothers Douglas, Brennan, and Marshall would at one fell swoop invalidate laws enacted by Congress and 40 of the 50 state legislatures, and would consign to the limbo of unconstitutionality under a single rubric penalties for offenses as varied and unique as murder, piracy, mutiny, highjacking, and desertion in the face of the enemy. My Brothers Stewart and White, asserting reliance on a more limited rationale — the reluctance of judges and juries actually to impose the death penalty in the majority of capital cases — join in the judgments in these cases. Whatever its precise rationale, today's holding necessarily brings into sharp relief the fundamental question of the role of judicial review in a democratic society. How can government by the elected representatives of the people co-exist with the power of the federal judiciary, whose members are constitutionally insulated from responsiveness to the popular will, to declare invalid laws duly enacted by the popular branches of government?...

If there can be said to be one dominant theme in the Constitution, perhaps more fully articulated in the Federalist Papers than in the instrument itself, it is the notion of checks and balances. The Framers were well aware of the natural desire of office holders as well as others to seek to expand the scope and authority of their particular office at the expense of others. They sought to provide against success in such efforts by erecting adequate checks and balances in the form of grants of authority to each branch of the government in order to counteract and prevent usurpation on the part of the others....

While overreaching by the Legislative and Executive Branches may result in the sacrifice of individual protections that the Constitution was designed to secure against action of the State, judicial over-reaching may result in sacrifice of the equally important right of the people to govern themselves. The Due Process and Equal Protection Clauses of the Fourteenth Amendment were "never intended to destroy the States' power to govern themselves."

3

Double Jeopardy and Ex Post Facto

The right against re-prosecution when there has been an acquittal and that right against being prosecuted for conduct that was not a crime when committed are fundamental Anglo-American rights. The material that follows examines the broad federal constitutional double jeopardy and ex post facto prohibitions. The chapter concludes with a few remarks on the Bill of Attainder Clause, trial in absentia and law of the case doctrine.

Double Jeopardy

The Fifth Amendment to the Federal Constitution declares that no person shall "be subject for the same offence to be twice put in jeopardy of life or limb[.]" The constitutional prohibition against double jeopardy was designed to protect an individual from being subjected to the hazards of trial and possible conviction more than once for an alleged offense. Under the common law double jeopardy was grounded in the plea of autrefois acquit or convict (former acquittal or conviction), which represented the universal maxim that no person was to be brought into jeopardy of his or her life more than once for the same offense.[1]

The principle of autrefois was part of the legal tradition of the American colonists. The Massachusetts Body of Liberties of 1641, a compilation of legal principles taken from the common law and English statutes, provided: "No man shall be twise sentenced by Civill Justice for one and the same Crime, offence, or Trespasse," and that "Everie Action betweene partie and partie, and proceedings against delinquents in Criminall causes shall be briefly and distinctly entered on the Rolles of every Court by the Recorder thereof. That such actions be not afterwards brought againe to the vexation of any man."[2]

Although the Colonists were aware of principles against double jeopardy from the common law and English statutes, New York was the lone jurisdiction to propose an amendment to the Constitution that included a prohibition against double jeopardy. The bill of rights adopted at the New York convention and transmitted to Congress included a declaration that "no Person ought to be put twice in Jeopardy of Life or Limb for one and the same Offence, nor, unless in case of impeachment, be punished more than once for the same Offence."[3]

James Madison was influenced by New York's double jeopardy clause when he drafted the constitutional amendments to be proposed to the states. The words Madison introduced into the House of Representatives were: "No person shall be subject, except in cases of impeachment, to more than one punishment or one trial for the same offence[.]" The double jeopardy principle worded by Madison caused some concern. Representatives feared that, as proposed by Madison, double jeopardy might be taken to prohibit a second trial of a defendant who had his or her conviction reversed on appeal. Representative Benson of New York argued that the double jeopardy principle had to express the idea "that no man's life should be more than once put in jeopardy for the same offence; yet it was well known, that they were entitled to more than one trial." The provision that was ratified as part of the Fifth Amendment was substantially in the language used by Representative Benson.[4]

Under Anglo-American jurisprudence the Double Jeopardy Clause has been interpreted as protecting against (1) a second prosecution for the same offense after acquittal, (2) a second prosecution for the same offense after conviction, and (3) multiple punishments for the same offense. The Supreme Court observed in *Schiro v. Farley*, 510 U.S. 222 (1994) that these protections stem from the underlying premise that a defendant should not be twice tried or punished for the same offense. The Double Jeopardy Clause operates as a bar against repeated attempts to convict, with consequent subjection of the defendant to embarrassment, expense, anxiety, and insecurity, and the possibility that he or she may be found guilty even though innocent. Therefore, when a defendant has been acquitted the Double Jeopardy Clause guarantees that the state shall not be permitted to make repeated attempts to convict him or her. Of course, when there is no threat of either multiple punishment or successive prosecutions, the Double Jeopardy Clause is not offended.

Under double jeopardy principles, when the same criminal act or transaction constitutes a violation of two distinct statutory provisions, the test to be applied to determine whether there are two offenses or only one is whether each provision requires proof of an additional fact which the other does not. If additional proof is not required, then the two offenses are the same and double jeopardy may prohibit dual punishment. In *Williams v. Oklahoma*, 358 U.S. 576 (1959), it was held that the Double Jeopardy Clause did not prohibit Oklahoma from prosecuting the defendant for capital kidnapping, after prosecuting him for murder of the victim who was kidnapped.

A capital penalty phase proceeding has been deemed comparable to a trial on the issue of guilt, thereby making the Double Jeopardy Clause relevant to such proceeding.

Concurrent Jurisdiction

Under the concurrent jurisdiction or dual sovereignty doctrine, when a defendant in a single act violates the law of two sovereign jurisdictions, he or she has committed two distinct offenses and may be prosecuted by both jurisdictions. For constitutional purposes, the United States government and each of the fifty state governments are sovereign jurisdictions. A political subdivision of a state is not a sovereign jurisdiction.

In the context of capital punishment, the concurrent jurisdiction doctrine permits the death penalty to be imposed on a defendant in two jurisdictions for the murder of one victim. This may occur where sufficient acts take place in both jurisdictions concerning the murder, though the victim actually dies in only one of the jurisdictions.

The idea behind concurrent jurisdiction, in the context of capital punishment, is simply that more than one jurisdiction may prosecute a defendant for the same capital offense under certain circumstances.[5] The discretion of prosecutors in this area is based upon the sovereignty of each jurisdiction. An extended excerpt from the case of *Heath v. Alabama*, 474 U.S. 82 (1985), will provide a realistic illustration of the issues involved when prosecutors in different jurisdictions seek to prosecute a defendant for the same capital crime.

The state of Georgia convicted the defendant of capital murder and sentenced him to life imprisonment. The state of Alabama also prosecuted the defendant for the same capital murder, but sentenced him to death. The defendant's argument to the United States Supreme Court was that Alabama's prosecution of him, for the same capital murder, violated the Double Jeopardy Clause.[6] The Supreme Court disagreed as follows:

In August 1981, petitioner, Larry Gene Heath, hired [two men] to kill his wife, Rebecca Heath, who was then nine months pregnant, for a sum of $2,000. On the morning of August 31, 1981, petitioner left the Heath residence in Russell County, Alabama, to meet with [the two men] in Georgia, just over the Alabama border from the Heath home. Petitioner led them back to the Heath residence, gave them the keys to the Heath's car and house, and left the premises in his girlfriend's truck. [The two men] then kidnapped Rebecca Heath from her home. The Heath car, with Rebecca Heath's body inside, was later found on the side of a road in Troup County, Georgia. The cause of death was a gunshot wound in the head. The estimated time of death [was] consistent with the theory that the murder took place in Georgia[.]

Georgia and Alabama authorities pursued dual investigations in which they cooperated to some extent. On September 4, 1981, petitioner was arrested by Georgia authorities. Petitioner waived his Miranda rights and gave a full confession admitting that he had arranged his wife's kidnapping and murder. In November 1981, the grand jury of Troup County, Georgia, indicted petitioner for the offense of malice murder.... On February 10, 1982, petitioner pleaded guilty to the Georgia murder charge in exchange for a sentence of life imprisonment, which he understood could involve his serving as few as seven years in prison.

On May 5, 1982, the grand jury of Russell County, Alabama, returned an indictment against petitioner for the capital offense of murder during a kidnapping. Before trial on this indictment, petitioner [filed a motion] arguing that his conviction and sentence in Georgia barred his prosecution in Alabama for the same conduct [under double jeopardy principles]. Petitioner also [contested] the jurisdiction of the Alabama court on the ground that the crime had occurred in Georgia.

After a hearing, the trial court rejected petitioner's double jeopardy claims....

On January 12, 1983, the Alabama jury convicted petitioner of murder during a kidnapping in the first degree. After a sentencing hearing, the jury recommended the death penalty [which was subsequently imposed by the trial judge].

Petitioner sought a writ of certiorari from this Court, raising double jeopardy claims....

Successive prosecutions are barred by the Fifth Amendment only if the two offenses for which the defendant is prosecuted are the "same" for double jeopardy purposes.... We [will] assume, arguendo, that, had [the offenses petitioner was convicted of had] arisen under the laws of one State ... the second conviction would have been barred by the Double Jeopardy Clause.

The sole remaining question ... is whether the dual sovereignty doctrine permits successive prosecutions under the laws of different States[.]

The dual sovereignty doctrine is founded on the common-law conception of crime as an offense against the sovereignty of the government. When a defendant in a single act violates the "peace and dignity" of two sovereigns by breaking the laws of each, he has committed two distinct offenses[.]

In applying the dual sovereignty doctrine, then, the crucial determination is whether the two entities that seek successively to prosecute a defendant for the same course of conduct can be termed separate sovereigns. This determination turns on whether the two entities draw their authority to punish the offender from distinct sources of power. [This] Court has uniformly held [in prior cases] that the States are separate sovereigns with respect to the federal Government because each State's power to prosecute is derived from its own "inherent sovereignty," not from the Federal Government....

The States are no less sovereign with respect to each other than they are with respect to the Federal Government. Their powers to undertake criminal prosecutions derive from separate and independent sources of power and authority ... preserved to them by the Tenth Amendment.

Foremost among the prerogatives of sovereignty is the power to create and enforce a criminal code. To deny a state its power to enforce its criminal laws because another State has won the race to the courthouse would be a shocking and untoward deprivation of the historic right and obligation of the states to maintain peace and order within their confines.... [Conviction affirmed.]

Seeking Death After Reversal of a Life Imprisonment Sentence

Conviction of a capital crime does not mean that a sentence of death will be imposed. Life imprisonment is an option in capital prosecutions. Invariably a defendant convicted of a capital offense will seek to overturn the conviction, whether or not the death penalty was imposed. The issue presented now involves prosecutorial discretion to seek the death penalty, at a retrial of a defendant, when the overturned sentence in the first trial was life imprisonment.[7]

This section does not discuss the issue of a defendant being convicted of non-capital murder, but on retrial receives a capital conviction. This issue is straightforward and barred by the Double Jeopardy Clause. The Supreme Court specifically held in *Green v. United States*, 355 U.S. 184 (1957), a defendant's conviction for capital murder, on retrial from the reversal of his first conviction, violated double jeopardy principles because he was convicted of second degree murder — a non-capital crime — in his first trial.

The Stroud ruling. In the case of *Stroud v. United States*, 251 U.S. 15 (1919), the defendant was convicted of the capital offense of first degree murder and was sentenced to life imprisonment. The defendant appealed his conviction. The appellate court overturned the conviction and granted the defendant a new trial. At the second trial the defendant was again convicted of first degree murder; however, this time he was sentenced to die. The defendant appealed his second conviction to the United States Supreme Court.

The defendant's argument to the Supreme Court was that the Double Jeopardy Clause of the Fifth Amendment prohibited imposition of the death penalty at his second trial, because the first trial determined that the death penalty was inappropriate. This argument was rejected. The Supreme Court held that the death penalty may be constitutionally sought by a prosecutor at a retrial of a defendant, even though the punishment was not imposed at the first trial.

The Bullington ruling. The ruling in *Stroud* remained unchallenged law until the Supreme Court heard the case of *Bullington v. Missouri*, 451 U.S. 430 (1981).

The defendant in *Bullington* was indicted in 1977 for the capital murder of a woman during the commission of a kidnapping. After a lengthy trial the jury returned a verdict of guilty of capital murder. The prosecutor indicated he would seek the death penalty, therefore a sentencing hearing was held to determine the penalty. The sentencing jury returned a verdict of life imprisonment.

Shortly after the sentencing verdict was returned, the defendant filed post-verdict motions. In the motions he asked the trial court to set aside the guilty verdict and acquit him or, in the alternative, set aside the guilty verdict and grant him a new trial. Due to a constitutional error at the trial, the presiding judge set aside the guilty verdict and granted the defendant a new trial. Prior to the start of the second trial, the prosecutor filed a notice that he would again seek the death penalty. The defendant objected to this and filed a motion asking the trial court to quash the notice. The defendant argued that the Double Jeopardy Clause prevented the prosecutor from seeking the death penalty, after the jury rejected this in the first trial.

The trial court agreed with the defendant and prohibited the prosecutor from seeking the death penalty in the second trial. The prosecutor thereafter made an interlocutory appeal of the trial court's ruling to the Missouri Supreme Court. The state high court agreed with the prosecutor that the Double Jeopardy Clause did not prevent him from seeking the death penalty in the second trial. The state high court then set aside the trial court's ruling.

Before the second trial began, the defendant made an interlocutory appeal of the state high court decision to the United States Supreme Court. The essence of the Supreme Court's response to the issue of seeking death in a retrial is as follows:

> It is well established that the Double Jeopardy Clause forbids the retrial of a defendant who has been acquitted of the crime charged. This Court, however, has resisted attempts to extend that principle to sentencing. The imposition of a particular sentence usually is not regarded as an "acquittal" of any more severe sentence that could have been imposed. The Court generally has concluded, therefore, that the Double Jeopardy Clause imposes no absolute prohibition against the imposition of a harsher sentence at retrial after a defendant has succeeded in having his original conviction set aside.
>
> The procedure that resulted in the imposition of life imprisonment upon [the defendant] at his first trial, however, differs significantly from those employed in any of the Court's cases where the Double Jeopardy Clause has been held inapplicable to sentencing. The jury in this case was not given unbounded discretion to select an appropriate punishment from a wide range authorized by statute. Rather, a separate hearing was required and was held, and the jury was presented both a choice between two alternatives and standards to guide the making of that choice. Nor did the prosecution simply recommend what it felt to be an appropriate punishment. It undertook the burden of establishing certain facts ... in its quest to obtain the harsher of the two alternative verdicts. The presentence hearing resembled ... the immediately preceding trial on the issue of guilt or innocence. It was itself a trial on the issue of punishment[.]
>
> In contrast, the sentencing procedures in [*Stroud*] did not have the hallmarks of the trial on guilt or innocence. In ... *Stroud*, there was no separate sentencing proceeding at which the prosecution was required to prove ... facts in order to justify the particular sentence. In [*Stroud*] the sentencer's discretion was essentially unfettered[.]
>
> By enacting a capital sentencing procedure that resembles a trial on the issue of guilt or innocence ... Missouri explicitly requires the jury to determine whether the prosecution has proved its case[.]...
>
> Because the sentencing proceeding at [the defendant's] first trial was like the trial on the question of guilt or innocence, the protection afforded by the Double Jeopardy clause to one acquitted by a jury also is available to him, with respect to the death penalty, at his retrial. We therefore refrain from extending the reasoning of *Stroud* to this very different situation.
>
> The judgment of the Supreme Court of Missouri is reversed[.]

Under *Bullington* a prosecutor is prohibited from seeking the death penalty in a retrial, when the death penalty was rejected in the first trial.

The Rumsey ruling. *Bullington* was applied in *Arizona v. Rumsey*, 467 U.S. 203 (1984). In *Rumsey* the defendant was tried and convicted of capital murder by the state of Arizona.

At a non-jury penalty phase, the trial judge found that no statutory aggravating circumstances were present. Accordingly, the defendant was sentenced to life imprisonment. The defendant appealed the conviction. During the appeal the Arizona Supreme Court held that the trial judge erred during the penalty phase. Consequently, that court reversed the sentence and remanded for a new death penalty hearing. The defendant was given a death sentence on remand. The United States Supreme Court found that the death sentence in *Rumsey* violated *Bullington* and held that that the defendant's initial life sentence constituted an acquittal of the death penalty, and the trial court could not subsequently sentence him to death on a retrial of the penalty phase proceeding.

The Poland ruling. In *Poland v. Arizona*, 476 U.S. 147 (1986), the defendants, two brothers, were convicted and sentenced to death for capital murder during the course of a robbery by the state of Arizona. On appeal the Arizona Supreme Court reversed the convictions and death sentences. The appellate court found that the evidence was insufficient to support the trial judge's finding that the murder was "especially heinous, cruel, or depraved" (a statutory aggravating circumstance). It was determined by the appellate court that the trial judge erred in finding the "pecuniary gain" statutory aggravating circumstance did not apply to robbery of a bank. The appellate court remanded the case for a new trial.

At the second trial the defendants were again convicted of capital murder. At the second non-jury penalty phase proceeding, the trial judge found the existence of both, the "pecuniary gain" and "especially heinous, cruel, or depraved" statutory aggravating circumstances. The sentence of death was again imposed on each defendant. The Arizona Supreme Court affirmed the convictions and death sentences. In doing so, the appellate court found that the evidence did not support finding the existence of the "especially heinous, cruel, or depraved" factor, but the evidence did sustain finding the existence of the "pecuniary gain" factor. The appellate court also rejected the defendants' argument that the Double Jeopardy Clause barred re-imposition of the death penalty. The United States Supreme Court granted certiorari to consider the issue.

The Supreme Court held in *Poland* that re-imposing the death penalty on the defendants did not violate the Double Jeopardy Clause. The opinion stated that the decision in the case was not inconsistent with *Bullington* and *Rumsey*, because under those cases the relevant inquiry is whether there was a determination made that the prosecutor failed to prove its case for the death penalty, which meant that there was an acquittal on the sentence of death. The opinion addressed this issue as follows:

> At no point during [the defendants'] first capital sentencing hearing and appeal did either the sentencer or the reviewing court hold that the prosecution had "failed to prove its case" that [the defendants] deserved the death penalty. Plainly, the sentencing judge did not acquit, for he imposed the death penalty. While the Arizona Supreme Court held that the sentencing judge erred in relying on the "especially heinous, cruel, or depraved" aggravating circumstance, it did not hold that the prosecution had failed to prove its case for the death penalty. Indeed, the court clearly indicated that there had been no such failure, by remarking that "the trial court mistook the law when it did not find that the defendants 'committed the offense as consideration for the receipt, or in expectation of the receipt, of anything of pecuniary value,'" and that "[u]pon retrial, if the defendants are again convicted of first degree murder, the court may find the existence of this aggravating circumstance[.]"

The Sattazahn ruling. In *Sattazahn v. Pennsylvania*, 537 U.S. 101 (2003), the penalty phase jury was deadlocked on the punishment. As a result, the trial judge sentenced the defendant to life in prison. The defendant appealed his conviction on the merits of guilt finding and was given a new trial. During the second trial the defendant was found guilty and sentenced to death. The defendant argued before the Supreme Court that the Double Jeopardy and Due Process Clauses of the Constitution prohibited imposition of the death penalty on a retrial. The Supreme Court disagreed and held that when a jury does not make a determination of whether the death penalty should be imposed, a defendant may face such punishment after a retrial of the guilt phase. Specifically, the following was held in *Sattazahn*:

> [T]he relevant inquiry for double-jeopardy purposes was not whether the defendant received a life sentence the first time around, but rather whether a first life sentence was an "acquittal" based on findings sufficient to establish legal entitlement to the life sentence — *i.e.,* findings that the government failed to prove one or more aggravating circumstances beyond a reasonable doubt....
>
> But that is not what happened. Petitioner was convicted in the guilt phase of his first trial of ... first-degree murder. During the sentencing phase, the jury deliberated without reaching a decision on death or life, and without making any findings regarding aggravating or mitigating circumstances. After 3½ hours the judge dismissed the jury as hung and entered a life sentence in accordance with Pennsylvania law. As explained, neither judge nor jury "acquitted" petitioner of ... "first-degree murder plus aggravating circumstance(s)." Thus, when petitioner appealed and succeeded in invalidating his conviction..., there was no double-jeopardy bar to Pennsylvania's retrying petitioner [and seeking the death penalty].

Collateral Estoppel

In *Schiro v. Farley*, 510 U.S. 222 (1994), the state of Indiana charged the defendant with one count of committing capital murder "intentionally," and a second count of committing capital murder during the course of a rape, i.e., felony-murder. A guilt phase jury convicted the defendant of the second count of committing capital murder during a rape, but did not return a verdict on the first count. At the penalty phase the trial court imposed the death sentence, after finding that the prosecutor proved the statutory aggravating circumstance that the defendant committed the murder by "intentionally" killing the victim while committing rape. The judgment was affirmed on direct appeal and during a state habeas corpus proceeding.

The defendant in *Schiro* subsequently filed a habeas corpus petition in a federal district court. The defendant argued that the jury acquitted him of "intentionally" murdering the victim and that as a result, the doctrine of collateral estoppel precluded the trial judge from finding the existence of the aggravating circumstance that he "intentionally" killed the victim while committing rape. The district court rejected the argument and dismissed the petition. A federal court of appeals affirmed the dismissal. The United States Supreme Court granted certiorari to consider the issue.

The Supreme Court ruled that the Double Jeopardy Clause incorporates the doctrine of collateral estoppel in criminal proceedings. It was said that collateral estoppel, or issue preclusion, means simply that when an issue of ultimate fact has once been determined by a valid and final judgment, that issue cannot again be litigated between the same parties in any future lawsuit. The opinion held that it need not address whether collateral estoppel could bar the use of the "intentional" murder aggravating circumstance, because the defendant did not meet his burden of establishing the factual predicate for the application of the doctrine, if it were applicable, namely that an issue of ultimate fact has once been determined in his favor. It was said the failure to return a verdict does not have collateral estoppel effect, unless the record establishes that the issue was actually and necessarily decided in the defendant's favor. The record in the case did not show that the jury was required to return a verdict on all the charges on the verdict form. Therefore, failure to return any verdict on the intentional murder charge could not be interpreted as an acquittal.

In *Bobby v. Bies*, 556 U.S. 825 (2009), the Supreme Court also rejected a collateral estoppel claim. The defendant in *Bobby* was convicted by an Ohio jury of capital murder. During the sentencing phase the defendant put on mitigating evidence suggesting he was mentally retarded. The jury sentenced the defendant to death. During the automatic review by the Ohio Supreme Court, that court said the defendant's mild-to-borderline mental retardation merited some weight in mitigation, but concluded that the aggravating circumstances outweighed the mitigating factors beyond a reasonable doubt. The Ohio high court affirmed the judgment.

Several years after the defendant's conviction in *Bobby*, the United States Supreme Court issued the decision in *Atkins v. Virginia*, 536 U.S. 304 (2002). *Atkins* held that the Eighth Amendment's prohibition of cruel and unusual punishments bars execution of mentally retarded offenders. As a result of *Atkins* an Ohio trial court ordered a hearing be held to determine whether the defendant in *Bobby* was mentally retarded. Thereafter the defendant filed a federal habeas corpus petition seeking to stop the Ohio court from holding a hearing to determine whether he was mentally retarded. The defendant argued that the penalty phase jury and Ohio Supreme Court already found that he was mentally retarded, therefore the collateral estoppel doctrine precluded relitigating the issue. The federal district court and a court of appeals agreed with the defendant. The United States Supreme Court granted certiorari and reversed.

In *Bobby* the Supreme Court noted that collateral estoppel bars successive litigation of an issue of fact or law that is actually litigated and determined by a valid and final judgment, and is essential to the judgment. If a judgment does not depend on a given determination, relitigation of that determination is not precluded. In addition, *Bobby* said that even where the core requirements of collateral estoppel are met, an exception to the general rule may apply when a change in the applicable legal context intervenes. In finding that Ohio could hold a hearing to decide whether the defendant was mentally retarded, the opinion in *Bobby* stated:

> The Sixth Circuit, in common with the District Court, fundamentally misperceived the application of the Double Jeopardy Clause and its issue preclusion (collateral estoppel) component. First, [the defendant] was not "twice put in jeopardy." He was sentenced to death, and Ohio sought no further prosecution or punishment. Instead of serial prosecutions by the government[,] this case involves serial efforts by the defendant to vacate his capital sentence. Further, mental retardation for purposes of *Atkins*, and mental retardation as one mitigator to be weighed against aggravators, are discrete issues. [I]issue preclusion is a plea available to prevailing parties. The doctrine bars relitigation of determinations necessary to the ultimate outcome of a prior proceeding. The Ohio courts' recognition of [defendant's] mental state as a mitigating factor was hardly essential to the death sentence he received. On the contrary, the retardation evidence cut against the final judgment. Issue preclusion, in short, does not transform final judgment losers, in civil or criminal proceedings, into partially prevailing parties.

Mistrial

A trial judge is vested with the authority to grant a mistrial over the defendant's objection, and discharge a jury whenever in his or her opinion there is a manifest necessity for the mistrial. A retrial after a mistrial properly granted is not prohibited by double jeopardy principles. However, an improperly granted mistrial to which the defendant objected precludes a second prosecution for the same offense and acts as an acquittal.

In *Thompson v. United States*, 155 U.S. 271 (1894), the Supreme Court addressed the issue of whether the Double Jeopardy Clause bars a second capital prosecution when the trial judge declares a mistrial during the first trial. *Thompson* held that principles of double jeopardy did not prevent the retrial of a defendant after the trial court granted a mistrial of the first prosecution, when manifest necessity for the mistrial is shown. Specifically the following was said in *Thompson*:

> As to the question raised by the plea of former jeopardy ... courts of justice are invested with the authority to discharge a jury from giving any verdict whenever, in their opinion, taking all the circumstances into consideration, there is a manifest necessity for the act, or the ends of public justice would otherwise be defeated, and to order a trial by another jury; and that the defendant is not thereby twice put in jeopardy, within the meaning of the Fifth Amendment to the Constitution of the United States.

The Supreme Court, in *United States v. Perez*, 22 U.S. 579 (1824), observed that "the power [to declare a mistrial] ought to be used with the greatest caution, under urgent circumstances, and for very plain and obvious causes; and, in capital cases especially, Courts should be extremely careful how they interfere with any of the chances of life, in favor of the prisoner."

Executing a Defendant Twice for the Same Crime

The Double Jeopardy Clause generally prohibits punishing a defendant twice for the same offense. However, implementing the death penalty is not an exact science. Mistakes are made wherein a capital felon is not put to death after the method of death is inflicted. When this occurs, authorities may make a second or subsequent attempt at executing the capital felon. The crucial constitutional issue in making subsequent attempts to carry out an execution involves the reason for the initial failure. So long as the initial or any subsequent failure is due to an honest mistake, further attempts may ensue. The federal Constitution prohibits authorities from purposely tormenting a capital felon by intentionally botching an initial attempt at execution.

TABLE 3.0 MODERN DAY BOTCHED ELECTROCUTIONS

Inmate Name	Execution Date	Jurisdiction	Problem
Frank J. Coppola	October 10, 1982	Virginia	electrocuted twice
John Evans	April 22, 1983	Alabama	electrocuted twice
Alpha O. Stephens	December 12, 1984	Georgia	electrocuted twice
William E. Vandiver	October 16, 1985	Indiana	electrocuted thrice
Horace F. Dunkins	July 14, 1989	Alabama	electrocuted twice
Derick L. Peterson	August 22, 1991	Virginia	electrocuted twice

SOURCE: Louis J. Palmer, Jr., *Encyclopedia of Capital Punishment in the United States* (2008).

For example, in *Francis v. Resweber*, 329 U.S. 459 (1947), the defendant was electrocuted but did not die. The state of Louisiana sought to electrocute him a second time. The defendant presented three constitutional arguments as to why Louisiana should be prohibited from carrying out a second execution of him. The United States Supreme Court responded to and rejected the arguments as follows:

> First. Our minds rebel against permitting the same sovereignty to punish an accused twice for the same offense. But where the accused successfully seeks review of a conviction, there is no double jeopardy upon a new trial.... When an accident, with no suggestion of malevolence, prevents the consummation of a sentence, the state's subsequent course in the administration of its criminal law is not affected on that account by any requirement of due process under the Fourteenth Amendment. We find no double jeopardy here which can be said to amount to a denial of federal due process in the proposed execution.
>
> Second. We find nothing in what took place here which amounts to cruel and unusual punishment in the constitutional sense.... The traditional humanity of modern Anglo-American law forbids the infliction of unnecessary pain in the execution of the death sentence....
>
> Petitioner's suggestion is that because he once underwent the psychological strain of preparation for electrocution, now to require him to undergo this preparation again subjects him to a lingering or cruel and unusual punishment. Even the fact that petitioner has already been subjected to a current of electricity does not make his subsequent execution any more cruel in the constitutional sense than any other execution. The cruelty against which the Constitution protects a convicted man is cruelty inherent in the method of punishment, not the necessary suffering involved in any method employed to extinguish life humanely. The fact that an unforeseeable accident prevented the prompt consummation of the sentence cannot, it seems to us, add an element of cruelty to a subsequent execution. There is no purpose to inflict unnecessary pain nor any unnecessary pain involved in the proposed execution.... We cannot agree that the hardship imposed upon the petitioner rises to that level of hardship denounced as denial of due process because of cruelty.
>
> Third. The Supreme Court of Louisiana also rejected petitioner's contention that death inflicted after his prior sufferings would deny him the equal protection of the laws, guaranteed by the Fourteenth Amendment. This suggestion ... is based on the idea that execution, after an attempt at execution has failed, would be a more severe punishment than is imposed upon others guilty for a like offense. That is, since others do not go through the strain of preparation for execution a second time or have not experienced a non-lethal current in a prior attempt at execution, as petitioner did, to compel petitioner to submit to execution after these prior experiences denies to him equal protection. Equal protection does not protect a prisoner ... against accidents during his detention for execution. Laws cannot prevent accidents nor can a law equally protect all against them. So long as the law applies to all alike, the requirements of equal protection are met. We have no right to assume that Louisiana singled out Francis for a treatment other than that which has been or would generally be applied.

Louisiana successfully executed the defendant by electrocution on May 9, 1947.

Ex Post Facto

In Article I, Section 9 of the federal Constitution it is expressly stated that "[n]o ... ex post facto Law shall be passed." *Kring v. Missouri*, 107 U.S. 221 (1883), noted that there are four distinct classes of laws prohibited by the Ex Post Facto Clause: (1) every law that makes an action done before the passing of the law, and which was innocent when done, criminal, and punishes such action; (2) every law that aggravates the crime or makes it greater than it was when committed; (3) every law that changes the punishment and inflicts a greater punishment than was annexed to the crime when committed; and (4) every law that alters the legal rules of evidence, and receives less or different testimony than the law required at the time of the commission of the offense in order to convict the offender.[8]

A frequent issue raised in capital prosecutions involves changing the method of execution. Capital felons have contended that when the method of execution changes after the commission of their crimes, the Ex Post Facto Clause prevents the new method of execution from being applied to them. The argument is further extended by the assertion that since the initial method of execution was repealed, their executions cannot be carried out because no valid law exists stating the method of execution. Consistent with *Malloy v. South Carolina*, 237 U.S. 180 (1915), (allowing hanging to be replaced with electrocution), courts have unanimously rejected these arguments. Whatever method of execution is provided for by statute when it is time to execute a capital felon may be imposed regardless of when the method was authorized.

In *Dobbert v. Florida*, 432 U.S. 282 (1977), it was held that changes in Florida's death penalty laws could apply to the defendant, because the changes were only procedural. It was said in *Dobbert* that "[e]ven though it may work to the disadvantage of a defendant, a procedural change is not ex post facto." The decision in *Rooney v. North Dakota*, 196 U.S. 319 (1905), found that application of a new death penalty statute to the defendant did not violate ex post facto principles, because the new law only made minor procedural changes that did not adversely impact the defendant. The Supreme Court indicated in *Duncan v. Missouri*, 152 U.S. 377 (1894), that application to the defendant of changes in the appellate procedure of Missouri's high court did not violate ex post facto principles. *Holden v. Minnesota*, 137 U.S. 483 (1890), held that the Ex Post Facto Clause does not bar enforcement of a death penalty statute that was repealed and reenacted after the date of the defendant's crime, but does not alter the substantive law existing at the time of the crime. *McNulty v. California*, 149 U.S. 645 (1893), said that when the Ex Post Facto Clause prevents application of a new death penalty law, the repeal of the former death penalty procedure did not prevent the defendant from being executed according to the repealed law. It was said in *Thompson v. Missouri*, 171 U.S. 380 (1898), that application to the defendant of a new rule of evidence, admitting handwriting samples that was not the law at the time of his offense, did not violate ex post facto principles.

The Supreme Court held in *In re Medley*, 134 U.S. 160 (1890), that the defendant's conviction and sentence were invalid because he was prosecuted under a statute that was not in existence at the time of his crime. Although the changes in the law appeared to be procedural, the majority went out of its way to reverse the death sentence. The dissenting opinion in the case addressed the matter as follows:

> The substantial punishment imposed by each statute is death by hanging. The differences between the two, as to the manner in which this sentence of death shall be carried into execution, are trifling.... Yet, on account of these differences, a convicted murderer is to escape the death he deserves, and be turned loose in society.

Bill of Attainder Clause

In Article I, Section 9.3 of the federal Constitution it is expressly stated that "[n]o Bill of Attainder ... shall be passed." The Bill of Attainder Clause has been interpreted as prohibiting legislatures from enacting laws that impose capital punishment without any conviction within the ordinary course of a judicial proceeding.[9]

Capital felons have unsuccessfully argued that when jurisdictions enact legislation providing for alternative methods of execution, such laws violate the Bill of Attainder Clause. This argument has always been made in the context of a pending constitutional attack on the existing method of execution used by a jurisdiction. That is, capital felons contend that by enacting legislation creating an alternative method of execution while a capital felon has a pending challenge to the constitutionality of the existing method of execution, the new law effectively moots the pending constitutional challenge on the existing method of execution. Courts have consistently ruled that this reasoning stretches the meaning and intent of the Bill of Attainder Clause and, therefore, has been uniformly rejected.

Tried in Absentia

The federal Constitution guarantees every defendant the right to be present at criminal proceedings against him or her; this includes both the trial and sentencing.[10] It was observed by a dissenting judge in *Rice v. Wood*, 77 F.3d 1138 (9th Cir. 1996), that "[t]he pronouncement of the death sentence is the most solemn moment in the lives of both the jurors and the defendant; to say that the person facing death has no connection to the people and proceedings charged with deciding his fate is to say that we are no longer human." Of course, the right to be present during a trial does not prevent the prosecution of a defendant for capital murder or any crime, in absentia, so long as his or her absence was voluntary and for the purpose of evading prosecution.[11] For example, it was held in *Smith v. State*, 465 N.E.2d 1105 (Ind. 1984), that the defendant could not claim that he received ineffective assistance of counsel based on the fact that his counsel presented no evidence during death penalty phase of prosecution, because the defendant refused to be present during the death penalty phase of his trial and insisted on being tried in absentia during that phase.

Law of the Case Doctrine

The law of the case doctrine provides that when a court renders a decision on a legal issue in a case, the court will not revisit the issue previously decided by it, in any subsequent proceeding involving the case. Courts have recognized, in the context of capital punishment cases, a manifest injustice exception to the law of the case doctrine. Under this exception, a court is obligated to revisit an issue it previously decided in the case in order to prevent a manifest injustice from occurring.

The manifest injustice principle was applied in *Dobbs v. Zant*, 506 U.S. 357 (1993). The defendant in *Dobbs* was convicted and sentenced to death for capital murder by the state of Georgia. After the defendant exhausted his state post-conviction remedies, he filed a habeas corpus petition in a federal district court. In the habeas the defendant alleged ineffective assistance of counsel at the penalty phase of his trial. In rejecting the defendant's claim, the district court was forced to rely upon representations by defense counsel regarding his trial performance, because the penalty phase transcript was not available. A court of appeals affirmed the district court's decision.

After the court of appeals affirmed the denial of relief, the defendant located a transcript of the penalty phase hearing which contradicted defense counsel's account of what occurred at the proceeding. At the time of the discovery of the transcript, the court of appeals was reviewing another matter presented to it by the defendant. Consequently, the defendant motioned the court of appeals to supplement the appellate record with the transcript. The court of appeals denied his motion to supplement the appellate record with the transcript. The court of appeals reasoned that the "law of the case doctrine" prevented it from revisiting its prior rejection of the ineffective assistance claim. The United States Supreme Court granted certiorari to consider the issue.

The Supreme Court opinion held that the court of appeals erred by refusing to consider the sentencing hearing transcript. It was said that the transcript was no doubt relevant, because it called into serious question the factual predicate on which the lower courts relied in deciding the defendant's ineffective assistance claim. The Supreme Court rejected the assertion that the law of the case doctrine precluded the court of appeals from revisiting the issue. The manifest injustice exception to the law of the case doctrine allowed the court of appeals to revisit the issue.

4

Right to Counsel and
Right to Remain Silent

Two of the greatest components of Anglo-American criminal jurisprudence may be found in the constitutional right to counsel and the right to remain silent. These two rights are central to the integrity of the criminal justice system and to the continued acceptance of that system by the American people. The material that follows examines the broad federal constitutional guarantees of the right to counsel and the right to remain silent.

Right to Counsel

Under the common law of England a defendant charged with treason or other felony was denied the aid of counsel. At the same time, however, parties in civil cases and defendants accused of misdemeanors were entitled to the full assistance of counsel. After 1688 the rule was abolished as to treason, but was otherwise adhered to until 1836, when by act of the English Parliament the full right to counsel was granted with respect to felonies generally.[1]

The common law rule denying the right of counsel for felonies was rejected by the American colonies. Before the adoption of the federal Constitution, the constitution of Maryland had declared: "That, in all criminal prosecutions, every man hath a right ... to be allowed counsel[.]" The right to counsel provided by Maryland was adopted by other Colonies as follows: the constitution of Pennsylvania in 1776; the constitution of New York in 1777; the constitution of Massachusetts in 1780; and the constitution of New Hampshire in 1784.[2]

In the case of Pennsylvania, as early as 1701, the Penn Charter declared that "all Criminals shall have the same Privileges of Witnesses and Council as their Prosecutors." There was also a provision in the Pennsylvania statute of May 31, 1718, which provided that in capital cases counsel should be assigned to the prisoners. The 1776 constitution of New Jersey contained a provision like that of the Penn Charter, to the effect that all criminals should be admitted to the same privileges of counsel as their prosecutors.

In Delaware's constitution of 1776 it adopted the common law of England, but expressly excluded such parts as were repugnant to the rights and privileges contained in the Declaration of Rights. The Declaration of Rights, which was adopted on September 11, 1776, provided: "That in all Prosecutions for criminal Offences, every Man hath a Right ... to be allowed Counsel[.]"

North Carolina's constitution of 1776 did not contain the guaranty to counsel, but a statute provided: "That every person accused of any crime or misdemeanor whatsoever, shall be entitled to council in all matters which may be necessary for his defense, as well to facts as to law[.]" Similarly, the 1776 constitution of South Carolina did not contain a provision as to counsel, but it was provided as early as 1731 by statute that every person charged with treason, murder, felony, or other capital offense should be admitted to make full defense by counsel learned in the law. In Virginia there was no original constitutional provision on the subject of right to counsel, but as early as 1734, there was an act declaring that in all trials for capital offenses the prisoner, upon petition to the court, should be allowed counsel. In Connecticut's constitution of 1818 it provided that "in all criminal prosecutions, the accused shall have a right to be heard by himself and by counsel." However, it appears that the English common law rule had been rejected by Connecticut in practice prior to 1796. The 1777 constitution of Georgia did not contain a guarantee with respect to counsel, but its constitution of 1798 provided that "no person shall be debarred from advocating or defending his cause before any court or tribunal, either by himself or counsel, or both." The first constitution adopted by Rhode Island in 1842 contained the guaranty with respect to the assistance of counsel in criminal prosecutions. However, as early as 1798, Rhode Island provided by statute that "in all criminal prosecutions, the accused shall enjoy the right ... to have the assistance of counsel for his defence[.]"

The above cursory review of the right to counsel in the early history of the nation demonstrates "that in at least twelve of the thirteen colonies the rule of the English common law ... had been definitely rejected and the right to counsel fully recognized in all criminal prosecutions, save that in one or two instances the right was limited to capital offenses or to the more serious crimes[.]"[3]

Sixth Amendment Right to Counsel

The Sixth Amendment to the federal Constitution embodies the guarantee of the right to counsel. It is provided in the Sixth Amendment that: "In all criminal prosecutions, the accused shall ... have the Assistance of Counsel for his defence." The Supreme Court recognized in *Powell v. Alabama*, 287 U.S. 45 (1932), the constitutional right to counsel in capital cases as follows:

[W]e are of opinion that ... the necessity of counsel [in these capital cases] was so vital and imperative that the failure of the trial court to make an effective appointment of counsel was ... a denial of due process within the meaning of the Fourteenth Amendment. Whether this would be so in other criminal prosecutions, or under other circumstances, we need not determine. All that it is necessary now to decide, as we do decide, is that in a capital case, where the defendant is unable to employ counsel, and is incapable adequately of making his own defense because of ignorance, feeble mindedness, illiteracy, or the like, it is the duty of the court, whether requested or not, to assign counsel for him as a necessary requisite of due process of law; and that duty is not discharged by an assignment at such a time or under such circumstances as to preclude the giving of effective aid in the preparation and trial of the case. To hold otherwise would be to ignore the fundamental postulate, already adverted to, that there are certain immutable principles of justice which inhere in the very idea of free government which no member of the Union may disregard. In a case such as this, whatever may be the rule in other cases, the right to have counsel appointed, when necessary, is a logical corollary from the constitutional right to be heard by counsel.

The constitutional right to counsel in capital cases means that, if a capital defendant cannot afford to retain counsel, the prosecuting jurisdiction must appoint an attorney to represent the defendant.

Thirty years after *Powell* the right to counsel was extended to all criminal proceedings when incarceration was possible. The Supreme Court imposed the broad right to counsel upon states in the case of *Gideon v. Wainwright*, 372 U.S. 335 (1963). *Gideon* reasoned as follows:

> [R]eason and reflection require us to recognize that in our adversary system of criminal justice, any person hauled into court, who is too poor to hire a lawyer, cannot be assured a fair trial unless counsel is provided for him. This seems to us to be an obvious truth. Governments, both state and federal, quite properly spend vast sums of money to establish machinery to try defendants accused of crime. Lawyers to prosecute are everywhere deemed essential to protect the public's interest in an orderly society. Similarly, there are few defendants charged with crime, few indeed, who fail to hire the best lawyers they can get to prepare and present their defenses. That government hires lawyers to prosecute and defendants who have the money hire lawyers to defend are the strongest indications of the widespread belief that lawyers in criminal courts are necessities, not luxuries. The right of one charged with crime to counsel may not be deemed fundamental and essential to fair trials in some countries, but it is in ours. From the very beginning, our state and national constitutions and laws have laid great emphasis on procedural and substantive safeguards designed to assure fair trials before impartial tribunals in which every defendant stands equal before the law. This noble ideal cannot be realized if the poor man charged with crime has to face his accusers without a lawyer to assist him. A defendant's need for a lawyer is nowhere better stated than in the moving words of Justice Sutherland in *Powell* v. *Alabama*:
>
> > The right to be heard would be, in many cases, of little avail if it did not comprehend the right to be heard by counsel. Even the intelligent and educated layman has small and sometimes no skill in the science of law. If charged with crime, he is incapable, generally, of determining for himself whether the indictment is good or bad. He is unfamiliar with the rules of evidence. Left without the aid of counsel he may be put on trial without a proper charge, and convicted upon incompetent evidence, or evidence irrelevant to the issue or otherwise inadmissible. He lacks both the skill and knowledge adequately to prepare his defense, even though he has a perfect one. He requires the guiding hand of counsel at every step in the proceedings against him. Without it, though he be not guilty, he faces the danger of conviction because he does not know how to establish his innocence.

The decision in *Gideon* held that the Sixth Amendment required indigent criminal defendants be provided with legal counsel paid for by the government. The right to counsel extends to trial proceedings and a first appeal of right. The constitutional right to counsel does not extend to post-conviction habeas proceedings.[4] In *Murray v. Giarratano*, 492 U.S. 1 (1989), the Supreme Court held that neither the Eighth Amendment nor the Due Process Clause requires states to appoint counsel for indigent death row inmates seeking state habeas relief.

Court Appointed Counsel

An indigent capital defendant's right to court appointed counsel does not mean that he or she will have competent counsel. Studies have shown that one of the primary factors that determine whether a capital defendant will receive the death penalty is the nature of the legal representation, i.e., court appointed counsel or retained counsel.[5] A defendant convicted of a capital offense will, more likely than not, receive a death sentence if he or she is represented by court appointed counsel. On the other hand, studies have shown that a defendant convicted of a capital offense, but represented by retained counsel, will more likely than not receive a life sentence.[6]

It is unquestioned that capital prosecutions present the most difficult criminal cases to defend. Capital prosecutions are more complex than any noncapital prosecution. As a result of the complexity of a capital prosecution, it is imperative that experienced counsel represent a capital felon and that adequate financial resources be made available for the defense. All studies that have evaluated capital prosecutions concluded that inexperienced counsel and inadequate financial resources were the norm. This situation exists because the overwhelming majority of capital defendants are poor and must obtain court appointed counsel.[7]

In a study done of Mississippi court appointed attorneys, it was found that 83 percent of the attorneys appointed in capital cases indicated they would refuse any subsequent appointment because of inadequate financial resources. It is generally recognized that a properly conducted capital trial should take a month or more to complete. A random sampling of capital trials in Louisiana for the period 1978–1987 revealed the average length of a trial was three days. Another study of Louisiana revealed that in 85 percent of the capital trials held between 1976–1994, defense counsel failed to present the type of mitigating evidence during the penalty phase that is essential for obtaining a life sentence.

A few capital punishment jurisdictions have begun to address the problem of inexperienced counsel and inadequate financial resources. Statutes and court rules have been promulgated in a few capital punishment jurisdictions that require legal counsel to have a minimum number of years of experience, and which make available greater financial resources.[8]

Right to Effective Assistance of Counsel

The Sixth Amendment right to counsel carries with it the right to have effective assistance of counsel. In *Strickland v. Washington*, 466 U.S. 668 (1984), the Supreme Court outlined the test for determining whether a defendant received effective assistance of counsel.[9] *Strickland* held that a convicted defendant's claim that defense counsel's assistance was so defective as to require reversal of a capital conviction or setting aside of a death sentence requires that the defendant show: (1) that defense counsel's performance was deficient and (2) that the deficient performance prejudiced the defense so as to deprive the defendant of a fair trial or sentencing. Failure to make the required showing of either deficient performance or sufficient prejudice defeats the ineffectiveness claim. Contemporary assessment of defense counsel's conduct is used when determining the deficient performance component of the test; the prejudice component is not dependent upon analysis under the law existing at the time of the deficient performance.[10] For example, *Burger v. Kemp*, 483 U.S. 776 (1987), it was held that the defendant failed to show that his counsel's decision not to put on the sparse available mitigating evidence was an unreasonable decision. In *Florida v. Nixon*, 543 U.S. 175 (2004), it was held that counsel was not ineffective by conceding defendant's guilt. In *Mickens v. Taylor*, 535 U.S. 162 (2002), it was said that a trial judge who knows or should know that a defendant's attorney has a conflict of interest must find that the conflict adversely affected counsel's performance before a defendant is entitled to a new trial.

In *Bell v. Cone*, 535 U.S. 685 (2002), it was noted that there are only a few situations in which a presumption of prejudice arises in a claim of ineffective assistance of counsel. For example, a trial would be presumptively unfair where the accused is denied the presence of counsel at a critical stage, or where counsel is called upon to render assistance under circumstances where competent counsel very likely could not. *Bell* found that no presumption of prejudice arises merely because counsel did not put on specific types of mitigating evidence and waived the right to closing argument.

Lockhart v. Fretwell, 506 U.S. 364 (1993), stated that because the law which formed the basis of the defendant's ineffective assistance claim was overruled, so that the complained of deficient performance of his counsel no longer existed, the defendant suffered no prejudice from the deficient performance within the meaning of Strickland. The Supreme Court found the defendant was not prejudiced by counsel's performance in *Woodford v. Visciotti*, 537 U.S. 19 (2002), *Wong v. Belmontes*, 130 S.Ct. 383 (2009), *Bobby v. Van Hook*, 130 S.Ct. 13 (2009), and *Cullen v. Pinholster*, 131 S.Ct. 1388 (2011).

It was held in *Coleman v. Thompson*, 501 U.S. 722 (1991), that an attorney's errors in a state habeas proceeding did not qualify as cause for procedural default of the errors in a federal habeas proceeding. However, in the noncapital punishment case of *Martinez v. Ryan*, 132 S.Ct. 1309 (2012), the Supreme Court qualified *Coleman*. It was said in *Martinez* that ineffective assistance of counsel at a state habeas proceeding may establish cause for a prisoner's procedural default of a claim of ineffective assistance of counsel at trial.

Competency of the defendant to be a witness. The disqualification of a defendant as a witness in his or her own trial characterized a common law principle for centuries. The remote origins of this principle are traced to the contest for judicial hegemony between the developing common law jury trial and the older modes of trial such as compurgation and wager of law. Under those old forms, a defendant's oath itself was a means of decision in a case. The jury trial replaced judgment by oath, with judgment of the jury based upon the testimony of witnesses. A result of this change was that a defendant was deemed incapable of being a witness at his or her trial. In time the principal justification for the rule was the potential untrustworthiness of the defendant's testimony.

By the sixteenth century it became necessary for a defendant to conduct his or her own defense; a defendant was neither allowed to call witnesses nor permitted the assistance of counsel. In the seventeenth century rules changed and a defendant was permitted to call witnesses in his or her behalf. The common law drew a distinction between the accused and his or her witnesses — the defendant's witnesses gave evidence, but the defendant did not.

Disqualification for interest was entrenched in the common law when the United States was formed. The early courts in America followed the common law and held that defendants were deemed incompetent as witnesses in their own trial. The greatest negative impact of the disqualification rule was manifested in capital prosecutions, where defendants could not testify to their own defense. Legal historians believe the disqualification rule resulted in countless death sentences being imposed on innocent defendants.

In the early nineteenth century American courts began to abandon the disqualification rule. In 1859 Maine created the first statute to permit a defendant to give sworn evidence in the trial of a few crimes. Maine followed in 1864 with a general competency statute for criminal defendants. Within 20 years most of the states had followed Maine's lead. Before the end of the century every state except Georgia had abolished the common law disqualification rule. Georgia retained the rule well into the 1960s.

Georgia's retention of the incompetency rule was taken up by the Supreme Court in *Ferguson v. Georgia*, 365 U.S. 570 (1961). In that case the state of Georgia charged the defendant with capital murder. At the time, Georgia had a statute which prohibited defendants from testifying in their own behalf. Defendants could only offer unsworn written statements. During the defendant's trial defense counsel called the defendant as a witness to give oral unsworn testimony, but the trial court precluded the defendant from actually testifying. The jury convicted the defendant and sentenced him to death. The United States Supreme Court granted certiorari to consider the issue of the denial of the defendant's right to testify.

Ferguson observed that Georgia was the only state to retain the common law rule that a person charged with a criminal offense was incompetent to testify under oath in his or her own behalf at his or her trial. It was said that Georgia had two distinct disqualification rules. Under one rule a defendant could not give testimony under oath. Under the second rule, a defendant could give a written unsworn statement, but could not give live unsworn testimony. During the defendant's trial he sought to testify under the rule regarding unsworn statements.

Because the defendant invoked the unsworn statement rule, the Court in *Ferguson* did not believe it had jurisdiction to render a decision on the constitutionality of Georgia's rule which prohibited sworn testimony by a defendant. The opinion, therefore, limited its holding to the second rule. The Supreme Court held that the part of the Georgia statute which denied the defendant the right to give live "unsworn" testimony and to be questioned by his counsel also denied the defendant his constitutional right to effective assistance of his counsel.

Right to Self-Representation

The constitutional right to counsel carries with it the right of self-representation. This right was first recognized by the Supreme Court in the case of *Faretta v. California*, 422 U.S. 806 (1975). The *Faretta* right, as it is called, may be exercised by a defendant charged with a capital offense. A capital defendant may waive his or her right to counsel and represent himself or herself.[11] The *Faretta* right is not absolute. It was held in *Godinez v. Moran*, 509 U.S. 389 (1993), that the competency standard for waiving the right to counsel is whether the defendant has sufficient present ability to consult with his or her lawyer with a reasonable degree of rational understanding, and a rational as well as factual understanding of the proceedings against him or her. Even when a trial court determines that a defendant is competent to waive the right to counsel and represent him/herself, the court may still appoint "standby" counsel for the defendant to consult with as needed.[12] Courts unanimously agree that a defendant who represents him/herself cannot raise, on appeal, the issue of ineffective assistance of counsel. Some cases have permitted defendants who have utilized stand-by counsel to raise an ineffective assistance of counsel claim on issues that the stand-by counsel was consulted on.

Right to Remain Silent

The Fifth Amendment guarantees the right against self-incrimination. This constitutional provision provides that: "No person ... shall be compelled in any criminal case to be a witness against himself." In *Jackson v. Denno*, 378 U.S. 368 (1964), the Supreme Court held that the voluntariness of a confession should be determined by the trial judge and not a jury.

In Court Silence

The right to remain silent is an expansive right. During a criminal trial the right to remain silent permits a defendant to sit mute during the trial. That is, a defendant cannot be compelled to testify against him/herself. Part of the protection of the constitutional right to remain silent is that the failure of a defendant to testify in his or her own defense does not create any presumption against the defendant. If a defendant chooses not to testify at trial, no comment or argument about his or her failure to testify is permitted. In *Stewart v. United States*, 366 U.S. 1 (1961), it was held that it was constitutional error for the trial court to deny the defendant's request for a mistrial after the prosecutor informed the jury the defendant did not testify at his first two trials.[13]

A defendant's right not to be compelled to testify in a court proceeding is qualified. If a trial court grants the defendant immunity from prosecution, he or she may be compelled to testify or may be subject to being held in contempt of court. In *Hardy v. United States*, 186 U.S. 224 (1902), it was held that incriminating statements made by the defendant to a magistrate during a preliminary hearing were admissible at trial, because the statements were voluntary and made after the defendant was warned against making any statements. The decision in *Thomas v. Arizona*, 356 U.S. 390 (1958), found that the defendant's confession, given before a justice of the peace, was voluntary.

Out of Court Silence

In addition to a defendant's right to remain silent in court, he or she also has a right not to be forced or tricked into making incriminating statements by government officials outside of a courtroom. For example, in *Bram v. United States*, 168 U.S. 532 (1897), it was held that the defendant's confession was not voluntarily given, even though physical force was not used against him, as it was enough that he was in a situation that precluded him from exercising free will. The decision in *Fikes v. Alabama*, 352 U.S. 191 (1957), held that the defendant's confession was involuntary based upon long periods of isolation, even though no physical force was used against him. *Sims v. Georgia*, 389 U.S. 404 (1967), held that the defendant established that his confession was the product of physical violence. The Supreme Court held in *Leyra v. Denno*, 347 U.S. 556 (1954), that the initial involuntary confession by the defendant tainted subsequent confessions, so as to preclude their use against the defendant. The convictions and death sentences in *Malinski v. New York*, 324 U.S. 401 (1945), *Harris v. South Carolina*, 338 U.S. 68 (1949), *Turner v. Pennsylvania*, 338 U.S. 62 (1949), *Watts v. Indiana*, 338 U.S. 49 (1949), *Payne v. Arkansas*, 356 U.S. 560 (1958), *Spano v. New York*, 360 U.S. 315 (1959), and *Rogers v. Rishmond*, 365 U.S. 534 (1961), were reversed because the confessions were not voluntary.

In *Lisenba v. California*, 314 U.S. 219 (1941), the Supreme Court held that the defendant's confessions were not obtained or used in violation of the Constitution, even though the police used tactics that came close to the line of being constitutionally unacceptable. The decision in *Stroble v. California*, 343 U.S. 181 (1952), also found that the defendant's confession was not shown to be involuntary.

A case which illustrates the use of extreme measures to extract an involuntary confession is *Ziang v. United States*, 266 U.S. 1 (1924). The defendant, Sung Wan Ziang, was convicted of capital murder and sentenced to death by the District of Columbia. On appeal, the District of Columbia Court of Appeals affirmed the judgment. In doing so, the appellate court rejected the defendant's argument that his confession and incriminating statements were obtained illegally. The United States Supreme Court granted certiorari to consider the issue. The Supreme Court found that defendant's confession and incriminating statements were involuntary. In granting the defendant a new trial, the Court gave the following account of how the confession and incriminating statements came about:

> [T]he detectives took [the defendant] to Hotel Dewey; and, without entering his name in the hotel registry, placed him in a bedroom on an upper floor. In that room he was detained continuously one week. Throughout the period, he was sick and, most of the time, in bed. A physician was repeatedly called. It was a police surgeon who came. In vain [the defendant] asked to see his brother, with whom he lived in New York, who had nursed him in his illness, who had come to Washington at his request in January, who had returned with him to New York, and whom, as he later learned, the detectives had also brought to Washington, were detaining in another room of the hotel, and were subjecting to like interrogation.

> [The defendant] was held in the hotel room without formal arrest, incommunicado. But he was not left alone. Every moment of the day, and of the night, at least one member of the police force was on guard inside his room. Three ordinary policemen were assigned to this duty. Each served eight hours; the shifts beginning at midnight, at 8 in the morning, and at 4 in the afternoon. Morning, afternoon, and evening (and at least on one occasion after midnight) the prisoner was visited by the superintendent of police and/or one or more of the detectives. The sole purpose of these visits was to interrogate him. Regardless of [the defendant's] wishes and protest, his condition of health, or the hour, they engaged him in conversation. He was subjected to persistent, lengthy, and repeated cross-examination. Sometimes it was subtle, sometimes severe. Always the examination was conducted with a view to entrapping [the defendant] into a confession of his own guilt and/or that of his brother. Whenever these visitors entered the room, the guard was stationed outside the closed door.

> On the eighth day, the accusatory questioning took a more excruciating form. A detective was in attendance throughout the day. In the evening, [the defendant] was taken from Hotel Dewey to [the crime scene]. There, continuously for ten hours, this sick man was led from floor to floor minutely to examine and re-examine the scene....

> On the ninth day, at 20 minutes past 5 in the morning, [the defendant] was taken ... to the station house and placed formally under arrest. There the interrogation was promptly resumed. Again the detectives were in attendance, day and evening, plying their questions, pointing out alleged contradictions, arguing with the prisoner, and urging him to confess, lest his brother be deemed guilty of the crime. Still the statements secured failed to satisfy the detectives' craving for evidence. On the tenth day, [the defendant] was bundled up, was again taken to the [crime scene and], was again questioned there for hours.... On the eleventh day, a formal interrogation of [the defendant] was conducted at the station house by the detectives in the presence of a stenographer. On the twelfth day, the verbatim typewritten report of the interrogation (which occupies 12 pages of the printed record) was read to [the defendant], in his cell at the jail. There he signed the report and initialed each page. On the thirteenth day, for the first time, [the defendant] was visited by the chief medical officer of the jail, in the performance of his duties.

The Miranda ruling. In the case of *Miranda v. Arizona*, 384 U.S. 436 (1966), the Supreme Court held that a suspect who has been formally arrested must be warned prior to any questioning (1) that he or she has the right to remain silent, (2) that anything he or she says can be used against him or her in a court of law, (3) that he or she has the right to the presence of an attorney, and (4) that if he or she cannot afford an attorney one will be appointed for him or her prior to any questioning if he or she so desires. After *Miranda* warnings have been given, a suspect may knowingly and intelligently waive these rights and agree to answer questions or make a statement. However, unless and until such warnings and waiver are demonstrated by the prosecution, no evidence obtained as a result of interrogation can be used against a suspect. The voluntariness of a confession or incriminating statements must be determined by the trial judge and may not be submitted to the jury for determination. In *Texas v. Cobb*, 532 U.S. 162 (2001), it was held that a defendant represented by counsel on a burglary charge may unilaterally waive his *Miranda* rights with respect to a charge for capital murder that occurred during the burglary.

It was noted in *Bobby v. Dixon*, 132 S.Ct. 26 (2011), that if a defendant is not in custody then *Miranda* and its progeny do not apply. In determining whether an individual was in custody, for Fifth Amendment purposes, a court must examine all of the circumstances surrounding the interrogation, but the ultimate inquiry is simply whether there was a formal arrest or restraint on freedom of movement of the degree associated with a formal arrest. In *Stansbury v. California*, 511 U.S. 318 (1994), it was held that the initial determination of custody depends on the objective circumstances of the interrogation, not on the subjective views harbored by either the interrogating officers or the person being questioned. A police officer's subjective view that the individual under questioning is a suspect, if undisclosed, does not bear upon the question of whether the individual is in custody for purposes of *Miranda*.

An officer's knowledge or beliefs may bear upon the custody issue if they are conveyed, by word or deed, to the individual being questioned. Those beliefs are relevant only to the extent they would affect how a reasonable person in the position of the individual being questioned would gauge the breadth of his or her freedom of action. Even a clear statement from an officer that the person under interrogation is a prime suspect is not, in itself, dispositive of the custody issue. The weight and pertinence of any communications regarding the officer's degree of suspicion will depend upon the facts and circumstances of the particular case. In sum, an officer's views concerning the nature of an interrogation, or beliefs concerning the potential culpability of the individual being questioned, may be one among many factors that bear upon the assessment of whether that individual was in custody, but only if the officer's views or beliefs were somehow manifested to the individual under interrogation and would have affected how a reasonable person in that position would perceive his or her freedom to leave.[14]

In *Montejo v. Louisiana*, 556 U.S. 778 (2009), the Supreme Court overruled its decision in *Michigan v. Jackson*, 475 U.S. 625 (1986), which had held that if the police initiate interrogation of a defendant after he or she asserts, at an arraignment or similar proceeding, his or her right to counsel, any waiver of the defendant's right to counsel for that interrogation is presumed invalid. *Montejo* held instead that when a court appoints counsel for an indigent defendant in the absence of any request on his or her part, there is no basis for a presumption that any subsequent waiver of the right to counsel will be involuntary. The opinion stated that no reason exists to assume that a defendant who has done nothing at all to express his or her intentions with respect to the right to counsel would not be perfectly amenable to speaking with the police without having counsel present.

The prophylactic safeguards of *Miranda* have been extended to pretrial court ordered psychiatric examinations of defendants charged with capital offenses.[15] This issue was first addressed by the Supreme Court in *Estelle v. Smith*, 451 U.S. 454 (1981). In that case the defendant was indicted in Texas for capital murder. Prior to trial the judge ordered a psychiatric examination to determine the defendant's competency to stand trial. A psychiatrist conducted the examination at the jail where the defendant was being held and determined that the defendant was competent. Thereafter, the defendant was tried by a jury and convicted of capital murder. One of the statutory issues the penalty phase jury had to resolve was the future dangerousness of the defendant, i.e., whether there was a probability that he would commit criminal acts of violence that would constitute a continuing threat to society. At the sentencing hearing, the doctor who had conducted the pretrial psychiatric examination was allowed to testify for the prosecutor over defense counsel's objection. The doctor testified that the defendant would be a danger to society. The jury then returned a sentence of death. After the defendant's direct appeal failed, he filed a federal habeas corpus petition. A federal district court vacated the death sentence because it found constitutional error in admitting the doctor's testimony at the penalty phase. A court of appeals affirmed. The United States Supreme Court granted certiorari to consider the issue.

The Supreme Court held in *Estelle* that the defendant was not advised before the pretrial psychiatric examination that he had a right to remain silent, and that any statement he made could be used against him at a capital sentencing proceeding. The opinion held that there was no basis for distinguishing between the guilt and penalty phases of the defendant's trial, so far as the protection of the Fifth Amendment privilege was concerned. It was said that the prosecutor's attempt to establish the defendant's future dangerousness, by relying on the unwarned statements the defendant made to the examining doctor, infringed the Fifth Amendment just as much as would have any effort to compel the defendant to testify against his will at the sentencing hearing.

It was further held in *Estelle* that merely because the defendant's statements were made in the context of a psychiatric examination, this did not automatically remove them from the reach of the Fifth Amendment. The opinion reasoned that the considerations calling for the accused to be warned prior to custodial interrogation apply with no less force to a pretrial psychiatric examination. The opinion ruled that an accused that neither initiated a psychiatric evaluation nor attempted to introduce any psychiatric evidence may not be compelled to respond to a psychiatrist if his or her statements can be used against him or her at a capital sentencing proceeding. When faced with a court ordered psychiatric inquiry, the defendant's statements to the doctor were not given freely and voluntarily without any compelling influences and, as such, could only be used by the prosecutor at the penalty phase if the defendant had been apprised of his rights and had freely and knowingly decided to waive them.

The decision in *Estelle* was applied in *Satterwhite v. Texas*, 486 U.S. 249 (1988) (death sentence reversed), and *Powell v. Texas*, 492 U.S. 680 (1989) (death sentenced reversed).

Courts have ruled that the inherent unreliability of an involuntary confession requires its exclusion from the penalty phase of a capital prosecution as a proffered non-statutory aggravating circumstance. The exclusion of such evidence is not diminished by the mere fact that a capital felon pled guilty to the crimes related to the confessions.

5

Capital Felon's Defense Team

In the case of *Rompilla v. Beard*, 545 U.S. 374 (2005), the Supreme Court held that even though defense counsel believes no mitigating evidence exists to present during the penalty phase of a capital prosecution, defense counsel is still "bound to make reasonable efforts to obtain and review material that counsel knows the prosecution will probably rely on as evidence of aggravation at the sentencing phase of trial." The Court in *Rompilla* reversed the defendant's death sentence on the grounds that his trial attorneys failed to reasonably investigate areas that could have revealed mitigating penalty phase evidence. The opinion in the case addressed these areas as follows:

> When new counsel entered the case to raise Rompilla's postconviction claims ... they identified a number of likely avenues the trial lawyers could fruitfully have followed in building a mitigation case. School records are one example, which trial counsel never examined in spite of the professed unfamiliarity of the several family members with Rompilla's childhood, and despite counsel's knowledge that Rompilla left school after the ninth grade. Other examples are records of Rompilla's juvenile and adult incarcerations, which counsel did not consult, although they were aware of their client's criminal record. And while counsel knew from police reports provided in pretrial discovery that Rompilla had been drinking heavily at the time of his offense, and although one of the mental health experts reported that Rompilla's troubles with alcohol merited further investigation, counsel did not look for evidence of a history of dependence on alcohol that might have extenuating significance.

The decision in *Rompilla* provides an example of the complexity of defending a person charged with a capital offense. One of the factors that make a capital prosecution extremely difficult is the fact that it is composed of two trials — the guilt phase trial and the penalty phase trial. As a result of the dual trials (and other reasons) that make up a capital prosecution, the American Bar Association (ABA) promulgated the *Guidelines for the Appointment and Performance of Defense Counsel in Death Penalty Cases*. The *Guidelines* recommend that every defendant charged with a capital offense be represented by a defense team that consists of no fewer than two attorneys, an investigator, mitigation specialist, and a mental health evaluator.[1]

This chapter explores some of the components of a capital felon's defense team. In reviewing this material it should be kept in mind that the unique facts of every capital prosecution will dictate what type of expert services are needed, e.g., DNA expert, ballistic expert, fingerprint expert, or others. A defendant must show a "particularized need" for the appointment of an expert. To prove "particularized need" a defendant must establish that he or she cannot receive a fair trial without the expert's assistance and that there exists a reasonable likelihood that the expert will materially assist preparation of the defense.[2]

Defense Attorneys

It should be clearly understood that "[t]here is no constitutional right per se to the appointment of co-counsel in a capital case."[3] Even so, as was previously mentioned, the ABA *Guidelines* recommend that every capital felon be represented by at least two attorneys. The *Guidelines* suggest that the legal representation should be broken down into a lead counsel and co-counsel. Both attorneys should have meaningful criminal defense experience. The *Guidelines* indicate that lead counsel has overall responsibility for the performance of the defense team. Lead counsel should allocate, direct, and supervise the work.[4] Many capital punishment jurisdictions have set out specific qualifications for attorneys appointed to represent capital felons. The material below involving Arizona provides an example of how some jurisdictions have attempted to insure that capital felons obtain competent legal representation.

Arizona Rule 6.8.
Standards for Appointment and Performance of Counsel in Capital Cases
    a. General. To be eligible for appointment in a capital case, an attorney
        (1) Shall have been a member in good standing of the State Bar of Arizona for at least five years immediately preceding the appointment;
        (2) Shall have practiced in the area of state criminal litigation for three years immediately preceding the appointment; and
        (3) Shall have demonstrated the necessary proficiency and commitment which exemplify the quality of representation appropriate to capital cases.
    b. Trial Counsel.
        (1) Lead counsel. To be eligible for appointment as lead counsel, an attorney must meet the qualifications set forth in section (a) of this rule and the following:
            (i) Shall have practiced in the area of state criminal litigation for five years immediately preceding the appointment;
            (ii) Shall have been lead counsel in at least nine felony jury trials that were tried to completion and have been lead counsel or co-counsel in at least one capital murder jury trial;
            (iii) Shall be familiar with and guided by the performance standards in the 2003 American Bar Association *Guidelines for the Appointment and Performance of Defense Counsel in Death Penalty Cases*; and
            (iv) Shall have attended and successfully completed, within one year prior to the initial appointment, at least six hours of relevant training or educational programs in the area of capital defense, and within one year prior to any subsequent appointment, at least twelve hours of relevant training or educational programs in the area of criminal defense.
        (2) Co-counsel. To be eligible for appointment as co-counsel, an attorney must be a member in good standing of the State Bar of Arizona and shall have attended and successfully completed, within one year prior to the initial appointment, at least six hours of relevant training or educational programs in the area of capital defense, and within one year prior to any subsequent appointment, at least twelve hours of relevant training or educational programs in the area of criminal defense. Section (b)(1)(iii) applies to co-counsel.
    c. Appellate and Post-conviction Counsel. To be eligible for appointment as appellate or post-conviction counsel, an attorney must meet the qualifications set forth in section (a) of this rule and the following:
        (1) Within three years immediately preceding the appointment have been lead counsel in an appeal or post-conviction proceeding in a case in which a death sentence was imposed, as well as prior experience as lead counsel in the appeal of at least three felony convictions and at

least one post-conviction proceeding that resulted in an evidentiary hearing. Alternatively, an attorney must have been lead counsel in the appeal of at least six felony convictions, at least two of which were appeals from first or second degree murder convictions, and lead counsel in at least two post-conviction proceedings that resulted in evidentiary hearings.

(2) Have attended and successfully completed, within one year prior to the initial appointment, at least six hours of relevant training or educational programs in the area of capital defense, and within one year prior to any subsequent appointment, at least twelve hours of relevant training or educational programs in the area of criminal defense.

(3) Shall be familiar with and guided by the performance standards in the 2003 American Bar Association *Guidelines for the Appointment and Performance of Defense Counsel in Death Penalty Cases.*

d. Exceptional Circumstances. In exceptional circumstances and with the consent of the Supreme Court, an attorney may be appointed who does not meet the qualifications set forth in sections (a)(1) and (2), (b) and (c) of this rule, providing that the attorney's experience, stature and record enable the Court to conclude that the attorney's ability significantly exceeds the standards set forth in this rule and that the attorney associates with himself or herself a lawyer who does meet the standards set forth in this rule. Section (b)(1)(iii) and (c)(3) shall apply to attorneys appointed under this section.

Investigator

The defense of any capital felon will depend greatly upon the "nuts-and-bolts" pretrial investigation of potential witnesses, including fact and character witnesses, and other evidence gathering.[5] The ABA has suggested that in capital punishment cases these duties should be handled by a specially trained investigator.[6] The role of the investigator should be viewed broadly so as to encompass seeking out evidence specifically designed to counter evidence the prosecutor intends to use during both the guilt phase and penalty phase.[7]

An investigator should be used to ferret out all exculpatory and/or mitigating evidence regardless of any admission by the defendant concerning the facts of the crime. Under the ABA's *Guidelines* such an investigation should occur even when the defendant indicates that evidence bearing upon guilt or punishment should not to be collected or presented.

The decision in *Williams v. Taylor*, 529 U.S. 362 (2000), illustrates the importance of employing an investigator in capital prosecutions. The defendant in *Williams* was sentenced to death by a Virginia jury for a murder committed in 1985. The United States Supreme Court reversed the death sentence in a habeas corpus appeal in 2000. The Supreme Court reversed the death sentence because the defendant's trial counsel failed to perform an investigation to uncover and present evidence for the defendant during the penalty phase. The evidence defense counsel failed to investigate included the abuse the defendant suffered as a child from his parents, and that the defendant was borderline mentally retarded.

Mitigation Specialist

In *Wiggins v. Smith*, 539 U.S. 510 (2003), the Supreme Court observed that the ABA *Guidelines* provide that investigations into mitigating evidence "should comprise efforts to discover *all reasonably available* mitigating evidence and evidence to rebut any aggravating evidence that may be introduced by the prosecutor."[8] In this regard the ABA *Guidelines* suggest that a capital defense team employ a mitigation specialist.[9] "The commentary to ... the ABA *Guidelines* explains the role of a mitigation specialist, calling this person 'an indispensable member of the defense team throughout all capital proceedings' and stating that '[m]itigation specialists possess clinical and information-gathering skills and training that most lawyers simply do not have.'"[10]

It has been noted that "[m]itigation specialists serve to fill the significant blind spot [that] existed between the roles played by the private investigator and the psychiatrist, the two standard information-getters in the trial process."[11] The Court in *Burns v. State*, 2005 WL 3504990 (Tenn.Crim.App.), described the role of the mitigation specialist as follows:

> The primary role of the mitigation specialist is to assist the attorney by conducting a comprehensive social history evaluation of the client. Other roles that the mitigation expert may play are to educate the attorneys about areas concerning mental health issues, issues of working with impaired clients and their family members and individuals who know them and have information about them, working with developing a team that's going to be best suited for the needs of the client, [and] conducting research into special topics.[12]

There is no specific educational background required for a person to be a mitigation specialist. This specialist may have a professional background that includes prior work as a mental health professional, social worker, lawyer, probation officer, private investigator, journalist, etc. The task of a mitigation specialist is to uncover detailed information about the defendant from his or her family, friends, employers, teachers, and anyone else who has had relevant contact with the defendant. This information is gathered in order to construct a compelling mitigating life story of the defendant that can be used in working out a plea deal or during the penalty phase. In addition, the mitigation specialist can be instrumental in identifying the need for expert assistance and in locating appropriate experts.[13] It has been suggested "that the average number of hours needed to complete a mitigation investigation is ideally between 2,500 and 5,000[;] but as a practical matter between 1,000 and 1,500 hours ... begins to approach a competent test and reliability."[14]

The Sixth Circuit Court of Appeals reversed the death sentence of the defendant in *Jells v. Mitchell*, 538 F.3d 478 (6th Cir. 2008), in part because defense counsel failed to employ a mitigation specialist. The *Jells* court held:

> We ... conclude that Jells's counsel were ineffective in failing to use a mitigation specialist who would have gathered information about Jells's educational, medical, psychological, and social background necessary to prepare a proper mitigation defense. In a post-conviction affidavit, Dr. Susan Shorr, a mitigation specialist for the Cuyahoga County Public Defender's Office, stated that Jells's trial counsel initially requested her assistance but "never followed through on their request by formally involving [her] in the case." Had her assistance—which she was willing to give—been obtained, she would have gathered evidence pertaining to Jells's developmental experiences, family dynamics and functioning, academic capacities and concomitant academic success or failure, interpersonal relationships and social adjustments, history of drug and alcohol abuse, and general psychological functioning....
>
> Jells's counsel failed to fulfill their duty to investigate Jells's background prior to the mitigation hearing. That Jells's counsel conducted some investigation of Jells's background is evident from their limited presentation during the mitigation hearing of Jells's unstable childhood and academic difficulties. However, while counsel generally has the discretion to determine that further investigation into available mitigating evidence is unnecessary, counsel's awareness of Jells's unstable home environment and academic difficulties should have alerted them that further investigation by a mitigation specialist might proved fruitful.

Mental Health Expert

The role of a mental health expert in capital prosecutions gained greater importance when the United States Supreme Court overruled *Penry v. Lynaugh*, 492 U.S. 302 (1989). The decision in *Penry* held that the constitution did not prohibit executing a person who was mentally retarded at the time of execution. *Penry* was overruled by the decision in *Atkins v. Virginia*, 536 U.S. 304 (2002). The decision in *Atkins* yielded to public pressure and held that the constitution prohibited executing mentally retarded prisoners.

The ABA *Guidelines* suggest that a capital defense team employ at least one person qualified by training and experience to screen the defendant for the presence of mental or psychological disorders or impairments. The *Guidelines* recognize that mental health experts, i.e., psychologists, psychiatrists, and others, while not unique to death penalty cases, are relied upon to a much greater degree in capital punishment cases than in non-death penalty cases. A mental health expert may be used in a variety of ways that include evaluating a defendant, reviewing mental health records, consulting with counsel, and testifying during the guilt phase or penalty phase.

The testimony of a mental health expert could prevent a defendant from being convicted of capital murder through evidence that the defendant was insane at the time of the offense. Further, even if a defendant is convicted of capital murder, a mental health expert could prevent imposition of the death penalty through evidence showing the defendant was mentally retarded.

In *Ake v. Oklahoma*, 470 U.S. 68 (1985), the Supreme Court held that when an indigent defendant has made a preliminary showing that his or her sanity at the time of the offense is likely to be a significant factor at trial, the Constitution requires the government provide the defendant with court appointed psychiatric expert assistance. *Ake* reasoned that "without the assistance of a psychiatrist to conduct a professional examination on issues relevant to the defense, to help determine whether the insanity defense is viable, to present testimony, and to assist in preparing the cross-examination of a State's psychiatric witnesses, the risk of an inaccurate resolution of sanity issues is extremely high. With such assistance, the defendant is fairly able to present at least enough information to the jury, in a meaningful manner, as to permit it to make a sensible determination."[15]

Future Dangerousness Expert

During the penalty phase of a capital trial the jury must decide between a sentence of life in prison and a sentence of death. Prosecutors will typically present evidence showing that a defendant is too dangerous to be confined in prison.[16] Such an argument is consistent with the Supreme Court's determination in *Barefoot v. Estelle*, 463 U.S. 880 (1983), that predicting future dangerousness "is a constitutionally acceptable criterion for imposing the death penalty." This type of evidence should be countered by a defense expert who can inform the jury about the conditions of life in prison and to provide information about whether the defendant will be dangerous to others if incarcerated for life.[17] In *Skipper v. South Carolina*, 476 U.S. 1 (1986), the Supreme Court held that "evidence that the defendant would not pose a danger if spared (but incarcerated) must be considered potentially mitigating." In *Skipper* the Supreme Court ruled that the trial court should have permitted the testimony of former jailers who would have opined on the defendant's good jail behavior. What should be understood is that the *Skipper* Court said nothing about the need for *expert* testimony on this subject. Therefore, a defendant does not have a per se constitutional right to appointment of a future dangerousness expert.[18]

However, in *Ake v. Oklahoma*, 470 U.S. 68 (1985), future dangerousness was a significant factor at the sentencing phase. The state psychiatrist who treated the defendant at the state mental hospital testified at the guilt phase that the defendant posed a threat of continuing criminal violence. This testimony raised the issue of the defendant's future dangerousness, which was an aggravating factor under Oklahoma's capital sentencing scheme, and on which the prosecutor relied at sentencing. As a consequence of these circumstances, the Supreme Court held that the defendant "was entitled to the assistance of a psychiatrist on this issue and that the denial of that assistance deprived him of due process."

Jury Consultant

A jury consultant can provide a wide range of services to a capital felon, including matters such as developing questionnaires for jurors and participating in voir dire.[19] This assistance can be critical in a death penalty prosecution because the jury selection process is more complicated in a capital trial. In spite of the tremendous assistance a jury consultant can provide to a defense team, a defendant does not have a constitutional right to such a consultant.[20] In *Moore v. Johnson*, 225 F.3d 495 (5th Cir. 2000), the defendant argued that he had a right to a jury consultant during his capital prosecution. The Fifth Circuit disagreed as follows:

> [A] defendant cannot expect the state to provide him a most-sophisticated defense; rather, he is entitled to access to the raw materials integral to the building of an effective defense. Most of those raw materials come to the defendant in the form of his court-appointed lawyer — in his expert knowledge about how to negotiate the rules of court, how to mount an effective defense, and so forth....
>
> [J]ury selection is not a mysterious process to be undertaken by those learned in the law only with the assistance of outside professionals. All competent lawyers are endowed with the "raw materials" required to pick a jury fairly disposed toward doing substantive justice. While the wealthiest of defendants might elect to spend their defense funds on jury consultants, indigent defendants are not privileged to force the state to expend its funds on this exercise in bolstering an attorney's fundamental skills. Meanwhile, of course, a defendant does not lack "an adequate opportunity to present [his] claims fairly" because he has been denied a jury consultant. Communicating with the jury is a quintessential responsibility of counsel.[21]

Charging Discretion
of a Prosecutor

The legal system in the United States may be divided into two broad categories: civil and criminal. In civil litigation individual citizens hire private attorneys to represent their interests. In criminal litigation a defendant has a constitutional right to be represented by private counsel (appointed or retained). However, the victim of a crime does not have a constitutional right to have a private attorney prosecute his or her case against a defendant. In criminal cases, government attorneys, called prosecutors, represent the interests of a crime victim.

This chapter will provide a brief historical review of the development of the prosecutor in the United States. The emphasis is on understanding why prosecutors have almost absolute discretion in criminal matters. The chapter will also provide a discussion on specific issues involving a prosecutor's discretion in capital punishment cases.

Historical Development of the Public Prosecutor

To properly consider and understand the deference courts give to prosecutorial discretion, it is necessary to review the origin of the office of public prosecutor. This section will briefly trace the path that has given Anglo-American jurisprudence the public prosecutor.

The Prosecutor Under Common Law

The English Crown made criminal prosecution an unregulated for-profit business. All crimes in England were punishable by fine, in addition to physical forms of punishment. Under the common law a fine included cash, as well as other personal and real property. Depending upon the nature of the offense, a convicted defendant's land could be confiscated by the Crown, as well as everything else he or she may have owned.[1]

Although the English Parliament existed during the common law era, the Crown was the true sovereign authority. As the sovereign authority, it was the duty and responsibility of the Crown to maintain the peace and enforce the laws of the realm. This duty and responsibility meant apprehending and prosecuting law breakers. The Crown delegated, in large part, both its arrest and prosecution duties to the general public.[2] In other words, both the Crown and common citizens carried out criminal prosecutorial duties.

Prosecution by the Crown. The English Crown employed numerous legal advisors.

Some of the legal offices created by the Crown included: (1) King's advocate general, (2) King's attorney general, (3) King's solicitor general and (4) King's serjeants.[3] Legal advisors employed by the Crown enjoyed the benefits of the inherent prerogative of the Crown, due to their association with the Crown. This meant that, in practice, legal advisors of the Crown were viewed literally as being above all other attorneys and treated with absolute deference in courts of law. It was said by one scholar that the Crown's attorney did not represent the Crown in court, because the Crown was theoretically always present. The attorney merely followed a case on behalf of the Crown.[4] This framework of absolute deference to the Crown's attorneys laid the seeds of prosecutorial discretion that is present in Anglo-American jurisprudence today.

As pointed out, the Crown was the sovereign authority under the common law. In fulfilling its duty of prosecuting criminal offenders, the Crown relied primarily upon its attorney general, though the king's serjeants are said to have played a minor role in this area of litigation as well.

The Crown's attorney general did not prosecute all crimes, although it had the authority to do so. Instead, the attorney general limited its attention to major felony crimes like treason, murder, outlawry and robbery. The crime of murder and treason were of particular interest to the Crown, because the real property of defendants convicted of either offense escheated to the Crown. Enormous fines were appended to other major felony offenses.

The fact that the attorney general selected the cases it would prosecute (those bringing the greatest bounty to the Crown) was a prerogative act of discretion that could not be challenged by the courts or anyone, except the Crown itself. The attorney general represented the Crown and, as one court put it, "[i]f the agent of the sovereign desired that a prosecution should [not occur], that was the end of the matter. The pubic subjects had no interest and could not be heard to complain."[5]

Additionally, if the attorney general began a prosecution and decided it did not wish to proceed further, or if the prosecution was begun by a private citizen and the attorney general desired to terminate the action, it could do so by filing a *nolle prosequi*. The *nolle prosequi* was "a statement by the [attorney general] that he would proceed no further in a criminal case.... The discretion to discontinue prosecution rested solely with the [attorney general] and it was unnecessary to obtain the permission of the court to give legal effect to this decision."[6]

The attorney general had absolute discretion in determining the fate of a prosecution because the Crown, as sovereign authority, "was theoretically the only party interested in the prosecution."[7]

Prosecution by citizens. It was previously noted that criminal prosecution under the common law was an unregulated for-profit business. The validity of this assertion is nowhere more evident than in the Crown's relinquishment of its prosecutorial duties to all private citizens.

Under the common law all citizens were permitted to prosecute criminal offenders in the name of the Crown. This privilege was monstrously abused because of the benefits that could be reaped by successful prosecutions. A citizen bringing a successful criminal prosecution could share in the proceeds of the invariably imposed fine.[8]

Private prosecutors were also able to monetarily take advantage of the common law's rule that an acquittal could be appealed (rejected by Anglo-American jurisprudence). A defendant, acquitted of a crime, could be confined in jail pending an appeal of the acquittal. This situation usually resulted in the defendant entering a settlement agreement with the private prosecutor. The private prosecutor would agree to forgo an appeal in exchange for a monetary payment by the defendant.[9]

Evolution of the Public Prosecutor in America

The common law did not have a public prosecutor, as that term is understood today.[10] Instead, the common law tolerated gross selective prosecution by the Crown's attorney general and wholesale prosecution by private citizens. Unfortunately this chaotic method of prosecuting criminals was transplanted to the American colonies. Fortunately, however, another method of prosecuting criminal defendants also took root in North America. This second method came not from England and the common law. When the Dutch founded the colony of New Netherland during the seventeenth century, they brought with them their system of prosecuting criminal defendants. A review of both methods of prosecution will follow.

Common law prosecution in the colonies. The Crown appointed attorney generals in all of the colonies. The first appointment was made in Virginia in 1643.[11] The primary task of colonial attorney generals was to promote and protect the financial interests of the Crown. This meant that the bulk of the legal work performed by the colonial attorney generals was civil in nature.

Colonial attorney generals were also responsible for prosecuting criminal defendants. However, this duty was neglected. Rarely did colonial attorney generals prosecute criminal defendants. They intervened in this area only when a notorious major felony occurred. A routine murder was not considered notorious, unless it affected a colonial aristocrat.[12]

The attitude of colonial attorney generals was the same as their brethren in England, i.e., if the Crown did not obtain a substantial benefit from criminal prosecutions, there would be no prosecution by the sovereign authority whose duty it was to prosecute all crimes. Colonial judges did not challenge the discretion exercised by colonial attorney generals.

Two factors caused colonial judges to defer to the prosecutorial discretion of colonial attorney generals. First, the judges followed the legal principles of the common law. Under the common law it was held that the Crown's prosecutors had absolute discretion in deciding what course, if any, to take regarding a criminal offense. This common law principle was echoed in modern times in the case of *Newman v. United States*, 382 F.2d 479 (D.C. Cir. 1967), where it was said that "[f]ew subjects are less adapted to judicial review than the exercise by the [prosecutor] of his discretion in deciding when and whether to institute criminal proceedings, or what precise charge shall be made, or whether to dismiss a proceeding once brought."

The second factor which caused colonial judges to bow to the whim of colonial attorney generals was the Crown. Colonial attorney generals were not ordinary attorneys. The Crown's prerogative was vested in colonial attorney generals when they carried out their legal duties. No colonial judge could muster the death-certain courage to tell the Crown when it should prosecute a criminal case.

The fact that colonial attorney generals rarely prosecuted criminal defendants did not mean that vigorous criminal prosecutions were nonexistent in the colonies. Crime was routinely prosecuted. The citizens of the colonies prosecuted the vast majority of crimes.

The chaotic private prosecutorial method that existed in England was allowed to flourish in the colonies. The inducement used to encourage colonists to prosecute criminals was the same carrot used in England. Private prosecutors reaped monetary rewards for successfully prosecuting criminals. They also reaped rewards by intimidating defendants into settling criminal charges, prior to trial, by paying them monetary sums.[13]

Criminal prosecution in New Netherland. The Dutch ventured to North America and settled a colony in the seventeenth century. They called their colony New Netherland (this colony comprised parts of Delaware, New Jersey, New York, Pennsylvania, and Connecticut).[14] As would be expected, Dutch colonists brought with them the Dutch culture, social norms and system of government.

One aspect of the Dutch system of government that was brought with the colonists had a profound effect on Anglo-American jurisprudence. The legal system of the Dutch had an office called the "schout." Legal scholars rarely acknowledge the point, but it was the principles undergirding the office of schout which shaped the prosecutorial system that America would eventually adopt and utilize to this day.[15]

The schout was a public prosecutor. Unlike the chaotic system of prosecution tolerated by the common law, Dutch law entrusted the task of prosecuting criminals in a single office—the office of schout. Dutch colonists did not haul their neighbors into criminal courts on real or monetarily imagined charges. If a criminal offense occurred, the office of schout prosecuted the crime.[16]

When the English eventually took New Netherland from the Dutch, the term schout was buried. However, the idea of entrusting a public prosecutor with the responsibility for prosecuting all crimes took root and blossomed in America. The public prosecutor of today is a distant cousin of the common law and the first cousin of the schout.[17]

Modern day public prosecutor. The nation's prosecutorial system is a hybrid of the common law and the schout. It was pointed out that the schout was a public prosecutor. When the American colonists threw off the yoke of the Crown, they also tossed out the common law's ad hoc approach to prosecuting criminal defendants. The nation unanimously moved in the direction of imposing the duty of prosecuting criminal defendants upon individual governments. Neither the nation nor its legal system was prepared to continue depending upon private citizens to prosecute criminals. Crime would be prosecuted, but it would be under the schout model.

Today all jurisdictions have schouts, though they go by various names: district attorney, county prosecutor, state attorney, attorney general, or simply public prosecutor. A majority of jurisdictions provide for the election of prosecutors on a local, usually county, level.[18]

In spite of the rejection of the common law's prosecutorial method, the judiciary continued to adhere to the common law principle that a prosecutor has broad discretion regarding the disposition of criminal cases. Although the nation is not governed by a Crown, the judiciary continues to allow prosecutors to have almost unassailable prosecutorial power and authority.

The Powell Propositions

In the case of *Wayte v. United States*, 470 U.S. 598 (1985), Justice Powell articulated the modern day justification for adhering to the common law's deference to prosecutors. Justice Powell reasoned as follows:

This broad discretion rests largely on the recognition that the decision to prosecute is particularly ill-suited to judicial review. Such factors as the strength of the case, the prosecution's general deterrence value, the Government's enforcement priorities, and the case's relationship to the Government's overall enforcement plan are not readily susceptible to the kind of analysis the courts are competent to undertake. Judicial supervision in this area, moreover, entails systemic costs of particular concern. Examining the basis of a prosecution delays the criminal proceeding, threatens to chill law enforcement by subjecting the prosecutor's motives and decisionmaking to outside inquiry, and may undermine prosecutorial effectiveness by revealing the Government's enforcement policy. All these are substantial concerns that make the courts properly hesitant to examine the decision whether to prosecute.

Five propositions were offered by Justice Powell for the modern day deference to prosecutors:

(1) inability to systematically analyze the prosecutor's decision making process;
(2) oversight would be too costly;
(3) wholesale review would clog up the system;
(4) oversight would discourage prosecutions; and
(5) oversight could make public otherwise hidden agendas.

The concerns expressed in the Powell Propositions have merit. However, numerous commentators challenge the Powell Propositions and the unbridled prosecutorial discretion they permit.[19] At the core of the arguments taken against deference to prosecutorial discretion stands one idea: prosecutors frequently abuse their discretion.

Death Penalty Charging Discretion

The determination of whether to charge a person with a capital offense rests with the prosecutor. The power vested in the prosecutor is almost without limit. In this section a review is given on specific issues related to a prosecutor's discretion in death penalty cases.

Discretion to Seek the Death Penalty

Traditionally the determination of what penalty a convicted defendant will receive is made by the presiding judge, based upon the penalty range provided by statute. For example, if a prosecutor obtains a conviction for rape and the penalty for the offense is from five to fifteen years' imprisonment, the prosecutor cannot absolve the defendant from being subject to this penalty. At most, a prosecutor may recommend to the trial judge that the defendant receive probation or some other disposition. The court can accept or reject the recommendation.[20] In other words, once a prosecutor charges a defendant with a crime, the penalty automatically attaches and the prosecutor cannot, sua sponte, remove the defendant from exposure to the penalty (short of dismissing the charge).

Tradition is abandoned, however, in capital murder prosecutions. In this context the prosecutor can invade the traditionally exclusive domain of the trial judge. All capital punishment jurisdictions give prosecutors statutory discretion to waive the death penalty, sua sponte, for any death-eligible offense. One appellate court said the exercise of this discretion does not violate "the separation of powers provision of [federal or state constitutions], in that the prosecutor is given power to exercise a part of the sentencing process, which should properly be a judicial function."[21]

A note of caution is in order with respect to waiving the death penalty. The fact that a prosecutor waives or gives up the right to seek the death penalty in a case does not mean that the case will not be prosecuted. The prosecution continues, but the maximum penalty a defendant would face upon conviction would be life imprisonment.

The McCleskey Ruling

In the case of *McCleskey v. Kemp*, 481 U.S. 279 (1987), the defendant argued that the state of Georgia's capital punishment statute was unconstitutional, because it gave unfettered discretion to prosecutors to determine when they would seek the death penalty for capital offenses. The defendant contended that the constitution required that death penalty statutes set out guidelines to control the circumstances in which a prosecutor may seek, or decline to seek, the death penalty. The Supreme Court disagreed with the defendant as follows:

[T]he policy considerations behind a prosecutor's traditionally wide discretion suggest the impropriety of our requiring prosecutors to defend their decisions to seek death penalties....

Our refusal to require that the prosecutor provide an explanation for his decisions ... is completely consistent with this Court's longstanding precedents that hold that a prosecutor need not explain his decisions unless the criminal defendant presents a prima facie case of unconstitutional conduct with respect to his case....

Similarly, the capacity of prosecutorial discretion to provide individualized justice is firmly entrenched in American law. As we have noted, a prosecutor can ... decline to seek a death sentence in any particular case. Of course, the power to be lenient [also] is the power to discriminate, but a capital punishment system that did not allow for discretionary acts of leniency would be totally alien to our notions of criminal justice[.]

We have held that discretion in a capital punishment system is necessary to satisfy the Constitution.... Prosecutorial decisions necessarily involve both judgmental and factual decisions that vary from case to case. Thus, it is difficult to imagine guidelines that would produce ... predictability ... without sacrificing the discretion essential to a humane and fair system of criminal justice.

The import of *McCleskey* is that "the federal Constitution does not mandate guidelines for prosecutors in administering the death penalty statute[.]"[22] In fact, *McCleskey* pronounced, in dicta, that it would be unconstitutional for a prosecutor not to have discretion in determining whom to seek the death penalty against and whom to show mercy.

The broad sweep of *McCleskey* has been tempered by other Supreme Court cases, so that the decision to seek the death penalty cannot be done in a discriminatory manner that violated constitutional rights of defendants, e.g., basing the decision to waive or not waive the death penalty on racial, gender or religious grounds. Ultimately, however, the Supreme Court has indicated that "[a]bsent facts to the contrary, it cannot be assumed that prosecutors will be motivated in their charging decision by factors other than the strength of their case and the likelihood that a jury would impose the death penalty if it convicts."[23] In *United States v. Bass*, 536 U.S. 862 (2002), the Supreme Court held the defendant failed to establish a claim for racially selective death penalty prosecution by the United States, for the purpose of conducting pretrial discovery on the issue.

7

Capital Murder
Charging Instruments

The intent of this chapter is to provide a review of the instruments prosecutors use to charge defendants with capital offenses. The chapter will also present material regarding specific issues that relate to capital charging instruments. Its two major sections are based upon the two charging instruments used by prosecutors, i.e., the indictment and information.

The Indictment

Depending upon the requirements of a particular jurisdiction, capital murder is prosecuted by an indictment or information. This section will explore prosecution of a capital felon under an indictment. The material starts out with a summation of a preliminary hearing and the grand jury and its role with an indictment. Following that discussion the section will examine specific capital punishment indictment issues.

Preliminary Hearing

The phrase "preliminary hearing" is typically used to describe any type of criminal hearing held before trial. However, the phrase has a technical meaning. In its strictest use, the term refers to a specific hearing held to determine whether sufficient evidence exists to submit a case to the grand jury for indictment consideration.

In all grand jury jurisdictions, a preliminary hearing is usually presided over by a court of limited jurisdiction, such as a magistrate court. At the preliminary hearing the magistrate must determine without a jury (1) whether there is probable cause to believe a felony crime was committed, and (2) whether there is probable cause to believe that the named defendant committed the felony. If probable cause is found for both issues presented to the magistrate, the case is bound over to a court of general jurisdiction for the purpose of having a grand jury consider the matter. If the magistrate finds that probable cause is lacking for one or both of the dispositive issues, the charge must be dismissed.

During a preliminary hearing a defendant has a right to be represented by counsel, to present evidence, and to cross examine witnesses. Generally trial court rules of evidence are relaxed at preliminary hearings.

The Grand Jury

An indictment is an instrument that is drawn up by a grand jury. The origin of the grand jury is traditionally traced back to England, during the reign of King Henry II. Legal scholars report that in the year 1166, King Henry II created an institution called the Assize of Clarendon. The assize consisted of twelve men who were given the duty of informing the local sheriff, or an itinerant justice of the peace, of any criminal conduct in their community. The assize operated in this fashion until the end of the fourteenth century.[1]

The assize split into two separate institutions by the end of the fourteenth century. One institution was called the petit jury and the other was called *le grande inques*t or grand jury.[2] The concern here, of course, is with the grand jury. At its inception the grand jury had two purposes: (1) prevent unjust prosecutions and (2) initiate just prosecutions.

The grand jury was incorporated into Anglo-American jurisprudence by the American colonists. During the early development of the nation, all jurisdictions required felony prosecutions be initiated by the grand jury. The document used by the grand jury to initiate a prosecution was called an indictment. The grand jury issues an indictment against a person only if it finds (1) probable cause existed that a crime was committed, and (2) probable cause existed that a named person committed the crime.

As a result of a decision by the Supreme Court in *Hurtado v. California*, 110 U.S. 516 (1884) (discussed in the information section), only a minority of jurisdictions now require felony offenses be prosecuted by a grand jury indictment.[3] In *Talton v. Mayes*, 163 U.S. 376 (1896), it was held that an indictment returned against the defendant was not invalid due to the grand jury being composed of only five people, because the composition of the grand jury was a matter exclusively within the control of each jurisdiction.

Fatal Variance in Indictment

Allegations in a capital indictment must be proven at trial. There are times, however, when a prosecutor will prove an essential issue at a trial that was not alleged in the indictment or fail to prove a matter that was alleged in the indictment. This situation is called a variance. Jurisdictions differ on how they treat specific capital indictment variances. Some variances are deemed fatal variances. A fatal variance in a capital indictment will result in a conviction being overturned. As a practical matter, most capital indictment variances are deemed nonfatal.

A few examples of fatal capital indictment variances are as follows. In *Borrego v. State*, 800 S.W.2d 373 (Tex.App.–Corpus Christi 1990), it was said that if an indictment alleged specific means of committing murder, failure to prove such means is a fatal variance. The court in *Alford v. State*, 906 P.2d 714 (Nev. 1995), held that where an indictment charged a defendant only with malice aforethought murder, the prosecutor could not pursue at trial the alternative theory of felony-murder. In *Fairchild v. State*, 459 S0.2d 793 (Miss. 1984), it was held that the prosecutor must prove that the victim allegedly murdered is the same person named in the indictment as having been killed. The court in *Chavez v. State*, 657 S.W.2d 146 (Tex.Cr.App. 1983), said that when an indictment fails to recite use of a deadly weapon, but proof at trial establishes a deadly weapon, a fatal variance occurs.

Nonfatal Variance in Indictment

It was previously noted that in practice, courts tend to overlook capital indictment variances. The case-specific examples that follow (some cases are from jurisdictions that no longer have the death penalty) represent indictment variances that were found to be nonfatal, i.e., the convictions were not overturned.

The court in *People v. Nitz*, 610 N.E.2d 1289 (Ill.App. 5 Dist. 1993), found that there was no fatal variance in the indictment and proof at trial, where the indictment charged the defendant with shooting the victim to death, but the prosecutor did not present any evidence of a shooting. The *Nitz* court held that the indictment adequately informed the defendant that she was charged with murder and that the defendant was not prejudiced by the variance, because her theory of defense was that she was not present during the murder. In *Battles v. State*, 420 S.E.2d 303 (Ga. 1992), the court held that there was no fatal variance in the indictment and proof at trial, where the indictment alleged the defendant struck the murder victim with a wrench, but the evidence proved that the victim was struck with a gun. In *Commonwealth v. Robertson*, 563 N.E.2d 223 (Mass. 1990), the court indicated that the defendant was not deprived of fair trial as a result of the indictment alleging that the murder victim died from a beating, but the evidence at trial revealed no beating took place. The court in *Manna v. State*, 440 N.E.2d 473 (Ind. 1982), held that where the indictment charged that murder occurred with a deadly weapon, the exact nature unknown, there was no material variance when proof established that no deadly weapon was used. The *Manna* court reasoned that the allegation of a weapon was mere surplusage that did not mislead the defendant in preparation of a defense.

In *Stephens v. Borg*, 59 F.3d 932 (9th Cir. 1995), it was said that a jury may be instructed on felony-murder even though the indictment did not expressly set out such theory. The court in *Commonwealth v. Shelton*, 643 N.E.2d 48 (Mass.App. 1994), held that there was no fatal variance in an indictment charging the defendant with malice murder, merely because a felony-murder instruction is given to the trial jury. The courts in *People v. Wilkins*, 31 Cal.Rptr. 764 (1994), and *Dunn v. State*, 434 S.E.2d 60 (Ga. 1993), held that the defendants in those cases were not denied due process of law simply because the indictments alleged malice aforethought murder, but proof and convictions were based on felony-murder. In *Bush v. State*, 461 S0.2d 936 (Fla. 1984), it was held that there was no material variance in charging the defendant with premeditated murder and proof of felony-murder.

The court in *Williams v. Collins*, 16 F.3d 626 (5th Cir. 1994), found that there was no fatal variance in an indictment alleging the defendant killed the victim during a robbery of the victim, and proof at trial that the victim was killed during the defendant's robbery of a convenience store where the victim worked. In *Commonwealth v. Daughtry*, 627 N.E.2d 928 (Mass. 1994), the court said that a defendant may be prosecuted as an accomplice in a capital murder indictment which indicated the defendant acted as a principal.

In *Crawford v. State*, 863 S.W.2d 152 (Tex.App.–Houston 1993), the court held that there was no fatal variance in an indictment charging the defendant with hiring a person to commit murder for remuneration "and" a promise of remuneration, but the jury was instructed that it may convict the defendant on a finding of remuneration "or" a promise of remuneration. The court in *McCall v. State*, 501 S0.2d 496 (Ala.Cr.App. 1986), found that there was no fatal variance in an indictment alleging a specific individual paid the defendant to kill the victim, and failure of the prosecutor to prove that a specific individual paid the defendant.

Turner v. State, 406 S0.2d 1066 (Ala.Cr.App. 1981), held that a variance in the middle name of the person named in the indictment as the victim and the actual middle name established at trial is not fatal. The court in *Johnson v. Estelle*, 704 F.2d 232 (5th Cir. 1983), found that there was no fatal variance in an indictment listing the victim's name as "Carol" and proof at trial that the victim was known as "Carlyn." In *Koehler v. State*, 653 S.W.2d 617 (Tex.App. 4 Dist. 1983), the court held that there was no fatal variance in an indictment calling the victim "Yolanda," and proof at trial showing the victim was known as "Yolando."

In *Roberts v. State*, 314 S.E.2d 83 (Ga. 1984), it was held that there was no fatal variance in an indictment alleging the murder weapon was a .38-caliber handgun and proof at trial showing that it was a .38 Special. The court in *Stevenson v. State*, 404 S0.2d 111 (Ala.Cr.App. 1981), found that there was no material variance between an indictment charging murder with a pistol and proof at trial that the weapon used was a shotgun. In *Trest v. State*, 409 S0.3d 906 (Fla.Cr.App. 1981), it was said that there was no material variance in an indictment charging murder by use of a .38-caliber pistol and proof at trial that the weapon was a .357 caliber. The court in *Weaver v. State*, 407 S0.2d 568 (Ala.Cr.App. 1981), held that there was no fatal variance in an indictment alleging that death was caused by a .25-caliber automatic rifle and proof at trial that death resulted from a .25-caliber automatic pistol.

Alleging Capital Felony-Murder

The issue of indicting a defendant on a capital felony-murder charge can be problematic, depending upon the dictates of the particular jurisdiction. The examples that follow illustrate issues defendants have argued regarding capital felony-murder indictments (some cases are from jurisdictions that no longer have the death penalty).

In *Davis v. State*, 782 S.W.2d 211 (Tex.Cr.App. 1989), it was said that a capital felony-murder indictment predicated on two underlying felonies does not require the prosecutor prove both underlying felonies. The court in *State v. Jones*, 475 A.2d 1087 (Conn. 1984), indicated that an indictment may allege two underlying felonies in the alternative, in a felony-murder prosecution. In *Gray v. State*, 441 A.2d 209 (Del. 1981), the court held that a felony-murder indictment is not defective in failing to recite the degree of the underlying felony. The court in *State v. Williams*, 292 S.E.2d 243 (N.C. 1982), held that an indictment for felony-murder is not defective in failing to charge the defendant with committing the underlying felony. In *Hogue v. State*, 711 S.W.2d 9 (Tex.Cr.App. 1986), it was determined that an indictment that fails to set out the manner in which the underlying felony occurred, in a felony-murder prosecution, is not vague or invalid for that reason.

The court in *Armstrong v. State*, 642 S0.2d 730 (Fla. 1994), held that even though the indictment failed to provide notice of a felony-murder theory, a prosecution on that theory may proceed. In *State v. Bockorny*, 866 P.2d 1230 (Or.App. 1993), it was held that a felony-murder indictment need not set out all of the elements of the underlying crime, nor the manner in which the crime occurred. In *State v. Flanders*, 572 A.2d 983 (Conn. 1990), the court said that a felony-murder indictment is valid even though it does not specify whether the defendant or a participant in the underlying felony caused the victim's death.

Stephenson v. State, 593 S0.2d 160 (Ala.Cr.App. 1991), held that an indictment which merely states that force causing physical injury was used against the murder victim in the course of committing theft was sufficient to charge the defendant with felony-murder predicated on first degree robbery. The court in *Beathard v. State*, 767 S.W.2d 423 (Tex.Cr.App. 1989), held that an indictment for capital murder predicated on burglary did not have to set out the elements of burglary. In *Hunt v. State*, 659 S0.2d 933 (Ala.Cr.App. 1994), the court held that a felony-murder indictment which erroneously alleged that sexual abuse in the second degree was a felony, when in fact it was a misdemeanor, did not invalidate the indictment in light of the fact that the aggravating component of the capital offense was burglary.

Alleging Alternative Theories or Multiple Offenses

A capital murder indictment is not infirm in setting out several ways in which the murder was committed.[4] An indictment may assert alternative means by which murder is alleged to have been committed, so long as the theories are not "stacked" to increase penalty phase aggravating circumstances.[5] Courts have held that merely because an indictment alleges more than one theory of murder does not mean the prosecutor must prove all the theories alleged.[6]

An indictment may set out more than one offense. In *Pointer v. United States*, 151 U.S. 396 (1894), the Supreme Court held that an indictment may set out two murder offenses, in separate counts, which occurred close in time.

Excluded Matters Fatal to Indictment

In *State v. Clemmons*, 682 S.W.2d 843 (Mo.App. 1984), it was held that a capital murder indictment which fails to allege the element of deliberation is fatally defective. The court in *Brown v. State*, 410 A.2d 17 (Md.App. 1979), held that an indictment for murder is fatally defective when it omits the element malice aforethought. In *Peck v. State*, 923 S.W.2d 839 (Tex.App.–Tyler 1996), it was said that an indictment charging murder must allege the means used to commit the crime, if known by the grand jury. The court in *State v. Brown*, 651 A.2d 19 (N.J. 1994), held that a murder indictment must specify that the homicide was committed by the defendant's own conduct. In *Janecka v. State*, 823 S.W.2d 232 (Tex.Cr.App. 1990), the court indicated that an indictment is fatally defective if it charges a defendant with murder-for-hire, but fails to include the name of the person providing the remuneration.

The court in *Ridgely v. State*, 756 S.W.2d 870 (Tex.App.–Fort Worth 1988), determined that an indictment was fatally defective in failing to allege the manner and means by which the victim was strangled, because of testimony by a medical examiner that death could have occurred by choking with hands, suffocation with a paper towel or by ligature. In *Crawford v. State*, 632 S.W.2d 800 (Tex.App. 14 Dist. 1982), the court held that a capital murder indictment was constitutionally defective in merely alleging the defendant committed murder in the course of committing rape, when the statute required the underlying offense be "aggravated rape." *King v. State*, 594 S.W.2d 425 (Tex.Cr.App. 1980), held that an indictment charging capital murder premised on rape is materially defective when it fails to recite the identity of the victim of the rape. The court in *Rougeau v. State*, 738 S.W.2d 651 (Tex.Cr.App. 1987), held that the indictment was defective in failing to provide the identity of the intended robbery victim in a prosecution of the defendant for murder predicated on robbery and attempted robbery. In *Welch v. State*, 331 S.E.2d 573 (Ga. 1985), the court held that the defendant's conviction for felony-murder could not stand, where the indictment charging him with two counts of malice murder did not charge him with committing the underlying felony of burglary.

Excluded Matters Not Fatal to Indictment

In *Mitchell v. Esparza*, 540 U.S. 12 (2003), it was held that the failure of an indictment to charge the defendant as a principal offender was not error, where the defendant was the only person charged with committing the crime. An indictment need not specify the theory of murder on which the prosecutor intends to rely.[7] It was held in *St. Clair v. United States*, 154 U.S. 134 (1894), that an indictment against the defendant was not invalid due to its failure to state where the offense occurred, because allegations of crimes committed on the high seas do not need the specificity required of crimes committed on land. It was said in *Westmoreland v. United States*, 155 U.S. 545 (1895), that the indictment against the defendant was not defective in failing to allege he knew that he was giving the victim poison and that the poison was ingested in the victim's stomach, because the absence of such allegations did not prevent the defendant from preparing a defense to the charge against him.

Allegations as to the means used to commit murder is a formal, not an essential part of an indictment.[8] It has been held that the failure of an indictment to allege the means in which the murder occurred did not render it fatally defective, where the defendant did not object to it until the prosecutor rested at the end of its case-in-chief.[9] An indictment is not fatally defective where it recites disjunctively phrased causes of death, because allegations of the means used to cause death are not an essential part of indictment.[10] It is not required that an indictment charge the specific subsection of the murder statute identifying the mental state consistent with felony-murder.[11] In a prosecution for malice murder an indictment does not have to set out facts the prosecutor will rely on to prove express or implied malice.[12]

A capital murder indictment does not have to specify the precise instrument used to cause the victim's death.[13] An indictment that alleges the defendant killed a police officer while the officer was lawfully discharging his or her official duties does not have to allege specific acts of the officer which constituted his or her official duties.[14] An indictment is not fatally defective because it does not allege which of two guns killed the victim.[15] A murder indictment is not fatally defective in failing to allege the cause of death, when medical testimony establishes that decomposition of the victim's body made it impossible to determine the cause of death.[16]

An indictment charging the defendant with capital murder committed in the course of burglary of a habitation is sufficient even though it does not state burglarious intent.[17] A felony-murder indictment is not fatally defective in failing to allege the specific address of a burglarized dwelling in which the victim was killed.[18]

An indictment alleging the defendant murdered the victim while engaged in the commission of robbery is not fatally defective in omitting to allege an overt act for the robbery.[19] An indictment charging the defendant with committing murder during the course of theft of currency is not fatally defective in failing to specify the value or amount of the currency.[20] A capital murder indictment predicated on remuneration does not have to specify the object of value.[21] A capital murder indictment premised on homicide during robbery is not constitutionally defective in failing to allege the time of the offense.[22] An indictment charging capital murder premised on robbery is not defective in failing to allege the ownership of the property taken.[23]

An indictment charging the defendant with capital murder is not defective in failing to use the phrase "capital offense."[24] A capital murder indictment is not invalid in using the phrase "cause the death of," instead of the statutory word "kill," because the phrase is not misleading.[25] An indictment is not fatally defective in omitting the words "after deliberation upon the matter" when charging first-degree murder.[26] An indictment charging capital murder that fails to allege the defendant "knowingly" killed is not fatally defective when the indictment contains words of similar import.[27] Although "malice" must be alleged in a capital murder indictment when required by the jurisdiction, that exact word need not be used.[28] An indictment failing to allege "premeditated" is not fatally defective in a capital murder prosecution, where the essence of the term is conveyed through the use of other words.[29]

The fact that the an indictment only charges premeditated murder does not preclude the prosecutor from seeking a felony-murder conviction.[30] Where a murder indictment recites the name of the victim it need not state that the victim is a human being.[31] A murder indictment is not fatally defective in failing to allege that the defendant is a human being.[32]

An indictment charging the defendant with killing the victim by stomping and kicking is not invalid in failing to allege the defendant was wearing shoes at the time.[33] Failure of a murder indictment to allege that a rifle is a "gun" is not a fatal omission.[34]

Adequate Notice

A capital murder indictment is not constitutionally invalid in failing to give notice that the charge carries the possibility of a death sentence.[35] Where an indictment charges the defendant with purposeful killing, it sufficiently apprises him or her that the charge includes specific intent to cause the victim's death.[36] The prosecutor has no obligation to give notice of the underlying felony that it will rely on to prove felony-murder.[37]

In the case of *Johnson v. State*, 815 S.W.2d 707 (Tex.Cr.App. 1991), the court held an indictment alleging the defendant caused the victim's death by striking him with his feet and hands gave the defendant adequate notice that the prosecutor would seek an affirmative finding that the defendant's feet and hands were deadly weapons. In *Long v. State*, 820 S.W.2d 888 (Tex.App.–Houston 1991), it was said that although the indictment did not state explicitly that the named weapon used in the murder, a knife, was a deadly weapon, the defendant was not deprived of adequate notice that the prosecutor would seek an affirmative finding of the use of a deadly weapon in killing the victim.

The Information

This section examines issues involving prosecution of a capital felon under an information. The material begins with a brief comment on how the information came into use in felony prosecutions generally. The remainder of the section reviews specific issues related to an information charging capital murder.

The Hurtado Ruling

Utilization of the grand jury and indictment to prosecute felony offenses began to lose favor by mid–1800. It has been reported that in 1859 Michigan became the first jurisdiction to permit felony prosecutions without a grand jury handing down an indictment. The path taken by Michigan was followed initially by only a few jurisdictions. The trend started by

Michigan, however, picked up steam after the decision of the Supreme Court in *Hurtado v. California*, 110 U.S. 516 (1884).

In *Hurtado* the defendant was prosecuted and convicted of murder based upon a charging document, an information, drawn up by the prosecutor. The defendant argued to the Supreme Court that the Fifth Amendment guaranteed him the right to be prosecuted by a grand jury indictment, and that the prosecutor's information was therefore unconstitutional. The Supreme Court disagreed with the defendant. The *Hurtado* opinion made clear that the requirement under the Fifth Amendment, that all felony prosecutions be initiated by a grand jury indictment, was applicable only to federal prosecutions. Therefore, utilization of the grand jury and indictment was a discretionary matter for each state to determine. The ruling in *Hurtado* was reaffirmed in *Lem Woon v. Oregon*, 229 U.S. 586 (1913).

In the final analysis, the *Hurtado* ruling permitted use of a prosecutor's information to prosecute felony offenses generally. Today a majority of jurisdictions utilize the information exclusively in all felony prosecutions.

Fatal Variance in Information

If an information alleges a named murder victim, the prosecutor must prove the victim's identity.[38] Where an information states the means in which a homicide occurred, the prosecutor must prove that death occurred through those means.[39] An information charging the defendant with malice aforethought murder only is fatally defective in sustaining a conviction for felony-murder.[40]

Alleging Capital Felony-Murder

It is not necessary in a felony-murder prosecution to place in the information the elements of the underlying felony nor the specific means of committing that felony.[41] A prosecutor is required to charge felony-murder and its attendant facts, if it chooses to pursue a felony-murder conviction.[42] An information is not constitutionally vague because it recites two underlying felonies in a felony-murder prosecution, without identifying which underlying felony would be relied upon.[43]

Alleging Alternative Matters

An information charging premeditated murder or felony-murder is sufficient without specifically referring to either theory.[44] A prosecutor is required to charge felony-murder and its attendant facts, as an alternative theory, if it chooses to pursue a felony-murder conviction.[45]

Excluded Matters Fatal to Information

An information is fatally defective if it does not charge a defendant with felony-murder explicitly and the prosecutor obtains a conviction for felony-murder.[46] An information is fatally defective in charging a defendant with felony-murder, if it fails to recite facts that allege every element of the capital murder offense and every element of the underlying felony.[47] Where an information fails to set out a mental state in a homicide charge, it is fatally defective.[48] An information is constitutionally inadequate where it charges a defendant with murder by torture, but fails to provide the defendant with notice that prosecutor has to prove he acted for the purpose of revenge, extortion, or persuasion.[49] It has been held that an information is invalid where it purports to charge murder during the course of an armed robbery, but fails to allege facts constituting armed robbery.[50]

Excluded Matters Not Fatal to Information

Courts have held that an information need not specify the theory of murder on which the prosecutor intends to rely.[51] An information need not recite cause or manner of death.[52] It has been determined that an information need not recite method of murder, so long as it states the elements of the offense with sufficient clarity to apprise the defendant of what he or she must defend against.[53] Courts have held that an information is not fatally defective in failing to narrate the mental state of the underlying offense in a felony-murder prosecution.[54] It has also been held that an information charging felony-murder does not have to charge underlying felony.[55]

An information charging a defendant as a principal includes a charge as an accessory; therefore, the information does not have to explicitly charge the defendant as an accessory in order for a conviction as an accessory to occur.[56] Courts have said that an information charging malice murder does not have to recite facts that will be used to prove malice.[57]

Where probable cause affidavits apprised defendant of the means and manner in which the murder occurred, the information is not fatally defective in failing to specify how the murder occurred.[58] An information charging the defendant as an aider and abettor in felony-murder is not fatally defective in not explicitly stating that the victim died.[59] The failure of an information to allege the caliber of weapon used in a murder does not require dismissing it, because the matter is not an element of the offense.[60] A capital murder information is not fatally defective because it failed to recite the exact place of the victim's death.[61]

8

Death Penalty
Notice Requirements

In the case of *In re Oliver*, 333 U.S. 257 (1948), the Supreme Court held that the Due Process Clause of the Constitution demanded that a defendant be given "reasonable notice of a charge against him, and an opportunity to be heard in his defense[.]" The constitutional notice requirement is generally satisfied at the arraignment stage of a prosecution. At an arraignment a defendant is formally given a copy of the charging instrument and is informed by the trial court of the nature of the accusation against him or her.

In the context of a capital prosecution, a charging instrument will inform the defendant that he or she is accused of an offense that may be punished with death. As a general matter, the Constitution does not require death penalty notice beyond that which is provided in the charging instrument and explained during an arraignment. The intent of this chapter is to show that some capital punishment jurisdictions have additional death penalty notice requirements that are not constitutionally required.

Two types of notice requirements are discussed below: notice that the death penalty will be sought, and notice involving aggravating circumstances.

Notice of Intent to Seek the Death Penalty

This section looks at three aspects of providing notice that the death penalty will be sought: (1) statutory notice, (2) notice in multiple death cases, and (3) the *Lankford* notice exception.

Statutory Notice Requirement

A minority of capital punishment jurisdictions statutorily require prosecutors to provide defendants notice of the intent to seek the death penalty, prior to the trial and independent of the notice provided at the arraignment in the charging instrument.[1] Several justifications have been proffered for the stringent statutory notice requirement: (1) it is an acknowledgment that the death penalty is unlike any other form of punishment in its finality, (2) it insures that the plea bargaining process is effectively and fairly carried out, and (3) it enables a defendant to timely make a more intelligent determination of what evidence to present at trial.[2]

Notice in Multiple Murder Prosecution

In the case of *Grandison v. State*, 670 A.2d 398 (Md. 1995), the court addressed the issue of notice to seek the death penalty in a multiple murder prosecution. The defendant in *Grandison* was prosecuted for committing two homicides. The prosecutor provided the defendant with statutory notice that the death penalty would be sought. However, the notice did not state that the death penalty would be sought for both homicides.

Subsequent to the defendant's convictions for multiple homicides, he appealed the convictions on the basis that statutory death penalty notice he received was inadequate. The defendant contended that he should have received notice that the death penalty would be sought for each murder. The *Grandison* court disagreed with the defendant in a cautious way. The court indicated that the record in the case revealed that the defendant was aware, before the trial started, that the death penalty would be sought for both murders. The court did not indicate what its decision on the issue would have been, if the record did not show that the defendant was aware before the trial that the death penalty was going to be sought for both murders.

The Lankford Notice Exception

The Supreme Court had an opportunity to address the issue of death penalty notice in the case of *Lankford v. Idaho*, 500 U.S. 110 (1991). The defendant in *Lankford* was convicted and sentenced to death for committing two murders. The record revealed that "[a]t the [defendant's] arraignment, the trial judge advised [him] that the maximum punishment that [he] may receive if ... convicted on either of the two charges [was] imprisonment for life or death."

Subsequent to the defendant's double murder convictions, his penalty phase hearing was postponed until after the trial of a co-defendant in the case. During this hiatus the defendant asked the trial judge to order the prosecutor to disclose whether the death penalty would in fact be sought at the sentencing hearing. The trial court issued the requested order and the prosecutor responded that it "will not be recommending the death penalty as to either count of first degree murder for which the defendant was earlier convicted."

When the sentencing hearing was finally held, no discussion or evidence was presented in contemplation of the death penalty. The prosecutor recommended a sentence of life for both convictions, to run concurrently. The defendant put on evidence to support concurrent life sentences. To the surprise of both parties, the trial court imposed two death sentences on the defendant.

The defendant appealed the death sentences to the Supreme Court. In the appeal the defendant argued that he did not have notice that he would be subject to the death penalty. In responding to this issue, the Supreme Court initially noted that "the advice received at [defendant's] arraignment, provided such notice." The Court went on to point out, however, that subsequent conduct in the prosecution nullified the notice given at the arraignment. The Court ultimately held that:

Notice of issues to be resolved by the adversary process is a fundamental characteristic of fair procedure.... If notice is not given ... the adversary process is not permitted to function properly [and] there is an increased chance of error, and with that, the possibility of an incorrect result. [The defendant's] lack of adequate notice that the judge was contemplating the imposition of the death sentence created an impermissible risk that the adversary process may have malfunctioned in this case.

The opinion in *Lankford* established two things.[3] First, a properly conducted arraignment will constitutionally satisfy the notice requirement in capital murder cases. Second, if subsequent to an arraignment a prosecutor explicitly indicates it will not seek the death penalty, such a punishment may not be imposed, absent a timely notice that the punishment will in fact be sought.

Notice of Aggravating Circumstances

As a general matter, aggravating circumstances refers to factors that a prosecutor must prove at a penalty phase hearing in order for the death penalty to be imposed. This section addresses the issue of providing a defendant notice of aggravating circumstances before the trial starts and before the penalty phase hearing begins.

Notice Before Trial

In response to the critical role of aggravating circumstances in death penalty cases, a minority of capital punishment jurisdictions statutorily require prosecutors to provide defendants with pretrial notice of the aggravating circumstances that will be used against them.[4] In the case of *People v. Arias*, 913 P.2d 980 (Cal. 1996), it was held that pretrial notice of aggravating circumstances is adequate, if it gives a defendant a reasonable understanding of what to expect and prepare for at the penalty phase hearing.

Two primary concerns are addressed by the requirement of giving pretrial notice of aggravating circumstances.[5] First, the requirement provides a defendant with sufficient time to prepare a penalty phase defense to the aggravating circumstances. Second, this requirement can facilitate the plea bargaining process by letting the defendant know the strength of the prosecutor's penalty phase evidence.[6]

Notice Prior to Penalty Phase

The penalty phase of a capital offense prosecution is the sentencing hearing. This proceeding follows the guilt phase of a prosecution.

A minority of capital punishment jurisdictions statutorily require prosecutors to provide defendants with notice of aggravating circumstances, prior to the start of the penalty phase of a capital murder prosecution.[7] This requirement means that the notice does not have to be given until after the trial.

9

Prosecuting a Nontriggerman

Determining under what circumstances a convicted nontriggerman may be sentenced to death is not at issue in this chapter. The material in this chapter is narrowly confined to exploring circumstances that allow a prosecutor to charge and obtain a conviction of a non-triggerman for capital murder. Various legal theories are available which permit a prosecutor to charge and convict a defendant for capital murder, even though he or she did not actually perform the act which resulted in the victim's death. The legal theories in question include: law of parties, accomplice liability, theory of accountability, felony-murder, common design rule, and joint venture theory. Some discussion regarding each theory follows.

Law of Parties

Under the law of parties it is immaterial that the defendant did not participate in the actual murder.[1] Additionally, even where the actual killer is only convicted of a lesser included offense of murder, a co-felon may be prosecuted for murder on the theory that he or she aided, abetted, counseled or procured the actual perpetrator who committed the homicide.[2]

The law of parties is circumscribed by the limitation that the lethal force act must be (1) in furtherance of a crime, (2) in prosecution of a common design, or (3) an unlawful act the parties set out to accomplish.[3] In determining whether a defendant should be prosecuted for murder as a party to a homicide, courts look at events occurring before, during and after the offense, as well as to the conduct of the parties which show an understanding and common design to kill the victim.[4] The law of parties consists of four types of actors: (1) principal in the first degree; (2) principal in the second degree; (3) accessory before the fact; and (4) accessory after the fact. Remarks about each follow.

Principal in the First Degree

A principal in the first degree is the actor who, with the requisite mental state or *mens rea*,[5] actually performs the act which directly inflicts death upon a victim.[6] Some examples of the application of the principal in the first degree rule follow.

In the cases of *Smith v. Farley*, 59 F.3d 659 (7th Cir. 1995), *Ex Parte Simmons*, 649 So.2d 1282 (Ala. 1994), and *People v. Pock*, 23 Cal.Rptr.2d 900 (1993), it was held that a prosecution for murder may be sustained against the defendant as a principal when the defendant and a co-felon both shoot the victim, but it is not known which of the two actually fired the bullet that killed the victim. The courts in *Strickler v. Commonwealth*, 404

S.E.2d 227 (Va. 1991), and *People v. Vernon*, 152 Cal.Rptr. 765 (1979), held that when two or more persons take direct part in a fatal beating of the victim, each participant is a principal for capital murder prosecution. In *Purifoy v. State*, 822 S.W.2d 374 (Ark. 1991), it was held that even though a co-felon fired the shot which killed the victim, it would not preclude the defendant's liability as a principal for murder, where the defendant and the co-felon both had guns and both fired at the victim. The court in *Darden v. State*, 758 S.W.2d 264 (Tex.Cr.App. 1988), ruled that where a defendant intentionally took arms to a police station to engage in a gun battle with the police, he may be prosecuted for capital murder as a principal even though the officer killed was shot by a fellow officer. It was held in *State v. Forrest*, 356 So.2d 945 (La. 1978), and *State v. Thomas*, 595 S.W.2d 325 (Mo. App. 1980), that a defendant who drives a co-felon and the victim to the murder scene, and gives the co-felon the weapon used to kill the victim, is a principal in the first degree to murder.

Principal in the Second Degree

To be a principal in the second degree an actor must (1) be present at the scene of the crime and (2) aid, abet, counsel, command or encourage the commission of the offense.[7] The general rule is that one who aids and abets murder with the intent to assist the murder to completion may be prosecuted for capital murder.[8] An aider and abettor can be said to share the principal's intent to murder, when he or she knowingly intends to assist the principal in the commission of a crime and the murder is a natural and probable consequence of that crime.[9] The constitution does not prohibit jurisdictions from making aiders and abettors equally responsible, as a matter of law, with principals.[10]

A defendant may be convicted of first degree murder premised on aiding and abetting, even though no other party was convicted of first degree murder.[11] To establish a murder charge premised on aiding and abetting, the prosecutor must show that (1) the defendant knew the crime was occurring, (2) the defendant associated himself or herself with the effort to murder, (3) the defendant took part in the murder as something he or she wished to bring about, and (4) the defendant committed some overt act to make the murder a success.[12]

To prosecute a defendant for murder as a principal in the second degree, it is not necessary to prove an agreement between the defendant and another in advance of the criminal act or even at the time of the act.[13] A defendant may be found constructively present and acting in concert with the principal murderer, if the defendant shared the criminal intent with the principal and the principal knew it.[14] The fact that a prosecutor cannot prove with certainty who pulled the trigger of the gun that killed the victim will not preclude prosecution of a defendant as an aider and abettor.[15] While mere presence of a defendant at a murder scene, without more, is insufficient to deem him or her a party to crime, when combined with other incriminating evidence, presence at the murder scene may be sufficient to sustain a murder prosecution.[16]

Where the evidence does not establish the defendant was present at the time of the killing, and aided and abetted the crime, a charge of being a principal in the second degree fails.[17] Liability for a homicide will not attach to a defendant who becomes an aider and abettor to robbery, after the victim has already been killed.[18] In *State v. Raines*, 606 A.2d 265 (Md. 1992), it was held that where there was no evidence that (1) the driver of a car knew or believed that the passenger intended to shoot and kill from the car, or (2) that the driver himself acted with such intent, or (3) that the victim was shot in furtherance of the commission of a criminal offense which the driver and passenger had undertaken, (4) the driver could not be convicted of murder as a principal in the second degree. The case of *Rogers v. Commonwealth*, 410 S.E.2d 621 (Va. 1991), held that a principal in the second degree cannot be prosecuted for capital murder when the principal commits capital murder willfully, deliberately and premeditated while in the commission of armed robbery or while in the commission of or subsequent to rape.

Accessory Before the Fact

The general rule is that an accessory before the fact of murder may be prosecuted for murder.[19] To be prosecuted as an accessory before the fact to murder (1) the defendant must have counseled, procured, commanded, encouraged, or aided the principal in killing the victim, (2) the principal must have murdered the victim, and (3) the defendant must not have been present when the killing occurred.[20]

To successfully prosecute a defendant for murder as an accessory, the prosecutor must show the defendant had the intent to aid the principal and, in doing so, must have intended to commit the offense.[21] A charge of accessory before the fact of murder will be sustained where the defendant counseled, procured or planned a robbery during the course of which the victim is killed.[22] A defendant may be prosecuted for first degree murder as an accessory before the fact, even though the principal pled guilty to second degree murder.[23] The mere fact that the defendant is in jail when the murder occurred will not preclude his or her conviction for murder where it is shown that he or she was involved in planning the murder.[24] A person who procures another to commit murder is an accessory before the fact of murder.[25]

Accessory After the Fact

To sustain a charge of accessory after the fact, the prosecutor must show that (1) the principal committed murder, (2) the defendant aided the principal in evading arrest, punishment or escape, and (3) the defendant knew that principal committed the murder.[26] An accessory after the fact may not constitutionally be punished with death. However, the common law rule that an accessory after the fact cannot also be a principal in the same crime is inapplicable, where the defendant is charged as an accessory after the fact to murder of one victim, and as a principal on a charge of assault with intent to murder a second victim, as the two offenses represent separate felonies.[27]

Accomplice Liability

For all practical purposes, accomplice liability is nothing more than a legal phrase that describes conduct of a principal in the second degree and accessory before the fact, without distinguishing presence or absence at the crime scene. As a general matter, a person is liable as an accomplice if he or she (1) provided assistance or encouragement, or failed to perform a legal duty, (2) with the intent thereby to facilitate or promote the commission of a crime.

A defendant can be an accomplice to murder even though his or her participation in the killing, when compared to that of the principal, is relatively passive.[28] To hold a defendant liable as an accomplice to a homicide committed by another, the prosecutor needs only show that the defendant intended to promote or facilitate a crime, and there is no need to show that the defendant specifically intended to promote or facilitate a murder.[29] A murder prosecution under the accomplice liability theory does not require the defendant to participate in the actual murder.[30]

Where an accomplice purposely aids in the commission of murder, he or she is said to have the same intent as the principal.[31] However, in determining whether murder is the appropriate charge against an accomplice to a homicide, it is necessary to look at his or her state of mind and not that only of the principal.[32] Moreover, under the accomplice liability theory, it is not necessary that the defendant be shown to have the intent to commit murder after deliberation and premeditation, it is enough to establish the defendant had the intent purposely to promote the commission of murder.[33]

In *State v. Gordon*, 915 S.W.2d 393 (Mo.App. 1996), it was said that proof that a defendant fired the fatal shot which killed a victim is not essential where the defendant is prosecuted under the theory of accomplice liability. The court in *State v. Langford*, 837 P.2d 1037 (Wash.App. 1992), held that by assisting in promoting a fist fight between the victim and principal, the defendant could be held liable as an accomplice, even though he alleged not be to aware that the principal was carrying the knife used in the killing. In *State v. Dees*, 916 S.W.2d 287 (Mo.App. 1995), it was said that a defendant who aided and encouraged a co-felon to hire a third party to kill the victim may be held liable for murder, even though she did not personally perform each act constituting the elements of murder.[34]

Theory of Accountability

The theory of accountability is nothing more than a restatement of the liability theories of principal in the second degree and accessory before the fact, without a distinction being made as to presence or absence at the crime scene. To sustain a murder charge under the theory of legal accountability, the prosecutor must show (1) the defendant solicited, aided, abetted, agreed or attempted to aid another person in planning or committing murder, (2) the defendant's act or conduct occurred before or during the commission of murder, and (3) the defendant acted with concurrent specific intent to promote or facilitate the murder.[35] In *People v. Watts*, 525 N.E.2d 233 (Ill.App. 4 Dist. 1988), it was said that under legal accountability principles it is not necessary that the defendant be shown to have had the specific intent to kill or that he took part in a preconceived plan to commit murder. The court in *People v. Richards*, 413 N.E.2d 5 (Ill.App. 1980), held that where individuals conspire to commit a crime wherein they contemplate violence may be necessary to carry out the plan, all such felons are liable for acts done in furtherance of the plan, so that if death occurs all are liable for murder whether present or not during the commission of the crime.

To sustain a prosecution for murder premised on legal accountability principles it is not necessary to have a disposition against the principal.[36] The fact that the actual killer of the victim is acquitted will not preclude prosecution of the defendant under the theory of accountability, when it is shown the defendant cooperated in planning the felony which resulted in the victim's death and was an active participant in the felony.[37] Liability may attach for murder under the theory of accountability even though the criminal act committed does not result from a preconceived plan, so long as evidence indicates the defendant was involved in the spontaneous act of the group.[38] Mere presence, without more, will not sustain liability under the theory of accountability.[39] However, it was said by the courts in

People v. Taylor, 646 N.E.2d 567 (Ill. 1995), and *Commonwealth v. Lendon*, 622 N.E.2d 1394 (Mass.App. 1993), that under the theory of accountability a defendant who is a passenger in a vehicle and knows that one of its occupants has a weapon and is looking for the victim for the purpose of killing the victim, and the defendant remains in the vehicle with such knowledge, as well as remains with the occupants after the killing, such a defendant may be prosecuted for murder though he or she did not actively participate.

The theory of accountability will sustain a charge of murder when a defendant and a co-felon enter a common design to commit battery and the co-felon kills the victim during the course of battery.[40] The theory of accountability permits a defendant to be convicted under a capital multiple-victim murder statute, regardless of whether the defendant personally killed more than one person.[41] Where the defendant knew that a co-felon intended to rob a victim and the defendant acted as a lookout, he or she can be held accountable for intentional murder of the victim.[42] Even though evidence is not definite that a defendant intended for co-felons to kill the victim, clear proof that the defendant played an integral role in the plan to harm the victim by bringing the victim to the co-felons will support a murder charge under the accountability theory.[43]

Felony-Murder

The law of parties and the felony-murder doctrine merge in order to make a defendant liable for the acts of his or her co-felons. Both doctrines are circumscribed by the limitation that the lethal force act must be (1) in furtherance of the crime, (2) in prosecution of a common design, or (3) an unlawful act the parties set out to accomplish.[44] The Supreme Court's decision in *Enmund v. Florida*, 458 U.S. 782 (1982), prohibits imposition of the death penalty upon a defendant "who aids and abets a felony in the course of which a murder is committed by others[,] but who does not himself kill, attempt to kill, or intend that a killing take place or that lethal force will be employed." The Supreme Court's ruling in *Enmund* applies only to the penalty phase of a capital prosecution, not the guilt phase, therefore a nontriggerman who is a major participant in the underlying felony may be prosecuted for murder under felony-murder theory.[45]

In *Presnell v. Georgia*, 439 U.S. 14 (1978), it was held that the Due Process Clause prohibits imposition of a death sentence under a felony-murder theory, when the underlying non-capital offense conviction is invalid.

When a conspiracy is formed to commit a crime and any of the conspirators commits murder in perpetration or attempted perpetration of the crime, all conspirators actually or constructively present, aiding and abetting the actual perpetrators of the crime, may be prosecuted for murder under the felony-murder theory.[46] In order to hold a defendant liable for murder as an aider and abettor in a felony-murder prosecution, the prosecutor must show either that the defendant had the intent to kill or acted with reckless indifference to human life while participating in the underlying felony.[47] Under the felony-murder doctrine all participants in the underlying crime are regarded as principals, irrespective of whether they can be classified as aiders, abettors or principals.[48]

The felony-murder rule was applied in the fact situations that follow. In *State v. Littlejohn*, 459 S.E.2d 629 (N.C. 1995), it was held that when the defendant accompanied his confederate to commit armed robbery, he could be prosecuted for felony-murder, although he opposed killing and was not in the room when the victim was stabbed. The court in *Hagood v. State*, 588 So.2d 526 (Ala.Cr.App. 1991), said that the defendant may be prosecuted for capital murder, even though he did not stab the victim, but had the intent to aid in the murder of the victim during the course of robbery. In *State v. Johnson*, 365 So.2d 1267 (La. 1978), the court held that when the defendant is responsible for providing escape from a robbery by accomplices, he may be held liable for a homicide committed during the course of the robbery or attempt of the same. In *Wallace v. Lockart*, 701 F.2d 719 (8th Cir. 1983), the court said that evidence showing the defendant was an accomplice to kidnapping the victim is sufficient to sustain a capital felony-murder prosecution, even though the co-defendant actually caused the victim's death.

Common Design Rule

Under the common design rule (also known as concert of action theory), when two or more persons act in concert in the commission of a felony, and a victim is killed by one of the felons, that felon's intent is transferred to the other felon(s) as principal(s) in the second degree.[49] The court in *Price v. State*, 362 So.2d 204 (Miss. 1978), addressed the matter by stating that where two or more individuals act in concert, with a common design to commit a crime of violence against another and a homicide is committed by one of them as incident to the execution of the common design, all participants are criminally liable for the homicide. The court in *State v. Blankenship*, 447 S.E.2d 727 (N.C. 1994), however, held that criminal liability for murder under the common design rule will not attach unless the defendant has the requisite specific intent to commit murder.[50]

In general, proof of a common design to commit an unlawful act which results in death may be inferred from circumstances such as: (1) presence at scene of crime without opposition or disapproval, (2) continued close association with perpetrator after criminal act, (3) failure to inform authorities of incident, or (4) concealment or destruction of evidence after the crime.[51]

Joint Venture Theory

To convict a defendant for murder under the joint venture theory, the prosecutor must prove (1) the defendant was present at the scene of the crime, (2) the defendant had knowledge another intended to commit a crime, and (3) by agreement the defendant was willing and available to help the confederate if necessary.[52] The theory of joint venture murder requires more than mere knowledge of planned criminal conduct or a failure to take affirmative steps to prevent it; rather, a defendant must intend that the victim be killed or know that there is a substantial likelihood of the victim being killed.[53] A joint venturer may be prosecuted for murder if he or she intended that the victim be killed or knew that there was a substantial likelihood that the victim would be killed.[54] The joint venture theory requires that each participant share the requisite mens rea or mental state of the principal.[55]

To sustain a charge of felony-murder premised on the joint venture theory, the prosecutor must show (1) the defendant was a joint venturer with another, (2) the defendant intentionally assisted the principal in the underlying felony, (3) the defendant shared the principal's mental state regarding the underlying felony, (4) the homicide occurred in the commission or attempted commission of the underlying felony, and (5) the homicide flowed naturally from carrying out the joint enterprise.[56]

Murder by joint venture does not require the defendant have an unwavering intent to commit murder; it will suffice if the purpose of murder was a conditional or contingent one.[57] To sustain a joint venture theory of murder in which another person carried and used the weapon, the prosecutor must establish that the defendant knew the other person had the weapon with him or her.[58] A defendant who takes part in a robbery as a joint venturer is responsible for the natural and probable consequences of the robbery, and when a homicide results therefrom, will not escape liability by asserting that he or she was unaware that violence was preplanned by his or her accomplices without his or her knowledge.[59]

10

Foreign Nationals and Capital Punishment

For the purpose of capital punishment, a foreign national is a defendant having citizenship in another country, but is a resident in the United States. The critical issue that has consistently clouded capital prosecution of foreign nationals is their right to communicate with their consular representatives in the United States. This right has unfortunately been routinely violated, so that consular representatives are rarely notified until long after foreign nationals have been prosecuted. In several instances foreign nations have sought to halt the execution of foreign nationals in the United States because of the failure of local officials to notify consular representatives. In no instance has such pressure actually halted an execution.[1] As discussed below, the right of foreign nationals to communicate with their consular representatives is set out in the Vienna Convention on Consular Relations. This chapter will also provide summary discussion of the International Court of Justice and extradition.

Vienna Convention on Consular Relations

The United States ratified the Vienna Convention on Consular Relations in 1969.[2] Article 36 of the Convention expressly requires local officials to timely inform consular officers when foreign nationals are arrested, and to inform arrested foreign nationals of their right to consular assistance.[3] Along with the Vienna Convention, the United States ratified the Optional Protocol Concerning the Compulsory Settlement of Disputes. The Optional Protocol provides that disputes arising out of the interpretation or application of the Convention will lie within the jurisdiction of the International Court of Justice (ICJ), and allows parties to the Protocol to bring such disputes before the ICJ. In response to a decision by the ICJ, in the case of *Mexico v. United States*, 2004 I.C.J. 128, President George W. Bush issued a February 28, 2005, memorandum for the attorney general that said local authorities had to give effect to the *Mexico v. United States* decision. The decision in *Mexico v. United States* required local judicial review of the convictions and death sentences of 51 Mexican nationals, who were not informed of their right to have consular assistance.[4]

The Supreme Court was called upon in *Medellin v. Texas*, 128 S.Ct. 1346 (2008), to decide whether the ICJ decision in *Mexico v. United States* could be enforced in a Texas court by one of the 51 Mexican nationals. The Texas courts found that the defendant could not raise the issue of a violation of the Vienna Convention because he waited too long to raise the issue. When the case reached the Supreme Court the defendant argued that the ICJ decision was enforceable in Texas because of the Vienna Convention and President Bush's memorandum. The Supreme Court rejected both grounds.

First, it was said in *Medellin* that "while the ICJ's judgment ... creates an international law obligation on the part of the United States, it does not of its own force constitute binding federal law that pre-empts state restrictions on the filing of successive habeas petitions." In other words, the Supreme Court found that nothing in the Vienna Convention pre-empted compliance with criminal procedural laws of a government. Thus, the defendant's failure to comply with Texas' procedural rule of timely raising an issue could not be overcome merely because of the ICJ's decision. Second, the Court in *Medellin* found that there was no authority in the Vienna Convention or federal law which gave the president the right to force states to be bound by the decision of the ICJ. Specifically, the following was said in *Medellin*:

> The President's Memorandum is not supported by a "particularly longstanding practice" of congressional acquiescence, but rather is what the United States itself has described as "unprecedented action." Indeed, the Government has not identified a single instance in which the President has attempted (or Congress has acquiesced in) a Presidential directive issued to state courts, much less one that reaches deep into the heart of the State's police powers and compels state courts to reopen final criminal judgments and set aside neutrally applicable state laws. The Executive's narrow and strictly limited authority to settle international claims disputes pursuant to an executive agreement cannot stretch so far as to support the current Presidential Memorandum.

In the decision of *Sanchez-Llamas v. Oregon*, 548 U.S. 331 (2006), the Supreme Court was asked to decide whether evidence of a foreign national's crime should be suppressed when the government fails to inform his or her consular officers of his or her arrest. The Court found that insofar as the Vienna Convention did not set out a remedy for its violation, one could not be created by the courts of the United States. Specifically, it was said in the opinion that "[i]f we were to require suppression for Article 36 violations without some authority in the Convention, we would in effect be supplementing those terms by enlarging the obligations of the United States under the Convention. This is entirely inconsistent with the judicial function."[5]

At least one capital punishment jurisdiction attempted to recognize the consular notification right of foreign nationals. Florida enacted a statute known as the "Recognition of International Treaties Act." This statute obligated Florida officials to assure that contact with consular representatives was timely made when a foreign national was arrested by the state. This statute, however, was repealed in 2001 and replaced with the following:

Florida Code § 901.26 Arrest and Detention of Foreign Nationals
Failure to provide consular notification under the Vienna Convention on Consular Relations or other bilateral consular conventions shall not be a defense in any criminal proceeding against any foreign national and shall not be cause for the foreign national's discharge from custody.

Box 10.0 Article 36 Vienna Convention on Consular Relations

Communication and Contact with Nationals of the Sending State

1. With a view to facilitating the exercise of consular functions relating to nationals of the sending State:

(a) consular officers shall be free to communicate with nationals of the sending State and to have access to them. Nationals of the sending State shall have the same freedom with respect to communication with and access to consular officers of the sending State;

(b) if he so requests, the competent authorities of the receiving State shall, without delay, inform the consular post of the sending State if, within its consular district, a national of that State is arrested or committed to prison or to custody pending trial or is detained in any other manner. Any communication addressed to the consular post by the person arrested, in prison, custody or detention shall also be forwarded by the said authorities without delay. The said authorities shall inform the person concerned without delay of his rights under this subparagraph;

(c) consular officers shall have the right to visit a national of the sending State who is in prison, custody or detention, to converse and correspond with him and to arrange for his legal representation. They shall also have the right to visit any national of the sending State who is in prison, custody or detention in their district in pursuance of a judgment. Nevertheless, consular officers shall refrain from taking action on behalf of a national who is in prison, custody or detention if he expressly opposes such action.

2. The rights referred to in paragraph 1 of this Article shall be exercised in conformity with the laws and regulations of the receiving State, subject to the proviso, however, that the said laws and regulations must enable full effect to be given to the purposes for which the rights accorded under this Article are intended.

Table 10.0 Foreign Nationals Executed 1976–2011

Name	Nationality	State	Date of Execution
Leslie Lowenfield	Guyana	Louisiana	April 13, 1988
Carlos Santana	Dominican Republic	Texas	March 23, 1993
Ramon Montoya	Mexico	Texas	March 25, 1993
Pedro Medina	Cuba	Florida	March 25, 1997
Irineo Tristan Montoya	Mexico	Texas	June 18, 1997
Mario Murphy	Mexico	Virginia	September 18, 1997
Angel Breard	Paraguay	Virginia	April 14, 1998
Jose Villafuerte	Honduras	Arizona	April 22, 1998
Tuan Nguyen	Viet Nam	Oklahoma	December 10, 1998
Jaturun Siripongs	Thailand	California	February 9, 1999
Karl LaGrand	Germany	Arizona	February 24, 1999
Walter LaGrand	Germany	Arizona	March 3, 1999
Alvaro Calambro	Philippines	Nevada	April 5, 1999
Joseph Stanley Faulder	Canada	Texas	June 17, 1999
Miguel Angel Flores	Mexico	Texas	November 9, 2000
Sebastian Bridges	South Africa	Nevada	April 21, 2001
Sahib al-Mosawi	Iraq	Oklahoma	December 6, 2001
Javier Suarez Medina	Mexico	Texas	August 14, 2002
Rigoberto Sanchez Velasco	Cuba	Florida	October 2, 2002
Mir Aimal Kasi	Pakistan	Virginia	November 14, 2002
Hung Thanh Le	Viet Nam	Oklahoma	March 23, 2004
Angel Maturino Resendiz	Mexico	Texas	June 27, 2006
Jose Ernesto Medellin	Mexico	Texas	August 5, 2008
Heliberto Chi Aceituno	Honduras	Texas	August 7, 2008
Edward Nathaniel Bell	Jamaica	Virginia	February 29, 2009

Name	*Nationality*	*State*	*Date of Execution*
Yosvanis Valle	Cuba	Texas	November 10, 2009
Humberto Leal	Mexico	Texas	July 7, 2011
Manuel Valle	Cuba	Florida	September 28, 2011

SOURCE: Death Penalty Information Center, Foreign Nationals (2012).

International Court of Justice

The International Court of Justice (Court) is the primary judicial organ of the United Nations. The Court is located in Netherland at the Peace Palace in The Hague. The Court was established in 1946, after it replaced its predecessor, the Permanent Court of International Justice. The Court was founded for the purpose of resolving legal disputes submitted to it by countries, and to provide advisory opinions on international legal questions. The membership of the Court consists of 15 judges, who are elected to nine-year terms by the United Nations General Assembly and Security Council. Under the rules governing the Court each judge must be from a different country. If the Court hears a case in which a judge is not of the nationality of a country that is a party to the litigation, that country may appoint someone to sit as a judge ad hoc solely for that case. Seats on the Court are filled for one-third of its membership every three years. To qualify for membership on the Court a person must be eligible for appointment to the highest judicial office of his or her country, or be a jurist with recognized competency in international law.

Under its rules the Court may only hear cases that are brought in the name of a country. Neither individuals nor organizations may be a party. The Court may hear a dispute only if the countries involved have accepted its jurisdiction in one or more of the following ways: (1) by special agreement between the parties to submit their dispute to the Court; (2) by a treaty in which both parties are signatories and such treaty authorizes the countries to submit a dispute involving the treaty to the Court; or (3) through the United Nations' Statute wherein both parties have made a declaration that jurisdiction of the Court is compulsory in the event of a dispute.

The procedure used by the Court requires both parties to file and exchange pleadings. Oral arguments are made to the Court at public hearings by agents and counsels for the parties. (The Court utilizes English and French as its official languages for speaking and writing.) After oral arguments are concluded, the Court deliberates in chambers to vote on a decision and then delivers its judgment at a public hearing. The Court decides each case in accordance with international treaties, international custom and general principles of law. The judgment of the Court is final and cannot be appealed. The Court's judgment may be enforced by the Security Council of the United Nations.

During the period 1946 to 2006 the Court delivered 92 judgments that include disputes involving land frontiers and maritime boundaries, territorial sovereignty, interference in the internal affairs of countries, diplomatic relations, hostage-taking, the right of asylum, nationality, and economic rights. As discussed below, two of the cases decided by the Court involved defendants sentenced to death in the United States.[6]

In one case, *Federal Republic of Germany v. United States*, 2001 I.C.J. 466 (June 27), Germany filed a complaint against the United States on March 2, 1999. It was alleged by Germany that the United States violated Article 36 of the Vienna Convention on Consular

Relations, with respect to convictions and death sentences of two German nationals, Karl and Walter LaGrand by the State of Arizona. The violations involved the failure to inform the German consular of the LaGrand brothers' arrest, and the failure to inform the LaGrand brothers of their right to consular assistance, as required by Article 36.

The Court rendered a judgment in the case on June 27, 2001. In that judgment the Court found that the United States did not deny that it had violated Article 36 as alleged by Germany. As for a remedy, the Court pointed out that the United States had agreed to implement a program to ensure that the notification requirements of Article 36 were followed in all jurisdictions. The Court ended its judgment by warning that should future notification problems be brought against the United States, the Court would require the convictions and sentences of affected individuals be reconsidered in light of noncompliance with Article 36. Arizona executed the LaGrand brothers in 1999.

Mexico filed a complaint against the United States on January 9, 2003, in the case of *Mexico v. United States*, 2004 I.C.J. 128 (March 31). In that case Mexico alleged that the United States violated Article 36, with respect to 52 (originally 54) Mexican nationals who were sentenced to death in various jurisdictions. The Court rendered its judgment in the case on March 31, 2004. It held that Article 36 required countries to provide consular information as soon as it is known that an arrested person is a foreign national. The Court concluded that 51 of the 52 Mexican nationals in the case were not given consular information as required by Article 36. It was also found that in 49 of the cases the United States violated its obligation under Article 36 to allow Mexican consular officials to communicate with the arrested individuals. Further, the Court held that in 34 of the cases the United States failed to permit consular officials to arrange for their legal representation. Although Mexico sought, as a remedy for the violations, to have the convictions and death sentences of the prisoners vacated, the Court declined to impose such a penalty. Instead, the Court held that the each prisoner's conviction and death sentence had to be reviewed by the appropriate United States court, in light of the violations of Article 36.

In response to the decision of the Court, President George W. Bush issued a February 28, 2005, memorandum for the attorney general, which said that local authorities had to give effect to the Court's decision. Additionally, the Court's decision was recognized by the United States Supreme Court in the case of *Medellin v. Dretke*, 544 U.S. 660 (2005). The defendant in *Medellin*, a Mexican national, asked the Supreme Court to set aside his conviction and death sentence because the State of Texas violated Article 36 during his prosecution. The Supreme Court dismissed the appeal to permit a Texas court to review the issue in light of President Bush's memorandum. The resolution of the matter is discussed in the previous section.

Extradition

Extradition refers to the involuntary or voluntary removal of a suspect from one jurisdiction to another jurisdiction for criminal prosecution. Two contentions are frequently raised regarding extradition.

First, usually when a capital murder suspect is apprehended in a state that does not have capital punishment, he or she will argue against being extradited to the demanding state because of the prospect of being put to death if found guilty. Under modern capital punishment jurisprudence, non–capital punishment states will not refuse to extradite a capital murder suspect to a capital punishment state for prosecution. On the international level during the late 1990s, Israel refused to extradite Samuel Sheinbein to Maryland to face a capital murder prosecution. Sheinbein and another suspect (the other suspect committed suicide in a Maryland jail while awaiting prosecution) were accused of killing and dismembering the body of 19 year old Alfredo Enrique Tello in 1997. Sheinbein, 17 years old at the time, fled the United States to Israel. The highest court in Israel refused to permit Sheinbein to be extradited to Maryland because he would face a capital punishment prosecution. Sheinbein was eventually prosecuted in Israel for the Maryland murder and sentenced to prison.

The second extradition argument that finds frequent use involves defendants sentenced to death in one state but temporarily extradited to another state for prosecution on other charges. In this situation defendants have argued that the state which imposed the death sentence no longer has jurisdiction to carry out the death penalty, as a result of the temporary extradition. Courts unanimously have held that authority to carry out the death penalty is not lost by a state that temporarily extradites a defendant for further prosecution.

11

Death-Eligible Offenses

As a result of the Supreme Court's interpretation of the Cruel and Unusual Punishment Clause, capital punishment today does not resemble its common law counterpart. A principal alteration has been the drastic reduction in the number of crimes that are punishable as capital offenses. Under the guidance of *Coker v. Georgia*, 433 U.S. 584 (1977) and *Kennedy v. Louisiana*, 554 U.S. 407 (2008) capital punishment for any offense that does not involve the death of a victim may be found unconstitutional by the United States Supreme Court.

Crimes that are punishable with death are called *death-eligible offenses*. The distinguishing feature of death-eligible offenses is that they are created with *special circumstances*. The intent of this chapter is two-fold. First, it will explain the significance of special circumstances. Second, this chapter will provide a detailed look at the vast majority of death-eligible offenses that are used in capital punishment jurisdictions.

BOX 11.0 CAPITAL PUNISHMENT JURISDICTIONS 2012

Alabama	Indiana	Nevada	Texas
Arizona	Kansas	New Hampshire	Utah
Arkansas	Kentucky	Ohio	Virginia
California	Louisiana	Oklahoma	Washington
Colorado	North Carolina	Oregon	Wyoming
Delaware	Mississippi	Pennsylvania	Federal System
Florida	Missouri	South Carolina	
Georgia	Montana	South Dakota	
Idaho	Nebraska	Tennessee	

The Nature of Special Circumstances

The United States Supreme Court has held that the Cruel and Unusual Punishment Clause requires "narrowing the categories of murders for which a death sentence may ... be imposed[.]"[1] This means the death penalty may not be imposed merely because a murder occurred. Legislatures are constitutionally required to add meaningful *special circumstances* that accompany murder in order to justify the imposition of the death penalty.

In the case of *Jurek v. Texas*, 428 U.S. 262 (1976), the Supreme Court held that the special circumstances narrowing of murder for imposition of the death penalty may occur at the guilt phase or penalty (sentencing) phase of a capital prosecution. Subsequent chapters will show that the vast majority of capital punishment jurisdictions impose the constitutional special circumstances narrowing requirement at both the guilt phase and sentencing phase. This situation has unnecessarily added to the complexity of capital punishment.

As a result of the dual narrowing of murder at the guilt phase and penalty phase, the special circumstances requirement has taken on the unintended limited meaning of merely creating death-eligible offenses. Special circumstances do not perform the task of actually causing the imposition of the death penalty. The decision of whether to impose death is controlled by what are called statutory *aggravating circumstances* that are used at the penalty phase.

An underlying premise of special circumstances is that not every murder justifies capital punishment consideration.[2] That is, in keeping with constitutional requirements, special circumstances seek to limit the class of murders that will be exposed to death penalty prosecution. In an effort to pull out a subclass of death-eligible murders from among all murders, legislators have carved out specific factors or conduct that may appear in some murders. These specific factors or conduct are called special circumstances and form the basis of all death-eligible offenses.[3] As a result of forming the basis of death-eligible offenses, a special circumstance actually constitutes an element of the capital offense. As an element of an offense, the constitution requires a special circumstance be proven at the guilt phase beyond a reasonable doubt.

In the final analysis, the crime of murder is the only offense that is punished with death. However, by applying special circumstances to murder, this single offense is transformed into numerous death-eligible offenses, as the material that follows demonstrates.

Death-Eligible Offenses

Only one offense acts as the catalyst for the creation of all constitutionally valid capital crimes: murder. Capital punishment jurisdictions have taken the offense of murder and surrounded it with a variety of special circumstances that culminate in what are referred to as death-eligible offenses. A brief review of some of the current statutory death-eligible offenses follows.

TABLE 11.0 MURDER TIME CLOCK 1999–2010

Year	Frequency of Murder	Year	Frequency of Murder
1999	every 34 minutes	2005	every 31 minutes
2000	every 33 minutes	2006	every 30 minutes
2001	every 32 minutes	2007	every 31 minutes
2002	every 32 minutes	2008	every 32 minutes
2003	every 31 minutes	2009	every 34 minutes
2004	every 32 minutes	2010	every 35 minutes

SOURCE: U.S. Department of Justice, Federal Bureau of Investigation, Uniform Crime Reports (1999–2010).

Murder-Without-More

The phrase murder-without-more refers generally to the intentional killing of a single human being. A majority of capital punishment jurisdictions authorize death penalty consideration for the crime of murder-without-more.[4] A variety of names are used to describe this offense: first-degree murder,[5] murder,[6] deliberate homicide,[7] and aggravated murder.[8]

The special circumstance that is used to make murder-without-more a death-eligible offense is the mental state of a defendant at the time of the commission of the murder. Capital punishment jurisdictions differ on how they describe the mental state. The following are the words that are found in statutes: intentional, willful, deliberate, premeditated, malice, or prior calculation and design. Comments about each mental state will follow.

Intentional murder-without-more. To establish intent to kill, the prosecutor must do more than show an intentional act by the defendant; the prosecutor must establish that the defendant intended for his or her act to result in death.[9] In determining whether a defendant possessed the requisite intent to commit murder, relevant factors that are looked at include the disparity in size and strength between the defendant and victim, and the nature and extent of the victim's injuries.[10]

In proving intent to kill it is not necessary to establish that a specific intent existed for any particular period of time before the homicide occurred.[11] The length of time during which intent to kill is needed varies with the individual defendant and circumstances, but need only be long enough to permit a defendant to maturely and meaningfully contemplate the gravity of his or her intended act.[12] Courts have held that, depending upon a given set of circumstances, intent to murder may occur as instantaneously as successive thoughts.[13]

A capital murder prosecution will be sustained provided the intent to kill is formed before the act is committed and not simultaneously with such act.[14]

Examples of how intentional murder-without-more may be established from the circumstances of the offense include the following. In *State v. McConnaughey*, 311 S.E.2d 26 (N.C.App. 1984), it was held that when a defendant intentionally fires a gun in the direction of a person, thereby causing the death of the person, the killing is intentional. In *Commonwealth v. Lacava*, 666 A.2d 221 (Pa. 1995), it was held that intent to kill may be inferred by the defendant's use of a deadly weapon on a vital part of the victim's body. The court in *State v. Golson*, 658 So.2d 225 (La.App. 2 Cir. 1995), indicated that intent to kill may be inferred from the fact that the defendant pointed the gun at the victim and fired three shots.

Willful murder-without-more. In the context of killing of a human being, willful simply means intentional.[15] To commit willful murder, the defendant must possess the intent to kill.[16]

Deliberate murder-without-more. In the context of capital murder, deliberate refers to something more than intentional, but less than premeditation, and represents a conscious decision that is greater than the mere will to cause the death of the victim.[17] For murder to be deliberate there must be a full and conscious knowledge of the purpose to kill.[18] If a homicide results from a choice made as a consequence of thought, the offense is deemed deliberate murder.[19] Deliberation requires that the defendant consider the probable consequences of his or her act before doing it.[20] Factors that courts consider in determining whether a killing was done with deliberation include: lack of provocation by victim; conduct and statements of defendant before, during and after killing; ill will or previous difficulties between the parties; whether the victim continued to be assaulted after falling and being rendered helpless; and evidence that the killing was done in a brutal manner.[21]

More than a split-second of reflection is required to satisfy a homicide premised on deliberation.[22] Deliberation requires substantially more reflection than the mere amount of thought necessary to form the element of intent to kill.[23] Deliberation requires reflection and judgment, but does not require a long period of time.[24] The deliberation required to support murder-without-more is found when the act done is performed with a cool and deliberate state of mind.[25]

Deliberate intent will not be sustained when the killing is the result of mere unconsidered and rash impulse, even though it includes intent to kill.[26] However, deliberation is not negated merely because the defendant was angry or emotional at the time of the killing, unless evidence establishes that the anger or emotion was strong enough to displace the defendant's ability to reason.[27]

Premeditated murder-without-more. For murder to be premeditated the design to kill must have preceded the killing by an appreciable length of time.[28] In *Jackson v. Virginia*, 413 U.S. 307 (1979), the Supreme Court indicated that premeditation need not exist for any particular length of time and that the decision to kill may be formed at the moment of the commission of the homicide. The appellate court in *DeAngelo v. State*, 616 So.2d 440 (Fla. 1993), held that premeditation can be formed at any moment, and need only exist long enough for a defendant to be conscious of the danger of his or her act and the probable result therefrom. In *State v. Martin*, 702 S.W.2d 560 (Tenn. 1985), it was held that the decision to kill the victim, made during a struggle with the victim, would support finding premeditation; as only a moment of time was required between the plan to kill and execution of that plan.[29] However, *State v. West*, 388 N.W.2d 823 (Neb. 1986), held that no particular length of time was required for premeditation, provided that the decision to kill is formed before the act is committed and not simultaneously with it.[30] In *People v. Van Ronk*, 217 Cal.Rptr. 581 (1985), it was said that premeditation requires substantially more reflection than the mere amount of thought necessary to form the intent to kill.

To determine whether a defendant killed with premeditation, courts are obliged to determine whether, at the time of killing, the defendant had a settled and fixed purpose to take the victim's life.[31] Factors that may be considered in determining whether a defendant engaged in premeditation include: the brutality of the attack, the number of blows inflicted, disparity in size and strength of the defendant and victim, concealment of the corpse, lack of remorse, motive and efforts to avoid detection.[32] Additionally, courts will seek to determine if a deadly weapon was used, the conduct of the defendant before and after the killing, and the presence or absence of provocation.[33]

In the case of *People v. Pride*, 833 P.2d 643 (Cal. 1992), it was held that premeditation may be inferred from a violent and bloody homicide as a result of stab wounds. The court in *Hays v. State*, 599 So.2d 1230 (Ala.Cr.App. 1992), stated that the mere fact that a homicide was unskillfully and haphazardly conceived will not exclude a finding that it was premeditated. In *People v. Edwards*, 819 P.2d 436 (Cal. 1991), the court indicated that a homicide that is senseless and random but premeditated is capital murder. It was held in *Hays v. State*, 85 F.2d 1492 (11th Cir. 1996), that the mere fact that a defendant did not initially set out to kill the victim is irrelevant, when the victim is beaten with a tree limb, dragged by a noose and has his throat slit. Under such facts premeditation can be found.

Malice murder-without-more. The term malice is not the same as, nor interchangeable with, the phrase malice aforethought.[34] Malice aforethought may be defined as intentionally doing a wrongful act, without just cause or excuse, after thinking about it beforehand for any length of time.[35] Malice refers to hatred, ill will or spite; in addition to meaning the condition of mind which prompts a person to take the life of another intentionally without just cause, excuse or justification.[36] Malice aforethought is not an essential element of the crime of murder.[37] Malice is an essential element of murder-without-more and its presence, either directly or inferentially, must be established to sustain a conviction.[38]

Malice, as an element of murder-without-more, may be express or implied.[39] Proving express malice means establishing deliberate intent to kill, whereas proving implied malice requires establishing the commission of a wrongful act from which an abandoned and malignant heart may be inferred.[40] Additionally, malice may be implied from evidence showing wanton disregard for life and the subjective awareness of the risk created by the a defendant's conduct.[41] It has also been held that malice is implied when no considerable provocation appears.[42]

Implied malice may be regarded as constructive malice in that it has not been proven directly to have existed, but the law regards the circumstances of the defendant's act to be so harmful that it is treated as malice. The circumstances must show the defendant's act was done willfully or purposefully.[43]

Implied malice has a physical and mental component. The physical component is met by performance of an act, the natural consequences of which are dangerous to human life. The mental component is met where an act is deliberately performed by a defendant who knows that the act endangers human life, but proceeds with conscious disregard.[44]

Malice refers generally to having knowledge that there is a plain and strong likelihood, based upon the surrounding circumstances, that death will follow contemplated conduct. As a general rule, malice exists as a matter of law whenever there is an unlawful and intentional homicide without justification.[45] The mere fact that a defendant acted on an irrational motive does not preclude a finding of malice.[46]

Malice may be formed just prior to the commission of a homicide.[47] There is no particular length of time required for malice to be generated in the mind of the defendant, and it may be formed in a moment or the instant a mortal blow is given or fatal shot fired.[48] Factors which establish proof of malice in a homicide will vary depending upon the actual circumstances of each case.[49] Malice may be established by proof in one of three ways: (1) the defendant intended to the kill victim without justification or legal excuse; (2) the defendant intended to cause grievous bodily harm; or (3) the defendant acted in circumstances that a reasonably prudent person would know poses a plain and strong likelihood that death would follow the contemplated act.[50]

In *Crossley v. State*, 420 So.2d 1376 (Miss. 1982), it was held that a pistol, even if not loaded or capable of being fired, is a deadly weapon and, as such, its use supplied the element of malice in a murder-without-more prosecution. The court in *State v. Gandy*, 324 S.E.2d 65 (S.C. 1984), held that malice was inferred from the defendant's intent to kill a specific person by firing a gun through a door. In *Commonwealth v. Williams*, 650 A.2d 420 (Pa. 1994), it was held that malice may be established by showing the defendant used a dangerous weapon on a vital part of the victim's body. Malice may be shown by proof that, under circumstances known to the defendant, a reasonably prudent person would have known that there was a plain and strong likelihood that death would follow the contemplated conduct.

Prior calculation and design murder-without-more. It was said in *State v. Cotton*, 381 N.E.2d 190 (Ohio 1978), that in Ohio *prior calculation and design* replaced deliberate and premeditation in capital murder. The court in *Cotton* stated that prior calculation and design was a more stringent element, which meant that instantaneous deliberation was not sufficient to constitute this new element.

Prior calculation and design means that the purpose to kill was reached by a definite process of reasoning in advance of the killing, including a mental plan involving studied consideration of the method or instrument with which to kill.[51] Factors that are considered in determining whether homicide was the result of prior calculation and design include: (1) whether the defendant knew the victim prior to the homicide and, if so, whether the relationship had been strained; (2) whether thought and preparation were given by the defendant to the weapon used and the site where the homicide occurred; and (3) whether the homicide was drawn out over a period of time, as opposed to an instantaneous eruption of events.

The mere fact that a defendant did not know the homicide victim is not conclusive on the issue of whether there was prior calculation and design, if the evidence establishes the defendant planned to kill someone at random.[52] For murder committed with prior calculation and design, reflection need not be long, nor the plan elaborate, but both must have existed.[53]

Homicide in the Commission of Another Offense

Most capital punishment jurisdictions make it a death-eligible offense when anyone causes the death of another during the course of committing a crime.[54] This offense, of course, is nothing more than felony-murder. A few capital punishment jurisdictions do not refer to the offense as such, though they adhere to the principles attendant to felony-murder. The following three statutes illustrate how this death-eligible offense is provided for.

Delaware Code Annotated 11 § 636(a)(2):
While engaged in the commission of, or attempt to commit, or flight after committing or attempting to commit any felony, the person recklessly causes the death of another person.

Georgia Code Annotated § 16-5-1(c):
A person also commits the offense of murder when, in the commission of a felony, he causes the death of another human being irrespective of malice.

Indiana Statutes Annotated § 35-42-1-1(2):
Kills another human being while committing or attempting to commit arson, burglary, child molesting, consumer product tampering, criminal deviate conduct, kidnapping, rape, robbery, human trafficking, promotion of human trafficking, sexual trafficking of a minor, or carjacking.

Capital felony-murder statutes are not unconstitutional on the basis that it relieves the prosecutor of the burden of proving the mental element of murder, because the mental element is established by the prosecutor's proof of intent in the underlying felony.[55] In *State v. McLoughlin*, 679 P.2d 504 (Ariz. 1984), the court said that it is constitutionally permissible to expose a defendant who causes death while seeking to accomplish one of several enumerated felonies, each of which requires a showing of intent or knowledge for a conviction, to the same criminal charge and punishment as a person who causes death with premeditation.

The justification for making homicide during the commission of a crime, a death-eligible offense, is to try and deter the taking of life when homicide is not the motive of a crime.

Victim-Specific Murder

At present, a large minority of capital punishment jurisdictions provide that victim-specific murder is a death eligible offense.[56] Victim-specific murder refers to the intentional killing of an individual who has been officially recognized by a statute. The following statutory illustrations will help in understanding this type of capital crime.

Idaho Code § 18-4003(b):
Any murder of any peace officer, executive officer, officer of the court, fireman, judicial officer or prosecuting attorney who was acting in the lawful discharge of an official duty, and was known or should have been known by the perpetrator of the murder to be an officer so acting[.]

Arkansas Code Annotated § 5-10-101(a)(3):
A person commits capital murder if ... [w]ith the premeditated and deliberated purpose of causing the death of any law enforcement officer, jailer, prison official, fire fighter, judge, or other court official, probation officer, parole officer, any military personnel, or teacher or school employee, when such person is acting in the line of duty[.]

Washington Revised Code § 10.95.020(12):
The victim was regularly employed or self-employed as a newsreporter and the murder was committed to obstruct or hinder the investigative, research, or reporting activities of the victim.

Victim-specific murder statutes seek to provide additional protection for the lives of individuals whose occupations expose them to potential revenge by criminals. Federal statutes provide such additional protection for the president, vice-president,[57] members of Congress and other federal officials.[58]

It will also be noted that victim-specific murder statutes are not confined exclusively to particular occupations. The statute that follows illustrates this point.

Virginia Code § 18.2-31(11):
The willful, deliberate, and premeditated killing of a pregnant woman by one who knows that the woman is pregnant and has the intent to cause the involuntary termination of the woman's pregnancy without a live birth[.]

TABLE 11.1 MURDER CIRCUMSTANCES BY RELATIONSHIP 2010

Victim Relation to Murderer	Victims
Husband	110
Wife	603
Mother	107
Father	135
Son	256
Daughter	197
Brother	88
Sister	19
Boyfriend	131
Girlfriend	492

SOURCE: U.S. Department of Justice, Federal Bureau of Investigation, Uniform Crime Reports, Homicides, Table 10 (2010).

Murder-for-Hire

A minority of capital punishment jurisdictions allow imposition of the death penalty for a homicide committed pursuant to a contract, i.e., exchange of something of pecuniary value for killing a person.[59] Murder-for-hire is generally thought of as conduct engaged in by organized crime. This is especially true after the 1992 trial and conviction of John Gotti, reputed former head of the largest Mafia organization in the United States, the Gambino Crime Family.[60] During Gotti's trial, one of his underbosses, Salvatore "Sammy the Bull" Gravano, testified that he killed 19 people pursuant to contracts issued by John Gotti.[61]

Murder-for-hire is not, however, confined to organized crime. Husbands hire people to kill their wives, as in the case of *Parker v. State*, 610 So.2d 1181 (Ala. 1992), and wives hire people to kill their husbands, as in the cases of *Nunley v. State*, 660 P.2d 1052 (Okla. 1983), and *Coker v. State*, 911 S.W.2d 357 (Tenn. 1995). This, of course, is in addition to nonspousal murder-for-hire crimes, as in the cases of *Grandison v. State*, 670 A.2d 398 (Md. 1995), *State v. DiFrisco*, 662 A.2d 442 (N.J. 1995), and *State v. Kolbe*, 838 P.2d 612 (Ore. 1992). Two illustrations of death-eligible murder-for-hire statutes follow.

Kansas Statutes Annotated § 21-3439(a)(2):
[I]ntentional and premeditated killing of any person pursuant to a contract or agreement to kill such person or being a party to the contract or agreement pursuant to which such person is killed.

Oregon Revised Statutes § 163.095(1):
(a) The defendant committed the murder pursuant to an agreement that the defendant receive money or other thing of value for committing the murder.
(b) The defendant solicited another to commit the murder and paid or agreed to pay the person money or other thing of value for committing the murder.

Len Bias Murder

On June 18, 1986, University of Maryland basketball standout Len Bias signed a lucrative contract to play professional basketball with the Boston Celtics. On June 19, 1986, Len Bias was found dead after allegedly ingesting cocaine. The nation was stunned over the way in which the basketball world had lost a promising superstar.[62]

Before national outrage reached its peak over the death of Len Bias, another senseless tragedy struck the sports world. On June 27, 1986, Cleveland Browns defensive back Don Rogers was found dead after allegedly ingesting cocaine.

After the death of Bias and Rogers, a national call rang out demanding special punishment for drug pushers if death resulted from the use of their drugs. All jurisdictions responded to this call, one way or another, by toughening their drug laws. A small minority of jurisdictions took the ultimate step by enacting specific death-eligible offenses for deaths that occur from the use of illegal drugs.

Colorado Revised Statutes § 18-3-102(1)(e):
He or she commits unlawful distribution, dispensation, or sale of a controlled substance to a person under the age of eighteen years on school grounds…, and the death of such person is caused by the use of such controlled substance.

Florida Statutes Annotated § 782.04(1)(a)(3):
The unlawful killing of a human being … [w]hich resulted from the unlawful distribution of any … cocaine … or opium or any synthetic or natural salt, compound, derivative, or preparation of opium, or methadone by a person 18 years of age or older, when such drug is proven to be the proximate cause of the death of the user[.]

Drive-By Shooting Murder

At the height of the Prohibition Era, traffickers in the sale of illegal alcohol were famous for taking the lives of competitors by firing machine guns and pistols from vehicles. This brazen public method of handling disputes lost its luster and subsided as a national problem in part because of the iron-like determination of law enforcement folk hero Elliot Ness.[63]

Drive-by shooting resurfaced as a national problem during the 1990s. The perpetrators of this deadly resurrection are not bootleggers, however. Drug dealers have taken up this reckless method of handling disputes among themselves. An unfortunate side effect of the current drive-by shooting problem is that innocent bystanders (too often children) have been gunned downed from Los Angeles to Chicago to Atlanta to New York and to every major city in the nation.[64]

A minority of capital punishment jurisdictions have responded to drive-by shooting murder by making it a death-eligible offense.[65] Examples of drive-by-shooting murder statutes follows.

Alabama Code § 13A-5-40(a)(18):
Murder committed by or through the use of a deadly weapon fired or otherwise used within or from a vehicle.

Arkansas Code Annotated § 5-10-101(a)(10):
The person:
(A) Purposely discharges a firearm from a vehicle at a person or at a vehicle, conveyance, or a residential or commercial occupiable structure that he or she knows or has good reason to believe to be occupied by a person; and
(B) Thereby causes the death of another person under circumstances manifesting extreme indifference to the value of human life.

Specific-Device Murder

A federal judge in Alabama opened a package received in the mail and the package exploded, killing him. A civil rights lawyer in Georgia received a package at his office, opened it and it exploded, killing him. These are two real and tragic illustrations of specific-device murders.

A strong and sturdy federal building sits placidly in the heart of America. The building holds children and the laughter of youth. Adults are in the building working toward their American dream. A van sits outside the building. The van explodes and the strong, sturdy federal building falls. Death is everywhere. Oklahoma and the nation are brought to tears. This devastating crime involved specific-device murders.

In New York City, Atlanta, Detroit or Small Town U.S.A., a police officer is in a shoot-out with a desperate drug dealer. The police officer is wearing a bullet-proof vest. The drug dealer takes aim at the officer's heart, fires a shot and the police officer falls to the ground, dead. The drug dealer was using special bullets designed to penetrate metal. This hypothetical scenario represents a potential reality for every police officer in the nation. The scenario is also a specific-device murder.

A large minority of capital punishment jurisdictions have addressed specific-device murder by making this crime a death-eligible offense.[66] The following statute illustrates this offense.

Utah Code Annotated § 76-5-202(1)(n):
[T]he homicide was committed ... (i) by means of a destructive device, bomb, explosive, incendiary device, or similar device which was planted, hidden, or concealed in any place, area, dwelling, building, or structure, or was mailed or delivered; or (ii) by means of any weapon of mass destruction[.]

TABLE 11.2 MURDER WEAPON USED 2006–2010
Year and Number of Victims

Weapon Used	2006	2007	2008	2009	2010
Firearm	10,177	10,086	9,484	9,146	8,775
Knife	1,822	1,796	1,897	1,825	1,704
Blunt object	607	647	614	611	540
Poison	11	10	10	6	11
Explosive	1	1	10	2	4
Fire	115	130	86	99	74
Narcotics	42	49	33	45	n/a

SOURCE: U.S. Department of Justice, Federal Bureau of Investigation, Uniform Crime Reports, Homicide (2006–2010).

Hostage/Human-Shield Murder

The offense of hostage taking must be distinguished from kidnapping. The traditional definition of kidnapping refers to the abduction or transportation of a person against his or her will, for the purpose of holding the victim until a ransom has been paid.[67] Hostage taking, on the other hand, refers to the seizure or detention of a person against his or her will, for the purpose of obtaining some political goal in exchange for the release of the hostage.[68] The two offenses are overlapping, but they are legally distinct forms of conduct.

The human-shield offense describes conduct that may occur in a kidnapping or hostage taking situation. In the case of *People v. Casseus*, 606 N.Y.S.2d 21 (1993), the human-shield offense was described thus:

On February 1, 1989, at approximately 12:30 P.M., a shooting erupted at the Cypress Hills Housing Projects in Brooklyn. While a mother and her two small children were seeking cover between two cars in a parking lot, the defendant grabbed one of the children and held the child up in front of him, using the child as a human shield to block the line of gunfire. The child was shot and seriously wounded.

One jurisdiction, Utah, has specifically provided that hostage-murder and human-shield murder are death-eligible offenses. The Federal System has made hostage-murder a death eligible-offense. The federal statute is set out below.

Federal System 18 U.S.C. § 1203(a):
[W]hoever ... seizes or detains and threatens to kill, to injure, or to continue to detain another person in order to compel a third person or a governmental organization to do or abstain from doing any act as an explicit or implicit condition for the release of the person ... shall ... if the death of any person results ... be punished by death or life imprisonment.

In the case of *United States v. Yunis*, 681 F.Supp. 896 (D.D.C. 1988), it was stated that the federal hostage murder statute "imposes liability on any individual who takes an American national hostage irrespective of where the seizure occurs." *Yunis* further indicated that the purpose of the statute is to "demonstrate to other governments and international forums that the United States is serious about its efforts to deal with international terrorism."

Multiple-Victim Murder

In *State v. Copeland*, 300 S.E.2d 63 (S.C. 1983) three service station attendants were abducted and taken to a secluded area and shot to death. In the case of *State v. Pizzuto*, 810 P.2d 680 (Idaho 1989), two victims were beaten in the head until they were dead. In the case of *State v. Lavers*, 814 P.2d 333 (Ariz. 1991), a mother was shot to death, while her daughter was stabbed to death.

The homicides committed in *Copeland, Pizzuto* and *Lavers* involved the killing of more than one victim. A minority of capital punishment jurisdictions provide that multiple-victim murder is a death-eligible offense.[69] The following are illustrations of multiple-victim murder statutes.

Virginia Code § 18.2-31(7):
The willful, deliberate and premeditated killing of more than one person as part of the same act or transaction.

Texas Penal Code § 19.03(a)(7):
[T]he person murders more than one person:
(A) during the same criminal transaction; or
(B) during different criminal transactions but the murders are committed pursuant to the same scheme or course of conduct.

Drug-Trafficking Murder

During the period 2006 through 2010, an average of 571 murders per year occurred in the context of the illegal drug trade.[70] The staggering impact of drug-trafficking murder[71] may help in understanding why a minority of capital punishment jurisdictions have made this a death-eligible offense.[72]

The case of *United States v. Darden*, 70 F.3d 1507 (8th Cir. 1995), provides a gritty example of the violent context in which drug-trafficking occurs in the nation. There were seven defendants in *Darden*. The defendants were charged with violating various federal drug laws and with committing several murders. The excerpt from the case centers on the murderous path of one of the defendants — Gerald Hopkins:

> The United States presented evidence at the appellants' trial tending to show that Jerry Lee Lewis participated in and became the leader of a powerful criminal racketeering enterprise that for over ten years controlled a large percentage of the market for ... heroin and cocaine in north St. Louis. Lewis obtained and maintained his position by murdering competitors and others who threatened his organization (the Jerry Lewis Organization or JLO). The profitable but bloody activities of the appellants in this case, all members of the JLO, were described by other JLO members who eventually cooperated with the government.... In essence, the investigation and prosecution of Jerry Lee Lewis and his associates produced evidence of a long-term, violent drug-trafficking enterprise....
>
> Jerry Lewis called Gerald Hopkins "my little hitman," and the evidence supports Lewis' conclusion. Earl Parnell testified that both he and [Gerald] Hopkins were involved in the 1985 murder of a deputy sheriff. The deputy, Antar Tiari, was attempting to evict Jerry Lewis ... from ... rented space in St. Louis ... from which JLO conducted operations. [Gerald] Hopkins and Jerry Lewis, dressed in army fatigues, met with Parnell ... to plan the murder.... Parnell testified that [Gerald] Hopkins said, "I shot that [expletive omitted]. Every time I hit him, he just jumped around and danced like this."
>
> Ruby Weaver testified that [Gerald] Hopkins participated in the planning of the 1987 killing of Harold "Court" Johnson, a rival drug dealer, and Ronnie Thomas testified that [Gerald] Hopkins helped to plan the 1988 killing of Ronald Anderson....
>
> Ronnie Thomas also testified that [Gerald] Hopkins participated in the JLO's March 28, 1988 surveillance of Billy Patton, a rival drug dealer who was eventually killed. Andrea Patton, Billy Patton's niece, was rendered a quadriplegic when the car she was driving was riddled with bullets. She had left her uncle's apartment in the car, and ... Thomas ... testified that JLO members

shot at the car in the mistaken belief that Billy Patton was inside. [It was] testified that [Gerald] Hopkins fired the shots....

The drug related killings by the JLO and Gerald Hopkins illustrate why a minority of capital punishment jurisdictions have made drug-trafficking murder an independent death-eligible offense. The following statutes illustrate this offense.

Louisiana Revised Statutes 14 § 30(A)(6):
When the offender has the specific intent to kill or to inflict great bodily harm while engaged in the distribution, exchange, sale, or purchase ... of a controlled dangerous substance[.]

Oklahoma Code tit. 21 § 701.7(B):
A person also commits the crime of murder in the first degree ... if the death of a human being results from, the ... unlawful distributing or dispensing of controlled dangerous substances, or trafficking in illegal drugs.

Murder-on-the-Run

During the 1980s penal institution reformers were successful in their efforts to bring greater civility into correctional institutions. One such achievement in this area was that of allowing model inmates to work outside the grounds of institutions and to have weekend passes to leave confinement. Experience has shown that many model inmates have taken advantage of release privileges by escaping from custody. Too often such escapes have ended with innocent people being killed by inmates on the run.[73]

A large minority of capital punishment jurisdictions have responded to homicides committed by escaped inmates, by making murder-on-the-run a death-eligible offense.[74] Examples of this statutory offense follows.

Idaho Code § 18-4003(f):
Any murder committed by a person while escaping or attempting to escape from a penal institution is murder of the first degree.

Oregon Revised Statutes §163.095(2)(f):
The murder was committed after the defendant had escaped from a state, county or municipal penal or correctional facility and before the defendant had been returned to the custody of the facility.

Grave-Risk Murder

It was held in *State v. Fierro*, 804 P.2d 72 (Ariz. 1990), that for a grave-risk murder to occur the person endangered by the conduct of the defendant must not have been the intended victim of the crime. The capital offense of grave-risk murder is triggered when unintended victims are endangered by a capital felon's conduct. A minority of capital punishment jurisdictions have made grave-risk murder a death-eligible offense.[75] The following statutes illustrate this offense.

Colorado Revised Statutes § 18-3-102(1)(d):
Under circumstances evidencing an attitude of universal malice manifesting extreme indifference to the value of human life generally, he knowingly engages in conduct which creates a grave risk of death to a person, or persons, other than himself, and thereby causes the death of another.

Utah Code Annotated § 76-5-202(1)(c):
[T]he actor knowingly created a great risk of death to a person other than the victim and the actor.

Perjury/Subornation of Perjury Murder

The offense of perjury may be defined as giving false testimony, while under oath, in a matter that involves a felony offense.[76] Subornation of perjury, on the other hand, involves inducing another person to testify falsely, while under oath, in a matter that involves a felony or misdemeanor offense.[77] A minority of capital punishment jurisdictions make perjury murder and subornation of perjury murder death-eligible offenses.[78] The statute that follows illustrates perjury and subornation of perjury murder.

Colorado Revised Statutes § 18-3-102(1)(c):
A person commits the crime of murder in the first degree if ... [b]y perjury or subornation of perjury he procures the conviction and execution of any innocent person.

Forced-Suicide Murder

The death-eligible offense of forced-suicide murder is distinguishable from the crime of assisted suicide, though both produce the same result. Assisted suicide involves intentionally or knowingly making an instrument available for someone who wants to voluntarily commit suicide. Forced-suicide murder, on the other hand, involves intentionally compelling someone to commit suicide, when the victim does not want to die. One capital punishment jurisdiction, Delaware, has made forced-suicide murder a death-eligible offense. The statutory offense is provided for as follows.

Delaware Code Annotated 11 § 636(a)(3):
A person is guilty of murder in the first degree when ... [t]he person intentionally causes another person to commit suicide by force or duress.

Gang-Status Murder

Organized crime flourishes, in large part, because of the existence of a hierarchy in each particular crime gang. The structural essence of any organizational hierarchy is tripartite — top, middle and bottom. Those at the top wish to stay there. Those in the middle and bottom wish to move up. How does one, at the bottom or in the middle, move up in a criminal enterprise? Better still, how does one become a member of a criminal enterprise? There are, no doubt, an unlisted number of ways to advance in a criminal enterprise or become a lethal member of a criminal enterprise. The concern here is with one method of advancement or entrance — murder.

Gang-status murder involves killing someone as a rite of passage into a criminal organization, or killing someone in order to advance in the hierarchy of a criminal organization. At present, the state of Washington is the only capital punishment jurisdiction that makes gang-status murder an independent death-eligible offense. The following statute sets out this offense.

Washington Revised Code § 10.95.020(6):
The person committed the murder to obtain or maintain his or her membership or to advance his or her position in the hierarchy of an organization, association, or identifiable group.

Perpetrator-Status Murder

Not infrequently homicide is committed by someone who is on parole or probation, or has had a previous homicide conviction, or is incarcerated at the time of the commission of the homicide. In any of the latter situations the perpetrator has a legally recognizable status, i.e., parolee, probationer, ex-offender or inmate.

The crime of perpetrator-status murder has as its focal point, the particular status of the perpetrator at the time of the commission of a murder. The significance of status, in this context, is that it implies that the person is a threat to society.

For example, John Dillinger is a respected banker in Small Town, U.S.A. Mr. Dillinger, for one reason or another, shoots and kills a teller in his bank. At the time of the homicide, Mr. Dillinger's status was that of banker. This status does not convey or imply a threat to society. For all practical purposes, Mr. Dillinger's status is irrelevant in determining the offense to charge him with. The law is not concerned with how it should punish bankers, as opposed to anyone else who commits a homicide.

However, a minority of capital punishment jurisdictions has singled out particular statuses and created death-eligible perpetrator-status murder offenses.[79] The following statutes illustrate perpetrator-status murder offenses.

Kansas Statutes Annotated § 21-5401(a)(3):
[I]ntentional and premeditated killing of any person by an inmate or prisoner confined in a state correctional institution, community correctional institution or jail or while in the custody of an officer or employee of a state correctional institution, community correctional institution or jail.

Mississippi Code § 97-3-19(2)(b):
Murder which is perpetrated by a person who is under sentence of life imprisonment.

Oregon Revised Statutes § 163.095(1)(c):
The defendant committed murder after having been convicted previously in any jurisdiction of any homicide[.]

Torture-Murder

The murder committed in *Penick v. State*, 659 N.E.2d 484 (Ind. 1995), provides some understanding of the death-eligible crime of torture-murder. The defendant in *Penick* and three other accomplices were satanic ritualists. On September 25, 1991, the defendant and his accomplices tricked a young man into going to a secluded area with them. The defendant wanted to kill the young man because he had knowledge that the defendant had previously killed someone.

Upon tying up the young man and putting him on the ground, the defendant and his accomplices did the following: "[T]he victim's chest and abdomen were cut open, [an accomplice] tried to cut out the victim's heart before he died.... [T]he victim remained conscious throughout this and responded to questions from the defendant. Only after [the] defendant slit the victim's neck did the torture end.... Finally [they engaged in the] dismemberment of [the] victim's head and hands."

The murder in *Penick* was not clean and quick. Death came only after the victim endured excruciating pain and suffering. Additionally, the victim sustained post-death mutilation. It will be noted that torture and post-death mutilation are legally distinct. Torture means the infliction of severe physical or mental pain upon the victim while he or she remains alive and conscious.[80] Post-death mutilation refers to the dismemberment or disfigurement of a corpse.[81]

A minority of capital punishment jurisdictions have isolated torture-murder and made it a death-eligible offense.[82] The statute that follows illustrates this offense.

Utah Code Annotated § 76-5-202(r):
[T]he homicide was committed in an especially heinous, atrocious, cruel, or exceptionally depraved manner, any of which must be demonstrated by physical torture, serious physical abuse, or serious bodily injury of the victim before death.

Lying-in-Wait Murder

The elements of lying-in-wait murder were set out in the case of *People v. Sims*, 20 Cal.Rptr.2d 537 (1993), as follows: (1) concealment of purpose, (2) substantial period of watching and waiting for an opportune time to act, and (3) immediately thereafter, a surprise attack on an unsuspecting victim from a position of advantage. In *Sims* two defendants were charged and convicted of lying-in-wait murder. The defendants rented a motel room for the purpose of committing the crime. The victim was a young man who worked for a pizza restaurant. The defendants called the restaurant and ordered pizza, knowing that the intended victim would make the delivery. Once the victim arrived he was attacked by the defendants and drowned in a prepared bathtub filled with water.

A small minority of capital punishment jurisdictions have isolated lying-in-wait murder and made it a death-eligible offense.[83] The statute that follows illustrates this offense.

Nevada Revised Statutes § 200.030(1)(a):
Murder in the first degree is murder which is [p]erpetrated by means of ... lying in wait[.]

Victim-Age Murder

The full force of the concern embedded in victim-age murder may be grasped by a review of the salient facts in the case of *State v. Simpson*, 462 S.E.2d 191 (N.C. 1995). The murder victim in this case was named the Reverend Jean E. Darter. Most of the facts presented stemmed from a confession given by the defendant:

> Defendant confessed that ... he and his pregnant, sixteen-year old girlfriend, Stephanie Eury, went for a walk to look for some money. Stephanie went to the front door of the Reverend Darter's house and rang the doorbell. She told the Reverend Darter she was hungry, so he brought her a diet soft drink and gave the defendant a glass of milk. Stephanie asked if they could come inside, so the three went into the front living room. Stephanie told the Reverend that she and defendant were traveling to Florida and had gotten stuck in Reidsville. The Reverend suggested they contact the Salvation Army or the police. Stephanie asked the [Reverend] Darter if he could give them some money, and the Reverend Darter gave her four dollars, explaining that was all the money he had in cash.... Defendant told the police that before he and Stephanie left the house, the Reverend gave them some sponge cake and peaches to take with them....
> The next day ... defendant said that he and Stephanie "both talked about going back to preacher Darter's house to get some money. Stephanie and I decided we would go back to Darter's house and we would not come back empty-handed no matter what[.]" Once it was dark enough, the two walked to the Reverend Darter's house, looking around to make sure no one saw them. They rang the doorbell, and when the Reverend Darter answered the door, they forced their way inside. The Reverend Darter ran to the telephone, but defendant "pulled the preacher's hands off the telephone." Defendant told Stephanie to cut the telephone cords, and in the meantime, he was "struggling with Preacher Darter holding onto the preacher's arms to control him and force him back in his bedroom so he would tell me where some money was." Defendant held the Reverend down on the bed, with his hands around his neck, telling him he wanted money "or else," but the Reverend told defendant he did not have any money.
> Defendant reached across the bed and got a belt and "looped it around his neck and tightened

the belt.... Then I called Stephanie to bring me something in the bedroom to kill this preacher with."

When defendant did not receive any weapon to his liking, he called for Stephanie to come and hold the belt while he "went in the kitchen and looked for some device to beat the old preacher and finish him off." He picked up a full pop bottle and then decided to put it back and get an empty bottle. He returned to the bedroom, pulled tight on the belt, and "hit the old preacher hard three times with this bottle and on the third blow the soft drink bottle broke." Defendant then decided to tie the end of the belt to the bedpost, and he went into the bathroom and got a double-edged razor blade. "I held this double-edged razor blade between my right index finger and right thumb and then I sliced the preacher's arms from the biceps all of the way down the underside of the forearms to the wrist. I cut both of the preacher's arms." Stephanie gathered a bag of food, a porcelain lamp, a radio, and boxes of Kleenex and packed them in a plastic laundry bag. "The last thing we did before leaving the preacher's house was to turn off all the lights except the bathroom light[.]"

Pathologist Michael James Shkrum performed an autopsy on the Reverend Darter and testified the Reverend sustained blunt-trauma injuries to his face causing swelling and bruising. The bone between the eye socket and the brain was fractured, the cheek and the jaw bone were broken, and the Reverend's tongue was torn....

At first impression the murder of the Reverend Darter may appear to be an example of torture-murder. This was, of course torture-murder. However, the focus at this point is not on torture-murder. Victim-age murder is the offense under consideration now. Should the fact that the Reverend Darter was ninety-two years old factor in on the decision to make his homicide a death-eligible offense?

In the case of *People v. Memro*, 47 Cal.Rptr.2d 219 (1996), the defendant slit the throats of two boys aged ten and twelve. In *Harrison v. State*, 644 N.E.2d 1243 (Ind. 1995), the defendant burned alive a child age three and a half years and another age twenty-one months. Should the age of the victims be the determining factor in *Simpson*, *Memro* and *Harrison*, in deciding whether to hold the defendants under the pressure of death-eligible prosecutions?

Victim-age murder has begun to carve out a path as a distinct death-eligible offense. A minority of capital punishment jurisdictions currently have some form of a death-eligible victim-age murder statute.[84] The statute that follows illustrates this offense.

Louisiana Revised Statutes 14 § 30(A)(5):
First degree murder is the killing of a human being ... [w]hen the offender has the specific intent to kill or to inflict great bodily harm upon a victim under the age of twelve or sixty-five years of age or older.

12

Determining Guilt Before
Penalty Phase Hearing

The federal Constitution prohibits imposing capital punishment upon any defendant without there first being a lawful determination that he or she is guilty of committing a capital offense. This determination is made at the guilt phase of a capital prosecution. A capital felon's guilt may be determined in one of three ways: (1) verdict by plea, (2) verdict by the court, or (3) verdict by jury. This chapter examines the legal devices that are used to determine whether a defendant committed a capital offense.

Burden of Proof at Guilt Phase

The doctrine of burden of proof is concerned with the degree of evidence that the law requires to be produced in order to persuade the factfinder of the truth of an allegation. If proffered evidence does not rise to the level required by the law, then the burden has not been sustained and the allegation is deemed not proven. Burden of proof, as a general proposition, means having the obligation of presenting a specific level of evidence to persuade a factfinder of the truth of an allegation.[1] In *Yates v. Aiken*, 484 U.S. 211 (1988), it was held that the Constitution prohibited states from shifting the burden of persuasion on an element of an offense to the defendant.

At the guilt phase of a trial the federal Constitution has been interpreted as requiring prosecutors to prove beyond a reasonable doubt every element of a charged offense. This burden can never shift to a defendant. The significance in having the prosecutor prove a defendant's guilt beyond a reasonable doubt is best understood through the presumption of innocence doctrine.[2]

Anglo-American jurisprudence affords a person charged with a crime a presumption of innocence. The presumption of innocence is a conclusion drawn by the law in favor of the defendant. The burden of proof is never upon the defendant to establish his or her innocence, or to disprove the facts necessary to establish the crime for which he or she is charged. The burden of proof is on the prosecution from the beginning to the end of the trial, and applies to every element necessary to constitute the crime. What this means is that a defendant is not obligated to present any evidence at trial in order to be acquitted of a crime. For example: (1) if the prosecutor presents no evidence during a trial a defendant must be set free; (2) if evidence by a prosecutor only shows that a defendant might have committed a charged crime, the defendant must be acquitted; (3) if a the prosecutor's evidence only establishes that a defendant probably committed a charged crime, a verdict of acquittal must be rendered. In each of the latter three situations the presumption of innocence is combined with the beyond a reasonable doubt standard in order to render an acquittal.[3]

Capital felons frequently challenge their convictions based upon alleged erroneous instructions to juries on the meaning of "beyond a reasonable doubt." Occasionally this challenge has proven successful. For example, in *Cage v. Louisiana*, 498 U.S. 39 (1990), the Supreme Court reversed a capital conviction after concluding the trial court did not correctly define "reasonable doubt" to the jury, because its definition allowed a conviction based on less evidence than the Constitution required to sustain a conviction. However, in most instances challenges to the definition of beyond a reasonable doubt have failed. This is primarily true because the federal Constitution does not dictate that any particular form of words to be used in advising the jury of the government's burden of proof at the guilt phase, so long as, taken as a whole, the instructions correctly convey the concept of reasonable doubt. The proper inquiry into the constitutional validity of a jury instruction on the meaning of "beyond a reasonable doubt" is not whether the instruction "could have" been applied unconstitutionally, but whether there was a reasonable likelihood that the jury in fact applied it unconstitutionally.[4] This was the holding in two consolidated capital cases in *Victor v. Nebraska*, 511 U.S. 1 (1994).

In spite of placing the burden of proof of guilt on prosecutors, defendants are generally required to prove any affirmative defense that is offered. Examples of affirmative defenses include insanity, alibi, self-defense, intoxication and defense of another. In most instances a defendant must prove an affirmative defense by a preponderance of the evidence. Failure to prove an affirmative defense does not mean that a defendant is guilty of a crime. The prosecutor must always prove a defendant's guilt beyond a reasonable doubt regardless of the evidence submitted on an affirmative defense.[5] It will also be noted that, as held in *Johnson v. United States*, 157 U.S. 320 (1895), defendant's conviction and death sentence are not invalid as a result of the prosecutor's failure to prove a motive for the crime, because motive is not an element of a crime. Further, in *Snyder v. Massachusetts*, 291 U.S. 97 (1934) — overruled in other grounds by *Malloy v. Hogan*, 378 U.S. 1 (1964) — it was held that federal Constitution does not require a defendant be permitted to accompany a jury to view the crime scene, because such observations do not constitute evidence. Further, in *Valdez v. United States*, 244 U.S. 432 (1917), it was said that the absence of the defendant during the trial judge's visit to the crime scene did not deny him due process of law.

Verdict by Plea

The Fifth Amendment protects a capital felon from being compelled to confess to committing the offense charged against him or her. Under the Sixth Amendment a capital offender has the right to have his or her guilt determined by a jury. Although the constitutional right against self-incrimination and the right to trial by jury are unshakable rights when invoked, a capital felon may constitutionally waive both.[6]

A capital felon who waives the right against self-incrimination and the right to trial by jury usually intends to enter an adverse plea. The Supreme Court has held that in order for a defendant to enter an adverse plea, he or she must knowingly, voluntarily and intelligently waive the guarantees provided by the constitution.[7] It is only after the latter three elements have been judicially determined that a trial court may accept an adverse plea from a capital felon.

A capital offender does not have a constitutional right to enter an adverse plea. In the case of *North Carolina v. Alford*, 400 U.S. 25 (1970), the Supreme Court pointed out emphatically that "[a] criminal defendant does not have an absolute right under the Constitution to have his ... plea accepted by the court[.]" The privilege of entering an adverse plea is a matter determined by the laws of each jurisdiction.[8]

Up to now the phrase "adverse plea" has been used without distinguishing its components. There are two types of adverse pleas: (1) a nolo contendere plea and (2) a guilty plea. A few comments about each follow.

Nolo Contendere Plea

The phrase "nolo contendere" means no contest. In criminal prosecutions a nolo contendere plea has the effect of a guilty plea, insofar as the punishment for a crime may be imposed based upon the plea. However, a nolo contendere plea is technically not a plea of guilty, nor a plea of innocence. The nolo contendere plea was originally designed to permit a defendant to avoid civil consequences that might result from a plea of guilty. For example, a defendant who assaults a victim is subject to both criminal and civil prosecution. Thus, if a defendant entered a plea of guilty to the criminal charge of assault, the victim could merely take the record of the guilty plea into a civil court and use it as conclusive evidence in a civil case against the defendant for the same conduct. By entering a plea of nolo contendere, a defendant does not give the victim conclusive proof of his or her guilt for use in a civil case. The nolo contendere plea is rare in capital prosecutions, but it has been used.[9] A minority of capital punishment jurisdictions statutorily permit a capital offender to enter a plea of nolo contendere.[10]

Guilty Plea

As recognized in *Bradshaw v. Stumpf*, 545 U.S. 175 (2005), the federal Constitution does not prohibit a court from accepting a defendant's plea of guilty to a capital offense. However, several constitutional rights are implicated and waived when a defendant enters a valid plea of guilty, including the (1) privilege against compulsory self-incrimination, (2) right to trial by jury, and (3) right to confront one's accusers. For a guilty plea to be valid it is constitutionally required that the trial record reflect an affirmative showing that the guilty plea was intelligently and voluntarily made. In *Godinez v. Moran*, 509 U.S. 389 (1993), it was held that the competency standard for pleading guilty is whether the defendant has sufficient present ability to consult with his or her lawyer with a reasonable degree of rational understanding, and a rational as well as factual understanding of the proceedings against him or her.[11] In *Smith v. Baldi*, 344 U.S. 561 (1953), it was held that the Constitution permitted the state to allow the defendant to plead guilty before a determination of his sanity was made, because a procedure was in place to allow the defendant to plead not guilty by reason of insanity.

The plea of guilty ends all discussion concerning who did what, when, where, and how. A capital felon who enters a plea of guilty terminates the adversarial essence of the prosecutorial system. The net effect of such a plea, figuratively speaking, places a defendant on his or her knees in supplication for mercy. In the context of a plea of guilty to a capital offense, mercy means a sentence to life imprisonment.[12]

Generally prosecutors have discretion to enter into any type of constitutionally permissible plea agreement with a capital felon. However, a few courts have held that a prosecutor cannot enter a plea agreement wherein a defendant agrees to enter a plea of guilty to capital murder in exchange for an agreement by the prosecutor to recommend life imprisonment to the penalty phase jury. Courts reason that so long as there is evidence of the existence of at least one statutory aggravating circumstance, a prosecutor is obligated to seek the death penalty once a valid capital offense conviction has been obtained.

Some courts have held that if a plea agreement is made whereby a capital defendant agrees to enter a plea of guilty to non-capital murder, but the agreement is broken, the prosecutor may not thereafter seek a capital murder conviction and sentence. It has been said that regardless of the propriety of increasing an offense charge following a breach of a plea agreement, imposition of the death penalty in such circumstances offends the constitutional principle that capital sentencing determinations require special treatment. When the predictable result of a breach of a plea agreement is the death penalty, imposition of that penalty is arbitrary and in violation of the federal Constitution.

A majority of capital punishment jurisdictions statutorily permit a plea of guilty to a capital offense.[13] Statistics show that while over 90 percent of all non-capital prosecutions are resolved by pleas of guilty, less than 50 percent of all capital offense prosecutions terminate by guilty pleas. Obviously this disparity is reflective of the finality that is incident to a sentence of death. Prosecutors may seek the death penalty against capital felons who reject a plea agreement offer.[14]

Alford plea. In the context of capital punishment, an *Alford* plea is a protestation by a defendant that he or she is innocent, but will plead guilty to avoid the death penalty. The name "*Alford* plea" refers to the case in which the rule of law was announced, *North Carolina v. Alford*, 400 U.S. 25 (1970). The United States Supreme Court has found that an *Alford* plea does not violate the federal Constitution.[15]

Verdict by the Court

A capital offender may waive the right to trial by jury, but nonetheless have a trial. A trial without a jury is called a bench trial. The factfinder in a bench trial is the presiding judge. All capital punishment jurisdictions afford a capital offender the privilege of waiving the right to trial by jury and having a bench trial instead.[16] One jurisdiction, Ohio, requires that a capital punishment bench trial be presided over by a three-judge panel. In all other jurisdictions a single judge sits as factfinder in a bench trial.

A bench trial usually will not occur unless three factors are met: (1) the capital felon validly waives his or her right to trial by jury, (2) the prosecutor consents to trial by the bench, and (3) the judge agrees to hold a bench trial.

Verdict by Jury

The Sixth Amendment to the federal Constitution provides that "[i]n all criminal prosecutions, the accused shall enjoy the right to ... an impartial jury[.]" Qualifications have been made to the constitutional right to trial by jury. The right to trial by jury may be understood more clearly in the context of petty offenses, i.e., offenses that carry a maximum incarceration punishment of six months. In *Baldwin v. New York*, 399 U.S. 66 (1970), and *Codispoti v. Pennsylvania*, 418 U.S. 506 (1974), the Supreme Court held that the Sixth Amendment did not require use of a jury for offenses that carried no more than six months' confinement. Any offense carrying a penalty greater than six months of incarceration must be presided over by a jury, unless a defendant validly waives the right to trial by jury.[17] Capital offenses are punishable by life imprisonment or death. In the final analysis, no capital offender may be prosecuted without a jury unless he or she validly waives the constitutional right to trial by jury.[18]

Number of Jurors

All capital punishment jurisdictions require capital offense juries be composed of twelve members. This privilege is crucial in light of the Supreme Court's pronouncement in *Williams v. Florida*, 399 U.S. 78 (1970), that the Sixth Amendment does not require use of a twelve person jury in felony prosecutions. The Supreme Court also held in *Ballew v. Georgia*, 435 U.S. 223 (1978), however, that a jury composed of fewer than six persons violates the Constitution.

Jury Selection

The Supreme Court also made clear in *Lewis v. United States*, 146 U.S. 370 (1892), that a defendant has a right to be present when jurors are selected for his or her trial, and a violation of that right invalidates his or her conviction and death sentence.

In determining who will be a juror in a trial, the defendant has a right, along with the prosecutor, to challenge persons summoned as potential jurors. The challenge and removal of prospective jurors are done in two ways: (1) for cause, and (2) by peremptory strikes.

Removal for cause. Removal of a prospective juror for "cause" is done by the trial judge. In order to remove a prospective juror for "cause," it must be shown that the juror has a bias or prejudice which prevents him or her from fairly and impartially deciding the issues in the case.

Peremptory strike. Removal of a juror by a peremptory strike is done by the defendant and prosecutor independently. Both the defendant and prosecutor will have a limited number of peremptory strikes which they may use to remove potential jurors for any reason (other than for racial, religious or gender reasons).

Voir dire. In order to utilize peremptory strikes and challenges for cause, potential jurors are questioned. The questioning process is called voir dire examination. The right of challenge comes from the common law, and has always been held essential to the fairness of trial by jury. Under Anglo-American jurisprudence, it is constitutional error to conduct jury selection out of the presence of the defendant. In *Mu'Min v. Virginia*, 500 U.S. 415 (1991), it was held that a trial judge's refusal to question prospective jurors about the specific contents of pretrial news reports of the crime to which they had been exposed did not violate the defendant's constitutional rights.

Race, gender or religious discrimination. A criminal defendant is denied the equal protection of the laws guaranteed by the Fourteenth Amendment of the federal Constitution if he or she is indicted by a grand jury or tried by a petit jury from which members of his or her race, gender or religion have been excluded because of their race, gender or religion. Procedures used to select grand or petit juries may not systematically exclude persons because of their race, gender or religion. A claim of discrimination in grand or petit jury selection cannot be sustained on bare allegations. A defendant must present evidence in support of the claim.

During the early history of the development of capital punishment jurisprudence, the Supreme Court was called upon on numerous occasions to address the issue of racial discrimination in the composition of grand and petit juries. Beginning with the decision in *Strauder v. West Virginia*, 100 U.S. 303 (1879), the Supreme Court has been inflexible in holding that, because of the finality of capital punishment prosecutions, racial discrimination cannot be tolerated in the selection of grand or petit juries. In addition to *Strauder*, other capital punishment cases in which the Supreme Court addressed the issue of racial discrimination in jury selection include: *Akins v. Texas*, 325 U.S. 398 (1945) (no discrimination found); *Arnold v. North Carolina*, 376 U.S. 773 (1964) (discrimination found); *Bush v. Kentucky*, 107 U.S. 110 (1883) (discrimination found); *Carter v. Texas*, 177 U.S. 442 (1900) (discrimination found); *Cassell v. Texas*, 339 U.S. 282 (1950) (discrimination found); *Coleman v. Alabama*, 389 U.S. 22 (1967) (discrimination found); *Eubanks v. Louisiana*, 356 U.S. 584 (1958) (discrimination found); *Franklin v. South Carolina*, 218 U.S. 161 (1910) (no discrimination found); *Gibson v. Mississippi*, 162 U.S. 565 (1896) (no discrimination found); *Hale v. Kentucky*, 303 U.S. 613 (1938) (discrimination found); *Hill v. Texas*, 316 U.S. 400 (1942) (discrimination found); *In re Jugiro*, 140 U.S. 291 (1891) (issue not properly raised); *In Re Wood*, 140 U.S. 278 (1891) (issue not properly raised); *Martin v. Texas*, 200 U.S. 316 (1906) (no discrimination found); *Miller-El v. Dretke*, 545 U.S. 231 (2005) (discrimination found); *Murray v. Louisiana*, 163 U.S. 101 (1896) (no discrimination found); *Neal v. Delaware*, 103 U.S. 370 (1880) (discrimination found); *Norris v. Alabama*, 294 U.S. 587 (1935) (discrimination found); *Patterson v. Alabama*, 294 U.S. 600 (1935) (discrimination found); *Patton v. Mississippi*, 332 U.S. 463 (1948) (discrimination found); *Pierre v. Louisiana*, 306 U.S. 354 (1939) (discrimination found); *Reece v. Georgia*, 350 U.S. 85 (1955) (discrimination found); *Rogers v. Alabama*, 192 U.S. 226 (1904) (discrimination found); *Shepherd v. Florida*, 341 U.S. 50 (1951) (discrimination found); *Sims v. Georgia*, 389 U.S. 404 (1967) (discrimination found); *Smith v. Mississippi*, 162 U.S. 592 (1896) (no discrimination found); *Snyder v. Louisiana*, 128 S.Ct. 1203 (2008) (discrimination found); *Swain v. Alabama*, 380 U.S. 202 (1965) (no discrimination found); *Thomas v. Texas*, 212 U.S. 278 (1909) (no discrimination found); *Whitus v. Georgia*, 385 U.S. 545 (1967) (discrimination found); *Williams v. Georgia*, 349 U.S. 375 (1955) (discrimination found); *Williams v. Mississippi*, 170 U.S. 213 (1898) (no discrimination found).

The Supreme Court pointed out in the case of *Batson v. Kentucky*, 476 U.S. 79 (1986), that a three part procedure is used in order for a defendant to show that a prosecutor used peremptory strikes to remove potential jurors because of their race. First, a defendant must make a prima facie showing that a peremptory strike was made based upon race. Second, if such a showing is made, the prosecutor must come forward and offer a race-neutral basis for striking the juror. Third, the trial court must determine, based upon the parties' submission, whether the defendant has demonstrated intentional discrimination.[19] In *Snyder v. Louisiana*, 128 S.Ct. 1203 (2008), the Supreme Court noted a trial court has a pivotal role in evaluating *Batson* claims. *Snyder* indicated that step three of the *Batson* inquiry involves an evaluation of the prosecutor's credibility, and the best evidence of discriminatory intent often will be the demeanor of the attorney who exercises the challenge. In addition, race-neutral reasons for peremptory challenges often invoke a juror's demeanor (e.g., nervousness, inattention), making the trial court's first-hand observations of even greater importance. In this situation, the trial court must evaluate not only whether the prosecutor's demeanor belies a discriminatory intent, but also whether the juror's demeanor can credibly be said to have exhibited the basis for the strike attributed to the juror by the prosecutor.

In *Thaler v. Haynes*, 130 S.Ct. 1171 (2010), the Supreme Court clarified that neither *Batson* nor *Snyder* held that a demeanor-based explanation for a peremptory challenge must be rejected, unless the judge personally observed and recalls the relevant aspect of the prospective juror's demeanor. Thus, where the explanation for a peremptory challenge is based on a prospective juror's demeanor, the trial judge should take into account, among other things, any observations of the juror that the judge was able to make during the voir dire. *Thaler* concluded that *Batson* and *Snyder* plainly did not go further and hold that a demeanor-based explanation must be rejected if the judge did not observe or cannot recall the juror's demeanor.

Death-qualified jury. Selecting jurors for capital prosecutions presents greater difficulties than the selection process in non-capital cases. In non-capital prosecutions jury selection merely involves selecting a fair and impartial panel. In capital prosecutions the jury selection involves selecting a fair, impartial and death-qualified panel. The death-qualified component of jury selection in capital cases is the factor which imposes greater stress in the jury selection process.

Two unique legal principles have developed and become a part of the process of selecting a petit jury to decide the facts in a capital offense prosecution. The two legal principles in question were developed for the purpose of having death-qualified juries preside over the trial of a capital punishment prosecution.[20] A death-qualified jury is one that can fairly and impartially hear the evidence of a capital offense prosecution and return a verdict that serves the interests of justice.[21] It was said in *Morgan v. Illinois*, 112 S.Ct. 2222 (1992), that a trial court's refusal to inquire whether potential jurors would automatically impose the death penalty upon convicting a capital felon is inconsistent with and violates the Due Process Clause of the Fourteenth Amendment.

The first death-qualified jury principle was developed by the Supreme Court in *Witherspoon v. Illinois*, 391 U.S. 510 (1968). The decision in *Witherspoon* held that the Constitution prohibited enforcement of an Illinois statute which authorized the prosecutor to exclude from the jury, for cause, any venire person who voiced general objections to capital punishment and who indicated that he or she had conscientious scruples against inflicting the death penalty. The Supreme Court found that *Witherspoon* was violated in *Davis v. Georgia*, 429 U.S. 122 (1976), when a prospective juror was struck for cause for merely expressing scruples against the death penalty. In *Adams v. Texas*, 448 U.S. 38 (1980), it was held that *Witherspoon* was violated by a statute used by Texas to exclude members of the venire from jury service because they were unable to take an oath that the automatic penalty of death would not affect their deliberations on any issue of fact. In *Wainwright v. Witt*, 469 U.S. 412 (1985), the Supreme Court held that the *Witherspoon* standard for determining when a prospective juror may be excused for cause, due to his or her views on capital punishment, is whether the juror's views would prevent or substantially impair the performance of his or her duties as a juror in accordance with his or her instructions and oath. This standard does not require that a juror's bias be proved with unmistakable clarity. The decision in *Gray v. Mississippi*, 481 U.S. 648 (1987), reversed a death sentence based upon a violation of *Witherspoon*. Finally, in *Uttecht v. Brown*, 551 U.S. 1 (2007), the Supreme Court made clear that a defendant waives the issue of error in a *Witherspoon* removal of a juror, if the defendant fails to make a timely objection during the jury selection.

The second death-qualified jury principle was announced by the Supreme Court in *Morgan v. Illinois*, 112 S.Ct. 2222 (1992). Under the *Morgan* principle a trial judge may exclude from the venire panel any potential juror who has made known that he or she would automatically vote for imposition of the death penalty, regardless of the evidence in the case.[22] The decision in *Morgan* undermined the ruling in *Ross v. Oklahoma*, 487 U.S. 81 (1988), which held the defendant's right to a fair trial was not violated because the trial court refused to remove a juror who indicated he would automatically vote for the death penalty if the defendant was found guilty.

Courts have held that jurors in capital prosecutions have an obligation to apply the law which mandates death under certain circumstances. Jurors may not ignore their oath or affirmation and obligation to apply the law by choosing to reject the death penalty due to moral opposition to capital punishment. Consequently, the federal Constitution does not prohibit the removal for "cause" of prospective jurors whose opposition to the death penalty is so strong that it would prevent or substantially impair the performance of their duties as jurors at the penalty phase of the trial. This is so even though death-qualification may produce juries somewhat more conviction-prone than non-death-qualified juries. However, a sentence of death cannot be carried out if the jury that imposed or recommended the sentence was chosen by excluding potential jurors for "cause," simply because they voiced general objections to the death penalty or expressed conscientious or religious scruples against its infliction.[23] Of course, as in *Darden v. Wainwright*, 477 U.S. 168 (1986), a court may properly strike for cause a juror who voices strong religious opposition to the death penalty, and a clear statement that such religious views on capital punishment would prevent or substantially impair the performance of his or her duties as a juror.

It was observed in *Lockhart v. McCree*, 476 U.S. 162 (1986), that "[i]t is important to remember that not all who oppose the death penalty are subject to removal for cause in capital cases; those who firmly believe that the death penalty is unjust may nevertheless serve as jurors in capital cases so long as they state clearly that they are willing to temporarily set aside their own beliefs in deference to the rule of law."[24]

In *Uttecht v. Brown*, 127 S.Ct. 2218 (2007), it was held that appellate courts must accord deference to death-qualifying jury decisions made by trial judges. It was said in *Uttecht* that the need to defer to the trial court's ability to perceive jurors' demeanor does not foreclose the possibility that an appellate court may reverse the trial court's decision where the record discloses no basis for a finding of substantial impairment. But where there is lengthy questioning of a prospective juror and the trial court has supervised a diligent and thoughtful voir dire, the trial court has broad discretion.

Race-qualified jury. In *Aldridge v. United States*, 283 U.S. 308 (1931), it was held that the trial court committed reversible error in refusing a request to ask the prospective jury, during jury selection, if they had racial prejudices that would prevent them from fairly deciding the case because the defendant was black and the victim was white. In *Turner v.*

Murray, 476 U.S. 28 (1986), it was said that the constitutional guarantee of an impartial jury entitles a defendant, in a capital case involving interracial violence, to have prospective jurors questioned on the issue of racial bias. This right includes informing the prospective jurors of the race of the victim. This right is not automatic. To invoke the right of having a race-qualified jury, a defendant must specifically request the trial judge make an inquiry into racial opinions and beliefs. The requirements of this rule have not been extended outside of interracial violence criminal prosecutions.[25]

Jury Instructions

Jury instructions embody the law which jurors must apply to the evidentiary facts presented during a prosecution. The trial judge has the exclusive authority to give jury instructions. However, the actual instructions given may incorporate legal principles proffered by the defendant and the prosecutor.[26]

In capital prosecutions separate jury instructions must be given to the guilt phase jury and penalty phase jury. The jury instructions given at the guilt phase encompass legal doctrines concerned with determining guilt or innocence. The penalty phase jury instructions embody legal principles associated with determining whether to impose a sentence of death or grant mercy and impose a sentence of life imprisonment.[27]

Jury Deliberation

The phrase "jury deliberation" refers to the sequestration of a jury for the purpose of deciding issues presented to it during a trial. In capital punishment prosecutions two distinct jury deliberations occur. First, the jury must deliberate to determine whether a defendant is guilty of a capital offense. This deliberation occurs at the guilt phase. Second, if the guilt phase jury renders a verdict finding the defendant guilty of capital murder, the jury must then hear evidence on the issue of punishment. This occurs at the penalty phase. Once the penalty phase jury has heard the evidence on the issue of punishment, it will retire to deliberate on the punishment the defendant should receive.

During jury deliberation no one is allowed in the jury room. In *Mattox v. United States*, 146 U.S. 140 (1892), it was held that improper contact with the jury during its deliberations will result in setting aside a capital conviction. In *Wellons v. Hall*, 130 S.Ct. 727 (2010), the Supreme Court remanded the case to the court of appeals to determine whether the defendant was entitled to discovery and an evidentiary hearing before the district judge, based upon the following misconduct involving the jury:

> Petitioner Marcus Wellons was convicted in Georgia state court of rape and murder and sentenced to death. Although the trial looked typical, there were unusual events going on behind the scenes. Only after the trial did defense counsel learn that there had been unreported *ex parte* contacts between the jury and the judge, that jurors and a bailiff had planned a reunion, and that either during or immediately following the penalty phase, some jury members gave the trial judge chocolate shaped as male genitalia and the bailiff chocolate shaped as female breasts. The judge had not reported any of this to the defense.

Voting Requirement

The Supreme Court indicated in *Johnson v. Louisiana*, 406 U.S. 356 (1972), that there is no constitutional right to have a twelve person jury return a unanimous verdict. However, in the case of *Burch v. Louisiana*, 441 U.S. 130 (1979), the Court held that the constitution required verdict unanimity when a six person jury is used. The majority of capital punishment jurisdictions require a unanimous verdict in capital offense prosecutions.

Mental Impairment Verdicts

A defendant who committed a capital murder while suffering from a mental illness or disease may be found guilty but mentally ill or not guilty by reason of insanity. Both types of verdicts are discussed below.

The Supreme Court held in *Riggins v. Nevada*, 504 U.S. 127 (1992), that forcing the defendant to use the antipsychotic drug Mellaril during his trial infringed upon his due process right to a fair trial. In *Riggins* the state of Nevada charged the defendant with capital murder. Prior to trial the defendant complained of hearing voices and having sleep problems. The trial court ordered a psychiatric examination of the defendant's competency to stand trial. The defendant was found competent, but the examining psychiatrist prescribed the antipsychotic drug Mellaril for the defendant. Defense counsel made a motion to suspend the administration Mellaril until after the defendant's trial, arguing that its use infringed upon his freedom, that its effect on his demeanor and mental state during trial would deny him due process, and that he had the right to show jurors his true mental state when he offered an insanity defense. The trial court denied the motion. The defendant was tried, convicted and sentenced to death. On appeal, the Nevada Supreme Court affirmed the conviction and sentence. In doing so, the appellate court rejected the defendant's contention that forced use of the Mellaril drug violated his constitutional rights. The United States Supreme Court granted certiorari and reversed the defendant's conviction and sentence.

The opinion in *Riggins* held that a defendant has an interest in avoiding involuntary administration of antipsychotic drugs that is protected under the Due Process Clause. The opinion reasoned that once the defendant motioned the trial court to terminate his treatment, the state became obligated to establish both the need for Mellaril and its medical appropriateness. It was indicated that due process would have been satisfied had the state shown that the treatment was medically appropriate and, considering less intrusive alternatives, essential for the defendant's own safety or the safety of others. Additionally, the opinion noted that the state also might have been able to justify the treatment, if medically appropriate, by showing that an adjudication of guilt or innocence could not be obtained by using less intrusive means. However, the opinion found that the trial court allowed the drug's administration to continue without making any determination of the need for its continuation or any findings about reasonable alternatives, and it failed to acknowledge the defendant's liberty interest in freedom from antipsychotic drugs.

Guilty but Mentally Ill

The defense of guilty but mentally ill is a public policy response to societal frustration with criminal defendants who successfully assert the defense of insanity. The height of public disfavor with the result of a verdict of not guilty by reason of insanity reached its apogee in 1982, when John Hinckley was found not guilty by reason of insanity. Hinckley wounded President Ronald Reagan during an assassination attempt in 1980. Hinckley's acquittal by reason of insanity spurred lawmakers around the nation to adopt the seldom previously used verdict of guilty but mentally ill.[28] A minority of capital punishment jurisdictions have adopted the verdict of guilty but mentally ill.[29]

Capital punishment jurisdictions that utilize the verdict of guilty but mentally ill also retain insanity as a defense. Unlike the insanity defense, which provides for acquittal, the defense of guilty but mentally ill will not remove a capital felon from the punishment prescribed by law. Capital felons found guilty but mentally ill are held criminally responsible and may be sentenced to death. Several state high court decisions have upheld the imposition of the death penalty upon capital felons who have been found guilty but mentally ill.[30]

South Carolina Code § 17-24-20
Guilty but Mentally Ill General Requirements for Verdict
(A) A defendant is guilty but mentally ill if, at the time of the commission of the act constituting the offense, he had the capacity to distinguish right from wrong or to recognize his act as being wrong as defined in Section 17-24-10(A), but because of mental disease or defect he lacked sufficient capacity to conform his conduct to the requirements of the law.

(B) To return a verdict of "guilty but mentally ill" the burden of proof is upon the State to prove beyond a reasonable doubt to the trier of fact that the defendant committed the crime, and the burden of proof is upon the defendant to prove by a preponderance of evidence that when he committed the crime he was mentally ill as defined in subsection (A).

(C) The verdict of guilty but mentally ill may be rendered only during the phase of a trial which determines guilt or innocence and is not a form of verdict which may be rendered in the penalty phase.

(D) A court may not accept a plea of guilty but mentally ill unless, after a hearing, the court makes a finding upon the record that the defendant proved by a preponderance of the evidence that when he committed the crime he was mentally ill as provided in Section 17-24-20(A).

Not Guilty by Reason of Insanity

The insanity defense is an affirmative defense. Capital punishment jurisdictions vary in the burden of proof imposed on a capital felon asserting the insanity defense. Most jurisdictions impose a preponderance of the evidence burden. However, in *Leland v. Oregon,* 343 U.S. 790 (1952), the Supreme Court approved of requiring a defendant to prove insanity beyond a reasonable doubt. Notwithstanding the burden placed on a defendant, the prosecutor must still prove guilt beyond a reasonable doubt.

The issue of insanity as a defense is centered on the defendant's state of mind precisely at the time of the commission of the offense. If during the guilt phase of trial the prosecutor fails to show beyond a reasonable doubt that a defendant was sane at the time the offense was being committed, then a verdict of not guilty by reason of insanity must be returned by the jury. The ultimate result of acquittal that follows a successful assertion of the insanity defense caused two capital punishment jurisdictions, Idaho and Montana, to actually abolish the defense by statute.

The first step in a capital punishment prosecution wherein the defendant asserts the insanity defense is for the trial court to determine whether the defendant is competent for trial purposes. To make this determination the trial court will order a psychiatric evaluation of the defendant. The overwhelming majority of defendants who assert the insanity defense are found to be competent for trial purposes.[31] In *Cooper v. Oklahoma*, 517 U.S. 314 (1996), it was held that the Constitution does not permit a state to require a defendant to prove incompetency to stand trial by clear and convincing evidence.

Legal definitions of insanity. The most perplexing issue involving the insanity defense has been that of finding a workable legal definition for the defense. Numerous definitions for legal insanity have been crafted by judges, legislators and commentators on the law. The most reported upon legal definitions of insanity include the *M'Naghten* rule, *Durham* rule, Irresistible Impulse test, and the Substantial Capacity test.

M'Naghten rule. The *M'Naghten* rule was imported to the United States from England. This test for insanity was developed in an English judicial decision styled *M'Naghten's Case*, 8 Eng.Rep. 718 (1843). Under the *M'Naghten* rule a trial court instructs the jury that the defendant may be found not guilty by reason of insanity if the evidence shows that, at the time of committing the act, the defendant was suffering under such a defect of reason, from disease of the mind, as not to know the nature and quality of the act he or she was doing; or, if he or she did know it, that he or she did not know what he or she was doing was wrong.

When the *M'Naghten* rule first hit the legal shores of the United States, it was quickly adopted by almost every court in the nation. Time, however, proved the test to be cumbersome and unworkable.

Durham rule. The *Durham* rule represented the initial break with the unworkable *M'Naghten* rule. The *Durham* rule was fashioned in the case of *Durham v. United States*, 214 F.2d 862 (D.C. Cir. 1954). Under the *Durham* rule the jury is instructed by the trial court that in order to find the defendant not guilty by reason of insanity, the evidence must establish that the defendant was suffering from a diseased or defective mental condition at the time of the commission of the act charged and that there was a causal relation between such disease or defective condition and the act. The *Durham* rule has never been widely adopted.

Irresistible Impulse test. The Irresistible Impulse test was developed by courts as an alternative to the *M'Naghten* rule. In the final analysis, the Irresistible Impulse test is broader than the *M'Naghten* Rule. The Irresistible Impulse test is defined as an impulse to commit a criminal act which cannot be resisted, because a mental disease has destroyed a defendant's freedom of will, power of self-control and choice of actions. Under this test a defendant may avoid criminal responsibility for his or her conduct, even though he or she is capable of distinguishing between right and wrong and is fully aware of the nature and quality of his or her conduct, provided he or she establishes that he or she was unable to refrain from acting. A number of courts utilize this test.

Substantial Capacity test. The Substantial Capacity test was developed by the American Law Institute in 1962 and set out under § 4.01 of the Model Penal Code. Under the Substantial Capacity test a defendant is not responsible for criminal conduct if at the time of such conduct, as a result of mental disease or defect, he or she lacks substantial capacity either to appreciate the wrongfulness of his or her conduct or to conform his or her conduct to the requirement of the law. The Substantial Capacity test has been widely adopted.

Separation of guilt and insanity issues. A few capital punishment jurisdictions have, by statute, separated the issue of guilt and insanity. The legislatures in Arizona, California, Colorado, and Wyoming created a procedure requiring a separate trial for the issue of insanity. In Arizona and Wyoming the statutes were found unconstitutional by the supreme courts of each state. The basic idea behind such statutes is simple. First, a trial on the issue of the defendant's guilt is held. Second, if the defendant is found guilty, a trial on the issue of insanity is held. (This procedure is discussed more fully in the next chapter.)

Civil commitment. Although being found not guilty by reason of insanity acquits a defendant of the offense, this does not mean that the defendant will freely leave the courtroom upon hearing the verdict of the factfinder. A defendant found not guilty by reason of insanity will usually be confined to a secure mental institution under the civil commitment laws of the jurisdiction. This is accomplished through a post-acquittal civil commitment proceeding wherein a determination is made as to whether the defendant is a substantial danger to him/herself or society, by reason of a mental defect that is short of insanity.[32]

13

Structure and Nature
of Penalty Phase

The intent of this chapter is to provide a review of the structure and nature of a capital penalty phase hearing. The material is presented in four sections. The first section looks at the impact of two Supreme Court cases that changed the structure and nature of capital prosecutions in the nation. In the second section an examination of the basic structural components of the penalty phase is provided. The third section gives a general review of the evidentiary nature of a penalty phase proceeding. The final section looks at the non-death penalty punishment that may be imposed for capital murder.

Impact of Furman and Gregg

Capital punishment was fundamentally altered in the nation as a result of decisions by the Supreme Court in two cases. This section reviews both cases.

Furman Abolished Unitary Capital Trials

The Supreme Court decision in *Furman v. Georgia*, 408 U.S. 238 (1972), repudiated almost two hundred years of American capital punishment jurisprudence.[1] In the final analysis, *Furman* indirectly voided and invalidated every capital punishment statute in the nation.

The decision in *Furman* implicated only one capital punishment issue: The constitutionality of the method used by capital punishment jurisdictions to impose the death penalty.[2] *Furman* did not address the issue of whether an offense could have death as a penalty, or whether the method of executing the death penalty was valid. *Furman*'s challenge was confined exclusively to the decision making process that was used to determine who would be sentenced to death and who would be spared death.[3]

Furman concluded that the capital punishment decision making process used in the nation, which was in substance unitary, violated the Cruel and Unusual Punishment Clause of the Eighth Amendment.[4]

The *Furman* decision put an end to the death penalty in the nation. In doing so, the opinion only held that the arbitrary and capricious method by which all capital punishment jurisdictions imposed the death penalty violated the Cruel and Unusual Punishment Clause. As a result of this narrow holding, the door was left open for a rebirth of capital punishment, if a method could be found that would impose death in a constitutionally fair and impartial manner.[5]

Bifurcation Under Gregg

Perhaps it was only appropriate that the state of Georgia developed a new method of imposing capital punishment, which resurrected the death penalty. Georgia devised a scheme which called for a bifurcation of the guilt and penalty phases of a capital offense prosecution. Under this approach, a capital offender's guilt would first be determined. Once the guilt of a capital felon was determined by the jury, a totally separate proceeding would be held wherein aggravating and mitigating circumstances would be presented for consideration by the jury in determining whether the death penalty was the appropriate punishment.

Georgia's new bifurcated scheme was challenged in the case of *Gregg v. Georgia*, 428 U.S. 152 (1976). The Supreme Court held in *Gregg* that Georgia's new method of imposing the death penalty passed constitutional muster. With this monumental ruling the death penalty took on new life and once again became an active part of Anglo-American jurisprudence. Georgia's bifurcated, guilt phase–penalty phase death-penalty procedure became the model for all capital punishment jurisdictions.[6]

Trifurcated trial. The legal concept of a trifurcated trial has its origin in civil litigation. In the context of civil litigation a trifurcated trial involves holding a trial on liability, a separate trial on general damages, and a separate trial on the issue of punitive damages. This civil law trial scheme has found its way into criminal law in a few jurisdictions.

In the context of capital punishment, a trifurcated trial occurs when a capital felon raises the defense of insanity. A trial involving the defense of insanity would take place as follows. First, a trial on the issue of the capital felon's guilt would take place. Next, if the jury rendered a verdict of guilty of a capital offense, another proceeding would be held to determine whether the defendant was insane at the time he or she committed the capital offense. Finally, if the jury determined the capital felon was sane at the time of the offense, a penalty phase proceeding would be held to determine whether the capital felon should be sentenced to death. Currently only the capital punishment jurisdictions of California and Colorado employ a trifurcated trial when a capital felon raises the defense of insanity.

It will be noted that in opinions issued by a few courts, the term trifurcated trial is used to describe a capital prosecution that involves an advisory penalty phase jury. In this situation, a defendant's guilt is determined at the guilt phase proceeding. Next, a penalty phase proceeding is held wherein an advisory jury is used. After the advisory jury renders its recommendation to the trial judge, the trial judge then makes specific findings of fact and conclusions of law as to the penalty to be imposed. It is the separate roles of the advisory jury and the trial court in conjunction with the guilt phase that has caused some courts to describe the process as a trifurcated trial.

Penalty Phase Structure

The decisions of the United States Supreme Court have fashioned a unique capital punishment penalty phase. This section explores the basic skeleton of the penalty phase.

Time Between Guilt Phase and Penalty Phase

The guilt phase of a capital prosecution can last for several weeks. Following the guilt phase, of course, is the penalty phase. At present no jurisdiction provides by statute for a specific time between the end of the guilt phase proceeding and the start of the penalty phase hearing.[7] As a general matter, a recess occurs between the two phases in order to allow the parties to review their notes and strategies, as well as to allow the jury to freshen up.

A recess between the guilt phase and penalty phase is not the equivalent of a continuance. A continuance involves a relatively long period of time. An exceptional and prejudicial circumstance must present itself before a trial court grants a continuance between the two phases. For example, in *State v. Hines*, 919 S.W.2d 573 (Tenn. 1995), the issue of continuance was addressed. The defendant in *Hines* argued on appeal that the trial court abused its discretion in not allowing him a continuance between the two phases. The defendant wanted the continuance in order to arrange for material out-of-state witnesses to appear and testify at the penalty phase hearing. The appellate court rejected the argument that the trial court should have granted a continuance, because prior to the guilt phase the trial court had granted the defendant time to have the witnesses appear.

Presentence Report

A presentence report represents a descriptive history of a defendant who has been convicted of a crime. Presentence reports are compiled by probation officers and submitted to trial judges for consideration prior to imposing sentences. The purpose of a presentence report is to give a trial judge an individualized assessment of a defendant, which includes a review of the defendant's family background and criminal history.

In the context of capital punishment, the United States Supreme Court has held that there is no federal constitutional right to have a presentence report prepared in a capital prosecution. As a general rule, however, presentence reports are prepared prior to the start of a capital penalty phase proceeding. Courts permit penalty phase juries to consider relevant mitigating and aggravating aspects of a presentence report.

In *Williams v. New York*, 337 U.S. 241 (1949), the Supreme Court held that a capital defendant did not have a constitutional right to see and contest information contained in a presentence report that was considered in imposing a death sentence. However, the Court eventually reversed its position and has held that information in a presentence report, to the extent it is relied upon to impose a sentence, must seen by the defendant and an opportunity given to him or her to challenge information in the report. Specifically, in *Gardner v. Florida*, 430 U.S. 349 (1977), the Supreme Court reversed a death sentence because the defendant was not given an opportunity to contest information the trial judge considered in a presentence report.

Basic Outline of Penalty Phase

The format for conducting a penalty phase hearing generally follows that of a trial: opening statements, case-in-chief, rebuttal, closing arguments, and charge to the jury. A few remarks regarding each stage in the hearing follows.

Opening statements. The prosecutor and defense counsel are afforded an opportunity to make opening statements to the penalty phase jury. The opening statement is a nonargumentative summary presentation of the type of evidence each party intends to present to the jury. The prosecutor's opening statement generally is given first.[8] The capital felon will usually give his or her opening statement immediately after the prosecutor concludes. For strategic reasons, however, a capital felon may delay giving his or her opening statement until after the prosecutor's evidence has actually been presented.

Case-in-chief. Once opening statements have been given, the actual evidence of both parties will be presented. This stage is called case-in-chief. Generally the prosecutor will present its case-in-chief first.[9] The prosecutor's case-in-chief will consist of testimonial and physical evidence on the issue of aggravating circumstances. The prosecutor's examination of witnesses that it calls will be through direct examination. What this means is that the questioning must generally be open-ended and not leading. The capital felon will be afforded an opportunity to cross examine all witnesses called by the prosecutor. Leading questions are permitted on cross examination.

At the conclusion of the prosecutor's case-in-chief, the capital felon will be allowed to put on his or her case-in-chief. The evidence presented by the capital felon will consist of testimonial and physical evidence on the issue of mitigating circumstances. The capital felon's questioning of witnesses called by him or her will be through direct examination. The prosecutor will be given an opportunity to cross examine witnesses called by the capital felon.

Rebuttal. In the event that an issue was brought out during the capital felon's case-in-chief that was not addressed during the prosecutor's case-in-chief, the trial court has the discretion to allow the prosecutor to present rebuttal evidence.[10] Rebuttal evidence refers to evidence that is proffered to explain, repel, counteract, or disprove facts given in evidence by the opposing party.[11]

The court in *Johnson v. State*, 660 So.2d 637 (Fla. 1995), noted as a general matter that when a defendant proffers evidence of his or her good character, the prosecutor may rebut such evidence with other character evidence, including collateral crimes that tend to undermine the defendant's character evidence.[12] It was said in *People v. Bounds*, 662 N.E.2d 1168 (Ill. 1995), that a defendant is not denied a fair penalty phase hearing because the prosecutor is permitted to present rebuttal evidence. The court in *State v. Murray*, 906 P.2d 542 (Ariz. 1995), held that a prosecutor may call rebuttal witnesses who did not testify at the guilt phase, so long as such witnesses are timely disclosed to the defendant.

In *State v. Barrett*, 469 S.E.2d 888 (N.C. 1996), it was held that where the defendant's mother testified to his good character, the prosecutor could offer as rebuttal testimony evidence of rumors that the defendant had killed two other people and wounded a third. In *State v. Sepulvado*, 672 So.2d 158 (La. 1996), it was said that where the defendant offered evidence to show that he was a deeply religious man, the prosecutor could rebut the same with evidence concerning details of the defendant's past relationships with women and physical abuse of his stepson. The court in *People v. Medina*, 906 P.2d 2 (Cal. 1995), held that where a defendant proffered evidence that he had a loving relationship with his family, the prosecutor could rebut such testimony with evidence that the defendant had threatened his father when confronted about a stolen truck.

The court in *Greene v. State*, 469 S.E.2d 129 (Ga. 1996), held that where the defendant called a sheriff to testify that he acted as a model prisoner while in jail, the prosecutor was permitted to show in rebuttal that the defendant's model prisoner conduct was merely a ploy to avoid the death penalty. In *Jenkins v. State*, 912 S.W.2d 793 (Tex.Cr.App. 1993), the court held that where a defendant proffers evidence that he would not pose a danger in the future if given a life sentence, because drugs would be unavailable to him in prison, the prosecutor may rebut such testimony by calling a prison narcotics investigator to testify to the availability of drugs in prison.

In *State v. Roscoe*, 910 P.2d 635 (Ariz. 1996), the court held that while a prosecutor may offer rebuttal evidence testimony from the victim's father that focused on the impact of the victim's death, it would be improper rebuttal for the prosecutor to solicit the victim's father's recommendation of punishment. It was said in *People v. Medina*, 906 P.2d 2 (Cal. 1995), that where a defendant proffers evidence that his violent acts began when he was released from prison, it is improper rebuttal for the prosecutor to introduce evidence that the defendant was arrested for violent conduct before he was released from prison.

Closing arguments. At the conclusion of the presentation of all evidence, both sides are given an opportunity to give closing arguments. The purpose is to allow both parties to argue reasons why the jury should reject the evidence of the other party. The general rule is that the prosecutor gives its closing argument last. However, a minority of jurisdictions statutorily require the capital felon give his or her closing argument last.[13]

Charge to the jury. The trial judge will read instructions on the law to the jury before it retires to deliberate. The charge to the jury informs it of the law that must be applied to the facts presented during the penalty phase proceeding.

Jury Penalty Phase Hearing

The penalty phase of a capital offense prosecution is a distinct, trial-like proceeding that allows aggravating and mitigating factors to be introduced and argued. The arguments presented at the penalty phase may be heard by a jury or the court, if the defendant waives the right to have a jury determine the issues. The brief remarks here concern issues involving participation by a jury at the penalty phase.

Right to have penalty phase jury. The federal Constitution guarantees a capital felon the right to trial by jury at the guilt phase of a capital offense prosecution. With that point in mind, it would seem logical that the Constitution would guarantee a capital felon the right to have a jury determine, at the penalty phase, whether the death penalty should be imposed.[14] The Constitution is not always interpreted in a logical manner. In *Walton v. Arizona*, 497 U.S. 639 (1990), and *Clemons v. Mississippi*, 494 U.S. 738 (1990), the Supreme Court held that a capital felon did not have a constitutional right to have a jury determine the issues presented at the capital penalty phase.

The *Walton-Clemons* line of cases were effectively overruled by the Supreme Court in *Ring v. Arizona*, 536 U.S. 584 (2002). The decision in *Ring* held that the federal Constitution required that a jury determine the presence or absence of aggravating and mitigating circumstances at the penalty phase. The decision in *Ring* did not preclude a defendant from waiving the right to a jury trial at the penalty phase. Consequently, a judge may determine the presence or absence of aggravating and mitigating circumstances at the penalty phase, when there has been a valid waiver of the right to a jury. A majority of capital punishment jurisdictions utilize a twelve person jury at the penalty phase.[15]

In *Hildwin v. Florida*, 490 U.S. 638 (1989), it was held that the Constitution does not require a jury specify the aggravating factors that permit the imposition of capital punishment. It was held in *Odle v. Calderon*, 919 F.Supp. 1367 (N.D.Cal. 1996), that there is no constitutional bar to having the jury that presided at the guilt phase also preside at the penalty phase of a capital prosecution.[16] In *United States v. Walker*, 910 F.Supp. 837 (N.D.N.Y. 1995), the court held that a capital felon does not have a right to have a non–death qualified jury for the guilt phase and a separate death-qualified jury for the penalty phase.

The defendant in *People v. Lucas*, 907 P.2d 373 (Cal. 1995), contended that he was entitled to a separate penalty phase jury because the trial court had informed the guilt phase jury that he would put on mitigating evidence at the guilt phase, when in fact he did not put on any evidence at the penalty phase. The *Lucas* court acknowledged that it may have been error for the trial court to inform the guilt phase jury that the defendant was going to introduce mitigating evidence at the penalty phase; however, the error did not warrant a separate penalty phase jury because the trial court purged any prejudice from the error by instructing the jury that the defendant was not obligated to put on mitigating evidence.

Special jury instructions. The material that follows discusses special types of instructions that are given to penalty phase juries, and an instruction that is prohibited.

Non-discrimination jury instruction. A trend has begun wherein capital punishment statutes are expressly requiring trial judges to instruct penalty phase juries that they are not to consider the race, color, religious belief, national origin or sex of capital felons when deliberating on their fate. Courts have been quick to observe that statutory non-discrimination jury instructions are not intended to eliminate jury consideration of legitimate mitigating factors, such as inferences which can be drawn from a capital felon who had a culturally difficult and deprived background.

Nullification jury instruction. The vast majority of jurisdictions limit juries to making findings of fact, and not conclusions of law. However, it is known that juries oftentimes disregard instructions and engage in what is called jury nullification. That is, determining the outcome of an issue based upon their personal beliefs, instead of the dictates of the law. In the area of capital punishment the Supreme Court has been called upon on two occasions to address the issue of trial judges giving nullification instructions to juries. That is, instructing the jury to make a decision that is inconsistent with the law. In *Smith v. Texas*, 543 U.S. 37 (2004), and *Penry v. Johnson*, 532 U.S. 782 (2001), the Supreme Court reversed death sentences because the juries in the cases were instructed in a manner that permitted them to disobey the law in deciding whether the death penalty should be imposed.

Parole ineligibility jury instruction. In *Ramdass v. Angelone*, 530 U.S. 156 (2000), it was held that the trial court was not required to inform the penalty phase jury that the defendant was ineligible for parole, when no evidence made this fact relevant. However, the Supreme Court indicated in *Kelly v. South Carolina*, 534 U.S. 246 (2002), that the prosecutor's evidence showing the defendant took part in an attempt to escape from jail required the penalty phase jury to be informed that he was not eligible for parole. *Kelly* is consistent with the Supreme Court's holding in *Shafer v. South Carolina*, 532 U.S. 36 (2001), and *Simmons v. South Carolina*, 512 U.S. 154 (1994), that a parole ineligibility instruction is required during the penalty phase when evidence of a defendant's future dangerousness is presented by a prosecutor. No such instruction is required if a defendant would, in fact, be eligible for parole.

Rule against double-counting aggravators. Courts prohibit double-counting of certain statutory aggravating circumstances when both factors relate to the same aspect of the crime. For example, it is improper for the trial court to utilize both a felony murder aggravator and a pecuniary gain aggravator when the murder occurred during a robbery. The reason is that the same evidence would support the "monetary" aspect of both aggravators.

Some courts prohibit giving the jury instructions on statutory aggravating circumstances that relate to the same aspect of the crime, and require the prosecutor to make an election between the aggravators the jury will consider. The general approach of most courts, however, is simply to give the jury a list of relevant statutory aggravating circumstances from which to choose, in making their assessment as to whether death is the proper sentence in light of any mitigating circumstances presented in the case. The trial judge must set out in his or her final order the statutory aggravating circumstances found to exist without double-counting. Criticism has been launched against this procedure because it still permits the jury to double-count, even though the trial court removes the double-counting in the sentencing judgment order.

When requested, a capital felon is entitled to a limiting instruction advising the jury not to double-count the weight of multiple aggravating circumstances supported by a single aspect of the crime. Courts have held that the same facts may be used to support more than one statutory aggravating circumstance as long the facts reveal different characteristics of the crime.

Death request generally. The federal Constitution does not prohibit a capital felon from waiving his or her right to put on mitigating evidence during the penalty phase and requesting to be sentenced to death. However, before a capital defendant is permitted to waive his or her right to put on mitigating evidence at the penalty phase and request a sentence of death, a trial court must evaluate the possible mitigating circumstances and inform the defendant of any potential merit they may have.

In addition to having the right to request a death sentence at the penalty phase, a capital felon may request or volunteer to be executed once he or she is on death row. From 1976 to 2011, a request to be put to death was made by and granted to 137 death row inmates.

Jury unanimity. The Constitution does not require jury unanimity at the guilt phase of a capital prosecution. For the sake of consistency, if nothing else, the Constitution does not require jury unanimity at the penalty phase.

In spite of the position of the Constitution, a majority of capital punishment jurisdictions statutorily require jury unanimity in the decision to impose the death penalty.[17] One jurisdiction, Alabama, requires that at least 10 jurors must concur in the decision that the death penalty is appropriate. Additionally, another jurisdiction, Florida, requires only that a "majority" of jurors agree that the death penalty is appropriate.

In *Mills v. Maryland*, 486 U.S. 367 (1988), and *McKoy v. North Carolina*, 494 U.S. 433 (1990), it was held that death penalty statutes could not require a jury to unanimously find the existence of mitigating circumstances, because this would prevent the sentencer from considering all relevant mitigating evidence.

Jury deadlock. In the context of capital punishment, a deadlocked jury is one that is unable to reach a verdict on a defendant's guilt or punishment. In the case of *Allen v. United States*, 164 U.S. 492 (1896), the Supreme Court approved of an instruction to use when a jury is deadlocked. The instruction, called an *Allen* charge, advises the jury to give deference to each other's opinions and informs the minority holdout to reconsider the reasonableness of their position, in light of the position taken by the majority. The *Allen* charge was in great favor for some time, but has been increasingly rejected by state and federal courts as intruding too much on the deliberation process.

In *Weeks v. Angelone*, 528 U.S. 225 (2000), it was said that the trial court acted correctly in responding to a penalty phase jury question about not imposing the death penalty, by informing the jury to reconsider a previously given instruction.

During the guilt phase of a capital trial if the jury is deadlocked and unable to reach a verdict, the trial court will declare a mistrial. A defendant may be reprosecuted after a mistrial caused by a deadlocked jury.

It is not uncommon for a penalty phase jury to be hopelessly deadlocked, i.e., unable to render a verdict based upon the requirements of the jurisdiction. In *Jones v. United States*, 527 U.S. 373 (1999), it was held that the Constitution does not require the penalty phase jury be instructed as to the effect of a jury deadlock on the issue of punishment. The Supreme Court has not declared that the Constitution requires a particular procedure be used or disposition rendered, when a penalty phase jury is deadlocked. The Constitution's silence on this issue means that capital punishment jurisdictions have the discretion to determine this issue as they deem fair.

A majority of capital punishment jurisdictions require that a capital felon be sentenced by the trial judge to prison for life, if the jury is deadlocked.[18] As shown by the statute below, Alabama departs from the majority position.

Alabama Code § 13A-5-46(g):
If the jury is unable to reach [a] verdict recommending a sentence ... the trial court may declare a mistrial of the sentence hearing. Such a mistrial shall not affect the conviction. After such a mistrial or mistrials another sentence hearing shall be conducted before another jury, selected according to the laws and rules governing the selection of a jury for the trial of a capital case.

In *Sattazahn v. Pennsylvania*, 537 U.S. 101 (2003), the penalty phase jury was deadlocked on the punishment. As a result, the trial judge sentenced the defendant to life in prison. The defendant appealed his conviction on the merits of guilt and was given a new trial. During the second trial the defendant was found guilty and sentenced to death. The defendant argued before the Supreme Court that the Double Jeopardy and Due Process Clauses of the Constitution prohibited imposition of the death penalty on a retrial. The Supreme Court disagreed and held that when a jury does not make a determination of whether the death penalty should be imposed, a defendant may face such punishment after a retrial of the guilt phase.

The issue of a deadlocked penalty phase jury was the basis for the decision by the highest court in New York to invalidate that state's death penalty laws. Under the former death penalty laws of New York, a trial judge was required to instruct the penalty phase jury that they had to unanimously decide whether a defendant should be sentenced to death or to life without parole. The trial court was further required to inform the jury that if they failed to agree, the court would have to sentence the defendant to life imprisonment with parole eligibility. In *People v. LaValle*, 3 N.Y.3d 88 (2004), the high court of New York declared that this deadlock instruction coerced juries into voting for the death penalty. As a consequence, New York's death penalty laws were invalidated.

Binding/nonbinding jury sentencing determination. In *Ring v. Arizona*, 536 U.S. 584 (2002), the Supreme Court held that the federal Constitution gave a defendant a right to have a penalty phase jury determine the presence or absence of aggravating and mitigating circumstances. Although under *Ring* a defendant has a right to have a jury at the penalty phase, the actual decision made by a capital penalty phase jury is not constitutionally required to be followed the trial judge. That is, there has been no express authority which overruled the decisions in *Baldwin v. Alabama*, 472 U.S. 372 (1985), and *Spaziano v. Florida*,

468 U.S. 447 (1984). The *Baldwin-Spaziano* decisions stand for the proposition that there is no constitutional right to have a penalty phase jury return a binding recommendation. Thus, the Constitution does not prohibit a trial judge from overriding a jury's recommendation to sentence a capital felon to life imprisonment and impose a sentence of death instead. As a general rule, it is only when facts suggesting a sentence of death are so clear and convincing that virtually no reasonable person could differ on a sentence of death may a trial judge override a jury's recommendation of life imprisonment and impose death.

While there is no constitutional right to have a penalty phase jury's decision followed, a majority of jurisdictions require that judges impose the verdict returned by the jury. These jurisdictions are called binding jurisdictions. Three capital punishment jurisdictions — Alabama, Delaware, and Florida — permit trial judges to override the penalty phase jury's verdict and impose a different sentence. These jurisdictions are called nonbinding jurisdictions. In *Harris v. Alabama*, 513 U.S. 504 (1995), it was held that the Constitution does not require a state to define the weight the sentencing judge must give to an advisory jury verdict.

The Capital Jury Project. In *McCleskey v. Kemp*, 481 U.S. 279 (1987), the Supreme Court held that statistical evidence could not be used to prove racial discrimination in death penalty cases in federal courts. In response to the decision in *McCleskey*, social scientists from eight different states collaborated to determine whether arbitrariness, in the form of racial bias, was still present in capital prosecutions. The research collaboration is called the Capital Jury Project (CJP).

CJP was officially founded in 1991 and is supported by the National Science Foundation. The CJP was designed to: (1) systematically describe jurors' exercise of capital sentencing discretion; (2) assess the extent of arbitrariness in jurors' exercise of such discretion; and (3) evaluate the efficacy of capital statutes in controlling such arbitrariness.[19]

Since its founding the CJP has completed almost 1,200 interviews from jurors in 353 capital trials in 14 states. Jurors were interviewed in Alabama, California, Florida, Georgia, Indiana, Kentucky, Louisiana, Missouri, North Carolina, Pennsylvania, South Carolina, Tennessee, Texas, and Virginia. As a result of its work the CJP produced a report which concluded that the decision making process of death penalty jurors was at odds with the constitution in seven respects: (1) deciding on the death penalty before hearing any penalty phase evidence, (2) pro-death predisposition, (3) failure to understand sentencing requirements, (4) believing that the death penalty is mandatory, (5) evading responsibility for the defendant's punishment, (6) depreciating the death penalty alternative, and (7) racial bias.[20]

Right to Counsel at Penalty Phase

It was not until the case of *Gideon v. Wainwright*, 372 U.S. 335 (1963), that the Supreme Court held that criminal defendants in all jurisdictions have a Sixth Amendment right to counsel at criminal trials. The right to counsel at trial means that, if a defendant cannot afford to retain counsel, the prosecuting jurisdiction must provide an attorney to the defendant. *Gideon*, however, addressed only the guilt phase of a prosecution.

It was not until the case of *Mempa v. Rhay*, 389 U.S. 128 (1967), that the Supreme Court addressed the issue of a defendant's right to counsel during sentencing by the trial judge. (*Mempa* was not decided in the context of bifurcated death penalty proceedings.) In *Mempa* the Court eloquently reasoned that "the necessity for the aid of counsel in marshaling the facts, introducing evidence of mitigating circumstances and in general aiding and assisting the defendant to present his case as to [the] sentence is apparent." The *Mempa* opinion went on to hold that the Sixth Amendment guaranteed a defendant a right to counsel during the sentencing hearing of any criminal prosecution.

Under the *Mempa* precedent, a capital felon has a constitutional right to have an attorney represent him at a capital penalty phase proceeding.[21] This right requires appointment of an attorney for the penalty phase by the prosecuting jurisdiction, if the capital felon is indigent.

Appointment of co-counsel. All capital punishment jurisdictions provide trial courts with discretion to appoint co-counsel for indigent capital felons (a few jurisdictions require this by statute).[22] However, it was pointed out in *Hatch v. Oklahoma*, 58 F.3d 1447 (10th Cir. 1995), and *United States v. Chandler*, 996 F.2d 2083 (11th Cir. 1993), that the constitution does not require appointment of more than one attorney for an indigent capital felon. Notwithstanding *Hatch* and *Chandler*, trial courts will in fact appoint co-counsel for an indigent capital felon if the prosecution involves complex factual and legal issues.[23]

Nature of Evidence at Penalty Phase

The common law developed a body of rules that were used to determine the type of facts that could be introduced as evidence at an actual trial. The common law evidence rules served the purpose of reasonably assuring that a defendant's guilt or innocence would be determined fairly and justly. The rules were not developed to give the prosecutor an advantage at trial, nor were they developed to give the defendant a trial advantage. Fundamental fairness and basic justice were the twin engines that drove common law evidence rules.

The common law evidence rules were adopted, developed and modified by Anglo-American jurisprudence. Presently a majority of jurisdictions have taken the common law evidence rules and, with varying degrees of modification, compiled them into what are known today as rules of evidence. A minority of jurisdictions continue to utilize evidentiary rules that are not in a systemic compilation.

Prior to the Supreme Court's monumental decision in *Furman v. Georgia*, 408 U.S. 238 (1972), the rules of evidence had no real significance outside of the guilt phase of a capital prosecution. This was because the capital sentencing hearing in most jurisdictions involved nothing more than the formality of the trial judge imposing a previously determined sentence. In other words, the pre–*Furman* sentencing hearing was not adversarial. It was because of the nonadversarial nature of the pre–*Furman* sentencing hearing that the rules of evidence had no real application.

Part of the Supreme Court's acceptance of Georgia's penalty phase proceeding in *Gregg v. Georgia*, 428 U.S. 153 (1976), was due to the adversarial nature of the proceeding. As a result of the adversarial nature of the penalty phase, the rules of evidence have now been extended, to some degree, from the guilt phase to the capital penalty phase. However, the rules of evidence generally are relaxed at the penalty phase and evidence is admissible so long as it is relevant and reliable.[24]

Capital felons have argued that the federal Constitution requires that the standard for introducing evidence at the penalty phase be higher than that which is used at the guilt phase. Courts have rejected this contention. As a general rule, any relevant evidence may be introduced during the penalty phase. Wide latitude is granted to parties in introducing evidence in aggravation and mitigation during the capital penalty phase. The evidence, generally, need not satisfy the more restrictive rules of evidence that govern the guilt phase. Such evidence must have a direct bearing on the statutory prerequisites for imposition of the death penalty.

Capital punishment jurisdictions are split on the issue of the application of the rules of evidence at capital penalty phase proceedings.[25] A majority of the jurisdictions do not apply the rules of evidence (at least by statute) to the penalty phase.[26] The remaining jurisdictions have addressed the issue in three different ways. First, in three jurisdictions the rules of evidence apply only against the prosecutor.[27] In these jurisdictions the defendant can introduce any evidence, but the prosecutor's evidence must comply with the rules of evidence. Second, two jurisdictions apply the rules of evidence to both the defendant and prosecutor.[28] Finally, in ten jurisdictions the prosecutor is prohibited from introducing evidence that was obtained in violation of the federal or respective state constitution.[29]

At the penalty phase the prosecutor and defense counsel may introduce and comment upon (1) any evidence raised at the guilt phase that is relevant to the special circumstances found in the indictment or information for which the capital felon was found guilty; (2) any other testimony or evidence relevant to the special circumstances found in the indictment or information; (3) evidence rebutting the existence of an aggravating or mitigating circumstance; (4) any presentence report that was produced; and (5) any mental examination report that was produced.

Physical Evidence

For purposes here, physical evidence is limited to documents and photographs. Examples of decisional law on the admissibility of such evidence follows.

Documentary evidence. In *Barbour v. State*, 673 So.2d 461 (Ala.Cr.App. 1994), the appellate court sustained the trial court's exclusion of a letter proffered by the defendant at the penalty phase. The letter was written by the murder victim's brother and requested that the defendant be sentenced to life imprisonment instead of death. In *Grandison v. State*, 670 A.2d 398 (Md. 1995), it was held that a trial court may exclude court docket entries and an indictment involving an unrelated crime against a co-felon, proffered by the defendant as mitigating evidence, because such evidence had no relevancy and did not concern the defendant's character, background or circumstances of his offense.

In *Ballenger v. State*, 667 So.2d 1242 (Miss. 1995), the appellate court held that the trial court could exclude as irrelevant a psychological report alleging that it was probable that a confederate, rather than the defendant, masterminded the plan in which the victim was killed. In *Johnson v. State*, 660 So.2d 637 (Fla. 1995), the court upheld exclusion of medical records pertaining to the defendant's psychological problems, on the grounds that the records were not authenticated, were incomplete, and required interpretation to be understood by the jury. The court in *McKenna v. McDaniel*, 65 F.3d 1483 (9th Cir. 1995), held that excluding defendant's autobiography from evidence did not violate his constitutional right to individualized sentencing, when witnesses testified as to the substance of the facts contained in the autobiography, thereby making the autobiography cumulative evidence.

Photographic evidence. In *State v. Williams*, 468 S.E.2d 626 (S.C. 1996), the appellate court held that in determining whether to admit photographs of a murder victim's body, a trial court should perform a balancing test to ascertain the prejudicial effect of the pictures against their probative value, with an understanding that probative value has a greater scope at the penalty phase than at the guilt phase. In *Cargle v. State*, 909 P.2d 806 (Okl.Cr. 1995), it was held that a photograph showing the victim holding one of his art works was not admissible, though arguably relevant, because its probative value was substantially outweighed by its prejudicial effect. The back of the photograph had the victim's date of birth and death inscribed on it.[30]

The appellate court in *Pennington v. State*, 913 P.2d 1356 (Okl.Cr. 1995), held that the trial court properly excluded, as irrelevant mitigating evidence, the defendant's proffer of a photograph of himself while in military uniform. In *Johnson v. State*, 660 So.2d 637 (Fla. 1995), it was said that the trial court properly excluded, as mitigating evidence, a photograph of the defendant's stillborn daughter; as the photograph was of little relevance, had the potential to unduly disturb the jury, and was cumulative in light of the fact that the jury was told of the photograph's existence. In *Cargle v. State*, 909 P.2d 806 (Okl.Cr. 1995), the court held that for the purpose of showing victim impact evidence by the prosecutor, a photograph of two murder victims was irrelevant and inadmissible, because it did not show financial, psychological or physical impact of the deaths on the family or any particular information about the victims.

Video recording. In *Cave v. State*, 660 So.2d 705 (Fla. 1995), it was held that a video recording, which dramatized the route taken by the defendant when the victim was kidnapped and the location where the victim was killed, was irrelevant, cumulative and unduly prejudicial; when defendant's guilt was unquestioned and witnesses had testified to the distance between the scene of the abduction and murder, as well as the time it took to travel the distance. However, in *Whittlesey v. State*, 665 A.2d 223 (Md. 1995), it was said that the trial court properly admitted a video recording of the murder victim playing a piano, as this evidence provided relevant information not already in evidence; such as the victim's appearance near the time of death and the victim's skill at playing the piano.

Testimonial Evidence

It was articulated in *People v. McDonald*, 660 N.E.2d 832 (Ill. 1995), that only evidence having a direct impact on statutory prerequisites for imposing the death penalty should be admitted at the penalty phase. In *Commonwealth v. Stevens*, 670 A.2d 623 (Pa. 1996), it was said that testimony regarding one victim's status as an off-duty police officer and a pathologist's testimony regarding his examination of all the victims and medical conclusions were admissible, where the evidentiary value of such evidence (1) clearly outweighs any likelihood of inflaming the minds and passions of the jury, (2) assists the jury in understanding the circumstances surrounding the victims' death and (3) forms the history and natural development of events for which the defendant is being sentenced. In *State v. Sepulvado*, 672 So.2d 158 (La. 1996), it was said that the general rule which prohibits the prosecutor from initiating character evidence about the defendant at the guilt phase is inapplicable at the penalty phase because the defendant's character is the central focus at the penalty phase.

Hearsay testimony. Hearsay is a legal technical term that means a statement, other than one made by a declarant while testifying at trial or hearing, offered in evidence to

prove the truth of the matter asserted by the statement. Under Anglo-American jurisprudence hearsay is generally not allowed at a trial or hearing. The basis of the hearsay exclusion
is that the opposing party will not have had an opportunity to cross examine the declarant
making the out-of-court statement. Thus, the veracity of an out-of-court statement is
deemed questionable.

In capital prosecutions the hearsay rule is followed by all jurisdictions during the guilt
phase. However, jurisdictions are split on the admissibility of hearsay during the penalty
phase. Some jurisdictions generally permit hearsay at the penalty phase, while others apply
the hearsay rule at the penalty phase.

In *Green v. Georgia*, 442 U.S. 95 (1979), it was held that the Constitution prohibited
Georgia from using its hearsay rules to preclude a defense witness' testimony at the penalty
phase of the defendant's capital trial. *Green* found that excluded testimony was highly
relevant to a critical issue in the punishment phase of the trial, and substantial reasons
existed to assume its reliability. It was noted in *Whittlesey v. State*, 665 A.2d 223 (Md.
1995), that it would be error for a trial court to rule that all hearsay evidence is inadmissible
at the penalty phase. The proper course, instead, is for a trial court to make individual
determinations of the reliability of proffered hearsay.

The court in *People v. Moore*, 662 N.E.2d 1215 (Ill. 1996), found that hearsay testimony
by a deputy sheriff that a correction officer told him that the defendant had attacked two
correction officers, had threatened a third officer, and that other law enforcement officers
informed him that while the defendant was being escorted back to the state for trial the
defendant threatened to grab a gun and escape, was properly admitted at the penalty phase
because such hearsay was sufficiently reliable and the information was compiled for security
precautions for those officers who had to guard the defendant. The court in *Moore* also
approved of hearsay testimony by police officers that the defendant committed the uncharged
crimes of rape and attempted rape, on the grounds that the officers had actually investigated
the offenses, the victims had immediately reported the incidents and the officers were thoroughly cross examined.[31]

The court in *Russell v. State*, 670 So.2d 816 (Miss. 1995), held that when prosecution
witnesses testify at the guilt phase, but are unavailable to testify during the penalty phase,
their guilt phase testimony may be introduced into evidence at the penalty phase under the
former testimony exception to the hearsay rule.[32] The court in *Miles v. State*, 918 S.W.2d
511 (Tex.Cr.App. 1996), held that statements made by a deceased declarant which implicated
defendant in the murder were not admissible at the penalty phase under the exception to
the hearsay rule for statements against penal interest, when the declarant had maintained
that he was not a participant in the crime.

Alternatives to Death Sentence

A defendant convicted of a capital offense does not have to be sentenced to death. The
majority of capital punishment jurisdictions provide the alternative sentence of life imprisonment without parole, while a minority of jurisdictions permits the possibility of parole
or a term of years.

There are several ways in which a convicted capital felon may receive a sentence other
than death. First, the penalty phase jury may determine that the prosecutor failed to establish

any statutory aggravating circumstances, in which case a sentence other than death is statutorily automatic. Second, the penalty phase jury, after finding at least one statutory aggravating circumstance exists, may nevertheless reject imposition of the death penalty and recommend or impose a sentence other than death. Third, the penalty phase jury may recommend the death penalty, but the trial judge may decide that based upon the evidence that a sentence other than death is appropriate. Finally, appellate courts may impose a sentence other than death, after finding an incurable prejudicial error occurred at the penalty phase when the capital felon was sentenced to death.

TABLE 13.0 ALTERNATIVES TO DEATH SENTENCE FOR CONVICTION OF CAPITAL OFFENSE

Jurisdiction	Life Without Parole	Life with Parole	Term of Years
Alabama	X		
Arizona	X	X	
Arkansas	X		
California	X		X
Colorado	X		
Delaware	X		
Florida	X		
Georgia	X		
Idaho	X	X	
Indiana	X		
Kansas	X		
Kentucky	X	X	X
Louisiana	X		
Mississippi	X	X	
Missouri	X		
Montana	X		X
Nebraska	X		
Nevada	X	X	X
New Hampshire	X		
North Carolina	X		
Ohio	X	X	
Oklahoma	X	X	
Oregon	X	X	
Pennsylvania	X		
South Carolina	X		X
South Dakota	X		
Tennessee	X	X	
Texas	X		
Utah	X		X
Virginia	X		
Washington	X		
Wyoming	X	X	
Federal System	X		X

The argument has been made by capital felons, in life imprisonment without parole jurisdictions, that they have a right to have the penalty phase jury informed that if they are sentenced to life imprisonment, instead of death, they will not be eligible for parole. Capital felons argue that such information is a valid non-statutory mitigating circumstance for the jury to consider and that the federal Constitution demands the penalty phase jury be informed about parole. Courts have responded, in general, that parole ineligibility is not a mitigating circumstance and, therefore, the federal Constitution does not require penalty phase juries be informed about parole ineligibility, absent the introduction by the prosecutor of evidence of future dangerousness.

14

Statutory Aggravating Circumstances

This chapter will provide a review of statutory aggravating circumstances. The material on statutory aggravating circumstances is divided initially under three broad headings: (1) criminal offense statutory aggravators, (2) identity of victim statutory aggravators, and (3) other statutory aggravators. Some preliminary discussion is required in order to place statutory aggravating circumstances in the proper perspective.

The Meaning of Statutory Aggravating Circumstances

Statutory aggravating circumstances refers to unique factors created by legislators which, if found to exist by the penalty phase factfinder, will constitutionally permit the death penalty to be imposed upon capital offenders.[1] In the case of *Zant v. Stephens*, 462 U.S. 862 (1983), the Supreme Court held that no capital felon may validly be sentenced to death unless at least one statutory aggravating circumstance was proven against him or her. The statutory aggravating circumstance requirements have replaced the pre–*Furman v. Georgia*, 408 U.S. 238 (1972), arbitrariness in imposing the death penalty, and are the sole criteria that permit the death penalty to be imposed.

In the case of *Tuilaepa v. California*, 512 U.S. 967 (1994), the Supreme Court established two conditions that must be satisfied in order for a statutory aggravating circumstance to be constitutionally valid.[2] First, the statutory aggravating circumstance must not be a factor that could be applied to every defendant convicted of murder. For example, the mere fact that a victim died could not be a constitutionally valid statutory aggravating circumstance that allows imposition of the death penalty. The reason being, in every murder the victim dies. A statutory aggravating circumstance must be some factor that would have application to only a subclass of murders.[3]

The second requirement announced in *Tuilaepa* is that a statutory aggravating circumstance cannot be set out in a manner that makes it vague, i.e., it must have a common sense meaning that a jury would understand.[4] For example, in *Espinosa v. Florida*, 505 U.S. 1079 (1992), it was held that the "especially wicked, evil, atrocious or cruel" aggravating circumstance used at the penalty phase of the defendant's trial was constitutionally vague and therefore required his death sentence be vacated. In *Godfrey v. Georgia*, 446 U.S. 420 (1980), it was held that the vague statutory aggravating circumstance of "outrageously or wantonly vile, horrible or inhuman" was not properly defined so as to sustain the defendant's death sentence.

The Supreme Court has held that a vague aggravating circumstance may be cured through judicial guidelines. For example, in *Arave v. Creech*, 507 U.S. 463 (1993), it was held that the state of Idaho placed a constitutionally acceptable limiting construction on the statutory aggravating circumstance of "utter disregard for human life," which cured the vagueness of its meaning. Similarly, in *Bell v. Cone*, 543 U.S. 447 (2005), it was found that the Tennessee Supreme Court placed a narrowing interpretation upon the statutory aggravating circumstance of "heinous, atrocious or cruel." Further, in *Lewis v. Jeffers*, 497 U.S. 764 (1990), and *Walton v. Arizona*, 497 U.S. 639 (1990), overruled on other grounds by *Ring v. Arizona*, 536 U.S. 584 (2002), it was said that the construction given to the statutory aggravating circumstance "especially heinous, cruel or depraved manner" was not vague as applied to the defendant in those cases. The Supreme Court held in *Richmond v. Lewis*, 506 U.S. 40 (1992), *Stringer v. Black*, 503 U.S. 22 (1992), *Shell v. Mississippi*, 498 U.S. 1 (1990), and *Maynard v. Cartwright*, 486 U.S. 356 (1988), that the statutory aggravating circumstance "especially heinous, atrocious, depraved, or cruel" was constitutionally vague as applied to the defendants in those cases.

TABLE 14.0 MURDER TOTALS 2006–2010

Year	Total Murders
2006	15,087
2007	14,916
2008	14,224
2009	13,752
2010	12,996

SOURCE: U.S. Department of Justice, Federal Bureau of Investigation, Uniform Crime Reports, Homicides, Table 8 (2010).

Distinguishing Special Circumstances from Statutory Aggravators

Special circumstances and statutory aggravating circumstances are factors that are created by legislators. The purpose of special circumstances and statutory aggravating circumstances are the same. Both seek to narrow the class of murders subject to death penalty treatment. The function of special circumstances and aggravating circumstances are different. The function of a special circumstance is that of merely triggering death penalty consideration for those whose conduct falls within their sphere of proscriptions. The function of a statutory aggravating circumstance, on the other hand, is that of causing the death penalty to be imposed.

Special circumstances are elements of capital offenses and, as such, are constitutionally required to be proven beyond a reasonable doubt at the guilt phase; if a special circumstance is not so proven at the guilt phase, then a defendant could not be subject to capital sentencing for a homicide. Statutory aggravating circumstances are not elements of capital offenses. They are not constitutionally required to be proven beyond a reasonable doubt, and the proof of their existence is made at the penalty phase.

Many special circumstances are also duplicated as statutory aggravating circumstances. In *Lowenfield v. Phelps*, 484 U.S. 231 (1988), it was held that the Constitution does not prohibit use of a guilt phase special circumstance as a penalty phase statutory aggravating circumstance. Most jurisdictions utilize only a few special circumstances that are the same as some of their statutory aggravating circumstances. However, a few capital punishment jurisdictions duplicate all of their special circumstances as statutory aggravating circumstances.[5] Notwithstanding such duplication, each of the jurisdictions requires proof of both types of "circumstances" at the guilt phase and penalty phase.

Distinguishing Special Statutory Issues from Statutory Aggravators

Four capital punishment jurisdictions do not utilize statutory aggravating circumstances.[6] These jurisdictions allow special circumstances to fulfill the constitutional narrowing at the guilt phase. In *Jurek v. Texas*, 428 U.S. 262 (1976), the Supreme Court indicated that the constitution permitted the narrowing process to occur at the guilt phase and did not require more. Notwithstanding *Jurek*, the four jurisdictions utilize, at the penalty phase, special statutory issues that must be addressed by the factfinder in deciding whether to impose the death penalty. *Jurek* upheld the constitutionality of using special statutory issues, instead of statutory aggravators, at the penalty phase. In *Johnson v. Texas*, 509 U.S. 350 (1993), it was held that the penalty phase special issues used by Texas adequately allowed the jury to consider the defendant's age as a mitigating factor.

Although special statutory issues and statutory aggravators serve the same purpose, i.e., they both are used to determine whether to impose the death penalty, they differ in one respect. Special statutory issues are constant for all capital felons, in that special statutory issues are a series of questions that are asked in all capital prosecutions. However, statutory aggravators vary with the circumstances of each capital homicide. The statute set out below illustrates penalty phase special statutory issues.

Oregon Revised Statutes § 163.150(1)(b):
(A) Whether the conduct of the defendant that caused the death of the deceased was committed deliberately and with the reasonable expectation that death of the deceased or another would result;
(B) Whether there is a probability that the defendant would commit criminal acts of violence that would constitute a continuing threat to society;
(C) If raised by the evidence, whether the conduct of the defendant in killing the deceased was unreasonable in response to the provocation, if any, by the deceased; and
(D) Whether the defendant should receive a death sentence.

Distinguishing Non-Statutory from Statutory Aggravators

Statutory aggravators are a limited number of factors that are created by legislators to narrow the class of persons that may be sentenced to death. The constitution demands this narrowing process. However, oftentimes a murder will involve "aggravating" factors that are not codified. These non-codified aggravators are called non-statutory aggravating circumstances.

The most significant difference between non-statutory and statutory aggravators is that the death penalty cannot be imposed solely upon a non-statutory aggravator, but it can be imposed upon a finding of a single statutory aggravator. In this context, non-statutory aggravators serve only to support imposing the death penalty, upon finding the existence of a statutory aggravator. As a general matter, non-statutory aggravators must have relevance to the case. In *Romano v. Oklahoma*, 512 U.S. 1 (1994), it was held that admission of evidence of an unrelated prior death sentence at the defendant's penalty phase proceeding did not violate the Constitution.

Criminal Offense Statutory Aggravators

In this section a review will be given of felony offenses which constitute statutory aggravating circumstances. As statutory aggravators, these offenses permit the imposition of the death penalty, if they are found to exist by the penalty phase factfinder.

TABLE 14.1 AGGRAVATING CIRCUMSTANCES OF MURDER 2006-2010

Year and Number of Murder Incidents

Circumstance	2006	2007	2008	2009	2010
Rape	32	32	22	24	41
Robbery	1,053	935	930	857	780
Burglary	80	86	88	110	80
Larceny	16	10	18	13	20
Vehicle theft	16	20	20	23	37
Arson	27	59	27	38	35
Drug law violation	806	590	500	496	463

SOURCE: U.S. Department of Justice, Federal Bureau of Investigation, Uniform Crime Reports, Homicides, Table 12 (2010).

Sexual Offenses

Sexual offenses include rape, statutory rape, compelled anal and oral intercourse, sodomy and deviant sexual behavior with a minor. In and of themselves, sexual offenses are not offenses that are punishable by death. However, a majority of capital punishment jurisdictions have made sexual offenses statutory aggravating circumstances.[7] As statutory aggravating circumstances, sexual offenses are crimes that may constitutionally cause the death penalty to be imposed when it is shown that the offense occurred during the course of a murder.

TABLE 14.2 GENDER OF VICTIM OF AGGRAVATING CIRCUMSTANCES MURDER 2010

Circumstance	Total Victims	Gender Male	Female
Rape	41	0	41
Robbery	780	696	84
Burglary	80	60	20
Larceny	20	16	4
Motor vehicle theft	37	27	10
Arson	35	24	11
Drug law violation	463	431	32

SOURCE: U.S. Department of Justice, Federal Bureau of Investigation, Uniform Crime Reports, Homicides, Table 13 (2010).

Robbery

The crime of robbery is nothing more than forcible larceny. It is not necessary that force actually be used; mere display of force, i.e., showing a victim a weapon while his or her property is being taken, also constitutes robbery. Robbery alone is not a crime punishable with death. A majority of capital punishment jurisdictions, however, make robbery a statutory aggravating circumstance.[8] In such jurisdictions when robbery and murder combine a defendant may be sentenced to death at the penalty phase.

Burglary

Under the common law burglary was defined as breaking and entering the dwelling of another, at night, with the intent to commit a felony. The common law definition of burglary makes it an inchoate crime, in the sense that completion of the intended felony is not necessary. Although most jurisdictions have modified the common law definition of burglary, its essence is still retained by all jurisdictions, i.e., intent to commit a felony. Burglary, in and of itself, is not an offense that permits the punishment of death. However, a majority of capital punishment jurisdictions make burglary a statutory aggravating circumstance.[9] In this posture, burglary can cause the imposition of the death penalty.

Kidnapping

The most notorious criminal prosecution in the first half of the twentieth century involved the 1934 prosecution of the man responsible for kidnapping and murdering the child of Charles Lindbergh. The defendant in that case was Bruno Richard Hauptmann. Mr. Hauptmann was executed, not because kidnapping was then considered a statutory aggravating circumstance, but because of the murder itself. Today a majority of capital punishment jurisdictions have made kidnapping a statutory aggravating circumstance.[10] When this statutory aggravator accompanies murder, a capital felon may lawfully be executed in a majority of capital punishment jurisdictions.

Arson

The crime of arson, like burglary, is an offense that has outgrown its common law roots. Common law arson meant merely the intentional burning of an occupied dwelling of another. Modern statutes have expanded this narrow definition to include the burning of one's own dwelling, personal property, commercial buildings, boats, trains — and most things under the sun. There were several catalysts that brought about the expansion of arson, principal among them was the fact that some people began the practice of purposely insuring "everything under the sun" with the intent of burning it to collect insurance proceeds.

Arson is not an offense that, without more, would permit the imposition of the death penalty. However, arson is a statutory aggravating circumstance in the majority of capital punishment jurisdictions.[11] Thus, this offense can cause the imposition of death when it accompanies murder.

Escape

A person incarcerated or in the custody of a law enforcement officer, who flees from such confinement or custody, commits the offense of escape. A majority of capital punishment jurisdictions have made this offense a statutory aggravating circumstance when it accompanies murder.[12] The death penalty may be imposed when this statutory aggravator is proven to exist.

Other Crimes

In addition to the criminal offenses highlighted above, capital punishment jurisdictions have other offenses which constitute statutory aggravating circumstances when accompanied by murder. The other offenses, however, do not enjoy majority capital punishment jurisdiction status. They are minority status statutory aggravating circumstances. The following is a representative sample of such statutory aggravating circumstances.

Train wrecking. The offense of train wrecking is a statutory aggravating circumstance when death results therefrom. Two capital punishment jurisdictions have made this offense a statutory aggravating circumstance.[13]

Carjacking. The crime of carjacking involves forcibly taking a vehicle from its owner or possessor. The crime of carjacking has been elevated to a statutory aggravating circumstance when accompanied by murder. Two capital punishment jurisdictions have made this crime a statutory aggravating circumstance.[14]

Plane hijacking. The crime of plane hijacking has taken on the status of a statutory aggravating circumstance when murder results therefrom. This offense has been made a statutory aggravating circumstance in nine capital punishment jurisdictions.[15]

Train hijacking. The offense of train hijacking has been made a statutory aggravating circumstance when accompanied by murder. Two capital punishment jurisdictions have made this offense a statutory aggravating circumstance.[16]

Aggravated battery. The crime of aggravated battery is not the same as the crime of battery. Aggravated battery occurs when there is serious injury to a victim. The crime of battery can be a mere touching of a victim. Aggravated battery has been made a statutory aggravating circumstance when murder occurs. Two capital punishment jurisdictions have made this offense a statutory aggravating circumstance.[17]

Ship hijacking. In former days ship hijacking went under the name of pirating. As an offense, ship hijacking has been made a statutory aggravating circumstance when accompanied by murder. One capital punishment jurisdiction has made this offense a statutory aggravating circumstance.[18]

Bus hijacking. The offense of bus hijacking has been made a statutory aggravating circumstance when murder accompanies it. One capital punishment jurisdiction has made this offense a statutory aggravating circumstance.[19]

Drug trafficking. Although the crime of drug trafficking is a monumental problem in the nation, it does not enjoy majority status as a statutory aggravating circumstance. Only eight capital punishment jurisdictions have made this offense a statutory aggravating circumstance.[20]

Identity of Victim Statutory Aggravators

In the case of *Brecht v. Abrahamson*, 944 F.2d 1363 (7th Cir. 1991), a federal court of appeals ruled that it was permissible for evidence to be introduced which showed that the murder victim disliked homosexuals and, as a result, the defendant (who was a homosexual) killed the victim. The victim in *Brecht* may be classified as a homophobic and, as such, had a unique identity. While no capital punishment jurisdiction currently makes the murder of a homophobic a statutory aggravating circumstance, the *Brecht* decision is instructive of the compassion a victim's unique identity may engender when it is the motive for murder.

Legislators in capital punishment jurisdictions are not oblivious to the compassionate concerns citizens have when a person is murdered solely because of that person's unique identity. Many capital punishment jurisdictions have responded to this concern by enacting various statutory aggravating circumstances that are based upon a victim's unique identity. This section will examine some of those statutory aggravating circumstances.

TABLE 14.3 AVERAGE ANNUAL WORKPLACE HOMICIDES 1993–1996

SOURCE: Bureau of Labor Statistics, Census of Fatal Occupational Injuries, 1993–96.

Correction Officer

A majority of capital punishment jurisdiction legislators have acknowledged the necessary and dangerous work of correction officers. This recognition is evident in that a majority of capital punishment jurisdictions provide that the murder of a correction officer while he or she is on duty is a statutory aggravating circumstance.[21]

Law Enforcement Officer

The vast majority of capital punishment jurisdictions are sensitive to the vital role the police have in society and the dangerous nature of their work. Consequently, the vast majority of capital punishment jurisdictions have made murdering a police officer, while on duty or off duty but because of his or her work, a statutory aggravating circumstance.[22]

Firefighter

Firefighters perform a critical service in society. The indispensable role of firefighters has caused nearly a majority of capital punishment jurisdictions to provide that the murder of a firefighter while on duty is a statutory aggravating circumstance.[23]

Witness

Crime is successfully prosecuted because of witnesses. A slight majority of capital punishment jurisdictions have attempted to protect and encourage witnesses to criminal conduct by making the murder of a witness a statutory aggravating circumstance.[24]

Prosecutor

During the criminal prosecution of O.J. Simpson, at least one member of the team of prosecutors, Chris Darden, reported that threats on his life were made because of his role in the case. The threats Mr. Darden received are the potential companion of every prosecutor in the nation. A significant minority of capital punishment jurisdictions have sought to protect prosecutors from personal attacks attributed to their work.[25] This protection is manifested through statutes that make the murder of a prosecutor a statutory aggravating circumstance.

Judge

Judges play a critical role in the prosecution of criminals. This role exposes them to reprisals by criminals. Nearly a majority of capital punishment jurisdictions have sought to protect judges by making the murder of a judge a statutory aggravating circumstance.[26]

Age of Victim

A large minority capital punishment jurisdictions provide that the age of a victim of murder is a statutory aggravating circumstance that permits the imposition of the death penalty. There is no unity among the jurisdictions regarding the age which constitutes a statutory aggravating circumstance.[27]

TABLE 14.4 AGE OF VICTIM THAT CONSTITUTES AN AGGRAVATING CIRCUMSTANCE

Age	Number of Jurisdictions
5 or younger[28]	1
11 or younger[29]	7
14 or younger[30]	2
16 or younger[31]	1
62 or older[32]	1
65 or older[33]	1
66 or older[34]	1
70 or older[35]	1

TABLE 14.5 AGE AND GENDER OF MURDER VICTIM 2010

Age of Victim	Total Victims	Victim Gender	
		Male	Female
Under 1	185	91	94
1 to 4	313	192	121
5 to 8	85	44	41
9 to 12	43	28	15
13 to 16	363	288	75
17 to 19	1,231	1,065	166
20 to 24	2,256	1,944	312
25 to 29	1,964	1,627	337
30 to 34	1,539	1,286	253
35 to 39	1,072	820	252
40 to 44	882	635	247
45 to 49	838	589	249
50 to 54	686	508	178
55 to 59	472	329	143

Age of Victim	Total Victims	Victim Gender	
		Male	*Female*
60 to 64	325	199	126
65 to 69	189	125	64
70 to 74	136	80	56
75 & over	259	109	150

SOURCE: U.S. Department of Justice, Federal Bureau of Investigation, Uniform Crime Reports, Homicides, Table 2 (2011).

Other Identities

The major players in victim identity statutory aggravating circumstances are correction officials, police officers, firefighters, witnesses, prosecutors, judges and age. All of the latter enjoy the distinction of having a majority or near majority of capital punishment jurisdictions recognizing their identities as statutory aggravating circumstances. There are, however, other victim identity statutory aggravating circumstances, most of which do not enjoy significant recognition by capital punishment jurisdictions.

Parole/probation officer. The work of parole and probation officers, while essentially the same, is carried out under different circumstances. Parole officers monitor convicted criminals who have been released from confinement prior to the expiration of their sentence. Probation officers monitor convicted criminals who have had their sentence suspended. Parole and probation officers have authority to cause their respective parolees and probationers to be incarcerated for violating conditions of release. A few capital punishment jurisdictions have seen the need for making the murder of a parole or probation officer a statutory aggravating circumstance.[36]

Pregnant woman. A few capital punishment jurisdiction have made the murder of a pregnant woman a statutory aggravating circumstance.[37]

Juror. In routine criminal prosecutions the identity of jurors is not kept from the public. In high profile criminal prosecutions, like that of former mafia kingpin John Gotti or O.J. Simpson, it may be necessary to keep the identity of jurors from the public — at least until after verdicts are returned. Juror intimidation is always a potential impediment to justice. A few capital punishment jurisdictions have taken this matter seriously and made the murder of a juror a statutory aggravating circumstance.[38]

Informant. Informants are people who provide information to the police that implicates criminal suspects. A few capital punishment jurisdictions have made the murder of an informant a statutory aggravating circumstance.[39]

Elected official. Elected officials cannot please all constituents on all issues. This fact carries with it the potential for violent retaliation by a disgruntled constituent. A minority of capital punishment jurisdictions have expressed sensitivity to the ever present threat elected officials face, by making the murder of an elected official a statutory aggravating circumstance.[40]

Handicap person. In 1985 religious extremists attacked a cruise ship called the *Achille Lauro*, off the Egyptian coast, and killed a helpless wheelchair-bound victim.[41] A few capital punishment jurisdictions have sought to curb violence against handicapped persons by making the murder of a handicap person a statutory aggravating circumstance.[42]

Race, religion and gender. In the case of *Barclay v. Florida*, 463 U.S. 939 (1983), the trial judge considered, as a non-statutory aggravating circumstance, the fact that the murder victim was killed for no other reason than his race. The defendant contested consideration of the victim's race during the penalty phase. The Supreme Court found no constitutional impediment to the trial judge's consideration of this non-statutory aggravating circumstance. A few capital punishment jurisdictions have embraced the *Barclay* ruling by making murder motivated by race, religion, or gender a statutory aggravating circumstance.[43]

Other Statutory Aggravators

Experience has shown that not all murders will occur in the commission of another offense and, too, not all murder victims will have statutorily recognized identities that permit imposition of the death penalty. The fact that a murder may not fit either of the latter two situations does not mean that the death penalty is barred as a form of punishment.

Legislators in all capital punishment jurisdictions have carved out a variety of situations that will allow the death penalty to be imposed, even though a particular murder did not occur during the commission of another felony or the victim did not have a statutory identity. The necessity of having to create additional types of statutory aggravating circumstances is in keeping with the constitutional requirement of "justify[ing] the imposition of a more severe sentence on the defendant compared to others found guilty of murder."[44] The statutory aggravating circumstances to follow permit the imposition of the death penalty in jurisdictions that recognize them.

TABLE 14.6 OTHER MURDER CIRCUMSTANCES 2006–2010

Year and Number of Murder Incidents

Circumstance	2006	2007	2008	2009	2010
Gangland killing	121	78	135	177	176
Juvenile gang killing	864	678	700	715	673
Institutional killing	22	11	14	12	17
Sniper attack	2	1	7	1	3
Drug induced killing	53	65	70	94	58
Alcohol induced killing	106	118	130	117	121

SOURCE: U.S. Department of Justice, Federal Bureau of Investigation, Uniform Crime Reports, Homicides, Table 12 (2011).

Heinous, Atrocious, Cruel or Depraved

Jeffrey Dahmer's method of killing his victims illustrates what is contemplated by the terms heinous, atrocious, cruel and depraved. Dahmer's victims were cut into pieces, acid was used to remove skin and some were cannibalized. To meet death in such a manner is the height of heinous, atrocious, cruel and depraved. A slight majority of capital punishment jurisdictions have responded to Dahmer-type homicides by making murder committed in a heinous, atrocious, cruel or depraved manner a statutory aggravating circumstance.[45]

Pecuniary Gain

During the 1996 drug possession prosecution of professional football player Michael Irvin, authorities learned that a Texas police officer attempted to pay someone to kill Mr. Irvin. Fortunately, authorities were able to intervene and prevent the murder-for-hire plot from coming full circle.

The Irvin affair is instructive on the point that human life is like an item in a department store, i.e., a price can be attached to it. The stark reality of this point has not gone unnoticed by legislators. The extreme seriousness and frequency of murder taking place for pecuniary gain has caused all capital punishment jurisdictions, except Montana, to make murder for pecuniary gain a statutory aggravating circumstance.

Multiple Homicides

A single murder is a tragedy. A defendant who murders more than one person in a single episode or series of incidents compounds the tragedy of murder. Legislators have sought to deter the tragedy of multiple homicides by making such conduct a statutory aggravating circumstance. A slight majority of capital punishment jurisdictions make multiple homicides a statutory aggravating circumstance.[46]

Great Risk to Others

The statutory aggravator "great risk to others" seeks to punish with death those who, while committing murder, expose unintended persons to death or great bodily harm. A majority of capital punishment jurisdictions make murder involving a great risk to others a statutory aggravating circumstance.[47]

In Custody

Custody refers to confinement in prison or jail, or both, depending upon the jurisdiction. A majority of capital punishment jurisdictions make murder committed while in custody a statutory aggravating circumstance.[48]

Prior Felony or Homicide

In an attempt to prevent recidivist conduct, legislators have made murder committed by a defendant who was previously convicted of a serious felony involving violence or a prior homicide a statutory aggravator. A majority of capital punishment jurisdictions make murder committed by a defendant with a prior felony or homicide conviction a statutory aggravating circumstance.[49]

Explosives or Chemicals

Explosives refer to any type of device that causes an incendiary-like explosion. A minority of capital punishment jurisdictions make murder committed with the use of explosives or chemicals a statutory aggravating circumstance.[50]

Torture

Torture refers to the infliction of great pain and suffering. A minority of capital punishment jurisdictions make murder that involved torture to the victim a statutory aggravating circumstance.[51]

Additional Factors

In addition to the above statutory aggravators, capital punishment jurisdictions have created a few other, minority status, statutory aggravating circumstances. A review of these follows.

Disrupting governmental function. The 1995 Oklahoma bombing can be viewed from many perspectives. One is disruption of a governmental function. That is, the deaths that occurred in the bombing resulted from efforts to disrupt the federal governmental operations that took place in the building that was bombed.

Conduct which seeks to disrupt a governmental function does not have to end in tragic deaths. Each day some patriotic libertarian engages in a form of peaceful conduct that seeks to disrupt a governmental function. Peaceful protest has constitutional backing. The Oklahoma incident does not fall under constitutional protection. Currently, a minority of capital punishment jurisdictions have decided to make disruption of a governmental function a statutory aggravating circumstance when death results therefrom.[52]

TABLE 14.7 GENDER OF VICTIM OF OTHER MURDER CIRCUMSTANCES 2010

Circumstance	Total Victims	Gender	
		Male	Female
Gangland killing	176	164	12
Juvenile gang killing	671	639	33
Institutional killing	17	15	2
Sniper attack	3	3	0
Drug induced killing	58	44	14
Alcohol induced killing	121	103	18

SOURCE: U.S. Department of Justice, Federal Bureau of Investigation, Uniform Crime Reports, Homicides, Table 13 (2010).

Parole or probation. As a fundamental matter, parole is the legal status given to someone who has served time in prison and been released before the full sentence has been served. Probation is the legal status given to someone who has not been sentenced to confinement or the sentence to confinement has been suspended and incarceration has not been imposed.[53] Parole and probation are privileges bestowed by sovereign jurisdictions upon guilty defendants.

As a result of parole and probation being privileges and not rights, society demands nothing short of model behavior by defendants placed on parole or probation. A few capital punishment jurisdictions have elevated the expectations demanded of parolees and probationers, by making murder committed by a person on parole or probation a statutory aggravating circumstance.[54]

It will be noted that in the case of *Lindsey v. Smith*, 820 F.2d 1137 (11th Cir. 1987), the Eleventh Circuit pointed out in dicta that being on parole was a weak factor, standing alone, to permit the imposition of the death penalty. The *Lindsey* opinion has waved a yellow flag of caution indicating that a sentence of death grounded solely on a parole or probation statutory aggravating circumstance probably requires an additional statutory aggravating circumstance in order to pass constitutional muster. The Supreme Court has not addressed this issue. Therefore, as of now, parole or probation may constitutionally stand alone as a statutory aggravating circumstance which causes the death penalty to be imposed.

Authorized release from custody. At first blush, parole and probation may seem to be indistinguishable from authorized release from custody. The three legal concepts, however, are different. Authorized release from custody refers to an inmate who has been allowed to leave confinement for a stated period of time and for a specific reason, but must return to confinement according to the terms of release.

An example of authorized release from custody would be an inmate who is allowed to leave confinement during the day to work for a private employer. This is a typically practiced form of release that is called work-release. Another example of authorized release from custody is that of furlough programs. Under a furlough program an inmate is allowed to leave confinement for a day or two, as a result of good behavior while incarcerated. A few capital punishment jurisdictions have made authorized release from custody a statutory aggravating circumstance.[55]

Unlawfully at liberty. The crime of escape may come to mind when looking at the phrase "unlawfully at liberty." The two matters are different. Unlawfully at liberty can be understood by looking at "authorized release from custody." An inmate on authorized release from custody has a specific time in which to report back to confinement. If an inmate does not return to confinement as required by the terms of the release, the inmate is then unlawfully at liberty. The issue of escape does not come into play, because the inmate was lawfully released from custody. A few capital punishment jurisdictions have made murder committed by an inmate unlawfully at liberty a statutory aggravating circumstance.[56]

Drive-by shooting. A few capital punishment jurisdictions provide that murder involving drive-by shooting is a statutory aggravating circumstance.[57]

Ordering killing. A minority of capital punishment jurisdictions provide that murder committed upon the order of another is a statutory aggravating circumstance.[58]

Lying-in-wait. A minority of capital punishment jurisdictions provide that murder committed while lying-in-wait is a statutory aggravating circumstance.[59]

15

Mitigating Circumstances

In her concurring opinion in *California v. Brown*, 479 U.S. 538 (1987), Justice O'Connor wrote that "evidence about the defendant's background and character is relevant because of the belief, long held by this society, that defendants who commit criminal acts that are attributable to a disadvantaged background, or to emotional and mental problems, may be less culpable than defendants who have no such excuse." Therefore, she continued, "the sentence imposed at the penalty stage should reflect a reasoned moral response to the defendant's background, character, and crime."

The carefully thought out words of Justice O'Connor appropriately express the narrow scope of this chapter. The focus here is limited to reviewing issues related to the nature and extent of penalty phase mitigating circumstances. As a general proposition, mitigating circumstances involve any relevant evidence that may justify imposition of a sentence that is less than the maximum possible sentence. Placed in the context of capital punishment, mitigating circumstances involve any relevant evidence that may justify imposition of a less severe penalty than death.[1]

Distinguishing Mitigating and Aggravating Circumstances

The outcome of a penalty phase proceeding will be death or imprisonment for a capital felon. Determining what this outcome will be turns on the jury's interpretation of the mitigating and statutory aggravating circumstances presented by the two actors in the proceeding, i.e., the capital felon and the prosecutor.

BOX 15.0 PENALTY PHASE ACTORS, EVIDENCE AND CONSEQUENCES

Actor	Evidence	Consequence
Prosecutor	aggravating circumstances	death
Capital felon	mitigating circumstances	imprisonment

Statutory aggravating circumstances are the tools of the prosecutor.[2] Mitigating circumstances are the tools of the capital felon. Aggravating circumstances which permit the imposition of the death penalty are required to be placed in statutes. Mitigating circumstances are not required to be enacted into law. The function of statutory aggravating circumstances is that of imposing death on the capital felon. Mitigating circumstances serve the function of placing the capital felon in prison for life.

The underlying rationale for utilizing statutory aggravating circumstances is to narrow the class of capital felons who should receive the death penalty. The narrowing process involves utilizing a small number of factors that have been determined to merit the death penalty whenever any of such factors are present in a murder. The underlying rationale for permitting mitigating circumstances to enter the death penalty equation is that of expanding the class of capital felons who should not be put to death. This expansion process involves the utilization of any relevant factor that tends to justify imprisoning, rather than executing, a capital felon.

Significant Supreme Court Decisions

The issue of mitigating circumstances has generated a great deal of issues and litigation. This section examines several Supreme Court cases that addressed some of those issues.

The Lockett Principles

There is no requirement that mitigating circumstances be enacted into law. This issue was squarely addressed by the Supreme Court in *Lockett v. Ohio*, 438 U.S. 586 (1978). In *Lockett* the state of Ohio had provided for three mitigating circumstances in its death penalty statute. The three mitigating circumstances operated in such a manner as to preclude use of any other mitigating circumstance. In its initial response to this issue the Supreme Court made the following observations:

> There is no perfect procedure for deciding in which cases governmental authority should be used to impose death. But a statute that prevents the sentencer in all capital cases from giving independent mitigating weight to aspects of the defendant's character and record and to circumstances of the offense proffered in mitigation creates the risk that the death penalty will be imposed in spite of factors which may call for a less severe penalty.

Mitigating circumstances may be statutory. The inference to be made from the language in the above quote is the first of three principles that came out of *Lockett*. The first principle holds that a death penalty statute may create mitigating circumstances. The importance of this principle is that it fostered two categories of mitigating circumstances: (1) statutory mitigating circumstances and (2) non-statutory mitigating circumstances. A majority of capital punishment jurisdictions have created statutory mitigating circumstances. However, because of *Lockett* such statutory mitigating circumstances co-exist with non-statutory mitigating circumstances. From a constitutional standpoint, statutory and non-statutory mitigating circumstances stand on equal footing.

Relevant mitigating circumstances cannot be excluded. In addressing the issue of the limitations imposed by the Ohio death penalty statute in *Lockett*, the Supreme Court held that "[t]he limited range of mitigating circumstances which may be considered by the sentencer under the Ohio statute is incompatible with the Eighth and Fourteenth Amendments."

At first impression the above statement by the Supreme Court could be interpreted to mean that all mitigating circumstances are constitutionally required to be admitted into evidence at the penalty phase. Such an interpretation is incorrect. The second principle coming out of *Lockett* states that a death penalty statute must not preclude consideration of any "relevant" mitigating circumstances. For example, in the companion case of *Bell v. Ohio*, 438 U.S. 637 (1978), it was held that the Ohio death penalty statute violated the Constitution because it prevented the penalty phase factfinder from considering relevant non-statutory mitigating evidence. In *Hitchcock v. Dugger*, 481 U.S. 393 (1987), the Supreme Court reversed a death sentence because the trial court instructed the jury not to consider any mitigating circumstance that was not enumerated by statute.

In *Mills v. Maryland*, 486 U.S. 367 (1988), and *McKoy v. North Carolina*, 494 U.S. 433 (1990), it was held that death penalty statutes could not require a jury to unanimously find the existence of mitigating circumstances, because this would prevent the sentencer from considering all relevant mitigating evidence. In *Smith v. Spisak*, 130 S.Ct. 676 (2010), and *Bobby v. Mitts*, 131 S.Ct 1762 (2011), the Supreme Court rejected the argument that the *Mills-McKoy* prohibition was violated in those cases.

It was held in *Buchanan v. Angelone*, 522 U.S. 269 (1998), that the Constitution does not require that a capital penalty phase jury be instructed on the concept of mitigating evidence generally, or on particular statutory mitigating factors, when the jury is instructed to consider all relevant mitigating evidence. In *Johnson v. Texas*, 509 U.S. 350 (1993), it was held that the penalty phase special issues used by Texas adequately allowed the jury to consider the defendant's age as a mitigating factor. In *Parker v. Dugger*, 498 U.S. 308 (1991), it was held that the Florida Supreme Court had to consider evidence of non-statutory mitigating circumstances during its review of sentencing evidence.

BOX 15.1 THE LOCKETT PRINCIPLES

1. A death penalty statute may create mitigating circumstances.
2. To meet constitutional requirements, a death penalty statute must not preclude consideration of relevant mitigating circumstances.
3. Irrelevant mitigating circumstances may constitutionally be barred from use at capital penalty phase proceedings.

The *Lockett* principles were applied in *Ayers v. Belmontes*, 127 S.Ct. 469 (2006) (finding jury properly considered evidence defendant would lead a constructive life if sentenced to prison), *Brown v. Payton*, 544 U.S. 133 (2005) (finding harmless error in prosecutor wrongly telling jury to ignore defendant's post-crime mitigating evidence); *Boyde v. California*, 494 U.S. 370 (1990) (finding jury properly considered defendant's pre and post-crime mitigating evidence); *Skipper v. South Carolina*, 476 U.S. 1 (1986) (finding error in not allowing witnesses to testify defendant was well-behaved in jail); and *Eddings v. Oklahoma*, 455 U.S. 104 (1982) (finding error in trial court's exclusion of relevant mitigating evidence).

It was held in *Tennard v. Dretke*, 542 U.S. 274 (2004), that a federal appeals court could not condition issuance of a certificate of appealability on the defendant establishing that his alleged mitigating evidence was constitutionally relevant.

Irrelevant mitigating circumstances may be excluded. By holding that the constitution will not tolerate exclusion of any relevant mitigating circumstances, *Lockett* implicitly approved of excluding irrelevant mitigating circumstances.[3] Therefore, the third principle coming out of *Lockett* provides that irrelevant mitigating circumstances may be constitutionally precluded from use at penalty phase proceedings.

The third principle from *Lockett* was operationalized in *Robison v. Maynard*, 943 F.2d 1216 (10th Cir. 1991). In *Robison* the court of appeals upheld exclusion of proffered testimony by the murdered victim's sister. The victim's sister wanted to testify that the defendant should not be sentenced to die. The court of appeals held that such testimony was not a relevant mitigating circumstance and could therefore be excluded.[4]

The mere fact that proffered mitigating circumstances are statutory or non-statutory is of no consequence to the issue of relevancy. Both statutory and non-statutory mitigating circumstances may be excluded from the penalty phase if they are irrelevant.[5] There is no magical formula used to determine when mitigating circumstances are relevant or irrelevant. The issue is determined on a case-by-case basis by the presiding judge.[6]

Residual Doubt of Guilt

The phrase "residual doubt of guilt" is used to refer to evidence submitted at the penalty phase of a capital prosecution which implies that a defendant is innocent of the crime. In several cases, *Oregon v. Guzek*, 126 S.Ct. 1226 (2006), and *Franklin v. Lynaugh*, 487 U.S. 164 (1988), the United States Supreme Court has made clear that a capital felon does not have a federal constitutional right to present residual doubt of guilt evidence at the penalty phase. In *Guzek* the Supreme Court addressed the issue by stating that "the parties previously litigated the issue to which the evidence is relevant — whether the defendant committed the basic crime [of murder]. The evidence thereby attacks a previously determined matter in a [sentencing] proceeding at which, in principle, that matter is not at issue." Some courts expressly preclude introduction of residual doubt of guilt evidence at the penalty phase for mitigation purposes. However, other courts, such as *State v. McKinney*, 74 S.W.3d 291 (Tenn. 2002), and *State v. Garner*, 656 N.E.2d 623 (Ohio 1995), hold that residual doubt of guilt is a valid non-statutory mitigating circumstance for the penalty phase jury to consider.

Although there is no constitutional right to present residual doubt of guilt during the penalty phase, the Supreme Court made clear in *Holmes v. South Carolina*, 126 S.Ct. 1727 (2006), that evidence of innocence cannot be excluded at the guilt phase. Specifically, it was said in *Holmes* that the Constitution prohibited use of a South Carolina evidence rule that barred a defendant from introducing evidence of third-party guilt, if the prosecution has introduced forensic evidence that strongly supports a guilty verdict.

The Delo Rule

In the case of *Delo v. Lashley*, 113 S.Ct. 1222 (1993), a 17 year old defendant beat and stabbed to death his cousin, who was physically handicapped, during a robbery attempt. The defendant was convicted of capital murder by a Missouri jury. At the close of the penalty phase the defendant asked the court to inform the penalty phase jury that they could consider, as a statutory mitigating circumstance, the fact that he did not have a significant criminal history. The court refused to give the instruction because no evidence was proffered on the issue of the defendant's criminal history. The defendant was subsequently sentenced to die.

During the course of many appeals the defendant was able to get a federal court of appeals to set aside the death sentence. The court of appeals did so after interpreting the *Lockett* decision as requiring the trial court to give the requested statutory mitigating circumstance instruction. The state of Missouri appealed the case to the Supreme Court.

The issue confronting the Supreme Court in *Delo* was whether *Lockett* required a penalty phase jury be instructed to consider any type of relevant mitigating circumstance, even though evidence was not proffered on it. The Supreme Court responded to the issue raised by *Delo* as follows:

> [W]e never have suggested that the Constitution requires a state trial court to instruct the jury on mitigating circumstances in the absence of any supporting evidence.... [T]o comply with due process state courts need give jury instructions in capital cases only if the evidence so warrants.... Nothing in the Constitution obligates state courts to give mitigating circumstance instructions when no evidence is offered to support them.

The above quote articulates the *Delo* rule. It should be understood that the *Delo* rule is not inconsistent with *Lockett*. The decision in *Lockett* prohibits exclusion of any relevant mitigating circumstance. The *Delo* rule merely states that if no evidence is presented on a relevant statutory or non-statutory mitigating circumstance, the trial court does not have to instruct the penalty phase jury to consider what was never offered as evidence.[7]

The Ake Rule

In the case of *Ake v. Oklahoma*, 470 U.S. 68 (1985), the prosecutor relied on expert testimony from a psychiatrist to establish, as a statutory aggravating circumstance, that the defendant would be dangerous in the future. The defendant was indigent and, as a consequence, he was not able to present mitigating circumstance evidence from an independent psychiatrist. The defendant was eventually sentenced to die.

The defendant in *Ake* appealed his sentence to the Supreme Court. The defendant argued that the Due Process Clause required Oklahoma provide him with a psychiatrist to present mitigating circumstance evidence on the issue of his future dangerousness. The Supreme Court agreed with the defendant using the following language:

> Without a psychiatrist's assistance, the defendant cannot offer a well-informed expert's opposing view, and thereby loses a significant opportunity to raise in the juror's minds questions about the State's proof of an aggravating factor. In such a circumstance, where the consequence of error is so great, the relevance of responsive psychiatric testimony so evident, and the burden on the state so slim, due process requires access to a psychiatric examination on relevant issues, to the testimony of the psychiatrist, and to assistance in preparation at the sentencing phase.

The *Ake* rule provides that when evidence of psychiatric mitigating circumstances is relevant, an indigent capital felon has a constitutional right to be provided with a psychiatrist by the government to prepare and present such evidence.

The Penry Rule

The case of *Penry v. Lynaugh*, 492 U.S. 302 (1989), overruled on other grounds by *Atkins v. Virginia*, 536 U.S. 304 (2002), involved a capital felon who was sentenced to death in a jurisdiction that did not have statutory mitigating circumstances. The defendant, however, was allowed to present non-statutory mitigating circumstances to the penalty phase jury. The mitigating circumstances included testimony about the defendant's mental problems and childhood abuse.

One of the issues that the defendant in *Penry* presented to the Supreme Court concerned an omission in the jurisdiction's death penalty statute. The statute did not indicate that the penalty phase jury had to be instructed on the effect of mitigating circumstances on the decision to impose the death penalty. As a result of this omission, the trial court did not instruct the penalty phase jury that it could refuse to impose the death penalty, if the mitigating circumstances were found to justify this outcome.

The problem posed by the lack of such an instruction was that the jury could have interpreted the defendant's mental problem and childhood abuse to mean that he would always be dangerous and therefore should be put to death. The defendant believed that he had a right to have the jury instructed that it had to interpret all of his mitigating circumstances as a justification for a sentence of life imprisonment, and not as support for imposing the death penalty. The Supreme Court responded to the issue as follows:

> [P]unishment should be directly related to the personal culpability of the defendant [therefore] the jury must be allowed to consider and give effect to mitigating evidence relevant to a defendant's character or record or the circumstances of the offense. Rather than creating the risk of an unguided emotional response, full consideration of evidence that mitigates against the death penalty is essential if the jury is to be given a reasoned moral response to the defendant's background, character, and crime. In order to ensure reliability in the determination that death is the appropriate punishment in a specific case, the jury must be able to consider and give effect to any mitigating evidence relevant to a defendant's background and character or the circumstances of the crime.
>
> In this case, in the absence of instructions informing the jury that it could consider and give effect to the mitigating evidence of Penry's mental [problem] and abused background by declining to impose the death penalty, we conclude that the jury was not provided with a vehicle for expressing its reasoned moral response to that evidence in rendering its sentencing decision.

The initial interpretation of *Penry* was that it created a rule requiring special instructions be given to penalty phase juries on the effects of each and every tendered mitigating circumstance.[8] However, the *Penry* rule was restricted by the decisions in *Graham v. Collins*, 113 S.Ct. 892 (1993), and *Johnson v. Texas*, 113 S.Ct. 2658 (1993).[9] The meaning now given to the *Penry* rule is that, when a capital felon proffers a mitigating circumstance which has the potential for being interpreted for and against the death penalty, a special instruction must be given to the jurors that informs them of the effect they must give such evidence.[10] The *Penry* rule was applied to reverse death sentences in *Smith v. Texas*, 127 S.Ct. 1686 (2007), *Abdul-Kabir v. Quarterman*, 127 S.Ct. 1654 (2007), and *Brewer v. Quarterman*, 127 S.Ct. 1706 (2007).

The Rompilla/Wiggins/Williams Rule

The Rompilla case. In the case of *Rompilla v. Beard*, 545 U.S. 374 (2005), the state of Pennsylvania charged the defendant with the 1988 capital murder of James Scanlon. A jury convicted the defendant of the crime. During the penalty phase the prosecutor sought to establish several aggravating circumstances, one of which included the defendant's prior criminal record. Although the defendant's court appointed counsel knew that the prosecutor was going to use the prior conviction record at the penalty phase, counsel failed to obtain and review the prior conviction file before the penalty phase proceeding began. At the conclusion of the penalty phase the jury recommended the death sentence for the defendant. The conviction and sentence were upheld on direct appeal. The defendant eventually filed a federal habeas corpus petition. The defendant alleged in the petition that he was denied his constitutional right to effective assistance of counsel during the penalty phase, because his trial counsel failed to timely obtain and review his prior conviction file before the penalty phase proceeding began. A federal district judge agreed with the defendant and set aside the death sentence. However, a court of appeals found that there was no ineffective assistance of counsel and reversed the district judge's decision. The Supreme Court granted certiorari to consider the issue.

The Supreme Court found that the defendant established ineffective assistance of counsel. The opinion in *Rompilla* set out detailed information that was in the prior conviction file, which could have been used as mitigating evidence and which could have better prepared defense counsel to rebut the aggravating information in the file. The opinion addressed the issue as follows:

> The notion that defense counsel must obtain information that the State has and will use against the defendant is not simply a matter of common sense. As the District Court points out, the American Bar Association Standards for Criminal Justice in circulation at the time of [the] trial describes the obligation in terms no one could misunderstand in the circumstances of a case like this one:
>
>> It is the duty of the lawyer to conduct a prompt investigation of the circumstances of the case and to explore all avenues leading to facts relevant to the merits of the case and the penalty in the event of conviction. The investigation should always include efforts to secure information in the possession of the prosecution and law enforcement authorities. The duty to investigate exists regardless of the accused's admissions or statements to the lawyer of facts constituting guilt or the accused's stated desire to plead guilty.
>
> It flouts prudence to deny that a defense lawyer should try to look at a file he knows the prosecution will cull for aggravating evidence, let alone when the file is sitting in the trial courthouse, open for the asking. No reasonable lawyer would forgo examination of the file thinking he could do as well by asking the defendant or family relations whether they recalled anything helpful or damaging in the prior victim's testimony. Nor would a reasonable lawyer compare possible searches for school reports, juvenile records, and evidence of drinking habits to the opportunity to take a look at a file disclosing what the prosecutor knows and even plans to read from in his case. Questioning a few more family members and searching for old records can promise less than looking for a needle in a haystack, when a lawyer truly has reason to doubt there is any needle there. But looking at a file the prosecution says it will use is a sure bet: whatever may be in that file is going to tell defense counsel something about what the prosecution can produce.

Based upon the failure of defense counsel to conduct adequate review of penalty phase evidence, the Supreme Court reversed the death sentence and remanded the case for a new sentencing hearing.

The Wiggins case. In *Wiggins v. Smith*, 539 U.S. 510 (2003), the state of Maryland charged the defendant with the 1988 capital murder of Florence Lacs. During a bench trial on the issue of guilt, the defendant was found guilty of capital murder. A jury presided over the penalty phase. During the penalty phase the defendant's two court appointed attorneys presented evidence suggesting that the defendant did not actually kill the victim. The defense attorneys did not present mitigating evidence of defendant's life history, which included physical abuse, foster care placement, being homosexually raped on numerous occasions, and borderline mental retardation. The jury returned a death sentence. The conviction and sentence were upheld on direct appeal.

The defendant in *Wiggins* subsequently filed a federal habeas petition, alleging ineffective assistance of counsel during the penalty phase. A federal district court agreed with the defendant and reversed the death sentence. However, a federal court of appeals reinstated the death sentence, after finding the defendant's attorneys provided effective assistance of counsel. The Supreme Court granted certiorari to consider the issue.

The opinion in *Wiggins* held that the defendant was denied his constitutional right to effective assistance of counsel during the penalty phase, because his attorneys failed to investigate and present evidence of his life history:

> Counsel's investigation into Wiggins' background did not reflect reasonable professional judgment. Their decision to end their investigation when they did was neither consistent with the professional standards that prevailed in 1989, nor reasonable in light of the evidence counsel uncovered in the social services records — evidence that would have led a reasonably competent attorney to investigate further....
>
> The mitigating evidence counsel failed to discover and present in this case is powerful.... Wiggins experienced severe privation and abuse in the first six years of his life while in the custody of his alcoholic, absentee mother. He suffered physical torment, sexual molestation, and repeated rape during his subsequent years in foster care. The time Wiggins spent homeless, along with his diminished mental capacities, further augment his mitigation case. Petitioner thus has the kind of troubled history we have declared relevant to assessing a defendant's moral culpability....
>
> We further find that had the jury been confronted with this considerable mitigating evidence, there is a reasonable probability that it would have returned with a different sentence....
>
> Wiggins' sentencing jury heard only one significant mitigating factor — that Wiggins had no prior convictions. Had the jury been able to place petitioner's excruciating life history on the mitigating side of the scale, there is a reasonable probability that at least one juror would have struck a different balance.

The judgment of the Court of Appeals was reversed and the case was remanded for the defendant to be given a new sentencing hearing.

The Williams case. The decision in *Williams v. Taylor*, 529 U.S. 362 (2000), involved a defendant who was convicted by a Virginia jury for a murder committed in 1985. During the penalty phase the defendant's counsel presented limited mitigating evidence and informed the jury "that it was difficult to find a reason why the jury should spare Williams' life." The jury found that the defendant should be sentenced to death. The defendant's conviction and death sentence were upheld on direct appeal.

The defendant in *Williams* filed a habeas petition in federal court. The federal district judge found that the defendant was denied effective assistance of counsel, because his attorney failed to investigate and present mitigating evidence. The federal judge vacated the death sentence. A federal court of appeals reversed the district judge's decision. The Supreme Court granted certiorari to consider the ineffective assistance of counsel issue.

The opinion in *Williams* found that the defendant was denied effective assistance of counsel at the penalty phase, because of his counsel's failure to investigate and present mitigating evidence. That mitigating evidence was highlighted as follows:

> Although ... counsel competently handled the guilt phase of the trial, ... their representation during the sentencing phase fell short of professional standards — a judgment barely disputed by the State in its brief to this Court. The record establishes that counsel did not begin to prepare for that phase of the proceeding until a week before the trial. They failed to conduct an investigation that would have uncovered extensive records graphically describing Williams' nightmarish childhood.... Had they done so, the jury would have learned that Williams' parents had been imprisoned for the criminal neglect of Williams and his siblings, that Williams had been severely and repeatedly beaten by his father, that he had been committed to the custody of the social services bureau for two years during his parents' incarceration (including one stint in an abusive foster home), and then, after his parents were released from prison, had been returned to his parents' custody.

Counsel failed to introduce available evidence that Williams was "borderline mentally retarded" and did not advance beyond sixth grade in school. They failed to seek prison records recording Williams' commendations for helping to crack a prison drug ring and for returning a guard's missing wallet, or the testimony of prison officials who described Williams as among the inmates "least likely to act in a violent, dangerous or provocative way." Counsel failed even to return the phone call of a certified public accountant who had offered to testify that he had visited Williams frequently when Williams was incarcerated as part of a prison ministry program, that Williams "seemed to thrive in a more regimented and structured environment," and that Williams was proud of the carpentry degree he earned while in prison.

The judgment of the Court of Appeals was reversed on the ineffective assistance of counsel issue and the case was remanded.

The meaning of Rompilla/Wiggins/Williams. The principle of law that was followed in *Rompilla*, *Wiggins* and *Williams* is straightforward. Those cases impose a duty on defense attorneys to use all reasonable means to uncover and present all relevant mitigating evidence at the penalty phase. The decisions in *Sears v. Upton*, 130 S.Ct. 3259 (2010), and *Porter v. McCollum*, 130 S.Ct. 447 (2009), applied the principles of *Rompilla*, *Wiggins* and *Williams* to set aside the death sentences in those cases.

Statutory Mitigating Circumstances

All capital punishment jurisdictions, except for six, have created various statutory mitigating circumstances.[11] The mere fact that mitigating circumstances are embodied in statutes does not mean that they are automatically made a part of a penalty phase proceeding. If a statutory mitigating circumstance is not relevant to the proceeding, or no evidence is proffered on it, there is no constitutional requirement for its use. This section sets out the vast majority of statutory mitigating circumstances.

No Significant Prior Criminal History

A majority of capital punishment jurisdictions have made "no significant prior criminal record" a statutory mitigating circumstance.[12] Note that this mitigating factor, by using the word "significant," leaves room for a capital felon to have some minor prior brushes with the law.[13]

Extreme Mental or Emotional Disturbance

A majority of capital punishment jurisdictions provide that "extreme mental or emotional disturbance," at the time of the commission of murder, is a statutory mitigating circumstance.[14] This statutory mitigating circumstance does not refer to or include mental retardation or mental impairment due to a foreign substance. Its meaning lies somewhere between mental retardation and mental impairment due to a foreign substance. It does not reach insanity, because that is a defense to a prosecution.[15]

Some guidance in fashioning an understanding of this statutory mitigating circumstance was provided by the Kentucky Supreme Court in *McClellan v. Commonwealth*, 715 S.W.2d 464 (Ky. 1986). The *McClellan* court held that "Extreme emotional disturbance is a temporary state of mind so enraged, inflamed, or disturbed as to overcome one's judgment, and to cause one to act uncontrollably from the impelling force of the extreme emotional disturbance rather than from evil or malicious purposes; it is not a mental disease in itself[.]"

The definition provided by *McClellan* raises more questions than it answers. However, the definition does nail home the point that mental or emotional disturbance is not a mental disease.

Victim's Consent

"Consent" is a universally recognized defense to many crimes. However, consent as a defense to a murder prosecution has never been accepted in Anglo-American jurisprudence. Although consent is not recognized as a defense to a murder prosecution, it has taken on a mitigating perspective in the context of a penalty phase proceeding. A majority of capital punishment jurisdictions provide that a victim's consent to being killed, or participation in the conduct leading to the murder is a statutory mitigating circumstance.[16]

Minor Participation

For the crime of murder, the degree of involvement by a defendant can be significant in determining punishment. A majority of capital punishment jurisdictions have provided by statute that minor participation in a capital offense is a mitigating circumstance.[17]

Extreme Duress

A majority of capital punishment jurisdictions have provided that being under extreme duress or substantial domination of another is a statutory mitigating circumstance that may preclude imposition of the death penalty.[18]

Capacity Substantially Impaired

In the case of *State v. Stuard*, 863 P.2d 881 (Ariz. 1993), the Arizona Supreme Court found that the defendant's mental impairment—which included organic brain damage, dementia and a low I.Q.—established that his "capacity to appreciate the wrongfulness of his conduct or to conform his conduct to the requirements of the law was substantially impaired." Therefore, the court determined that it was justified in reducing the defendant's three death sentences to consecutive life terms in prison.

The decision in *Stuard* gave recognition to the following statutory mitigating circumstance: the capacity to appreciate the wrongfulness of one's conduct or to conform one's conduct to the requirements of law was substantially impaired at the time of the offense. This statutory mitigating circumstance has been adopted in the statutes of a majority of capital punishment jurisdictions.[19]

The impairment mitigating circumstance is subject to being interpreted differently by courts. It was pointed out in *State v. Cooey*, 544 N.E.2d 895 (Ohio 1989), that some jurisdictions allow impairment to be triggered by alcohol consumption or drug usage. However, in *State v. Apelt*, 861 P.2d 654 (Ariz. 1993), it was said that other jurisdictions require showing that the impairment was initiated by a mental disease or psychological disorder.

Age of Capital Felon

A majority of capital punishment jurisdictions have provided by statute that age is a mitigating circumstance.[20] Three jurisdictions specifically require that a capital felon must be under 18 at the time of the murder in order to invoke the statutory age mitigating circumstance.[21] However, the decision in *Roper v. Simmons*, 543 U.S. 551 (2005), which prohibited executing defendants who committed capital murder while under eighteen, has nullified the effects of the statutes in those three jurisdictions. The majority of capital punishment jurisdictions that utilize age as a statutory mitigating circumstance do not specify any specific age.[22]

TABLE 15.0 AGE AND GENDER OF MURDERER 2010

Age of Murderer	Total Murderers	Murderer Gender	
		Male	*Female*
Under 1	0	0	0
1 to 4	0	0	0
5 to 8	2	2	0
9 to 12	9	6	3
13 to 16	437	395	42
17 to 19	1,575	1,445	130
20 to 24	2,544	2,315	229
25 to 29	1,641	1,478	163
30 to 34	1,107	971	136
35 to 39	778	685	93
40 to 44	606	529	77
45 to 49	526	459	67
50 to 54	405	338	67
55 to 59	247	223	24
60 to 64	155	144	11
65 to 69	83	75	8
70 to 74	48	39	9
75 & over	71	64	7

SOURCE: U.S. Department of Justice, Federal Bureau of Investigation, Uniform Crime Reports, Homicides, Table 3 (2011).

Other Statutory Mitigating Circumstances

The preceding statutory mitigating circumstances had majority consensus. The mitigating circumstances with minority status are the following.

No reasonable foreseeability. The doctrine of foreseeability is a civil law doctrine that occasionally finds application in criminal law. The foreseeability doctrine states that an actor may not be held liable for his or her conduct in harming another, if it was not reasonably foreseeable that his or her conduct would bring about such harm. Two capital punishment jurisdictions have taken the foreseeability doctrine and made it a statutory mitigating circumstance.[23]

Moral justification. Murder committed by a capital felon who believed the killing was morally justified is a statutory mitigating circumstance in five capital punishment jurisdictions.[24]

Cooperation with authorities. Two capital punishment jurisdictions provide by statute that cooperation with authorities is a statutory mitigating circumstance.[25] This mitigating circumstance involves two types of cooperation: (1) cooperation by a capital felon with authorities investigating the murder for which the capital felon was charged, and (2) cooperation with authorities concerning a felony offense for which the capital felon was not charged with or suspected of committing.

Many defendants have unsuccessfully challenged this statutory mitigating circumstance as being unconstitutional, in that it purportedly "allows for imposition of the death penalty based upon the exercise of the right to remain silent."[26] This is to say that the statutory mitigating circumstance indirectly punishes a capital felon who remains silent and does not cooperate in bringing about his or her own conviction. This situation, it is contended, violates a capital felon's constitutional right to remain silent.

On the other hand, capital felons also demand the right to take advantage of this statutory mitigating circumstance. In the case of *State v. Bacon*, 390 S.E.2d 327 (N.C. 1990), the defendant argued that the trial court committed error by failing to instruct the penalty phase jury that his cooperation in helping authorities apprehend another capital felon was a statutory mitigating circumstance. The North Carolina Supreme Court agreed with the defendant in *Bacon* and reversed his death sentence.

No future threat. If it is determined at the penalty phase proceeding that a capital felon should not be sentenced to death, then he or she will be sentenced to prison for life. What are the chances that a capital felon, sentenced to prison for life, will not commit murder while in prison? This question, not answered here, forms the heart of the "no future threat" mitigating circumstance. Three capital punishment jurisdictions have made "no future threat" a statutory mitigating circumstance.[27]

Victim-caused post-traumatic stress syndrome. Post-traumatic stress syndrome describes a state of mind that is disoriented due to some extreme emotional experience.[28] Clinical studies have revealed that people who acquire post-traumatic stress syndrome, because of conduct by another, occasionally strike back at the person who caused the syndrome. One capital punishment jurisdiction has recognized the latter fact, and provided by statute that victim-caused post-traumatic stress syndrome is a statutory mitigating circumstance.[29]

Co-defendant spared death penalty. It is not unusual for equally culpable co-defendants to receive different sentences for the same offense. This situation occurs most often when one defendant agrees to testify against the co-defendant. This situation can result in a capital felon being sentenced to life in prison, while his or her co-felon is sentenced to death. Two capital punishment jurisdictions have made "co-defendant spared death penalty" a statutory mitigating circumstance.[30]

16

Penalty Phase Burden of Proof

The doctrine of burden of proof is concerned with the degree of evidence that the law requires to be produced in order to persuade the factfinder of the truth of an allegation. If proffered evidence does not rise to the level required by the law, then the burden has not been sustained and the allegation is deemed not proven. Burden of proof, as a general proposition, means having the obligation of proffering a specific level of evidence to persuade a factfinder of the truth of an allegation.

At the penalty phase of a capital prosecution, the burden of proof doctrine governs the determination of whether mitigating or statutory aggravating circumstances actually exist. And, to a large degree, burden of proof determines the process for comparing mitigating and statutory aggravating circumstances, as well as the process used in reaching a result from such comparison.

The issue of burden of proof at the penalty phase of a capital prosecution is not simplistic for several reasons. First, the federal Constitution does not require the burden of proof be imposed upon the prosecutor at the penalty phase. The primary reason is that no presumption of innocence exists for a defendant at the penalty phase; his or her guilt has been determined at the guilt phase. Second, the penalty phase only involves evidence of aggravating circumstances and mitigating circumstances. The prosecutor has the burden of presenting aggravating circumstances and the defendant has the burden of presenting mitigating circumstances. As a result of both parties having the burden of presenting some evidence on their respective issue, a mechanism must be used for the jury to determine how to interpret the evidence of both parties. Third, each jurisdiction is free to devise any mechanism it desires, within the limits of due process of law, for determining the interpretation to give to proven mitigating and aggravating circumstances.

The material in this chapter will unravel the complex nature of burden of proof at the penalty phase under three broad headings: (1) establishing the existence of aggravators and mitigators, (2) comparing proven aggravators and mitigators, and (3) determining the result of comparing proven aggravators and mitigators.

Establishing the Existence of Aggravators and Mitigators

Proving Aggravating Circumstances Exist

In the case of *Woratzeck v. Lewis*, 863 F.Supp. 1079 (D.Ariz. 1994), the federal District Court of Arizona enumerated three key points regarding statutory aggravating circumstances.[1]

First, the District Court pointed out that "[a]n aggravating factor in the penalty phase of a capital proceeding is not an element of the offense." Second, it was pointed out "that the federal constitution does not require that aggravating factors in a capital sentencing proceeding be proven beyond a reasonable doubt." The final point made by *Woratzeck* is that "the Supreme Court ... has [not] determined what burden of proof must be satisfied when proving the existence of aggravating factors."

Whenever the constitution is deemed silent on an issue, jurisdictions are generally free to address the matter as they deem appropriate. Capital punishment jurisdictions have responded to the constitution's silence on the standard of proof needed to establish the existence of statutory aggravating circumstances. The vast majority of capital punishment jurisdictions demand, by statute, that the existence of statutory aggravating circumstances be proven beyond a reasonable doubt.[2]

Proving Mitigating Circumstances Exist

In the capital case of *Walton v. Arizona*, 497 U.S. 639 (1990), overruled on other grounds by *Ring v. Arizona*, 536 U.S. 584 (2002), the Supreme Court held that "a defendant's constitutional rights are not violated by placing on him the burden of proving mitigating circumstances sufficiently substantial to call for leniency." The potential harshness of imposing a burden of proof on capital felons was ameliorated by two other Supreme Court rulings which held that requiring jury unanimity on whether a mitigating circumstance existed was unconstitutional.[3] The Supreme Court has taken the position that requiring unanimity on the existence of mitigating circumstances would result in juries not considering relevant mitigating circumstances if just one juror dissented.[4] This situation would conjure up an indirect violation of the requirement in *Lockett v. Ohio*, 438 U.S. 586 (1978), that all relevant mitigating circumstance evidence be allowed into evidence at the penalty phase.[5] Thus, under the current law, as articulated in *Mills v. Maryland*, 486 U.S. 367 (1988), and *McKoy v. North Carolina*, 494 U.S. 433 (1990), if only one penalty phase juror finds that a capital felon carried his or her burden of persuasion on the existence of a mitigating circumstance, then the circumstance is deemed proven.

No capital punishment jurisdiction requires capital felons to prove the existence of mitigating circumstances beyond a reasonable doubt.[6] A minority of capital punishment jurisdictions require by statute that capital felons prove the existence of mitigating circumstances by a preponderance of evidence.[7] One capital punishment jurisdiction, Alabama, provides by statute that the prosecutor must disprove the existence of mitigating circumstances by a preponderance of evidence. The statutes of a majority of capital punishment jurisdictions do not provide any standard of proof for establishing the existence of mitigating circumstances.[8] This statutory silence means that capital felons merely have to raise the issue of mitigating circumstances, i.e., present some evidence on the issue. Only one jurisdiction explicitly provides by statute that a capital felon merely has to raise the issue of mitigating circumstances.[9]

In the case of *State v. Sivak*, 806 P.2d 413 (Idaho 1990), the Idaho Supreme Court held that "[t]he defendant's burden is merely to raise, in the aggravation-mitigation hearing, any factors which might possibly tend to mitigate his culpability for the offense." The holding in *Sivak*, that the capital felon does not bare the burden of persuasion on the existence of mitigating circumstances, is in total harmony with the requirement of *Lockett* that all relevant mitigating evidence be allowed into evidence at the penalty phase. *Sivak* is representative of the majority of capital punishment jurisdictions in not providing any standard of proof for establishing the existence of mitigating circumstances.

Comparing Proven Aggravators and Mitigators

Determining the existence of mitigating and statutory aggravating circumstances does not end the burden of proof process. Once the existence hurdle is overcome, a second process is triggered: mitigating and statutory aggravating circumstances must be compared with each other. The comparison process is carried out in one of two manners: weighing or non-weighing.[10]

Weighing Jurisdictions

The Utah Supreme Court described the weighing process in *State v. Wood*, 648 P.2d 71 (Utah 1981), as follows:

> [This] standard require[s] that the sentencing body compare the totality of the mitigating against the totality of the aggravating factors, not in terms of the relative numbers of the aggravating and the mitigating factors, but in terms of their respective substantiality and persuasiveness. Basically, what the sentencing authority must decide is how ... persuasive the totality of the mitigating factors are when compared against the totality of the aggravating factors. The sentencing body [is] making the judgment that aggravating [or mitigating] factors "outweigh," or are more [persuasive] than, the mitigating [or aggravating] factors[.]

Wood points out that the weighing process does not involve determining if more mitigating circumstances exist than statutory aggravating circumstances. Mere tallying is not the purpose of the weighing process. It matters not that, for example, five statutory aggravating circumstances were proven to exist, but only one mitigating circumstance is found to exist. The factfinder could still determine the mitigating circumstance outweighed the five statutory aggravating circumstances.

The Supreme Court noted in *Harris v. Alabama*, 115 S.Ct. 1031 (1995), that no "specific method for balancing mitigating and aggravating factors in a capital sentencing proceeding is constitutionally required." The "balancing" referred to in *Harris* is the weighing process. The result of *Harris'* pronouncement is that capital punishment jurisdictions may devise weighing processes as they see fit.[11] This discretion has led to the development of two classes of weighing jurisdictions: (1) no standard of proof jurisdictions and (2) standard of proof jurisdictions. A separate discussion of both follows.

No standard of proof jurisdictions. There are two types of weighing jurisdictions that do not impose a standard of proof on the weighing process. Each type is set out separately below.

Aggravating must outweigh mitigating. Statutes in a minority of capital punishment jurisdictions require statutory aggravating circumstances outweigh mitigating circumstances.[12] Two important consequences flow from this particular weighing process.

First, under this process the prosecutor has the burden of showing that statutory aggravating circumstances are more credible than mitigating circumstances. This situation is favorable to the capital felon.

Second, under this weighing process no standard of proof is imposed on the prosecutor.

That is, in weighing mitigating and statutory aggravating circumstances, the factfinder is free to use its own judgment as to why statutory aggravating circumstances appear more creditable than mitigating circumstances.

Mitigating must outweigh aggravating. A minority of capital punishment jurisdictions require that mitigating circumstances outweigh statutory aggravating circumstances.[13] Under this process the capital felon is given the burden of establishing that mitigating circumstances are more credible than statutory aggravating circumstances. This situation is favorable to the prosecutor.

The burden on the capital felon under this weighing process is lessened by the fact that no specific standard of proof is imposed upon the capital felon. The factfinder uses its own judgment in determining why more credibility should be given to mitigating circumstances. Further, under this process if the evidence of aggravating and mitigating circumstances is in equipoise, the death penalty may be imposed. The equipoise possibility was found constitutional in *Kansas v. Marsh*, 126 S.Ct. 2516 (2006).

Standard of proof jurisdictions. There are two types of weighing jurisdictions that impose a standard of proof on the weighing process. Each type is reviewed separately below.

Aggravating outweighs by a preponderance of evidence. In one capital punishment jurisdiction statutory aggravating circumstances are required to outweigh mitigating circumstances by a preponderance of evidence.[14] This jurisdiction imposes the burden of proof on the prosecutor. More significantly, the prosecutor is required to persuade the factfinder by a preponderance of evidence that the statutory aggravating circumstances outweigh the mitigating circumstances. The standard of proof imposed on the prosecutor makes it more difficult to obtain a sentence of death.

Aggravating outweighs beyond a reasonable doubt. The final weighing process is extremely formidable. This process demands that statutory aggravating circumstances outweigh mitigating circumstances beyond a reasonable doubt. Four capital punishment jurisdictions use this weighing process.[15] Under this process the prosecutor is strapped with the burden of proof. The prosecutor must persuade the factfinder beyond a reasonable doubt that the statutory aggravating circumstances outweigh the mitigating circumstances. This situation inures to the advantage of the capital felon.

Non-Weighing Jurisdictions

The South Carolina Supreme Court held in *State v. Bellamy*, 359 S.E.2d 63 (S.C. 1987), that the penalty phase jury should not be instructed to weigh statutory aggravating circumstances against mitigating circumstances. Instead, the jury had to be instructed to merely consider the mitigating and statutory aggravating circumstances. The holding in *Bellamy* was in accord with a ruling by the United States Supreme Court in *Zant v. Stephens*, 462 U.S. 862 (1983), that the Constitution does not require weighing mitigating and statutory aggravating circumstances. The decision in *Zant* fostered what are called non-weighing capital punishment jurisdictions.[16] There are currently eight non-weighing capital punishment jurisdictions.[17]

In non-weighing jurisdictions the factfinder is not instructed or guided on how to compare mitigating and statutory aggravating circumstances. As explained in *Bellamy*, the factfinder in a non-weighing jurisdiction is instructed to merely consider the proffered circumstances for sufficiency. The non-weighing process has developed along two different lines.[18] Each will be discussed separately below.

Determine whether mitigating is sufficient. Seven capital punishment jurisdictions require nothing more than that the penalty phase factfinder determine whether sufficient mitigating circumstances exist to warrant leniency.[19] The method for making this "sufficiency determination" is left up to the factfinder. Additionally, this particular non-weighing process does not have a standard of proof for measuring sufficiency. The factfinder is allowed to determine for itself what constitutes sufficiency. Finally, the burden of proving sufficiency in these jurisdictions is on the capital felon.

Mitigating not sufficient beyond a reasonable doubt. Under this non-weighing process the factfinder must determine whether sufficient mitigating circumstances do not exist beyond a reasonable doubt. One capital punishment jurisdiction utilizes this process.[20]

Two matters distinguish this particular non-weighing process. First, in making its sufficiency determination, the factfinder is provided with a standard of proof for measuring sufficiency. The beyond a reasonable doubt standard of proof is used. Second, the burden of proof is placed on the prosecutor. The prosecutor must persuade the factfinder that mitigating circumstances are not sufficient beyond a reasonable doubt.

Determining the Result of Comparing Proven Aggravators and Mitigators

The previous sections were concerned with how mitigating and statutory aggravating circumstances are compared to determine which "outweighed" or was more "sufficient" than the other. This section looks at what happens once a weighing or sufficiency determination has been made that is favorable to the prosecutor.[21]

In *Boyde v. California*, 494 U.S. 370 (1990), the Supreme Court held that there was no constitutional requirement that a penalty phase jury must be instructed that it can decline to impose the death penalty, even if it decided that statutory aggravating circumstances outweighed mitigating circumstances. The *Boyde* holding has been interpreted to mean that, once a weighing or sufficiency determination has been made that is favorable to the prosecutor, the Constitution permits the death penalty to be imposed. Nothing further is constitutionally required. The *Boyde* decision has promoted two types of jurisdictions: (1) death automatic jurisdictions and (2) death discretionary jurisdictions. Both are presented below after a brief discussion of an argument raised about presumption of death.

Presumption That Death Is the Proper Sentence

Capital felons have argued that death penalty statutes which provide that the trial court "shall impose" the death penalty if one or more aggravating circumstances are found and mitigating circumstances are held insufficient to call for leniency creates an unconstitutional presumption that death is the proper sentence. This argument has been rejected as an improper reading of the phrase "shall impose." In *Walton v. Arizona*, 497 U.S. 639 (1990), overruled on other grounds by *Ring v. Arizona*, 536 U.S. 584 (2002), it was said that the phrase merely directs trial courts as to what they must do, if the evidence proves that a death sentence is appropriate. The phrase does not require trial courts to presume that death is appropriate.

Death Automatic Jurisdictions

A large minority of capital punishment jurisdictions require that death must be imposed once a weighing or sufficiency determination is made that is favorable to the prosecutor. These jurisdictions are broken down into weighing and non-weighing jurisdictions and are discussed below.

Weighing jurisdictions that require death. There are thirteen weighing capital punishment jurisdictions that require the death penalty be imposed, if the weighing process is favorable to the prosecutor.[22] What this means, of course, is that the factfinder is not given any discretion once it plugs in the weighing formula and makes a determination that is favorable to the prosecutor. The capital felon in *Boyde* contended that this lack of factfinder discretion was cruel and unusual punishment. The Supreme Court rejected the argument.

Non-weighing jurisdictions that require death. In two non-weighing jurisdictions no discretion is given to the factfinder once a pro-prosecutor determination is made.[23] The death penalty must be imposed once a sufficiency determination is made that is favorable to the prosecutor.

Death Discretionary Jurisdictions

Notwithstanding a weighing or sufficiency determination that is favorable to the prosecutor, a majority of all capital punishment jurisdictions provide discretion to the factfinder. The factfinder can refuse to impose the death penalty even though the weighing or sufficiency determination was favorable to the prosecutor. The jurisdictions providing such discretion are divided into three types and are discussed below.

Weighing jurisdictions that permit discretion. The Supreme Court indicated in *Boyde* that the constitution did not require giving the factfinder discretion to reject the death penalty, even though the weighing or sufficiency determination was favorable to the prosecutor. This holding by *Boyde* does not mean that the constitution prohibited giving the factfinder such discretion.

Twelve weighing capital punishment jurisdictions have taken advantage of *Boyde's* "window of opportunity" and given discretion to the factfinder.[24] In these jurisdictions the factfinder may reject imposing the death penalty on the capital felon, even though the weighing process called for imposition of the death penalty.

Jurisdictions requiring beyond a reasonable doubt. In the majority of weighing capital punishment jurisdictions that give the factfinder death discretion, no standard of proof is used in determining whether that discretion should be exercised. However, two weighing jurisdictions that afford death discretion to the factfinder impose a standard of proof in determining whether to exercise that discretion.[25] The two jurisdictions in question require the factfinder to determine beyond a reasonable doubt that imposing the death penalty is justified, even though the weighing process was favorable to the prosecutor.

Non-weighing jurisdictions that permit discretion. In four non-weighing capital punishment jurisdictions the factfinder is given death discretion once it makes a sufficiency determination that is favorable to the prosecutor.[26] In these jurisdictions the capital felon may be spared the death penalty, notwithstanding the fact that the sufficiency determination called for death.

17

Automatic Appellate Review of Death Sentence

It is commonly understood in the legal community that no trial is ever error free. Consequently, courts recognize two types of trial court errors: harmless error and prejudicial error. It was noted in *Calderon v. Coleman*, 119 S.Ct. 500 (1998), that under the harmless error standard a defendant must show that the error had a substantial and injurious effect or influence in determining the jury's verdict. Under this rule, if the prosecutor can prove beyond a reasonable doubt that a constitutional error did not contribute to the verdict, the error is harmless and the verdict may stand.

Every capital conviction and sentence carries with it the potential for being infected with harmless error or prejudicial error. If the final word in a criminal prosecution rested at the trial level, then actual prejudicial errors would go undetected.[1]

BOX 17.0 TYPES OF TRIAL ERROR

1. **Prejudicial Error**—an error is deemed prejudicial if it had the potential of causing the outcome that resulted from a criminal prosecution.
2. **Harmless Error**—an error is considered harmless if it had no impact on the outcome of a criminal prosecution.

Anglo-American jurisprudence has long rejected allowing a trial court to have the final word in criminal prosecutions. This rejection is manifested in appellate courts. Part of the function of appellate courts is that of examining criminal convictions and sentences for prejudicial error.[2] All jurisdictions, capital and non-capital, have appellate courts.

There is no constitutional right to have a conviction or sentence examined by an appellate court. Over one hundred years ago, in the case of *McKane v. Durston*, 153 U.S. 684 (1894) (and the companion case of *Bergemann v. Backer*, 157 U.S. 655 [1895]), the Supreme Court indicated that "a State is not required by the Federal Constitution to provide appellate courts or a right to appellate [examination of errors] at all."[3] While *McKane* is still good law today, its pronouncement is meaningless because all jurisdictions do in fact provide appellate courts.

In *Schwab v. Berggren*, 143 U.S. 442 (1892), and *Fielden v. Illinois*, 143 U.S. 452 (1892), the Supreme Court held that a defendant did not have a constitutional right to be present in person when the state appellate court reviewed his or her death sentence, because such right was only accorded at the trial court level when the original sentence was pronounced.

167

This chapter outlines the procedures used by appellate courts to review death sentences. The material has been divided into five sections. The first section provides a discussion of the differences that exist between appellate review of a death sentence and the traditional appeal of a conviction and sentence. The second section looks at the issue of procedural type errors that may occur in a capital prosecution. In the third section a discussion is given on how appellate courts review aggravating and mitigating circumstance issues. The fourth section is concerned with factors appellate courts look at to determine whether a death sentence is appropriate. The fifth and final section examines disposition alternatives available to appellate courts once a sentencing review is completed.

Distinguishing Automatic Review from Appeal

Prior to capital punishment being abolished by *Furman v. Georgia*, 408 U.S. 238 (1972), all capital punishment jurisdictions allowed capital felons to bring their conviction and sentence to appellate courts by way of an appeal (or writ of error, as it was sometimes called). When the Supreme Court resurrected the death penalty in *Gregg v. Georgia*, 428 U.S. 152 (1976), by approving of the capital punishment scheme Georgia created, one feature of the new procedures it approved of was stated as follows:

> Finally, the Georgia statute has an additional provision designed to assure that the death penalty will not be imposed on a capriciously selected group of convicted defendants. The new sentencing procedures require that the [Georgia] Supreme Court review every death sentence....
> The provision for appellate review in the Georgia capital-sentencing system serves as a check against the random or arbitrary imposition of the death penalty. In particular, the proportionality review substantially eliminates the possibility that a person will be sentenced to die by the action of an aberrant jury. If a time comes when juries generally do not impose the death sentence in a certain kind of murder case, the appellate review procedures assure that no defendant convicted under such circumstances will suffer a sentence of death.

Georgia's automatic appellate review of death sentences is not the traditional appeal. In approving of this new review process in *Gregg*, the Supreme Court did not hold that the constitution required such a process. The Supreme Court indicated merely that the automatic review process was constitutionally acceptable.[4]

Gregg's acceptance of Georgia's automatic appellate review of death sentences was quickly adopted by other capital punishment jurisdictions. As it stands now, Utah is the only capital punishment jurisdiction that does not utilize automatic appellate review of a death sentence.[5] That is, in all other jurisdictions a capital felon does not have to request review of his or her death sentence. The review will occur as a matter of law, absent a valid waiver by the capital felon.[6]

It was previously noted that the traditional appeal involved both guilt phase and penalty phase assignments of error. The automatic death sentence appellate review process, on the other hand, involves ostensibly only penalty phase issues. What this means is that, the question of whether a capital felon was erroneously found guilty of the offense is not considered during automatic appellate review of a death sentence. The only issue at stake in the automatic review process is whether a capital felon was sentenced to die in accordance with the law. Guilt phase issues are brought to the appellate level by way of the traditional appeal.

A minority of capital punishment jurisdictions that utilize automatic appellate review of death sentences provide by statute that if a capital felon prosecutes a guilt phase appeal, the appeal is to be consolidated with the penalty phase review issues.[7]

A capital felon whose sentence is under automatic review may assign as error any matter he or she believes affected the sentence. However, in all but five review jurisdictions, statutes set out specific issues that appellate courts must address in making a review.[8]

Procedural Type Errors

The phrase "procedural type errors" is used here to refer to a catch-all category of purported trial and sentencing errors. This catch-all category of alleged errors is as expansive as the imagination of appellate defense attorneys. That is, the alleged errors that fall under this category have no limit. While it would not be practical to examine all of the alleged trial and sentencing errors that have, heretofore been placed under this category, a representative sample of the issues is warranted.

Self-Representation

The Sixth Amendment guarantees every defendant the right to self-representation (barring mental incompetency). Occasionally capital felons will choose to give up their right to legal counsel and represent themselves. Invariably self-represented capital felons are found guilty and sentenced to death. Usually at this point self-represented capital felons will request and obtain legal counsel to represent them in appellate court.

In the case of *Townes v. Commonwealth*, 362 S.E.2d 650 (Va. 1987), the defendant represented himself and was sentenced to death. One of the issues he raised during appellate review of the sentence was that it was cruel and unusual punishment to impose the death penalty on a defendant who represented himself. The Virginia Supreme Court rejected the argument that a defendant who voluntarily represents himself cannot have the death penalty imposed.

The case of *Bloom v. California*, 774 P.2d 698 (Cal. 1989), also involved a defendant who decided to represent himself. During the penalty phase of his prosecution the defendant chose not to put on any evidence. He was sentenced to death. During appellate review of the sentence the defendant contended that his death sentence was not reliable, because the factfinder was not presented with any evidence by him. The California Supreme Court disagreed with the defendant and held that intentionally failing to put on evidence at the penalty phase does not render a sentencing verdict unreliable.

Requesting Death

One argument that has been raised in opposition to the death penalty is that life imprisonment has greater retribution potential than the death penalty. Proponents of this argument contend that the death penalty provides a relatively quick and painless end to life for people who should "suffer" in prison. Occasionally capital felons agree that death is less retributive than life imprisonment, and will request at penalty phase proceedings that the factfinder impose death.

Requesting death and actually having the request granted brings astonishingly swift sobriety to capital felons. The case examples that follow illustrate this.

In the case of *People v. Grant*, 755 P.2d 894 (Cal. 1988), the defendant exercised his right of allocution and addressed the penalty phase factfinder. With great bravado the defendant demanded the factfinder return a verdict of death. The factfinder obliged the defendant and returned a verdict of death. When the defendant got his wish, he sought to retract his request.

A central issue raised by the defendant in *Grant* during appellate review of his sentence was that it was cruel and unusual punishment to sentence a person to death based upon a request to die. The appellate court had little trouble rejecting this argument, after finding that the sentence of death was imposed based upon compliance with statutory criteria. One can only speculate what would happen at penalty phase proceedings, if it was unconstitutional to sentence a defendant to death should he or she request death.

The case of *People v. Guzman*, 755 P.2d 917 (Cal. 1988), presented another death requesting defendant. As in *Grant*, the defendant in *Guzman* realized that asking the factfinder to sentence him to death was not a rational thing to do. Unlike *Grant*, however, the defendant in *Guzman* did not contend, during appellate review of his sentence, that death could not be imposed on a death requesting defendant.

The defendant in *Guzman* sought to get out of his predicament by arguing that the trial judge should have instructed the factfinder that it could not base its decision on the imprudent request of the defendant. The appellate court agreed with the defendant that such an instruction should have been given. However, the appellate court reasoned that the burden was on the defendant to request such an instruction from the trial judge. Since the instruction request was not made, the appellate court concluded that it was not error in failing to provide the instruction.

The case of *State v. Hightower*, 577 A.2d 99 (N.J. 1990), stretches to the limit attempts to undo death requests. The defendant in that case calmly and voluntarily addressed the factfinder during the penalty phase and implored it to sentence him to death. The factfinder did not disappoint the defendant.

During appellate review of the death sentence in *Hightower*, the defendant offered the novel argument that the trial court had an affirmative duty to prevent him from requesting the death penalty. The defendant contended that failure of the trial court to carry out this purported duty made the imposition of the death penalty cruel and unusual. The appellate court disagreed with the defendant. The appellate court reasoned that the law does not require judges to "gag" defendants who wish to request the death penalty. To do this would infringe upon a defendant's right to allocution, i.e., the right to address the factfinder.

In *Demosthenes v. Baal*, 495 U.S. 731 (1990), the defendant withdrew his request for state habeas corpus review of his conviction and indicated he wished to be executed. A few hours before his execution the defendant's parents filed a petition for federal habeas corpus relief as his "next friend," contending that the defendant was not competent to waive review of his conviction and sentence. A federal district court denied relief. However, an appellate court reversed and remanded the case for a full evidentiary hearing. The United States Supreme Court reversed the appellate court decision. It was said in *Demosthenes* that the prerequisite for litigating as a "next friend" is that the real party in interest be unable to litigate his or her own cause due to mental incapacity. The opinion held that this prerequisite was not satisfied where an evidentiary hearing showed that the defendant gave a knowing, intelligent, and voluntary waiver of his right to proceed in a state habeas proceeding. The opinion also stated:

We realize that last minute petitions from parents of death row inmates may often be viewed sympathetically. But federal courts are authorized by the federal habeas statutes to interfere with the course of state proceedings only in specified circumstances. Before granting a stay, therefore, federal courts must make certain that an adequate basis exists for the exercise of federal power. In this case, that basis was plainly lacking. The State is entitled to proceed without federal intervention.

It was also said in *Whitmore v. Arkansas,* 495 U.S. 149 (1990), that a third party does not have standing to challenge the validity of a death sentence imposed on a capital defendant who has knowingly, intelligently, and voluntarily elected to forgo the right of appeal to the state supreme court.

Retrial of a Penalty Phase Proceeding

Not infrequently a capital defendant sentenced to death will have his or her sentence reversed by an appellate court, and the case remanded to the trial court solely for a second penalty phase proceeding. Defendants have argued against being subjected to a second penalty phase hearing when the initial penalty phase proceeding is invalidated. In the case of *People v. Davenport,* 906 P.2d 1068 (Cal. 1995), it was pointed out that subjecting a defendant to retrial of the penalty phase hearing does not violate his or her constitutional rights to due process, equal protection, fair trial, or proportional sentencing, in view of the fact that a defendant has an opportunity to present a significant portion of his or her guilt phase evidence during the second penalty phase proceeding.

Rebuttal by the Prosecutor

Capital felons frequently, and usually unsuccessfully, argue during appellate review that improper rebuttal occurred during the penalty phase. In the case of *Pickens v. State,* 783 S.W.2d 341 (Ark. 1990), the appellate court rejected the defendant's contention that it was improper for the prosecutor to rebut his evidence, since the prosecutor had the burden of proof. The exact same argument was raised and rejected in *People v. Douglas,* 788 P.2d 640 (Cal. 1990), and *Wood v. State,* 547 N.E.2d 772 (Ind. 1989).

The gist of the argument raised in cases like *Pickens, Douglas* and *Wood* is that the prosecutor has the burden of proof (in the jurisdictions where the argument was raised), therefore the prosecutor should present all its evidence during its case-in-chief. This argument is sound; however, capital felons apply it to situations that are inapplicable, as in the above cited cases. Usually a prosecutor will not be aware of every issue that a capital felon intends to present during the penalty phase. Therefore, a prosecutor will frequently fail to address, during its case-in-chief, an issue that a capital felon presents in his or her case-in-chief. When this situation occurs, fairness requires the prosecutor have an opportunity to rebut the issue.

In both *People v. West,* 560 N.E.2d 594 (Ill. 1990), and *Ex Parte Wilson,* 571 So.2d 1251 (Ala. 1990), the defendants argued that it was improper rebuttal by the prosecutors to call psychiatric expert witnesses that had evaluated them. The thrust of this argument was that self-incriminating statements were given to the psychiatrists by the defendants, therefore the Fifth Amendment protected the statements from disclosure. The appellate courts rejected the argument, principally because the defendants had been made aware of their Fifth Amendment rights before speaking to the psychiatrists, and secondarily because the issue of guilt had already been determined — thus the right against self-incrimination was a moot issue.

In *Caldwell v. Mississippi*, 472 U.S. 320 (1985), the defendant argued that the prosecutor gave improper rebuttal by informing the jury that responsibility for determining the appropriateness of a death sentence rests not with the jury, but with the appellate court which later reviews the case. The Supreme Court agreed with the defendant that the rebuttal was improper:

> This Court has always premised its capital punishment decisions on the assumption that a capital sentencing jury recognizes the gravity of its task and proceeds with the appropriate awareness of its "truly awesome responsibility." In this case, the State sought to minimize the jury's sense of responsibility for determining the appropriateness of death. Because we cannot say that this effort had no effect on the sentencing decision, that decision does not meet the standard of reliability that the Eighth Amendment requires. The sentence of death must therefore be vacated.

The Supreme Court made clear in *Parker v. Matthews*, 132 S.Ct. 2148 (2012), that its decision in *Darden v. Wainwright*, 477 U.S. 168 (1986), held "that a prosecutor's improper comments will be held to violate the Constitution only if they so infected the trial with unfairness as to make the resulting conviction a denial of due process."

Sentence for Non-Capital Crime

It is often the situation that a capital defendant will be convicted of non-capital crimes during the trial of a capital offense. Occasionally trial courts do not sentence capital felons on the non-capital convictions until after a penalty phase capital verdict is returned. Capital defendants sentenced to death under such circumstances have argued that their federal constitutional due process rights are violated by not being sentenced on the non-capital crimes before the capital penalty phase proceeding begins.

This argument is raised by capital felons convicted in the few jurisdictions that allow a sentence of life imprisonment with the possibility of parole, as an option to a sentence of death for capital murder. Capital felons in such jurisdictions seek to have trial judges impose punishment for the non-capital convictions, prior to the start of the capital penalty phase, so that they can argue to the penalty phase jury that, in view of the sentence for the non-capital crimes, they will not be released on parole if the jury recommended a sentence of life imprisonment. Courts have rejected this due process argument as a basis for invalidating death sentences.

Wearing Shackles During Prosecution

The Due Process Clause of the federal Constitution prohibits routine use of visible shackles on capital defendants during their trial. In *Deck v. Missouri*, 544 U.S. 622 (2005), the Supreme Court held that a defendant may be required to wear visible shackles only when it has been shown that there is a specific security need or escape risk. The general prohibition against the use of visible shackles has slightly different justifications for the guilt phase and penalty phase of a capital prosecution.

With respect to the guilt phase of a capital prosecution, three reasons support the general bar against visible shackles. First, insofar as the criminal justice system presumes that a defendant is innocent, forcing a defendant to wear visible shackles undermines the presumption of innocence. It suggests to the jury that the defendant is guilty. Second, the use of physical restraints diminishes a defendant's constitutional right to counsel, because shackles can interfere with a defendant's ability to communicate with his or her lawyer. Third, the routine use of shackles in the presence of juries would undermine the formal dignity of the courtroom.

In regards to the penalty phase, the primary concern with the use of visible shackles involves factors juries consider in deciding whether to impose the death penalty or life imprisonment. The appearance of a defendant during the penalty phase in shackles inevitably implies to a jury that court officials consider the defendant a danger to the community. This impression has concrete negative consequences. First, many jurisdictions make "danger to the community" a statutory aggravating circumstance that permits the imposition of the death penalty. Therefore, requiring a defendant to wear visible shackles can assist the prosecutor in proving a statutory aggravating circumstance. Second, in an effort to have a jury impose life imprisonment, instead of death, defendants invariably put on mitigating evidence to show that they are no longer a threat to society. This mitigating evidence would become meaningless if capital defendants were routinely required to wear visible shackles at the penalty phase.

Denial of Right to Confront Accusers

The Confrontation Clause of the Sixth Amendment of the federal Constitution requires a defendant be permitted to confront witnesses against him or her. The purpose of the Confrontation Clause is to ensure the reliability of evidence against a defendant, by subjecting the evidence to rigorous testing in a criminal trial through cross examination of an adverse witness. The Confrontation Clause generally forbids the introduction of hearsay into a trial unless the evidence falls within a firmly rooted hearsay exception or otherwise possesses particularized guarantees of trustworthiness.

The Confrontation Clause was addressed in *Lilly v. Virginia*, 527 U.S. 116 (1999). In *Lilly* the defendant was charged by the state of Virginia with capital murder in the commission of a robbery. Two accomplices were also charged. The three men had separate trials. During the guilt phase of the defendant's trial the prosecutor called one of the accomplices as a witness against the defendant. The accomplice invoked his Fifth Amendment privilege against self-incrimination and refused to testify. Consequently, the prosecutor was allowed to introduce into evidence a written confession by the accomplice that implicated the defendant as the person who killed the robbery victim. The jury convicted the defendant of capital murder and a sentence of death was imposed. The Supreme Court found that the defendant's rights under the Confrontation Clause were violated.

The opinion in *Lilly* said that exceptions to the general exclusion of hearsay statements exist only where (1) the statements fall within a firmly rooted hearsay exception or (2) they contain particularized guarantees of trustworthiness such that adversarial testing would be expected to add little, if anything, to their reliability. *Lilly* indicated that hearsay statements are admissible under a firmly rooted hearsay exception when they fall within a hearsay category whose conditions have proven over time to remove all temptation to falsehood, and to enforce as strict an adherence to the truth as would the obligation of an oath and cross examination at a trial. One such firmly rooted hearsay exception involves statements that are against the declarant's penal or criminal interest. However, it was held that this exception cannot be extended to include admission of statements by an accomplice that shifts or spreads blame to a criminal defendant.

Improper Consideration of Aggravating Circumstance

During the penalty phase of a capital prosecution, the prosecutor may present evidence of statutory and non-statutory aggravating circumstances. However, the death penalty may only be imposed based upon evidence establishing the existence of statutory aggravating circumstances. The issue presented to the Supreme Court in *Barclay v. Florida*, 463 U.S. 939 (1983), was whether a state may constitutionally impose the death penalty when one of the aggravating circumstances relied upon by the factfinder to support the sentence was not among those established by the state's death penalty statute. In *Barclay* the penalty phase factfinder, the trial judge, relied upon the defendant's prior criminal record to support imposing the death penalty. However, prior criminal record was not a statutory aggravating circumstance under Florida law. The Supreme Court applied a harmless error test in *Barclay* to determine whether the death sentence should be reversed. It was held in *Barclay* that a death sentence is not constitutionally invalid because of the improper consideration of a non-statutory aggravating circumstance, if an appellate court performs an analysis that removes the improper factor and finds that with the improper factor removed, the sentence of death is supported by the remaining permissible aggravating factors. Applying this test to the facts of the case, it was held in *Barclay* that the error was harmless because sufficient evidence was present to support the existence of statutory aggravating circumstances.

In *Zant v. Stephens*, 462 U.S. 862 (1983), it was held that the Constitution permits appellate courts to sustain a death sentence, when an invalid statutory aggravating circumstance is used, so long as at least one of several statutory aggravating circumstances found by the jury is valid and supports the sentence. It was said in *Tuggle v. Netherland*, 516 U.S. 10 (1995), that *Zant* did not permit a death sentence to be upheld on the basis of one valid aggravating circumstance, regardless of the reasons another aggravating factor may have been found to be invalid. *Tuggle* held that under *Zant* courts are required to analyze the possible prejudicial effect on the sentencing decision by the evidence used to establish the invalid aggravating factor. It was said in *Wainwright v. Goode*, 464 U.S. 78 (1983), where the record indicates the state's highest court reweighed aggravating and mitigating circumstances, excluding the impermissible aggravator, and thereafter affirms the death sentence, any error in a trial court's consideration of an impermissible aggravator is harmless error. In *Sochor v. Florida*, 504 U.S. 527 (1992), it was held that when a state appellate court finds that one or more of several statutory aggravators are invalid, the court must re-weigh the evidence or apply harmless error analysis to the evidence. Under *Sochor*, failure to perform either test will result in the sentence being vacated.

In *Brown v. Sanders*, 126 S.Ct. 884 (2006), the Supreme Court was concerned with whether the invalidity of two out of four special circumstances found by a jury to make a defendant eligible for the death penalty affected the constitutionality of the death sentence ultimately imposed. *Brown* held that the invalidity of two special circumstances found by a jury to make a defendant eligible for the death penalty did not affect the constitutionality of the death sentence ultimately imposed, because the facts relied upon for those two special circumstances were also used to find other valid aggravating circumstances. In *Clemons v. Mississippi*, 494 U.S. 738 (1990), it was said that the Constitution does not prevent a state appellate court from upholding a death sentence that is based in part on an invalid or improperly defined aggravating circumstance, either by reweighing of the aggravating and mitigating evidence or by harmless error review.

In *Dawson v. Delaware*, 503 U.S. 159 (1992), the Supreme Court reversed a death sentence because of the introduction of evidence that the defendant was a member of a prison gang, where the evidence had no relevance to the issues being decided in the proceeding. It was held in *Johnson v. Mississippi*, 486 U.S. 578 (1988), that the reversal of the defendant's prior rape conviction by a New York court rendered his Mississippi death sentence unconstitutional, because the death sentence was imposed in part due to the prosecutor's use of the rape conviction to establish the "prior felony conviction" statutory aggravating circumstance. The Supreme Court indicated in *Jones v. United States*, 527 U.S. 373 (1999), that two non-statutory aggravating circumstances were not duplicative, vague, or overbroad; and, assuming arguendo, that they were duplicative, vague, and overbroad, submission of them to the jury was harmless error beyond a reasonable doubt.

Failure to Give Lesser Included Offense Instruction

The decision in *Beck v. Alabama*, 447 U.S. 625 (1980), addressed the issue of a trial court's refusal to give a lesser included offense instruction to the jury. In *Beck* the defendant was charged by the state of Alabama with capital murder. At the time of the prosecution Alabama's death penalty statute provided that the trial judge was prohibited from giving the guilt phase jury the option of convicting the defendant of any lesser included offense. Instead, the jury had to either convict the defendant of the capital crime or acquit him. During the trial the defendant presented evidence tending to show that he was guilty of a lesser included offense to capital murder. However, because of Alabama's statute, the trial court refused to instruct the jury that they could return a verdict of guilty of a lesser included offense. The defendant was convicted of capital murder and sentenced to death.

The Supreme Court reversed the conviction and sentence. It was said in *Beck* that a death sentence may not constitutionally be imposed after a jury verdict of guilty of a capital offense, where the jury was not permitted to consider a verdict of guilty of a lesser included offense. The opinion reasoned that providing the jury with the option of convicting on a lesser included offense gave assurances that the jury would accord the defendant the full benefit of the reasonable doubt standard. *Beck* stated that when the evidence establishes that the defendant is guilty of a serious and violent offense, but leaves some doubt as to an element justifying conviction of a capital offense, the failure to give the jury such a lesser included instruction inevitably enhances the risk of an unwarranted conviction. *Beck* ruled that such a risk could not be tolerated in a case in which the defendant's life was at stake.

In *Hopkins v. Reeves*, 524 U.S. 88 (1998), it was held that *Beck* did not require the trial court to instruct the guilt phase jury on offenses that were not lesser included offenses of capital felony murder under Nebraska law. The Supreme Court held in *Hopper v. Evans*, 456 U.S. 605 (1982), that the invalidation of a state law which precluded instructions on lesser included offenses in the defendant's capital case did not require a new trial because the defendant's own evidence negated the possibility that such an instruction might have been warranted. In *Schad v. Arizona*, 501 U.S. 624 (1991), it was held that the defendant was not entitled to a jury instruction on the lesser included offense of robbery when the jury was instructed on the lesser included offense of second-degree murder.

Victims' Opinion About the Death Penalty

In a few capital prosecutions, victims of capital murder have left behind documented opinions about their views on the death penalty. Such views have been for and against the death penalty. Courts have prohibited capital defendants from introducing victim opinions that opposed capital punishment. And, too, courts have barred prosecutors from introducing as victim impact evidence documented statements by capital murder victims approving of the death penalty. Courts have precluded such evidence on both sides, because it goes to the issue of the appropriate sentence to be imposed. The determination of the appropriate sentence must be made purely upon factors that aggravated a murder, as well as factors surrounding the character of the capital defendant and the circumstances of the crime that mitigate the punishment.

Victim Impact Evidence

Victim impact evidence involves personal characteristics of the victim and the emotional, economic and social impact of the crime on the victim's immediate family. In *Booth v. Maryland*, 482 U.S. 496 (1987), and *South Carolina v. Gathers*, 490 U.S. 805 (1989), this type of evidence was once found to violate the federal Constitution as being too prejudicial for use at the penalty phase of a capital prosecution. However, *Booth* and *Gathers* were overruled by *Payne v. Tennessee*, 501 U.S. 808 (1991), where it was held that victim impact evidence does not offend the federal Constitution and may be admissible at a capital penalty phase proceeding for the penalty phase jury to consider as non-statutory aggravating evidence.

As a result of the emotional appeal and prejudice of victim impact evidence, courts are generally strict in the type of victim evidence they will permit the jury to consider. Highly inflammatory or irrelevant victim impact evidence is usually barred from introduction at the penalty phase. Victim impact evidence is admitted at the penalty phase proceeding only after there is present in the record evidence of one or more statutory aggravating circumstances.

Anti-Sympathy Instruction

In *California v. Brown*, 479 U.S. 538 (1987), a California jury convicted the defendant of capital murder. During the penalty phase the defendant presented the testimony of several family members who recounted the defendant's peaceful nature and expressed disbelief that he was capable of such a brutal crime. The defendant also presented the testimony of a psychiatrist, who stated that the defendant killed the victim because of his shame and fear over sexual dysfunction. The defendant testified, stating that he was ashamed of his prior criminal conduct and asked the jury for mercy. The trial court instructed the penalty phase jury that it must not be swayed by mere sentiment, conjecture, sympathy, passion, prejudice, public opinion or public feeling. The defendant was sentenced to death. On automatic appeal, the California Supreme Court reversed the defendant's death sentence on the grounds that the anti-sympathy instruction violated federal constitutional law by denying the defendant the right to have sympathy factors raised by the evidence considered by the jury when determining the appropriate penalty. The United States Supreme Court held that the California high court wrongly interpreted federal constitutional law:

Reading the instruction as a whole, as we must, it is no more than a catalog of the kind of factors that could improperly influence a juror's decision to vote for or against the death penalty. [A] rational juror could hardly hear this instruction without concluding that it was meant to confine the jury's deliberations to considerations arising from the evidence presented, both aggravating and mitigating.

An instruction prohibiting juries from basing their sentencing decisions on factors not presented at the trial, and irrelevant to the issues at the trial, does not violate the United States Constitution. It serves the useful purpose of confining the jury's imposition of the death sentence by cautioning it against reliance on extraneous emotional factors, which, we think, would be far more likely to turn the jury against a capital defendant than for him....

We hold that the instruction challenged in this case does not violate the provisions of the Eighth and Fourteenth Amendments to the United States Constitution.

Reviewing Aggravating and Mitigating Findings

Appellate review of whether evidence supported the determination made regarding the existence of mitigating and statutory aggravating circumstances does not involve "weighing" or "sufficiency" determinations (those issues comes a different stage in the review process). The focus of review at this point is limited to a determination of whether the jury properly found the "existence" of statutory aggravating circumstances and correctly found the "lack of existence" of mitigating circumstances. These two issues are treated separately in the two subsections that follow.

Review of Aggravating Circumstance Finding

Appellate courts engage in two types of aggravating circumstance review: (1) determine whether an aggravating circumstance is invalid because of vagueness and (2) determine whether an aggravating circumstance was actually proven to exist. Both matters are presented below.

Determining vagueness. Statutory aggravating circumstances permit imposition of the death penalty, therefore, statutory aggravating circumstances must be constitutionally valid. That is, statutory aggravators cannot be vague in their meaning nor have an overinclusive application. Statutory aggravating circumstances are not unconstitutionally vague if they have some common sense core of meaning that the jury is capable of understanding. It was pointed out by the South Carolina Supreme Court, in *State v. Smith*, 381 S.E.2d 724 (S.C. 1989), that a statutory aggravating circumstance is unconstitutionally vague if it does not properly channel or limit the jury's discretion in imposing the death penalty.

When faced with a "vagueness" challenge to a statutory aggravating circumstance, courts must determine whether the aggravator is vague on its face and, if so, whether appellate case law decisions have adequately defined the aggravator so as to provide guidance for the penalty phase jury. If a particular statutory aggravating circumstance leaves the jury without sufficient guidance for determining its evidentiary presence or absence, it will be constitutionally vague and invalid.

Infrequently a jurisdiction will have a statutory aggravating circumstance that is constitutionally invalid for one reason or another. If a capital felon is sentenced to death based upon presentation of only one statutory aggravating circumstance, and that aggravator is found to be constitutionally invalid, the death sentence must be vacated. On the other hand, when multiple aggravators have been used, and only one is found to be invalid, the general rule is that a death sentence supported by multiple aggravating circumstances need not always be set aside if one aggravator is found to be invalid. This rule is predicated on the fact that even after elimination of the invalid aggravator, the death sentence rests on firm ground. In the case of *Brown v. Sanders*, 126 S.Ct. 884 (2006), the Supreme Court abolished the case law distinction between "weighing" and "nonweighing" jurisdictions, with respect to determining whether consideration of an invalid guilt phase special circumstance or penalty phase aggravating circumstance warrants setting aside a death sentence. The decision in *Brown* held that "[a]n invalidated sentencing factor (whether an eligibility factor or not) will render the sentence unconstitutional by reason of its adding an improper element to the aggravation scale in the weighing process unless one of the other sentencing factors enables the sentencer to give aggravating weight to the same facts and circumstances." In other words, so long as the evidence used for an invalid factor was also used to support another valid factor, a death sentence will be upheld.

Capital felons have mounted a legion of arguments challenging statutory aggravating circumstances as being vague. While vagueness challenges, for the most part, are frivolous, appellate courts must nevertheless make independent evaluations of all arguments. Some of the vagueness arguments made include the examples that follow.

In *People v. Bunyard*, 756 P.2d 795 (Cal. 1988), the defendant argued that the "multiple victims" statutory aggravating circumstance was vague in its application to the murder of a pregnant woman and the fetus she carried. This argument was rejected by the appellate court primarily because the fetus was viable. In *People v. Edelbacher*, 766 P.2d 1 (Cal. 1989), the "pecuniary gain" statutory aggravating circumstance was challenged as being vague, in that it did not provide a fair warning of what conduct was prohibited. The appellate court rejected this argument on the grounds that it had previously limited this statutory aggravating circumstance to mean: the victim's death is the consideration for, or an essential prerequisite to, the financial gain sought by the defendant. The statutory aggravating circumstance "under sentence of imprisonment" was challenged in *People v. Davis*, 794 P.2d 159 (Colo. 1990), as being vague in its application to a paroled defendant. The appellate court rebuffed the defendant's argument by holding that the legislature intended for this statutory aggravating circumstance to apply to incarcerated and paroled felons.

The statutory aggravating circumstance that capital felons have been able to successfully challenge as vague is that of "heinous, atrocious, cruel or depraved." This statutory aggravating circumstance was found unconstitutionally vague in *Wilcher v. Hargett*, 978 F.2d 872 (5th Cir. 1992), and *Moore v. Clarke*, 951 F.2d 895 (8th Cir. 1991), because no definitions for the terms were provided.

Determining if an aggravating circumstance is proven. Failure of a vagueness challenge does not end appellate review of statutory aggravating circumstances. One of the most critical findings that must be made by an appellate court is whether a statutory aggravating circumstance was properly proven to exist. This determination is made by a thorough and careful review of all evidence in support of and in opposition to the establishment of each proffered statutory aggravating circumstance.

In *State v. Fierro*, 804 P.2d 72 (Ariz. 1990), one of the issues confronting the appellate court was determining whether the statutory aggravating circumstance "prior felony using or threatening violence" was properly established. Two prior felony convictions were used by the prosecutor to establish this statutory aggravating circumstance: aggravated assault and robbery. The appellate court examined how each prior felony was statutorily defined. This analysis revealed that both crimes could be committed, under their statutory definitions, without using or threatening violence. As a result of the broad definition given the offenses, the appellate court found that evidence of the prior offenses did not establish the existence of the statutory aggravating circumstance.

The defendant in *State v. Commer*, 799 P.2d 333 (Ariz. 1990), argued that the statutory aggravating circumstance "pecuniary gain" was not established. The defendant contended that this statutory aggravating circumstance could only be proven by evidence showing that he actually received money or other valuable goods, and that the prosecutor failed to prove this. The appellate court rejected this argument and held that merely establishing the defendant's intent to receive, or expectation of receiving pecuniary gain, was adequate. The prosecutor presented evidence to establish such an intent or expectation, therefore the statutory aggravating circumstance was proven to exist.

In the case of *People v. Young*, 538 N.E.2d 461 (Ill. 1989), the defendant contended that the statutory aggravating circumstance "other crimes" was not established because hearsay testimony was used in presenting the issue. The appellate court rejected this argument (noting that the rules of evidence were relaxed in penalty phase proceedings), primarily because the hearsay evidence had a strong indicia of reliability. The hearsay was presented by a police officer.

Review of Mitigating Circumstance Finding

All relevant mitigating evidence must be allowed into evidence at the penalty phase. Relevant mitigating evidence, for appellate review purposes, is divided into two issues: (1) evidence offered to establish the existence of a non-statutory mitigating circumstance and (2) evidence submitted to establish the existence of a statutory mitigating circumstance. Both issues are examined by appellate courts from the perspective that a determination was made that a mitigating circumstance was not established. At this stage appellate review is not concerned with examining mitigating circumstances that were proven to exist. Analysis of mitigating circumstances proven to exist at the penalty phase is the subject of "weighing" or "sufficiency" determinations, which is discussed in the next section.

Non-statutory mitigating circumstance review. In the case of *Morrison v. State*, 500 So.2d 36 (Ala. 1985), the defendant contended that evidence presented to show that he was well-behaved during the investigation of his crime and the trial was a non-statutory mitigating circumstance. The appellate court rejected the argument and held that such evidence did not constitute a non-statutory mitigating circumstance.

The case of *Underwood v. State*, 535 N.E.2d 507 (Ind. 1989), presented a novel attempt at creating a non-statutory mitigating circumstance. In *Underwood* the defendant put on evidence concerning the method of execution of the death penalty. The defendant contended that the evidence on this issue established a non-statutory mitigating circumstance. The appellate court rejected this argument, not because the evidence failed to establish how the execution of the death penalty was carried out, but on the grounds that "method of execution" was an improper non-statutory mitigating circumstance.

In *People v. Christiansen*, 506 N.E.2d 1253 (Ill. 1987), the defendant contended that he proffered evidence to establish that he was an alcoholic. The defendant argued that "alcoholism" was a non-statutory mitigating circumstance. The appellate court agreed with the defendant that alcoholism was a bona fide non-statutory mitigating circumstance. However, the appellate court found that the defendant failed to establish that he was an alcoholic.

In the case of *State v. Wallace*, 773 P.2d 983 (Ariz. 1989), the defendant argued that "family background" was a non-statutory mitigating circumstance. The defendant presented evidence during the penalty phase to show that he had a very difficult family background. The appellate court agreed that "family background" was a recognized non-statutory mitigating circumstance in the jurisdiction. However, the appellate court disagreed with the defendant's contention that this factor should not have been rejected by the factfinder. The appellate court reasoned that "family background" was not a mitigating circumstance in this case, because the defendant failed to show that his family background contributed to the murders he committed.

Statutory mitigating circumstance review. A majority of capital punishment jurisdictions have statutory mitigating circumstances, however, only a small percentage provide by statute that statutory mitigating circumstance rulings must be reviewed by appellate courts.[9] As a practical matter, however, appellate courts address the issue of statutory mitigating circumstances, with or without a statutory mandate.

The statutory mitigating circumstance "extreme mental or emotional disturbance" was the subject in *People v. Crews*, 522 N.E.2d 1167 (Ill. 1988). To support this statutory mitigating circumstance, the defendant proffered evidence at the penalty phase that he was found guilty but mentally ill of the crime charged. The defendant contended that this evidence established the statutory mitigating circumstance of extreme mental or emotional disturbance. The appellate court rejected the argument. The court held that mental illness and extreme mental or emotional disturbance were statutorily defined differently. Therefore, proof of mental illness did not establish the statutory mitigating circumstance.

The case of *State v. Dickerson*, 543 N.E.2d 1250 (Ohio 1989), presented the duress statutory mitigating circumstance. The defendant presented evidence to show that at the time of the murder, he was under stress due to the death of his mother and breakup with his girlfriend. The defendant argued that this evidence established the duress statutory mitigating circumstance. The appellate court rejected the contention that stress evidence established the duress statutory mitigating circumstance. In hindsight, the defendant should have argued that stress was an independent non-statutory mitigating circumstance.

In *State v. Cummings*, 404 S.E.2d 849 (N.C. 1991), the defendant contended that he established the existence of the impairment statutory mitigating circumstance. The defendant argued that evidence he proffered to show that he was intoxicated at the time of his capital crime established that he lacked the capacity to conform his conduct to the requirements of the law. The appellate court agreed with the defendant. The appellate court found that the trial court instructed the penalty phase jury in an erroneous manner which precluded consideration of the impairment statutory mitigating circumstance.

Determining Whether Death Is the Proper Sentence

Once an appellate court determines that at least one statutory aggravating circumstance was validly found by the jury and makes its statutory and non-statutory mitigating circumstance analysis, the next stage in the review process is triggered. At this stage the appellate court must determine whether the sentence of death was proper. This determination involves three separate issues: (1) did passion, prejudice or other arbitrary factor cause death to be imposed; (2) was the sentence excessive or disproportionate compared to other cases; and (3) the outcome of an independent weighing or sufficiency determination.

Passion, Prejudice or Other Arbitrary Factor

The decision to impose death upon a capital felon must be made without the influence of passion, prejudice or any other arbitrary factor. If the sentence of death is to be imposed, this result must be the product of evidentiary facts. The decision in *Furman v. Georgia*, 408 U.S. 238 (1972), nullified the death penalty in the nation because it was being imposed for arbitrary reasons that had no nexus with evidentiary facts.

In an effort to assure that pre–*Furman* era arbitrariness did not infect a sentence of death, appellate courts review capital sentences to determine whether passion, prejudice or any other arbitrary factor played a role in the sentencing decision. A majority of capital punishment jurisdictions require by statute that this issue be addressed during appellate review.[10]

Notwithstanding statutory requirements, engaging in a review for arbitrariness (this term is being used to encompass passion and prejudice) is largely dependent upon the capital felon making an allegation that a specific arbitrary factor influenced the decision in the case. This is so because an arbitrary factor will rarely stand out on the record in a case. Of course, the mere fact that a capital felon alleges that an arbitrary factor infected the sentencing decision does not mean that the allegation is true. Such an assertion, however, will focus the review to the specific factor alleged. Commonly asserted arbitrary factors include race, gender, indigence, ethnicity, victim sympathy, adverse publicity and fear of community response.

Excessive or Disproportionate Sentence

It was pointed out in *People v. Hayes*, 564 N.E.2d 803 (Ill. 1990), that, for purposes of imposing the death penalty, the Eighth Amendment demands that a defendant's punishment be proportionate to his or her personal culpability or blameworthiness. *Hayes* correctly stated the law as it presently stands. However, it was pointed out in *People v. Belmontes*, 755 P.2d 310 (Cal. 1988), that appellate court determination of whether imposition of the death penalty on a defendant was disproportionate (or excessive), compared to other cases, is not required by the Eighth Amendment.[11] In fact, in *Pulley v. Harris*, 465 U.S. 37 (1984), the Supreme Court expressly held that the Constitution does not require proportionality review of death sentences by appellate courts. In spite of *Pulley*, a majority of capital punishment jurisdictions statutorily require appellate courts to review each death sentence to determine whether it is excessive or disproportionate, when compared to other cases in the jurisdiction imposing the sentence.[12]

Several matters need to be underscored regarding excessive and disproportionate review. First, *excessive* and *disproportionate* are terms that are used interchangeably by courts, but the terms actually refer to different points of analysis. A review of the extent of a capital felon's role in a crime seeks to determine whether the punishment of death is excessive. A comparison of a capital felon's sentence with similar cases seeks to determine whether the death sentence is disproportionate. In between these two points of analysis, a variety of determinations are made wherein the terms *excessive* and *disproportionate* are used interchangeably.

Second, comparative excessive or disproportionate review is usually confined to cases within an appellate court's jurisdiction. This limitation is necessary for no other reason than the impracticality of comparing a single death sentence with all other similar death penalty cases in other jurisdictions. Too many capital murder convictions rest in the annals of Anglo-American jurisprudence.[13]

The final point to be noted is that getting a death sentence vacated as a result of excessive or disproportionate review — while not impossible — comes within a hair of being impossible.

Weighing or Sufficiency Determination

Provided that an appellate court does not find that a sentence was infected with an arbitrary factor, or discern an excessive or disproportionate problem in a case, it may then engage in an independent weighing or sufficiency determination. Currently non-weighing jurisdictions do not statutorily require appellate courts conduct a sufficiency determination. A minority of weighing jurisdictions do statutorily require appellate courts to engage in an independent weighing process.[14]

Disposition by Appellate Court

Once appellate court review of a death sentence is completed, the case must be disposed of based upon the conclusions reached from the review process. Since the exclusive focus of this chapter has been on the penalty phase, it will be assumed, for the purpose of this section, that the issue of guilt was not appealed or was upheld by the appellate court after consolidation. In this context, review of a sentencing determination may be disposed of in four ways: (1) affirm; (2) vacate and remand for further proceedings; (3) vacate and remand for imposition of life sentence; or (4) vacate and impose life sentence. Each disposition alternative is examined below.

Affirm

All capital punishment jurisdictions allow appellate courts to affirm death sentences. When a death sentence is affirmed it means that the sentence was validly imposed and may be carried out. The fact that a sentence has been affirmed does not, in and of itself, mean that no errors were committed during the penalty phase. If a death sentence is affirmed even though errors occurred in the penalty phase proceeding, the errors reflected one of two possibilities.

First, it was previously noted that penalty phase errors may be prejudicial or harmless. If errors occurred during a penalty phase proceeding, but the appellate court determined that the errors were harmless, then the sentence will be affirmed — notwithstanding the errors.

Second, not infrequently capital felons receive more than one death sentence. This occurs when there has been more than one murder victim in a single incident. It is possible for an appellate court to find that one of several death sentences was imposed as a result of prejudicial error. When the latter situation presents itself, an appellate court may affirm the sentence that was imposed validly and dispose of the invalidly imposed sentence in one of the disposition alternatives that follow.

Vacate and Remand for Further Proceedings

A sentence of death that was reached as a result of prejudicial error is not valid. A capital felon sentenced to death cannot be executed based upon an invalid death sentence. One option available to appellate courts, when it is determined that a death sentence is invalid, is to vacate the sentence and remand the case for further penalty phase proceedings. A majority of capital punishment jurisdictions provide for this option by statute.[15]

When a death sentence is vacated it means that the sentence has been set aside or reversed and is no longer legally valid. Remanding means sending the sentencing issue back to the lower court.

A death sentence that has been vacated and remanded for further proceedings involves one of two things. First, the appellate court may remand the case with instructions that a new penalty phase proceeding be held. Second, an appellate court may remand the case with instructions that the lower court "reweigh" the mitigating and statutory aggravating circumstances or make another "sufficiency" determination (depending on the type of jurisdiction). The latter option would mean that the appellate court found that at least one statutory aggravating circumstance was invalid, or a statutory or non-statutory mitigating circumstance existed which had not been previously recognized.

Vacate and Remand for Imposition of Life Sentence

A minority of capital punishment jurisdictions provide by statute that appellate courts may, when appropriate, vacate a death sentence and remand the case with instructions to the trial court to impose a life sentence.[16] One of two factors will usually trigger this type of disposition.

First, the appellate court may determine from its review that the sentence of death is simply improper. Second, an appellate court may find that, as a result of noncorrectable prejudicial error, life imprisonment must be imposed.

Vacate and Impose Life Sentence

The final appellate court disposition option is to vacate a death sentence and impose a life sentence. A minority of capital punishment jurisdictions provide for this option by statute.[17] This method of disposition involves imposition of a life sentence directly by the appellate court. An appellate court will utilize this option when it finds the sentence of death improper, or an egregious error was committed that is not correctable.

18

Habeas Corpus, Coram Nobis and Section 1983 Proceedings

Once a capital felon unsuccessfully exhausts his or her direct review/appeal of a conviction and sentence, he or she will then initiate habeas corpus proceedings. If a defendant is convicted in a state court, habeas relief can be sought on two tracks. First, the capital felon can mount a habeas proceeding in state court — which ultimately can be appealed to the United States Supreme Court. Second, if the defendant is denied relief in a state habeas proceeding, he or she can then begin a new habeas proceeding in a federal district court. On the other hand, if the defendant was convicted in a federal court, he or she can only seek habeas relief in federal court.

If a capital felon has exhausted all habeas attacks on his or her conviction and sentence, an attack may be made in some states using the writ of coram nobis. The writ of coram nobis is infrequently used, but it is available. The Supreme Court has indicated that "it is difficult to conceive of a situation in a federal criminal case today where [a writ of *coram nobis*] would be necessary or appropriate."[1]

In addition to mounting an attack on a death sentence using habeas corpus and coram nobis petitions, under appropriate circumstances a capital felon may utilize 42 U.S.C. § 1983 of the Civil Right Act to challenge the method of execution. The nature of the writ of habeas corpus, coram nobis, and § 1983 are discussed in the material below.

Habeas Corpus

The term "habeas corpus" is Latin and means "you have the body." Habeas corpus is a writ or legal device designed to permit a person incarcerated to challenge his or her detention. Habeas corpus cannot be sought by a person who is not under confinement.

The origin of habeas corpus is traceable to the common law. English jurist William Blackstone called habeas corpus the most celebrated writ in English law. American jurists have called habeas corpus "the Great Writ."[2]

The legal history of habeas corpus in Anglo-American jurisprudence began with the founding of the nation. In Article I, Section 9, Clause 2, of the federal Constitution it is proclaimed that "[t]he Privilege of the Writ of Habeas Corpus shall not be suspended, unless when in Cases of Rebellion or Invasion the public Safety may require it." Only once in the nation's history, during the Civil War, was habeas corpus suspended.[3]

Congress codified habeas corpus in Section 14 of the Judiciary Act of 1789. The Judiciary

Act authorized federal courts to grant habeas corpus when prisoners were "in custody, under or by colour of the authority of the United States, or [were] committed for trial before some court of the same."

In addition to habeas corpus relief under federal law, habeas corpus is provided directly by constitutions, statutes or court rules in every state. Both federal and state laws provide limitations on the grounds upon which habeas corpus may be sought. Generally, a petition for habeas corpus relief must assert that (1) confinement is in violation of a constitutional right, (2) the court involved lacked jurisdiction to confine the petitioner, or (3) a sentence was imposed in excess of that provided for by law.[4]

Habeas corpus may be used to challenge pretrial or post-conviction confinement. The greatest use of habeas comes at the post-conviction confinement stage. Except for the issue of post-conviction bail, all jurisdictions generally limit post-conviction use of habeas corpus until after direct review or appeal of the judgment imposing confinement.[5]

It was noted in *Brown v. Allen*, 344 U.S. 443 (1953), that no weight is to be given to the United States Supreme Court's former refusal of certiorari in a case on direct appeal, when a lower federal court receives the case again in a habeas corpus proceeding. In *Lonchar v. Thomas*, 517 U.S. 314 (1996), it was held that a federal court may not deny a stay of execution and dismiss a first federal habeas petition for general equitable reasons. In *McFarland v. Scott*, 512 U.S. 849 (1994), superseded by statute, it was held that a capital defendant is not required to file a formal federal habeas corpus petition in order to obtain appointment of counsel and to establish a federal court's jurisdiction to enter a stay of execution. It was said in *Miller-El v. Cockrell*, 537 U.S. 322 (2003), that a habeas prisoner does not have to show that a state court decision was objectively unreasonable by clear and convincing evidence, before a federal court of appeals may issue a certificate of appealability of a federal district judge's decision. In *Murray v. Giarratano*, 492 U.S. 1 (1989), the Supreme Court held that neither the Eighth Amendment nor the Due Process Clause requires states to appoint counsel for indigent death row inmates seeking state habeas relief.

As a general matter, a defendant must establish "good cause" to conduct discovery for a habeas proceeding. For example, *Bracy v. Gramley*, 520 U.S. 899 (1997), it was held that in showing that his trial judge was convicted of taking bribes from criminal defendants, the defendant established "good cause" to conduct discovery during his habeas corpus proceeding.

Antiterrorism and Effective Death Penalty Act

Congress enacted significant changes to federal habeas laws in 1996, through its enactment of the Antiterrorism and Effective Death Penalty Act (AEDP).[6] The AEDP provides for expedited review of habeas petitions and limits the scope of review of the merits of habeas petitions. Senator Orrin Hatch stated during a Senate Judiciary Committee hearing that the purpose of AEDP was "to ensure that a ... capital sentence imposed by a state court could be carried out without awaiting the disruptive, dilatory tactics of counsel for condemned prisoners."[7] In *Felker v. Turpin*, 518 U.S. 651 (1996), the AEDP was held constitutional. In *Woodford v. Garceau*, 538 U.S. 202 (2003), it was said that the AEDP applied to the defendant's case even though he filed a motion for appointment of habeas counsel before the effective date of the statute.

The strictest provision under the AEDP is Chapter 154.[8] This provision revises procedural rules for federal habeas proceedings in capital cases. Most notably, it provides for an expedited review process in proceedings brought against qualifying states. It imposes a 180-day limitation period for filing a federal habeas petition. It treats an untimely petition as a successive petition for purposes of obtaining a stay of execution, and it allows a prisoner to amend a petition after an answer is filed only where the prisoner meets the requirements for a successive petition. Chapter 154 also obligates a federal district court to render a final judgment on any petition within 180 days of its filing, and a court of appeals to render a final determination within 120 days of the briefing.[9]

Chapter 154 will apply in state capital cases only to states that meet certain conditions.[10] A state must establish a mechanism for the appointment, compensation, and payment of reasonable litigation expenses of competent counsel in state postconviction proceedings, and must provide standards of competency for the appointment of such counsel. The state must offer counsel to all capital defendants, and the state court must enter an order concerning appointment of counsel. If a state meets these criteria, then it may invoke Chapter 154.[11] In other words, Chapter 154 establishes a quid-pro-quo relationship. In *Calderon v. Ashmus*, 523 U.S. 740 (1998), it was held that a defendant could not maintain a federal class action lawsuit to determine whether California complied with Chapter 154.

A state seeking greater federal deference to its habeas decisions in capital cases must, by appointing competent counsel to represent indigent defendants, further ensure that its own habeas proceedings are meaningful.[12] Of course, the federal Constitution does not require that a capital felon have legal representation to mount a collateral or habeas corpus attack on his or her conviction and sentence.[13] The Constitution only demands that an indigent defendant be appointed counsel at the trial level and at the first appeal of right.[14]

Federal Habeas Relief for Person in Federal Custody

A separate statute provides generally for habeas corpus relief for an inmate confined in a federal institution. This statute was modified by the AEDP to impose a 1 year statute of limitations for seeking habeas relief.[15] The federal habeas statute is set out below.

28 U.S.C. § 2255
Federal Custody; Remedies on Motion Attacking Sentence
    A prisoner in custody under sentence of a court established by Act of Congress claiming the right to be released upon the ground that the sentence was imposed in violation of the Constitution or laws of the United States, or that the court was without jurisdiction to impose such sentence, or that the sentence was in excess of the maximum authorized by law, or is otherwise subject to collateral attack, may move the court which imposed the sentence to vacate, set aside or correct the sentence.
    Unless the motion and the files and records of the case conclusively show that the prisoner is entitled to no relief, the court shall cause notice thereof to be served upon the United States attorney, grant a prompt hearing thereon, determine the issues and make findings of fact and conclusions of law with respect thereto. If the court finds that the judgment was rendered without jurisdiction, or that the sentence imposed was not authorized by law or otherwise open to collateral attack, or that there has been such a denial or infringement of the constitutional rights of the prisoner as to render the judgment vulnerable to collateral attack, the court shall vacate and set the judgment aside and shall discharge the prisoner or resentence him or grant a new trial or correct the sentence as may appear appropriate.
    A court may entertain and determine such motion without requiring the production of the prisoner at the hearing.

An appeal may be taken to the court of appeals from the order entered on the motion as from a final judgment on application for a writ of habeas corpus.

An application for a writ of habeas corpus in behalf of a prisoner who is authorized to apply for relief by motion pursuant to this section, shall not be entertained if it appears that the applicant has failed to apply for relief, by motion, to the court which sentenced him, or that such court has denied him relief, unless it also appears that the remedy by motion is inadequate or ineffective to test the legality of his detention.

A 1-year period of limitation shall apply to a motion under this section. The limitation period shall run from the latest of—

(1) the date on which the judgment of conviction becomes final;

(2) the date on which the impediment to making a motion created by governmental action in violation of the Constitution or laws of the United States is removed, if the movant was prevented from making a motion by such governmental action;

(3) the date on which the right asserted was initially recognized by the Supreme Court, if that right has been newly recognized by the Supreme Court and made retroactively applicable to cases on collateral review; or

(4) the date on which the facts supporting the claim or claims presented could have been discovered through the exercise of due diligence.

Except as provided in section 408 of the Controlled Substances Act, in all proceedings brought under this section, and any subsequent proceedings on review, the court may appoint counsel, except as provided by a rule promulgated by the Supreme Court pursuant to statutory authority. Appointment of counsel under this section shall be governed by section 3006A of title 18.

A second or successive motion must be certified as provided in section 2244 by a panel of the appropriate court of appeals to contain —

(1) newly discovered evidence that, if proven and viewed in light of the evidence as a whole, would be sufficient to establish by clear and convincing evidence that no reasonable factfinder would have found the movant guilty of the offense; or

(2) a new rule of constitutional law, made retroactive to cases on collateral review by the Supreme Court, that was previously unavailable.

Federal Habeas Relief for Person in State Custody

Congress provided for state prisoners to have access to habeas relief in federal courts through an amendment to the Judiciary Act in 1867. Under this amendment federal courts were authorized to grant habeas corpus "in all cases where any person may be restrained of his or her liberty in violation of the constitution, or of any treaty or law of the United States." The authority of federal courts to grant habeas corpus relief to persons in state custody was not significantly exercised until well into the twentieth century, when the United States Supreme Court decided that federal habeas relief was available to determine whether a state criminal process satisfied the due process requirements of the Fourteenth Amendment.

The Supreme Court observed in *Wilson v. Corcoran*, 131 S.Ct. 13 (2010), that "it is only noncompliance with *federal* law that renders a State's criminal judgment susceptible to collateral attack in the federal courts." A state prisoner's use of federal habeas corpus is authorized under 28 U.S.C § 2254 of the AEDP. In *Cullen v. Pinholster*, 131 S.Ct. 1388 (2011), the Supreme Court summarized the requirements of that statute. *Cullen* noted that 28 U.S.C. § 2254 sets several limits on the power of a federal court to grant an application for a writ of habeas corpus on behalf of a state prisoner. Section 2254(a) permits a federal court to entertain only those applications alleging that a person is in state custody in violation of the Constitution or laws or treaties of the United States. Sections 2254(b) and (c) provide that a federal court may not grant such applications unless, with certain exceptions, the applicant has exhausted state remedies. If an application includes a claim that has been adjudicated on the merits in state court proceedings, an additional restriction applies. Under § 2254(d) federal courts are prohibited from granting an application for a writ of habeas corpus with respect to a claim adjudicated on the merits in state court, unless that adjudication resulted in a decision that was contrary to, or involved an unreasonable application of, clearly established federal law, as determined by the United States Supreme Court, or resulted in a decision that was based on an unreasonable determination of the facts in light of the evidence presented in the State court proceeding.[16] This standard is difficult to satisfy and has been criticized by many scholars as effectively curtailing federal habeas relief for capital defendants.[17] The federal habeas statute utilized by state prisoners is set out below.

28 U.S.C. § 2254
State Custody; Remedies in Federal Courts

(a) The Supreme Court, a Justice thereof, a circuit judge, or a district court shall entertain an application for a writ of habeas corpus in behalf of a person in custody pursuant to the judgment of a State court only on the ground that he is in custody in violation of the Constitution or laws or treaties of the United States.

(b)(1) An application for a writ of habeas corpus on behalf of a person in custody pursuant to the judgment of a State court shall not be granted unless it appears that—

(A) the applicant has exhausted the remedies available in the courts of the State; or

(B)(i) there is an absence of available State corrective process; or (ii) circumstances exist that render such process ineffective to protect the rights of the applicant.

(2) An application for a writ of habeas corpus may be denied on the merits, notwithstanding the failure of the applicant to exhaust the remedies available in the courts of the State.

(3) A State shall not be deemed to have waived the exhaustion requirement or be estopped from reliance upon the requirement unless the State, through counsel, expressly waives the requirement.

(c) An applicant shall not be deemed to have exhausted the remedies available in the courts of the State, within the meaning of this section, if he has the right under the law of the State to raise, by any available procedure, the question presented.

(d) An application for a writ of habeas corpus on behalf of a person in custody pursuant to the judgment of a State court shall not be granted with respect to any claim that was adjudicated on the merits in State court proceedings unless the adjudication of the claim—

(1) resulted in a decision that was contrary to, or involved an unreasonable application of, clearly established Federal law, as determined by the Supreme Court of the United States; or

(2) resulted in a decision that was based on an unreasonable determination of the facts in light of the evidence presented in the State court proceeding.

(e)(1) In a proceeding instituted by an application for a writ of habeas corpus by a person in custody pursuant to the judgment of a State court, a determination of a factual issue made by a State court shall be presumed to be correct. The applicant shall have the burden of rebutting the presumption of correctness by clear and convincing evidence.

(2) If the applicant has failed to develop the factual basis of a claim in State court proceedings, the court shall not hold an evidentiary hearing on the claim unless the applicant shows that—

(A) the claim relies on—(i) a new rule of constitutional law, made retroactive to cases on collateral review by the Supreme Court, that was previously unavailable; or (ii) a factual predicate that could not have been previously discovered through the exercise of due diligence; and

(B) the facts underlying the claim would be sufficient to establish by clear and convincing evidence that but for constitutional error, no reasonable factfinder would have found the applicant guilty of the underlying offense.

(f) If the applicant challenges the sufficiency of the evidence adduced in such State court proceeding to support the State court's determination of a factual issue made therein, the applicant, if able, shall produce that part of the record pertinent to a determination of the sufficiency of the evidence to support such determination. If the applicant, because of indigency or other reason is unable to produce such part of the record, then the State shall produce such part of the record and the Federal court shall direct the State to do so by order directed to an appropriate State official. If the State cannot provide such pertinent part of the record, then the court shall determine under the existing facts and circumstances what weight shall be given to the State court's factual determination.

(g) A copy of the official records of the State court, duly certified by the clerk of such court to be a true and correct copy of a finding, judicial opinion, or other reliable written indicia showing such a factual determination by the State court shall be admissible in the Federal court proceeding.

(h) Except as provided in section 408 of the Controlled Substances Act, in all proceedings brought under this section, and any subsequent proceedings on review, the court may appoint counsel for an applicant who is or becomes financially unable to afford counsel, except as provided by a rule promulgated by the Supreme Court pursuant to statutory authority. Appointment of counsel under this section shall be governed by section 3006A of title 18.

(i) The ineffectiveness or incompetence of counsel during Federal or State collateral post-conviction proceedings shall not be a ground for relief in a proceeding arising under section 2254.

Statute of Limitations

Under the 28 U.S.C. § 2244(d) of the AEDP, a one year statute of limitations applies to an application for habeas corpus relief by an inmate in state custody. The statute provides that the limitations period is tolled during the period that a state habeas proceeding is pending. In *Lawrence v. Florida*, 127 S.Ct. 1079 (2007), the Supreme Court held that the one year statute of limitations period is not tolled during the time that it is deciding whether to grant an appeal from a state high court habeas corpus denial. It was also said in *Allen v. Siebert*, 128 S.Ct. 2 (2007) that when a habeas petition is untimely filed under state law, that is the end of the matter for purposes of § 2244(d). That is, when a petition for state habeas relief is rejected as untimely by a state court, a federal habeas petition is not properly filed under § 2244(d).

In *Holland v. Florida*, 130 S.Ct. 2549 (2010), it was held "that the timeliness provision in the federal habeas corpus statute is subject to equitable tolling." *Holland* pointed out that an inmate is entitled to equitable tolling only if the inmate shows (1) that he or she has been pursuing his or her rights diligently, and (2) that some extraordinary circumstance stood in his or her way and prevented timely filing.

Appointment of Habeas Counsel

It was noted by the Supreme Court in *Murray v. Giarratano*, 492 U.S. 1 (1989), that the Constitution does not require states to appoint counsel for indigent death row inmates seeking habeas relief. In 1988 Congress enacted 18 U.S.C. § 3599 to govern appointment of counsel in capital cases. It is provided under § 3599(a)(2) that in any habeas proceeding brought by a federal or state prisoner under a sentence of death, such "defendant who is or becomes financially unable to obtain adequate representation or investigative, expert, or other reasonably necessary services shall be entitled to the appointment of one or more attorneys and the furnishing of such other services[.]" The statute also provides that an attorney appointed under it may be replaced by a qualified counsel upon the appointed attorney's own motion or upon motion of the inmate. In *Martel v. Clair*, 132 S.Ct. 1276 (2012), the Supreme Court was called upon to determine how a district court should decide such a motion to replace counsel.

The defendant in *Martel* was convicted of committing capital murder in 1984 by the state of California. After the defendant exhausted state appeal rights, he filed a federal habeas petition. The defendant requested and was appointed legal counsel. On two occasions in 2005 the defendant wrote the court a letter requesting appointment of new counsel. The defendant's chief complaint was that counsel sought only to overturn the death sentence, but the defendant also wanted to attack the conviction. The district court denied both substitution motions. The defendant appealed the denial of substitution of counsel. A court of appeals reversed and allowed substitution of counsel. The Supreme Court disagreed with the court of appeals and reinstated the district court's order denying substitution of counsel.

The Supreme Court indicated in *Martel* that the standard to apply in reviewing a request to substitute habeas counsel is the "interests of justice" standard. *Martel* indicated that factors appellate courts should look at under this standard include the timeliness of the motion; the adequacy of the district court's inquiry into the defendant's complaint; and the asserted cause for that complaint, including the extent of the conflict or breakdown in communication between lawyer and client (and the client's own responsibility, if any, for that conflict). It was pointed out by *Martel* that "[b]ecause a trial court's decision on substitution is so fact-specific, it deserves deference; a reviewing court may overturn it only for an abuse of discretion."

In *Harbison v. Bell*, 129 S.Ct. 1481 (2009), the Supreme Court held that a plain reading of § 3599 indicates that Congress authorized federal courts to appoint counsel to represent state prisoners in clemency proceedings.

Decision to Hold an Evidentiary Hearing

An inmate filing a federal habeas corpus petition can have the matter resolved with or without an evidentiary hearing. Under the AEDP a federal district court judge must review the pleadings and any transcripts and records of the state court proceedings to determine whether an evidentiary hearing is warranted. It was held in *Schriro v. Landrigan*, 127 S.Ct. 1933 (2007), that in deciding whether to grant an evidentiary hearing, a federal court must consider whether such a hearing could enable an inmate to prove the petition's factual allegations, which, if true, would entitle the inmate to federal habeas relief. If the record refutes the inmate's factual allegations or otherwise precludes habeas relief, a district court is not required to hold an evidentiary hearing. In other words, an evidentiary hearing is not required on issues that can be resolved by reference to the state court record.

It was observed in *Cullen v. Pinholster*, 131 S.Ct. 1388 (2011), that 28 U.S.C. § 2254(e)(2) of the AEDP imposes a limitation on the discretion of federal habeas courts to take new evidence in an evidentiary hearing. It is provided under 28 U.S.C. § 2254(e)(2) that if the inmate failed to develop the factual basis of a claim in state court proceedings, the federal court cannot hold an evidentiary hearing on the claim unless the inmate shows that the claim relies on (i) an applicable new rule of constitutional law; or (ii) a factual predicate that could not have been previously discovered through the exercise of due diligence; and the facts underlying the claim would be sufficient to establish by clear and convincing evidence that but for constitutional error, no reasonable factfinder would have found the applicant guilty of the underlying offense.

In *Jefferson v. Upton*, 130 S.Ct. 2217 (2010), the Supreme Court applied an older version of 28 U.S.C. 2254 to find that a federal court of appeals failed to consider all of the statute's former eight factors in deciding whether an evidentiary hearing is required. The current version of the statute does not contain the eight factors.

The Basis for Granting Relief

The opinions in *Williams v. Taylor, 529 U.S. 362 (2000)*, and *Thaler v. Haynes*, 130 S.Ct. 1171 (2010), noted that under the AEDP, 28 U.S.C. § 2254(d), a habeas inmate may obtain relief (1) if the state court arrives at a conclusion opposite to that reached by the United States Supreme Court on a question of law, or the state court decides a case differently than United States Supreme Court has on a set of materially indistinguishable facts; or (2) if the state court identifies the correct governing legal principle from the United States Supreme Court's decisions but unreasonably applies that principle to the facts of the inmate's case.

In *Cullen v. Pinholster*, 131 S.Ct. 1388 (2011), it was held that review under § 2254(d)(1) is limited to the record that was before the state court that adjudicated the claim on the merits. Review under § 2254(d)(1) focuses on what a state court knew and did. State court decisions are measured against the Supreme Court's precedents as of the time the state court renders its decision. *Cullen* held that to determine whether a particular decision is contrary to then-established law, a federal court must consider whether the decision applies a rule that contradicts such law and how the decision confronts the set of facts that were before the state court. If the state court decision identifies the correct governing legal principle in existence at the time, a federal court must assess whether the decision unreasonably applies that principle to the facts of the inmate's case. It was said in *Wetzel v. Lambert*, 132 S.Ct. 1195 (2012), that "[u]nder § 2254(d), a habeas court must determine what arguments or theories supported ... the state court's decision; and then it must ask whether it is possible fairminded jurists could disagree that those arguments or theories are inconsistent with the holding in a prior decision of this Court."

In *Wood v. Allen*, 130 S.Ct. 841 (2010), the Supreme Court noted that under 28 U.S.C. § 2254(e)(1) of the AEDP, a determination of a factual issue made by a state court is be presumed to be correct and the inmate has the burden of rebutting the presumption of correctness by clear and convincing evidence. The *Wood* decision noted that the Supreme Court has not determined whether this standard applies in every claim asserted under 28 U.S.C. § 2254(d)(2).

Mixed Petition for Habeas Corpus Relief

A "mixed petition for habeas corpus relief" involves the filing of a federal habeas petition by a state inmate that raises claims addressed by a state court, and claims which were not addressed by a state court. This situation presents several problems. First, as a general matter, federal courts may not address state claims that were not presented to a state court.

Second, under federal law, a one year statute of limitations is placed upon the presentation of state claims to a federal court, once a state court has addressed the claim. As a result of the one year statute of limitations, a state prisoner runs the risk of not being able to present a federal court with claims that were addressed by a state court, if a federal petition is dismissed because it raised claims that were not addressed by a state court.

In the case of *Rhines v. Weber*, 544 U.S. 269 (2005), the Supreme Court set out guidelines for addressing a mixed petition. *Rhines* held that a federal court should stay and hold in abeyance claims that were addressed by a state court, in order to permit a prisoner to file the unaddressed claims with a state court, if (1) a prisoner had good cause for failing to initially present the claims to a state court; (2) the claims are potentially meritorious, and (3) there is no indication that the prisoner engaged in intentionally dilatory litigation tactics. It was also said in *Rhines* that if a court determines that issuance of a stay and abeyance is inappropriate, the court should allow the prisoner to delete the unaddressed claims and to proceed with the previously addressed claims, if dismissal of the entire petition would unreasonably impair the prisoner's right to obtain federal relief.

Exhaustion of State Remedies Doctrine

Federal courts have power to grant writs of habeas corpus for the purpose of inquiring into the cause of restraint of liberty of any person in custody under the authority of a state in violation of the federal Constitution. However, under the doctrine of exhaustion of state remedies, federal courts will not, except in cases of peculiar urgency, exercise habeas corpus jurisdiction by a discharge of the person in advance of a final determination of his or her case in the courts of the state. This includes all appellate remedies in the state courts and direct appeal for certiorari in the United States Supreme Court. The doctrine of exhaustion of state remedies is frequently invoked in capital punishment cases, when defendants seek federal habeas intervention before exhausting all state avenues of legal redress. For example, in *Phyle v. Duffy*, 334 U.S. 431 (1948), the Supreme Court was presented with the issue of whether the Due Process Clause required California provide the capital defendant with a judicial hearing to determine if he had returned to sanity as reported by a doctor in a non-judicial setting. However, the opinion held in *Phyle* that the constitutional issue presented would not be addressed in a habeas proceeding, because the defendant had another adequate remedy, mandamus, under state law. On the other hand, in *Irvin v. Dowd*, 359 U.S. 394 (1959), it was held that the doctrine of exhaustion of state remedies did not preclude the defendant from bringing a federal habeas corpus proceeding, because his federal constitutional claim was addressed by the Indiana Supreme Court on direct appeal.

State courts also utilize a version of the exhaustion of remedies doctrine. At the state level defendants are generally prohibited from bringing collateral constitutional issues, such as ineffective assistance of counsel, on direct appellate review. Alleged collateral errors are usually deferred for habeas corpus proceedings, which follow direct appeals.

Procedural Default of Constitutional Claims

Smith v. Murray, 477 U.S. 527 (1986), said that under the procedural default doctrine a defendant may forfeit any alleged error in a prosecution by failing to present the issue to a court in the manner provided by general criminal procedural rules. That is, as stated in *Magwood v. Patterson*, 130 S.Ct. 2788 (2010), "[i]f a petitioner does not satisfy the procedural requirements for bringing an error to the state court's attention — whether in trial, appellate, or habeas proceedings, as state law may require — procedural default will bar federal review." The Supreme Court clarified in *Cone v. Bell*, 129 S.Ct. 1769 (2009), that a claim is procedurally barred when it has not been fairly presented to the state courts for their initial consideration — not when the claim has been presented to state courts more than once. It has been held that the procedural default doctrine protects the integrity of the criminal justice system by imposing a forfeiture sanction for failure to follow applicable procedural rules, thereby deterring defendants from deviating from the jurisdiction's scheme.

The procedural default doctrine can be used to prevent a capital felon convicted in a state court from raising a federal constitutional claim in a federal habeas court. That is, if a capital felon does not follow the procedures for presenting alleged constitutional errors to the attention of a state court, a federal court may employ the procedural default doctrine to preclude raising the issues in federal court. For example, in *Dugger v. Adams*, 489 U.S. 401 (1989), the Florida Supreme Court determined that the defendant's failure to raise an issue in state court on direct appeal and initial habeas proceeding resulted in a default of the issue, and this precluded federal courts from addressing the defaulted issue. The procedural default doctrine was applied in *In re Jugiro*, 140 U.S. 291 (1891) (the merits of the defendant's jury discrimination claim could not be addressed by federal courts because the defendant failed to raise the issue before the courts of New York); *In re Wood*, 140 U.S. 278 (1891) (the jury discrimination issue could not be addressed by federal courts because the defendant failed to raise the issue in the state courts of New York); *Stewart v. Smith*, 536 U.S. 856 (2002) (defendant waived issue of penalty phase ineffective assistance of counsel claim in state court); and *Howell v. Mississippi*, 543 U.S. 440 (2005) (holding that issue presented would not be addressed because of failure to present it in state court).

In *Breard v. Greene*, 523 U.S. 371 (1998), it was held that the defendant was not entitled to raise the issue of a violation of the Vienna Convention on Consular Relations for the first time in federal court:

> [I]t has been recognized in international law that, absent a clear and express statement to the contrary, the procedural rules of the forum State govern the implementation of the treaty in that State. This proposition is embodied in the Vienna Convention itself, which provides that the rights expressed in the Convention "shall be exercised in conformity with the laws and regulations of the receiving State[.]" It is the rule in this country that assertions of error in criminal proceedings must first be raised in state court in order to form the basis for relief in habeas. Claims not so raised are considered defaulted. By not asserting his Vienna Convention claim in state court, Breard failed to exercise his rights under the Vienna Convention in conformity with the laws of the United States and the Commonwealth of Virginia. Having failed to do so, he cannot raise a claim of violation of those rights now on federal habeas review....

In *Schlup v. Delo*, 513 U.S. 298 (1995), *Herrera* v. *Collins*, 506 U.S. 390 (1993), and *Sawyer* v. *Whitley*, 505 U.S. 333 (1992), the Supreme Court held that in certain exceptional cases involving a compelling claim of actual innocence, the state procedural default rule is not a bar to a federal habeas corpus petition. It was said in *Coleman v. Thompson*, 501 U.S. 722 (1991), and *Maples v. Thomas*, 132 S.Ct. 912 (2012), that federal courts may not review federal habeas corpus claims that were defaulted on by a defendant in a state habeas corpus proceeding, unless the defendant can demonstrate (1) cause for the default; (2) actual prejudice as a result of the alleged violation of federal law; or (3) that failure to consider the claims will result in a fundamental miscarriage of justice. The decision in *Maples* also pointed out that good cause for procedural default may be shown when an inmate's attorney abandons him or her and the inmate does not know until after claims are defaulted. Specifically, *Maples* said that "a client cannot be charged with the acts or omissions of an attorney who has abandoned him. Nor can a client be faulted for failing to act on his own behalf when he lacks reason to believe his attorneys of record, in fact, are not representing him."

It was held in *Coleman v. Thompson,* 501 U.S. 722 (1991), that an attorney's errors in a state habeas proceeding did not qualify as cause for a default. However, in the noncapital punishment case of *Martinez v. Ryan,* 132 S.Ct. 1309 (2012), the Supreme Court qualified *Coleman.* It was said in *Martinez* that ineffective assistance of counsel at a state habeas proceeding may establish cause for a prisoner's procedural default of a claim of ineffective assistance of counsel at trial.

In *House v. Bell,* 547 U.S. 518 (2006), the Supreme Court noted that a defendant may seek relief in a federal habeas proceeding after defaulting constitutional claims at the state level, if the defendant establishes that, in light of new evidence, it is more likely than not that no reasonable juror would have found the defendant guilty beyond a reasonable doubt. In *Williams v. Taylor,* 529 U.S. 420 (2000), it was held that the defendant could raise issues in a federal habeas proceeding for the first time where it was shown that the defendant could not have reasonably discovered the issues when the case was in state court.

Although a tactical or intentional decision to forgo a procedural opportunity in state court normally cannot constitute cause to excuse a default on a claim, the failure of counsel to raise a constitutional issue reasonably unknown to him or her is a situation in which the "cause for the default" requirement is met. Establishing that the factual or legal basis for a claim was not reasonably available to counsel or that some interference by public officials made compliance impracticable constitutes cause for the default. For example, in *Amadeo v. Zant,* 486 U.S. 214 (1988), it was held that the evidence supported a federal district court's conclusion that the defendant successfully established "good cause" for his failure to raise in the state trial court a constitutional challenge to the composition of the jurors that convicted and sentenced him to death.

Successive Habeas Application

Under the AEDP, 28 U.S.C. § 2244(b)(1), a claim presented in a second or successive habeas corpus application by state prisoner that was presented in a prior application must be dismissed by the district court. It is also provided under the AEDP, 28 U.S.C. § 2244(b)(2), that a claim presented in a second or successive habeas corpus application by a state prisoner that was not presented in a prior application must be dismissed unless (1) the applicant shows that the claim relies on a new rule of constitutional law, made retroactive to cases on collateral review by the Supreme Court, that was previously unavailable, or (2) the factual predicate for the claim could not have been discovered previously through the exercise of due diligence, and the facts underlying the claim would be sufficient to establish by clear and convincing evidence that, but for constitutional error, no reasonable factfinder would have found the applicant guilty of the underlying offense. Under the AEDP, 28 U.S.C. § 2244(b)(3), a second or successive application for a writ of habeas corpus requires authorization from a court of appeals.

In *Stewart v. Martinez-Villareal,* 523 U.S. 637 (1998), it was held that the defendant's incompetency claim was not a second or successive habeas application under the AEDP, because the district court failed to address the merits of the issue during its resolution of the defendant's initial habeas petition. In *Magwood v. Patterson*, 130 S.Ct. 2788 (2010), it was held that the defendant's first habeas application challenging his new sentence was not a second or successive application.

Independent and Adequate State Ground Doctrine

It was said in *Cone v. Bell*, 129 S.Ct. 1769 (2009), federal courts will not review questions of federal law presented in a habeas petition when the state court's decision rests upon a state-law ground that is independent of the federal question and adequate to support the judgment. In the context of federal habeas proceedings, the independent and adequate state ground doctrine is designed to ensure that a state's interest in correcting its own mistakes is respected in all federal habeas cases. *Cone* noted that when a defendant fails to properly raise his or her federal claims in state court, the defendant deprives the state of an opportunity to address those claims in the first instance and frustrates the state's ability to honor the defendant's constitutional rights. *Cone* held that when a defendant fails to raise a federal claim in compliance with relevant state procedural rules, the state court's refusal to adjudicate the claim ordinarily qualifies as an independent and adequate state ground for denying federal review.

It was held in *Beard v. Kindler*, 130 S.Ct. 612 (2009), that a discretionary state procedural rule can serve as an adequate ground to bar federal habeas review. *Beard* found that nothing inherent in such a rule renders it inadequate for purposes of the adequate state ground doctrine. To the contrary, a discretionary rule can be firmly established and regularly followed — even if the appropriate exercise of discretion may permit consideration of a federal claim in some cases but not others.

Actual Innocence Claim

An "actual innocence claim" is a legal theory that is used by a capital felon who has exhausted direct appeals and initial collateral or habeas corpus attacks on the judgment rendered against him or her. The actual innocence claim permits a court to hear the merits of a successive, abusive, or defaulted claim for relief, if failure to do so would result in a miscarriage of justice. The miscarriage of justice exception applies where a capital felon alleges he or she is "actually innocent" of the capital crime for which he or she was convicted or the death penalty which was imposed. In *Schlup v. Delo*, 513 U.S. 298 (1995), *Herrera v. Collins*, 506 U.S. 390 (1993), and *Sawyer v. Whitley*, 505 U.S. 333 (1992), the Supreme Court held that in certain exceptional cases involving a compelling claim of actual innocence, the state procedural default rule is not a bar to a federal habeas corpus petition.

The Supreme Court observed in *House v. Bell*, 547 U.S. 518 (2006), that in order for a capital felon to establish actual innocence of the "crime" for which he or she was convicted, it must be shown that, in light of new evidence, it is more likely than not that no reasonable jury would have found the defendant guilty beyond a reasonable doubt. To show actual innocence of the "punishment" imposed, a capital felon must show by clear and convincing evidence that, but for a constitutional error, no reasonable jury would have found him or her eligible for the death penalty.

Retroactive Application of a New Constitutional Rule

Capital punishment decisions by the United States Supreme Court often proclaim new constitutional rules. A principle becomes a new rule if it breaks new ground, imposes a new obligation on the states or the federal government, or was not dictated by precedent existing at the time the defendant's conviction became final. This issue has been addressed in numerous Supreme Court capital cases, including *Beard v. Banks*, 542 U.S. 406 (2004) (holding that appellate court incorrectly found prior case applied retroactively); *Schriro v. Summerlin*, 542 U.S. 348 (2004) (holding that prior case requiring a jury preside over the penalty phase of a capital prosecution did not apply retroactive to cases that were final when the decision was handed down); *Horn v. Bank*, 536 U.S. 266 (2002) (holding that federal court of appeals was required to do an analysis of whether a new rule of law applied retroactive to the defendant's case, before applying the new rule); *Lambrix v. Singletary*, 520 U.S. 771 (1997) (holding that inmate whose conviction became final before the decision in new case was rendered is foreclosed from relying on that decision in a habeas corpus proceeding because the decision announced a new rule); *O'Dell v. Netherland*, 521 U.S. 151 (1997) (holding that the rule announced in new case was a new rule and therefore inapplicable to the defendant's case); *Gray v. Netherland*, 518 U.S. 152 (1996) (holding that creation of a requirement obligating prosecutors to give adequate notice of penalty phase evidence of uncharged crimes constitutes a new constitutional rule, and therefore may not be created and applied in the defendant's case); *Graham v. Collins*, 506 U.S. 461 (1993) (holding that the issue presented by the defendant was brought after his conviction became final, the merit of the claim could not be reached insofar as granting relief to him would require creation of a new constitutional rule); *Stringer v. Black*, 503 U.S. 22 (1992) (holding that the rule announced in prior case was not a new rule and therefore was applicable to the defendant's case); *Butler v. McKellar*, 494 U.S. 407 (1990) (holding new constitutional rule could not apply to defendant's case); *Saffle v. Parks*, 494 U.S. 484 (1990) (holding that the defendant cannot obtain habeas relief, when to do so required the creation of a new constitutional rule after the defendant's capital conviction became final); and *Sawyer v. Smith*, 497 U.S. 227 (1990) (holding that defendant could not challenge his death sentence under a new constitutional rule announced after his conviction became final).

A primary issue involving a new constitutional rule is whether it may be applied retroactively to capital cases decided prior to the announcement of the new rule. The general rule regarding retroactivity of a new constitutional rule is that, after a defendant's conviction has become final, he or she may not use a subsequently created constitutional rule to attack the conviction in a federal habeas corpus proceeding. This prohibition has been applied to prevent the adoption of a new rule in cases actually being decided by the Supreme Court.

Two narrow exceptions have been carved out from the general prohibition against applying a new constitutional rule to convictions that have become final. A new rule may be applied retroactively if it: (1) placed an entire category of primary conduct beyond the reach of criminal law or prohibited imposition of a certain type of punishment for a class of defendants because of their status or offense; or (2) was a watershed rule of criminal procedure implicating a criminal proceeding's fundamental fairness and accuracy.

Failure to Disclose Evidence

The Supreme Court held in *Brady v. Maryland*, 373 U.S. 83 (1963), that the Constitution provides a defendant with the right to have a prosecutor reveal all material evidence that may tend to show the defendant's innocence or that could be used by a defendant to attack the credibility of a witness. Failure of prosecutors to abide by this constitutional right is called a *Brady* violation, and may result in a conviction being reversed. There are three essential components of a *Brady* violation: (1) withheld evidence must be favorable to the defendant, either because it is exculpatory, or because it is impeaching; (2) the evidence must have been suppressed by the prosecutor, either willfully or inadvertently; and (3) prejudice must have been caused to the defendant.

The Supreme Court applied *Brady* in the case of *Banks v. Dretke*, 540 U.S. 668 (2004). In *Banks* the state of Texas prosecuted the defendant for the 1980 murder of Richard Whitehead. Prior to trial the defendant requested the prosecutor turn over all information that was exculpatory. The prosecutor informed the defendant that he would receive all such information. However, the prosecutor failed to turn over information regarding two critical witnesses, Charles Cook and Robert Farr. During the trial, Cook and Farr lied about certain matters, but only the prosecutor knew of the lies because it failed to turn over information to the defendant which would have shown that the witnesses lied. The defendant was convicted and sentenced to death. In a habeas corpus appeal to the Supreme Court it was held that the evidence withheld concerning Farr was material and relevant to the penalty phase, therefore the death sentence would be reversed. The Supreme Court further determined that the withheld evidence regarding Cook was relevant to the guilt phase. However, because the federal court of appeals did not address the Cook issue, the Supreme Court remanded the issue for further development.

Additionally, in *Kyles v. Whitley*, 514 U.S. 419 (1995), and *Smith v. Cain*, 132 S.Ct. 627 (2012), it was held that the suppression of exculpatory evidence of the possible innocence of the defendants in those cases required reversal of their convictions and death sentences, and new trials. However, in *Strickler v. Greene*, 119 S.Ct. 1936 (1999), it was held that the defendant was not prejudiced by the prosecutor's failure to reveal evidence that the defendant could have used to impeach the prosecutor's star witness against him.

Coram Nobis

The term "coram nobis" is Latin and means "our court." The writ of coram nobis is an extraordinary remedy known more for its denial than its approval. The writ was developed by the common law during the sixteenth century. Insofar as there was no right to move for a new trial or the right to appeal under the common law, the writ of coram nobis was developed as a procedural mechanism to allow courts to provide relief under limited circumstances. Essentially, the writ of coram nobis allowed a trial court to reopen and correct its judgment upon discovery of a substantial factual error not appearing in the record which, if known at the time of judgment, would have prevented the judgment from being pronounced. Therefore, the writ of coram nobis was addressed to the very court which had rendered the judgment rather than to an appellate or other reviewing court.[18]

The grounds on which a litigant could obtain relief via a writ of coram nobis were narrower than by habeas corpus. The writ of coram nobis secured relief where no other remedy existed, from a judgment rendered while there existed some fact which would have prevented its rendition if the trial court had known it and which, through no negligence or fault of the defendant, was not then known to the court.[19] As such, the writ of coram nobis did not encompass complaints about errors or mistakes in the judgment, but instead alleged that because of something that never came before the court, it was a mistake to proceed to judgment at all. Though more frequently employed in civil cases, coram nobis relief was available in criminal proceedings under the common law. Generally at common law the only time limitation upon the filing of the writ of coram nobis was the requirement that a petitioner show that he or she had exercised due diligence in advancing the claim and seeking the remedy.[20]

The common law writ of coram nobis was brought over from England to the thirteen colonies and later incorporated into the jurisprudence of the United States. The writ was not often utilized in criminal cases and, with the advent of the right to seek a new trial and the right to appeal, use of the writ in both civil and criminal cases declined well into the twentieth century.[21]

The court in *People v. Kim*, 45 Cal.4th 1078 (2009), set out the general modern day requirements for obtaining a writ of coram nobis.[22] It was said in *Kim* that the writ would grant relief only when three requirements are met: (1) petitioner must show that some fact existed which, without any fault or negligence on his or her part, was not presented to the court at the trial on the merits, and which if presented would have prevented the rendition of the judgment; (2) petitioner must also show that the newly discovered evidence does not go to the merits of issues tried; and (3) petitioner must show that the facts upon which he or she relies were not known and could not in the exercise of due diligence have been discovered at any time substantially earlier than the time of his or her motion for the writ.[23]

Today federal courts take the position that "[c]oram nobis is an extraordinary remedy that [can only be] used to attack [federal] convictions with continuing consequences when the petitioner is no longer in custody for purposes of 28 U.S.C. § 2255."[24] That is, "[b]ecause federal prisoners ... may make use of the statutory remedy of 28 U.S.C. § 2255, *coram nobis* relief is unavailable to them."[25]

Some states that impose the death penalty, like Arkansas, continue to recognize the writ of coram nobis.[26] The court in *Coulter v. State*, 227 S.W.3d 904 (Ark. 2006), set out the following principles of law applicable to the writ of coram nobis in Arkansas:

> We have held that a writ of *error coram nobis* was available to address certain errors of the most fundamental nature that are found in one of four categories: (1) insanity at the time of trial, (2) a coerced guilty plea, (3) material evidence withheld by the prosecutor, or (4) a third-party confession to the crime during the time between conviction and appeal. *Coram nobis* proceedings are attended by a strong presumption that the judgment of conviction is valid. Newly discovered evidence in itself is not a basis for relief under *coram nobis*.[27]

Other states with capital punishment, like Kentucky, have adopted a rule of civil procedure that allows for an independent action to attack a judgment "as a substitute for the common law writ of coram nobis[.]"[28]

In *Lane v. Brown*, 372 U.S. 477 (1963), it was said that the state of Indiana may not, consistent with the Constitution, deny the defendant the right to have a free transcript of his coram nobis hearing for appeal purposes, solely because of his indigency. It was held in *Taylor v. Alabama*, 335 U.S. 252 (1948), that the defendant was not deprived of due process when the Alabama Supreme Court denied him permission to file a petition for a writ of coram nobis in the trial court.

Section 1983 of the Civil Rights Act of 1871

Under the federal Civil Rights Act of 1871, 42 U.S.C. § 1983, a lawsuit may be filed against any person who — pursuant to a statute, ordinance, regulation, custom, or usage —

subjects any citizen to the deprivation of any rights, privileges, or immunities secured by the federal laws. In the context of capital punishment, inmates have invoked § 1983 in order to challenge some procedure in the method chosen to execute them. In two cases, *Hill v. McDonough*, 126 S.Ct. 2096 (2006), and *Nelson v. Campbell*, 541 U.S. 637 (2004), the Supreme Court has held that § 1983 may be used by inmates to challenge some aspect of the method in which they are to be executed. *Hill* and *Nelson* indicated that § 1983 may not be used to challenge the legality of a death sentence. That is, if an inmate seeks to prevent his or her execution outright, § 1983 cannot be used; instead a traditional habeas corpus petition must be used. Moreover, if for any reason a state capital felon is denied a request for post-conviction DNA testing, he or she may file a § 1983 petition in federal court to secure DNA testing.[29]

19

The Innocence Protection Act
and Post-Conviction DNA Testing

An inherent flaw in the criminal justice system is that innocent people are sometimes found guilty and sentenced to death.[1] For example, during the period 1973 through June of 2012, a total of 140 inmates sentenced to die were found to be innocent.[2] These individuals were lucky, to the extent that they were found to be innocent before being executed.[3] Out of that 140 inmates, 17 inmates were found innocent as a result of post-conviction DNA testing.[4]

In response to the relatively new forensic technology of DNA testing, Congress decided to encourage post-conviction DNA testing in capital punishment litigation. It did so through enactment of the Innocence Protection Act of 2004 (Act). The Act includes procedures for post-conviction DNA testing in federal court. The Act also established a federal grant program to provide money to states to defray the costs of post-conviction DNA testing.[5] Additionally, the Act set out provisions for increasing the quality of legal representation for capital felons and for increasing compensation for wrongfully convicted federal defendants.[6]

This chapter reviews the salient aspects of the Act, including a general discussion concerning DNA testing.

What Is DNA Testing

DNA is the abbreviation for "deoxyribonucleic acid." DNA is the genetic material present in the nucleus of cells in all living organisms. DNA has been referred to as the "blueprint of life," because it contains all of the information required to make an organism grow and develop. Researchers have found that the majority of the DNA is identical from one human to another, but there are locations in the DNA that have been found to differ from one individual to another, with the exception of twins. These locations are the regions of DNA that are used to compare the DNA obtained from an unknown evidence sample to the DNA of a known individual. DNA samples may be taken from liquid blood or bloodstains, liquid saliva or saliva stains, liquid semen or dried semen stains, pieces of tissue or skin, fingernails, plucked and shed hairs, bone, teeth, fingernails, or tissues from internal organs (including brain).[7]

In 1986 the first known use of DNA to solve a criminal identification occurred in Narborough, England. Authorities there had arrested a 17 year old mentally disturbed youth for a rape-murder incident. Approximately 3 months after the youth confessed to the crime, authorities used DNA testing to apprehend the true perpetrator. DNA was first introduced into evidence in a United States court in 1986.[8] In little more than a decade DNA testing became the foremost forensic technique for identifying criminals, eliminating suspects, and freeing convicted defendants who were innocent.[9]

There are three basic types of forensic DNA tests: (1) Restriction Fragment Length Polymorphism Testing; (2) Polymerase Chain Reaction Testing — Nuclear DNA; and (3) Polymerase Chain Reaction Testing — Mitochondrial DNA. While there are different types of DNA testing done, a few basic steps are performed regardless of the type of test used. The general procedure includes: (1) isolating the DNA from an evidence sample containing DNA of unknown origin; (2) processing the DNA so that test results may be obtained; (3) determination of the DNA test results from specific regions of the DNA; and (4) comparison and interpretation of the test results to determine whether the known individual is excluded as the source of the DNA or is included as a possible source of the DNA.[10]

In a typical criminal case, investigators obtain samples of DNA from the crime scene and have it analyzed with DNA taken from the crime suspect. If the crime scene DNA does not match the suspect's DNA, the suspect did not contribute the DNA found at the crime scene. However, if the DNA patterns match, the suspect may have contributed the evidence sample found at the crime scene.[11]

As a result of the creation of DNA databases, law enforcement officers are now able to compare crime scene DNA with DNA profiles stored in databases.[12] The use of DNA databases has been instrumental in solving crimes.[13]

Post-Conviction DNA Testing

In *District Attorney's Office v. Osborne*, 557 U.S. 52 (2009), the Supreme Court held that there is no constitutional right to post-conviction DNA testing. Notwithstanding *Osborne's* denial of constitutional support for post-conviction DNA testing, under 18 U.S.C. § 3600 of the Innocence Protection Act, federal capital felons may file a motion seeking post-conviction DNA testing of possible exculpatory evidence. It is provided in the Act that the court that entered the capital conviction shall order DNA testing of specific evidence if the court finds that all of the following apply: (1) the applicant asserts, under penalty of perjury, that the applicant is actually innocent of the federal offense for which the applicant is under a sentence of death; (2) the evidence to be tested was secured in relation to the investigation or prosecution of the federal capital offense; (3) the evidence to be tested was not previously subjected to DNA testing and the applicant did not knowingly and voluntarily waive the right to request DNA testing of that evidence, or was previously subjected to DNA testing and the applicant is requesting DNA testing using a new method or technology that is substantially more probative than the prior DNA testing; (4) the evidence is in the possession of the Government and has been subject to a chain of custody and retained under conditions sufficient to ensure that such evidence has not been substituted, contaminated, tampered with, replaced, or altered in any respect material to the proposed DNA testing; (5) the proposed DNA testing is reasonable in scope, uses scientifically sound methods, and is consistent with accepted forensic practices; (6) the applicant identifies a theory of defense that is not inconsistent with an affirmative defense presented at trial and would establish the actual innocence of the applicant; (7) if the applicant was convicted following a trial, the identity of the perpetrator was at issue in the trial; (8) the proposed DNA testing of the evidence may produce new material evidence that would support the theory of defense and raise a reasonable probability that the applicant did not commit the offense; (9) the applicant certifies that the applicant will provide a DNA sample for purposes of comparison; (10) the motion seeking DNA testing is made in a timely fashion.[14]

All capital punishment jurisdictions, except Oklahoma, provide by statute for some form of post-conviction DNA testing.[15] Capital felons in Oklahoma are not without a means of obtaining post-conviction DNA testing. Oklahoma provides through judicial rules for post-conviction DNA testing.[16] Moreover, if for any reason a state capital felon is denied post-conviction DNA testing, he or she may file a petition in federal court under the Civil Rights Act, 42 U.S.C. § 1983, to secure DNA testing.[17]

In *Harvey v. Horan*, 285 F.3d 298 (4th Cir. 2002), Judge Luttig filed a concurring opinion in which he argued that inmates should have a post-conviction right to DNA testing. Several federal courts adopted Judge Luttig's position and found that inmates do have a constitutional right to post-conviction DNA testing.[18] It was not until the decision in *Skinner v. Switzer*, 131 S.Ct. 1289 (2011), that the Supreme Court squarely addressed the issue. It was held in *Skinner* "that a post-conviction claim for DNA testing is properly pursued in a § 1983 action. Success in the suit gains for the prisoner only access to the DNA evidence, which may prove exculpatory, inculpatory, or inconclusive. In no event will a judgment that simply orders DNA tests necessarily imply the unlawfulness of the State's custody."[19]

Improving the Quality of Representation in State Capital Cases

Under 42 U.S.C. §§ 14163–14163e of the Innocence Protection Act, the United States attorney general is authorized to administer a grant program to improve the quality of legal representation for capital felons.[20] Grants awarded under the Act must be used to establish, implement, or improve an effective system for providing competent legal representation to (1) indigents charged with an offense subject to capital punishment; (2) indigents who have been sentenced to death and who seek appellate or collateral relief in state court; (3) and indigents who have been sentenced to death and who seek review in the Supreme Court of the United States. The Act expressly prohibits using grant money to fund, directly or indirectly, representation in specific capital cases.[21]

Compensation of the Wrongfully Convicted

Under 28 U.S.C. § 2513 of the Innocence Protection Act, a federal prisoner wrongfully convicted of a capital offense may be compensated up to $100,000 per year of incarceration for the capital conviction.[22] In debating this specific provision of the Act, members of Congress spoke about the need to provide justice to certain individuals who had suffered wrongful convictions. Representative William Delahunt noted that "[t]hose charged with false accusations and imprisoned based on wrongful convictions are also victims.... Ultimately, this bill is ... about justice for all victims. And it's about innocent people like ... Kirk Bloodsworth" who had previously been wrongfully convicted and later cleared of the charges.[23]

To obtain monetary compensation under the Act a person must allege and prove that: (1) his or her conviction has been reversed on the ground that he or she is not guilty of the offense, or during a new trial he or she was found not guilty of such offense, or that he or she has been pardoned upon the stated ground of innocence and unjust conviction; and (2) he or she did not commit any of the acts charged, and he or she did not by misconduct or neglect cause or bring about his or her own prosecution.[24]

Statutes providing for some form of compensation for the wrongly convicted defendants are in place in 17 capital punishment states.[25] The compensation awarded ranges from direct monetary awards to paid educational expenses.[26]

Seeking Compensation Under 42 U.S.C. § 1983

Under 42 U.S.C. § 1983, a municipality or other local government may be held liable if the governmental body itself subjects a person to a deprivation of rights or causes a person to be subjected to such deprivation. However, under § 1983 local governments are responsible only for their own illegal acts. They are not vicariously liable for their employees' actions. A litigant who seeks to impose liability on local governments under § 1983 must prove that action pursuant to official municipal policy caused their injury. Official municipal policy includes the decisions of a government's lawmakers, the acts of its policymaking officials, and practices that are so persistent and widespread as to practically have the force of law. These are actions for which the municipality is actually responsible. It was recognized in *Connick v. Thompson*, 131 S.Ct. 1350 (2011), that in limited circumstances, a local government's decision not to train certain employees about their legal duty to avoid violating citizens' rights may rise to the level of an official government policy for purposes of § 1983. To satisfy the statute, a municipality's failure to train its employees in a relevant respect must amount to deliberate indifference to the rights of persons with whom the untrained employees come into contact.

The decision in *Connick* involved a civil law suit against a Louisiana prosecutor's office by a former death row inmate, John Thompson. In the criminal case Mr. Thompson was charged by the state of Louisiana with committing capital murder in 1985. Prior to the murder trial, victims of an unrelated armed robbery attempt identified Mr. Thompson as their assailant. The prosecutor thereafter charged Mr. Thompson with attempted arm robbery. During attempted arm robbery investigation the prosecutor was given a piece of bloodstained cloth from one of the attempted robbery victims. The bloodstain was from the assailant. The prosecutor had the blood analyzed and the test result came back showing the blood was type B. The prosecutor never disclosed the bloodstained cloth or the blood test result to Mr. Thompson.

Mr. Thompson was tried on the attempted robbery charge first. During the trial the prosecutor did not reveal it had uncovered the bloodstained cloth and obtained a blood test result. The jury convicted Mr. Thompson of the attempted armed robbery charge. When capital murder trial began Mr. Thompson chose not to testify, because the attempted armed robbery conviction would be introduced if he testified. The jury convicted Mr. Thompson of capital murder and he was sentenced to death.

While Mr. Thompson was on death row in 1999, a private investigator discovered the bloodstain test result in the files of the New Orleans Police Crime Laboratory. Subsequently Mr. Thompson was tested and found to have blood type O, proving that the blood on the piece of cloth was not his. Mr. Thompson's attorneys presented this evidence to the prosecutor's office, which, in turn, moved to stay the execution and vacate Mr. Thompson's attempted armed robbery conviction. The Louisiana court of appeals then reversed Mr. Thompson's murder conviction, concluding that the attempted armed robbery conviction unconstitutionally deprived Mr. Thompson of his right to testify in his own defense at the murder trial. In 2003, the prosecutor's office retried Mr. Thompson for capital murder. The jury found Mr. Thompson not guilty.

After the acquittal of capital murder Mr. Thompson filed a § 1983 civil lawsuit against the prosecutor's office. A jury found the prosecutor's office guilty of failing to train its attorneys to disclose exculpatory evidence as required by *Brady v. Maryland,* 373 U.S. 83 (1963), and awarded Mr. Thompson $14 million in damages. The verdict in *Connick* was appealed to the United States Supreme Court. The Supreme Court reversed the verdict and concluded that "showing merely that additional training would have been helpful in making difficult decisions does not establish municipal liability."

20

Challenging Death Sentence
Under Racial Justice Acts

In *McCleskey v. Kemp*, 481 U.S. 279 (1987), the defendant, an African American, was convicted of capital murder by a Georgia jury and sentenced to die. After his conviction was affirmed on direct review, the defendant filed a habeas corpus petition in federal court that eventually reached the United States Supreme Court. The defendant argued to the Supreme Court that imposition of the death penalty against him violated the Constitution, because it was imposed as a result of his race. The defendant presented statistical evidence compiled by Professor David Baldus which demonstrated that Georgia juries imposed the death penalty more frequently when the murder victim was a non–African American.[1] Five members of the Supreme Court — Justices Powell, Scalia, White, Rehnquist and O'Connor — decided that statistical evidence could not be used to prove racial discrimination in death penalty cases in federal courts. Four justices — Brennan, Blackmun, Stevens and Marshall — dissented.

In 1994, in response to the decision in *McCleskey*, the United States House of Representatives passed the Racial Justice Act, which would have allowed statistical proof of racial discrimination to be introduced in capital punishment cases.[2] However, a Senate Republican filibuster prevented the Act from becoming law.[3]

Although the Supreme Court has refused to permit statistical evidence of racial discrimination to be introduced into evidence in capital punishment litigation in federal courts, states are free to decide the issue.[4] As a consequence, in 1998, Kentucky became the first state in the country to adopt a Racial Justice Act applicable to death penalty prosecutions.[5] In 2009, North Carolina became the second state to enact a Racial Justice Act.[6]

The first application of North Carolina's Racial Justice Act came in April of 2012. At that time a decision was rendered by North Carolina Superior Court Judge Gregory Weeks which held that death row prisoner Marcus Robinson succeeded in showing that racial bias had influenced his death sentence. Judge Weeks vacated Robinson's death sentence and resentenced him to life in prison without the possibility of parole.[7] Immediately after Judge Weeks' decision was handed down, the North Carolina legislature rewrote the state's Racial Justice Act, in an effort to make it more difficult for racial discrimination to be proven by statistical evidence alone. The rewritten Racial Justice Act was vetoed by North Carolina Governor Beverly Perdue; however, the veto was overridden by the legislature on July 2, 2012.

The North Carolina and Kentucky laws, although they share the same name, are different in many respects. For example, the Kentucky statute cannot be applied retroactive for defendants sentenced to death before 1998; a discrimination claim can only be raised before a trial; and the law also prohibits defendants from claiming racial discrimination in a jury's decision to impose the death penalty.[8] On the other hand, North Carolina's rewritten law narrows the statistical evidence death penalty defendants are allowed to use to that of the county or prosecutorial district where the death penalty was imposed; limits the use of statistics from ten years before the crime and two years after sentencing; and provides that statistical evidence alone is insufficient to establish that race was a significant factor in seeking or imposing the death penalty.

Kentucky Racial Justice Act

Kentucky Revised Statutes § 532.300. Prohibition against death sentence being sought or given on the basis of race; procedures for dealing with claims

(1) No person shall be subject to or given a sentence of death that was sought on the basis of race.

(2) A finding that race was the basis of the decision to seek a death sentence may be established if the court finds that race was a significant factor in decisions to seek the sentence of death in the Commonwealth at the time the death sentence was sought.

(3) Evidence relevant to establish a finding that race was the basis of the decision to seek a death sentence may include statistical evidence or other evidence, or both, that death sentences were sought significantly more frequently:

(a) Upon persons of one race than upon persons of another race; or

(b) As punishment for capital offenses against persons of one race than as punishment for capital offenses against persons of another race.

(4) The defendant shall state with particularity how the evidence supports a claim that racial considerations played a significant part in the decision to seek a death sentence in his or her case. The claim shall be raised by the defendant at the pre-trial conference. The court shall schedule a hearing on the claim and shall prescribe a time for the submission of evidence by both parties. If the court finds that race was the basis of the decision to seek the death sentence, the court shall order that a death sentence shall not be sought.

(5) The defendant has the burden of proving by clear and convincing evidence that race was the basis of the decision to seek the death penalty. The Commonwealth may offer evidence in rebuttal of the claims or evidence of the defendant.

North Carolina Racial Justice Act

North Carolina General Statutes § 15A-2011. Proof of racial discrimination; hearing procedure

(a) A finding that race was the basis of the decision to seek or impose a death sentence may be established if the court finds that race was a significant factor in decisions to seek or impose the death penalty in the defendant's case at the time the death sentence was sought or imposed. For the purposes of this section, "at the time the death sentence was sought or imposed" shall be defined as the period from 10 years prior to the commission of the offense to the date that is two years after the imposition of the death sentence.

(b) It is the intent of this Article to provide for an amelioration of the death sentence. It shall be a condition for the filing and consideration of a motion under this Article that the defendant knowingly and voluntarily waives any objection to the imposition of a sentence to life imprisonment without parole based upon any common law, statutory law, or the federal or State constitutions that would otherwise require that the defendant be eligible for parole. The waiver shall be in writing, signed by the defendant, and included in the motion seeking relief under this Article. If the court determines that a hearing is required pursuant to subdivision (3) of subsection (f) of this section, the court shall make an oral inquiry of the defendant to confirm the defendant's waiver, which shall be part of the record. If the court grants relief under this Article, the judgment shall include a finding that the defendant waived any objection to the imposition of a sentence of life imprisonment without parole.

(c) The defendant has the burden of proving that race was a significant factor in decisions to seek or impose the sentence of death in the county or prosecutorial district at the time the death sentence was sought or imposed. The State may offer evidence in rebuttal of the claims or evidence of the defendant, including statistical evidence. The court may consider evidence of the impact upon the defendant's trial of any program the purpose of which is to eliminate race as a factor in seeking or imposing a sentence of death.

(d) Evidence relevant to establish a finding that race was a significant factor in decisions to seek or impose the sentence of death in the county or prosecutorial district at the time the death sentence was sought or imposed may include statistical evidence derived from the county or prosecutorial district where the defendant was sentenced to death, or other evidence, that either (i) the race of the defendant was a significant factor or (ii) race was a significant factor in decisions to exercise peremptory challenges during jury selection. The evidence may include, but is not limited to, sworn testimony of attorneys, prosecutors, law enforcement officers, judicial officials, jurors, or others involved in the criminal justice system. A juror's testimony under this subsection shall be consistent with Rule 606(b) of the North Carolina Rules of Evidence, as contained in G.S. 8C-1.

(e) Statistical evidence alone is insufficient to establish that race was a significant factor under this Article. The State may offer evidence in rebuttal of the claims or evidence of the defendant, including, but not limited to, statistical evidence.

(f) In any motion filed under this Article, the defendant shall state with particularity how the evidence supports a claim that race was a significant factor in decisions to seek or impose the sentence of death in the defendant's case in the county or prosecutorial district at the time the death sentence was sought or imposed.

(1) The claim shall be raised by the defendant at the pretrial conference required by the General Rules of Practice for the Superior and District Courts or in postconviction proceedings pursuant to Article 89 of Chapter 15A of the General Statutes.

(2) If the court finds that the defendant's motion fails to state a sufficient claim under this Article, then the court shall dismiss the claim without an evidentiary hearing.

(3) If the court finds that the defendant's motion states a sufficient claim under this Article, the court shall schedule a hearing on the claim and may prescribe a time prior to the hearing for each party to present a forecast of its proposed evidence.

(g) If the court finds that race was a significant factor in decisions to seek or impose the sentence of death in the defendant's case at the time the death sentence was sought or imposed, the court shall order that a death sentence not be sought, or that the death sentence imposed by the judgment shall be vacated and the defendant resentenced to life imprisonment without the possibility of parole.

21

Barriers to Execution

In a practical sense, a death sentence is never final until a capital felon is actually executed. In between imposition of a death sentence and its execution stand a number of factors that may temporarily or permanently delay the execution. This chapter focuses on factors that can temporarily or permanently forestall execution of a death sentence.

The issues addressed in this chapter are: (1) youth of a capital felon; (2) physical condition of a female capital felon; (3) mental condition of a capital felon; (4) judicial stays; and (5) executive clemency.

Youth of a Capital Felon

Until relatively recently, youths age 7 to 17 did not play a dispositive role in capital punishment. The historical insignificance of youth in capital punishment has its roots embedded in the common law.[1]

The Common Law Executed Minors

The Supreme Court made the following observation in the case of *In re Gault*, 387 U.S. 1 (1967): "At common law, children under seven were considered incapable of possessing criminal intent. Beyond that age, they were subjected to arrest, trial, and in theory to punishment like adult offenders." In other words, the common law permitted the death penalty to be imposed and executed on youth. One commentator reported that between 1801 and 1836, a London court, called Old Bailey, sentenced to death 103 youths under age fourteen.[2]

Prior to the 1900s, 95 youths were executed in the United States. It was reported that two were ten years old. From 1900 to 1983, there were 192 executions of youths in the United States. Of these, the youngest defendant was thirteen years old.[3]

Extending Constitutional Mercy to Juveniles — Thompson/Stanford/Roper

Thompson rejects death penalty for certain minors. In 1988 the United States Supreme Court addressed the issue of whether the Eighth Amendment prohibited imposition

209

and execution of the death penalty on youth who were fifteen years old or younger at the time of their offense. This issue was presented in the case of *Thompson v. Oklahoma*, 487 U.S. 815 (1988). In its analysis of the issue in *Thompson*, the Supreme Court made the following observations:

> The line between childhood and adulthood is drawn in different ways by various States. There is, however, complete or near unanimity among all 50 States and the District of Columbia in treating a person under 16 as a minor for several important reasons. In no State may a 15-year-old vote or serve on a jury. Further, in all but one State a 15-year-old may not drive without parental consent, and in all but four States a 15-year-old may not marry without parental consent. Additionally, in those States that have legislated on the subject, no one under age 16 may purchase pornographic materials (50 States), and in most States that have some form of legalized gambling, minors are not permitted to participate without parental consent (42 States). Most relevant, however, is the fact that all States have enacted legislation designating the maximum age for juvenile court jurisdiction at no less than 16. All of this legislation is consistent with the experience of mankind, as well as the long history of our law, that the normal 15-year-old is not prepared to assume the full responsibilities of an adult....
>
> Inexperience, less education, and less intelligence make the teenager less able to evaluate the consequences of his or her conduct while at the same time he or she is much more apt to be motivated by mere emotion or peer pressure than is an adult. The reasons why juveniles are not trusted with the privileges and responsibilities of an adult also explain why their irresponsible conduct is not as morally reprehensible as that of an adult.

Based upon the above observations, and more, *Thompson* came to the sober conclusion that the Eighth Amendment "prohibit[ed] the execution of a person who was under 16 years of age at the time of his or her offense."[4] The *Thompson* decision stood for the proposition that if a defendant committed a capital offense while he or she was under the age of sixteen, the death penalty could not be imposed or executed on him or her.[5]

Stanford permitted the death penalty for certain minors. In *Stanford v. Kentucky*, 492 U.S. 361 (1989), the Supreme Court consolidated two cases from different jurisdictions that concerned youth and the imposition and execution of the death penalty. In one case the defendant was sixteen when he committed capital murder, and in the second case the defendant was seventeen. Both defendants contended that execution of the death penalty on them was cruel and unusual punishment because of their ages when their capital crimes were committed.[6] The Court responded to their argument as follows.

> Neither petitioner asserts that his sentence constitutes one of those modes or acts of punishment that had been considered cruel and unusual at the time that the Bill of Rights was adopted. Nor could they support such a contention. At that time, the common law set the rebuttable presumption of incapacity to commit any felony at the age of 14, and theoretically permitted capital punishment to be imposed on anyone [7 or older]. In accordance with the standards of this common-law tradition, at least 281 offenders under the age of 18 have been executed in this country, and at least 126 under the age of 17....
>
> We discern neither a historical nor a modern societal consensus forbidding the imposition of capital punishment on any person who murders at 16 or 17 years of age. Accordingly, we conclude that such punishment does not offend the Eighth Amendment's prohibition against cruel and unusual punishment.

The decision in *Stanford* stood for the proposition that the Eight Amendment did not prohibit imposition and execution of the death penalty on defendants who were sixteen or seventeen at the time of their crimes.

Roper rejects the death penalty for all minors. The decision in *Stanford* was overruled by the decision in *Roper v. Simmons*, 543 U.S. 551 (2005). In *Roper* the Supreme Court held that "[t]he Eighth and Fourteenth Amendments forbid imposition of the death penalty on offenders who were under the age of 18 when their crimes were committed." Under the decision in *Roper* no jurisdiction may impose capital punishment on a person who commits a capital offense while under the age of 18.

TABLE 21.0 JUVENILES BETWEEN THE AGES 12 AND 15 WHEN EXECUTED

Name	Date Executed	Age When Executed	Jurisdiction
Hannah Ocuish	December 20, 1786	12	Connecticut
Clem "Doe"	May 11, 1787	12	Virginia
James Guild	November 28, 1828	13	New Jersey
Alfred "Doe"	July 16, 1858	12	Alabama
Henry "Doe"	April 20, 1866	15	Alabama
Susan Eliza	February 7, 1868	13	Kentucky
Samuel Orr	December 11, 1873	15	Missouri
Jack Thomasson	July 6, 1877	15	Georgia
Perry Homer	November 7, 1884	15	Georgia
Jim Conelm	February 3, 1888	14	Louisiana
Milbry Brown	October 7, 1892	14	South Carolina
Willie Bell	November 29, 1892	15	Georgia
Brad Beard	December 17, 1897	14	Alabama
John Berry	June 16, 1899	15	Maryland
Buck High	May 29, 1907	15	Georgia
Irving Hanchett	May 6, 1910	15	Florida
George Stinney, Jr.	June 16, 1944	14	South Carolina
James Lewis, Jr.	July 23, 1947	15	Mississippi

SOURCE: Victor L. Streib, Death Penalty for Juveniles (1987).

TABLE 21.1 INMATES EXECUTED WHO WERE UNDER 18 WHEN THEY COMMITTED MURDER 1976–2003

Name	Date Executed	Age at Time of Murder	Jurisdiction
Charles Rumbaugh	September 11, 1985	17	Texas
J. Terry Roach	January 10, 1986	17	South Carolina
Jay Pinkerton	May 15, 1986	17	Texas
Dalton Prejean	May 18, 1990	17	Louisiana
Johnny Garrett	February 11, 1992	17	Texas
Curtis Harris	July 1, 1993	17	Texas
Frederick Lashley	July 28, 1993	17	Missouri
Ruben Cantu	August 14, 1993	17	Texas
Chris Burger	December 7, 1993	17	Georgia
Joseph Cannon	April 22, 1998	17	Texas
Robert Carter	May 18, 1998	17	Texas
Dwayne A. Wright	October 14, 1998	17	Virginia
Sean Sellers	February 4, 1999	16	Oklahoma
Douglas C. Thomas	January 10, 2000	17	Virginia
Steven Roach	January 13, 2000	17	Virginia
Glen McGinnis	January 25, 2000	17	Texas
Gary Graham	June 22, 2000	17	Texas

Name	Date Executed	Age at Time of Murder	Jurisdiction
Gerald Mitchell	October 22, 2001	17	Texas
Napoleon Beazley	May 28, 2002	17	Texas
T.J. Jones	August 8, 2002	17	Texas
Toronto Patterson	August 28, 2002	17	Texas
Scott A. Hain	April 3, 2003	17	Oklahoma

SOURCE: Louis J. Palmer, Jr., Encyclopedia of Capital Punishment in the United States (2d ed. 2008).

Physical Condition of a Female Capital Felon

Crime is gender neutral. In 2010 a total of 112,822 women were imprisoned in state and federal facilities.[7] Out of the 3,199 capital felons on death row in 2011, there were 58 females.[8] Although crime is gender neutral, for female capital felons sentenced to death, gender may temporarily forestall execution of the death penalty.[9]

A Female Cannot be Executed While Pregnant

The Supreme Court has not been given an opportunity to rule upon the following question: May a female capital felon be executed while pregnant? A majority of capital punishment jurisdictions have addressed this question by enacting statutes that prohibit executing female capital felons while they are pregnant.[10]

Statutes vary in how they address the issue of a female capital felon who alleges she is pregnant. The following two statutes illustrate this point.

Alabama Code § 15-18-86:

(a) If there is reason to believe that a female convict is pregnant, the sheriff must, with the concurrence of a judge of the circuit court, summon a jury of six disinterested persons, as many of whom must be physicians as practicable. The sheriff must also give notice to the district attorney or, in his absence, to any attorney who may be appointed by a circuit judge to represent the state and who has authority to issue subpoenas for witnesses.

(b) The jury, under the direction of the sheriff or officer acting in his place, must proceed to ascertain the fact of pregnancy and must state their conclusion in writing, signed by them and the sheriff. If such jury is of opinion, and so find, that the convict is with child, the sheriff or officer acting in his place must suspend the execution of the sentence and transmit the finding of the jury to the Governor.

(c) Whenever the Governor is satisfied that such convict is no longer with child, he must issue his warrant to the sheriff appointing a day for her to be executed according to her sentence, and the sheriff or other officer must execute the sentence of the law on the day so appointed.

Wyoming Statutes Annotated § 7-13-912:

(a) If there is good reason to believe that a female sentenced to death is pregnant, the director of the department of corrections shall immediately give written notice to the court in which the judgment of death was rendered and to the district attorney. The execution of the death sentence shall be suspended pending further order of the court.

(b) Upon receiving notice as provided in subsection (a) of this section, the court shall appoint a jury of three (3) physicians to inquire into the supposed pregnancy and to make a written report of their findings to the court.

Wyoming Statutes Annotated § 7-13-913:

(a) If the court determines the female is not pregnant, the director of the department of corrections shall execute the death sentence.

(b) If the court determines the female is pregnant, the court shall order the execution of the sentence suspended until it is determined that the female is no longer pregnant at which time the court shall issue a warrant appointing a new date for the execution of the sentence.

Pregnancy is not a permanent barrier to the execution of the death penalty. Once the pregnancy has ended, the death penalty may be carried out. None of the capital punishment jurisdictions that have statutes addressing the issue of a pregnant capital felon indicate what happens to the child that is born to a pregnant capital felon.

Mental Condition of a Capital Felon

The mental condition of a capital felon has legal significance at various stages in a criminal prosecution. If a capital felon is found by proper proof to be insane prior to trial, the trial cannot occur until competent expert testimony indicates his or her sanity has returned. Should a capital felon be competent at the start of his or her trial, but becomes insane during the trial, the proceeding must terminate in a mistrial. A subsequent trial may not occur until the capital felon's sanity is re-established. If a capital felon is tried, but the factfinder determines that he or she was insane at the time of the offense, it must render a verdict of not guilty by reason of insanity (or guilty but mentally ill in jurisdictions recognizing such verdict). Should a capital felon be tried and convicted of the offense charged, but becomes insane before the sentence is imposed, the penalty phase proceeding must be continued until the capital felon's sanity returns. Two issues not mentioned, insanity and mental retardation at the time of execution, are addressed in the subsections that follow

Insanity and Capital Punishment Under the Common Law

Many of the most painful forms of capital punishment were approved of by the common law. The common law did not twinge at the sight of a defendant being quartered or beheaded. Ice flowed, in a manner of speaking, through the veins of the common law when it came to methods of carrying out capital punishment.

In view of the common law's tolerance of cruel forms of capital punishment, it would not come as a surprise if the common law condoned executing insane capital felons. However, the common law prohibited executing an insane capital felon. It may appear, in the first instance, that it was not logical for the common law to revel in gruesome forms of capital punishment and yet show compassion for a condemned insane capital felon. This dichotomous position by the common law was perfectly logical.

Well developed principles form the foundation of criminal punishments. One such principle is embodied in the term "deterrence." The logic behind the common law's ghoulish methods of capital punishment was centered on the deterrent aspect of publicly executing a criminal in a hideous manner. The common law reasoned, however, that executing an insane capital felon would not deter rational or irrational people from committing crimes. The lack of deterrence value in executing insane capital felons was the primary reason for the common law's prohibition of such punishment for the insane.

Statutory Bar to Executing an Insane Capital Felon

The common law gave birth to Anglo-American jurisprudence. While many common law principles have been repudiated by jurisdictions, one common law principle that has stood the test of time in all jurisdictions is that an insane capital felon cannot be executed.[11]

A majority of capital punishment jurisdictions have codified the common law rule that insane capital felons should not be executed.[12] The two statutes that follow illustrate how this issue is addressed.

Mississippi Code § 99-19-57(2):

(a) If it is believed that an offender under sentence of death has become mentally ill since the judgment of the court, the following shall be the exclusive procedural and substantive procedure. The offender, or a person acting as his next friend, or the Commissioner of Corrections may file an appropriate application seeking post-conviction relief with the Mississippi Supreme Court. If it is found that the offender is a person with mental illness, as defined in this subsection, the court shall suspend the execution of the sentence. The offender shall then be committed to the forensic unit of the Mississippi State Hospital at Whitfield. The order of commitment shall require that the offender be examined and a written report be furnished to the court at that time and every month thereafter, stating whether there is a substantial probability that the offender will become sane under this subsection within the foreseeable future and whether progress is being made toward that goal. If at any time during the commitment, the appropriate official at the state hospital considers the offender to be sane under this subsection, the official shall promptly notify the court to that effect in writing and place the offender in the custody of the Commissioner of Corrections. The court then shall conduct a hearing on the sanity of the offender. The finding of the circuit court is a final order [that is] appealable[.]

(b) For the purposes of this subsection, a person shall be deemed to be a person with mental illness if the court finds that the offender does not have sufficient intelligence to understand the nature of the proceedings against him, what he was tried for, the purpose of his punishment, the impending fate that awaits him, and a sufficient understanding to know any fact that might exist that would make his punishment unjust or unlawful and the intelligence requisite to convey that information to his attorneys or the court.

Florida Code § 922.07

(1) When the Governor is informed that a person under sentence of death may be insane, the Governor shall stay execution of the sentence and appoint a commission of three psychiatrists to examine the convicted person. The Governor shall notify the psychiatrists in writing that they are to examine the convicted person to determine whether he or she understands the nature and effect of the death penalty and why it is to be imposed upon him or her. The examination of the convicted person shall take place with all three psychiatrists present at the same time. Counsel for the convicted person and the state attorney may be present at the examination. If the convicted person does not have counsel, the court that imposed the sentence shall appoint counsel to represent him or her.

(2) After receiving the report of the commission, if the Governor decides that the convicted person has the mental capacity to understand the nature of the death penalty and the reasons why it was imposed upon him or her, the Governor shall immediately lift the stay and notify the Attorney General of such action. Within 10 days after such notification, the Governor must set the new date for execution of the death sentence. When the new date for execution of the death sentence is set by the Governor under this subsection, the Attorney General shall notify the inmate's counsel of record of the date and time of execution.

(3) If the Governor decides that the convicted person does not have the mental capacity to understand the nature of the death penalty and why it was imposed on him or her, the Governor shall have the convicted person committed to a Department of Corrections mental health treatment facility.

(4) When a person under sentence of death has been committed to a Department of Corrections mental health treatment facility, he or she shall be kept there until the facility administrator determines that he or she has been restored to sanity. The facility administrator shall notify

the Governor of his or her determination, and the Governor shall appoint another commission to proceed as provided in subsection (1).

(5) The Governor shall allow reasonable fees to psychiatrists appointed under the provisions of this section which shall be paid by the state.

Under the Florida statute the state's governor controls the determination of whether a defendant is competent to be executed. Under the statute of Mississippi the state's Supreme Court makes that determination.

Ford Bars Executing an Insane Felon

In *Ford v. Wainwright*, 477 U.S. 399 (1986), the Supreme Court was asked for the first time to determine whether it is cruel and unusual punishment to execute an insane defendant. The decision in *Ford* responded by holding that the "Eighth Amendment prohibits a State from carrying out a sentence of death upon a prisoner who is insane." *Ford* reasoned as follows:

Today, no State in the Union permits the execution of the insane. It is clear that the ancient and human limitation upon the State's ability to execute its sentences has as firm a hold upon the jurisprudence of today as it had centuries ago in England. The various reasons put forth in support of the common-law restriction have no less logical, moral, and practical force than they did when first voiced. For today, no less than before, we may seriously question the retributive value of executing a person who has no comprehension of why he has been singled out and stripped of his fundamental right to life. Similarly, the natural abhorrence civilized societies feel at killing one who has no capacity to come to grips with his own conscience or deity is still vivid today. And the intuition that such an execution simply offends humanity is evidently shared across this Nation. Faced with such widespread evidence of a restriction upon sovereign power, this Court is compelled to conclude that the Eighth Amendment prohibits a State from carrying out a sentence of death upon a prisoner who is insane. Whether its aim be to protect the condemned from fear and pain without comfort of understanding, or to protect the dignity of society itself from the barbarity of exacting mindless vengeance, the restriction finds enforcement in the Eighth Amendment.

The decision in *Ford* also overruled the decision in *Solesbee v. Balkcom*, 339 U.S. 9 (1950), which had held that the Constitution did not require a judicial tribunal, rather than the office of a governor, to determine if a defendant is insane prior to execution.

In *Panetti v. Quarterman*, 127 S.Ct. 2842 (2007), it was held that *Ford*'s prohibition applies despite a prisoner's earlier competency to be held responsible for committing a crime and to be tried for it. Prior findings of competency do not foreclose a prisoner from proving he or she is incompetent to be executed because of his or her present mental condition. Under *Ford*, once an inmate makes the requisite preliminary showing that his or her current mental state would bar the execution, the Eighth Amendment entitles the inmate to an adjudication to determine his or her condition. These determinations are governed by the substantive federal baseline for competency set down in *Ford*. It was said in *Panetti* that under *Ford* an inmate is not automatically foreclosed from demonstrating incompetency once a court has found he or she can identify the stated reason for his or her execution. An inmate's awareness of the state's rationale for an execution is not the same as a rational understanding of it. *Panetti* rejected a strict test for competency that treats delusional beliefs as irrelevant once the prisoner is aware the state has identified the link between his or her crime and the punishment to be inflicted. *Panetii* emphasized that the conclusions of physicians, psychiatrists, and other experts in the field will bear upon the proper analysis. Expert evidence may clarify the extent to which severe delusions may render an inmate's perception of reality so distorted that he or she should be deemed incompetent.

Execution of Mentally Retarded Felons

In *Penry v. Lynaugh*, 492 U.S. 302 (1989), the Supreme Court was asked to decide whether it is cruel and unusual punishment to execute mentally retarded capital felons.[13] The Supreme Court responded as follows.[14]

> [M]ental retardation is a factor that may well lessen a defendant's culpability for a capital offense. But we cannot conclude today that the Eighth Amendment precludes the execution of any mentally retarded person.... While a national consensus against execution of the mentally retarded may someday emerge reflecting the evolving standards of decency that mark the progress of a maturing society, there is insufficient evidence of such a consensus today[.]

Penry was overruled by the decision in *Atkins v. Virginia*, 536 U.S. 304 (2002). The decision in *Atkins* yielded to public pressure and held that the constitution prohibited executing mentally retarded prisoners. In *Schriro v. Smith*, 126 S.Ct. 7 (2005), it was held that a jury was not required to determine whether a defendant was mentally retarded. The following Arizona statute illustrates how courts determine whether a capital felon is mentally retarded:

Arizona Code § 13-753
Mental Evaluations of Capital Defendants
   A. In any case in which the state files a notice of intent to seek the death penalty, a person who is found to have an intellectual disability pursuant to this section shall not be sentenced to death but shall be sentenced to life or natural life.
   B. If the state files a notice of intent to seek the death penalty, the court, unless the defendant objects, shall appoint a prescreening psychological expert in order to determine the defendant's intelligence quotient using current community, nationally and culturally accepted intelligence testing procedures. The prescreening psychological expert shall submit a written report of the intelligence quotient determination to the court within ten days of the testing of the defendant. If the defendant objects to the prescreening, the defendant waives the right to a pretrial determination of status. The waiver does not preclude the defendant from offering evidence of the defendant's intellectual disability in the penalty phase.
   C. If the prescreening psychological expert determines that the defendant's intelligence quotient is higher than seventy-five, the notice of intent to seek the death penalty shall not be dismissed on the ground that the defendant has an intellectual disability. If the prescreening psychological expert determines that the defendant's intelligence quotient is higher than seventy-five, the report shall be sealed by the court and be available only to the defendant. The report shall be released on the motion of any party if the defendant introduces the report in the present case or is convicted of an offense in the present case and the sentence is final. A prescreening determination that the defendant's intelligence quotient is higher than seventy-five does not prevent the defendant from introducing evidence of the defendant's intellectual disability or diminished mental capacity at the penalty phase of the sentencing proceeding.
   D. If the prescreening psychological expert determines that the defendant's intelligence quotient is seventy-five or less, the trial court, within ten days of receiving the written report, shall order the state and the defendant to each nominate three experts in intellectual disabilities, or jointly nominate a single expert in intellectual disabilities. The trial court shall appoint one expert in intellectual disabilities nominated by the state and one expert in intellectual disabilities nominated by the defendant, or a single expert in intellectual disabilities jointly nominated by the state and the defendant, none of whom made the prescreening determination of the defendant's intelligence quotient. The trial court, in its discretion, may appoint an additional expert

in intellectual disabilities who was neither nominated by the state nor the defendant, and who did not make the prescreening determination of the defendant's intelligence quotient. Within forty-five days after the trial court orders the state and the defendant to nominate experts in intellectual disabilities, or on the appointment of such experts, whichever is later, the state and the defendant shall provide to the experts in intellectual disabilities and the court any available records that may be relevant to the defendant's status. The court may extend the deadline for providing records on good cause shown by the state or defendant.

E. Not less than twenty days after receipt of the records provided pursuant to subsection D, or twenty days after the expiration of the deadline for providing the records, whichever is later, each expert in intellectual disability shall examine the defendant using current community, nationally and culturally accepted physical, developmental, psychological and intelligence testing procedures, for the purpose of determining whether the defendant has an intellectual disability. Within fifteen days of examining the defendant, each expert in intellectual disabilities shall submit a written report to the trial court that includes the expert's opinion as to whether the defendant has an intellectual disability.

F. If the scores on all the tests for intelligence quotient administered to the defendant are above seventy, the notice of intent to seek the death penalty shall not be dismissed on the ground that the defendant has an intellectual disability. This does not preclude the defendant from introducing evidence of the defendant's intellectual disability or diminished mental capacity at the penalty phase of the sentencing proceeding.

G. No less than thirty days after the experts in intellectual disabilities submit reports to the court and before trial, the trial court shall hold a hearing to determine if the defendant has an intellectual disability. At the hearing, the defendant has the burden of proving intellectual disability by clear and convincing evidence. A determination by the trial court that the defendant's intelligence quotient is sixty-five or lower establishes a rebuttable presumption that the defendant has an intellectual disability. This subsection does not preclude a defendant with an intelligence quotient of seventy or below from proving intellectual disability by clear and convincing evidence.

H. If the trial court finds that the defendant has an intellectual disability, the trial court shall dismiss the intent to seek the death penalty, shall not impose a sentence of death on the defendant if the defendant is convicted of first degree murder and shall dismiss one of the attorneys appointed under rule 6.2, Arizona rules of criminal procedure, unless the court finds that there is good cause to retain both attorneys. If the trial court finds that the defendant does not have an intellectual disability, the court's finding does not prevent the defendant from introducing evidence of the defendant's intellectual disability or diminished mental capacity at the penalty phase of the sentencing proceeding.

Judicial Stays

A total of 1,234 capital felons were executed between 1977 and 2010. It is estimated that these executed capital felons spent an average of ten years on death row.[15] The ability of a capital felon to remain on death row for an average of ten years is due to the Anglo-American appellate process. To shed some light on how the appellate process impacts on the period between sentence and execution, this section will review the path taken by the average "state" capital felon upon receiving a sentence of death.[16]

Before embarking upon the review that follows, a word must be said here regarding judicial stay and the structure of the court systems in the nation. A judicial stay involves entry of an order by a court which stops an event from occurring until the court examines an allegation that concerns the event. A judicial stay is temporary. In the context of capital punishment, a judicial stay is a court order halting the scheduled execution of a capital felon, pending the court's examination of allegations that the death penalty should not be executed.

The judicial systems in the nation may be broken down into two categories: (1) three-tier systems and (2) two-tier systems. Jurisdictions that utilize a three-tier system have a (1) court of general jurisdiction, (2) intermediate appellate court and (3) final appellate court. Two-tier system jurisdictions have a (1) court of general jurisdiction and (2) appellate court. The majority of capital punishment jurisdictions utilize a three-tier system.[17]

Box 21.0 Court Systems

Type of System	Trial Court	Intermediate Appellate Court	Final Appellate Court
Two-tier	yes	no	yes
Three-tier	yes	yes	yes

Stay During State Appellate Review and Appeal

The first judicial stay that surfaces when a capital felon is sentenced to death occurs immediately after the sentence is imposed. This stay is necessary to allow the capital felon to have his or her sentence and conviction examined by the state appellate court. The length of time involved at this stage depends upon several factors.

If the state has a two-tier judicial system, then the initial stay should be less than eight months. Also, if the state has a three-tier system, but the appeal and review go directly from the trial court to the final appellate court, then the initial stay in this system should also be less than eight months. However, if the state is a three-tier system and the intermediate appellate court is permitted to hear the review and appeal, before the matter is brought to the final appellate court, then there will be two stays. There will be an approximate eight month stay imposed for intermediate appellate court examination, and a stay of about five months imposed for final appellate court examination.

Stay During Supreme Court Appeal

Assuming that a capital felon did not obtain relief at the state appellate court level, the next step will usually be that of entering the federal system.[18] This initial journey in the federal system will usually be directly to the Supreme Court.[19] Provided that the Supreme Court grants a writ of certiorari, a stay will be imposed by it pending its review. This stay can remain in place up to a year.

Stay During State Habeas Corpus Proceedings

Provided that the capital felon is denied relief by the United States Supreme Court, the capital felon usually will begin an attack on his or her conviction and sentence, indirectly, by filing a petition for a writ of habeas corpus. A habeas corpus proceeding involves allegations by a capital felon that his or her conviction and sentence were imposed in violation of his or her constitutional rights.[20]

During this first round of habeas corpus proceedings, the capital felon usually will start out at the state level, though this process can begin in the federal system. Depending upon the requirements of the particular state, the habeas corpus petition will be filed in the trial court where the capital felon was convicted and sentenced, or in the state's highest court.

If the capital felon is permitted to file the habeas corpus petition in the trial court, a stay will be entered pending review by the trial court. The case could linger in the trial court for six months to a year.

Provided that the trial court did not grant the capital felon relief, he or she will appeal the denial of his or her requested relief. If the state has a three-tier judicial system, this appeal will usually go initially to the intermediate appellate court. A stay will be entered pending disposition by the intermediate appellate court. This stay will last up to eight months.

If the intermediate appellate court does not grant relief (or if the state has a two-tier judicial system) the capital felon will appeal to the highest court in the state. While the state high court reviews the habeas corpus appeal, a stay will be imposed that can last eight months.

If the state high court denies habeas relief, the capital felon may file a petition for appeal with the United States Supreme Court. Assuming the Supreme Court agreed to hear the case, a stay will be issued that could remain in place for a year.

Stay During Federal Habeas Corpus Proceedings

If the highest court in the state and the United States Supreme Court deny the capital felon state habeas corpus relief, he or she will enter the federal system again. This time, however, the capital felon will start out in a federal district court.[21] During this initial round of habeas corpus proceedings in the federal system, the district court will stay execution of the death penalty. This stay can last a year. It should be noted that in *Lonchar v. Thomas*, 517 U.S. 314 (1996), the Supreme Court made clear that a federal court may not deny a stay of execution and dismiss a first federal habeas petition for general equitable reasons. In *McFarland v. Scott*, 512 U.S. 849 (1994), superseded by statute, it was held that a capital defendant is not required to file a formal federal habeas corpus petition in order to obtain appointment of counsel and to establish a federal court's jurisdiction to enter a stay of execution.

Should the capital felon not obtain relief in the federal district court, he or she will appeal to a federal court of appeals. A stay will be granted by the court of appeals, which can last eight months. If the court of appeals denies relief, the capital felon will seek an appeal to the Supreme Court. If the Supreme Court grants certiorari, a stay will be in place for up to a year.[22]

In the case of *Barefoot v. Estelle*, 463 U.S. 880 (1983), superseded by statute, the Supreme Court provided a lengthy discussion of judicial stays. During the discussion the Court made the following observations regarding a stay of a death sentence by that Court:

> Stays of execution are not automatic pending the filing and consideration of a petition for a writ of certiorari from this Court to the Court of Appeals that has denied a writ of habeas corpus. It is well-established that there must be a reasonable probability that four members of the Court would consider the underlying issue sufficiently meritorious for the grant of certiorari or the notation of probable jurisdiction; there must be a significant possibility of reversal of the lower court's decision; and there must be a likelihood that irreparable harm will result if that decision is not stayed. Applications for stays of death sentences are expected to contain the information and materials necessary to make a careful assessment of the merits of the issue and so reliably to

determine whether plenary review and a stay are warranted. A stay of execution should first be sought from the Court of Appeals, and this Court generally places considerable weight on the decision reached by the circuit courts in these circumstances.

In *Bell v. Thompson*, 125 S.Ct. 2825 (2005), the Supreme Court scolded an appellate court for delaying the execution of an inmate by failing to issue a mandate or order denying relief. In *Bell* the defendant was convicted and sentenced to death by the state of Tennessee for the 1985 killing of Brenda Blanton Lane. The conviction and sentence were upheld on direct appeal, and during a state habeas corpus proceeding. The defendant eventually filed a federal habeas petition. A federal district court denied habeas relief. A federal court of appeals issued an opinion affirming the district judge's decision. However, the court of appeals stayed issuance of its mandate until the United States Supreme Court considered the case. The Supreme Court issued an order denying certiorari. The defendant thereafter asked the court of appeals to continue the stay of its mandate pending application for rehearing before the Supreme Court. The court of appeals granted the request. The Supreme Court eventually denied rehearing. Five months after the Supreme Court denied rehearing, the court of appeals issued an amended opinion that reversed the district court's decision and awarded the defendant a full evidentiary hearing before the district court. The Supreme Court granted certiorari to consider whether the court of appeals acted properly. The Supreme Court reversed the court of appeals decision and chastised it for withholding issuance of its mandate for five months:

> Tennessee expended considerable time and resources in seeking to enforce a capital sentence rendered 20 years ago, a sentence that reflects the judgment of the citizens of Tennessee that Thompson's crimes merit the ultimate punishment. By withholding the mandate for months — based on evidence that supports only an arguable constitutional claim — while the State prepared to carry out Thompson's sentence, the Court of Appeals did not accord the appropriate level of respect to that judgment.

Eleventh Hour Stay

The fact that a capital felon has unsuccessfully exhausted all avenues of appeal does not automatically mean that he or she will be executed on the appointed day and time for execution. Eleventh hour stays (last minute) are not uncommon. Various reasons may trigger an eleventh hour stay. For example, Alabama death row inmate Robert Lee Tarver had eaten his last meal and was about three hours away from execution on February 14, 2000, when the United States Supreme Court issued a stay of his execution to consider Tarver's challenge to the state's use of the electric chair. (The Supreme Court later decided not to review the matter. Tarver was eventually executed on April 14, 2000.)

Once the eleventh hour approaches, the most crucial factor in the execution process is the operation of the phone lines. It is imperative that split second communication is possible between the officials in the execution chamber and any potential judge or executive officer that has the authority to halt the execution.

It must be noted that the Supreme Court has made clear that it does not approve of eleventh hour stays by federal courts. Observations about the Supreme Court's position were made in *Clanton v. Muncy*, 845 F.2d 1238 (4th Cir. 1988), as follows:

> The situation we face here is similar to that in *Alabama v. Evans,* 461 U.S. 230 (1983), where the Supreme Court vacated a stay that had been entered by a district court for the purpose of

considering a last-minute habeas petition from a condemned inmate. What the Court said there is applicable here: "respondent's constitutional challenges ... have been reviewed exhaustively and repetitively by several courts in both the state and federal systems." Review of the Supreme Court's many opinions dealing with eleventh hour stay motions reveals a clear message: constitutional litigation is not to be conducted piecemeal, claims should be raised earlier rather than later, and considered resolution by state courts is far preferable to a last minute dash to federal habeas corpus. The claims presented in the habeas corpus petition underlying the stay before us violates each of these directives....

This eleventh hour attempt to repackage issues presented by Clanton at the time of his initial federal petition constitutes an abuse of the writ....

This case presents the situation addressed by the Supreme Court in *Woodard v. Hutchins,* 464 U.S. 377 (1984): "a last minute application for a stay of execution and a new petition for habeas corpus relief have been filed with no explanation as to why the claims were not raised earlier or why they were not all raised in one petition. It is another example of abuse of the writ."

The Great Writ War

If the capital felon fails to obtain habeas corpus relief from the Supreme Court, then the great writ war begins. At this stage a capital felon has argued all possible rational reasons for vacating his or her sentence and conviction, but has been denied relief. In order to continue to cling to life the capital felon will begin filing endless petitions for writs of mandamus, coram nobis, prohibition, and habeas corpus. Statistics indicate capital felons, in the past, were able to squeeze out an additional five or so years through judicial stays because of this great writ war. Recent changes in state and federal laws have cut the great writ war time in half.[23]

Executive Clemency

Between 1977 and 2010, a total of 302 death row inmates had their death sentences commuted to life imprisonment as a result of executive clemency.[24] It was said in *People v. Arellano,* 524 P.2d 305 (Colo. 1974), that once a defendant has exhausted all appellate remedies in seeking relief from a conviction and sentence, any further attempt at relief must be made not to the judiciary but to the executive department of government. *Arellano,* while correct, stated matters in part, not whole. Executive clemency may be obtained before or after exhausting all judicial appellate avenues.

As a general matter, executive clemency refers to granting a specific form of leniency from a conviction and sentence. Executive clemency is a matter of grace, not of right. No defendant has a right to obtain executive clemency.[25] In *Ohio Adult Parole Authority v. Woodard,* 523 U.S. 272 (1998), it was held that Ohio's clemency procedures for death row inmates did not violate the constitutional privilege against self-incrimination.

All capital punishment jurisdictions provide by statute or constitution for executive clemency. As pointed out by *Arellano,* executive clemency resides in the executive branch of government. Governors and the president control executive clemency. Jurisdictions vary as to the autonomy granted chief executive officers in making executive clemency decisions. A few jurisdictions attach no strings to the chief executive officer's authority in this area, while others require involvement of a council, board or commission. The following statutes are provided to illustrate how capital punishment jurisdictions address the matter.

Texas Code Annotated–C.C.P. Art. 48.01:

In all criminal cases, except treason and impeachment, the Governor shall have power, after conviction, on the written signed recommendation and advice of the Board of Pardons and Paroles, or a majority thereof, to grant reprieves and commutations of punishments and pardons; and upon the written recommendation and advice of a majority of the Board of Pardons and Paroles, he shall have the power to remit fines and forfeitures. The Governor shall have the power to grant one reprieve in any capital case for a period not to exceed 30 days; and he shall have power to revoke conditional pardons. With the advice and consent of the Legislature, the Governor may grant reprieves, commutations of punishment and pardons in cases of treason.

Washington Revised Code § 10.01.120:

Whenever a prisoner has been sentenced to death, the governor shall have power to commute such sentence to imprisonment for life at hard labor; and in all cases in which the governor is authorized to grant pardons or commute sentence of death, he or she may, upon the petition of the person convicted, commute a sentence or grant a pardon, upon such conditions, and with such restrictions, and under such limitations as he or she may think proper; and he or she may issue his or her warrant to all proper officers to carry into effect such pardon or commutation, which warrant shall be obeyed and executed, instead of the sentence, if any, which was originally given. The governor may also, on good cause shown, grant respites or reprieves from time to time as he or she may think proper.

Executive clemency may manifest itself in three ways: (1) reprieve (sometimes called "respite"), (2) commutation, or (3) pardon. Each type of executive clemency has its own unique consequence for a capital felon. The review of each form of executive clemency that follows will explain the consequences of each.

Executive Reprieve

A reprieve serves the same function as that of a judicial stay. It merely postpones an execution temporarily. Capital felon reprieves usually occur in one of two contexts.

First, if a capital felon has filed a habeas corpus or other type of petition with a court, but the court refuses to grant a stay while the matter is before it, the capital felon can request a reprieve while the court evaluates the matter. Second, if a capital felon requests a pardon or commutation, a reprieve may be granted while the application for pardon or commutation is under review.

In *Lambert v. Barrett*, 157 U.S. 697 (1895), it was said that the issue of whether the governor of New Jersey had authority to issue a reprieve of the defendant's execution and a subsequent death warrant for his execution did not present a federal question, therefore jurisdiction did not reside in federal courts to address the matter.

Executive Commutation

The court in *State ex rel. Maurer v. Steward*, 644 N.E.2d 369 (Ohio 1994), defined commutation as "the change of a punishment to which a person has been condemned into a less severe one." Most capital punishment jurisdictions limit commutation of a death sentence to that of life imprisonment.[26] In theory, when this limitation is not imposed, a capital felon can have his or her death sentence commuted to time served — which would mean immediate release.

However, as a practical matter commutations are usually confined to life imprisonment. Usually commutations are made with a condition that the capital felon will not seek parole. Commutations may also take on any other conditions deemed appropriate and in compliance with general laws. A violation of a condition of commutation can, in theory, result in the death penalty being reinstated and carried out. In *Biddle v. Perovich*, 274 U.S. 480 (1927), it was held that the president had authority to commute the defendant's death sentence to life imprisonment without the consent of the defendant. In *Schick v. Reed*, 419 U.S. 256 (1974), it was determined that the president may commute a death sentence to life imprisonment, with a condition that the defendant not be eligible for parole. In *California v. Ramos*, 463 U.S. 992 (1983), it was held that the Constitution permits a capital penalty phase jury to be instructed regarding a governor's power to commute a sentence of life without possibility of parole to one with parole. In *Rose v. Hodges*, 423 U.S. 19 (1975), it was held that the Constitution does not require that, following commutation of a death sentence by a state's governor, a defendant is entitled to have his or her sentence determined anew by a jury.

Executive Pardon

It was pointed out in *Ex Parte May*, 717 S.W.2d 84 (Tex.Cr.App. 1986), that, unlike commutation and reprieve, "a pardon may be granted by proper authority at any time — even before a criminal charge has been lodged against the offender." The court in *State ex rel. Maurer v. Steward*, 644 N.E.2d 369 (Ohio 1994), made the following observations regarding a pardon:

> A pardon discharges the individual designated from all or some specified penal consequences of his crime. It may be full or partial, absolute or conditional.
> A full and absolute pardon releases the offender from the entire punishment prescribed for his offense, and from all the disabilities consequent on his conviction.

Pardons for capital felons waiting to be executed have been rare. Usually a pardon in a capital prosecution is conditional. For example, in *Ex Parte Wells*, 59 U.S. 307 (1855), the defendant was granted a pardon by the president that was conditioned upon his remaining in prison for life. The defendant argued to the Supreme Court that a pardon could not be conditional — it had to be absolute. The Supreme Court disagreed:

> The counsel for the prisoner contends that the pardon is valid to remit entirely the sentence of the court for his execution, and that the condition annexed to the pardon, and accepted by the prisoner, is illegal....
> We think this is a mistake arising from the want of due consideration of the legal meaning of the word pardon. It is supposed that it was meant to be used exclusively with reference to an absolute pardon, exempting a criminal from the punishment which the law inflicts for a crime he has committed.
> But such is not the sense or meaning of the word, either in common parlance or in law....
> In the law it has different meanings, which were as well understood when the constitution was made as any other legal word in the constitution now is.
> Such a thing is a pardon without a designation of its kind is not known in the law. Time out of mind, in the earliest books of the English law, every pardon has its particular denomination. They are general, special, or particular, conditional or absolute, statutory, not necessary in some cases, and in some grantable of course....

Right to Counsel for Clemency Proceeding

In *Harbison v. Bell*, 129 S.Ct. 1481 (2009), the defendant in *Harbison* was convicted of capital murder by the state of Tennessee and sentenced to death. After failing to have state courts reverse the judgment, the defendant filed a federal habeas corpus petition. A federal court appointed counsel to represent the defendant in the federal habeas corpus proceeding. After the habeas proceedings ended unsuccessfully, the defendant requested counsel for state clemency proceedings. The Tennessee Supreme Court held that state law did not authorize the appointment of state public defenders as clemency counsel. Thereafter, the defendant's federally appointed counsel moved to expand the authorized scope of her representation to include state clemency proceedings. The federal district court denied the request. A court of appeals affirmed. The United States Supreme Court granted certiorari to address the issue.

The Supreme Court held in *Harbison* that a plain reading of 18 U.S.C. § 3599 indicates that Congress authorized federal courts to appoint counsel to represent state prisoners in clemency proceedings:

> Congress' decision to furnish counsel for clemency proceedings demonstrates that it ... recognized the importance of such process to death-sentenced prisoners.... Moreover, Congress' sequential enumeration suggests an awareness that clemency proceedings are not as divorced from judicial proceedings as the Government submits. [The statute] emphasizes continuity of counsel, and Congress likely appreciated that federal habeas counsel are well positioned to represent their clients in the state clemency proceedings that typically follow the conclusion of [habeas] litigation....
>
> [The defendant's] case underscores why it is entirely plausible that Congress did not want condemned men and women to be abandoned by their counsel at the last moment and left to navigate the sometimes labyrinthine clemency process from their jail cells. In authorizing federally funded counsel to represent their state clients in clemency proceedings, Congress ensured that no prisoner would be put to death without meaningful access to the "fail-safe" of our justice system.

Non-Capital and Capital Sentencing

Very often the situation arises where a capital felon will be convicted of capital murder, in addition to non-capital crimes during the same trial. An issue that arises frequently in this situation is whether the capital felon has a right to serve the non-capital prison sentence before having to be executed on the capital offense conviction. The universal rule on this issue is that a capital felon receiving a sentence of imprisonment, in addition to a sentence of death, does not have a right to serve the term of imprisonment before being executed. In fact, the Supreme Court has expressly held in *Kelley v. Oregon*, 273 U.S. 589 (1927), that a defendant does not have a constitutional right to serve out a prior imprisonment sentence before he or she can be executed for another crime.

22

Death Row

Death row is a phrase used to describe the place of incarceration for defendants sentenced to death. All death row facilities are maintained in maximum security prisons. For obvious reasons, intense and intimidating security is the operating principle for maintaining death row inmates. This chapter provides a summary of death row population and institutional characteristics.[1]

Death Row Population Characteristics

In 2009 a total of 3,173 inmates were on death row.[2] Of those, 60 or 1.9 percent were female.[3] The African American death row population for that period was 1,317 or 41.5 percent.[4] The mean age of all death row inmates in 2009 was 44.[5] More than half the population, 54.7 percent, was never married, and nearly half, 49.5 percent, failed to obtain a high school diploma or its equivalent.[6] The percentage of death row inmates in 2009 that had prior felony offenses when they committed their capital offense totaled 65.7 percent.[7]

TABLE 22.0 AVERAGE TIME ON DEATH ROW BEFORE EXECUTION 2000–2010

Year	Inmates Executed	Months
2000	85	137
2001	66	142
2002	71	127
2003	65	131
2004	59	132
2005	60	147
2006	53	145
2007	42	153
2008	37	139
2009	52	169
2010	46	178

SOURCE: U.S. Department of Justice, Bureau of Justice Statistics, Capital Punishment, Table 8 (2010).

TABLE 22.1 DEATH ROW INMATES BY JURISDICTION 2010

Jurisdiction	Inmates on Death Row	Jurisdiction	Inmates on Death Row
Alabama	201	California	699
Arizona	133	Colorado	3
Arkansas	42	Delaware	17

Jurisdiction	Inmates on Death Row	Jurisdiction	Inmates on Death Row
Florida	392	North Carolina	158
Georgia	100	Ohio	157
Idaho	16	Oklahoma	71
Indiana	13	Oregon	34
Kansas	8	Pennsylvania	215
Kentucky	34	South Carolina	56
Louisiana	84	South Dakota	2
Maryland	5	Tennessee	86
Mississippi	60	Texas	315
Missouri	49	Utah	9
Montana	2	Virginia	9
Nebraska	12	Washington	8
Nevada	81	Wyoming	1
New Hampshire	1	Federal	58

SOURCE: U.S. Department of Justice, Bureau of Justice Statistics, Capital Punishment, Table 4 (2010).

Death Row Institutional Characteristics

Death row cells generally comprise one or more wings in a prison. Each cell has a bed, a lavatory, commode, and a mounted writing table. Some institutions permit death row inmates to have cigarettes, food, radios and televisions in their cells.[8]

Death row inmates are served food three times a day. Some institutions require the meals be served in the cells, while others permit death row inmates to eat in dining halls. Most institutions do not permit inmates to leave their cells except for medical reasons, exercise, or for scheduled visits with outside visitors. Institutions provide a visiting area inside the prison where inmates and visitors may see and talk to each other, but have no physical contact. Death row inmates may receive mail.[9] In *McElvaine v. Brush*, 142 U.S. 155 (1891), and *Rogers v. Peck*, 199 U.S. 425 (1905), the Supreme Court held that detention in solitary confinement pending execution did not violate the Constitution.

Institutions do not assign prison jobs to death row inmates, other than a requirement that they keep their cells clean. Death row inmates have at least one hour per day for exercise. They are escorted in groups to outdoor or indoor exercise areas.[10]

Florida Death Row Information[11]

Death row and death watch cells: A death row cell is 6 × 9 × 9.5 feet high. Florida State Prison also has death watch cells to incarcerate inmates awaiting execution after the governor signs a death warrant for them. A death watch cell is 12 × 7 × 8.5 feet high. Men on death row are housed at Florida State Prison in Starke and Union Correctional Institution in Raiford. The women on death row are housed at Lowell Correctional Institution Annex in Lowell.

Meals: Death row inmates are served meals three times a day: at 5:00 A.M., from 10:30 A.M. to 11:00 A.M. and from 4:00 P.M. to 4:30 P.M. Food is prepared by Florida State Prison personnel and is transported in insulated carts to the cells. Inmates are allowed plates and spoons to eat their meals. Prior to execution, an inmate may request a last meal. To avoid extravagance, the food to prepare the last meal must cost no more than $20 and must be purchased locally.

Visitors: Visitors are allowed every weekend from 9 A.M. to 3 P.M. All visitors must be approved by prison officials before being placed on the inmate visitor list. Visitors traveling over 200 miles may visit both Saturday and Sunday. Members of the news media may request death row inmate interviews through the Department of Corrections. Inmates must agree to being interviewed. Because of safety and security concerns, the news media may not interview any prison personnel who are involved in executions except for official Department of Corrections spokespersons.

Showers: The inmates may shower every other day.

Security: Death row inmates are counted at least once an hour. They are escorted in handcuffs and wear them everywhere except in their cells, the exercise yard and the shower. They are in their cells at all times except for medical reasons, exercise, social or legal visits or media interviews. When a death warrant is signed the inmate is put under death watch status and is allowed a legal and social phone call.

Mail, Magazines and Entertainment: Inmates may receive mail every day except holidays and weekends. They may have cigarettes, snacks, radios and black and white televisions in their cells. They do not have cable television or air-conditioning and they are not allowed to be with each other in a common room. They can watch church services on closed circuit television. While on death watch, inmates may have radios and black and white televisions positioned outside their cell bars.

Clothing: Death row inmates can be distinguished from other inmates by their orange t-shirts. Their pants are the same blue colored pants worn by regular inmates.

Arizona Death Row Information[12]

Arizona's death row for men is in the Browning Unit at Arizona State Prison Complex–Eyman, located just outside the city of Florence. Female inmates on death row are housed at the Lumley Unit at the Arizona State Prison Complex–Perryville, near Goodyear. All executions are performed in Central Unit at the Arizona State Prison Complex–Florence.

All male and female inmates on death row are classified as maximum custody. All inmates are in single cells which are equipped with a toilet, sink, bed and mattress. Each death row inmate has no contact with any other inmate. Out-of-cell time is limited to outdoor exercise in a secured area, two hours a day, three times a week, and a shower, three times a week. All meals are delivered by correction officers at the cell front. Limited non-contact visitation is available. Death row inmates may place two ten minute telephone calls per week. Personal property is limited to hygiene items, two appliances, two books and writing materials, which can be purchased from the inmate commissary. Health care is provided at the Health Unit; medication is distributed at the cell front. Clergy contacts are provided at the cell.

North Carolina Death Row Information[13]

Location of men and woman inmates. The Division of Prisons houses male death row inmates at Central Prison and female death row inmates at the North Carolina Correctional Institution for Women. Both prisons are in Raleigh.

Male inmate cellblocks. At Central Prison, the men are housed in cellblocks of Unit III. Two correctional officers in a control center watch the inmates at all times. Each cell block is divided into eight pods with 24 single cells—12 cells on each level. The cells open into a dayroom area that has a television at one end, stainless steel tables in the middle and showers at the other end. Each cell has a bed, a lavatory, commode, and a wall-mounted writing table.

Female inmate cellblocks. Conditions are similar for female inmates on death row. The women are housed in a cellblock of the maximum security building at the North Carolina Correctional Institution for Women. Each of the single cells has a bed, lavatory and commode. The seven cells are side by side down a corridor. At the front of the cellblock is a dayroom with a television, table and chairs. This is where the women eat their meals.

Activities for inmates. Inmates on death row spend nearly all their time in either their cells or the adjacent dayroom. They may stay in their dayroom from 7 A.M. until 11 P.M. While in the dayroom, they may watch television. Death row inmates may be assigned incentive wage jobs in the canteen or clothes house, or may work as barbers or janitors within their housing areas. They are required to keep their cells and dayrooms clean. Inmates are allowed at least one hour per day for exercise and showers. Two days a week, officers escort death row inmates in groups from each cellblock pod to outdoor exercise areas, weather permitting, where the inmates can play basketball, walk or jog. Officers also escort the death row inmates by cellblock to the dining halls for each meal.

Visitation and religious worship. Death row inmates may receive one visit a week with a maximum of two visitors. In the visiting booths, visitors may see and talk with inmates, but physical contact is not possible. Inmates may participate in a one-hour Christian worship service each Sunday, or Islamic worship services for one hour each Friday. A Bible study class is also conducted by the prison's chaplain for 90 minutes each Tuesday morning.

Punishment for violating rules. If a death row inmate violates prison regulations, he may be placed in a segregation cellblock outside of the death row area. He must eat his meals in his cell and is separated from other death row inmates for his daily hour of exercise and shower.

Death Watch Cells

Most institutions have death watch cells to incarcerate death row inmates after an authorized official signs a death warrant setting the day and time for the execution. A death watch cell is usually larger than a regular death row cell. The death watch cell is usually adjacent to the execution chamber. The inmate remains in the death watch cell until receiving a stay or until escorted to the execution chamber. An inmate on death watch status is allowed a legal and social phone call while on death watch.[14] A few days before an inmate is scheduled to be executed he or she is moved from his or her death row cell and taken to a death watch cell. An example of death watch protocol is provided below.

North Carolina Death Watch Protocol[15]

When a death row inmate exhausts all appeals, the attorney general directs the secretary of correction to set an execution date. That inmate, male or female, is moved into the death watch area of Central Prison three to seven days prior to the execution date. The death watch area is adjacent to the execution chamber and is located in the prison's custody control building. The inmate moves all personal belongings from the death row cell to one of the four cells in the death watch area.

Each cell has a bed, lavatory, commode and a wall-mounted writing table. The cells are side by side and open into a dayroom where there is a table, a television and shower. With the exception of 15 minutes allowed for a shower, the inmate spends the entire day in the cell. A sergeant and a correctional officer are stationed just outside the cell in the dayroom 24 hours a day.

Visitation. The inmate may receive visits from his attorney, chaplains, psychologists and others authorized by the Division of Prisons and may receive non-contact family visits in the prison's regular visiting area. Contact visits may be allowed at the warden's discretion in the days immediately preceding execution. An inmate on death watch is not allowed contact with other inmates. The inmate remains in the death watch area until receiving a stay or until escorted to the execution chamber.

Last Meal

It is customary for a condemned inmate to be offered a last meal of choice before execution. Records show that most inmates request a last meal of choice, though a few reject the offer. Prisons generally have a budget limit. Some prisons restrict the food to that provided in the prison, while others will allow meals to be purchased outside the prison. Texas ended the last meal request ritual in 2011 as a result of an excessive meal ordered, but not eaten, by condemned inmate Lawrence Brewer.[16]

Last Meal of the LaGrand Brothers

Karl LaGrand executed by Arizona February 24, 1999
Two Bacon, Lettuce & Tomato sandwiches on white bread, Mayonnaise, 4 fried eggs, over-easy, Medium portion of hash-brown potatoes, 2 breakfast rolls, small portion of strawberry jelly. One half pint of pineapple sherbet ice cream, one 22 ounce of hot coffee, black, one medium slice of German chocolate cake with coconut-caramel icing, one 12 ounce cup of cold milk.

Walter LaGrand executed by Arizona March 3, 1999
Six fried eggs, cooked over-easy, 16 strips of bacon, one large portion of hash-browns, one pint of pineapple sherbet ice cream, one breakfast steak well done. One 16 ounce cup filled with ice, one 7UP, 1 Dr. Pepper, 1 Coke, one portion of hot sauce, one cup of coffee, two packets of sugar and four Rolaids tablets.

Last Statement

A ritual that has a long history in capital punishment is that of asking a condemned person if he or she has a last statement to make before being executed. The last statement ritual has continued under modern capital punishment.

As a general matter, if a condemned person has a last statement to make, the statement will be transcribed verbatim by an official present during the execution. Occasionally a prisoner will make a lengthy last statement, in which case only a summary of the statement will be transcribed.

Last Statement of Troy Davis

Troy Davis executed by Georgia September 21, 2011

Well, first of all I'd like to address the MacPhail family. I'd like to let you all know that despite the situation — I know all of you still are convinced that I'm the person that killed your father, your son and your brother, but I am innocent. The incidents that happened that night was not my fault. I did not have a gun that night. I did not shoot your family member. But I am so sorry for your loss. I really am — sincerely. All that I can ask is that each of you look deeper into this case, so that you really will finally see the truth. I ask to my family and friends that you all continue to pray, that you all continue to forgive. Continue to fight this fight. For those about to take my life, may God have mercy on all of your souls. God bless you all.

Last Statement of Karla Faye Tucker

Karla Faye Tucker executed by Texas February 3, 1998

Yes sir, I would like to say to all of you — the Thornton family and Jerry Dean's family that I am so sorry. I hope God will give you peace with this.

Baby, I love you. Ron, give Peggy a hug for me. Everybody has been so good to me.

I love all of you very much. I am going to be face to face with Jesus now. Warden Baggett, thank all of you so much. You have been so good to me. I love all of you very much. I will see you all when you get there. I will wait for you.

23

Witnessing an Execution

The primary focus of this chapter is to provide a review of statutes that control public access to executions. Prior to examining these laws some discussion is devoted to the origin of public executions, the movement away from them and efforts to make executions public again.

Origin of Public Executions

The common law tolerated, for reasons that are forthcoming, having capital felons executed in full view of the public. Attending an execution was a routine part of life in England, under the common law. People gathered, much as they gather today at sporting events, with joy and enthusiasm to watch the condemned be put to death.[1]

Anglo-American jurisprudence embraced England's practice of inviting the public to watch capital felons die. Public executions were an integral part of the early development of America. Prior to 1835 all capital punishments in the United States were open to the public.

Neither England nor the United States permitted public executions for the sake of entertaining citizens. Two fundamental reasons guided the decision to allow the public to observe capital felons being put to death. One was aimed at the capital felon and the other was centered on the public.

The first justification involved the dehumanization of the capital felon. Capital crimes were offenses that society deemed unforgivable. Due to the perceived reprehensible nature of capital crimes, it was felt necessary to humiliate and degrade a capital offender by parading him or her in front of the public before, during and after execution. Whether a capital felon felt humiliated and degraded — as opposed to feeling scared to death — is an issue for psychologist to digest. Penologists believed capital felons felt dehumanized by being brought before the public for execution.

The second justification for holding public executions was grounded in the deterrent principle underpinning criminal punishment in general. It was thought that exposing the public to executions would deter others from committing, at minimum, capital crimes.

Movement Away from Public Executions

New York is credited with being the first jurisdiction to permit nonpublic executions. It did so by enacting a statute in 1835 that allowed the sheriff to hold executions out of public view.[2] Without realizing it, New York set in motion a penological reform movement that would eventually engulf the nation.

The New York nonpublic execution statute was heralded as representing the evolving decency of society. Public executions were symbolic of a crude and unsophisticated society. Such a spectacle dehumanized not only the capital felon, it took away the humanity of those observing. In slow but steady fashion, the notion of evolving decency moved across the nation and jurisdictions began enacting statutes which took away the public's ability to view executions. The force of this movement touched down in England where, in 1868, that nation abolished the practice of holding public executions.

The theme of evolving decency came full circle in 1936. The last public execution occurred in the United States that year in Owensboro, Kentucky. It was said that between ten thousand and twenty thousand people came out to see the state of Kentucky hang 22 year old Ramsey Bethea.

Judicial Challenges to Nonpublic Executions

Removal of executions from the public's eye has not gone unchallenged. Numerous attacks, cloaked in diverse motives, have been made to remove secrecy from executions. Some of the legal battles waged to reopen executions to the public follow.

The Right of the Capital Felon and the Public

Penologists believed that public executions humiliated and degraded capital felons. This belief is difficult to digest when capital felons demand to have public executions. The first challenge to nonpublic executions came in 1890 and was made by a capital felon.

The Supreme Court picked up this challenge in the case of *Holden v. Minnesota*, 137 U.S. 483 (1890). The defendant in *Holden* had been sentenced to death for committing capital murder. At the time of his offense Minnesota permitted public executions (Minnesota currently does not allow capital punishment). However, shortly before his scheduled execution the state changed the law so that executions could no longer be held in public. The defendant argued that the change in law should not affect him, because at the time of his offense executions were public. The defendant contended that the federal Constitution's ban on ex post facto laws prohibited the new law from applying to him. The Supreme Court rejected the defendant's position:

> Whether a convicted, sentenced to death, shall be executed ... within or without the walls of the jail, or within or outside of some other enclosure, and whether the enclosure within which he is executed shall be higher than the gallows, thus excluding the view of persons outside, are regulations that do not affect [the defendant's] substantial rights. The same observation may be made touching the restriction ... as to the number and character of those who may witness the execution, and the exclusion altogether of reporters or representatives of newspapers. These are regulations which the legislature, in its wisdom, and for the public good, could legally prescribe in respect to executions occurring after the passage of the [law], and cannot, even when applied to offenses previously committed, be regarded as ex post facto within the meaning of the Constitution.

Holden has stood the test of time in championing the proposition that a capital felon does not have a constitutional right to a public execution. The case has also stood for the proposition that the general public does not have a right to attend an execution.

The Media's Right to Film Executions

The First Amendment is a powerful constitutional provision. In crystal clear words this amendment heralds the independence of the press (media) by proclaiming that "governments" cannot abridge the freedom of the press. Upon first impression it would seem that governments cannot bar the media from filming or photographing executions. This first impression has met a sad fate in judicial decisions.

In 1990 California was preparing to execute its first capital felon in twenty-three years. The recipient of this dubious distinction was named Robert Alton Harris. A local San Francisco television station, KQED, wanted to film the execution for posterity. The station approached California officials with a request to record the execution but was turned down. Unperturbed, the station filed an equity proceeding, styled *KQED v. Vasquez*, No. C-90-1383 (N.D.Cal. 1991), in a federal district court seeking to force California to allow it to film Harris' execution. The district court rebuffed the station and held that the state of California could constitutionally exclude cameras from its execution chamber.

In the case of *Halquist v. Dept. of Corrections*, 783 P.2d 1065 (Wash. 1989), a producer of radio and television documentaries asked officials in the state of Washington to allow him to videotape the execution of Charles Campbell. When the producer was turned down he filed an equity proceeding before the Washington Supreme Court. The producer contended that he had a right under the constitution of Washington to film the execution.

The state constitutional provision relied upon by the producer in *Halquist* provided that: "Every person may freely speak, write and publish on all subjects, being responsible for the abuse of that right." The producer argued that the latter state constitutional provision guaranteed him the right to film the execution. The court rebuffed this argument by noting that "the right to publish applies only to those who have previously and lawfully obtained information." The court also added that there was "a substantial difference between the right to publish already acquired information and the right to attend a proceeding for the purpose of news gathering." In placing the last nail in the producer's coffin, so to speak, the court observed that the United States Supreme Court took the position that "the First Amendment does not guarantee the press a constitutional right of special access to information not available to the public generally."

In *Garrett v. Estelle*, 556 F.2d 1274 (5th Cir. 1977), the state of Texas sought reversal of a federal district court's decision ordering it to permit a television news cameraman to film executions. In reversing the decision of the federal district court, the court of appeals held the following:

> Garrett asserts a first amendment right to gather news, which he contends can be limited only on account of a compelling state interest. He further argues that preventing him from using a motion picture camera to gather news denies him use of the tool of his trade and therefore denies him equal protection of the laws....
>
> News gathering is protected by the first amendment, for without some protection for seeking out the news, freedom of the press could be eviscerated. This protection is not absolute, however. As the late Chief Justice Warren wrote for the Supreme Court, "The right to speak and publish does not carry with it the unrestrained right to gather information[.]"
>
> [T]he press has no greater right of access to information than does the public at large and ... the first amendment does not require government to make available to the press information not available to the public. This principle marks a limit to the first amendment protection of the

press' right to gather news. Applying this principle to the present case, we hold that the first amendment does not invalidate nondiscriminatory prison access regulations.

While we agree that the death penalty is a matter of wide public interest, we disagree that the protections of the first amendment depend upon the notoriety of an issue. The Supreme Court has held that the first amendment does not protect means of gathering news in prisons not available to the public generally, and this holding is not predicated upon the importance or degree of interest in the matter reported....

Garrett next argues that to prevent his filming executions denies him equal protection of the law, since other members of the press are allowed free use of their usual reporting tools. This argument is also without merit. The Texas media regulation denies Garrett use of his camera, and it also denies the print reporter use of his camera, and the radio reporter use of his tape recorder. Garrett is free to make his report by means of anchor desk or stand-up delivery on the TV screen, or even by simulation. There is no denial of equal protection.

The Right of a Capital Felon to Videotape an Execution

Capital felons have argued that the methods used to execute the death penalty are cruel and unusual. Several capital felons have sought to prove this argument by offering into evidence videotapes of capital felons being put to death. To obtain such evidence capital felons have to establish that they have a "right" to videotape executions.

In the case of *Campbell v. Blodgett*, 982 F.2d 1356 (9th Cir. 1993),[3] a capital felon, Charles Campbell, filed an action in a federal district court seeking to force officials to allow him to videotape the hanging execution of Westley Allan Dodd. Campbell wanted to use the videotape in another proceeding where he had alleged that hanging was a cruel and unusual form of punishment. The federal district court denied the request. Campbell appealed to a federal court of appeals. The court of appeals stated that a videotape of Dodd's hanging would be insufficient proof that hanging was cruel and unusual, because it could not establish what degree of pain and suffering was endured. Therefore, the court of appeals affirmed the denial of relief.

The case of *Fierro v. Gomez*, 1993 U.S. Dist. LEXIS 14445 (N.D.Cal. 1993),[4] presented a ray of hope for capital felons seeking to prove death penalty methods were cruel and unusual. Three capital felons brought this case into federal court: David Fierro, Alejandro Gilbert Ruiz and Robert Alton Harris. In an effort to support their claim that California's use of lethal gas to execute capital felons was cruel and unusual punishment, the defendants asked a federal district court to issue an order permitting them to videotape the execution of Harris. The capital felons argued that the videotape would conclusively establish that death by lethal gas was cruel and unusual punishment. The district court held that such a videotape would have some relevancy on the defendants' claim. Therefore, the district court issued an order allowing the capital felons to videotape the execution of Harris. The court explicitly required that only Harris be videotaped and not anyone else attending the execution.

In the case of *Petition of Thomas*, 155 F.R.D. 124 (D.Md. 1994), a capital felon challenged the state of Maryland's method of execution as being cruel and unusual punishment. In an effort to prove his claim, the defendant asked a federal district court to allow him to conduct discovery on the state. Part of the discovery that the defendant wanted to engage in was that of videotaping the execution of another capital felon. The court in that case ultimately ruled that the defendant could conduct discovery to support his challenge to the state's method of execution and, as part of that discovery, he could videotape the execution of a consenting death row inmate.

Statutory Limitations on Access to Executions

Methodically detailed rules and regulations have been promulgated by correctional agencies that set out what the environment will consist of when an execution occurs. The overwhelming majority of capital punishment jurisdictions have provided, by statute, a few restrictions that help make up the rules and regulations for conducting an execution.[5]

This section will review most of the statutory guidelines for carrying out the death penalty. The bulk of the procedures for carrying out the death penalty are contained in administrative rules and regulations.

Attendance by Family Members of the Victim

Only four capital punishment jurisdictions allow, by statute, family members of a victim to attend the execution. Two of the jurisdictions allow only one family member of the victim to attend the execution.[6] Another jurisdiction sets the limit at three family members.[7] The fourth jurisdiction imposes no statutory limit on the number of family members that can attend the execution.[8]

Family and Friends of Capital Felon

Although the majority of capital punishment jurisdictions do not statutorily authorize members of a victim's family to attend the execution, the situation is different for the capital felon.[9] A majority of jurisdictions provide by statute that a capital felon's family and friends may attend the execution. Restrictions are placed on the number of family members and friends of the capital felon who may attend the execution.

TABLE 23.0 FAMILY/FRIENDS THAT MAY VIEW EXECUTION

Number of Jurisdictions	*Number of Family/friends*
Two[10]	10
Nine[11]	5
Four[12]	3
One[13]	2
Five[14]	no statutory limit

Media Representation

The majority of capital punishment jurisdictions do not provide by statute for media attendance at executions. The jurisdictions that do provide for media attendance by statute are divided into two types: (1) newspaper reporters only and (2) media (which includes newspaper, television and radio reporters).

Newspaper reporters only. Two capital punishment jurisdictions restrict, by statute, media presence at executions to newspaper reporters. One jurisdiction does not set a numerical limitation on the number of newspaper reporters,[15] while the other jurisdiction limits the number to eight.[16]

Media in general. The statutes in ten capital punishment jurisdictions provide for media representation at executions.

TABLE 23.1 MEDIA REPRESENTATION AT EXECUTIONS

Jurisdiction	Media Representation
Kentucky	9
Utah	9
Tennessee	7
Pennsylvania	6
South Carolina	5
Ohio	3
South Dakota	1
Florida	no statutory limit
Oklahoma	no statutory limit
Washington	no statutory limit

Audio-visual restrictions. Although no capital punishment jurisdiction currently allows executions to be televised, the unanimous bar is not found in statutes. Only four jurisdictions set out in statutes that audio-visual recorders are prohibited from being used at executions.[17]

Public Representation

A large minority of capital punishment jurisdictions provide by statute for limited "respectable citizen" representation at executions.[18] All of these jurisdictions, except for Delaware, authorize correctional officials to select the public representation.[19]

Citizen representation at an execution is voluntary. Persons selected by appropriate authority do not have to attend the execution. It should also be noted that the statutes use the phrase "respectable citizens," or "reputable citizens" to describe those who are selected as public representatives to attend executions.

Inmate Representation

Statutes that use the phrase "respectable citizens" or "reputable citizens" to describe who may view an execution do not define the terms. Doubtless, any definition given to the terms would exclude inmates. Does this mean that inmates are excluded, per se, from attending executions? Not necessarily.

Only four capital punishment jurisdictions specifically exclude, by statute, inmates from attending a capital felon's execution.[20] What this means, in theory, is that inmates in a majority of capital punishment jurisdictions may be able to attend executions as "friends" requested by capital felons. North Carolina, by statute, explicitly allows a capital felon to invite inmate friends to view the execution.

Spiritual Advisor

Hollywood popularized the notion of a capital felon going to the execution chamber with a priest close at hand. The classic depiction of this scenario involved Pat O'Brien playing a priest who attended James Cagney as he was ushered to the death chamber. Reality is not far behind Hollywood's fictional accounts of executions. A majority of capital punishment jurisdictions allow, by statute, spiritual advisors to be present at executions. Two types of spiritual advisors are provided for in statutes: (1) prison chaplains and (2) personal spiritual advisors.

Prison chaplain. All long-term correctional institutions have prison chaplains on staff.

Prison chaplains play a crucial role in fulfilling the "rehabilitation" goal of the criminal justice system. Of course, for capital felons awaiting execution, rehabilitation is not a goal in this life. Nonetheless, prison chaplains may provide some hope of spiritual rehabilitation for capital felons. This slim possibility has prompted five capital punishment jurisdictions to permit, by statute, prison chaplains to attend executions. Three of those jurisdictions limit prison chaplain representation to one.[21] The remaining two jurisdictions do not limit the number of prison chaplains that may attend executions.[22]

Personal spiritual advisor. A majority of capital punishment jurisdictions allow capital felons to invite their own personal spiritual advisors to be present at executions. These jurisdictions vary on the number of personal spiritual advisors that may be in attendance. Ten jurisdictions limit personal spiritual advisor representation to one.[23] Seven jurisdictions set the number at two.[24] Eight jurisdictions do not have a statutory limit.[25]

Physician Representation

The question of whether an execution is successful, i.e., is the capital felon dead, is important. For the majority of capital punishment jurisdictions the question is answered by a physician.[26]

Physician representation at executions vary.[27] Some jurisdictions limit that representation to one.[28] A few jurisdictions set the limit at two,[29] while others allow three physicians to be in attendance.[30] Finally, a few jurisdictions do not have a statutory limit.[31]

Age Restrictions

A minority of capital punishment jurisdictions provide statutory restrictions on the age of persons allowed to attend executions. Five jurisdictions provide that no "minors" are to be in attendance.[32] Two jurisdictions restrict attendance to persons 21 or over.[33]

Other Witnesses

All executions are attended by correctional commissioners or wardens (or their respective designated representatives), executioners, limited security personnel and, of course, the capital felon scheduled for execution. Statutes round out execution witnesses with a limited number of other individuals.

Capital felon's counsel. A minority of capital punishment jurisdictions allow legal counsel for a capital felon to attend the execution.[34]

Attorney general. The statutes in seven capital punishment jurisdictions allow the jurisdiction's attorney general to attend executions.[35]

Prosecutor. Four capital punishment jurisdictions allow the prosecutor responsible for bringing about the capital felon's conviction and sentence to attend the execution.[36]

Judge. It is provided in the statutes of three capital punishment jurisdictions that the judge who presided over the capital felon's case may attend the execution.[37]

Court clerk. New Hampshire is the only jurisdiction that allows the clerk of the court wherein the capital felon was convicted and sentenced to attend the execution.

24

Execution Methods
and Corpse Disposal

Under the common law a sentence of death was permitted to be carried out in a variety of painful and torturous ways, e.g., decapitation, quartering and burning. The Eighth Amendment of the Constitution has been used to bar methods of execution that involve torture or great pain and suffering.

This chapter offers a review of the five methods of execution utilized by capital punishment jurisdictions: (1) firing squad; (2) hanging; (3) lethal injection; (4) electrocution; and (5) lethal gas. The chapter will conclude with a review of execution preparation protocols and a look at how death penalty statutes provide for disposal of the corpses of executed felons.

TABLE 24.0 METHODS OF EXECUTION
USED DURING THE PERIOD 1977–2010

Method of Execution	Number of Executions
Firing squad	3
Hanging	3
Lethal gas	11
Electrocution	147
Lethal injection	1,060

SOURCE: U.S. Department of Justice, Bureau of Justice Statistics, Corrections, Capital Punishment, Table 10 (2011).

Execution Option Jurisdictions

As a preliminary to the individual treatment of death penalty methods, some discussion is in order regarding execution option jurisdictions. The phrase "execution option jurisdictions" refers to capital punishment jurisdictions that have statutes which provide for alternative methods of execution. The jurisdictions providing for more than one method of execution do so for a variety of reasons, including: (1) give inmate an option[1]; (2) use alternative if primary method found unconstitutional or if necessary for any reason[2]; (3) option for inmate sentenced before a certain date[3]; (4) option for inmate committing crime before a certain date.[4]

TABLE 24.1 NUMBER OF EXECUTIONS, U.S. 1990–2010

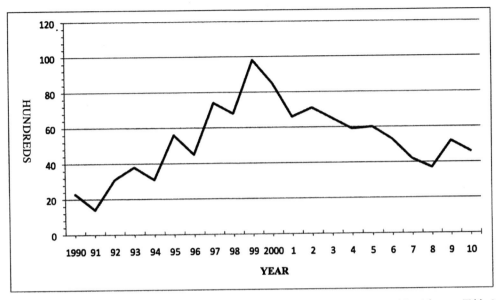

SOURCE: U.S. Department of Justice, Bureau of Justice Statistics, Corrections, Capital Punishment, Table 9 (2011).

TABLE 24.2 EXECUTION METHODS USED BY JURISDICTIONS

Jurisdiction	Lethal Injection	Electrocution	Hanging	Lethal Gas	Firing Squad
Alabama	X	X[1]			
Arizona	X			X[7]	
Arkansas	X	X[2]			
California	X			X[1]	
Colorado	X				
Delaware	X		X[2]		
Florida	X	X[1]			
Georgia	X				
Idaho	X				
Indiana	X				
Kansas	X				
Kentucky	X	X[4]			
Louisiana	X				
Mississippi	X				
Missouri	X			X[1]	
Montana	X				
Nebraska	X				
Nevada	X				
New Hampshire	X		X[3]		
North Carolina	X				
Ohio	X				
Oklahoma	X	X[2]			X[2]
Oregon	X				
Pennsylvania	X				
South Carolina	X	X[1]			
South Dakota	X				

Jurisdiction	Lethal Injection	Electrocution	Hanging	Lethal Gas	Firing Squad
Tennessee	X	X[5]			
Texas	X				
Utah	X				X[6]
Virginia	X	X[1]			
Washington	X		X[1]		
Wyoming	X			X[2]	
Federal System	X				

[1]Inmate's option. [2]Used if alternative method found unconstitutional. [3]If necessary for any reason. [4]Option for inmate sentenced before March 31, 1998. [5]Option for inmate committing crime before January 1, 1999. [6]Option for inmate sentenced before May 3, 2004, and used if alternative method found unconstitutional. [7]Option for inmate sentenced before November 23, 1992.

Executioner

Under modern capital punishment the role of the executioner varies with the method of execution used and the jurisdiction employing the method. For example, lethal injection involves injecting two or three (depending on the jurisdiction) chemicals in a condemned prisoner. Some jurisdictions employ a single person to perform the task, while others use a different person to inject each chemical.

The statutes in most jurisdictions require specially selected and trained correction officers to carry out the death penalty. However, prior to the year 2000, when Florida used only the electric chair to carry out the death penalty, its laws required a private individual be employed to carry out executions. Florida paid the executioner $150 for each execution.

The identity of capital punishment executioners is not made public for security reasons. Several challenges have been made by capital felons seeking to learn the identity of executioners. However, courts have been consistent in holding that capital felons do not have a constitutional right to know the identity of their executioners.

Prior to the shroud of secrecy engulfing executioners under modern capital punishment, executioners enjoyed some notoriety (albeit mostly negative). Robert G. Elliott was one of the most well-known executioners. In addition to executing 357 prisoners, Elliott performed the unusual feat of executing six prisoners by electrocution on the same day. He executed three prisoners in New York and three prisoners in Massachusetts.

One of the more tragic tales of executioners was that of John Hurlbert. He was the executioner at New York's Sing Sing Prison during the 1920s. Hurlbert executed over 120 prisoners in the electric chair at Sing Sing. The pressures of constantly executing prisoners took a toll. Hulbert unexpectedly resigned his job as executioner in 1926. Three years later, the depression that had engulfed him drove to him to commit suicide in the basement of his home.

Expiration of Execution Date

Generally statutes establish the time in which an execution should be carried out. However, under modern capital punishment law, an execution will rarely be carried out during a time period fixed by statute, because defendants usually file numerous appeals. The Supreme Court held in the case of *In re Cross*, 146 U.S. 271 (1892), that when an execution is not carried out in the time required by statute because of appeals by a defendant, the Constitution is not violated because the execution occurs outside the time set out by statute.

Execution by Firing Squad

Death by firing squad is traced to military tradition. Mutiny and desertion were among the offenses that the military punished with death by firing squad. The common law did not accept or reject execution by firing squad. Common law judges simply never resorted to this method of execution.

The exact date that execution by firing squad was adopted by civilian law in the United States is uncertain. Records reflect, however, that by the 1850s death by firing squad was a part of civilian law in the nation.

The most publicized firing squad execution in the last half of the twentieth century was the January 17, 1977, execution of Gary Gilmore by the state of Utah.[5] Gilmore was executed for having killed Ben Bushnell and Max Jensen. Two issues made Gilmore's execution noteworthy. First, Gilmore refused to appeal his conviction. However, his attorneys filed a state court appeal without his permission. Gilmore demanded the appeal be withdrawn. The appeal eventually reached the United States Supreme Court in the name of Gilmore's mother, who sought to halt his execution. The Supreme Court refused to stay the execution and denied the appeal in a memorandum opinion. However, a separate opinion was written by Chief Justice Warren Burger. In *Gilmore v. Utah*, 429 U.S. 238 (1972), Chief Justice Burger summed up the matter as follows:

> This case may be unique in the annals of the Court. Not only does Gary Mark Gilmore request no relief himself, but on the contrary he has expressly and repeatedly stated since his conviction in the Utah courts that he had received a fair trial and had been well treated by the Utah authorities. Nor does he claim to be innocent of the crime for which he was convicted. Indeed, his only complaint against Utah or its judicial process ... has been with respect to the delay on the part of the State in carrying out the sentence.

The second issue making Gilmore's case significant was the fact that the constitutionality of Utah's death penalty statute was still not determined. Utah had enacted a new death penalty statute in response to the moratorium placed on capital punishment by *Furman v. Georgia*, 408 U.S. 238 (1972). Although the Supreme Court had approved of lifting the moratorium in *Gregg v. Georgia*, 428 U.S. 153 (1976), no express determination had been made about the validity of Utah's new death penalty statute at the time of Gilmore's prosecution. Chief Justice Burger explained the problem in *Gilmore* as follows:

> [Gilmore's attorneys] informed the trial court that they had advised Gilmore ... that the constitutionality of the Utah death penalty statute had not yet been reviewed by either the Utah Supreme Court or the United States Supreme Court, and that in their view there was a chance that the statute would eventually be held unconstitutional. The trial court itself advised Gilmore ... that the constitutional issue had not yet been resolved, and that both counsel for the State and Gilmore's own counsel would attempt to expedite an appeal to avoid unnecessary delay. Gilmore stated that he did not "care to languish in prison for another day," that the decision was his own....[6]

Firing Squad Jurisdictions

Only two capital punishment jurisdictions, Utah and Oklahoma, allow execution by firing squad. In Utah the firing squad is an option for inmates sentenced before a specific date; the firing squad is also designated for use in the event the state's primary method of execution is found unconstitutional. Oklahoma provides for the use of a firing squad in the event that its other two designated methods of execution are found unconstitutional.

Constitutionality of Firing Squad

The constitutionality of execution by firing squad was answered by the United States Supreme Court in *Wilkerson v. Utah*, 99 U.S. 130 (1878). In *Wilkerson* the Supreme Court held that "[c]ruel and unusual punishments are forbidden by the Constitution, but the ... punishment of shooting as a mode of executing the death penalty ... is included in that category[.]" The decision in *Wilkerson* has stood unassailable for over 120 years. A major criticism of death by firing squad is that death is slow. A capital felon executed by firing squad literally has to bleed to death while in agony from the wounds.[7]

Firing Squad Protocol

The general procedure for carrying out death by firing squad involves the use of a multiple-person firing squad. The members of the firing squad use rifles (pistols have been known to be used), some of which have blanks. The use of blanks is done so that the firing squad team will not know who actually killed the prisoner.

The execution is carried out on prison grounds in an area not accessible to view by other prisoners or the public. The prisoner is strapped to a chair facing the firing squad. A hood is placed over the prisoner's head. A circular target is placed on the torso of the prisoner. A designated official gives a synchronized count, while the firing squad takes aim thirty to forty feet away from the prisoner. When the designated official shouts "Fire," the prisoner is put to death.

Utah Firing Squad Protocol

Firing Squad Team: Prior to any execution, executioners, Death Watch teams, tie-down teams, and escorts are selected and trained and rehearsals are conducted.

The firing squad is composed of six members. One of these members is the squad leader. The members of the firing squad are certified police officers selected from a list supplied by a law enforcement agency and are chosen by the executive director of the department or his designee. The weapons used are 30–30 caliber rifles. No special ammunition is used. The weapons are owned by the law enforcement agency where the squad member is employed and are serviced and maintained by that agency. Service on the firing squad is voluntary. The executive director and the warden are ultimately responsible for the execution team. The firing squad is compensated at the discretion of the executive director.

Execution: At the appropriate time, the condemned offender is led to the execution area or chamber, which is used for both lethal injection and firing squad executions. The offender is placed in a specially designed chair which has a pan beneath it to catch and conceal blood and other fluids. Restraints are applied to the offender's arms, legs, chest and head. A head restraint is applied loosely around the offender's neck to hold his neck and head in an upright position. The offender is dressed in a dark blue outfit with a white cloth circle attached by Velcro to the area over the offender's heart. Behind the offender are sandbags to absorb the volley and prevent ricochets. Dark sheets are draped over the sandbags.

When the offender is restrained, the warden asks the offender if he has any last statement to make. Following the offender's statement, a hood is placed over the offender's head. The warden leaves the room.

The firing squad members stand in the firing position. They support their rifles on the platform rests. With their rifle barrels in the firing ports, the team members sight through open sights on the white cloth circle on the offender's chest. On the command to fire, the squad fires simultaneously. One squad member has a blank charge in his weapon but no member knows which member is designated to receive this blank charge. Shortly after the shots are fired, death is determined. A physician and medical personnel from the Utah Department of Corrections stand right outside the execution area while the execution is taking place.

The estimated average length of time that elapses from the time that the offender is restrained to the time that death is determined is eight to ten minutes.

Execution by Hanging

The common law accepted death by hanging as a legitimate method of execution.[8] Hanging has also been a traditional part of Anglo-American jurisprudence as a result of its common law lineage. The American colonists used hanging as a form of punishment and the practice continued after the American Revolution.

Hanging Jurisdictions

Only three capital punishment jurisdictions employ hanging as a method of execution. One jurisdiction, Washington, provides hanging as an option for all capital felons. Another jurisdiction, Delaware, designated hanging as the method of execution in the event its primary method is found unconstitutional. The third jurisdiction, New Hampshire, utilizes hanging in the event its primary method of execution cannot be used for any reason.

Constitutionality of Hanging

The constitutionality of execution by hanging was addressed in dicta by the United States Supreme Court in *Wilkerson v. Utah*, 99 U.S. 130 (1878). The decision in *Wilkerson* was directly concerned with the constitutionality of death by firing squad. However, the Supreme Court discussed hanging by analogy as a constitutionally acceptable method of execution. In the decision of *Campbell v. Wood*, 18 F.3d 662 (1994), it was indicated on the merits that hanging did not violate the Constitution. However, in *Rupe v. Wood*, 863 F.Supp. 1307 (W.D.Wash. 1994), a federal district judge held that the state of Washington's use of hanging was unconstitutional, as a method of execution for the defendant in that case, because there was a substantial likelihood that he would be decapitated if hung, due to his weight (in excess of 400 pounds). In response to the decision in *Rupe*, Washington adopted lethal injection as a death penalty option.[9]

Two principal arguments are waged in opposition to hanging as a method of execution.[10] First, there is a risk that death will occur as a result of asphyxiation. This will happen if the execution is not properly done. Death by asphyxiation is slow and painful. As a result of the risk of asphyxiation and its attendant slow and agonizing pain, it is argued by some commentators that hanging should be prohibited as a method of execution.[11]

The second, and most profound, argument against hanging is that there is a risk of decapitation. If the hanging is done improperly the head of a capital felon could be torn from its trunk during the process. While decapitation was accepted and practiced under the common law as a method of execution, it has not been accepted by Anglo-American jurisprudence. Anti-hanging proponents contend that because of the risk of decapitation, hanging should not be used as a method of execution.[12]

Hanging Protocol

Hanging has evolved as a method of execution. The early gallows are not like those used today. In the past the gallows was nothing more than a large tree from which the condemned prisoner was hanged. In time the tree was replaced by an outdoor scaffold from which the condemned prisoner would be dropped.

Under modern capital punishment hanging is now performed inside of a prison building. A special room with a trapdoor and a ceiling fixture for a rope is used. The condemned prisoner is positioned on the trapdoor. The legs and arms of the condemned are fastened by restraints, and a hood placed over his or her head. If necessary (when a condemned has fainted), a metal frame is used to hold the condemned prisoner's body erect. A rope is lowered from the ceiling and placed around the condemned prisoner's neck. A button is then pushed to release the trapdoor and the condemned prisoner is dropped to his or her death.

When done correctly, the force of the drop and the stop caused by the length of the rope breaks the bones in the capital felon's neck and severs the spinal cord, causing him or her to go into shock and be rendered unconscious. At this point the capital felon strangles to death.

In carrying out a hanging the force of the drop is critical. The weight of the capital felon determines the force of the drop. Generally, the heavier the person is, the shorter the drop; and the lighter the person, the longer the drop. A drop that is of too short a distance will result in the spinal cord not being severed and, in turn, the capital felon will not go into shock and will be conscious during the strangulation period. A drop that is too long a distance will result in decapitation.

Washington Hanging Protocol

Execution Team: Washington does not have a designated "hangman" or executioner. The superintendent will appoint and provide a briefing to those individuals selected to implement the execution. No individual is required to participate in any part of the execution procedure. One member of the execution team pushes the button that releases the trap door.

Equipment Preparation: Prior to the execution, the gallows area trap door and release mechanisms are inspected for proper operation, and a determination of the proper amount of the drop of the condemned offender through the trap door is calculated using a standard military execution chart for hanging. The rope, which is of manila hemp of at least three-quarters of an inch and not more than one-and-one-quarter inch in diameter and approximately 30 feet in length, is soaked and then stretched while drying to eliminate any spring, stiffness, or tendency to coil. The hangman's knot, which is tied pursuant to military regulations, is treated with wax, soap, or clear oil to ensure that the rope slides smoothly through the knot. The end of the rope which does not contain the noose is tied to a grommet in the ceiling and then is tied off to a metal T-shaped bracket, which takes the force delivered by the offender's drop.

Examination of Inmate Prior to Execution: Prior to an execution, the condemned offender's file is reviewed to determine if there are any unusual characteristics the offender possesses that might warrant deviation from field instructions on hanging. If needed, a physical examination is conducted on the offender to determine if any special problems exist like obesity or deterioration of the bone or musculature structure that may affect the execution process. At this examination, the offender's height and weight are measured. Based upon this review of the offender's medical files and examination, the superintendent may consult with appropriate experts to determine whether deviation from policy is advisable to ensure a swift and humane death. For example, the offender may need a shoulder brace or have only one arm.

Execution: At the appropriate time on execution day, the condemned offender, in restraints, is escorted to the gallows area and is placed standing over a hinged trap door from which the offender will be dropped. Following the offender's last statement, a hood is placed over the offender's head. The hood is fashioned to have a rough outer surface of material and is split at the open end so that it comes well down over the offender's chest and back. Restraints are also applied. If the offender refuses to stand or cannot stand, he is placed on a collapse board. The noose is placed snugly around the offender's neck in such a manner that the knot is directly behind the offender's left ear.

Upon direction from the superintendent, a member of the execution team pushes a button that mechanically releases the trap door. The offender drops through the trap door. Escorts then move to the lower floor location to assist in the removal of the offender's body. After an appropriate time, the superintendent calls for the physician to make the pronouncement of death.

Execution by Lethal Injection

Lethal injection, as a method of execution, was not known to the common law. In the decision of *Ex Parte Granviel*, 561 S.W.2d 503 (Tex.Cr.App. 1978), the court noted that "[t]he intravenous injection of a lethal substance as a means of execution has not been heretofore utilized in this nation[.]" Injection of deadly chemicals into the bloodstream of a capital felon represents a new method of execution. Lethal injection, as this new method is called, is a child of the 1970s.

Oklahoma was the first jurisdiction to provide by statute for execution by lethal injection. It did so on May 10, 1977. The first state to actually execute a prisoner by lethal injection was Texas. It did so on December 7, 1982, when Charlie Brooks became the first inmate to die by this method.

Lethal Injection Jurisdictions

Lethal injection is provided as a method of execution in every capital punishment jurisdiction. The statutes in seven of those jurisdictions—Alabama, California, Florida, Missouri, South Carolina, Virginia, and Washington—provide for lethal injection as an option for all capital felons. Nine jurisdictions—Arizona, Arkansas, Delaware, Kentucky, New Hampshire, Oklahoma, Tennessee, Utah, and Wyoming—set out alternative methods of execution that are triggered upon the occurrence of a specific event. The remaining lethal injection jurisdictions utilize this method exclusively. The statutes set out below illustrate how jurisdictions provide for the infliction of lethal injection.

Colorado Revised Code §§ 18-1.3-1202 and 18-1.3-1204
The manner of inflicting the punishment of death shall be by the administration of a lethal injection.... For the purposes of this part ... "lethal injection" means a continuous intravenous

injection of a lethal quantity of sodium thiopental or other equally or more effective substance sufficient to cause death....

The execution shall be performed in the room or place by a person selected by the executive director and trained to administer intravenous injections. Death shall be pronounced by a licensed physician or a coroner according to accepted medical standards.

Oregon Code § 137.473

(1) The punishment of death shall be inflicted by the intravenous administration of a lethal quantity of an ultra-short-acting barbiturate in combination with a chemical paralytic agent and potassium chloride or other equally effective substances sufficient to cause death....

(2) The person who administers the lethal injection ... shall not thereby be considered to be engaged in the practice of medicine.

South Dakota Code § 23A-27A-32

The punishment of death shall be inflicted by the intravenous injection of a substance or substances in a lethal quantity. The warden ... shall determine the substances and the quantity of substances used for the punishment of death. An execution carried out by intravenous injection shall be performed by persons trained to administer the injection who are selected by the warden and approved by the secretary of corrections. The persons administering the intravenous injection need not be physicians, registered nurses, licensed practical nurses, or other medical professionals licensed or registered under the laws of this or any other state. Any infliction of the punishment of death by intravenous injection of a substance or substances in the manner required by this section may not be construed to be the practice of medicine.

Two issues need to be highlighted regarding the above statutes. First, none of the statutes require that a medical professional administer the lethal drug. This issue has been a source of litigation by capital felons, who contend that the use of non-medical professionals increases the risk that death will be slow and agonizing.[13]

A second matter involves the absence of a named ultra-short-acting barbiturate in the Oregon and South Dakota statutes. The Colorado statute designates (as an option) sodium thiopental as the lethal drug of choice. The majority of lethal injection jurisdictions follow Oregon and South Dakota in failing to name a specific lethal drug. This issue was litigated in *Ex Parte Granviel*, 561 S.W.2d 503 (Tex.Cr.App. 1978), where the defendant contended that failure to name a specific lethal drug made the death penalty statute vague and therefore constitutionally void. The defendant's position and the state's responses were set out in *Granviel* as follows:

[The defendant] argues it cannot be ascertained from the statute what substance or substances can be used in the injection and that the statute fails to offer any hint as to which substance or substances would be permissible. The State points out that the ... electrocution statutes throughout the United States have not prescribed the use of a chair, the amount of voltage, the volume of amperage, the place of attachment of electrodes, or whether or not AC or DC current shall be used. The earlier hanging statutes did not, the State argues, prescribe the type of gallows, the height of the fall, the type of rope or type of knot used, etc. Likewise, the State says, the laws relating to execution by firing squads did not specify the number of executioners, the muzzle velocity of the rifles, the type of bullets, or the distance of the guns to the condemned. The State urges the earlier execution statutes were never in any greater detail than the statute under attack and that none of them had been declared unconstitutional on the basis of being vague.

The *Granviel* court rejected the defendant's vagueness challenge and held:

While neither the exact substance to be injected nor the procedure surrounding the execution is expressly set forth in [the statute] we cannot conclude that failure to specify the exact substances and the procedure to be used render the statute unconstitutionally vague. The statute here, unlike penal statutes, was not intended to give fair notice of what specific behavior ... constitutes a criminal offense.... The context of the statute is a public statement of the general manner of execution. In this sense the statute is sufficiently definite....

So long as the statute is sufficiently complete to accomplish the regulation of the particular matters falling within the Legislature's jurisdiction, the matters of detail that are reasonably necessary for the ultimate application, operation and enforcement of the law may be expressly delegated to the authority charged with the administration of the statute.

The position of the *Granviel* court was not that the issue of the type of lethal drug used was irrelevant. The opinion acknowledged that the issue of the drug of choice was highly relevant and important. However, the court believed that the drug of choice was a matter that could be delegated to administrative officials to determine.

Constitutionality of Lethal Injection

Lethal injection was devised as a method of execution because it is believed to be the most humane method of executing inmates. However, lethal injection has been criticized on various fronts as being an unacceptable method of execution.[14] It has been argued that utilizing a needle to interject death can be painful and necessitate surgery to impart the needle.[15] When death comes slow, it is contended that capital felons endure psychological trauma and in some instances physical pain.

Capital felons have also attacked the constitutionality of the drugs used in carrying out lethal injection. One argument made is that the drugs used in lethal injection have not been approved by the Federal Food and Drug Administration for the purpose in which they are being used. This issue was litigated in the United States Supreme Court in the case of *Heckler v. Chaney*, 470 U.S. 821 (1985). The Supreme Court rejected the challenge on procedural grounds, thereby keeping the debate alive. In two subsequent cases, *Hill v. McDonough*, 126 S.Ct. 2096 (2006), and *Nelson v. Campbell*, 541 U.S. 637 (2004), the Supreme Court allowed inmates to challenge the constitutionality of lethal injection in lower courts.

In response to *Hill* and *Nelson*, a capital felon in *Harbison v. Little*, 511 F.Supp. 872 (M.D. Tenn. 2007), was able to get a federal judge to declare Tennessee's lethal injection protocol unconstitutional. The decision in *Harbison* was reversed on appeal in *Harbison v. Little*, 571 F.3d 531 (6th Cir. 2009), in response to the United States Supreme Court decision in *Baze v. Rees*, 128 S.Ct. 1520 (2008). In *Baze* the Supreme Court held that the lethal injection protocol used by Kentucky did not violate the Eight Amendment.[16] In doing so the following was said in *Baze*:

Kentucky has adopted a method of execution believed to be the most humane available, one it shares with 35 other States. Petitioners agree that, if administered as intended, that procedure will result in a painless death. The risks of maladministration they have suggested — such as improper mixing of chemicals and improper setting of IVs by trained and experienced personnel — cannot remotely be characterized as "objectively intolerable." Kentucky's decision to adhere to its protocol despite these asserted risks, while adopting safeguards to protect against them, cannot be viewed as probative of the wanton infliction of pain under the Eighth Amendment. Finally, the alternative that petitioners belatedly propose has problems of its own, and has never been tried by a single State.

Throughout our history, whenever a method of execution has been challenged in this Court as cruel and unusual, the Court has rejected the challenge. Our society has nonetheless steadily moved to more humane methods of carrying out capital punishment. The firing squad, hanging, the electric chair, and the gas chamber have each in turn given way to more humane methods, culminating in today's consensus on lethal injection. The broad framework of the Eighth Amendment has accommodated this progress toward more humane methods of execution, and our approval of a particular method in the past has not precluded legislatures from taking the steps they deem appropriate, in light of new developments, to ensure humane capital punishment. There is no reason to suppose that today's decision will be any different.

Although the decision in *Baze* found Kentucky's lethal injection protocol constitutional, it did not close the door completely to further legal challenges to lethal injection.

In the case of *Hobbs v. Jones*, 2012 Ark. 291 (2012), the Arkansas supreme court found that state's lethal injection protocol violated the state's constitution.

Lethal Injection Protocol

An inmate executed by lethal injection is brought into the execution chamber a few minutes prior to the appointed time of execution. The inmate is placed on a gurney and his or her wrists and ankles are then strapped to the gurney. Cardiac monitor leads and a stethoscope are attached. Two sets of intravenous tubes are then inserted in each arm. Three commonly used drugs include sodium pentothal (a sedative intended to put the inmate to sleep); pavulon (stops breathing and paralyzes the muscular system); and potassium chloride (causes the heart to stop). The sodium pentothal is injected first to put the inmate into a deep sleep. When the inmate is in a sedate mode, the other drugs are introduced into his or her body. (Some jurisdictions use a one-drug protocol.) When done properly death by lethal injection is not painful and the inmate goes to sleep prior to the fatal effects of the pavulon and potassium chloride.

Colorado Lethal Injection Protocol

After exhausting all mandatory appeals and other remedies, the sentencing judge will issue an execution warrant and [determine] a week during which the execution shall be carried out. The following is a breakdown of execution day:

- An approved spiritual advisor will meet with the inmate to assist the inmate in preparation for the execution. The inmate may elect to have the spiritual advisor present during the execution.
- The last meal will be served at normal meal time. The meal will consist of anything within reason that is stocked by the Food Service Department.
- The inmate will be offered the opportunity to shower and dress in clean clothes one and one-half hours prior to the scheduled execution time.
- Following the shower, the inmate will be dressed in green uniform pants, a green button-up front shirt, socks, and shoes.
- Thirty minutes prior to the scheduled execution time, the strap down team will remove the inmate from the holding cell and strap the inmate to the execution bed.
- Twenty minutes prior to the scheduled execution time or when instructed by the Warden, the IV team will insert two intravenous catheters into appropriate veins in the inmate's arms, one to deliver the lethal agents and the other to serve as a back-up in the event of injection failure into the primary catheter.
- The warden will read the execution warrant to the inmate.
- Approximately 8 minutes prior to the scheduled execution time, a select group of

witnesses, usually comprised of the victim's family, the prosecuting and defense attorneys, an official from the investigating law enforcement agency, and approved media representatives, are escorted to the witness viewing room.

- The warden will disconnect the telephone in the execution room after receiving the order from the governor and executive director to proceed with the execution. The witness viewing window curtain will then be opened.
- The warden will verify that the witness room curtain is open, enter the enclosed chemical room, and instruct the injection team, comprised of two anonymous DOC staff, to proceed with the injections.
- The injection team shall administer the chemical agents according to the department's lethal injection procedures, which provides the delivery of a lethal solution of sodium pentothol, pancuronium bromide, and potassium chloride. A saline solution is injected following each chemical injection. Anonymity is achieved in the execution process by requiring the injection team members to alternate in rendering each injection and by marking the chemical bottles by number only.
- Two minutes after the chemical agents are injected, the warden will ask the coroner to enter the room, examine the inmate, and pronounce death and the time.
- Immediately after the execution and pronouncement of death, the witness room curtain will be closed and the witnesses escorted from the viewing area to the lobby where they will sign the Record of Execution book.
- The media witnesses will then be transported as a group to the media area [where] they will brief the other media members.

Execution by Electrocution

The use of electricity to execute the death penalty dates back to the late nineteenth century. On January 6, 1885, the governor of New York gave the annual *State of the State Address* to the New York legislature. The governor made the following observation and suggestion: "The present mode of executing criminals by hanging has come down to us from the dark ages, and it may well be questioned whether the science of the present day cannot provide a means for taking the life of such as are condemned to die in a less barbarous manner. I commend this suggestion to the consideration of the legislature." As a result of prompting by the governor, the legislature assembled a commission to determine "the most humane and practical method known to modern science of carrying into effect the sentence of death in capital cases."

The New York commission evaluated several possible methods of execution, including lethal injection. Eventually the commission was persuaded by Thomas Edison's proposal to use DC current as the most efficient method for execution. The commission reported back that execution by electricity was the most humane method of imposing the death penalty. The New York legislature heeded the advice and in 1888 signed into law the first electrocution death penalty statute. The statute by its terms went into effect January 1, 1889.[17] One year later, on August 6, 1890, William Kemmler became the first person executed by electrocution when New York executed him for the crime of murder.

Electrocution Jurisdictions

A total of eight capital punishment jurisdictions permit electrocution to be used as a method of execution. Four of those jurisdictions—Alabama, Florida, South Carolina, and Virginia—provide electrocution as an option for all capital felons. Two jurisdictions, Arkansas and Oklahoma, utilize electrocution if their primary method of execution is ever found unconstitutional. Kentucky utilizes electrocution as an option for inmates sentenced prior to a specific date. Tennessee permits electrocution for inmates who committed their crime before a specific date.[18]

Constitutionality of Electrocution

The constitutionality of execution by electrocution was answered by the United States Supreme Court in *In re Kemmler*, 136 U.S. 436 (1890). In *Kemmler* the Supreme Court held that death by electrocution did not violate the federal Constitution. The decision in *Kemmler* has withstood countless challenges for over one hundred years.[19]

The two major criticisms of death by electrocution are that death is slow and the punishment disfigures the victim.[20] Both criticisms stem from executions that are not carried out properly. When done correctly, death by electrocution is relatively quick and disfigurement minimal. However, when problems arise, such as too much electrical current or not enough electrical current, the victim will suffer needlessly.[21]

Electrocution Protocol

The electric chair apparatus consists of a wooden chair, attached leg electrodes, a leather and sponge helmet with electrode, a drip pan, a Plexiglas seat and a non-incremental restraint system. The chair is connected to an electrical power supply. The leg electrodes, which are fabricated onto the leg stock, are composed of solid brass. The helmet consists of an outer helmet of leather and an inner helmet of copper mesh and sponge. The chair design includes a removable drip pan. The straps used include two ankle straps, two wrist straps and one chest harness.

The condemned inmate will be led to the chair and strapped in. One of the leg electrodes will be attached to a shaved leg. The helmet will be attached to the head (a leather strap may also be fastened to the condemned inmate's face). A hood will then be placed over the head of the condemned. The actual switch used ranges from a lever, switch or a three button system where three people will push each button (only one of them will push the real button). The condemned inmate will be given two sequences of electrical shocks. The initial voltage of electricity will be not less than 2200 volts for ten seconds; a five second interval must occur; followed by 750 volts or more for 22 seconds. The process is then repeated once. Actual voltage used is calculated by the weight of the condemned inmate. The heavier the inmate, the more voltage required. If the initial sequence is performed correctly, a physician will examine the condemned to proclaim him or her as heart dead.

Florida Electrocution Protocol

Testing the Chair: Prior to each execution, the execution equipment is tested. Additionally, testing of the execution equipment is performed a minimum of eight times each year. A "mock" execution is performed prior to each actual execution.

Phone Line Communication: At the direction of the superintendent, all calls are forwarded to the execution chamber from the governor's office through a switchboard extension. Should institutional telephone lines fail at any time during the process, the switchboard operator immediately advises the Command Center, which is located within hearing range of the switchboard operator. Telephones in the execution chamber are checked. Staff also ensures that a fully-charged cellular telephone is in the execution chamber. Sample telephone calls are placed to each telephone to ensure proper operation. The public address system is also checked to ensure its proper operation.

Staff establishes telephone communication with the governor's office on behalf of the superintendent. This phone line remains open during the entire execution proceeding.

Preparing Inmate: Staff at Florida State Prison supervises the shaving of the crown of the condemned offender's head and the offender's right leg from the knee to the ankle.

The offender is escorted to the shower area. Following the shower, the offender is returned to his assigned cell and issued underwear, a pair of trousers, a dress shirt or blouse (as appropriate) and socks. The offender wears no shoes. A suit coat is not worn by the offender during the execution but is placed on the offender's body after the execution proceedings.

Staff ensures that a salt-free, hypoallergenic, electrically-conducive gel is applied to the crown of the offender's shaven head and the calf of the offender's right leg in a total application of approximately 4 ounces.

Just prior to the execution, the superintendent reads the death warrant to the offender and the offender is allowed to make a last statement.

Staff applies restraints to the offender for escort into the execution chamber. Prior to the offender being escorted, security arrangements have been made for his movement from his Q-wing cell to the execution chamber in compliance with a schedule set by the superintendent. At the offender's request and subject to the approval of the superintendent or assistant superintendent, the chaplain may accompany the offender to the execution chamber. The time is recorded when the offender enters the chamber.

Execution: The offender enters the execution chamber and is placed in the electric chair. The chair is constructed of oak and is set on a rubber matting and bolted to a concrete floor. Lap, chest, arm, and forearm straps are secured. When the straps are secured, the restraints are removed and ankle straps are secured. A leg piece (anklet) is laced to the offender's right calf and a sponge and electrode is attached. Staff ensures that the sponge covers all areas of the electrode to prevent any contact of the electrode with the offender's skin, and also ensures that the sponge is sufficiently wet (slightly dripping). The headpiece is secured. The headgear consists of a metal headpiece covered with a leather hood which conceals the offender's face. The metal part of the headpiece consists of a copper wire mesh screen to which the electrode is brazened. A wet sponge is placed between the electrode and the offender's scalp. Excess saline solution from the sponge is dried with a clean towel. During the execution, two Department of Corrections staff members are posted in the execution chamber to ensure that the offender is seated and that the electrocution equipment is properly connected.

A staff member then proceeds to the outside open telephone line to inquire of any possible stays of execution. If there are no stays, the execution proceeds.

The safety switch is closed. The circuit breaker is engaged. The execution control panel is activated. The executioner is signaled either verbally or by gesture to engage the execution switch and the automatic cycle begins. While the automatic cycle has five cycles, only three are used. The automatic cycle begins with the programmed 2,300 volts (9.5 amps) for eight seconds, followed by 1,000 volts (4 amps) for 22 seconds, followed by 2,300 volts (9.5 amps) for eight seconds. When the cycle is complete, the electrician indicates that the current is off. Equipment is disconnected. The manual circuit behind the chair is disengaged. The safety switch is opened. The time in which the execution switch is disengaged is recorded.

Two minutes after the electrical current ceases, the physician examines the offender's body for vital signs. The physician pronounces the offender's death and the time of death. The estimated average length of time that elapses from the time the offender is restrained to the time that death is determined is 10 minutes. The physician signs the death certificate, and the physician and physician's assistant ensure that the proper documents are recorded. If the offender is not pronounced dead, the execution cycle is then ordered to be repeated.

Post-Execution: The governor is notified via the open phone line that the sentence has been carried out and that the offender has been pronounced dead. There is another announcement to the official witnesses and the media that the sentence has been carried out. Then, the witnesses and media are directed to exit the witness room. The official witnesses, except for the designated inspector general (IG) witness, and the media pool are escorted from the witness room by designated Department of Corrections escort staff. The designated IG witness remains in the witness room. After all other witnesses have exited the building, the IG designee is allowed entry into the execution chamber for evidence collection. The IG designee is authorized to collect both the head and leg sponges (which are placed in a plastic bag and securely sealed), inspect the execution equipment, make notes, and depart with these materials. If an unusual incident or problem should occur during an execution, the IG designee is also authorized to photograph the narrow and specific electrode contact points.

Staff coordinates the entry of hearse attendants for recovery of the offender's body. The offender is removed from the chair by the hearse attendants who are under supervision. The body is placed on a stretcher and then moved to a hallway outside the execution chamber. The executioner is compensated. A certification of death is obtained from the physician and is delivered to the hearse attendants prior to their departure.

As soon as possible after the execution proceeding, the superintendent forwards the death warrant to the governor indicating that the execution has been carried out and files a copy of the death warrant with the circuit court in which the condemned offender was convicted and sentenced to death. The correctional senior sentence specialist advises Central Records of the condemned offender's name and the date and time of death by execution.

Execution by Lethal Gas

The use of lethal gas as a method of execution is an early twentieth century Anglo-American jurisprudential phenomenon. The chemical agent used to carry out this method of execution is cyanide gas. Arizona was the first jurisdiction to actually have a gas chamber constructed.[22]

Lethal gas was first used by Nevada.[23] The first person to be executed by lethal gas was a condemned Nevada inmate named Gee Jon. He was executed, at age 29, on February 8, 1924. Gee Jon was born in China but spent most of his life in the United States.

Lethal Gas Jurisdictions

Only four capital punishment jurisdictions provide for the use of lethal gas to carry out the death penalty. Two jurisdictions, California and Missouri, utilize lethal gas as an option for all capital felons. One jurisdiction, Arizona, utilizes lethal gas as an option for inmates sentenced before a specific date. The fourth jurisdiction, Wyoming, has designated lethal gas as the method of execution in the event its primary method is found unconstitutional.

Constitutionality of Lethal Gas

Several state appellate courts had, prior to 1983, addressed the issue of whether execution by lethal gas was a cruel and unusual method of punishment. The first such court to do so was the Nevada Supreme Court in the case of *State v. Gee Jon*, 211 P. 676 (Nev. 1923). This case involved two defendants, Gee Jon and Hughie Sing (Sing's sentence was eventually commuted to life imprisonment), who had been convicted and sentenced to death for murder. At the time of their crime, the state of Nevada had but recently changed its method of execution to lethal gas. The defendants challenged the use of lethal gas as cruel and unusual punishment. The court in *Gee Jon* rejected this argument. In doing so the court made the following observations:

> What has been the punishment for centuries for the crime of murder, of the character we know as murder in the first degree? It has been death. For the state to take the life of one who perpetrates a fiendish murder has from time immemorial been recognized as proper. The [statute] in question authorizes the taking of the life of a murderer as a penalty for the crime which he commits. It is the same penalty which has been exacted for ages — sanctioned in the old biblical law of "an eye for an eye and a tooth for a tooth." It is true that the penalty has been inflicted in different ways; for instance, by hanging, by shooting, and by electrocution; but in each case the method used has been to accomplish the same end, the death of the guilty party. Our statute inflicts no new punishment; it is the same old punishment, inflicted in a different manner, and we think it safe to say that in whatever way the death penalty is inflicted it must of necessity be more or less cruel.
>
> But we are not prepared to say that the infliction of the death penalty by the administration of lethal gas would of itself subject the victim to either pain or torture.... For many years animals have been put to death painlessly by the administration of poisonous gas.... No doubt gas may be administered so as to produce intense suffering. It is also true that one may be executed by hanging, shooting, or electrocution in such a bungling fashion as to produce the same result. But this is no argument against execution by either method.
>
> It may be said to be a scientific fact that a painless death may be caused by the administration of lethal gas.[24]

Since 1983, several federal appellate courts have addressed the issue of whether lethal gas is a cruel and unusual punishment. The federal appellate courts are split on this issue. Two appellate courts, *Gray v. Lucas*, 710 F.2d 1048 (5th Cir. 1983), and *Hunt v. Nuth*, 57 F.3d 1327 (4th Cir. 1995), concluded that lethal gas was not cruel and unusual punishment, while the third court, *Fierro v. Gomez*, 77 F.3d 301 (9th Cir. 1996), *reversed*, 117 S.Ct. 285 (1996), came to the opposite conclusion. The United States Supreme Court eventually vacated the court of appeals decision in *Fierro*, however, it did so without any guidance on the issue it reversed. In a terse one paragraph memorandum opinion, the Court vacated the *Fierro* decision and merely remanded the case with instructions that the appellate court reconsider its judgment in light of the fact that the jurisdiction in controversy (California) amended its death penalty statute so that lethal gas would be used only if requested by a capital felon.

Two arguments are offered against the use of lethal gas as a method of execution. First, it is asserted that cyanide gas induces excruciating pain. Capital felons have been known to urinate, defecate, vomit and drool while undergoing death by lethal gas. Second, and the primary threat to continued use of lethal gas, death by this method can take over ten minutes. It is argued that such a span of time amounts to pure torture.

Lethal Gas Protocol

In carrying out death by lethal gas the condemned inmate will have a heart monitor attached to his or her chest prior to the execution. The inmate is then led into the gas chamber where he or she is strapped into a large chair. The chair used will have holes in it to permit the gas to flow upwards. The gas chamber itself is airtight and has windows so the witnesses can view the execution. The heart monitor is attached to an outside monitoring station so that the attending physician can declare the inmate dead.

Prison officials will place sulfuric acid in a large bowl below the inmate's chair. A small container of potassium cyanide is placed upon the sulfuric acid bowl. A switch located outside the gas chamber is used to empty the cyanide container into the bowl containing the sulfuric acid.

The effect of the cyanide gas will be to inhibit the body's ability to take in oxygen. The inmate will, in essence, strangle to death. The inmate will feel as if he or she is having a heart attack. Death will usually occur in 6 to 18 minutes.

After the execution ammonia gas will be pumped into the gas chamber to neutralize the cyanide gas. Prison officials wear gas masks when they enter the chamber to remove the body.

Arizona Lethal Gas Protocol

Receipt of Execution Warrant: When an inmate receives a warrant of execution, a schedule is developed for submission of related forms and inmate movement. From 24 to 48 hours prior to the scheduled execution, the inmate under a warrant of execution is transferred to the Death House.

Execution: One pound of sodium-cyanide is placed in a container underneath the gas chamber chair. The chair is made of perforated metal which allows the cyanide gas to pass through and fill the chamber. A bowl below the gas chamber contains sulfuric acid and distilled water. A lever is pulled and the sodium-cyanide falls into the solution, releasing the gas. It takes the prisoner several minutes to die. After the execution, the excess gas is released through an exhaust pipe which extends about 50 feet above Death House.

Return Death Warrant After Execution

One of the last legal technicalities that must be performed when an inmate is executed is that of placing an entry in the court record books that the order of execution was carried out. The statute below outlines the general procedure.

Oregon Code § 137.478

Not later than 30 days after the execution of a sentence of death ... the superintendent of the correctional institution where the sentence was executed shall return the death warrant to the clerk of the trial court from which the warrant was issued with the superintendent's return on the death warrant showing the time, place and manner in which the death warrant was executed.

Disposal of Executed Corpse

The present state of the law protects the corpse of a capital felon. There are five statutorily recognized dispositions for the bodies of executed capital felons.[25] Each disposition follows.

Permit Relatives to Take the Corpse

Twelve capital punishment jurisdictions provide, by statute, that the corpse of an executed felon is to be turned over to a requesting relative.[26] Five of those jurisdictions go so far as to pay the cost of shipping the corpse to a requesting relative, at the last residence of the capital felon.[27]

Permit a Friend to Take the Corpse

The statutes in eight capital punishment jurisdictions provide that the corpse of an executed felon may be turned over to a requesting friend.[28] In this situation the corpse would only be given to a friend of the capital felon if no relative made a request for the corpse.

A Person Designated by the Felon

Currently only two capital punishment jurisdictions provide, by statute, that the corpse of an executed felon may be turned over to a person designated by the capital felon prior to execution.[29] This type of disposal contemplates having the corpse sent to a medical facility for research.

Unclaimed Corpse Donated to Medical Center

The statutes in three capital punishment jurisdictions provide that the corpse of a capital felon may be turned over to a medical center for research.[30] This type of disposal is only triggered if neither relatives nor friends of the capital felon request the corpse.

Unclaimed Corpse Buried by the Jurisdiction

If no claim is made for the corpse of an executed felon, the statutes in eleven capital punishment jurisdictions provide for burial by the jurisdiction.[31] These statutes also provide that the cost of burial is borne by the jurisdiction.

25

Military Death Penalty Laws

The military has its own criminal code and, like some states, it imposes the death penalty for certain crimes. Although the military has its own trial courts and appellate courts, capital punishment prosecutions by the military are reviewable by the Supreme Court and by federal courts in general through habeas corpus proceedings.[1] The material in this chapter provides a limited review of military death penalty laws, including some discussion of the military's attempt to prosecute prisoners on Guantanamo Bay.

Early Development of Military Capital Punishment

From its inception, the United States military has had the power to decree capital punishment during wartime. This authority, however, does not have a long history of being able to prosecute members of the armed forces for capital offenses committed in the United States during peacetime.

In the early history of the nation, the powers of court-martial were fixed in the Articles of War. Congress enacted the first Articles of War in 1789. These placed significant restrictions on court-martial jurisdiction over capital offenses. While the death penalty was authorized for 14 military offenses, the Articles of War followed the English model of requiring the supremacy of civil court jurisdiction over ordinary capital crimes that were not special military offenses. In 1806 Congress debated and rejected a proposal to remove the death penalty from military jurisdiction.[2]

Over the next two centuries, Congress expanded military jurisdiction. In 1863 it granted court-martial jurisdiction to the military of common law capital crimes and the authority to impose the death penalty in wartime. In 1916 Congress granted to the military courts general jurisdiction over common law felonies committed by service members, except for murder and rape committed within the United States during peacetime. Military persons accused of murder or rape had to be turned over to the civilian authorities. In 1950, with the passage of the Uniform Code of Military Justice, Congress lifted the restriction on murder and rape.[3]

Military Capital Punishment Invalidated in Response to Furman v. Georgia

It was not until 1983 that the military confronted a challenge to the constitutionality of the military capital punishment scheme in light of the Supreme Court's 1972 decision in *Furman v. Georgia*, 408 U.S. 238 (1972).[4] In the case of *United States v. Matthews*, 16 M. J. 354 (1983), the military's highest court, the Court of Appeals for the Armed Forces (formerly the Court of Military Appeals), invalidated the military's capital punishment scheme. The court in *Matthews* found that the military's death penalty procedures failed to specifically identify the aggravating factors for which the death penalty could be imposed. In making its ruling, the court indicated that either Congress or the president could remedy the defect and that the new procedures could be applied retroactively.

President Ronald Reagan responded to the decision in *Matthews* on April 13, 1984, and reinstated capital punishment in the military. The president did so with an executive order promulgating the "Manual for Courts-Martial, United States, 1984."[5] The manual, as embodied in the Uniform Code of Military Justice and the Rules of Courts-Martial, reflects some of the concerns expressed by *Furman* in achieving a fair process for imposing capital punishment.[6]

The Loving ruling. A challenge to the reinstatement of the death penalty in the military was presented to the United States Supreme Court in *Loving v. United States*, 517 U.S. 748 (1996).[7]

On December 12, 1988 the defendant in *Loving*, Army Private Dwight Loving, murdered two taxicab drivers from the town of Killeen, Texas. He attempted to murder a third, but the driver disarmed him and escaped. Civilian and Army authorities arrested the defendant the next afternoon. He confessed to the murders and attempted murder. The defendant was prosecuted by the military and sentenced to death. The defendant appealed to the Supreme Court contesting the constitutional authority of the president to prescribe aggravating factors that permit the military to impose the death penalty upon a member of the armed forces convicted of murder.

The initial matter addressed in the opinion was the application of *Furman* and its progeny to military capital punishment. It was said that counsel for the military did not contest the application of the Supreme Court's death penalty jurisprudence to a court-martial, at least in the context of a conviction for capital murder committed in peacetime within the United States. Consequently, the Court assumed, without deciding, that *Furman* and the case law resulting from it were applicable to the offense and sentence in the case. With that "assumption" in place, the Court held that under the Eighth Amendment the military capital sentencing scheme must genuinely narrow the class of persons eligible for the death penalty, and must reasonably justify the imposition of a more severe sentence on a defendant compared to others found guilty of murder. It was said that the constitutional narrowing was not achieved in the statute authorizing capital punishment for murder by the military. However, it was found that the aggravating circumstances promulgated by the president satisfied the constitutional narrowing of the class of military defendants subject to capital punishment for murder.

In turning to the issue of the constitutional legitimacy of the president to promulgate aggravating circumstances used to impose the death penalty, the Court in *Loving* held that the president's congressionally authorized power to promulgate aggravating factors did not violate the separation of powers doctrine. The opinion pointed out that under the separation of powers doctrine, the federal lawmaking function belonged to Congress and could not be conveyed to another branch of government. The Court stated that the separation of powers doctrine did not mean, however, that only Congress could make a rule of prospective force.

It was said that although Congress could not delegate the power to make laws, Congress may delegate to others the authority or discretion to execute the law under and in pursuance of its terms. The opinion rejected the defendant's argument that Congress lacked power to delegate to the president the authority to prescribe aggravating factors in military capital murder cases. The Court concluded: "[I]t would be contrary to the respect owed the President as Commander in Chief to hold that he may not be given wide discretion and authority. Thus, in the circumstances presented here, Congress may delegate authority to the President to define the aggravating factors that permit imposition of a statutory penalty, with the regulations providing the narrowing of the death-eligible class that the Eighth Amendment requires."

Death Penalty Offenses

Under modern military capital punishment, crimes for which the death penalty may be imposed are set out under 10 U.S.C. § 881 et seq. and include conspiracy, desertion, assaulting or willfully disobeying a superior commissioned officer, mutiny, sedition, misbehavior before the enemy, subordinate compelling surrender, improper use of countersign, forcing a safeguard, aiding the enemy, spying, espionage, improper hazarding of a vessel, misbehavior of a sentinel or lookout, murder, felony murder, and rape. Most of the offenses punishable with death by the military are limited to wartime conduct.[8]

Death Penalty Procedures

A military capital prosecution is initiated by the convening authority, a high ranking commanding officer. The convening authority picks those service members who will serve as jurors.[9] The jury must consist of twelve members, unless twelve members are not reasonably available due to physical conditions or military exigencies, in which case the jury may consist of not less than five members.[10] The defendant is permitted to have at least one-third of the jury consist of enlisted personnel. A defendant is not permitted to have a bench (judge only) trial. Nor is a defendant permitted to plead guilty to a capital offense.

A defendant in a military capital trial cannot be convicted of a capital offense unless the jury unanimously finds him or her guilty beyond a reasonable doubt. If guilt is determined, the case proceeds to the penalty phase. At the penalty phase, the prosecution must prove the existence of at least one codified aggravating circumstance beyond a reasonable doubt. (One exception is a conviction for spying, which carries a mandatory death sentence.) The aggravating circumstances are set out under Rule 1004(c) of the Manual for Courts-Martial. For the offense of espionage, 10 U.S.C. § 906a(c) sets out specific aggravating circumstances.

The prosecution is required to give the defendant notice, prior to trial, of the aggravating circumstances that will be used at the penalty phase. During the penalty phase the prosecution presents its aggravating circumstances evidence, and the defendant submits his or her evidence in mitigation. The penalty phase jury is required to weigh all of the aggravating evidence in the case against evidence in mitigation. The death penalty may not be imposed unless the penalty phase jury unanimously concludes that the aggravating evidence substantially outweighs the mitigating evidence.[11] However, even if every juror agrees upon the existence of an aggravating circumstance and concludes that the evidence in aggravation outweighs the mitigating evidence, any juror is still free to choose a sentence less than death. This means that the jury must unanimously conclude that death is an appropriate sentence. If death is not imposed the defendant may be sentenced to life with or without the possibility of parole.

If a death sentence is imposed, the record is initially reviewed by the convening authority, which has the power to reduce the sentence. If the convening authority approves the death sentence, the defendant will be moved to the military death row at the United States Disciplinary Barracks, Fort Leavenworth, Kansas.

Once the convening authority reviews the death sentence, the record of trial then goes before one of the military justice system's four intermediate appellate courts: the Army, Navy-Marine Corps, Air Force, or Coast Guard Court of Criminal Appeals. The branch of service that the defendant is in dictates which intermediate appellate court reviews the sentence. If the intermediate appellate court affirms the death sentence, the case then goes before the military's highest court, the Court of Appeals for the Armed Forces.[12]

If the Court of Appeals for the Armed Forces affirms the sentence, the case may be reviewed by the United States Supreme Court. The Supreme Court's certiorari jurisdiction over military justice cases was authorized in 1983. If the Supreme Court affirms the death sentence or denies certiorari, the death sentence is then reviewed by the U.S. president. If the president approves the death sentence, the defendant may seek habeas corpus relief from the federal courts. If habeas relief is ultimately denied, the defendant may then be executed. The president has the power to commute a death sentence.

Lethal injection is used as the method of execution by the military. The last capital felon executed by the military in the twentieth century was Army Private John Arthur Bennett on April 13, 1961. He was executed by hanging. Bennett had been convicted of rape and attempted murder. As of July 2012 there were six inmates on military death row.[13]

Guantanamo Bay Prisoners

On September 11, 2001, members of the al Qaeda terrorist organization hijacked four commercial airplanes. Two of the planes were used to attack the World Trade Center in New York City; one was used to attack the national headquarters of the Department of Defense in Arlington, Virginia; and one plane crashed into a field near Shanksville, Pennsylvania. Nearly 3,000 civilians were killed. Congress responded to the attacks by authorizing the president to use all necessary and appropriate force against those nations, organizations, or persons responsible for the attacks. The president determined that the Taliban regime had supported al Qaeda and, therefore, ordered the military to invade Afghanistan. In the ensuing conflict, hundreds of individuals were captured and eventually detained at Guantanamo Bay Naval Base in Cuba.[14]

On November 13, 2001, the president issued a comprehensive military order intended to govern the prosecution of persons captured and detained at Guantanamo Bay. Under the order, any such individual "shall, when tried, be tried by military commission for any and all offenses triable that such individual is alleged to have committed, and may be punished in accordance with the penalties provided under applicable law, including life imprisonment or death." The order vested in the secretary of defense the power to appoint military commissions to try the prisoners.[15]

On July 3, 2003, the president announced his determination that Salim Ahmed Hamdan, a Yemeni national, and five other prisoners at Guantanamo Bay would be prosecuted by a military commission. On July 13, 2004, Hamdan was formally charged with conspiracy, to wit, he "willfully and knowingly joined an enterprise of persons who shared a common criminal purpose and conspired and agreed with [named members of al Qaeda] to commit the following offenses triable by military commission: attacking civilians; attacking civilian objects; murder by an unprivileged belligerent; and terrorism."

Prior to the formal charge Hamdan filed a petition for a writ of habeas corpus in a federal district court challenging his prosecution by a military commission.[16] The district judge found that the president did not have authority to create a military commission to prosecute Hamdan. A federal court of appeals reversed the decision of the district judge. The Supreme Court granted certiorari and issued a decision reversing the court of appeals in *Hamdan v. Rumsfeld*, 548 U.S. 557 (2006).[17]

The Hamdan ruling. The opinion in *Hamdan* recognized "a general Presidential authority to convene military commissions in circumstances where justified under the 'Constitution and laws,' including the law of war." With that acknowledgment in view, the Supreme Court addressed two substantive issues in *Hamdan*: (1) whether the charge of conspiracy was a recognized offense under the law of war, and (2) whether the structure and procedures of the military commission violated the Uniform Code of Military Justice and the Geneva Conventions.[18]

The conspiracy charge was not recognized by the law of war. After an exhaustive review of conspiracy as a crime during war, the opinion held that no valid crime was brought against the defendant:

Finally, international sources confirm that the crime charged here is not a recognized violation of the law of war. As observed above, none of the major treaties governing the law of war identifies conspiracy as a violation thereof. And the only "conspiracy" crimes that have been recognized by international war crimes tribunals are conspiracy to commit genocide and common plan to wage aggressive war, which is a crime against the peace and requires for its commission actual participation in a "concrete plan to wage war." The International Military Tribunal at Nuremberg, over the prosecution's objections, pointedly refused to recognize as a violation of the law of war conspiracy to commit war crimes, and convicted only Hitler's most senior associates of conspiracy to wage aggressive war. As one prominent figure from the Nuremberg trials has explained, members of the Tribunal objected to recognition of conspiracy as a violation of the law of war on the ground that "[t]he Anglo-American concept of conspiracy was not part of European legal systems and arguably not an element of the internationally recognized laws of war."

In sum, the sources that the Government ... [relies] upon to show that conspiracy to violate the law of war is itself a violation of the law of war in fact demonstrate quite the opposite. Far from making the requisite substantial showing, the Government has failed even to offer a "merely colorable" case for inclusion of conspiracy among those offenses cognizable by law-of-war military commission. Because the charge does not support the commission's jurisdiction, the commission lacks authority to try Hamdan....

Hamdan is charged not with an overt act for which he was caught redhanded in a theater of war and which military efficiency demands be tried expeditiously, but with an *agreement* the inception of which long predated the attacks of September 11, 2001.... That may well be a crime, but it is not an offense that "by the law of war may be tried by military commissio[n]." None of the overt acts alleged to have been committed in furtherance of the agreement is itself a war crime, or even necessarily occurred during time of, or in a theater of, war. Any urgent need for imposition or execution of judgment is utterly belied by the record; Hamdan was arrested in November 2001 and he was not charged until mid–2004. These simply are not the circumstances in which, by any stretch of the historical evidence or this Court's precedents, a military commission established by Executive Order under the authority of Article 21 of the UCMJ may lawfully try a person and subject him to punishment.

The structure and procedures of the military commission violated the Uniform Code of Military Justice and the Geneva Conventions. The Court in *Hamdan* next pointed out that "[t]he UCMJ conditions the president's use of military commissions on compliance not only with the American common law of war, but also with the rest of the UCMJ itself, insofar as applicable, and with the rules and precepts of the law of nations,— including, *inter alia,* the four Geneva Conventions signed in 1949." The opinion found that the rules promulgated by the president to prosecute the defendant permitted the prosecutor to present evidence that the defendant would not be allowed to hear, and permitted the prosecutor to present hearsay testimony in violation of the rules of evidence. The opinion found the president's rules violated the UCMJ and the Geneva Conventions:

> Nothing in the record before us demonstrates that it would be impracticable to apply court-martial rules in this case. There is no suggestion, for example, of any logistical difficulty in securing properly sworn and authenticated evidence or in applying the usual principles of relevance and admissibility. Assuming, *arguendo,* that the reasons articulated in the President's ... determination ought to be considered in evaluating the impracticability of applying court-martial rules, the only reason offered in support of that determination is the danger posed by international terrorism. Without for one moment underestimating that danger, it is not evident to us why it should require, in the case of Hamdan's trial, any variance from the rules that govern courts-martial.
>
> The absence of any showing of impracticability is particularly disturbing when considered in light of the clear and admitted failure to apply one of the most fundamental protections afforded not just by the Manual for Courts-Martial but also by the UCMJ itself: the right to be present. Whether or not that departure technically is "contrary to or inconsistent with" the terms of the UCMJ, the jettisoning of so basic a right cannot lightly be excused as "practicable."
>
> Under the circumstances, then, the rules applicable in courts-martial must apply....
>
> [T]he rules specified for Hamdan's trial are illegal....
>
> The procedures adopted to try Hamdan also violate the Geneva Conventions....
>
> [T]here is at least one provision of the Geneva Conventions that applies here.... Article 3, often referred to as Common Article 3 because ... it appears in all four Geneva Conventions, ... prohibits "the passing of sentences and the carrying out of executions without previous judgment pronounced by a regularly constituted court affording all the judicial guarantees which are recognized as indispensable by civilized peoples." ...
>
> While the term "regularly constituted court" is not specifically defined in either Common Article 3 or its accompanying commentary, other sources disclose its core meaning. The commentary accompanying a provision of the Fourth Geneva Convention, for example, defines "'regularly constituted'" tribunals to include "ordinary military courts" and "definitely exclud[e] all special tribunals." And one of the Red Cross' own treatises defines "regularly constituted court" as used in Common Article 3 to mean "established and organi[z]ed in accordance with the laws and procedures already in force in a country."
>
> The Government offers only a cursory defense of Hamdan's military commission in light of Common Article 3. [T]hat defense fails because "[t]he regular military courts in our system are the courts-martial established by congressional statutes." At a minimum, a military commission "can be 'regularly constituted' by the standards of our military justice system only if some practical need explains deviations from court-martial practice." As we have explained, no such need has been demonstrated here.

26

Native Americans and Capital Punishment

The Supreme Court stated in *Cherokee Nation v. Georgia*, 30 U.S. 1 (1831), that the United States recognizes Native American tribes as "domestic dependent nations." It was said in *Cherokee Nation* that Native American lands "are considered by foreign nations ... as being so completely under the sovereignty and dominion of the United States, that any attempt to acquire their lands, or to form a political [connection] with them, would be considered by all as an invasion of our territory, and an act of hostility." Under 8 U.S.C. § 1401(b), Native Americans born in the United States have been granted citizenship.[1]

In spite of the forced dependency recognized in *Cherokee Nation*, it was said in *United States v. Wheeler*, 435 U.S. 313 (1978) (superseded by statute), that Native American tribes "still possess those aspects of sovereignty not withdrawn by treaty or statute, or by implication as a necessary result of their dependent status." That is, Native American tribes still retain, in general, "inherent powers of a limited sovereignty which has never been extinguished."[2] It was held in *Duro v. Reina*, 495 U.S. 676 (1990) (superseded by statute), that among the inherent powers retained by Native American tribes is that of criminal jurisdiction over its members. However, Native American tribes only have the authority to arrest and deliver non–Native Americans to state or federal authorities for prosecution under federal or state laws.[3] As recognized in *Oliphant v. Suquamish Tribe*, 435 U.S. 191 (1978) (superseded by statute), Native American courts "do not have criminal jurisdiction over non–[Native Americans] absent affirmative delegation of such power by Congress."[4]

As a result of the inherent criminal jurisdiction of Native American tribes, rather than federal delegation, successive prosecution by a tribe and the federal government does not run afoul of the Double Jeopardy Clause, as the two are dual sovereigns.[5] However, Congress has statutorily forbidden a successive prosecution in federal court of an offense under the General Crimes Act (discussed later), if a tribe has prosecuted and imposed punishment for the offense.[6]

It has been observed that on Native American lands, "federal, state, and tribal governments all have a certain amount of authority to prosecute and try criminal offenses."[7] A complete understanding of criminal jurisdiction in Native American territory depends on a number of factors, including where the offense occurred, the status of the alleged offender and victim, and the type of offense.[8] As discussed infra, the criminal jurisdictional complexity engulfing Native American tribes is attributed to the Major Crimes Act, General Crimes Act and other federal statutes and federal court decisions.[9]

263

The determination of whether Native Americans are subject to the death penalty for committing murder will depend upon the circumstances of the crime and where it occurred. The material in this chapter will provide a brief overview of enforcement of criminal laws against Native Americans in general, and a discussion of capital punishment in particular.[10]

Proving That a Defendant Is a Native American for the Purpose of Criminal Prosecution

Under the federal Major Crimes Act and General Crimes Act, a defendant's Native American status is an essential element which the government must allege in the indictment and prove beyond a reasonable doubt at trial.[11] Although there are a variety of statutory definitions of Native American, Congress has not defined Native American as used in the Major Crimes Act and General Crimes Act. In the absence of a statutory definition, courts apply a two-part test for determining whether a person is a Native American for the purpose of establishing federal jurisdiction over crimes committed in Native American country: (1) the degree of Native American blood, and (2) whether the defendant has tribal or federal government recognition as a Native American.[12]

It has been held that a showing of as little as one-eighth Native American blood is sufficient to satisfy the first prong of the test. In determining whether a defendant has been recognized by the government or a tribe as a Native American, courts use four factors: (1) tribal enrollment, (2) government recognition formally and informally through receipt of assistance reserved only to Native Americans, (3) enjoyment of the benefits of tribal affiliation, and 4) social recognition as a Native American through residence on tribal land and participation in Native American social life.[13] Tribal enrollment is not required to establish recognition as a Native American. Indeed, the United States Supreme Court has declined to decide whether enrollment in an official tribe is an absolute requirement for federal jurisdiction, at least where the defendant lived on tribal land and maintained tribal relations.[14]

Federal courts have suggested that Native Americans emancipated from tribal relations or whose tribes have been terminated are not subject to the Major Crimes Act and General Crimes Act even if they are racially classified as Native Americans.[15]

General Crimes Act

The General Crimes Act, 18 U.S.C. § 1152, provides succinctly that the "general laws of the United States as to the punishment of offenses committed in any place within the sole and exclusive jurisdiction of the United States, except the District of Columbia, ... extend to [Native American] country."[16] The General Crimes Act has its roots in Congressional legislation of 1817, which "provided for general federal enclave jurisdiction over [Native American] and non-[Native Americans], except for crimes 'committed by one [Native American] against another,' within any '[Native American] boundary.'"[17] It has been said that "[u]nder the General Crimes Act if the [offense] occurs in [Native American] Country and the victim or perpetrator is non-[Native American], a crime can be charged and tried in federal court."[18] In other words, the General Crimes Act provides federal criminal jurisdiction over certain crimes committed in Native American country when either the defendant or the victim, but not both, is a Native American.[19] Thus, as indicated in *United States v. Doe,*

572 F.3d 1162 (10th Cir. 2009), "[a]bsent proof that the offense was 'interracial,' no federal crime has been committed" under the General Crimes Act.

The General Crimes Act does not authorize federal prosecution of three categories of offenses: crimes committed by one Native American against the person or property of another Native American; crimes committed by a Native American who has been punished by the tribe; and cases secured by treaty to the exclusive jurisdiction of a tribe. These exceptions do not exempt Native Americans from the general criminal laws of the United States that apply to acts that are federal crimes regardless of where committed, such as bank robbery, counterfeiting, sale of drugs, and assault on a federal officer.[20] Further, although the plain language of the General Crimes Act covers crimes in Native American lands committed by non–Native Americans against non–Native Americans, it was held in *United States v. McBratney*, 104 U.S. 621 (1882), that states retain exclusive jurisdiction over general crimes committed by non–Native Americans against non–Native Americans in tribal lands.[21]

The federal laws to which the General Crimes Act refers are commonly known as "federal enclave laws."[22] The federal enclave laws extended under the General Crimes Act are those that are applicable within the Special Maritime and Territorial Jurisdiction of the United States, as defined in 18 U.S.C. § 7.[23] Among these statutes are arson (18 U.S.C. § 81); assault (18 U.S.C. § 113); maiming (18 U.S.C. § 114); theft (18 U.S.C. § 661); receiving stolen property (18 U.S.C. § 662); murder (18 U.S.C. § 1111); manslaughter (18 U.S.C. § 1112); and sexual offenses (18 U.S.C. § 2241 *et seq.*). In order to prosecute a Native American under the General Crimes Act the government must prove, as jurisdictional requisite, that crime was in violation of a federal enclave law, and that the crime occurred between a Native American and a non–Native American within tribal lands.[24]

Ex Parte Crow Dog

As previously discussed, federal enclave laws were made applicable to Native American lands through the General Crimes Act of 1817. The second paragraph of this statute contains an exception to this jurisdictional authority. The second paragraph exempts from prosecution any Native American who commits a crime against another Native American. As early as 1883, the Supreme Court applied this exception to a capital murder prosecution in *Ex Parte Crow Dog*, 109 U.S. 556 (1883).

The defendant in *Crow Dog* was a Native American who killed another Native American on tribal land. The defendant was convicted of capital murder and sentenced to death by the Territory of Dakota. The Dakota Territory Supreme Court affirmed the judgment. In doing so, the appellate court rejected the defendant's contention that the courts of the Dakota Territory did not have jurisdiction over the offense committed by him. The United States Supreme Court granted certiorari to consider the issue.

The opinion in *Crow Dog* held that the courts established by the federal government for the Territory of Dakota did not have jurisdiction to prosecute the defendant for capital murder. The opinion stated that under federal statutes and treaties with Native Americans, crimes committed by Native Americans against other Native Americans had to be prosecuted by Native Americans. It was noted that the defendant was a member of the Brule Sioux tribe and the victim was also a member of the same tribe. The opinion concluded that jurisdiction to prosecute the defendant resided exclusively with the Brule Sioux tribe. The opinion justified its position as follows:

[This] is a case of life and death. It is a case where, against an express exception in the law itself, that law, by argument and inference only, is sought to be extended over aliens and strangers; over the members of a community separated by race, by tradition, by the instincts of a free ... life, from the authority and power which seeks to impose upon them the restraints of an external and unknown code, and to subject them to the responsibilities of civil conduct, according to rules and penalties of which they could have no previous warning; which judges them by a standard made by others and not for them, which takes no account of the conditions which should except them from its exactions, and makes no allowance for their inability to understand it. It tries them, not by their peers, nor by the customs of their people, nor the law of their land, but by [people] of a different race, according to the law of a social state of which they have imperfect conception, and which is opposed to the traditions of their history [and] to the habits of their lives....

To ... uphold the jurisdiction exercised in this case, would be to reverse in this instance the general policy of the government towards the [Native Americans], as declared in many statutes and treaties, and recognized in many decisions of this court, from the beginning to the present. To justify such a departure, in such a case, requires a clear expression of the intention of Congress, and that we have not been able to find.[25]

Major Crimes Act

In response to the United States Supreme Court decision in *Crow Dog*, Congress passed the Major Crimes Act of 1885, 18 U.S.C. § 1153.[26] The Major Crimes Act, in overruling *Crow Dog*, permits the federal government to prosecute Native Americans in federal courts for offenses committed on tribal lands by Native Americans against Native Americans.[27] Offenses listed under the Major Crimes Act include murder, manslaughter, kidnapping, maiming, a felony under chapter 109A, incest, assault with intent to commit murder, assault with a dangerous weapon, assault resulting in serious bodily injury, an assault against an person under 16, felony child abuse or neglect, arson, burglary, robbery, and a felony under section 661.[28]

The Supreme Court was called upon in *United States v. Kagama*, 118 U.S. 375 (1886), to determine whether the Major Crimes Act was constitutional. In *Kagama* two Native Americans were indicted by the federal government for murder of another Native American on tribal land in California. The murder charges were based upon authorization given by the Major Crimes Act. The federal district court certified questions to the Supreme Court that essentially asked whether the Major Crimes Act was constitutional. That is, did the federal government have constitutional authority to prosecute Native Americans for killing another Native American on Native American land? The Supreme Court found that the federal government had authority and a duty to prosecute crime by Native Americans against Native Americans on tribal land. The opinion set out the duty as follows:

It seems to us that this is within the competency of Congress. These [Native American] tribes are the wards of the nation. They are communities *dependent* on the United States. Dependent largely for their daily food. Dependent for their political rights. They owe no allegiance to the States, and receive from them no protection. Because of the local ill feeling, the people of the States where they are found are often their deadliest enemies. From their very weakness and helplessness, so largely due to the course of dealing of the Federal Government with them and the treaties in which it has been promised, there arises the duty of protection, and with it the power....

The power of the General Government over these remnants of a race once powerful, now weak and diminished in numbers, is necessary to their protection, as well as to the safety of those among whom they dwell. It must exist in that government, because it never has existed anywhere else, because the theatre of its exercise is within the geographical limits of the United States, because it has never been denied, and because it alone can enforce its laws on all the tribes.[29]

Although the Major Crimes Act does not expressly prohibit tribal jurisdiction over its enumerated crimes, it is arguable that the statute removes all jurisdiction over the enumerated crimes from Native American authorities.[30] In fact, because the Native American Civil Rights Act of 1968, discussed infra, essentially limits tribal jurisdiction to misdemeanor offenses, jurisdiction over Major Crimes Act offenses is, for all practical purposes, unenforceable by tribes.[31]

It has been held that the federal government may arrest a Native American for prosecution under the Major Crimes Act without notifying the tribal government so that formal extradition could take place.[32] It was held in *Keeble v. United States*, 412 U.S. 205 (1973), that when a Native American is prosecuted under the Major Crimes Act, he or she may seek an instruction on a lesser included offense, assuming that evidence warrants such instruction, even though the lesser included offense is not one of those offenses specified in the Major Crimes Act.

Public Law 280

From an historical perspective, criminal offenses between Native Americans have been subject only to federal or tribal laws, except where Congress has expressly provided that state laws govern.[33] State jurisdiction over offenses committed by or against Native Americans in tribal country may be obtained in one of two ways: (1) by a direct congressional grant[34], or (2) by a state's assumption of optional jurisdiction pursuant to Public Law 280.

In 1953 Congress enacted Public Law 280, 18 U.S.C. § 1162, which granted certain states, known as "mandatory states," criminal jurisdiction over offenses committed by or against Native Americans in specific areas of tribal land.[35] The mandatory states are Alaska, California, Minnesota, Nebraska, Oregon, and Wisconsin.[36] In these states the federal General Crimes Act and Major Crimes Act are not enforceable.[37] The mandatory states have the exclusive jurisdiction to enforce their criminal laws on tribal lands to the same degree as elsewhere in each state. Of course, federal criminal laws of general application throughout the nation continue to apply in tribal lands that are subject to Public Law 280.[38] "[T]hat is, actions that Congress has declared illegal regardless of where they occur — are not affected by the enactment of Public Law 280 and remain within the subject-matter jurisdiction of the federal courts."[39]

Section 7 of Public Law 280 also gave the option to other states to assume jurisdiction over Native American lands by affirmative legislative action.[40] However, in 1968 Congress passed the Native American Civil Rights Act, which repealed Section 7 of Public Law 280. Section 7 was replaced with 25 U.S.C. § 1321, which changed the method whereby a state could assume criminal jurisdiction over Native Americans for acts committed in tribal country.[41] Under 25 U.S.C. § 1321, "Congress has given its consent to any state assuming, with the consent of the affected tribe, criminal jurisdiction over Native Americans committing crimes on the tribe's land[.]"[42]

The federal government retains concurrent jurisdiction to prosecute under the Major

Crimes Act and General Crimes Act in the so-called "option states" under 25 U.S.C. § 1321.[43] Courts have also indicated that Public Law 280 does not divest tribes of concurrent criminal jurisdiction. In *Walker v. Rushing*, 898 F.2d 672 (8th Cir. 1990), the Eighth Circuit addressed the matter:

> [W]e agree with the district court's conclusion that Public Law 280 did not itself divest [Native American] tribes of their sovereign power to punish their own members for violations of tribal law. Nothing in the wording of Public Law 280 or its legislative history precludes concurrent tribal authority. As both the Supreme Court and this court have made clear, limitations on [a Native American] tribe's power to punish its own members must be clearly set forth by Congress. We find no such clear expression of congressional intent in Public Law 280.

The Washington Supreme Court in *State v. Schmuck*, 121 Wash. 2d 373 (1993), and the federal district court for the Central District of California in *Cabazon Band of Mission Indians v. Smith*, 34 F. Supp. 2d 1195 (C.D. Cal. 1998), reached the same conclusion as *Walker*.

Assimilative Crimes Act

The Assimilative Crimes Act, 18 U.S.C. § 13, is one of those federal enclave statutes that is extended to Native American country by the General Crimes Act.[44] The Assimilative Crimes Act provides that anyone who engages in conduct on a federal enclave which is not punishable under a law of Congress, but which is punishable under the law of the state where the enclave is located, shall be guilty of a federal crime based on the state law.[45] Under this statute anyone committing an act on Native American land that is a crime only under the laws of the state where the Native American land is situated may be prosecuted by the federal government for a violation of the assimilated state statute.[46] It has been said that the Assimilative Crimes Act "fills gaps in the law applicable to federal enclaves, ensures uniformity between criminal prohibitions applicable within the federal enclave and within the surrounding state, and provides residents of federal enclaves with the same protection as those outside its boundaries."[47]

Tribal Criminal Jurisdiction and the Native American Civil Rights Act of 1968

The passage of the Native American Civil Rights Act of 1968, 25 U.S.C. §§ 1301–1303, is the product of congressional concern that individual Native Americans had no guaranteed tribal constitutional rights.[48] Among the testimony heard by a congressional subcommittee were allegations of harassment, detention of political dissidents, corruption of tribal courts, and election fraud.[49] Through the enactment of the Civil Rights Act, Congress sought to achieve a balance between individual rights of tribal members on the one hand, and the continuation of tribal autonomy, customs, law and culture on the other.[50]

Among the rights addressed by the Civil Rights Act are specific provisions involving criminal punishment. The Civil Rights Act provides under 25 U.S.C. § 1302(a)(7) that no tribe shall (1) impose for conviction of any 1 offense any penalty or punishment greater than imprisonment for a term of 1 year or a fine of $5,000, or both; or (2) impose on a person in a criminal proceeding a total penalty or punishment greater than imprisonment for a term of 9 years. It is also provided by the Civil Rights Act, pursuant to 25 U.S.C. § 1302(b), that a tribal court may subject a defendant to a term of imprisonment greater than 1 year but not to exceed 3 years for any 1 offense, or a fine greater than $5,000 but not to exceed $15,000, or both, if the defendant is a person accused of a criminal offense who (1) has been previously convicted of the same or a comparable offense by any jurisdiction in the United States; or (2) is being prosecuted for an offense comparable to an offense that would be punishable by more than 1 year of imprisonment if prosecuted by the United States or any of the States.[51]

The Civil Rights Act, 25 U.S.C. § 1302(c), only requires the appointment of counsel for indigent criminal defendants in tribal court for prosecutions that result in a term of incarceration greater than one year. Accordingly, if a tribe elects not to provide for the right to appointed counsel through its own laws, Native American defendants in tribal court have no constitutional or statutory right to appointed counsel unless sentenced to a cumulative term of incarceration greater than one year.[52]

In 1990 the Civil Rights Act was amended in response to the Supreme Court's decision in *Duro v. Reina*, 495 U.S. 676 (1990) (superseded by statute). In *Duro* the Supreme Court confronted the issue of tribal jurisdiction over the criminal actions of non-member Native Americans (i.e., Native Americans who were members of a tribe other than the prosecuting tribe). The decision in *Duro* held that tribes do not have criminal jurisdiction over Native American non-members of the tribe. Within months of *Duro*, Congress amended the Civil Rights Act to legislatively overrule that decision and restore to the tribes the power to prosecute non-member Native Americans.[53] It was noted in *United States v. Enas*, 255 F.3d 662 (9th Cir. 2001), that a tribal court exercising its power to prosecute a non-member Native American under the Civil Rights Act does so as a separate sovereign, making a subsequent prosecution by the federal government permissible under the dual sovereignty doctrine.

The Federal Death Penalty Act's Opt-In Provision for Major Crimes Act Offenses

The Federal Death Penalty Act, 18 U.S.C. § 3598, conditionally eliminated the death penalty for Native American defendants prosecuted under the Major Crimes Act, subject to the penalty being reinstated by a tribe's governing body.[54] The statute provides specifically that "no person subject to the criminal jurisdiction of an [Native American] tribal government shall be subject to a capital sentence ... for any offense the Federal jurisdiction for which is predicated solely on Indian country and which has occurred within the boundaries of [Native American] country, unless the governing body of the tribe has elected that this chapter have effect over land and persons subject to its criminal jurisdiction."[55]

It was observed in *United States v. Martinez*, 505 F.Supp.2d 1024 (D.N.M. 2007), that the purpose of limiting the death penalty for offenses committed in Native American country to those areas in which the tribal government has elected to use the death penalty was to give tribes a sovereign right to elect whether the death penalty applies within their jurisdiction, similar to the right that states have to decide whether the death penalty applies to violations of state law.[56]

Application of Federal Laws of Nationwide Coverage Including Death Penalty Laws

Neither the Major Crimes Act nor General Crimes Act prohibit the application of federal laws of nationwide coverage that makes conduct criminal wherever committed.[57] Moreover, notwithstanding 18 U.S.C. § 3598 of the Federal Death Penalty Act, federal criminal laws of nationwide applicability, including death penalty laws, apply to Native Americans within tribal country just as they apply to non-death penalty states.[58] This issue was addressed in *United States v. Mitchell*, 502 F.3d 931 (9th Cir. 2007).

The defendant in *Mitchell*, a Navajo Native American, was charged by the federal government with capital murder and other crimes in causing the death of two Native American women in 2001. The murders occurred on Native American lands in Arizona. Non-death penalty crimes were brought against the defendant under the Major Crimes Act, and the death penalty crime, carjacking resulting in death, was brought under the Federal Death Penalty Act. The defendant was convicted of all charges and sentenced to death for the carjacking offense.

In the appeal, the defendant in *Mitchell* argued that the Federal Death Penalty Act did not extend to carjackings committed by one Native American against other Native Americans on tribal land. The defendant also contended that he could not be sentenced to death under the Federal Death Penalty Act because the Navajo Nation never opted into the federal capital punishment scheme. The opinion in *Mitchell* disposed of the first issue by noting that by virtue of judicial case law, federal court jurisdiction extends to intra–Native American violations of federal criminal laws of general, nationwide applicability.

The court in *Mitchell* rejected the second argument by pointing out that the Federal Death Penalty Act's opt-in provision for Native American tribes only applies to crimes listed under the Major Crimes Act. In affirming the death sentence, the court in *Mitchell* held:

> It is doubtful that Congress intended to carve out special exemptions to [Native American] tribes for the more than 40 death eligible federal offenses covered by the FDPA without expressly saying. Instead, the opt-in provision appears to afford [Native American] tribes as much authority as states in determining whether capital punishment may be imposed in circumstances not involving federal crimes of general applicability. The federal government seeks and obtains FDPA death sentences in states that have long since abandoned the death penalty themselves.

TABLE 26.0 NATIVE AMERICANS EXECUTED 1976–2012

Name	Date of Execution	Jurisdiction	Execution Method
James Allen	March 3, 1993	Delaware	Lethal Injection
Emmit Nave	July 31, 1996	Missouri	Lethal Injection
Scott D. Carpenter	May 8, 1997	Oklahoma	Lethal Injection
Robert West	July 29, 1997	Texas	Lethal Injection
Daniel Remeta	March 31, 1998	Florida	Electrocution
John Castro	January 7, 1999	Oklahoma	Lethal Injection
Darick Gerlaugh	February 3, 1999	Arizona	Lethal Injection
Domingo Cantu	October 28, 1999	Texas	Lethal Injection
Darrell K. Rich	March 15, 2000	California	Lethal Injection
James Robedeaux	June 1, 2000	Oklahoma	Lethal Injection
Dion Smallwood	January 18, 2001	Oklahoma	Lethal Injection

Name	Date of Execution	Jurisdiction	Execution Method
Terrance James	May 22, 2001	Oklahoma	Lethal Injection
Jerald W. Harjo	July 17, 2001	Oklahoma	Lethal Injection
Henry L. Hunt	September 12, 2003	North Carolina	Lethal Injection
Clarence R. Allen	January 19, 2006	California	Lethal Injection
Jeffrey Landrigan	October 26, 2010	Arizona	Lethal Injection

SOURCE: Deborah Fins, "Death Row U.S.A.," Criminal Justice Project, NAACP Legal Defense and Educational Fund (2012).

Murder Committed by Native Americans Outside of Native American Territory

There can be no question that federal and state courts have jurisdiction over Native Americans for crimes committed outside of Native American country.[59] A Native American who commits a criminal offense outside Native American territory is subject to the jurisdiction and punishment of the place of the offense. Thus, if a Native American commits murder in a state that does not have the death penalty, then he or she will not be subject to capital punishment by that state. On the other hand, if a Native American commits murder in a state that authorizes the death penalty, then he or she will be subject to capital punishment. As of January 2012 there were 36 Native Americans on death row.[60]

27

Inhabited American Territories and Capital Punishment

An issue that has haunted the United States since the 1800s concerns whether residents of United States territories are entitled to the full rights granted to citizens of the United States.[1] It has been said that the concurring opinion of Justice White in *Downes v. Bidwell*, 182 U.S. 244 (1901), answered that question when he discussed the doctrine of territorial incorporation. Justice White wrote that under this doctrine "territories can belong to the United States without necessarily being a part of the United States for all purposes."[2] This chapter briefly looks at the issue of capital punishment in five inhabited territories that belong to the United States, but are not part of the United States for all purposes. Those territories are Puerto Rico, U.S. Virgin Islands, Northern Mariana Islands, Guam and American Samoa.

Puerto Rico

Puerto Rico has been a territory of the United States since 1898. Although its residents are citizens of the United States, their rights as American citizens are limited, e.g., they cannot vote in a U.S. presidential election.[3] Puerto Rico has authority over its own local affairs. However, "Congress maintains similar powers over Puerto Rico as it possesses over the federal states."[4] All federal laws, criminal and civil in nature, apply to Puerto Rico as they apply to the states, unless otherwise provided by federal law.[5] The application of federal law to Puerto Rico is done pursuant to 48 U.S.C. § 734. This statute states that "[t]he statutory laws of the United States ... shall have the same force and effect in Puerto Rico as in the United States[.]"[6]

The local judicial system of Puerto Rico is based upon Spanish law. The Puerto Rico court system comprises a district court, superior court, appellate court and, supreme court. A federal district court sits in San Juan. The federal district court has original jurisdiction over matters involving federal questions (dispute arising out of a federal law) and diversity of citizenship (dispute between citizens of different states where matter in controversy exceeds $75,000.00). Appeals from a decision of the federal district court are taken to the United States Court of Appeals for the First Circuit seated in Boston. Appeals from that court are by *writ of certiorari* to the United States Supreme Court.[7]

Under Article II, § 7, of the constitution of Puerto Rico the death penalty is expressly prohibited.[8] While it is clear that local courts of Puerto Rico have no authority to impose the death penalty, this fact does not bar application of the death penalty under federal law by the federal district court sitting in Puerto Rico.[9] This issue was litigated in *United States v. Acosta-Martinez*, 252 F.3d 13 (1st Cir. 2001).

In *Acosta-Martinez* two defendants were charged with capital murder in a federal district court in Puerto Rico. The district court judge dismissed the death penalty notice and prohibited the federal prosecutor from seeking the death penalty. The district court prohibited the prosecutor from seeking the death penalty for two reasons: (1) Puerto Rico's constitution barred the death penalty and (2) the Federal Death Penalty Act did not expressly indicate that it applied to offenses committed in Puerto Rico. The prosecutor appealed to the First Circuit Court of Appeals. The First Circuit reversed and reinstated the death penalty. In doing so, the First Circuit held as follows:

> We ... conclude that Congress intended the death penalty to apply to these federal criminal prosecutions in Puerto Rico. The death penalty is intended to apply to Puerto Rico federal criminal defendants just as it applies to such defendants in the various states. This choice by Congress does not contravene Puerto Rico's decision to bar the death penalty in prosecutions for violations of crimes under the Puerto Rican criminal laws in the Commonwealth courts. The choice simply retains federal power over federal crimes. Congress has said that one purpose of the death penalty is to deter the commission of heinous crimes by prospective offenders. There is no reason to think that Congress did not intend the death penalty to serve this purpose in Puerto Rico as well.[10]

Although the federal government may prosecute a defendant in Puerto Rico for capital murder, it is up to a jury to impose the death penalty. From 1988, when the federal government reinstated capital punishment, to 2012, there were four federal capital prosecutions in Puerto Rico. Each prosecution ended with the jury refusing to impose the death penalty.

U.S. Virgin Islands

The United States purchased the Virgin Islands from the Danish in 1917.[11] Although the residents of the territory are citizens of the United States, their rights as American citizens are limited, e.g., they cannot vote in a U.S. presidential election. The Virgin Islands has authority over its own local affairs. However, all federal laws, criminal and civil in nature, apply in the territory. The application of federal law to the Virgin Islands is done pursuant to 48 U.S.C. § 1405q. This statute states that "[t]he laws of the United States applicable to the Virgin Islands on June 22, 1936, ... shall continue in force and effect[.]"[12]

The Virgin Islands local court system is comprised of a superior court and supreme court. A federal district court sits in St. Thomas and St. Croix. The federal district court has original jurisdiction over matters involving federal questions (dispute arising out of a federal law) and diversity of citizenship (dispute between citizens of different states where matter in controversy exceeds $75,000.00). Appeals from a decision of the federal district court are taken to the United States Court of Appeals for the Third Circuit seated in Philadelphia. Appeals from that court are by *writ of certiorari* to the United States Supreme Court.[13]

The Virgin Islands code provides that defendants convicted of first degree murder in local courts will receive life in prison without the possibility of parole, rather than the death penalty.[14] Thus, a defendant convicted of murder by a local Virgin Islands court cannot receive a death sentence. However, the death penalty may be imposed in the Virgin Islands by the federal district court for a conviction of a federal capital offense. For example, in *United States v. Casseus*, 282 F.3d 253 (3d Cir. 2002), the federal prosecutor indicted the defendants in the Virgin Islands for capital murder, but decided against invoking the punishment.

Northern Mariana Islands

In 1947 the Northern Mariana Islands, located in Micronesia in the Western Pacific, were governed by the United States as a United Nations–mandated Pacific trust territory.[15] It was not until 1975 that "the United States and the people of the Northern Mariana Islands entered into a Covenant of political union, which established a self-governing Commonwealth of the Northern Mariana Islands under the sovereignty of the United States."[16] Under this arrangement the Northern Mariana Islands have been guaranteed the right of self-government, but the United States maintains sovereignty.[17] Put another way, "[w]ith respect to their internal affairs, [the Northern Mariana Islands] are entitled to govern themselves according to their own Constitution. However, in the international arena, control of the Commonwealth's international affairs and security needs is delegated to the United States."[18] The residents of Northern Mariana Islands have been granted United States citizenship.[19]

The Northern Mariana Islands local court system is comprised of a superior court and supreme court. A federal district court has original jurisdiction over matters involving federal questions (dispute arising out of a federal law) and diversity of citizenship (dispute between citizens of different states where matter in controversy exceeds $75,000.00).[20] The district court is further authorized to exercise original jurisdiction over cases involving issues of local law which the Northern Mariana Islands local courts are not empowered by its constitution or laws to decide.[21] In this latter capacity only, the federal district court is considered to be a local court. Otherwise, the district court is a federal court. Appeals from a decision of the federal district court are taken to the Court of Appeals for the Ninth Circuit. Appeals from that court are by *writ of certiorari* to the United States Supreme Court.[22]

Article 1, § 4(i) of the Northern Mariana Islands prohibits capital punishment. However, the death penalty may be imposed in the Northern Mariana Islands by the federal district court for a conviction of a federal capital offense.

Guam

The island of Guam, located in the Western Pacific Ocean, became a territory of the United States in 1898 and was placed under the jurisdiction of the U.S. Navy.[23] It was in 1950 that Guam became a self-governing territory of the United States. The Guam Organic Act of 1950, 48 U.S.C. § 1421 et seq., established Guam as an unincorporated territory of the United States and transferred federal authority over the island from the Navy to the Department of the Interior.[24] The act conferred United States citizenship on residents of the island and gave the residents the right to establish a government.[25] The act also "created a 'Bill of Rights' for Guam paralleling the Bill of Rights in the federal Constitution."[26] Federal courts have indicated that "[t]he Organic Act serves the function of a constitution for Guam. Guam's self-government is constrained by the Organic Act, and the courts must invalidate Guam statutes in derogation of the Organic Act."[27]

The Guam local court system is comprised of a superior court and supreme court. A federal district court has original jurisdiction over matters involving federal questions (dispute arising out of a federal law) and diversity of citizenship (dispute between citizens of different states where matter in controversy exceeds $75,000.00). Appeals from a decision of the federal district court are taken to the Court of Appeals for the Ninth Circuit. Appeals from that court are by *writ of certiorari* to the United States Supreme Court. The death penalty is not authorized by the laws of Guam.[28] However, the death penalty may be imposed in Guam by the federal district court for a conviction of a federal capital offense.

American Samoa

American Samoa is comprised of five islands that lie in the South Pacific Ocean. The United States first acquired American Samoa as a territory in 1900.[29] Pursuant to 48 U.S.C. § 1661(c), the president of the United States was granted power to administer the islands. The president delegated the administration of the islands to the secretary of the interior.[30] A constitution was adopted by American Samoa in 1960 and approved by the secretary of the interior. Residents of American Samoa are nationals of the United States, but not citizens.[31]

There is a local judicial system in American Samoa. The local judicial system consists of an appellate High Court, which is composed of a chief justice and associate justices that are appointed by the secretary of the interior. The High Court has a trial court division that hears civil disputes over $10,000, probate cases, divorces, and felony criminal cases. A local district court hears small claims, traffic offenses, and misdemeanor crimes.[32] Unlike other United States territories, American Samoa does not have a federal district court.[33] Federal law applicable to the islands is enforced in district courts in Hawaii and Washington, D.C.[34]

Although the death penalty has not been carried out in American Samoa since the 1920s, the punishment is provided for by local law. The death penalty is set out under the code of American Samoa as follows:

American Samoa Code § 46.3513
Persons convicted of the offense of murder in the 1st degree shall, if the judge or jury so recommends ... be punished by death. If the judge or jury does not recommend the imposition of the death penalty on a finding of guilty of murder in the 1st degree, the convicted person is punished by imprisonment by the corrections division for life and is not to be eligible for probation or parole until he has served a minimum of 40 years of his sentence.

While the death penalty is on the books in American Samoa, the local government has not provided a method for carrying out the punishment.

28

Opposition to Capital Punishment

When the United States Supreme Court lifted the brief moratorium on capital punishment in 1976, it did so in the midst of strong opposition. During the ensuing decades anti-death penalty advocates have grown larger in numbers and in their scope. In a 2011 Gallup Poll it was indicated that more than one-third of Americans oppose capital punishment — the highest level of opposition in 40 years.[1] Further, research data suggests that a majority of Americans prefer alternatives to the death penalty as punishment for murder.[2] Today there are literally thousands of national and international organizations that have formed for the express purpose of abolishing capital punishment in the United States and the world. Some of the most influential organizations that seek to abolish capital punishment in the United States include Amnesty International USA, the American Civil Liberties Union, the NAACP Legal Defense and Education Fund, the National Coalition to Abolish the Death Penalty, and the World Coalition Against the Death Penalty.[3] The material in this chapter reviews the scope and direction of the opposition to capital punishment.

Reasons Given for Opposing Capital Punishment

Although the underlying motivation behind organizational and individual opposition to capital punishment varies, the few broad categories set out below capture much of the impetus.

Religious Grounds

Although the Judeo-Christian scriptures expressly endorses capital punishment for such offenses as murder, adultery, blasphemy, sodomy, idolatry, and incest, many organizations and individuals use religion as the basis for opposing the death penalty. Death penalty opponents point to Cain, the first biblical murderer, being punished with banishment and not death. They also cling strongly to biblical teachings on redemption and forgiveness, and the biblical admonishment "Thou shalt not kill," as cornerstones that make capital punishment inconsistent with their understanding of religious thought.

In 1999 the National Jewish/Catholic Consultation issued a joint statement calling for the abolishment of capital punishment, co-sponsored by the National Council of Synagogues and the National Conference of Catholic Bishops' Committee for Ecumenical and Interreligious Affairs. The joint statement of condemnation of capital punishment by the National

TABLE 28.0 PREFERRED PUNISHMENTS FOR MURDER

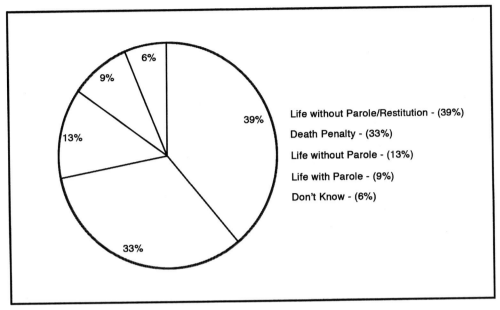

Life without Parole/Restitution - (39%)

Death Penalty - (33%)

Life without Parole - (13%)

Life with Parole - (9%)

Don't Know - (6%)

SOURCE: Death Penalty Information Center 2010.

Jewish/Catholic Consultation was in keeping with a growing national trend by religious institutions in the 1990s to publicly speak out against capital punishment. This trend was placed on the fast track by statements made by Pope John Paul II in the latter part of 1990s calling for a global end to capital punishment. There was also a statement issued in 1999 by the Dalai Lama calling for a moratorium on capital punishment in the United States.

In 2005 the United States Conference of Catholic Bishops issued a new statement of opposition to capital punishment, asserting that it contributes to a culture of death and violence in the United States.[4] It was the Bishops' first comprehensive statement on capital punishment in 25 years. The official website of the Bishops hosts a webpage entitled "Catholic Campaign to End the Use of the Death Penalty."[5] Other religious institutions that have issued statements calling for an end to capital punishment include American Baptist Churches in the U.S.A.; Benedictine Sisters of Cullman, Alabama; Christian Church (Disciples of Christ); Christian Reformed Church; Church of the Brethren; Church Women United; Episcopal Church; Evangelical Lutheran Church; Fellowship of Reconciliation; Moravian Church in America; National Council of Churches of Christ; Orthodox Church in America; Presbyterian Church; Rabbinical Assembly; Reorganized Church of Jesus Christ L.D.S.; Roman Catholic Church; Union for Reform Judaism; Unitarian Universalist Association; United Church of Christ; and United Methodist Church.

Philosophical Grounds

Many of the most influential philosophers — such as John Locke, Immanuel Kant, and Jean-Jacques Rousseau — did not oppose capital punishment, in spite of their development of and belief in the principle that human beings were born with a "natural right to life." Many opponents of the death penalty have taken the "natural right to life" principle as the basis for opposing capital punishment. It is argued that governmental taking of life as punishment violates the condemned person's "natural right to life." The fact that a condemned person took the "natural right to life" of another does not excuse or justify a government's actions in taking the life of the condemned.

One of the leading modern day writers on capital punishment, the late Hugo Adam Bedau, articulated the utilitarian philosophy against capital punishment. Bedau contended that punishment should be administered with the most efficient and socially benefiting sanction. He believed the death penalty is not the best means of punishment, because it is not the most efficient sanction and it does not benefit society — it in fact degrades society.[6]

Lack of Deterrence

One of the primary arguments made by proponents of capital punishment is that the punishment has a deterrent effect. Death penalty opponents contend that no supportable proof has ever been deduced which establishes that capital punishment has a meaningful deterrent effect. Death penalty opponents point to the historically consistent high level of homicides as irrefutable proof that capital punishment has no justifiable deterrent effect. For example, the Southern capital punishment states have carried out 80 percent of all executions, but they have a higher murder rate than the Northern capital punishment states. One study found that between 1989 and 2002, California (one execution), Texas (239 executions) and New York (no executions) all had almost identical patterns of murder rates — though overall, Texas' average murder rate was the highest.[7]

Discrimination

Death penalty opponents contend that capital punishment should be abolished because it is not meted out fairly in the nation. They point to statistics which show that capital punishment is disproportionately inflicted upon minorities and the poor. Justice Douglas made the following observation in his concurring opinion in *Furman v. Georgia*, 408 U.S. 238 (1972): "It is the poor, the sick, the ignorant, the powerless and the hated who are executed.[8] One searches our chronicles in vain for the execution of any member of the affluent strata of this society. The Leopolds and Loebs are given prison terms, not sentenced to death."

An example of Justice Douglas' observation can be found in the prosecution of Thomas Capano, a prominent Delaware lawyer. Capano was convicted of capital murder in 1999 and sentenced to death. However, the death sentence was overturned on appeal and Capano was thereafter sentenced to life in prison. Capano died in prison in September of 2011.[9]

TABLE 28.1 CHARACTERISTICS OF DEATH ROW INMATES 2005

Characteristic	Percentage
Male	98.4
Female	1.6
White	55.5
Black	42.2
Other race	2.4
8th grade or less	14.3
9th to 11th grade	36.9

Characteristic	Percentage
Diploma/GED	39.6
Some college	9.2

SOURCE: U.S. Department of Justice, Bureau of Justice Statistics, Corrections, Capital Punishment (2006).

Risk of Executing the Innocent

The justification for abolishing capital punishment that is embraced by most opponents is the risk of executing an innocent person. While no irrefutable evidence has ever been compiled to show that innocent persons were executed, a great deal of research has in fact given strong evidence that suggests many executed persons were in fact innocent. A study done in 1987 suggested that between 1900 and 1985, 23 were prisoners executed in the United States who were actually innocent of the crimes charged.[10]

It was reported that between 1973 and June of 2012, a total of 140 inmates sentenced to die were found to be innocent.[11] Amnesty International has suggested the following reasons for wrongful convictions in death penalty cases: inadequate legal representation; police and prosecutorial misconduct; perjured testimony and mistaken eyewitness testimony; racial prejudice; jailhouse "snitch" testimony; suppression or misinterpretation of mitigating evidence; and community or political pressure to solve a case.[12] In the final analysis, death penalty opponents argue that the risk of executing one innocent person is reason enough to abolish capital punishment.

Nations That Have Abolished Capital Punishment

A decisive trend was set in motion during the last decade of the twentieth century which saw the international community moving away from capital punishment. This trend carried over into the twenty-first century so that by May 2012, 141 nations had abolished capital punishment. That figure includes nations that abolished the death penalty for ordinary crimes only, or have not imposed the penalty in decades.[13]

Most of the nations of the world that have abolished capital punishment have done so through legislative acts. However, a few countries have taken the step of abolishing capital punishment per se, or limiting its application, through their constitutions. Nations that provide for the abolishment of capital punishment through their constitutions include Austria, Belgium, Cape Verde, Colombia, Dominican Republic, Ecuador, Finland, Germany, Haiti, Holland, Honduras, Iceland, Italy, Luxemburg, Marshall Islands, Federated States of Micronesia, Monaco, Mozambique, Namibia, Netherlands, Nicaragua, Panama, Portugal, Sao Tome and Principe, Spain, Sweden, Uruguay and Venezuela.

International Agreements Regarding Capital Punishment

The international arena has produced several documents that call for outright abolishment of capital punishment or limitations on its application.

Second Optional Protocol to the International Covenant on Civil and Political Rights

This instrument was sponsored by the United Nations. It provides for the abolishment of the death penalty. However, it allows nations to retain the death penalty in wartime.

Protocol to the American Convention on
Human Rights to Abolish the Death Penalty

The Organization of American States sponsored this instrument. Under this document capital punishment must be abolished by all nations, but may be retained in wartime.

Protocol No. 6 to the Convention for the Protection
of Human Rights and Fundamental Freedoms

The Council of Europe sponsored this covenant in 1983. It provides for the abolishment of the death penalty in peacetime.

Protocol No. 13 to the Convention for the Protection
of Human Rights and Fundamental Freedoms

The Council of Europe sponsored this covenant in 2002. It provides for the abolishment of the death penalty under all circumstances.

International Covenant on Civil
and Political Rights

The United Nations sponsored this agreement. It provides that capital punishment shall not be imposed for crimes committed by persons below 18 years of age and shall not be carried out on pregnant women.

Convention on the Rights of the Child

The United Nations sponsored this document. It provides that capital punishment shall not be imposed for offenses committed by persons below 18 years of age.

American Convention on Human Rights

The Organization of American States sponsored this instrument. It provides that capital punishment shall not be imposed upon persons who were under 18 or over 70 years of age at the time the crime was committed. It also prohibits imposition of the death penalty on pregnant women.

Safeguards Guaranteeing Protection
of the Rights of Those Facing the Death Penalty

A resolution entitled "Safeguards Guaranteeing Protection of the Rights of Those Facing the Death Penalty" was adopted by the United Nations Economic and Social Council by resolution May 25, 1984. The text of the resolution is set out below.

1. In countries which have not abolished the death penalty, capital punishment may be imposed only for the most serious crimes, it being understood that their scope should not go beyond intentional crimes with lethal or other extremely grave consequences.

2. Capital punishment may be imposed only for a crime for which the death penalty is prescribed by law at the time of its commission, it being understood that if, subsequent to the commission of the crime, provision is made by law for the imposition of a lighter penalty, the offender shall benefit thereby.

3. Persons below 18 years of age at the time of the commission of the crime shall not

be sentenced to death, nor shall the death sentence be carried out on pregnant women, or on new mothers, or on persons who have become insane.

4. Capital punishment may be imposed only when the guilt of the person charged is based upon clear and convincing evidence leaving no room for an alternative explanation of the facts.

5. Capital punishment may only be carried out pursuant to a final judgment rendered by a competent court after legal process which gives all possible safeguards to ensure a fair trial, at least equal to those contained in article 14 of the International Covenant on Civil and Political Rights, including the right of anyone suspected of or charged with a crime for which capital punishment may be imposed to adequate legal assistance at all stages of the proceedings.

6. Anyone sentenced to death shall have the right to appeal to a court of higher jurisdiction, and steps should be taken to ensure that such appeals shall become mandatory.

7. Anyone sentenced to death shall have the right to seek pardon, or commutation of sentence; pardon or commutation of sentence may be granted in all cases of capital punishment.

8. Capital punishment shall not be carried out pending any appeal or other recourse procedure or other proceeding relating to pardon or commutation of the sentence.

9. Where capital punishment occurs, it shall be carried out so as to inflict the minimum possible suffering.

United Nations Commission on Human Rights

On April 3, 1998, the United Nations Commission on Human Rights issued a resolution calling for a moratorium and eventual abolishment of executions in the United States. The resolution was prompted by a report generated by the United Nations Special Rapporteur on Extrajudicial, Summary or Arbitrary Executions. The special rapporteur, Bacre Waly Ndiaye (Senegal), visited the United States from September 21 to October 8, 1997, to investigate reports which suggested that compliance with international agreements relating to fair trials and specific restrictions on the death penalty were not being fully observed in the United States.

In his report, the special rapporteur found that the defendants who received the death penalty in the United States were not necessarily those who committed the most heinous crimes. The report indicated that factors other than the crime itself appeared to influence the imposition of a death sentence. The special rapporteur concluded that race and economic status, both of the victims and the defendants, were key factors in determining whether the death penalty was imposed.

The report was also critical of alleged political influences upon the use of the death penalty. It cited the election of judges as a compromise of the impartiality of the judicial system, which directly impacted on capital prosecutions. There was also criticism of the discretionary powers of the prosecutor in seeking the death penalty. The report found prosecutors often abused their discretion for political reasons when deciding whether to seek the death penalty in a given case.

The jury system also came under attack in the special rapporteur's report. It said that people with reservations regarding the death penalty were less likely to sit as jurors. Further, that jurors were most likely to be people predisposed to imposing capital punishment.

The special rapporteur noted that the practice of imposing capital punishment on juveniles by many jurisdictions was a direct violation international law (no longer permitted in U.S.). The special rapporteur also condemned the practice of executing mentally retarded (no longer permitted in U.S.).

World Coalition Against the Death Penalty

The World Coalition against the Death Penalty was created in Rome in May 2002. The Coalition brings together legal associations, unions, local governments, non-governmental organizations and others who are committed to the struggle against the death penalty, and who want to coordinate their lobbying and actions at an international level. It has declared October 10 the World Day against the death penalty. Article 1 of the Coalition's charter explains its purpose.

Article 1: Purpose of the World Coalition Against the Death Penalty
§1.1: The Coalition brings together various actors sharing a common objective, the universal abolition of the death penalty.

§1.2: The Coalition aims at strengthening the internationalisation of the fight against the death penalty, undertaking and coordinating international actions, including in particular lobbying efforts, that are complementary to those of its members, bringing together new abolitionists, and putting greater pressure on countries whose laws retain the death penalty.

§1.3: The Coalition's statements shall be aimed at complementing those of its members, who retain their full independence. The Coalition shall work primarily at the international level.

World Congress Against the Death Penalty

The World Congress Against the Death Penalty is an event that was started by a French anti-death penalty organization called Ensemble contre la Peine de Mort (Together Against the Death Penalty). The World Congress brings together non-governmental and governmental institutions and individuals opposed to the death penalty. The first World Congress took place in June of 2001 in Strasbourg. The second World Congress took place in Montreal in October of 2004. Paris hosted the third World Congress in February of 2007. At the first World Congress a Final Declaration was issued.

Final Declaration

We, citizens and abolitionist campaigners gathered in Strasbourg from 21 to 23 June 2001 for the Congress against the Death Penalty, organized by Ensemble contre la peine de mort, declare:

The death penalty means the triumph of vengeance over justice and violates the first right of any human being, the right to life. Capital punishment has never prevented crime. It is an act of torture and the ultimate cruel, inhuman and degrading treatment. A society that imposes the death penalty symbolically encourages violence. Every single society that respects the dignity of its people has to strive to abolish capital punishment.

We are pleased to note that many Speakers of Parliament have decided to launch on

22 June a "Solemn appeal for a world-wide moratorium on executions of those sentenced to death as a step towards universal abolition" at the European Parliament.

We demand the universal abolition of the death penalty. In this respect, we call on citizens, states and international organizations to act so that:

a. states ratify all abolitionist treaties and conventions on an international and regional level;

b. countries which have stopped executing people sentenced to death, remove the death penalty from their statute books;

c. states which sentence to death persons who were juveniles at the time of the crime, end this blatant violation of the international law;

d. mentally disabled people cannot be sentenced to death;

e. no states having abolished or suspended executions extradite anyone to third countries still applying the death penalty, irrespective of guarantees that it would not be imposed;

f. states regularly and openly publish information on death sentences, detention conditions and executions.

We support the investigation of the Council of Europe on the compatibility of the observer status of the United States and Japan with their adherence of the death penalty.

We call on the Council of Europe and the European Union to insist that Turkey, Russia and Armenia permanently abolish the death penalty for ALL crimes and commute all death sentences.

We call on the European Union to continue its efforts to achieve the abolition of the death penalty and thus, in the ordinary course of its international relations.

In addition to these general recommendations, we will issue specific recommendations, on a country-by-country basis, to support abolitionist campaigners.

We commit ourselves to creating a world-wide co-ordination of associations and abolitionist campaigners, whose first goal will be to launch a world-wide day for the universal abolition of the death penalty.

We call on the judicial and medical professions to confirm the utter incompatibility of their values with the death penalty and to intensify, country-by-country, their activities against the death penalty.

We associate ourselves with the petitions collected by Amnesty International, the Community of Sant' Egidio, Ensemble contre la peine de mort, the Federation of Human Rights League, Hands off Cain and any other organizations and call on all abolitionist campaigners to sign the following international petition:

"We, citizens of the world, call for an immediate halt of all executions of those sentenced to death and the universal abolition of the death penalty."

Lastly, we call upon every state to take all possible steps towards the adoption by the United Nations of a world-wide moratorium on executions, pending universal abolition.

Inter-American Commission on Human Rights

On August 3, 2012, the Inter-American Commission on Human Rights (IACHR) issued a press release calling for a moratorium in the application of the death penalty in the states of the region that still apply it. The press release was timed with the publication of

IACHR's report, "The Death Penalty in the Inter-American Human Rights System: From Restrictions to Abolition." The report made the following recommendations to its member states, which includes the United States:

The Commission makes the following recommendations to States:

- Impose a moratorium on executions as a step toward the gradual disappearance of this penalty;
- Ratify the Protocol to the American Convention on Human Rights to Abolish the Death Penalty;
- Refrain from any measure that would expand the application of the death penalty or reintroduce it;
- Take any measures necessary to ensure compliance with the strictest standards of due process in capital cases;
- Adopt any steps required to ensure that domestic legal standards conform to the heightened level of review applicable in death penalty cases; and
- Ensure full compliance with the decisions of the Inter-American Commission and Court, and specifically with decisions concerning individual death penalty cases and precautionary and provisional measures.[14]

29

The Costs of
Capital Punishment

Numerous factors make the cost of prosecuting capital felons more expensive than any other type of criminal case. Additional costs have been traced to complex pretrial motions, lengthy jury selections, and expenses for expert witnesses. Holding separate guilt phase and penalty phase proceedings factor tremendously in the increased costs. Once a defendant is convicted and sentenced to death, costs continue to incur through years of legal battles in appellate courts.[1] The ultimate truth of the extra expense imposed by death penalty prosecutions was shown in an article suggesting that prosecutors in poor counties and with limited budgets were less likely to seek the death penalty.[2] This chapter takes a brief look at the data which suggests that capital punishment is a money losing punishment.

The Death Penalty Is Not Cheap

Numerous studies have been conducted which all have concluded that prosecution of a capital felon is more expensive than any other type of criminal prosecution. A 2011 report said that from 1978 to 2011, California spent more than $4 billion on capital punishment cases.[3] A report issued in 2005 said that from 1983 to 2004, New Jersey spent more than $250 million to prosecute capital felons.[4] A 2003 study by Kansas noted that the median cost for prosecuting and executing a capital felon was $1.26 million. It was reported in 2000 that Florida could save $51 million annually by not having capital punishment. A 1992 report on Texas indicated that it spent an average of $2.3 million per death penalty case, which was about three times the cost of imprisoning someone for 40 years.

TABLE 29.0 MEDIAN COSTS FOR DEFENSE REPRESENTATION IN FEDERAL CAPITAL CASES 1998–2004

Type of Case	Total Cost	Attorney Cost	Attorney Total Hours	Attorney In-Court Hours	Attorney Out-of-Court Hours	Expert Cost	Transcript Cost
Death Penalty Not Sought	$44,809	$42,148	436	34	350	$5,275	$210
Death Penalty Sought	$353,185	$273,901	2,104	306	1,645	$83,029	$5,223

SOURCE: Jon B. Gould and Lisa Greenman, Report to the Committee on Defender Services Judicial Conference of the United States Update on the Cost and Quality of Defense Representation in Federal Death Penalty Cases (2010).

TABLE 29.1 TENNESSEE AVERAGE POST-CONVICTION DEFENSE COSTS 1993–2003

	Death Penalty	Life Without Parole	Life with Parole
Lead Counsel	$16,430	$1,281	$1,106
Co-counsel	$14,076	$0	$0
Expert Costs	$17,986	$0	$0
Total	$48,492	$1,281	$1,106

SOURCE: Office of Research Statistical Data Analysis of Administrative Office of the Courts, Indigent Defense Fund Data 1993–2003.

TABLE 29.2 INDIANA COSTS FOR MURDER CASES 2000–2007

Sentence Sought	Trial or Plea	Sentence Imposed	Number of Cases	Costs for Counsel, Experts, Appeals, Other	Cost of Incarceration	Combined Cost
Death	Trial	Death	6	$449,887	$55,886	$505,773
Death	Trial	Life w/o Parole	1	$518,002	$110,445	$628,447
Death	Plea	Life w/o Parole	19	$122,441	$109,072	$231,513
Life w/o Parole	Trial	Life w/o Parole	7	$42,658	$108,889	$151,547
Life w/o Parole	Plea	Life w/o Parole	7	$21,985	$108,721	$130,706
Life w/o Parole	Trial	Term of Years	3	$51,146	$107,439	$158,585
Life w/o Parole	Plea	Term of Years	2	$37,382	$111,416	$148,798

SOURCE: Indiana Legislative Services Agency, Office of Fiscal and Management Analysis 2010.

TABLE 29.3 NORTH CAROLINA EXTRA EXPENDITURES FOR DEATH PENALTY CASES 2005–2006

Purpose of Extra Expenditure	Amount of Extra Costs
Extra defense costs for trial phase	$13,180,385
Extra payments to jurors	$224,640
Post-conviction costs	$7,473,556
Resentencing hearings	$594,216
Prison system	$169,617
Total	$21,642,414

SOURCE: Philip J. Cook, "Potential Savings from Abolition of the Death Penalty in North Carolina," 2009.

As a result of the extraordinary costs imposed on Okanogan County, Washington, for a death penalty prosecution, the state of Washington enacted the Reimbursement of Extraordinary Criminal Justice Costs Act of 1999. The act was created to provide counties with financial relief from the extraordinary costs of investigating, prosecuting and defending aggravated murder cases.[5]

Washington Revised Code § 43.330.190
Reimbursement of Extraordinary Criminal Justice Costs Act
  Counties may submit a petition for relief to the office of public defense for reimbursement of extraordinary criminal justice costs. Extraordinary criminal justice costs are defined as those associated with investigation, prosecution, indigent defense, jury impanelment, expert witnesses, interpreters, incarceration, and other adjudication costs of aggravated murder cases.
  (1) The office of public defense, in consultation with the Washington association of prosecuting attorneys and the Washington association of sheriffs and police chiefs, shall develop procedures for processing the petitions, for auditing the veracity of the petitions, and for prioritizing the petitions. Prioritization of the petitions shall be based on, but not limited to,

such factors as disproportionate fiscal impact relative to the county budget, efficient use of resources, and whether the costs are extraordinary and could not be reasonably accommodated and anticipated in the normal budget process.

(2) Before January 1st of each year, the office of public defense, in consultation with the Washington association of prosecuting attorneys and the Washington association of sheriffs and police chiefs, shall develop and submit to the appropriate fiscal committees of the senate and house of representatives a prioritized list of submitted petitions that are recommended for funding by the legislature.

Time Spent Defending Capital Murder Defendants

A study of time spent defending capital murder defendants was reported in 2012 by Dr. Terance D. Miethe. The study examined murder prosecutions in Clark County, Nevada, during the period 2009 to 2011. Dr. Miethe's study was designed to provide average estimates of the time spent at various stages of criminal processing for the defense of capital and non-capital murder cases. A summary of the report's findings are set out below.[6]

Pretrial Phase Activities

The median time estimate as lead defense counsel for pretrial phase activities was 1,075 hours in a typical capital murder case and 461 hours in a typical non-capital murder case. The median time estimate as co-defense counsel for pretrial phase activities was 685 hours in a typical capital murder case and 351 hours in a typical noncapital murder case. The median time estimates as lead defense counsel and co-defense counsel for pretrial phase activities was 1,760 hours in a typical capital murder case and 812 hours in a typical non-capital murder case. This time differential as lead defense counsel and co-defense counsel was 948 hours longer for pretrial activities in capital than non-capital cases.

TABLE 29.4 TENNESSEE AVERAGE NUMBER OF DAYS
FROM OFFENSE DATE TO SENTENCE DATE 1993–2003

Type of Case	Average Days
Death Penalty	847
Life Without Parole	659
Life with Possibility of Parole	665

SOURCE: Office of Research, analysis of information from the Administrative Office of the Courts 1993–2003.

Trial Phase Activities

The median time estimate as lead defense counsel for trial phase activities was 168 hours in a typical capital murder case and 110 hours in a typical non-capital murder case. The median time estimate as co-defense counsel for trial phase activities was 180 hours in a typical capital murder case and 110 hours in a typical non-capital murder case. The median time estimates as lead defense counsel and co-defense counsel for trial phase activities was 348 hours in a typical capital murder case and 220 hours in a typical non-capital murder case. This time differential as lead defense counsel and co-defense counsel was 128 hours longer for trial activities in capital than noncapital cases.

Penalty Phase Activities

The median time estimate as lead defense counsel for penalty phase activities was 56 hours in a typical capital murder case and 12 hours in a non-capital murder case. The median time estimate as co-defense counsel for penalty phase activities was 58 hours in a typical capital murder case and 12 hours in a typical noncapital murder case. The median time estimates as lead defense counsel and co-defense counsel for penalty phase activities was 114 hours in a typical capital murder case and 24 hours in a typical non-capital murder case. This time differential as lead defense counsel and co-defense counsel was 90 hours longer for penalty phase activities in capital than non-capital cases.

Post-Conviction Phase Activities

The median time estimate as lead defense counsel for post-conviction phase activities was 48 hours in a typical capital murder case and 18 hours in a typical noncapital murder case. The median time estimate as co-defense counsel for post-conviction phase activities was 28 hours in a typical capital murder case and 13 hours in a typical non-capital murder case. The median time estimates as lead defense counsel and co-defense counsel for post-conviction phase activities was 76 hours in a typical capital murder case and 31 hours in a typical non-capital murder case. This time differential as lead defense counsel and co-defense counsel was 45 hours longer for post-conviction activities in capital than non-capital cases.

Appendix:
State and Federal
Death Penalty Laws

Alabama

General considerations. The state of Alabama is a capital punishment jurisdiction. The State reenacted its death penalty law after the United States Supreme Court decision in *Furman v. Georgia*, 408 U.S. 238 (1972), on March 5, 1976. It is provided under the laws of Alabama that, in capital cases, an indigent defendant must be appointed legal counsel having no less than five years of experience in the active practice of criminal law. Capital murder in Alabama is punishable by death or life imprisonment without parole. A capital prosecution in Alabama is bifurcated into a guilt phase and penalty phase. It is required at the penalty phase that at least 10 of 12 jurors must agree that a death sentence is appropriate before it can be imposed. If the penalty phase jury is unable to reach a verdict, the trial judge is required to declare a mistrial and convene another penalty phase jury. The decision of a penalty phase jury is not binding on the trial court under the laws of Alabama.

Under Alabama's capital punishment statute, a sentence of death is automatically reviewed by the Alabama Supreme Court. Alabama uses lethal injection to carry out death sentences, but a prisoner has the option of being put to death in the electric chair. The State's death row facility for men is in Atmore, while the facility for women is in Wetumpka. The governor has authority to grant clemency in capital cases. Capital felons who have their death sentences commuted to life imprisonment are eligible for a pardon from the state's Board of Pardons and Parole, if the board obtains sufficient evidence to indicate that the inmate is innocent of the crime and unanimously approves the pardon with the governor.

Death penalty offenses. Alabama's capital punishment offenses are set out under Alabama Code § 13A-5-40(a). This statute is triggered if a person commits a homicide under the following special circumstances:

(1) Murder by the defendant during a kidnapping in the first degree or an attempt thereof committed by the defendant.

(2) Murder by the defendant during a robbery in the first degree or an attempt thereof committed by the defendant.

(3) Murder by the defendant during a rape in the first or second degree or an attempt thereof committed by the defendant; or murder by the defendant during sodomy in the first or second degree or an attempt thereof committed by the defendant.

(4) Murder by the defendant during a burglary in the first or second degree or an attempt thereof committed by the defendant.

(5) Murder of any police officer, sheriff, deputy, state trooper, federal law enforcement officer, or any other state or federal peace officer of any kind, or prison or jail guard, while such officer or guard

is on duty, regardless of whether the defendant knew or should have known the victim was an officer or guard on duty, or because of some official or job-related act or performance of such officer or guard.

(6) Murder committed while the defendant is under sentence of life imprisonment.

(7) Murder done for a pecuniary or other valuable consideration or pursuant to a contract or for hire.

(8) Murder by the defendant during sexual abuse in the first or second degree or an attempt thereof committed by the defendant.

(9) Murder by the defendant during arson in the first or second degree committed by the defendant; or murder by the defendant by means of explosives or explosion.

(10) Murder wherein two or more persons are murdered by the defendant by one act or pursuant to one scheme or course of conduct.

(11) Murder by the defendant when the victim is a state or federal public official or former public official and the murder stems from or is caused by or is related to his official position, act, or capacity.

(12) Murder by the defendant during the act of unlawfully assuming control of any aircraft by use of threats or force with intent to obtain any valuable consideration for the release of said aircraft or any passenger or crewmen thereon or to direct the route or movement of said aircraft, or otherwise exert control over said aircraft.

(13) Murder by a defendant who has been convicted of any other murder in the 20 years preceding the crime; provided that the murder which constitutes the capital crime shall be murder as defined in subsection (b) of this section; and provided further that the prior murder conviction referred to shall include murder in any degree as defined at the time and place of the prior conviction.

(14) Murder when the victim is subpoenaed, or has been subpoenaed, to testify, or the victim had testified, in any preliminary hearing, grand jury proceeding, criminal trial or criminal proceeding of whatever nature, or civil trial or civil proceeding of whatever nature, in any municipal, state, or federal court, when the murder stems from, is caused by, or is related to the capacity or role of the victim as a witness.

(15) Murder when the victim is less than fourteen years of age.

(16) Murder committed by or through the use of a deadly weapon fired or otherwise used from outside a dwelling while the victim is in a dwelling.

(17) Murder committed by or through the use of a deadly weapon while the victim is in a vehicle.

(18) Murder committed by or through the use of a deadly weapon fired or otherwise used within or from a vehicle.

Under Alabama Code § 13A-10-152 the crime of terrorism is made a capital offense. This crime is committed when a person commits a homicide with the intent to intimidate or coerce a civilian population, influence the policy of a unit of government by intimidation or coercion, or affect the conduct of a unit of government by murder, assassination, or kidnapping.

Aggravating circumstances used to impose death penalty. In order to impose a death sentence upon a defendant, Alabama Code § 13A-5-49 requires that the prosecutor establishes the existence of at least one of the following statutory aggravating circumstances at the penalty phase:

(1) The capital offense was committed by a person under sentence of imprisonment;

(2) The defendant was previously convicted of another capital offense or a felony involving the use or threat of violence to the person;

(3) The defendant knowingly created a great risk of death to many persons;

(4) The capital offense was committed while the defendant was engaged or was an accomplice in the commission of, or an attempt to commit, or flight after committing, or attempting to commit, rape, robbery, burglary or kidnapping;

(5) The capital offense was committed for the purpose of avoiding or preventing a lawful arrest or effecting an escape from custody;

(6) The capital offense was committed for pecuniary gain;

(7) The capital offense was committed to disrupt or hinder the lawful exercise of any governmental function or the enforcement of laws;

(8) The capital offense was especially heinous, atrocious, or cruel compared to other capital offenses;

(9) The defendant intentionally caused the death of two or more persons by one act or pursuant to one scheme or course of conduct; or

(10) The capital offense was one of a series of intentional killings committed by the defendant.

Mitigating circumstances. Although the federal Constitution will not permit jurisdictions to prevent capital felons from presenting all relevant mitigating evidence at the penalty phase, Alabama has provided by statute, Alabama Code § 13A-5-51, the following statutory mitigating circumstances that permit a jury to reject imposition of the death penalty:

(1) The defendant has no significant history of prior criminal activity;

(2) The capital offense was committed while the defendant was under the influence of extreme mental or emotional disturbance;

(3) The victim was a participant in the defendant's conduct or consented to it;

(4) The defendant was an accomplice in the capital offense committed by another person and his participation was relatively minor;

(5) The defendant acted under extreme duress or under the substantial domination of another person;

(6) The capacity of the defendant to appreciate the criminality of his conduct or to conform his conduct to the requirements of law was substantially impaired; and

(7) The age of the defendant at the time of the crime.

Persons who may attend execution. Alabama law limits the number of persons who may be present at an execution. The following is provided by Ala. Code § 15-18-83:

(a) The following persons may be present at an execution and none other:

(1) The executioner and any persons necessary to assist in conducting the execution.

(2) The Commissioner of Corrections or his or her representative.

(3) Two physicians, including the prison physician.

(4) The spiritual advisor of the condemned.

(5) The chaplain of Holman Prison.

(6) Such newspaper reporters as may be admitted by the warden.

(7) Any of the relatives or friends of the condemned person that he or she may request, not exceeding six in number.

(8) The immediate family of the victim, over the age of 19, not exceeding eight in number and apportioned equally among the victim's immediate family members. If there are fewer than six total immediate family members of the deceased victim, additional immediate family members of a victim, for whose death the inmate is not sentenced to death.

(b) No convict shall be permitted by the prison authorities to witness the execution.

Arizona

General considerations. The state of Arizona is a capital punishment jurisdiction. The State reenacted its death penalty law after the United States Supreme Court decision in *Furman v. Georgia*, 408 U.S. 238 (1972), on August 8, 1973. Arizona requires the appointment of two attorneys to represent indigent capital felon defendants. The lead attorney is required to have practiced criminal law for at least five years and been counsel in at least one prior capital prosecution. Capital murder in Arizona is punishable by death or life imprisonment with or without parole. A capital prosecution in Arizona is bifurcated into a guilt phase and penalty phase. It is required at the penalty phase that the jury must unanimously agree that a death sentence is appropriate before it can be imposed. If the penalty phase jury is unable to reach a unanimous verdict, the defendant must be sentenced to imprisonment for life.

Under Arizona's capital punishment statute, a sentence of death is automatically reviewed by the Arizona Supreme Court. Arizona uses lethal injection to carry out death sentences. However, defendants sentenced to death for an offense committed prior to November 23, 1992, may elect between lethal gas or lethal injection as the means of execution. The state's death row facility for males is in Florence while the facility for females is in Perryville. The governor has authority to grant clemency in capital cases. The governor is required to obtain the consent of the state's Board of Pardons and Parole before a capital sentence may be commuted.

Death penalty offenses. Arizona's capital punishment offenses are set out under Arizona Code § 13-1105. This statute is triggered if a person commits a homicide under the following special circumstances:

1. Intending or knowing that the person's conduct will cause death, the person causes the death of another person, including an unborn child, with premeditation or, as a result of causing the death of another person with premeditation, causes the death of an unborn child.

2. Acting either alone or with one or more other persons the person commits or attempts to commit sexual conduct..., terrorism, ... narcotics offenses..., drive-by-shooting, kidnapping, burglary, arson, robbery, escape, child abuse, or unlawful flight from a pursuing law enforcement vehicle and in the course of and, in furtherance of the offense or immediate flight from the offense, the person or another person causes the death of any person.

3. Intending or knowing that the person's conduct will cause death to a law enforcement officer, the person causes the death of a law enforcement officer who is in the line of duty.

Aggravating circumstances used to impose death penalty. In order to impose a death sentence upon a defendant, Arizona Code § 13-751(F) requires that the prosecutor establishes the existence of at least one of the following statutory aggravating circumstances at the penalty phase:

1. The defendant has been convicted of another offense in the United States for which under Arizona law a sentence of life imprisonment or death was imposable.

2. The defendant has been or was previously convicted of a serious offense, whether preparatory or completed. Convictions for serious offenses committed on the same occasion as the homicide, or not committed on the same occasion but consolidated for trial with the homicide, shall be treated as a serious offense under this paragraph.

3. In the commission of the offense the defendant knowingly created a grave risk of death to another person or persons in addition to the person murdered during the commission of the offense.

4. The defendant procured the commission of the offense by payment, or promise of payment, of anything of pecuniary value.

5. The defendant committed the offense as consideration for the receipt, or in expectation of the receipt, of anything of pecuniary value.

6. The defendant committed the offense in an especially heinous, cruel or depraved manner.

7. The defendant committed the offense while: (a) In the custody of or on authorized or unauthorized release from the state department of corrections, a law enforcement agency or a county or city jail. (b) On probation for a felony offense.

8. The defendant has been convicted of one or more other homicides, as defined in § 13-1101, that were committed during the commission of the offense.

9. The defendant was an adult at the time the offense was committed or was tried as an adult and the murdered person was under fifteen years of age, was an unborn child in the womb at any stage of its development or was seventy years of age or older.

10. The murdered person was an on duty peace officer who was killed in the course of performing the officer's official duties and the defendant knew, or should have known, that the murdered person was a peace officer.

11. The defendant committed the offense with the intent to promote, further or assist the objectives of a criminal street gang or criminal syndicate or to join a criminal street gang or criminal syndicate.

12. The defendant committed the offense to prevent a person's cooperation with an official law enforcement investigation, to prevent a person's testimony in a court proceeding, in retaliation for a person's cooperation with an official law enforcement investigation or in retaliation for a person's testimony in a court proceeding.

13. The offense was committed in a cold, calculated manner without pretense of moral or legal justification.

14. The defendant used a remote stun gun or an authorized remote stun gun in the commission of the offense.

Mitigating circumstances. Although the federal Constitution will not permit jurisdictions to prevent capital felons from presenting all relevant mitigating evidence at the penalty phase, Arizona has provided by statute, Arizona Code § 13-751(G), the following statutory mitigating circumstances that permit a jury to reject imposition of the death penalty:

1. The defendant's capacity to appreciate the wrongfulness of his conduct or to conform his conduct to the requirements of law was significantly impaired, but not so impaired as to constitute a defense to prosecution.

2. The defendant was under unusual and substantial duress, although not such as to constitute a defense to prosecution.

3. The defendant was legally accountable for the conduct of another under § 13-303, but his participation was relatively minor, although not so minor as to constitute a defense to prosecution.

4. The defendant could not reasonably have foreseen that his conduct in the course of the commission of the offense for which the defendant was convicted would cause, or would create a grave risk of causing, death to another person.

5. The defendant's age.

Persons who may attend an execution. Arizona laws limit the number of persons who may be present at an execution. The following is provided by Arizona Code § 13-758:

The director of the state department of corrections or the director's designee shall be present at the execution of all death sentences and shall invite the attorney general and at least twelve reputable citizens of the director's selection to be present at the execution. The director shall, at the request of the defendant, permit clergymen, not exceeding two, whom the defendant names and any persons, relatives or friends, not exceeding five, to be present at the execution. The director may invite peace officers as the director deems expedient to witness the execution. No persons other than those set forth in this section shall be present at the execution nor shall any minor be allowed to witness the execution.

Arkansas

General considerations. Arkansas is a capital punishment jurisdiction. The state reenacted its death penalty law after the United States Supreme Court decision in *Furman v. Georgia*, 408 U.S. 238 (1972), on March 23, 1973. The laws of Arkansas, in capital cases, provide that an indigent defendant must be appointed two attorneys. Capital murder in Arkansas is punishable by death or life imprisonment without parole. A capital prosecution in Arkansas is bifurcated into a guilt phase and penalty phase. It is required at the penalty phase that jurors must unanimously agree that a death sentence is appropriate before it can be imposed. If the penalty phase jury is unable to reach a verdict, the trial judge is required to impose a sentence of life imprisonment.

Under Arkansas' capital punishment statute, a sentence of death is automatically reviewed by the Arkansas Supreme Court. Arkansas uses lethal injection to carry out death sentences. However, if that method is found unconstitutional, then death is imposed by electrocution. The state's death row facility for men is in Tucker; the facility for women is in Pine Bluff. Pursuant to the laws of Arkansas the governor has authority to grant clemency in capital cases. The state's parole board is permitted to make a nonbinding recommendation whether a death sentence should be commuted.

Death penalty offenses. Arkansas' capital punishment offenses are set out under Arkansas Code § 5-10-101(a). This statute is triggered if a person commits a homicide under the following special circumstances:

(1) Acting alone or with one or more other persons: (A) The person commits or attempts to commit: (i) Terrorism; (ii) Rape; (iii) Kidnapping; (iv) Vehicular piracy; (v) Robbery; (vi) Aggravated robbery; (vii) Residential burglary; (viii) Commercial burglary; (ix) Aggravated residential burglary; (x) A felony violation of the Uniform Controlled Substances Act, involving an actual delivery of a controlled substance; or (xi) First degree escape; and (B) In the course of and in furtherance of the felony or in immediate flight from the felony, the person or an accomplice causes the death of a person under circumstances manifesting extreme indifference to the value of human life;

(2) Acting alone or with one or more other persons: (A) The person commits or attempts to commit arson; and (B) In the course of and in furtherance of the felony or in immediate flight from the felony, the person or an accomplice causes the death of any person;

(3) With the premeditated and deliberated purpose of causing the death of any law enforcement officer, jailer, prison official, firefighter, judge or other court official, probation officer, parole officer, any military personnel, or teacher or school employee, when such person is acting in the line of duty, the person causes the death of any person;

(4) With the premeditated and deliberate purpose of causing the death of another person, the person causes the death of any person;

(5) With the premeditated and deliberate purpose of causing the death of the holder of any public office filled by election or appointment or a candidate for public office, the person causes the death of any person;

(6) While incarcerated in the Department of Correction or the Department of Community Correction, the person purposely causes the death of another person after premeditation and deliberation;

(7) Pursuant to an agreement that the person cause the death of another person in return for anything of value, he or she causes the death of any person;

(8) The person enters into an agreement in which a person is to cause the death of another person in return for anything of value, and a person hired pursuant to the agreement causes the death of any person;

(9)(A) Under circumstances manifesting extreme indifference to the value of human life, the person knowingly causes the death of a person fourteen (14) years of age or younger at the time the murder was committed if the defendant was eighteen (18) years of age or older at the time the murder was committed ... or

(10) The person: (A) Purposely discharges a firearm from a vehicle at a person or at a vehicle, conveyance, or a residential or commercial occupiable structure that he or she knows or has good reason to believe to be occupied by a person; and (B) Thereby causes the death of another person under circumstances manifesting extreme indifference to the value of human life.

It is provided in Arkansas Code § 5-51-201 that the crime of treason against the state is a capital offense. Treason is defined as levying war against the state, or adhering to the state's enemies by giving them aid and comfort.

Aggravating circumstances used to impose death penalty. In order to impose a death sentence upon a defendant, Arkansas Code § 5-4-604 requires that the prosecutor establishes the existence of at least one of the following statutory aggravating circumstances at the penalty phase:

(1) The capital murder was committed by a person imprisoned as a result of a felony conviction;

(2) The capital murder was committed by a person unlawfully at liberty after being sentenced to imprisonment as a result of a felony conviction;

(3) The person previously committed another felony, an element of which was the use or threat of violence to another person or the creation of a substantial risk of death or serious physical injury to another person;

(4) The person in the commission of the capital murder knowingly created a great risk of death to a person other than the victim or caused the death of more than one (1) person in the same criminal episode;

(5) The capital murder was committed for the purpose of avoiding or preventing an arrest or effecting an escape from custody;

(6) The capital murder was committed for pecuniary gain;

(7) The capital murder was committed for the purpose of disrupting or hindering the lawful exercise of any government or political function;

(8) (A) The capital murder was committed in an especially cruel or depraved manner ...;

(9) The capital murder was committed by means of a destructive device, bomb, explosive, or similar device that the person planted, hid, or concealed in any place, area, dwelling, building, or structure, or mailed or delivered, or caused to be planted, hidden, concealed, mailed, or delivered, and the person knew that his or her act would create a great risk of death to human life; or

(10) The capital murder was committed against a person whom the defendant knew or reasonably should have known was especially vulnerable to the attack because: (A) Of either a temporary or permanent severe physical or mental disability which would interfere with the victim's ability to flee or to defend himself or herself; or (B) The person was twelve (12) years of age or younger.

Mitigating circumstances. Although the federal Constitution will not permit jurisdictions to prevent capital felons from presenting all relevant mitigating evidence at the penalty phase, Arkansas has provided by statute, Arkansas Code § 5-4-605, the following statutory mitigating circumstances that permit a jury to reject imposition of the death penalty:

(1) The capital murder was committed while the defendant was under extreme mental or emotional disturbance;

(2) The capital murder was committed while the defendant was acting under an unusual pressure or influence or under the domination of another person;

(3) The capital murder was committed while the capacity of the defendant to appreciate the wrongfulness of his or her conduct or to conform his or her conduct to the requirements of law was impaired as a result of mental disease or defect, intoxication, or drug abuse;

(4) The youth of the defendant at the time of the commission of the capital murder;

(5) The capital murder was committed by another person and the defendant was an accomplice and his or her participation was relatively minor; or

(6) The defendant has no significant history of prior criminal activity.

Persons who may attend execution. Under the laws of Arkansas a limitation is imposed upon the number of persons who may be present at an execution. The following is provided by Arkansas Code § 16-90-502(d):

(1) No execution of any person convicted in this state of a capital offense shall be public, but shall be private.

(2) At the execution there shall be present the director or an assistant, the Department of Correction official in charge of medical services or his or her designee, and a number of respectable citizens numbering not fewer than six (6) nor more than twelve (12) whose presence is necessary to verify that the execution was conducted in the manner required by law. Counsel for the person being executed and the spiritual adviser to the person being executed may be present. Other persons designated by the director may be present, but the maximum number of persons at the execution shall not exceed thirty (30).

(3) (A) During the execution there shall be a closed-circuit audiovisual monitor placed in a location chosen by the director, and any close relatives of the deceased victim or any surviving innocent victims who desire to view the execution may be present. In no case shall the number of viewers exceed five (5) per execution. No audio or video recording shall be made of the execution.

California

General considerations. California is a capital punishment jurisdiction. The state reenacted its death penalty law after the United States Supreme Court decision in *Furman v. Georgia*, 408 U.S. 238 (1972), in 1977. In November of 1978 California voters approved Proposition 7 reaffirming the death penalty. Capital murder in California is punishable by death, life imprisonment without parole, or confinement in the state prison for a term of 25 years. A capital prosecution in California is bifurcated into a guilt phase and penalty phase. It is required at the penalty phase that the jury must unanimously agree that a death sentence is appropriate before it can be imposed. If the penalty phase jury is unable to reach a verdict, the trial judge is required to impanel a second penalty phase jury to decide the defendant's fate. If the second jury cannot reach a unanimous verdict, the trial judge is required to impanel a third penalty phase jury to decide the defendant's fate. If the third jury cannot reach a unanimous verdict, the trial judge is required to impose a punishment of confinement in prison for a term of 25 years. A unanimous decision by the penalty phase jury is binding on the trial court under the laws of California.

Under California's capital punishment statute, a sentence of death is automatically reviewed by the California Supreme Court. California uses lethal gas or lethal injection (a prisoner may choose) to carry out a death sentence. The state's death row facility for men is in San Quentin; the facility for female death row inmates is in Chowchilla. Pursuant to the laws of California the Governor has authority to grant clemency in capital cases. If a capital felon has two prior felony convictions, the governor must obtain a recommendation of the state's Supreme Court in order to grant clemency.

Death penalty offenses. California's capital punishment offenses are set out under California Penal Code § 189. This statute is triggered if a person commits a homicide under the following special circumstances:

[P]erpetrated by means of a destructive device or explosive, a weapon of mass destruction, knowing use of ammunition designed primarily to penetrate metal or armor, poison, lying in wait, torture, or by any other kind of willful, deliberate, and premeditated killing, or which is committed in the perpetration of, or attempt to perpetrate, arson, rape, carjacking, robbery, burglary, mayhem, kidnapping, train wrecking, or ... perpetrated by means of discharging a firearm from a motor vehicle, intentionally at another person outside of the vehicle with the intent to inflict death.

Under California Penal Code § 128 any person who, by willful perjury or subornation of perjury procures the conviction and execution of an innocent person, may be sentenced death.

Aggravating circumstances used to impose the death penalty. In order to impose a death sentence upon a defendant, California Penal Code § 190.2 requires that the prosecutor establishes the existence of at least one of the following statutory aggravating circumstances at the penalty phase:

(1) The murder was intentional and carried out for financial gain.

(2) The defendant was convicted previously of murder in the first or second degree.

(3) The defendant ... has been convicted [in the current prosecution] of more than one offense of murder in the first or second degree.

(4) The murder was committed by means of a destructive device, bomb, or explosive planted, hidden, or concealed in any place, area, dwelling, building, or structure, and the defendant knew, or reasonably should have known, that his or her act or acts would create a great risk of death to one or more human beings.

(5) The murder was committed for the purpose of avoiding or preventing a lawful arrest, or perfecting or attempting to perfect, an escape from lawful custody.

(6) The murder was committed by means of a destructive device, bomb, or explosive that the defendant mailed or delivered, attempted to mail or deliver, or caused to be mailed or delivered, and the defendant knew, or reasonably should have known, that his or her act or acts would create a great risk of death to one or more human beings.

(7) The victim was a peace officer.

(8) The victim was a federal law enforcement officer or agent.

(9) The victim was a firefighter.

(10) The victim was a witness to a crime who was intentionally killed for the purpose of preventing his or her testimony in any criminal or juvenile proceeding.

(11) The victim was a prosecutor or assistant prosecutor or a former prosecutor or assistant prosecutor of any local or state prosecutor's office.

(12) The victim was a judge or former judge of any court of record in the local, state, or federal system.

(13) The victim was an elected or appointed official or former official of the federal government, or of any local or state government.

(14) The murder was especially heinous, atrocious, or cruel, manifesting exceptional depravity.

(15) The defendant intentionally killed the victim by means of lying in wait.

(16) The victim was intentionally killed because of his or her race, color, religion, nationality, or country of origin.

(17) The murder was committed while the defendant was engaged in, or was an accomplice in, the commission of, attempted commission of, or the immediate flight after committing, or attempting to commit, the following felonies: (a) robbery, (b) kidnapping, (c) rape, (d) sodomy, (e) performance of a lewd or lascivious act upon the person of a child under the age of 14 years, (f) oral copulation, (g) burglary, (h) arson, (i) train wrecking, (j) mayhem, (k) rape with an instrument, or (l) carjacking.

(18) The murder was intentional and involved the infliction of torture.

(19) The defendant intentionally killed the victim by the administration of poison.

(20) The victim was a juror in any court of record in the local, state, or federal system.

(21) The murder was intentional and perpetrated by means of discharging a firearm from a motor vehicle, intentionally at another person or persons outside the vehicle with the intent to inflict death.

(22) The defendant intentionally killed the victim while the defendant was an active participant in a criminal street gang.

Mitigating circumstances. Although the federal Constitution will not permit jurisdictions to prevent capital felons from presenting all relevant mitigating evidence at the penalty phase,

California has provided by statute, California Penal Code § 190.3, the following statutory mitigating circumstances that permit a jury to reject imposition of the death penalty:

(a) The circumstances of the crime of which the defendant was convicted.

(b) The ... absence of criminal activity by the defendant which involved the use or attempted use of force or violence or the express or implied threat to use force or violence.

(c) The ... absence of any prior felony conviction.

(d) [T]he offense was committed while the defendant was under the influence of extreme mental or emotional disturbance.

(e) [T]he victim was a participant in the defendant's homicidal conduct or consented to the homicidal act.

(f) [T]he offense was committed under circumstances which the defendant reasonably believed to be a moral justification or extenuation for his conduct.

(g) [D]efendant acted under extreme duress or under the substantial domination of another person.

(h) [A]t the time of the offense the capacity of the defendant to appreciate the criminality of his conduct or to conform his conduct to the requirements of law was impaired as a result of mental disease or defect, or the effects of intoxication.

(i) The age of the defendant at the time of the crime.

(j) [T]he defendant was an accomplice to the offense and his participation in the commission of the offense was relatively minor.

(k) Any other circumstance which extenuates the gravity of the crime even though it is not a legal excuse for the crime.

Persons who may attend an execution. California law limits the number of persons who may be present at an execution. The following is provided by California Penal Code § 3605:

(a) The warden of the state prison where the execution is to take place shall be present at the execution and shall, subject to any applicable requirement or definition set forth in subdivision (b), invite the presence of the attorney general, the members of the immediate family of the victim or victims of the defendant, and at least 12 reputable citizens, to be selected by the warden. The warden shall, at the request of the defendant, permit those ministers of the gospel, not exceeding two, as the defendant may name, and any persons, relatives or friends, not to exceed five, to be present at the execution, together with those peace officers or any other Department of Corrections employee as he or she may think expedient, to witness the execution. But no other persons than those specified in this section may be present at the execution, nor may any person under 18 years of age be allowed to witness the execution.

(b)(1) For purposes of an invitation required by subdivision (a) to members of the immediate family of the victim or victims of the defendant, the warden of the state prison where the execution is to take place shall make the invitation only if a member of the immediate family of the victim or victims of the defendant so requests in writing. In the event that a written request is made, the warden of the state prison where the execution is to take place shall automatically make the invitation 30 days prior to the date of an imminent execution or as close to this date as practicable.

(2) For purposes of this section, "immediate family" means those persons who are related by blood, adoption, or marriage, within the second degree of consanguinity or affinity.

(c) No physician or any other person invited pursuant to this section, whether or not employed by the Department of Corrections, shall be compelled to attend the execution, and any physician's attendance shall be voluntary. A physician's or any other person's refusal to attend the execution shall not be used in any disciplinary action or negative job performance citation.

Colorado

General considerations. Colorado is a capital punishment jurisdiction. The state reenacted its death penalty law after the United States Supreme Court decision in *Furman v. Georgia*, 408 U.S. 238 (1972), on January 1, 1975. Capital murder in Colorado is punishable by death or life imprisonment without parole. A capital prosecution in Colorado is bifurcated into a guilt phase and penalty phase. It is required at the penalty phase that the jury must unanimously agree that a death sentence is appropriate before it can be imposed. If the penalty phase jury is unable to reach a unanimous verdict, the defendant must be sentenced to imprisonment for life.

Under Colorado's capital punishment statute, a sentence of death is automatically reviewed by the Colorado Supreme Court. Colorado uses lethal injection to carry out death sentences. The state's death row facilities for men and women are in Cannon City. Pursuant to the laws of Colorado the governor has authority to grant clemency in capital cases. Commutation may be life imprisonment or a term of not less than twenty years at hard labor.

Death penalty offenses. Colorado's capital punishment offenses are set out under Colorado Code § 18-3-102. This statute is triggered if a person commits a homicide under the following special circumstances:

(a) After deliberation and with the intent to cause the death of a person other than himself, he causes the death of that person or of another person; or

(b) Acting either alone or with one or more persons, he commits or attempts to commit arson, robbery, burglary, kidnapping, sexual assault, or the crime of escape and, in the course of or in furtherance of the crime that he is committing or attempting to commit, or of immediate flight therefrom, the death of a person, other than one of the participants, is caused by anyone; or

(c) By perjury or subornation of perjury he procures the conviction and execution of any innocent person; or

(d) Under circumstances evidencing an attitude of universal malice manifesting extreme indifference to the value of human life generally, he knowingly engages in conduct which creates a grave risk of death to a person, or persons, other than himself, and thereby causes the death of another; or

(e) He or she commits unlawful distribution, dispensation, or sale of a controlled substance to a person under the age of eighteen years on school grounds, and the death of such person is caused by the use of such controlled substance; or

(f) The person knowingly causes the death of a child who has not yet attained twelve years of age and the person committing the offense is one in a position of trust with respect to the victim.

Under Colorado Code § 18-3-107 the killing of a police officer or firefighter is a capital offense. This statute is triggered when police officer or firefighter is killed while engaged in the performance of his or her duties.

Aggravating circumstances used to impose death penalty. In order to impose a death sentence upon a defendant, Colorado Code § 18-1.3-1201(5) requires that the prosecutor establish the existence of at least one of the following statutory aggravating circumstances at the penalty phase:

(a) The murder was committed by a person under sentence of imprisonment for a felony; or

(b) The defendant was previously convicted of a felony; or

(c) The defendant intentionally killed any of the following persons while such person was engaged in the course of the performance of such person's official duties, and the defendant knew or reasonably should have known that such victim was such a person engaged in the performance of such person's official duties, or the victim was intentionally killed in retaliation for the performance of the victim's official duties: (I) A peace officer or former peace officer; or (II) A firefighter; or (III) A judge, referee, or former judge or referee of any court of record in the state or federal system or in any other state court system or a judge or former judge in any municipal court in this state or in any other state; or (IV) An elected state, county, or municipal official; or (V) A federal law enforcement officer or agent or former federal law enforcement officer or agent; or

(d) The defendant intentionally killed a person kidnapped or being held as a hostage by the defendant or by anyone associated with the defendant; or

(e) The defendant has been a party to an agreement to kill another person in furtherance of which a person has been intentionally killed; or

(f) The defendant committed the offense while lying in wait, from ambush, or by use of an explosive or incendiary device or a chemical, biological, or radiological weapon; or

(g) The defendant committed a felony and, in the course of or in furtherance of such or immediate flight therefrom, the defendant intentionally caused the death of a person other than one of the participants; or

(h) The murder was committed for pecuniary gain; or

(i) In the commission of the offense, the defendant knowingly created a grave risk of death to another person in addition to the victim of the offense; or

(j) The defendant committed the offense in an especially heinous, cruel, or depraved manner; or

(k) The murder was committed for the purpose of avoiding or preventing a lawful arrest or prosecution or effecting an escape from custody. This factor includes the intentional killing of a witness to a criminal offense.

(l) The defendant unlawfully and intentionally, knowingly, or with universal malice manifesting extreme indifference to the value of human life generally, killed two or more persons during the commission of the same criminal episode; or

(m) The defendant intentionally killed a child who has not yet attained twelve years of age; or

(n) The defendant committed the murder against the victim because of the victim's race, color, ancestry, religion, or national origin.

(o) The defendant's possession of the weapon used to commit the murder constituted a felony offense under the laws of this state or the United States; or

(p) The defendant intentionally killed more than one person in more than one criminal episode; or

(q) The victim was a pregnant woman, and the defendant intentionally killed the victim, knowing she was pregnant.

Mitigating circumstances. Although the federal Constitution will not permit jurisdictions to prevent capital felons from presenting all relevant mitigating evidence at the penalty phase, Colorado has provided by statute, Colorado Code § 18-1.3-1201(4), the following statutory mitigating circumstances that permit a jury to reject imposition of the death penalty:

(a) The age of the defendant at the time of the crime; or

(b) The defendant's capacity to appreciate wrongfulness of the defendant's conduct or to conform the defendant's conduct to the requirements of law was significantly impaired, but not so impaired as to constitute a defense to prosecution; or

(c) The defendant was under unusual and substantial duress, although not such duress as to constitute a defense to prosecution; or

(d) The defendant was a principal in the offense which was committed by another, but the defendant's participation was relatively minor, although not so minor as to constitute a defense to prosecution; or

(e) The defendant could not reasonably have foreseen that the defendant's conduct in the course of the commission of the offense for which the defendant was convicted would cause, or would create a grave risk of causing, death to another person; or

(f) The emotional state of the defendant at the time the crime was committed; or

(g) The absence of any significant prior conviction; or

(h) The extent of the defendant's cooperation with law enforcement officers or agencies and with the office of the prosecuting district attorney; or

(i) The influence of drugs or alcohol; or

(j) The good faith, although mistaken, belief by the defendant that circumstances existed which constituted a moral justification for the defendant's conduct; or

(k) The defendant is not a continuing threat to society; or

(l) Any other evidence which in the court's opinion bears on the question of mitigation.

Persons who may attend an execution. Colorado law limits the number of persons who may be present at an execution. The following is provided by Colorado Code § 18-1.3-1206:

The particular day and hour of the execution of said sentence within the week specified in said warrant shall be fixed by the executive director of the department of corrections or the executive director's designee, and the executive director shall be present thereat or shall appoint some other representative among the officials or officers of the correctional facilities at Canon City to be present in his or her place and stead. There shall also be present a physician and such guards, attendants, and other persons as the executive director or the executive director's designee in his or her discretion deems necessary to conduct the execution. In addition, there may be present such witnesses as the executive director or the executive director's designee in his or her discretion deems desirable, not to exceed eighteen persons. The executive director or the executive director's designee shall notify the governor of the day and hour for the execution as soon as it has been fixed.

Delaware

General considerations. Delaware is a capital punishment jurisdiction. The state reenacted its death penalty law after the United States Supreme Court decision in *Furman v. Georgia*, 408

U.S. 238 (1972), on March 29, 1974. Capital murder in Delaware is punishable by death or life imprisonment without parole. A capital prosecution in Delaware is bifurcated into a guilt phase and penalty phase. It is required at the penalty phase that the jury must unanimously agree that a death sentence is appropriate before it can be imposed. If the penalty phase jury is unable to reach a unanimous verdict, the defendant must be sentenced to imprisonment for life.

Under Delaware's capital punishment statute, a sentence of death is automatically reviewed by the Delaware Supreme Court. Delaware uses lethal injection to carry out death sentences. The state also provides that if lethal injection is found unconstitutional then a death sentence may be carried out by hanging. The state's death row facility for men is in Smyrna, while the facility for female death row inmates is in Claymont. Pursuant to the laws of Delaware the governor has authority to grant clemency in capital cases. The governor must obtain the consent of the state's Board of Pardons in order to grant clemency.

Death penalty offenses. Delaware's capital punishment offenses are set out under Delaware Code tit. 11 § 636. This statute is triggered if a person commits a homicide under the following special circumstances:

(1) The person intentionally causes the death of another person;

(2) While engaged in the commission of, or attempt to commit, or flight after committing or attempting to commit any felony, the person recklessly causes the death of another person.

(3) The person intentionally causes another person to commit suicide by force or duress;

(4) The person recklessly causes the death of a law-enforcement officer, corrections employee, fire fighter, paramedic, emergency medical technician, fire marshal or fire police officer while such officer is in the lawful performance of duties;

(5) The person causes the death of another person by the use of or detonation of any bomb or similar destructive device;

(6) The person causes the death of another person in order to avoid or prevent the lawful arrest of any person, or in the course of and in furtherance of the commission or attempted commission of escape in the second degree or escape after conviction.

Aggravating circumstances used to impose death penalty. In order to impose a death sentence upon a defendant, Delaware Code tit. 11 § 4209(e)(1) requires that the prosecutor establishes the existence of at least one of the following statutory aggravating circumstances at the penalty phase:

a. The murder was committed by a person in, or who has escaped from, the custody of a law-enforcement officer or place of confinement.

b. The murder was committed for the purpose of avoiding or preventing an arrest or for the purpose of effecting an escape from custody.

c. The murder was committed against any law-enforcement officer, corrections employee, firefighter, paramedic, emergency medical technician, fire marshal or fire police officer while such victim was engaged in the performance of official duties.

d. The murder was committed against a judicial officer, a former judicial officer, attorney general, former attorney general, assistant or deputy attorney general or former assistant or deputy attorney general, state detective or former state detective, special investigator or former special investigator, during, or because of, the exercise of an official duty.

e. The murder was committed against a person who was held or otherwise detained as a shield or hostage.

f. The murder was committed against a person who was held or detained by the defendant for ransom or reward.

g. The murder was committed against a person who was a witness to a crime and who was killed for the purpose of preventing the witness's appearance or testimony in any grand jury, criminal or civil proceeding involving such crime, or in retaliation for the witness's appearance or testimony in any grand jury, criminal or civil proceeding involving such crime.

h. The defendant paid or was paid by another person or had agreed to pay or be paid by another person or had conspired to pay or be paid by another person for the killing of the victim.

i. The defendant was previously convicted of another murder or manslaughter or of a felony involving the use of, or threat of, force or violence upon another person.

j. The murder was committed while the defendant was engaged in the commission of, or attempt to commit, or flight after committing or attempting to commit any degree of rape, unlawful sexual intercourse, arson, kidnapping, robbery, sodomy, burglary, or home invasion.

k. The defendant's course of conduct resulted in the deaths of 2 or more persons where the deaths are a probable consequence of the defendant's conduct.

l. The murder was outrageously or wantonly vile, horrible or inhuman in that it involved torture, depravity of mind, use of an explosive device or poison or the defendant used such means on the victim prior to murdering the victim.

m. The defendant caused or directed another to commit murder or committed murder as an agent or employee of another person.

n. The defendant was under a sentence of life imprisonment, whether for natural life or otherwise, at the time of the commission of the murder.

o. The murder was committed for pecuniary gain.

p. The victim was pregnant.

q. The victim was particularly vulnerable due to a severe intellectual, mental or physical disability.

r. The victim was 62 years of age or older.

s. The victim was a child 14 years of age or younger, and the murder was committed by an individual who is at least 4 years older than the victim.

t. At the time of the killing, the victim was or had been a nongovernmental informant or had otherwise provided any investigative, law enforcement or police agency with information concerning criminal activity, and the killing was in retaliation for the victim's activities as a nongovernmental informant or in providing information concerning criminal activity to an investigative, law enforcement or police agency.

u. The murder was premeditated and the result of substantial planning. Such planning must be as to the commission of the murder itself and not simply as to the commission or attempted commission of any underlying felony.

v. The murder was committed for the purpose of interfering with the victim's free exercise or enjoyment of any right, privilege or immunity protected by the First Amendment to the United States Constitution, or because the victim has exercised or enjoyed said rights, or because of the victim's race, religion, color, disability, national origin or ancestry.

Mitigating circumstances. Delaware does not provide by statute any mitigating circumstances to the imposition of the death penalty. Even though the state does not provide statutory mitigating circumstances, the United States Supreme Court has ruled that all relevant mitigating evidence must be allowed at the penalty phase.

Persons who may attend an execution. Under the laws of Delaware a limitation is imposed upon the number of persons who may be present at an execution. The following is provided by Delaware Code tit. 11 § 4209(f):

> The imposition of a sentence of death shall be upon such terms and conditions as the trial court may impose in its sentence, including the place, the number of witnesses, which shall not exceed 10, and conditions of privacy, and shall occur between the hours of 12:01 A.M. and 3:00 A.M. on the date set by the trial court. The trial court shall permit one adult member of the immediate family of the victim, or the victim's designee, to witness the execution of a sentence of death pursuant to the rules of the court, if the family provides reasonable notice of its desire to be so represented.

Florida

General considerations. Florida is a capital punishment jurisdiction. The state reenacted its death penalty law after the United States Supreme Court decision in *Furman v. Georgia*, 408 U.S. 238 (1972), on December 8, 1972. Capital murder in Florida is punishable by death or life imprisonment without parole. A capital prosecution in Florida is bifurcated into a guilt phase and penalty phase. It is required at the penalty phase that a majority of the jury must agree that a death sentence is appropriate before it can be imposed. If the penalty phase jury is unable to reach a verdict, the trial judge is required to sentence the defendant to life imprisonment. The decision of a penalty phase jury is not binding on the trial court under the laws of Florida. The trial court may accept or reject the jury's determination on punishment, and impose whatever sentence he or she believes the evidence established.

Under Florida's capital punishment statute, a sentence of death is automatically reviewed by the Florida Supreme Court. Florida permits capital felons to choose between death by lethal injection or the electric chair. The state's death row facility for men is located in Starke; the facility for female death row inmates is in Pembroke Pines. Pursuant to the laws of Florida the governor has authority to grant clemency in capital cases. The governor must obtain the consent of the state's Board of Executive Clemency in order to grant clemency.

Death penalty offenses. Florida's capital punishment offenses are set out under Florida Code § 782.04(1)(a). This statute is triggered if a person commits a homicide under the following special circumstances:

1. When perpetrated from a premeditated design to effect the death of the person killed or any human being;

2. When committed by a person engaged in the perpetration of, or in the attempt to perpetrate, any: (a) drug trafficking offense; (b) arson; (c) sexual battery; (d) robbery; (e) burglary; (f) kidnapping; (g) escape; (h) aggravated child abuse; (i) aggravated abuse of an elderly person or disabled adult; (j) aircraft piracy; (k) unlawful throwing, placing, or discharging of a destructive device or bomb; (l) carjacking; (m) home-invasion robbery; (n) aggravated stalking; (o) murder of another human being; (p) resisting an officer with violence to his or her person; (q) aggravated fleeing or eluding with serious bodily injury or death; (r) felony that is an act of terrorism or is in furtherance of an act of terrorism; or

3. Which resulted from the unlawful distribution of ... cocaine, opium or any synthetic or natural salt, compound, derivative, or preparation of opium, or methadone by a person 18 years of age or older, when such drug is proven to be the proximate cause of the death of the user.

Aggravating circumstances used to impose death penalty. In order to impose a death sentence upon a defendant, Florida Code § 921.141(5) requires that the prosecutor establishes the existence of at least one of the following statutory aggravating circumstances at the penalty phase:

(a) The capital felony was committed by a person previously convicted of a felony and under sentence of imprisonment or placed on community control or on felony probation.

(b) The defendant was previously convicted of another capital felony or of a felony involving the use or threat of violence to the person.

(c) The defendant knowingly created a great risk of death to many persons.

(d) The capital felony was committed while the defendant was engaged, or was an accomplice, in the commission of, or an attempt to commit, or flight after committing or attempting to commit, any: robbery; sexual battery; aggravated child abuse; abuse of an elderly person or disabled adult resulting in great bodily harm, permanent disability, or permanent disfigurement; arson; burglary; kidnapping; aircraft piracy; or unlawful throwing, placing, or discharging of a destructive device or bomb.

(e) The capital felony was committed for the purpose of avoiding or preventing a lawful arrest or effecting an escape from custody.

(f) The capital felony was committed for pecuniary gain.

(g) The capital felony was committed to disrupt or hinder the lawful exercise of any governmental function or the enforcement of laws.

(h) The capital felony was especially heinous, atrocious, or cruel.

(i) The capital felony was a homicide and was committed in a cold, calculated, and premeditated manner without any pretense of moral or legal justification.

(j) The victim of the capital felony was a law enforcement officer engaged in the performance of his or her official duties.

(k) The victim of the capital felony was an elected or appointed public official engaged in the performance of his or her official duties if the motive for the capital felony was related, in whole or in part, to the victim's official capacity.

(l) The victim of the capital felony was a person less than 12 years of age.

(m) The victim of the capital felony was particularly vulnerable due to advanced age or disability, or because the defendant stood in a position of familial or custodial authority over the victim.

(n) The capital felony was committed by a criminal gang member.

(o) The capital felony was committed by a person designated as a sexual predator or a person previously designated as a sexual predator who had the sexual predator designation removed.

(p) The capital felony was committed by a person subject to an injunction, or a foreign protection order accorded full faith and credit, and was committed against the petitioner who obtained the injunction or protection order or any spouse, child, sibling, or parent of the petitioner.

Florida has a separate statute that provides aggravating circumstances for a defendant convicted of a drug trafficking murder. The aggravating circumstances for drug trafficking murder are set out under Florida Code § 921.142(6).

Mitigating circumstances. Although the federal Constitution will not permit jurisdictions to prevent capital felons from presenting all relevant mitigating evidence at the penalty phase, Florida has provided by statute, Florida Code § 921.141(6), the following statutory mitigating circumstances that permit a jury to reject imposition of the death penalty:

(a) The defendant has no significant history of prior criminal activity.

(b) The capital felony was committed while the defendant was under the influence of extreme mental or emotional disturbance.

(c) The victim was a participant in the defendant's conduct or consented to the act.

(d) The defendant was an accomplice in the capital felony committed by another person and his or her participation was relatively minor.

(e) The defendant acted under extreme duress or under the substantial domination of another person.

(f) The capacity of the defendant to appreciate the criminality of his or her conduct or to conform his or her conduct to the requirements of law was substantially impaired.

(g) The age of the defendant at the time of the crime.

(h) The existence of any other factors in the defendant's background that would mitigate against imposition of the death penalty.

Florida has a separate statute that provides mitigating circumstances for a defendant convicted of a drug trafficking murder. The mitigating circumstances for drug trafficking murder are set out under Florida Code § 921.142(7).

Persons who may attend an execution. The laws of Florida limit the number of persons who may be present at an execution. The following is provided by Florida Code § 922.11:

(1) The warden of the state prison or a deputy designated by him or her shall be present at the execution. The warden shall set the day for execution within the week designated by the governor in the warrant.

(2) Twelve citizens selected by the warden shall witness the execution. A qualified physician shall be present and announce when death has been inflicted. Counsel for the convicted person and ministers of religion requested by the convicted person may be present. Representatives of news media may be present under rules approved by the secretary of corrections. All other persons, except prison officers and correctional officers, shall be excluded during the execution.

Georgia

General considerations. Georgia is a capital punishment jurisdiction. The state reenacted its death penalty law after the United States Supreme Court decision in *Furman v. Georgia*, 408 U.S. 238 (1972), on March 28, 1973. The state has created the Office of the Georgia Capital Defender to provide legal counsel to all indigent persons charged with a capital felony for which the death penalty is being sought. Capital murder in Georgia is punishable by death or life imprisonment without parole. A capital prosecution in Georgia is bifurcated into a guilt phase and penalty phase. It is required at the penalty phase that jury unanimously agree that a death sentence is appropriate before it can be imposed. If the penalty phase jury is unable to reach a verdict, the trial judge is required to impose a sentence of life imprisonment without parole.

Under Georgia's capital punishment statute, a sentence of death is automatically reviewed by the Georgia Supreme Court. Georgia uses lethal injection to carry out death sentences. The state's death row facility for men is in Jackson, Georgia; while the facility for women is in Atlanta. Pursuant to the laws of Georgia the state's Board of Pardons and Parole has exclusive jurisdiction to grant or deny clemency.

Death penalty offenses. Georgia's capital punishment offenses are set out under Georgia Code § 16-5-1. This statute is triggered if a person commits a homicide under the following special circumstances:

(a) A person commits the offense of murder when he unlawfully and with malice aforethought, either express or implied, causes the death of another human being.

(b) Express malice is that deliberate intention unlawfully to take the life of another human being which is manifested by external circumstances capable of proof. Malice shall be implied where no considerable provocation appears and where all the circumstances of the killing show an abandoned and malignant heart.

(c) A person also commits the offense of murder when, in the commission of a felony, he causes the death of another human being irrespective of malice.

In addition, Georgia Code § 16-11-1 makes the crime of treason a capital offense; Georgia Code § 16-5-44 makes the crime of aircraft highjacking a capital offense; Georgia Code § 16-6-1 makes the crime of rape punishable with death; Georgia Code § 16-5-40 makes the crime of kidnapping punishable with death; and Georgia Code § 16-8-41 makes the crime of armed robbery subject to the death penalty. However, under decisions by the United States Supreme Court, the death penalty cannot be imposed for aircraft highjacking, rape, kidnapping or armed robbery unless a homicide occurred.

Aggravating circumstances used to impose death penalty. In order to impose a death sentence upon a defendant, Georgia Code § 17-10-30(b) requires that the prosecutor establishes the existence of at least one of the following statutory aggravating circumstances at the penalty phase:

(1) The offense of murder, rape, armed robbery, or kidnapping was committed by a person with a prior record of conviction for a capital felony;

(2) The offense of murder, rape, armed robbery, or kidnapping was committed while the offender was engaged in the commission of another capital felony or aggravated battery, or the offense of murder was committed while the offender was engaged in the commission of burglary in any degree or arson in the first degree;

(3) The offender, by his act of murder, armed robbery, or kidnapping, knowingly created a great risk of death to more than one person in a public place by means of a weapon or device which would normally be hazardous to the lives of more than one person;

(4) The offender committed the offense of murder for himself or another, for the purpose of receiving money or any other thing of monetary value;

(5) The murder of a judicial officer, former judicial officer, district attorney or solicitor-general, or former district attorney, solicitor, or solicitor-general was committed during or because of the exercise of his or her official duties;

(6) The offender caused or directed another to commit murder or committed murder as an agent or employee of another person;

(7) The offense of murder, rape, armed robbery, or kidnapping was outrageously or wantonly vile, horrible, or inhuman in that it involved torture, depravity of mind, or an aggravated battery to the victim;

(8) The offense of murder was committed against any peace officer, corrections employee, or firefighter while engaged in the performance of his official duties;

(9) The offense of murder was committed by a person in, or who has escaped from, the lawful custody of a peace officer or place of lawful confinement;

(10) The murder was committed for the purpose of avoiding, interfering with, or preventing a lawful arrest or custody in a place of lawful confinement, of himself or another; or

(11) The offense of murder, rape, or kidnapping was committed by a person previously convicted of rape, aggravated sodomy, aggravated child molestation, or aggravated sexual battery.

Mitigating circumstances. Georgia does not provide by statute any mitigating circumstances to the imposition of the death penalty. Even though the state does not provide statutory mitigating circumstances, the United States Supreme Court has ruled that all relevant mitigating evidence must be allowed at the penalty phase.

Persons who may attend an execution. Georgia law limits the number of persons who may be present at an execution. The following is provided by Georgia Code § 17-10-41:

There shall be present at the execution of a convicted person the superintendent of the state correctional institution or a deputy superintendent thereof, at least three executioners, two physicians to determine when death supervenes, and other correctional officers, assistants, technicians, and witnesses as determined by the commissioner of corrections. In addition, the convicted person may request the presence of his or her counsel, a member of the clergy, and a reasonable number of relatives and friends, provided that the total number of witnesses appearing at the request of the convicted person shall be determined by the commissioner of corrections.

Idaho

General considerations. Idaho is a capital punishment jurisdiction. The state reenacted its death penalty law after the United States Supreme Court decision in *Furman v. Georgia*, 408 U.S. 238 (1972), on July 1, 1973. Capital murder in Idaho is punishable by death or life imprisonment with or without the possibility of parole. A capital prosecution in Idaho is bifurcated into a guilt phase and penalty phase. It is required at the penalty phase that the jury must unanimously agree that a death sentence is appropriate before it can be imposed. If the penalty phase jury is unable to reach a unanimous verdict, the defendant must be sentenced to imprisonment for life, or to a term of life imprisonment with a fixed term of not less than ten years.

Under Idaho's capital punishment statute, a sentence of death is automatically reviewed by the Idaho Supreme Court. Idaho uses lethal injection to carry out death sentences. The state's death row facility for men is in Boise, while the death row facility for women is in Pocatello. Pursuant to the laws of Idaho the state's Commission of Pardons and Paroles has authority to grant clemency. The governor may grant temporary reprieves.

Death penalty offenses. Idaho's capital punishment offenses are set out under Idaho Code tit. 18 § 4003. This statute is triggered if a person commits a homicide under the following special circumstances:

(a) All murder which is perpetrated by means of poison, or lying in wait, or torture....

(b) Any murder of any peace officer, executive officer, officer of the court, fireman, judicial officer or prosecuting attorney....

(c) Any murder committed by a person under a sentence for murder of the first or second degree, including such persons on parole or probation from such sentence....

(d) Any murder committed in the perpetration of, or attempt to perpetrate, aggravated battery on a child under twelve (12) years of age, arson, rape, robbery, burglary, kidnapping or mayhem, or an act of terrorism, or the use of a weapon of mass destruction, biological weapon or chemical weapon....

(e) Any murder committed by a person incarcerated in a penal institution upon a person employed by the penal institution, another inmate of the penal institution or a visitor to the penal institution....

(f) Any murder committed by a person while escaping or attempting to escape from a penal institution....

In addition, under Idaho Code tit. 18 § 5411 the death penalty may be imposed on any one who, by willful perjury or subornation of perjury, procures the conviction and execution of any innocent person. Further, Idaho Code tit. 18 § 4504 provides the punishment of death for kidnapping. However, the decisions of the United States Supreme Court have held that the death penalty may not be imposed unless a homicide occurred.

Aggravating circumstances used to impose death penalty. In order to impose a death sentence upon a defendant, Idaho Code tit. 19 § 2515(9) requires that the prosecutor establishes the existence of at least one of the following statutory aggravating circumstances at the penalty phase:

(a) The defendant was previously convicted of another murder.

(b) At the time the murder was committed the defendant also committed another murder.

(c) The defendant knowingly created a great risk of death to many persons.

(d) The murder was committed for remuneration or the promise of remuneration or the defendant employed another to commit the murder for remuneration or the promise of remuneration.

(e) The murder was especially heinous, atrocious or cruel, manifesting exceptional depravity.

(f) By the murder, or circumstances surrounding its commission, the defendant exhibited utter disregard for human life.

(g) The murder was committed in the perpetration of, or attempt to perpetrate, arson, rape, robbery, burglary, kidnapping or mayhem and the defendant killed, intended a killing, or acted with reckless indifference to human life.

(h) The murder was committed in the perpetration of, or attempt to perpetrate, an infamous crime against nature, lewd and lascivious conduct with a minor, sexual abuse of a child under sixteen (16) years of age, ritualized abuse of a child, sexual exploitation of a child, sexual battery of a minor child sixteen (16) or seventeen (17) years of age, or forcible sexual penetration by use of a foreign object, and the defendant killed, intended a killing, or acted with reckless indifference to human life.

(i) The defendant, by his conduct, whether such conduct was before, during or after the commission of the murder at hand, has exhibited a propensity to commit murder which will probably constitute a continuing threat to society.

(j) The murder was committed against a former or present peace officer, executive officer, officer of the court, judicial officer or prosecuting attorney because of the exercise of official duty or because of the victim's former or present official status.

(k) The murder was committed against a witness or potential witness in a criminal or civil legal proceeding because of such proceeding.

Mitigating circumstances. Idaho does not provide by statute any mitigating circumstances to the imposition of the death penalty. Even though the state does not provide statutory mitigating circumstances, the United States Supreme Court has ruled that all relevant mitigating evidence must be allowed at the penalty phase.

Indiana

General considerations. Indiana is a capital punishment jurisdiction. The state reenacted its death penalty law after the United States Supreme Court decision in *Furman v. Georgia*, 408 U.S. 238 (1972), on May 1, 1973. Capital murder in Indiana is punishable by death or life imprisonment without parole. A capital prosecution in Indiana is bifurcated into a guilt phase and penalty phase. It is required at the penalty phase that the jury unanimously agrees that a death sentence is appropriate before it can be imposed. The decision of a penalty phase jury is not binding on the trial court under the laws of Indiana. The trial court may accept or reject the jury's determination on punishment, and impose whatever sentence he or she believes the evidence established.

Under Indiana's capital punishment statute, a sentence of death is automatically reviewed by the Indiana Supreme Court. Indiana uses lethal injection to carry out death sentences. The state's death row facility for men is in Michigan City, while the facility for women is in Indianapolis. Pursuant to the laws of Indiana the governor has authority to grant clemency in capital cases. The governor is required to obtain the consent of the state's parole board before clemency may be granted.

Death penalty offenses. Indiana's capital punishment offenses are set out under Indiana Code § 35-42-1-1. This statute is triggered if a person commits a homicide under the following special circumstances:

(1) knowingly or intentionally kills another human being;

(2) kills another human being while committing or attempting to commit arson, burglary, child molesting, consumer product tampering, criminal deviate conduct, kidnapping, rape, robbery, human trafficking, promotion of human trafficking, sexual trafficking of a minor, or carjacking;

(3) kills another human being while committing or attempting to commit [a drug offense]; or

(4) knowingly or intentionally kills a fetus that has attained viability.

Aggravating circumstances used to impose death penalty. In order to impose a death sentence upon a defendant, Indiana Code § 35-50-2-9(b) requires that the prosecutor establishes the existence of at least one of the following statutory aggravating circumstances at the penalty phase:

(1) The defendant committed the murder by intentionally killing the victim while committing or attempting to commit any of the following: (A) arson; (B) burglary; (C) child molesting; (D) criminal deviate conduct; (E) kidnapping; (F) rape; (G) robbery; (H) carjacking; (I) criminal gang activity; (J) dealing in cocaine or a narcotic drug.

(2) The defendant committed the murder by the unlawful detonation of an explosive with intent to injure person or damage property.

(3) The defendant committed the murder by lying in wait.

(4) The defendant who committed the murder was hired to kill.

(5) The defendant committed the murder by hiring another person to kill.

(6) The victim of the murder was a corrections employee, probation officer, parole officer, community corrections worker, home detention officer, fireman, judge, or law enforcement officer.

(7) The defendant has been convicted of another murder.

(8) The defendant has committed another murder, at any time, regardless of whether the defendant has been convicted of that other murder.

(9) The defendant was at the time of the crime: (A) under the custody of the department of correction; (B) under the custody of a county sheriff; (C) on probation after receiving a sentence for the commission of a felony; or (D) on parole.

(10) The defendant dismembered the victim.

(11) The defendant burned, mutilated, or tortured the victim while the victim was alive.

(12) The victim of the murder was less than twelve (12) years of age.

(13) The victim was a victim of any of the following offenses for which the defendant was convicted: (A) battery; (B) kidnapping; (C) criminal confinement; (D) a sex crime.

(14) The victim of the murder was listed by the state or known by the defendant to be a witness against the defendant and the defendant committed the murder with the intent to prevent the person from testifying.

(15) The defendant committed the murder by intentionally discharging a firearm: (A) into an inhabited dwelling; or (B) from a vehicle.

(16) The victim of the murder was pregnant and the murder resulted in the intentional killing of a fetus that has attained viability.

Mitigating circumstances. Although the federal Constitution will not permit jurisdictions to prevent capital felons from presenting all relevant mitigating evidence at the penalty phase, Indiana has provided by statute, Indiana Code § 35-50-2-9(c), the following statutory mitigating circumstances that permit a jury to reject imposition of the death penalty:

(1) The defendant has no significant history of prior criminal conduct.

(2) The defendant was under the influence of extreme mental or emotional disturbance when the murder was committed.

(3) The victim was a participant in or consented to the defendant's conduct.

(4) The defendant was an accomplice in a murder committed by another person, and the defendant's participation was relatively minor.

(5) The defendant acted under the substantial domination of another person.

(6) The defendant's capacity to appreciate the criminality of the defendant's conduct or to conform that conduct to the requirements of law was substantially impaired as a result of mental disease or defect or of intoxication.

(7) The defendant was less than eighteen (18) years of age at the time the murder was committed.

(8) Any other circumstances appropriate for consideration.

Persons who may attend an execution. Indiana law limits the number of persons who may be present at an execution. The following is provided by Indiana Code § 35-38-6-6:

(a) Only the following persons may be present at the execution: (1) the superintendent of the state prison; (2) the person designated by the superintendent of the state prison and any assistants who are necessary to assist in the execution; (3) the prison physician; (4) one other physician; (5) the spiritual advisor of the convicted person; (6) the prison chaplain; (7) not more than five friends or relatives of the convicted person who are invited by the convicted person to attend; (8) except as provided in subsection (b), not more than eight of the following members of the victim's immediate family who are at least eighteen years of age: (A) the victim's spouse; (B) one or more of the victim's children; (C) one or more of the victim's parents; (D) one or more of the victim's grandparents; (E) one or more of the victim's siblings.

(b) If there is more than one victim, not more than eight persons who are members of the victims' immediate families may be present at the execution. The department shall determine which persons may be present in accordance with procedures adopted under subsection (c).

(c) The department shall develop procedures to determine which family members of a victim may be present at the execution if more than eight family members of a victim desire to be present or if there is more than one victim. Upon the request of a family member of a victim, the department shall establish a support room for the use of: (1) an immediate family member of the victim described in subsection (a) (8) who is not selected to be present at the execution; and (2) a person invited by an immediate family member of the victim described in subsection (a)(8) to offer support to the immediate family member.

(d) The superintendent of the state prison may exclude a person from viewing the execution if the superintendent determines that the presence of the person would threaten the safety or security of the state prison and sets forth this determination in writing.

Kansas

General considerations. Kansas is a capital punishment jurisdiction. The state reenacted its death penalty law after the United States Supreme Court decision in *Furman v. Georgia*, 408 U.S. 238 (1972), on April 22, 1994. In the 2004 decision of *State v. Marsh*, 102 P.3d 445 (Kan. 2004), the Kansas Supreme Court found that the state's death sentencing statute violated the federal constitution because it permitted a defendant to be sentenced to death when a jury gave equal weight to aggravating and mitigating circumstances. As a consequence of the state Supreme Court decision, the death penalty could not be imposed in Kansas. However, the case was appealed to the United States Supreme Court and in an opinion, *Kansas v. Marsh*, 126 S.Ct. 2516 (2006), the nation's highest court found that Kansas' death sentencing statute did not violate the federal constitution. This decision reinstated the death penalty in Kansas.

Capital murder in Kansas is punishable by death or life imprisonment without the possibility of parole. A capital prosecution in Kansas is bifurcated into a guilt phase and penalty phase. It is required at the penalty phase that the jury unanimously agrees that a death sentence is appropriate before it can be imposed. If the penalty phase jury is unable to reach a verdict, the trial judge is required to impose a sentence of life imprisonment.

Under Kansas' capital punishment statute, a sentence of death is automatically reviewed by the Kansas Supreme Court. Kansas uses lethal injection to carry out death sentences. The State's death row facility for males is in El Dorado, while the facility for women is in Topeka. The governor has exclusive authority to grant clemency in capital cases. The governor may commute a death sentence to life imprisonment without parole.

Death penalty offenses. Kansas' capital punishment offenses are set out under Kansas Code § 21-5401. This statute is triggered if a person commits a homicide under the following special circumstances:

(1) Intentional and premeditated killing of any person in the commission of kidnapping or aggravated kidnapping, when the kidnapping or aggravated kidnapping was committed with the intent to hold such person for ransom;

(2) intentional and premeditated killing of any person pursuant to a contract or agreement to kill such person or being a party to the contract or agreement pursuant to which such person is killed;

(3) intentional and premeditated killing of any person by an inmate or prisoner confined in a state correctional institution, community correctional institution or jail or while in the custody of an officer or employee of a state correctional institution, community correctional institution or jail;

(4) intentional and premeditated killing of the victim of one of the following crimes in the commission of, or subsequent to, such crime: Rape, criminal sodomy, or aggravated criminal sodomy, or any attempt thereof;

(5) intentional and premeditated killing of a law enforcement officer;

(6) intentional and premeditated killing of more than one person as a part of the same act or transaction or in two or more acts or transactions connected together or constituting parts of a common scheme or course of conduct; or

(7) intentional and premeditated killing of a child under the age of 14 in the commission of

kidnapping, or aggravated kidnapping, when the kidnapping or aggravated kidnapping was committed with intent to commit a sex offense upon or with the child or with intent that the child commit or submit to a sex offense.

Aggravating circumstances used to impose death penalty. In order to impose a death sentence upon a defendant, Kansas Code § 21-6624 requires that the prosecutor establishes the existence of at least one of the following statutory aggravating circumstances at the penalty phase:

(a) The defendant was previously convicted of a felony in which the defendant inflicted great bodily harm, disfigurement, dismemberment or death on another.

(b) The defendant knowingly or purposely killed or created a great risk of death to more than one person.

(c) The defendant committed the crime for the defendant's self or another for the purpose of receiving money or any other thing of monetary value.

(d) The defendant authorized or employed another person to commit the crime.

(e) The defendant committed the crime in order to avoid or prevent a lawful arrest or prosecution.

(f) The defendant committed the crime in an especially heinous, atrocious or cruel manner....

(g) The defendant committed the crime while serving a sentence of imprisonment on conviction of a felony.

(h) The victim was killed while engaging in, or because of the victim's performance or prospective performance of, the victim's duties as a witness in a criminal proceeding.

Mitigating circumstances. Although the federal Constitution will not permit jurisdictions to prevent capital felons from presenting all relevant mitigating evidence at the penalty phase, Kansas has provided by statute, Kansas Code § 21-6625, the following statutory mitigating circumstances that permit a jury to reject imposition of the death penalty:

(1) The defendant has no significant history of prior criminal activity.

(2) The crime was committed while the defendant was under the influence of extreme mental or emotional disturbances.

(3) The victim was a participant in or consented to the defendant's conduct.

(4) The defendant was an accomplice in the crime committed by another person, and the defendant's participation was relatively minor.

(5) The defendant acted under extreme distress or under the substantial domination of another person.

(6) The capacity of the defendant to appreciate the criminality of the defendant's conduct or to conform the defendant's conduct to the requirements of law was substantially impaired.

(7) The age of the defendant at the time of the crime.

(8) At the time of the crime, the defendant was suffering from posttraumatic stress syndrome caused by violence or abuse by the victim.

Persons who may attend an execution. Kansas law limits the number of persons who may be present at an execution. The following is provided by Kansas Code § 22-4003:

(a) In addition to the secretary of corrections or the warden designated by the secretary, the executioner and persons designated ... to assist in the execution, the following persons, and no others, may be present at the execution: (1) A member of the clergy attending the prisoner; (2) not more than three persons designated by the prisoner; and (3) not more than 10 persons designated by the secretary of corrections as official witnesses. The secretary shall consider the inclusion of members of the immediate family of any deceased victim of the prisoner as witnesses when designating official witnesses. The identity of persons present at the execution, other than the secretary or the warden designated by the secretary, shall be confidential. A witness may elect to reveal such witness' own identity, but in no event shall a witness reveal the identity of any other person present at the execution.

(b) All witnesses shall be 18 years of age or older.

(c) The secretary may deny the attendance of any person selected or designated as a witness when the secretary determines it is necessary for reasons of security and order of the institution.

(d) As used in this section, "members of the immediate family" means the spouse, a child by birth or adoption, stepchild, parent, grandparent, grandchild, sibling or the spouse of any member of the immediate family specified in this subsection.

Kentucky

General considerations. Kentucky is a capital punishment jurisdiction. The state reenacted its death penalty law after the United States Supreme Court decision in *Furman v. Georgia*, 408 U.S. 238 (1972), on January 1, 1975. Capital murder in Kentucky is punishable by death, life imprisonment without parole, or imprisonment for a term of years. A capital prosecution in Kentucky is bifurcated into a guilt phase and penalty phase. It is required at the penalty phase that the jury unanimously agrees that a death sentence is appropriate before it can be imposed. If the penalty phase jury is unable to reach a verdict, the trial judge is required to impose a sentence of life imprisonment without parole or a term of years.

Under Kentucky's capital punishment statute, a sentence of death is automatically reviewed by the Kentucky Supreme Court. Kentucky uses lethal injection to carry out death sentences. Defendants sentenced before March 31, 1998, have a choice of execution by lethal injection or electrocution. The state's death row facility for males is in Eddyville; the facility for female death row inmates is located in Pee Wee Valley. Pursuant to the laws of Kentucky the governor has exclusive authority to grant clemency in capital cases. The governor may commute a capital sentence to life imprisonment without parole.

Death penalty offenses. Kentucky's capital punishment offenses are set out under Kentucky Code § 507.020. This statute is triggered if a person commits a homicide under the following special circumstances:

(a) With intent to cause the death of another person, he causes the death of such person or of a third person...; or

(b) Including, but not limited to, the operation of a motor vehicle under circumstances manifesting extreme indifference to human life, he wantonly engages in conduct which creates a grave risk of death to another person and thereby causes the death of another person.

Under Kentucky Code § 509.040(2), kidnapping is a capital offense when the victim is not released alive or when the victim is released alive but subsequently dies as a result of: (a) serious physical injuries suffered during the kidnapping; (b) not being released in a safe place; or (c) being released in any circumstances which are intended, known or should have been known to cause or lead to the victim's death.

Aggravating circumstances used to impose death penalty. In order to impose a death sentence upon a defendant, Kentucky Code § 532.025(2)(a) requires that the prosecutor establish the existence of at least one of the following statutory aggravating circumstances at the penalty phase:

1. The offense of murder or kidnapping was committed by a person with a prior record of conviction for a capital offense, or the offense of murder was committed by a person who has a substantial history of serious assaultive criminal convictions;

2. The offense of murder or kidnapping was committed while the offender was engaged in the commission of arson in the first degree, robbery in the first degree, burglary in the first degree, rape in the first degree, or sodomy in the first degree;

3. The offender by his act of murder, armed robbery, or kidnapping knowingly created a great risk of death to more than one (1) person in a public place by means of a weapon of mass destruction, weapon, or other device which would normally be hazardous to the lives of more than one (1) person;

4. The offender committed the offense of murder for himself or another, for the purpose of receiving money or any other thing of monetary value, or for other profit;

5. The offense of murder was committed by a person who was a prisoner and the victim was a prison employee engaged at the time of the act in the performance of his duties;

6. The offender's act or acts of killing were intentional and resulted in multiple deaths;

7. The offender's act of killing was intentional and the victim was a state or local public official or police officer, sheriff, or deputy sheriff engaged at the time of the act in the lawful performance of his duties; and

8. The offender murdered the victim when an emergency protective order or a domestic violence order was in effect, or when any other order designed to protect the victim from the offender, such as

an order issued as a condition of a bond, conditional release, probation, parole, or pretrial diversion, was in effect.

Mitigating circumstances. Although the federal Constitution will not permit jurisdictions to prevent capital felons from presenting all relevant mitigating evidence at the penalty phase, Kentucky has provided by statute, Kentucky Code § 532.025(2)(b), the following statutory mitigating circumstances that permit a jury to reject imposition of the death penalty:

1. The defendant has no significant history of prior criminal activity;

2. The capital offense was committed while the defendant was under the influence of extreme mental or emotional disturbance even though the influence of extreme mental or emotional disturbance is not sufficient to constitute a defense to the crime;

3. The victim was a participant in the defendant's criminal conduct or consented to the criminal act;

4. The capital offense was committed under circumstances which the defendant believed to provide a moral justification or extenuation for his conduct even though the circumstances which the defendant believed to provide a moral justification or extenuation for his conduct are not sufficient to constitute a defense to the crime;

5. The defendant was an accomplice in a capital offense committed by another person and his participation in the capital offense was relatively minor;

6. The defendant acted under duress or under the domination of another person even though the duress or the domination of another person is not sufficient to constitute a defense to the crime;

7. At the time of the capital offense, the capacity of the defendant to appreciate the criminality of his conduct to the requirements of law was impaired as a result of mental illness or an intellectual disability or intoxication even though the impairment of the capacity of the defendant to appreciate the criminality of his conduct or to conform the conduct to the requirements of law is insufficient to constitute a defense to the crime; and

8. The youth of the defendant at the time of the crime.

Persons who may attend an execution. Under the laws of Kentucky a limitation is imposed upon the number of persons who may be present at an execution. The following is provided by Kentucky Code § 431.250:

> The following persons, and no others, may attend an execution: The executioner and the warden of the institution and his deputy or deputies and guards; the sheriff of the county in which the condemned was convicted; the commissioner of the Department of Corrections and representatives of the Department of Corrections designated by him; the physician and chaplain of the institution; a clergyman and three (3) other persons selected by the condemned; three (3) members of the victim's family designated by the commissioner from among the victim's spouse, adult children, parents, siblings, and grandparents; and nine (9) representatives of the news media as follows: one (1) representative from the daily newspaper with the largest circulation in the county where the execution will be conducted, one (1) representative from Associated Press wire service, one (1) representative from Kentucky Network, Inc., three (3) representatives for radio and television media within the state, and three (3) representatives for newspapers within the state. Use of audiovisual equipment by the representatives is prohibited during the execution. The Department of Corrections shall issue administrative regulations which govern media representation during the execution.

Louisiana

General considerations. Louisiana is a capital punishment jurisdiction. The state reenacted its death penalty law after the United States Supreme Court decision in *Furman v. Georgia*, 408 U.S. 238 (1972), on July 2, 1973. Capital murder in Louisiana is punishable by death or life imprisonment without parole. A capital prosecution in Louisiana is bifurcated into a guilt phase and penalty phase. It is required at the penalty phase that the jury unanimously agrees that a death sentence is appropriate before it can be imposed. If the penalty phase jury is unable to reach a verdict, the trial judge is required to sentence the defendant to life imprisonment without parole.

Under Louisiana's capital punishment statute, a sentence of death is automatically reviewed by the Louisiana Supreme Court. Louisiana uses lethal injection to carry out death sentences. The state's death row facility for males is in Angola; the facility for female death row inmates is in St. Gabriel, Louisiana. Pursuant to the laws of Louisiana the governor has authority to grant clemency in capital cases. The governor must obtain the consent of the state's Board of Pardons in order to grant clemency.

Death penalty offenses. Louisiana's capital punishment offenses are set out under Louisiana Code tit. 14 § 30. This statute is triggered if a person commits a homicide under the following special circumstances:

(1) When the offender has specific intent to kill or to inflict great bodily harm and is engaged in the perpetration or attempted perpetration of aggravated kidnapping, second degree kidnapping, aggravated escape, aggravated arson, aggravated rape, forcible rape, aggravated burglary, armed robbery, assault by drive-by shooting, first degree robbery, second degree robbery, simple robbery, terrorism, cruelty to juveniles, or second degree cruelty to juveniles.

(2) When the offender has a specific intent to kill or to inflict great bodily harm upon a fireman, peace officer, or civilian employee of the Louisiana State Police Crime Laboratory or any other forensic laboratory engaged in the performance of his lawful duties, or when the specific intent to kill or to inflict great bodily harm is directly related to the victim's status as a fireman, peace officer, or civilian employee.

(3) When the offender has a specific intent to kill or to inflict great bodily harm upon more than one person.

(4) When the offender has specific intent to kill or inflict great bodily harm and has offered, has been offered, has given, or has received anything of value for the killing.

(5) When the offender has the specific intent to kill or to inflict great bodily harm upon a victim under the age of twelve or sixty-five years of age or older.

(6) When the offender has the specific intent to kill or to inflict great bodily harm while engaged in the distribution, exchange, sale, or purchase, or any attempt thereof, of a controlled dangerous substance.

(7) When the offender has specific intent to kill and is engaged in ritualistic activities.

(8) When the offender has specific intent to kill or to inflict great bodily harm and there has been issued by a judge or magistrate any lawful order prohibiting contact between the offender and the victim in response to threats of physical violence or harm which was served on the offender and is in effect at the time of the homicide.

(9) When the offender has specific intent to kill or to inflict great bodily harm upon a victim who was a witness to a crime or was a member of the immediate family of a witness to a crime committed on a prior occasion and: (a) The killing was committed for the purpose of preventing or influencing the victim's testimony in any criminal action or proceeding whether or not such action or proceeding had been commenced; or (b) The killing was committed for the purpose of exacting retribution for the victim's prior testimony.

(10) When the offender has a specific intent to kill or inflict great bodily harm and the offender has previously acted with a specific intent to kill or inflict great bodily harm that resulted in the killing of one or more persons.

Aggravating circumstances used to impose death penalty. In order to impose a death sentence upon a defendant, Louisiana Code Cr.P.Art. 905.4 requires that the prosecutor establish the existence of at least one of the following statutory aggravating circumstances at the penalty phase:

(1) The offender was engaged in the perpetration or attempted perpetration of aggravated rape, forcible rape, aggravated kidnapping, second degree kidnapping, aggravated burglary, aggravated arson, aggravated escape, assault by drive-by shooting, armed robbery, first degree robbery, second degree robbery, simple robbery, cruelty to juveniles, second degree cruelty to juveniles, or terrorism.

(2) The victim was a fireman or peace officer engaged in his lawful duties.

(3) The offender has been previously convicted of an unrelated murder, aggravated rape, aggravated burglary, aggravated arson, aggravated escape, armed robbery, or aggravated kidnapping.

(4) The offender knowingly created a risk of death or great bodily harm to more than one person.

(5) The offender offered or has been offered or has given or received anything of value for the commission of the offense.

(6) The offender at the time of the commission of the offense was imprisoned after sentence for the commission of an unrelated forcible felony.

(7) The offense was committed in an especially heinous, atrocious or cruel manner.

(8) The victim was a witness in a prosecution against the defendant, gave material assistance to

the state in any investigation or prosecution of the defendant, or was an eye witness to a crime alleged to have been committed by the defendant or possessed other material evidence against the defendant.

(9) The victim was a correctional officer or any employee of the Department of Public Safety and Corrections who, in the normal course of his employment was required to come in close contact with persons incarcerated in a state prison facility, and the victim was engaged in his lawful duties at the time of the offense.

(10) The victim was under the age of twelve years or sixty-five years of age or older.

(11) The offender was engaged in the distribution, exchange, sale, or purchase, or any attempt thereof, of a controlled dangerous substance.

(12) The offender was engaged in [ritualistic activities].

(13) The offender has knowingly killed two or more persons in a series of separate incidents.

Mitigating circumstances. Although the federal Constitution will not permit jurisdictions to prevent capital felons from presenting all relevant mitigating evidence at the penalty phase, Louisiana has provided by statute, Louisiana Code Cr.P.Art. 905.5, the following statutory mitigating circumstances that permit a jury to reject imposition of the death penalty:

(a) The offender has no significant prior history of criminal activity;

(b) The offense was committed while the offender was under the influence of extreme mental or emotional disturbance;

(c) The offense was committed while the offender was under the influence or under the domination of another person;

(d) The offense was committed under circumstances which the offender reasonably believed to provide a moral justification or extenuation for his conduct;

(e) At the time of the offense the capacity of the offender to appreciate the criminality of his conduct or to conform his conduct to the requirements of law was impaired as a result of mental disease or defect or intoxication;

(f) The youth of the offender at the time of the offense;

(g) The offender was a principal whose participation was relatively minor;

(h) Any other relevant mitigating circumstance.

Persons who may attend an execution. Louisiana law limits the number of persons who may be present at an execution. The following is provided by Louisiana Code tit. 15 § 570:

A. Every execution of the death sentence shall take place in the presence of: (1) The warden of the Louisiana State Penitentiary at Angola, or a competent person selected by him. (2) The coroner of the parish of West Feliciana, or his deputy. (3) A physician summoned by the warden of the Louisiana State Penitentiary at Angola. (4) The operator of the electric chair, who shall be a competent electrician, who shall have not been previously convicted of a felony, or a competent person selected by the warden of the Louisiana State Penitentiary to administer the lethal injection. (5) A priest or minister of the gospel, if the convict so requests it. (6) Not less than five nor more than seven other witnesses.

B. No person under the age of eighteen years shall be allowed within the execution room during the time of execution.

C. Notwithstanding any other provision of law to the contrary, every execution of the death sentence shall take place between the hours of 6:00 P.M. and 9:00 P.M.

D. (1) The secretary of the Department of Public Safety and Corrections shall, at least ten days prior to the execution, either give written notice or verbal notice, followed by written notice placed in the United States mail within five days thereafter, of the date and time of execution to the victim's parents, or guardian, spouse, and any adult children who have indicated to the secretary that they desire such notice. The secretary, in such notice, shall give the named parties the option of attending the execution.

(2) The victim's parents or guardian, spouse, and any adult children who desire to attend the execution shall, within three days of their receipt of the secretary's notification, notify, either verbally or in writing, the secretary's office of their intention to attend. The number of victim relationship witnesses may be limited to two. If more than two of the aforementioned parties desire to attend the execution, then the secretary is authorized to select, from the interested parties, the two victim relationship witnesses who will be authorized to attend. In the case of multiple victims' families, the secretary shall determine the number of witnesses, subject to the availability of appropriate physical space.

(3) In no event shall failure to give notice to the victim's parents, or guardian, spouse, or any adult children have any effect as to execution of sentence.

Mississippi

General considerations. The state of Mississippi is a capital punishment jurisdiction. The state reenacted its death penalty law after the United States Supreme Court decision in *Furman v. Georgia*, 408 U.S. 238 (1972), on April 23, 1974. Capital murder in Mississippi is punishable by death or life imprisonment with or without parole. A capital prosecution in Mississippi is bifurcated into a guilt phase and penalty phase. It is required at the penalty phase that the jury unanimously agrees that a death sentence is appropriate before it can be imposed. If the penalty phase jury is unable to reach a verdict, the trial judge is required to impose a sentence of life imprisonment.

Under Mississippi's capital punishment statute, a sentence of death is automatically reviewed by the Mississippi Supreme Court. Mississippi uses lethal injection to carry out death sentences. The state's death row facility for men is in Parchman and the facility for women is in Pearl. Pursuant to state law the governor has exclusive authority to grant clemency in capital cases. The state's parole board investigates clemency requests.

Death penalty offenses. Mississippi's capital punishment offenses are set out under Mississippi Code § 97-3-19(2). This statute is triggered if a person commits a homicide under the following special circumstances:

(a) Murder which is perpetrated by killing a peace officer or fireman while such officer or fireman is acting in his official capacity or by reason of an act performed in his official capacity, and with knowledge that the victim was a peace officer or fireman;

(b) Murder which is perpetrated by a person who is under sentence of life imprisonment;

(c) Murder which is perpetrated by use or detonation of a bomb or explosive device;

(d) Murder which is perpetrated by any person who has been offered or has received anything of value for committing the murder, and all parties to such a murder, are guilty as principals;

(e) When done with or without any design to effect death, by any person engaged in the commission of the crime of rape, burglary, kidnapping, arson, robbery, sexual battery, unnatural intercourse with any child under the age of twelve (12), or nonconsensual unnatural intercourse with mankind, or in any attempt to commit such felonies;

(f) When done with or without any design to effect death, by any person engaged in the commission of the crime of felonious abuse and/or battery of a child, or in any attempt to commit such felony;

(g) Murder which is perpetrated on educational property;

(h) Murder which is perpetrated by the killing of any elected official of a county, municipal, state or federal government with knowledge that the victim was such public official.

Aggravating circumstances used to impose death penalty. In order to impose a death sentence upon a defendant, Mississippi Code § 99-19-101(5) requires that the prosecutor establishes the existence of at least one of the following statutory aggravating circumstances at the penalty phase:

(a) The capital offense was committed by a person under sentence of imprisonment.

(b) The defendant was previously convicted of another capital offense or of a felony involving the use or threat of violence to the person.

(c) The defendant knowingly created a great risk of death to many persons.

(d) The capital offense was committed while the defendant was engaged, or was an accomplice, in the commission of, or an attempt to commit, or flight after committing or attempting to commit, any robbery, rape, arson, burglary, kidnapping, aircraft piracy, sexual battery, unnatural intercourse with any child under the age of twelve (12), or nonconsensual unnatural intercourse with mankind, or felonious abuse and/or battery of a child, or the unlawful use or detonation of a bomb or explosive device.

(e) The capital offense was committed for the purpose of avoiding or preventing a lawful arrest or effecting an escape from custody.

(f) The capital offense was committed for pecuniary gain.

(g) The capital offense was committed to disrupt or hinder the lawful exercise of any governmental function or the enforcement of laws.

(h) The capital offense was especially heinous, atrocious or cruel.

In addition, in order to impose the death penalty, Mississippi Code § 99-19-101(7) requires the penalty phase jury find one of the following factors: (a) the defendant actually killed; (b) the defendant attempted to kill; (c) the defendant intended that a killing take place; (d) the defendant contemplated that lethal force would be employed.

Mitigating circumstances. Although the federal Constitution will not permit jurisdictions to prevent capital felons from presenting all relevant mitigating evidence at the penalty phase, Mississippi has provided by statute, Mississippi Code § 99-19-101(6), the following statutory mitigating circumstances that permit a jury to reject imposition of the death penalty:

(a) The defendant has no significant history of prior criminal activity.

(b) The offense was committed while the defendant was under the influence of extreme mental or emotional disturbance.

(c) The victim was a participant in the defendant's conduct or consented to the act.

(d) The defendant was an accomplice in the capital offense committed by another person and his participation was relatively minor.

(e) The defendant acted under extreme duress or under the substantial domination of another person.

(f) The capacity of the defendant to appreciate the criminality of his conduct or to conform his conduct to the requirements of law was substantially impaired.

(g) The age of the defendant at the time of the crime.

Persons who may attend an execution. Under the laws of Mississippi a limitation is imposed upon the number of persons who may be present at an execution. The following is provided by Mississippi Code § 99-19-55(2):

> When a person is sentenced to suffer death in the manner provided by law, it shall be the duty of the clerk of the court to deliver forthwith to the Commissioner of Corrections a warrant for the execution of the condemned person. It shall be the duty of the commissioner forthwith to notify the state executioner of the date of the execution and it shall be the duty of the said state executioner, or any person deputized by him in writing, in the event of his physical disability, as hereinafter provided, to be present at such execution, to perform the same, and have general supervision over said execution. In addition to the above designated persons, the commissioner of corrections shall secure the presence at such execution of the sheriff, or his deputy, of the county of conviction, at least one (1) but not more than two (2) physicians or the county coroner where the execution takes place, and bona fide members of the press, not to exceed eight (8) in number, and at the request of the condemned, such ministers of the gospel, not exceeding two (2), as said condemned person shall name. The commissioner of corrections shall also name to be present at the execution such officers or guards as may be deemed by him to be necessary to insure proper security. No other persons shall be permitted to witness the execution, except the commissioner may permit two (2) members of the condemned person's immediate family as witnesses, if they so request and two (2) members of the victim's immediate family as witnesses, if they so request. Provided further, that the governor may, for good cause shown, permit two (2) additional persons of good and reputable character to witness an execution. No person shall be allowed to take photographs or other recordings of any type during the execution. The absence of the sheriff, or deputy, after due notice to attend, shall not delay the execution.

Missouri

General considerations. Missouri is a capital punishment jurisdiction. The state reenacted its death penalty law after the United States Supreme Court decision in *Furman v. Georgia*, 408 U.S. 238 (1972), on September 28, 1975. Capital murder in Missouri is punishable by death or life imprisonment without parole. A capital prosecution in Missouri is bifurcated into a guilt phase and penalty phase. It is required at the penalty phase that the jury unanimously agrees that a death sentence is appropriate before it can be imposed. If the penalty phase jury is unable to reach a verdict, the trial judge is required to impose a sentence of life imprisonment without parole.

Under Missouri's capital punishment statute, a sentence of death is automatically reviewed by the Missouri Supreme Court. Missouri provides for the election of lethal injection or lethal gas to carry out death sentences. The state's death row facility for men is in Mineral Point while the facility for women is in Chillicothe. The governor has exclusive authority to grant clemency in capital cases. The governor has the discretion to appoint a board of inquiry to investigate a request for clemency.

Death penalty offenses. Missouri's capital punishment statute is triggered if a person commits a homicide under a single circumstance. It is provided by Missouri Code § 565.020 that capital murder occurs when the offender "knowingly causes the death of another person after deliberation upon the matter."

Aggravating circumstances used to impose death penalty. In order to impose a death sentence upon a defendant, Missouri Code § 565.032(2) requires that the prosecutor establishes the existence of at least one of the following statutory aggravating circumstances at the penalty phase:

(1) The offense was committed by a person with a prior record of conviction for murder in the first degree, or the offense was committed by a person who has one or more serious assaultive criminal convictions;

(2) The murder in the first degree offense was committed while the offender was engaged in the commission or attempted commission of another unlawful homicide;

(3) The offender by his act of murder in the first degree knowingly created a great risk of death to more than one person by means of a weapon or device which would normally be hazardous to the lives of more than one person;

(4) The offender committed the offense of murder in the first degree for himself or another, for the purpose of receiving money or any other thing of monetary value from the victim of the murder or another;

(5) The murder in the first degree was committed against a judicial officer, former judicial officer, prosecuting attorney or former prosecuting attorney, circuit attorney or former circuit attorney, assistant prosecuting attorney or former assistant prosecuting attorney, assistant circuit attorney or former assistant circuit attorney, peace officer or former peace officer, elected official or former elected official during or because of the exercise of his official duty;

(6) The offender caused or directed another to commit murder in the first degree or committed murder in the first degree as an agent or employee of another person;

(7) The murder in the first degree was outrageously or wantonly vile, horrible or inhuman in that it involved torture, or depravity of mind;

(8) The murder in the first degree was committed against any peace officer, or fireman while engaged in the performance of his official duty;

(9) The murder in the first degree was committed by a person in, or who has escaped from, the lawful custody of a peace officer or place of lawful confinement;

(10) The murder in the first degree was committed for the purpose of avoiding, interfering with, or preventing a lawful arrest or custody in a place of lawful confinement, of himself or another;

(11) The murder in the first degree was committed while the defendant was engaged in the perpetration or was aiding or encouraging another person to perpetrate or attempt to perpetrate a felony of any degree of rape, sodomy, burglary, robbery, kidnapping, or any felony offense;

(12) The murdered individual was a witness or potential witness in any past or pending investigation or past or pending prosecution, and was killed as a result of his status as a witness or potential witness;

(13) The murdered individual was an employee of an institution or facility of the department of corrections of this state or local correction agency and was killed in the course of performing his official duties, or the murdered individual was an inmate of such institution or facility;

(14) The murdered individual was killed as a result of the hijacking of an airplane, train, ship, bus or other public conveyance;

(15) The murder was committed for the purpose of concealing or attempting to conceal any felony offense;

(16) The murder was committed for the purpose of causing or attempting to cause a person to refrain from initiating or aiding in the prosecution of a felony offense;

(17) The murder was committed during the commission of a crime which is part of a pattern of criminal street gang activity.

Mitigating circumstances. Although the federal Constitution will not permit jurisdictions to prevent capital felons from presenting all relevant mitigating evidence at the penalty phase, Missouri has provided by statute, Missouri Code § 565.032(3), the following statutory mitigating circumstances that permit a jury to reject imposition of the death penalty:

(1) The defendant has no significant history of prior criminal activity;

(2) The murder in the first degree was committed while the defendant was under the influence of extreme mental or emotional disturbance;

(3) The victim was a participant in the defendant's conduct or consented to the act;

(4) The defendant was an accomplice in the murder in the first degree committed by another person and his participation was relatively minor;

(5) The defendant acted under extreme duress or under the substantial domination of another person;

(6) The capacity of the defendant to appreciate the criminality of his conduct or to conform his conduct to the requirements of law was substantially impaired;

(7) The age of the defendant at the time of the crime.

Persons who may attend an execution. Missouri law limits the number of persons who may be present at an execution. The following is provided by Missouri Code § 546.740:

The chief administrative officer of the correctional center or his duly appointed representative shall be present at the execution and the director of the department of corrections shall invite the presence of the attorney general of the state, and at least eight reputable citizens, to be selected by him; and he shall at the request of the defendant, permit such clergy or religious leaders, not exceeding two, as the defendant may name, and any person, other than another incarcerated offender, relatives or friends, not to exceed five, to be present at the execution, together with such peace officers as he may think expedient, to witness the execution; but no person under twenty-one years of age shall be allowed to witness the execution.

Montana

General considerations. Montana is a capital punishment jurisdiction. The state reenacted its death penalty law after the United States Supreme Court decision in *Furman v. Georgia*, 408 U.S. 238 (1972), on March 11, 1974. Capital murder in Montana is punishable by death, life imprisonment without parole, or imprisonment for a term of years. A capital prosecution in Montana is bifurcated into a guilt phase and penalty phase. Montana requires by statute that only a judge may preside over the penalty phase. However, this requirement is unconstitutional because the United States Supreme Court held in *Ring v. Arizona*, 536 U.S. 584 (2002), that a jury must be used at the penalty phase, absent a waiver by the defendant.

Under Montana's capital punishment statute, a sentence of death is automatically reviewed by the Montana Supreme Court. Montana uses lethal injection to carry out death sentences. The state's death row facility for men is located in Deer Lodge and the facility for women is in Warm Springs. Pursuant to the laws of Montana the governor has authority to grant clemency in capital cases. The governor must obtain the approval of the state's Board of Pardons in order to grant clemency.

Death penalty offenses. Montana's capital punishment offenses are set out under Montana Code § 45-5-102(1). This statute is triggered if a person commits a homicide under the following special circumstances:

(a) the person purposely or knowingly causes the death of another human being; or

(b) the person attempts to commit, commits, or is legally accountable for the attempt or commission of robbery, sexual intercourse without consent, arson, burglary, kidnapping, aggravated kidnapping, felonious escape, assault with a weapon, aggravated assault, or any other forcible felony and in the course of the forcible felony or flight thereafter, the person or any person legally accountable for the crime causes the death of another human being.

Aggravating circumstances used to impose death penalty. In order to impose a death sentence upon a defendant, Montana Code § 46-18-303 requires that the prosecutor establishes the existence of at least one of the following statutory aggravating circumstances at the penalty phase:

(1) (a) The offense was deliberate homicide and was committed: (i) by an offender while in official detention; (ii) by an offender who had been previously convicted of another deliberate homicide; (iii)

by means of torture; (iv) by an offender lying in wait or ambush; (v) as a part of a scheme or operation that, if completed, would result in the death of more than one person; or (vi) by an offender during the course of committing sexual assault, sexual intercourse without consent, deviate sexual conduct, or incest, and the victim was less than 18 years of age. (b) The offense was deliberate homicide and the victim was a peace officer killed while performing the officer's duty.

(2) The offense was aggravated kidnapping that resulted in the death of the victim or the death by direct action of the offender of a person who rescued or attempted to rescue the victim.

(3) The offense was attempted deliberate homicide, aggravated assault, or aggravated kidnapping committed while in official detention, by an offender who has been previously: (a) convicted of the offense of deliberate homicide; or (b) found to be a persistent felony offender.

(4) The offense was sexual intercourse without consent, the offender has a previous conviction of sexual intercourse without consent ... and the offender inflicted serious bodily injury upon a person in the course of committing each offense.

Mitigating circumstances. Although the federal Constitution will not permit jurisdictions to prevent capital felons from presenting all relevant mitigating evidence at the penalty phase, Montana has provided by statute, Montana Code § 46-18-304, the following statutory mitigating circumstances that permit a jury to reject imposition of the death penalty:

(a) The defendant has no significant history of prior criminal activity.

(b) The offense was committed while the defendant was under the influence of extreme mental or emotional disturbance.

(c) The defendant acted under extreme duress or under the substantial domination of another person.

(d) The capacity of the defendant to appreciate the criminality of the defendant's conduct or to conform the defendant's conduct to the requirements of law was substantially impaired.

(e) The victim was a participant in the defendant's conduct or consented to the act.

(f) The defendant was an accomplice in an offense committed by another person, and the defendant's participation was relatively minor.

(g) The defendant, at the time of the commission of the crime, was less than 18 years of age (federal law prohibits imposing death penalty in this situation).

Nebraska

General considerations. Nebraska is a capital punishment jurisdiction. The state reenacted its death penalty law after the United States Supreme Court decision in *Furman v. Georgia*, 408 U.S. 238 (1972), on April 20, 1973. Capital murder in Nebraska is punishable by death or life imprisonment without parole. Under the laws of Nebraska a capital prosecution is trifurcated into a guilt phase, aggravation phase and mitigation phase. A jury is used at the guilt phase and under Nebraska § 29-2520 a jury is used at the aggravation phase. However, under Nebraska § 29-2521, the mitigation phase is presided over by a three-judge panel. After a jury determines guilt, it must determine whether any statutory aggravating circumstance exists. If the jury finds that an aggravating circumstance exists, a three-judge panel hears mitigating evidence. The three-judge panel must unanimously agree that death is appropriate.

Under Nebraska's capital punishment statute, a sentence of death is automatically reviewed by the Nebraska Supreme Court. Nebraska uses lethal injection to carry out death sentences. The state's death row facility for males is in Lincoln, while the facility for female death row inmates is in York. An executive panel, which includes the governor, has authority to grant clemency in capital cases.

Death penalty offenses. Nebraska's capital punishment offenses are set out under Nebraska Code § 28-303. This statute is triggered if a person commits a homicide under the following special circumstances:

[H]e or she kills another person (1) purposely and with deliberate and premeditated malice, or (2) in the perpetration of or attempt to perpetrate any sexual assault in the first degree, arson, robbery, kidnapping, hijacking of any public or private means of transportation, or burglary, or (3) by administering poison or causing the same to be done; or if by willful and corrupt perjury or subornation of the same he or she purposely procures the conviction and execution of any innocent person.

Aggravating circumstances used to impose death penalty. In order to impose a death sentence upon a defendant, Nebraska Code § 29-2523(1) requires that the prosecutor establishes the existence of at least one of the following statutory aggravating circumstances:

(a) The offender was previously convicted of another murder or a crime involving the use or threat of violence to the person, or has a substantial prior history of serious assaultive or terrorizing criminal activity;

(b) The murder was committed in an effort to conceal the commission of a crime, or to conceal the identity of the perpetrator of such crime;

(c) The murder was committed for hire, or for pecuniary gain, or the defendant hired another to commit the murder for the defendant;

(d) The murder was especially heinous, atrocious, cruel, or manifested exceptional depravity by ordinary standards of morality and intelligence;

(e) At the time the murder was committed, the offender also committed another murder;

(f) The offender knowingly created a great risk of death to at least several persons;

(g) The victim was a public servant having lawful custody of the offender or another in the lawful performance of his or her official duties and the offender knew or should have known that the victim was a public servant performing his or her official duties;

(h) The murder was committed knowingly to disrupt or hinder the lawful exercise of any governmental function or the enforcement of the laws; or

(i) The victim was a law enforcement officer engaged in the lawful performance of his or her official duties as a law enforcement officer and the offender knew or reasonably should have known that the victim was a law enforcement officer.

Mitigating circumstances. Although the federal Constitution will not permit jurisdictions to prevent capital felons from presenting all relevant mitigating evidence at the penalty phase, Nebraska has provided by statute, Nebraska Code § 29-2523(2), the following statutory mitigating circumstances that permit a rejection of the imposition of the death penalty:

(a) The offender has no significant history of prior criminal activity;

(b) The offender acted under unusual pressures or influences or under the domination of another person;

(c) The crime was committed while the offender was under the influence of extreme mental or emotional disturbance;

(d) The age of the defendant at the time of the crime;

(e) The offender was an accomplice in the crime committed by another person and his or her participation was relatively minor;

(f) The victim was a participant in the defendant's conduct or consented to the act; or

(g) At the time of the crime, the capacity of the defendant to appreciate the wrongfulness of his or her conduct or to conform his or her conduct to the requirements of law was impaired as a result of mental illness, mental defect, or intoxication.

Persons who may attend execution. Under the laws of Nebraska a limitation is imposed upon the number of persons who may be present at an execution. The following is provided by Nebraska Code § 83-970:

Besides the director of Correctional Services and those persons required to be present under the execution protocol, the following persons, and no others ... may be present at the execution: (1) The member of the clergy in attendance upon the convicted person; (2) no more than three persons selected by the convicted person; (3) no more than three persons representing the victim or victims of the crime; and (4) such other persons, not exceeding six in number, as the director may designate. At least two persons designated by the director shall be professional members of the Nebraska news media.

Nevada

General considerations. Nevada is a capital punishment jurisdiction. The state reenacted its death penalty law after the United States Supreme Court decision in *Furman v. Georgia*, 408

U.S. 238 (1972), on July 1, 1973. Capital murder in Nevada is punishable by death, life imprisonment with or without parole, or imprisonment for a term of years. A capital prosecution in
Nevada is bifurcated into a guilt phase and penalty phase. It is required at the penalty phase
that the jury unanimously agrees that a death sentence is appropriate before it can be imposed.
The decision of a penalty phase jury is binding on the trial court under the laws of Nevada.

Under Nevada's capital punishment statute, a sentence of death is automatically reviewed
by the Nevada Supreme Court. Nevada uses lethal injection to carry out death sentences. The
state's death row facility for men is located in Ely, while the facility for women is in Carson
City. Pursuant to the laws of Nevada an executive panel that includes the governor has authority
to grant clemency in capital cases.

Death penalty offenses. Nevada's capital punishment offenses are set out under Nevada
Code § 200.030(1). This statute is triggered if a person commits a homicide under the following
special circumstances:

(a) Perpetrated by means of poison, lying in wait or torture, or by any other kind of willful, deliberate and premeditated killing;

(b) Committed in the perpetration or attempted perpetration of sexual assault, kidnapping, arson,
robbery, burglary, invasion of the home, sexual abuse of a child, sexual molestation of a child under
the age of 14 years, child abuse or abuse of an older person or vulnerable person;

(c) Committed to avoid or prevent the lawful arrest of any person by a peace officer or to effect the
escape of any person from legal custody;

(d) Committed on the property of a public or private school, at an activity sponsored by a public
or private school or on a school bus while the bus was engaged in its official duties by a person who
intended to create a great risk of death or substantial bodily harm to more than one person by means
of a weapon, device or course of action that would normally be hazardous to the lives of more than
one person; or

(e) Committed in the perpetration or attempted perpetration of an act of terrorism.

Aggravating circumstances used to impose death penalty. In order to impose a death
sentence upon a defendant, Nevada Code § 200.033 requires that the prosecutor establishes the
existence of at least one of the following statutory aggravating circumstances at the penalty
phase:

1. The murder was committed by a person under sentence of imprisonment.

2. The murder was committed by a person who, at any time before a penalty hearing is conducted for the murder, is or has been convicted of: (a) Another murder; or (b) A felony involving the
use or threat of violence to the person of another.

3. The murder was committed by a person who knowingly created a great risk of death to more
than one person by means of a weapon, device or course of action which would normally be hazardous to the lives of more than one person.

4. The murder was committed while the person was engaged, alone or with others, in the commission of, or an attempt to commit or flight after committing or attempting to commit, any robbery, arson in the first degree, burglary, invasion of the home or kidnapping in the first degree, and
the person charged: (a) Killed or attempted to kill the person murdered; or (b) Knew or had reason to
know that life would be taken or lethal force used.

5. The murder was committed to avoid or prevent a lawful arrest or to effect an escape from custody.

6. The murder was committed by a person, for himself or herself or another, to receive money or
any other thing of monetary value.

7. The murder was committed upon a peace officer or firefighter who was killed while engaged in
the performance of his or her official duty or because of an act performed in his or her official capacity, and the defendant knew or reasonably should have known that the victim was a peace officer or
firefighter.

8. The murder involved torture or the mutilation of the victim.

9. The murder was committed upon one or more persons at random and without apparent
motive.

10. The murder was committed upon a person less than 14 years of age.

11. The murder was committed upon a person because of the actual or perceived race, color, religion, national origin, physical or mental disability or sexual orientation of that person.

12. The defendant has, in the immediate proceeding, been convicted of more than one offense of murder in the first or second degree. For the purposes of this subsection, a person shall be deemed to have been convicted of a murder at the time the jury verdict of guilt is rendered or upon pronouncement of guilt by a judge or judges sitting without a jury.

13. The person, alone or with others, subjected or attempted to subject the victim of the murder to nonconsensual sexual penetration immediately before, during or immediately after the commission of the murder.

14. The murder was committed on the property of a public or private school, at an activity sponsored by a public or private school or on a school bus while the bus was engaged in its official duties by a person who intended to create a great risk of death or substantial bodily harm to more than one person by means of a weapon, device or course of action that would normally be hazardous to the lives of more than one person.

15. The murder was committed with the intent to commit, cause, aid, further or conceal an act of terrorism.

Mitigating circumstances. Although the federal Constitution will not permit jurisdictions to prevent capital felons from presenting all relevant mitigating evidence at the penalty phase, Nevada has provided by statute, Nevada Code § 200.035, the following statutory mitigating circumstances that permit a jury to reject imposition of the death penalty:

1. The defendant has no significant history of prior criminal activity.

2. The murder was committed while the defendant was under the influence of extreme mental or emotional disturbance.

3. The victim was a participant in the defendant's criminal conduct or consented to the act.

4. The defendant was an accomplice in a murder committed by another person and the defendant's participation in the murder was relatively minor.

5. The defendant acted under duress or under the domination of another person.

6. The youth of the defendant at the time of the crime.

7. Any other mitigating circumstance.

Persons who may attend execution. Under the laws of Nevada a limitation is imposed upon the number of persons who may be present at an execution. The following is provided by Nevada Code § 176.355(2)(e):

The director of the Department of Corrections shall: ...

Invite a competent physician, the county coroner, a psychiatrist and not less than six reputable citizens over the age of 21 years to be present at the execution. The director shall determine the maximum number of persons who may be present for the execution. The director shall give preference to those eligible members or representatives of the immediate family of the victim who requested to attend the execution.

New Hampshire

General considerations. New Hampshire is a capital punishment jurisdiction. The state reenacted its death penalty law after the United States Supreme Court decision in *Furman v. Georgia*, 408 U.S. 238 (1972), on January 1, 1991. Capital murder in New Hampshire is punishable by death or life imprisonment without parole. A capital prosecution in New Hampshire is bifurcated into a guilt phase and penalty phase. It is required at the penalty phase that the jury unanimously agrees that a death sentence is appropriate before it can be imposed. If the penalty phase jury is unable to reach a verdict, the trial judge is required to impose a sentence of life imprisonment without parole.

Under New Hampshire's capital punishment statute, a sentence of death is automatically reviewed by the New Hampshire Supreme Court. New Hampshire uses lethal injection to carry out death sentences. The state also provides for the use of hanging, if for any reason lethal injection cannot be used. The New Hampshire governor has exclusive authority to grant clemency in capital cases.

Death penalty offenses. Capital punishment offenses are set out under New Hampshire Code § 630:1. This statute is triggered if a person knowingly causes the death of:

(a) A law enforcement officer or a judicial officer acting in the line of duty or when the death is caused as a consequence of or in retaliation for such person's actions in the line of duty;

(b) Another before, after, while engaged in the commission of, or while attempting to commit kidnapping;

(c) Another by criminally soliciting a person to cause said death or after having been criminally solicited by another for his personal pecuniary gain;

(d) Another after being sentenced to life imprisonment without parole;

(e) Another before, after, while engaged in the commission of, or while attempting to commit aggravated felonious sexual assault;

(f) Another before, after, while engaged in the commission of, or while attempting to commit [a drug offense]; or

(g) Another, who is licensed or privileged to be within an occupied structure, or separately secured or occupied section thereof, before, after, or while in the commission of, or while attempting to commit, burglary.

Aggravating circumstances used to impose death penalty. In order to impose a death sentence upon a defendant, New Hampshire Code § 630:5(VII) requires that the prosecutor establishes the existence of at least one of the following statutory aggravating circumstances at the penalty phase:

(a) The defendant: (1) purposely killed the victim; (2) purposely inflicted serious bodily injury which resulted in the death of the victim; (3) purposely engaged in conduct which: (A) the defendant knew would create a grave risk of death to a person, other than one of the participants in the offense; and (B) resulted in the death of the victim.

(b) The defendant has been convicted of another state or federal offense resulting in the death of a person, for which a sentence of life imprisonment or a sentence of death was authorized by law.

(c) The defendant has previously been convicted of 2 or more state or federal offenses punishable by a term of imprisonment of more than one year, committed on different occasions, involving the infliction of, or attempted infliction of, serious bodily injury upon another person.

(d) The defendant has previously been convicted of 2 or more state or federal offenses punishable by a term of imprisonment of more than one year, committed on different occasions, involving the distribution of a controlled substance.

(e) In the commission of the offense of capital murder, the defendant knowingly created a grave risk of death to one or more persons in addition to the victims of the offense.

(f) The defendant committed the offense after substantial planning and premeditation.

(g) The victim was particularly vulnerable due to old age, youth, or infirmity.

(h) The defendant committed the offense in an especially heinous, cruel or depraved manner in that it involved torture or serious physical abuse to the victim.

(i) The murder was committed for pecuniary gain.

(j) The murder was committed for the purpose of avoiding or preventing a lawful arrest or effecting an escape from lawful custody.

Mitigating circumstances. Although the federal Constitution will not permit jurisdictions to prevent capital felons from presenting all relevant mitigating evidence at the penalty phase, New Hampshire has provided by statute, New Hampshire Code § 630:5(VI), the following statutory mitigating circumstances that permit a jury to reject imposition of the death penalty:

(a) The defendant's capacity to appreciate the wrongfulness of his conduct or to conform his conduct to the requirements of law was significantly impaired, regardless of whether the capacity was so impaired as to constitute a defense to the charge.

(b) The defendant was under unusual and substantial duress, regardless of whether the duress was of such a degree as to constitute a defense to the charge.

(c) The defendant is punishable as an accomplice in the offense, which was committed by another, but the defendant's participation was relatively minor, regardless of whether the participation was so minor as to constitute a defense to the charge.

(d) The defendant was youthful, although not under the age of 18.

(e) The defendant did not have a significant prior criminal record.

(f) The defendant committed the offense under severe mental or emotional disturbance.

(g) Another defendant or defendants, equally culpable in the crime, will not be punished by death.

(h) The victim consented to the criminal conduct that resulted in the victim's death.

(i) Other factors in the defendant's background or character mitigate against imposition of the death sentence.

Persons who may attend execution. Under the laws of New Hampshire a limitation is imposed upon the number of persons who may be present at an execution. The following is provided by New Hampshire Code § 630:6:

> The punishment of death shall be inflicted within the walls or yard of the state prison. The sheriff of the county in which the person was convicted, and 2 of his deputies, shall be present, unless prevented by unavoidable casualty. He shall request the presence of the attorney general or county attorney, clerk of the court and a surgeon, and may admit other reputable citizens not exceeding 12, the relations of the convict, his counsel and such priest or clergyman as he may desire, and no others.

North Carolina

General considerations. North Carolina is a capital punishment jurisdiction. The state reenacted its death penalty law after the United States Supreme Court decision in *Furman v. Georgia*, 408 U.S. 238 (1972), on June 1, 1977. Capital murder in North Carolina is punishable by death or life imprisonment without parole. A capital prosecution in North Carolina is bifurcated into a guilt phase and penalty phase. It is required at the penalty phase that the jury unanimously agrees that a death sentence is appropriate before it can be imposed. If the penalty phase jury is unable to reach a verdict, the trial judge is required to impose a sentence of life imprisonment without parole.

Under North Carolina's capital punishment statute, a sentence of death is automatically reviewed by the North Carolina Supreme Court. North Carolina uses lethal injection to carry out death sentences. The state's death row facility for men and women is in Raleigh. The North Carolina governor has exclusive authority to grant clemency in capital cases.

Death penalty offenses. North Carolina's capital punishment offenses are set out under North Carolina Code § 14-17. This statute is triggered if a person commits a homicide under the following special circumstances:

> A murder which shall be perpetrated by means of a nuclear, biological, or chemical weapon of mass destruction, poison, lying in wait, imprisonment, starving, torture, or by any other kind of willful, deliberate, and premeditated killing, or which shall be committed in the perpetration or attempted perpetration of any arson, rape or a sex offense, robbery, kidnapping, burglary, or other felony committed or attempted with the use of a deadly weapon....

Aggravating circumstances used to impose death penalty. In order to impose a death sentence upon a defendant, North Carolina Code § 15A-2000(e) requires that the prosecutor establishes the existence of at least one of the following statutory aggravating circumstances at the penalty phase:

(1) The capital felony was committed by a person lawfully incarcerated.

(2) The defendant had been previously convicted of another capital felony or had been previously adjudicated delinquent in a juvenile proceeding for committing an offense that would be a capital felony if committed by an adult.

(3) The defendant had been previously convicted of a felony involving the use or threat of violence to the person or had been previously adjudicated delinquent in a juvenile proceeding for committing an offense that would be a ... felony involving the use or threat of violence to the person if the offense had been committed by an adult.

(4) The capital felony was committed for the purpose of avoiding or preventing a lawful arrest or effecting an escape from custody.

(5) The capital felony was committed while the defendant was engaged, or was an aider or abettor, in the commission of, or an attempt to commit, or flight after committing or attempting to commit, any homicide, robbery, rape or a sex offense, arson, burglary, kidnapping, or aircraft piracy or the unlawful throwing, placing, or discharging of a destructive device or bomb.

(6) The capital felony was committed for pecuniary gain.

(7) The capital felony was committed to disrupt or hinder the lawful exercise of any governmental function or the enforcement of laws.

(8) The capital felony was committed against a law enforcement officer, employee of the Division of Adult Correction of the Department of Public Safety, jailer, fireman, judge or justice, former judge or justice, prosecutor or former prosecutor, juror or former juror, or witness or former witness against the defendant, while engaged in the performance of his official duties or because of the exercise of his official duty.

(9) The capital felony was especially heinous, atrocious, or cruel.

(10) The defendant knowingly created a great risk of death to more than one person by means of a weapon or device which would normally be hazardous to the lives of more than one person.

(11) The murder for which the defendant stands convicted was part of a course of conduct in which the defendant engaged and which included the commission by the defendant of other crimes of violence against another person or persons.

Mitigating circumstances. Although the federal Constitution will not permit jurisdictions to prevent capital felons from presenting all relevant mitigating evidence at the penalty phase, North Carolina has by North Carolina Code § 15A-2000(f) the following statutory mitigating circumstances that permit a jury to reject imposition of the death penalty:

(1) The defendant has no significant history of prior criminal activity.

(2) The capital felony was committed while the defendant was under the influence of mental or emotional disturbance.

(3) The victim was a voluntary participant in the defendant's homicidal conduct or consented to the homicidal act.

(4) The defendant was an accomplice in or accessory to the capital felony committed by another person and his participation was relatively minor.

(5) The defendant acted under duress or under the domination of another person.

(6) The capacity of the defendant to appreciate the criminality of his conduct or to conform his conduct to the requirements of law was impaired.

(7) The age of the defendant at the time of the crime.

(8) The defendant aided in the apprehension of another capital felon or testified truthfully on behalf of the prosecution in another prosecution of a felony.

(9) Any other circumstance arising from the evidence which the jury deems to have mitigating value.

Persons who may attend an execution. North Carolina law limits the number of persons who may be present at an execution. The following is provided by North Carolina Code § 15-190:

> At such execution there shall be present the warden or deputy warden or some person designated by the warden in the warden's place, and the surgeon or physician of the penitentiary. Four respectable citizens, two members of the victim's family, the counsel and any relatives of such person, convict or felon and a minister or member of the clergy or religious leader of the person's choosing may be present if they so desire. The identities, including the names, residential addresses, residential telephone numbers, and social security numbers of witnesses or persons designated to carry out the execution shall be confidential[.]

Ohio

General considerations. Ohio is a capital punishment jurisdiction. The state reenacted its death penalty law after the United States Supreme Court decision in *Furman v. Georgia*, 408 U.S. 238 (1972), on January 1, 1974. Capital murder in Ohio is punishable by death or life imprisonment with or without parole. It is provided under Rule 20 of the Rules of Superintendence for the Courts of Ohio that, in capital cases, an indigent defendant must be appointed two attorneys with experience in capital prosecutions. A capital prosecution in Ohio is bifurcated into a guilt phase and penalty phase. It is required at the penalty phase that the jury unanimously agrees that a death sentence is appropriate before it can be imposed. If the penalty phase jury is unable to reach a verdict, the trial judge is required to impose a sentence of life imprisonment with or without parole.

Under Ohio's capital punishment statute, a sentence of death is automatically reviewed by the Ohio Supreme Court. Ohio imposes death by lethal injection. The state's death row facility for men is in Mansfield and the facility for women is in Marysville. The governor has authority to grant clemency in capital cases. Requests for clemency are investigated by the state's Adult Parole Authority, which can make a nonbinding recommendation.

Death penalty offenses. Ohio's capital punishment offenses are set out under Ohio Code § 2903.01. This statute is triggered if a person commits a homicide under circumstances prohibited as follows:

(A) No person shall purposely, and with prior calculation and design, cause the death of another or the unlawful termination of another's pregnancy.

(B) No person shall purposely cause the death of another or the unlawful termination of another's pregnancy while committing or attempting to commit, or while fleeing immediately after committing or attempting to commit, kidnapping, rape, aggravated arson, arson, aggravated robbery, robbery, aggravated burglary, burglary, trespass in a habitation when a person is present or likely to be present, terrorism, or escape.

(C) No person shall purposely cause the death of another who is under thirteen years of age at the time of the commission of the offense.

(D) No person who is under detention as a result of having been found guilty of or having pleaded guilty to a felony or who breaks that detention shall purposely cause the death of another.

(E) No person shall purposely cause the death of a law enforcement officer whom the offender knows or has reasonable cause to know is a law enforcement officer when either of the following applies: (1) The victim, at the time of the commission of the offense, is engaged in the victim's duties. (2) It is the offender's specific purpose to kill a law enforcement officer.

Aggravating circumstances used to impose death penalty. In order to impose a death sentence upon a defendant, Ohio Code § 2929.04(A) requires that the prosecutor establish the existence of at least one of the following statutory aggravating circumstances at the guilt phase, and persuade the jury during the penalty phase that such proven aggravating circumstance outweighs any mitigating evidence:

(1) The offense was the assassination of the president of the United States or a person in line of succession to the presidency, the governor or lieutenant governor of this state, the president-elect or vice president-elect of the United States, the governor-elect or lieutenant governor-elect of this state, or a candidate for any of the offices described in this division.

(2) The offense was committed for hire.

(3) The offense was committed for the purpose of escaping detection, apprehension, trial, or punishment for another offense committed by the offender.

(4) The offense was committed while the offender was under detention or while the offender was at large after having broken detention.

(5) Prior to the offense at bar, the offender was convicted of an offense an essential element of which was the purposeful killing of or attempt to kill another, or the offense at bar was part of a course of conduct involving the purposeful killing of or attempt to kill two or more persons by the offender.

(6) The victim of the offense was a law enforcement officer....

(7) The offense was committed while the offender was committing, attempting to commit, or fleeing immediately after committing or attempting to commit kidnapping, rape, aggravated arson, aggravated robbery, or aggravated burglary, and either the offender was the principal offender in the commission of the aggravated murder or, if not the principal offender, committed the aggravated murder with prior calculation and design.

(8) The victim of the aggravated murder was a witness to an offense who was purposely killed to prevent the victim's testimony in any criminal proceeding and the aggravated murder was not committed during the commission, attempted commission, or flight immediately after the commission or attempted commission of the offense to which the victim was a witness, or the victim of the aggravated murder was a witness to an offense and was purposely killed in retaliation for the victim's testimony in any criminal proceeding.

(9) The offender, in the commission of the offense, purposefully caused the death of another who was under thirteen years of age at the time of the commission of the offense, and either the offender

was the principal offender in the commission of the offense or, if not the principal offender, committed the offense with prior calculation and design.

(10) The offense was committed while the offender was committing, attempting to commit, or fleeing immediately after committing or attempting to commit terrorism.

Mitigating circumstances. Although the federal Constitution will not permit jurisdictions to prevent capital felons from presenting all relevant mitigating evidence at the penalty phase, Ohio has provided by statute, Ohio Code § 2929.04(B), the following statutory mitigating circumstances that permit a jury to reject imposition of the death penalty:

[T]he nature and circumstances of the offense, the history, character, and background of the offender, and all of the following factors:

(1) Whether the victim of the offense induced or facilitated it;

(2) Whether it is unlikely that the offense would have been committed, but for the fact that the offender was under duress, coercion, or strong provocation;

(3) Whether, at the time of committing the offense, the offender, because of a mental disease or defect, lacked substantial capacity to appreciate the criminality of the offender's conduct or to conform the offender's conduct to the requirements of the law;

(4) The youth of the offender;

(5) The offender's lack of a significant history of prior criminal convictions and delinquency adjudications;

(6) If the offender was a participant in the offense but not the principal offender, the degree of the offender's participation in the offense and the degree of the offender's participation in the acts that led to the death of the victim;

(7) Any other factors that are relevant to the issue of whether the offender should be sentenced to death.

Persons who may attend execution. Under the laws of Ohio a limitation is imposed upon the number of persons who may be present at an execution. The following is provided by Ohio Code § 2949.25:

(A) At the execution of a death sentence, only the following persons may be present:

(1) The warden of the state correctional institution in which the sentence is executed or a deputy warden, any other person selected by the director of rehabilitation and correction to ensure that the death sentence is executed, any persons necessary to execute the death sentence by lethal injection, and the number of correction officers that the warden thinks necessary;

(2) The sheriff of the county in which the prisoner was tried and convicted;

(3) The director of rehabilitation and correction, or the director's agent;

(4) Physicians of the state correctional institution in which the sentence is executed;

(5) The clergyperson in attendance upon the prisoner, and not more than three other persons, to be designated by the prisoner, who are not confined in any state institution;

(6) Not more than three persons to be designated by the immediate family of the victim;

(7) Representatives of the news media as authorized by the director of rehabilitation and correction.

(B) The director shall authorize at least one representative of a newspaper, at least one representative of a television station, and at least one representative of a radio station to be present at the execution of the sentence under division (A)(7) of this section.

Oklahoma

General considerations. Oklahoma is a capital punishment jurisdiction. The state reenacted its death penalty law after the United States Supreme Court decision in *Furman v. Georgia*, 408 U.S. 238 (1972), on May 17, 1973. Capital murder in Oklahoma is punishable by death or life imprisonment with or without parole. A capital prosecution in Oklahoma is bifurcated into a guilt phase and penalty phase. It is required at the penalty phase that the jury unanimously agrees that a death sentence is appropriate before it can be imposed. If the penalty phase jury is unable to reach a verdict, the trial judge is required to impose imprisonment for life.

Under Oklahoma's capital punishment statute, a sentence of death is automatically reviewed by the Oklahoma Court of Criminal Appeals. Oklahoma uses lethal injection to carry out death sentences. The state provides for the use of electrocution should lethal injection be found uncon-stitutional, and provides for the use of a firing squad should electrocution and lethal injection be found unconstitutional. The state's death row facility for men is in McAlester; the facility for women is in Oklahoma City. The governor has authority to grant clemency in capital cases. The governor requires the approval of the state's Pardon and Parole Board in order to grant clemency.

Death penalty offenses. Oklahoma's capital punishment offenses are set out under Okla-homa Code tit. 21 § 701.7. This statute is triggered if a person commits a homicide under the following special circumstances:

A. A person commits murder in the first degree when that person unlawfully and with malice aforethought causes the death of another human being.

B. A person also commits the crime of murder in the first degree, regardless of malice, when that person or any other person takes the life of a human being during, or if the death of a human being results from, the commission or attempted commission of murder of another person, shooting or dis-charge of a firearm or crossbow with intent to kill, intentional discharge of a firearm or other deadly weapon into any dwelling or building, forcible rape, robbery with a dangerous weapon, kidnapping, escape from lawful custody, eluding an officer, first degree burglary, first degree arson, unlawful dis-tributing or dispensing of controlled dangerous substances or synthetic controlled substances, traffick-ing in illegal drugs, or manufacturing or attempting to manufacture a controlled dangerous substance.

C. A person commits murder in the first degree when the death of a child results from the willful or malicious injuring, torturing, maiming or using of unreasonable force by said person or who shall willfully cause, procure or permit any of said acts to be done upon the child.

D. A person commits murder in the first degree when that person unlawfully and with malice aforethought solicits another person or persons to cause the death of a human being in furtherance of unlawfully manufacturing, distributing or dispensing controlled dangerous substances, unlawfully possessing with intent to distribute or dispense controlled dangerous substances, or trafficking in ille-gal drugs.

E. A person commits murder in the first degree when that person intentionally causes the death of a law enforcement officer, correctional officer, or corrections employee while the officer or employee is in the performance of official duties.

Aggravating circumstances used to impose death penalty. In order to impose a death sentence upon a defendant, Oklahoma Code tit. 21 § 701.12 requires that the prosecutor estab-lishes the existence of at least one of the following statutory aggravating circumstances at the penalty phase:

1. The defendant was previously convicted of a felony involving the use or threat of violence to the person;

2. The defendant knowingly created a great risk of death to more than one person;

3. The person committed the murder for remuneration or the promise of remuneration or employed another to commit the murder for remuneration or the promise of remuneration;

4. The murder was especially heinous, atrocious, or cruel (this provision was found unconstitu-tional in *Maynard v. Cartwright*, 484 U.S. 356 [1988]);

5. The murder was committed for the purpose of avoiding or preventing a lawful arrest or prose-cution;

6. The murder was committed by a person while serving a sentence of imprisonment on convic-tion of a felony;

7. The existence of a probability that the defendant would commit criminal acts of violence that would constitute a continuing threat to society; or

8. The victim of the murder was a peace officer, or correctional employee of an institution under the control of the Department of Corrections, and such person was killed while in performance of official duty.

Mitigating circumstances. Oklahoma does not provide by statute any mitigating circum-stances to the imposition of the death penalty. Nonetheless, the United States Supreme Court has ruled that all relevant mitigating evidence must be allowed at the penalty phase.

Persons who may attend an execution. Oklahoma law limits the number of persons

who may be present at an execution. The following is provided by Oklahoma Code tit. 22 §
1015:

A. A judgment of death must be executed at the Oklahoma State Penitentiary at McAlester, Oklahoma, said prison to be designated by the court by which judgment is to be rendered.

B. The judgment of execution shall take place under the authority of the director of the Department of Corrections and the warden must be present along with other necessary prison and corrections officials to carry out the execution. The warden must invite the presence of a physician and the
district attorney of the county in which the crime occurred or a designee, the judge who presided at
the trial issuing the sentence of death, the chief of police of the municipality in which the crime
occurred, if applicable, and lead law enforcement officials of any state, county or local law enforcement agency who investigated the crime or testified in any court or clemency proceeding related to
the crime, including but not limited to the sheriff of the county wherein the conviction was had, to
witness the execution; in addition, the cabinet secretary of safety and security must be invited as well
as any other personnel or correctional personnel deemed appropriate and approved by the director.
The warden shall, at the request of the defendant, permit the presence of such ministers chosen by
the defendant, not exceeding two, and any persons, relatives or friends, not to exceed five, as the
defendant may name; provided, reporters from recognized members of the news media will be admitted upon proper identification, application and approval of the warden.

C. In the event the defendant has been sentenced to death in one or more criminal proceedings in
this state, or has been sentenced to death in this state and by one or more courts of competent jurisdiction in another state or pursuant to federal authority, or any combination thereof, and this state
has priority to execute the defendant, the warden must invite the prosecuting attorney or his or her
designee, the judge, and the chief law enforcement official from each jurisdiction where any death
sentence has issued. The above mentioned officials shall be allowed to witness the execution or view
the execution by closed circuit television as determined by the director of the Department of Corrections.

D. A place shall be provided at the Oklahoma State Penitentiary at McAlester so that individuals
who are eighteen (18) years of age or older and who are members of the immediate family of any
deceased victim of the defendant may witness the execution. The immediate family members shall be
allowed to witness the execution from an area that is separate from the area to which other nonfamily
member witnesses are admitted; provided, however, if there are multiple deceased victims, the
department shall not be required to provide separate areas for each family of each deceased victim. If
facilities are not capable or sufficient to provide all immediate family members with a direct view of
the execution, the Department of Corrections may broadcast the execution by means of a closed circuit television system to an area in which other immediate family members may be located.

Immediate family members may request individuals not directly related to the deceased victim but
who serve a close supporting role or professional role to the deceased victim or an immediate family
member, including, but not limited to, a minister or licensed counselor. The warden in consultation
with the director shall approve or disapprove such requests. Provided further, the department may set
a limit on the number of witnesses or viewers within occupancy limits.

E. Any surviving victim of the defendant who is eighteen (18) years of age or older may view the
execution by closed circuit television with the approval of both the director of the Department of
Corrections and the warden. The director and warden shall prioritize persons to view the execution,
including immediate family members, surviving victims, and supporting persons, and may set a limit
on the number of viewers within occupancy limits. Any surviving victim approved to view the execution of the defendant may have an accompanying support person as provided for members of the
immediate family of a deceased victim. As used in this subsection, "surviving victim" means any person who suffered serious harm or injury due to the criminal acts of the defendant of which the defendant has been convicted in a court of competent jurisdiction.

Oregon

General considerations. Oregon is a capital punishment jurisdiction. The state reenacted
its death penalty law after the United States Supreme Court decision in *Furman v. Georgia*, 408
U.S. 238 (1972), on December 7, 1978. Capital murder in Oregon is punishable by death or life
imprisonment with or without parole. A capital prosecution in Oregon is bifurcated into a guilt
phase and penalty phase. It is required at the penalty phase that the jury must unanimously

agree that a death sentence is appropriate before it can be imposed. If the penalty phase jury is unable to reach a verdict, the trial judge is required to impose life imprisonment with or without parole.

Under Oregon's capital punishment statute, a sentence of death is automatically reviewed by the Oregon Supreme Court. Oregon uses lethal injection to carry out death sentences. The state's death row facility is in Salem. Pursuant to the laws of Oregon the governor has exclusive authority to grant clemency in capital cases.

Death penalty offenses. Oregon's capital punishment offenses are set out under Oregon Code § 163.095. This statute is triggered if a person commits a homicide under the following special circumstances:

(1)(a) The defendant committed the murder pursuant to an agreement that the defendant receive money or other thing of value for committing the murder.

(b) The defendant solicited another to commit the murder and paid or agreed to pay the person money or other thing of value for committing the murder.

(c) The defendant committed murder after having been convicted previously in any jurisdiction of any homicide, the elements of which constitute the crime of murder or manslaughter.

(d) There was more than one murder victim in the same criminal episode.

(e) The homicide occurred in the course of or as a result of intentional maiming or torture of the victim.

(f) The victim of the intentional homicide was a person under the age of 14 years.

(2)(a) The victim was one of the following and the murder was related to the performance of the victim's official duties in the justice system: (A) A police officer; (B) A correctional, parole and probation officer or other person charged with the duty of custody, control or supervision of convicted persons; (C) A member of the Oregon State Police; (D) A judicial officer; (E) A juror or witness in a criminal proceeding; (F) An employee or officer of a court of justice; or (G) A member of the State Board of Parole and Post-Prison Supervision.

(b) The defendant was confined in a state, county or municipal penal or correctional facility or was otherwise in custody when the murder occurred.

(c) The defendant committed murder by means of an explosive.

(d) [T]he defendant personally and intentionally committed the homicide.

(e) The murder was committed in an effort to conceal the commission of a crime, or to conceal the identity of the perpetrator of a crime.

(f) The murder was committed after the defendant had escaped from a state, county or municipal penal or correctional facility and before the defendant had been returned to the custody of the facility.

Aggravating circumstances used to impose death penalty. Oregon does not set out separate aggravating circumstances for the penalty. Instead, Oregon Code § 163.150(1)(b) requires the jury, based upon any aggravating evidence the prosecutor presents, to answer the following issues affirmatively in order for the death penalty to be imposed:

(A) Whether the conduct of the defendant that caused the death of the deceased was committed deliberately and with the reasonable expectation that death of the deceased or another would result;

(B) Whether there is a probability that the defendant would commit criminal acts of violence that would constitute a continuing threat to society;

(C) If raised by the evidence, whether the conduct of the defendant in killing the deceased was unreasonable in response to the provocation, if any, by the deceased; and

(D) Whether the defendant should receive a death sentence.

Mitigating circumstances. Although the federal Constitution will not permit jurisdictions to prevent capital felons from presenting all relevant mitigating evidence at the penalty phase, Oregon has provided by statute, Oregon Code § 163.150(1)(c)(A), the following statutory mitigating circumstances that permit a jury to reject imposition of the death penalty: the defendant's age, the extent and severity of the defendant's prior criminal conduct and the extent of the mental and emotional pressure under which the defendant was acting at the time the offense was committed.

Persons who may attend an execution. Oregon law limits the number of persons who may be present at an execution. The following is provided by Oregon Code § 137.473(1):

The punishment of death shall be inflicted by the intravenous administration of a lethal quantity of an ultra-short-acting barbiturate in combination with a chemical paralytic agent and potassium chloride or other equally effective substances sufficient to cause death. The judgment shall be executed by the superintendent of the Department of Corrections institution in which the execution takes place, or by the designee of that superintendent. All executions shall take place within the enclosure of a Department of Corrections institution designated by the director of the Department of Corrections. The superintendent of the institution shall be present at the execution and shall invite the presence of one or more physicians or nurse practitioners, the attorney general, the sheriff of the county in which the judgment was rendered and representatives from the media. At the request of the defendant, the superintendent shall allow no more than two members of the clergy designated by the defendant to be present at the execution. At the discretion of the superintendent, no more than five friends and relatives designated by the defendant may be present at the execution. The superintendent shall allow the presence of any peace officers as the superintendent thinks expedient.

Pennsylvania

General considerations. Pennsylvania is a capital punishment jurisdiction. The state reenacted its death penalty law after the United States Supreme Court decision in *Furman v. Georgia,* 408 U.S. 238 (1972), on March 26, 1974. Capital murder in Pennsylvania is punishable by death or life imprisonment without parole. It is provided by Rule 801 of the Pennsylvania Rules of Criminal Procedure that, in capital cases, a retained or appointed attorney for a defendant must have no less than five years of experience in the active practice of criminal law. A capital prosecution in Pennsylvania is bifurcated into a guilt phase and penalty phase. It is required at the penalty phase that the jury unanimously agrees that a death sentence is appropriate before it can be imposed. If the penalty phase jury is unable to reach a verdict, the trial judge is required to impose a sentence of life imprisonment.

Under Pennsylvania's capital punishment statute, a sentence of death is automatically reviewed by the Pennsylvania Supreme Court. Pennsylvania uses lethal injection to carry out death sentences. The state has three sites for its death row facilities for men: Pittsburgh, Huntington and Graterford. The facility for women is in Muncy. Pursuant to the laws of Pennsylvania the governor has authority to grant clemency in capital cases. The governor is required to obtain the advice of the state's Board of Pardons.

Death penalty offenses. Pennsylvania's capital punishment statute, Pennsylvania Code tit.18 § 2502(a), is triggered if a person commits a homicide under the following special circumstance: The offender commits an intentional killing. It is also provided under Pennsylvania Code tit. 18 § 2507(a) that the intentional killing of a law enforcement officer while in the performance of duty is a capital offense.

Aggravating circumstances used to impose death penalty. In order to impose a death sentence upon a defendant, Pennsylvania Code tit. 42 § 9711(d) requires that the prosecutor establishes the existence of at least one of the following statutory aggravating circumstances at the penalty phase:

(1) The victim was a firefighter, peace officer, public servant concerned in official detention, judge of any court in the unified judicial system, the attorney general of Pennsylvania, a deputy attorney general, district attorney, assistant district attorney, member of the General Assembly, governor, lieutenant governor, auditor general, state treasurer, state law enforcement official, local law enforcement official, federal law enforcement official or person employed to assist or assisting any law enforcement official in the performance of his duties, who was killed in the performance of his duties or as a result of his official position.

(2) The defendant paid or was paid by another person or had contracted to pay or be paid by another person or had conspired to pay or be paid by another person for the killing of the victim.

(3) The victim was being held by the defendant for ransom or reward, or as a shield or hostage.

(4) The death of the victim occurred while defendant was engaged in the hijacking of an aircraft.

(5) The victim was a prosecution witness to a murder or other felony committed by the defendant and was killed for the purpose of preventing his testimony against the defendant in any grand jury or criminal proceeding involving such offenses.

(6) The defendant committed a killing while in the perpetration of a felony.

(7) In the commission of the offense the defendant knowingly created a grave risk of death to another person in addition to the victim of the offense.

(8) The offense was committed by means of torture.

(9) The defendant has a significant history of felony convictions involving the use or threat of violence to the person.

(10) The defendant has been convicted of another federal or state offense, committed either before or at the time of the offense at issue, for which a sentence of life imprisonment or death was imposable or the defendant was undergoing a sentence of life imprisonment for any reason at the time of the commission of the offense.

(11) The defendant has been convicted of another murder committed in any jurisdiction and committed either before or at the time of the offense at issue.

(12) The defendant has been convicted of voluntary manslaughter, or a substantially equivalent crime in any other jurisdiction, committed either before or at the time of the offense at issue.

(13) The defendant committed the killing or was an accomplice in the killing, while in the perpetration of a felony drug crime.

(14) At the time of the killing, the victim was or had been involved, associated or in competition with the defendant in the sale, manufacture, distribution or delivery of any controlled substance or counterfeit controlled substance, and the defendant committed the killing or was an accomplice to the killing and the killing resulted from or was related to that association, involvement or competition to promote the defendant's activities in selling, manufacturing, distributing or delivering controlled substances or counterfeit controlled substances.

(15) At the time of the killing, the victim was or had been a nongovernmental informant or had otherwise provided any investigative, law enforcement or police agency with information concerning criminal activity and the defendant committed the killing or was an accomplice to the killing and the killing was in retaliation for the victim's activities as a nongovernmental informant or in providing information concerning criminal activity to an investigative, law enforcement or police agency.

(16) The victim was a child under 12 years of age.

(17) At the time of the killing, the victim was in her third trimester of pregnancy or the defendant had knowledge of the victim's pregnancy.

(18) At the time of the killing the defendant was subject to a court order restricting in any way the defendant's behavior toward the victim.

Mitigating circumstances. Although the federal Constitution will not permit jurisdictions to prevent capital felons from presenting all relevant mitigating evidence at the penalty phase, Pennsylvania has provided by statute, Pennsylvania Code tit. 42 § 9711(e), the following statutory mitigating circumstances that permit a jury to reject imposition of the death penalty:

(1) The defendant has no significant history of prior criminal convictions.

(2) The defendant was under the influence of extreme mental or emotional disturbance.

(3) The capacity of the defendant to appreciate the criminality of his conduct or to conform his conduct to the requirements of law was substantially impaired.

(4) The age of the defendant at the time of the crime.

(5) The defendant acted under extreme duress, although not such duress as to constitute a defense to prosecution or acted under the substantial domination of another person.

(6) The victim was a participant in the defendant's homicidal conduct or consented to the homicidal acts.

(7) The defendant's participation in the homicidal act was relatively minor.

(8) Any other evidence of mitigation concerning the character and record of the defendant and the circumstances of his offense.

Persons who may attend an execution. Pennsylvania law limits the number of persons who may be present at an execution. The following is provided by Pennsylvania Code tit. 61 § 4305:

(a) No person except the following shall witness any execution under the provisions of this chapter:

(1) The chief administrator or his designee of the state correctional institution where the execution takes place.

(2) Six reputable adult citizens selected by the secretary.

(3) One spiritual adviser, when requested and selected by the inmate.

(4) Not more than six duly accredited representatives of the news media.

(5) Such staff of the department as may be selected by the secretary.

(6) Not more than four victims registered with and selected by the victim advocate.

(b) The secretary may refuse participation by a witness for safety or security reasons. The department shall make reasonable efforts to provide victims with a viewing area separate and apart from the area to which other witnesses are admitted.

South Carolina

General considerations. South Carolina is a capital punishment jurisdiction. The state reenacted its death penalty law after the United States Supreme Court decision in *Furman v. Georgia*, 408 U.S. 238 (1972), on July 2, 1974. Capital murder in South Carolina is punishable by death, life imprisonment without parole or imprisonment for a term of years. A capital prosecution in South Carolina is bifurcated into a guilt phase and penalty phase. It is required at the penalty phase that the jury unanimously agrees that a death sentence is appropriate before it can be imposed. If the penalty phase jury is unable to reach a verdict, the trial judge is required to impose a sentence of imprisonment for a term of years.

Under South Carolina's capital punishment statute, a sentence of death is automatically reviewed by the South Carolina Supreme Court. South Carolina provides for lethal injection or electrocution to carry out death sentences. The state's death row facility for males is located in Ridgeville, while the facility for female death row inmates is in Columbia. The South Carolina governor has exclusive authority to grant clemency in capital cases.

Death penalty offenses. South Carolina's capital punishment crimes are set out under several statutes. Under South Carolina Code § 16-3-10 a capital homicide occurs for murder committed with malice aforethought. Under South Carolina Code § 16-23-715 it is a capital offense for a person to commit a homicide by using a weapon of mass destruction in furtherance of an act of terrorism. A homicide that is caused by the use of a destructive device is a capital offense under South Carolina Code § 16-23-720.

Aggravating circumstances used to impose death penalty. In order to impose a death sentence upon a defendant, South Carolina Code § 16-3-20(C)(a) requires that the prosecutor establish the existence of at least one of the following statutory aggravating circumstances at the penalty phase:

(1) The murder was committed while in the commission of the following crimes or acts: (a) criminal sexual conduct in any degree; (b) kidnapping; (c) trafficking in persons; (d) burglary in any degree; (e) robbery while armed with a deadly weapon; (f) larceny with use of a deadly weapon; (g) killing by poison; (h) drug trafficking ; (i) physical torture; (j) dismemberment of a person; or (k) arson in the first degree.

(2) The murder was committed by a person with a prior conviction for murder.

(3) The offender by his act of murder knowingly created a great risk of death to more than one person in a public place by means of a weapon or device which normally would be hazardous to the lives of more than one person.

(4) The offender committed the murder for himself or another for the purpose of receiving money or a thing of monetary value.

(5) The murder of a judicial officer, former judicial officer, solicitor, former solicitor, or other officer of the court during or because of the exercise of his official duty.

(6) The offender caused or directed another to commit murder or committed murder as an agent or employee of another person.

(7) The murder of a federal, state, or local law enforcement officer or former federal, state, or local law enforcement officer, peace officer or former peace officer, corrections officer or former corrections officer, including a county or municipal corrections officer or a former county or municipal corrections officer, a county or municipal detention facility employee or former county or municipal

detention facility employee, or fireman or former fireman during or because of the performance of his official duties.

(8) The murder of a family member of an official listed in subitems (5) and (7) above with the intent to impede or retaliate against the official.

(9) Two or more persons were murdered by the defendant by one act or pursuant to one scheme or course of conduct.

(10) The murder of a child eleven years of age or under.

(11) The murder of a witness or potential witness committed at any time during the criminal process for the purpose of impeding or deterring prosecution of any crime.

(12) The murder was committed by a person deemed a sexually violent predator.

Mitigating circumstances. Although the federal Constitution will not permit jurisdictions to prevent capital felons from presenting all relevant mitigating evidence at the penalty phase, South Carolina has provided by South Carolina Code § 16-3-20(C)(b) the following statutory mitigating circumstances that permit a jury to reject imposition of the death penalty:

(1) The defendant has no significant history of prior criminal conviction involving the use of violence against another person.

(2) The murder was committed while the defendant was under the influence of mental or emotional disturbance.

(3) The victim was a participant in the defendant's conduct or consented to the act.

(4) The defendant was an accomplice in the murder committed by another person and his participation was relatively minor.

(5) The defendant acted under duress or under the domination of another person.

(6) The capacity of the defendant to appreciate the criminality of his conduct or to conform his conduct to the requirements of law was substantially impaired.

(7) The age or mentality of the defendant at the time of the crime.

(8) The defendant was provoked by the victim into committing the murder.

(9) The defendant was below the age of eighteen at the time of the crime (under federal law the death penalty may not be imposed in this situation).

(10) The defendant had mental retardation at the time of the crime (under federal law the death penalty may not be imposed in this situation).

Persons who may attend an execution. South Carolina law limits the number of persons who may be present at an execution. The following is provided by South Carolina Code § 24-3-550:

(A) To carry out an execution properly, the executioner and necessary staff must be present at the execution. In addition, the following persons may be present:

(1) three representatives, approved by the director, of the family of a victim of the crime for which a death penalty was imposed, provided that, if there is more than one victim, the director may reduce the number of family representatives to one representative for each victim's family; provided further, that, if there are more than two victims, the director may restrict the total number of victims' representatives present in accordance with the space limitations of the capital punishment facility;

(2) the solicitor, or an assistant solicitor or former solicitor designated by the solicitor, for the county where the offense occurred;

(3) a group of not more than three representatives of the South Carolina media, one of whom must represent the dominant wire service, one of whom must represent the print media, and one of whom must represent the electronic news media;

(4) the chief law enforcement officer, or an officer designated by the chief, from the law enforcement agency that had original jurisdiction in the case; and

(5) the counsel for the inmate and a religious leader. However, the inmate may substitute one person from his immediate family for either his counsel or a religious leader, or two persons from his immediate family for both his counsel and a religious leader.

(B) Other than those persons specified in subsection (A), no person is authorized to witness an execution.

(C) The department shall establish internal policies to govern the selection of media representatives.

(D) Witnesses authorized or approved pursuant to this section shall not possess telephonic equipment, cameras, or recording devices in the capital punishment facility during an execution.

(E) For security purposes, the director may exclude any person who is authorized or approved pursuant to this section from the capital punishment facility.

South Dakota

General considerations. South Dakota is a capital punishment jurisdiction. The state reenacted its death penalty law after the United States Supreme Court decision in *Furman v. Georgia*, 408 U.S. 238 (1972), on January 1, 1979. Capital murder in South Dakota is punishable by death or life imprisonment without parole. A capital prosecution in South Dakota is bifurcated into a guilt phase and penalty phase. It is required at the penalty phase that the jury unanimously agrees that a death sentence is appropriate before it can be imposed. If the penalty phase jury is unable to reach a verdict, the trial judge is required to impose a sentence of life imprisonment.

Under South Dakota's capital punishment statute, a sentence of death is automatically reviewed by the South Dakota Supreme Court. South Dakota uses lethal injection to carry out death sentences. The state's death row facility is located in Sioux Falls. The governor has exclusive authority to grant clemency in capital cases.

Death penalty offenses. South Dakota's capital punishment offenses are set out under South Dakota Code § 22-16-4. This statute is triggered if a person commits a homicide under the following special circumstances:

(1) If perpetrated without authority of law and with a premeditated design to effect the death of the person killed or of any other human being, including an unborn child; or

(2) If committed by a person engaged in the perpetration of, or attempt to perpetrate, any arson, rape, robbery, burglary, kidnapping, or unlawful throwing, placing, or discharging of a destructive device or explosive.

Homicide is also murder in the first degree if committed by a person who perpetrated, or who attempted to perpetrate, any arson, rape, robbery, burglary, kidnapping or unlawful throwing, placing or discharging of a destructive device or explosive and who subsequently effects the death of any victim of such crime to prevent detection or prosecution of the crime.

Aggravating circumstances used to impose death penalty. In order to impose a death sentence upon a defendant, South Dakota Code § 23A-27A-1 requires that the prosecutor establishes the existence of at least one of the following statutory aggravating circumstances at the penalty phase:

(1) The offense was committed by a person with a prior record of conviction for a Class A or Class B felony, or the offense of murder was committed by a person who has a felony conviction for a crime of violence;

(2) The defendant by the defendant's act knowingly created a great risk of death to more than one person in a public place by means of a weapon or device which would normally be hazardous to the lives of more than one person;

(3) The defendant committed the offense for the benefit of the defendant or another, for the purpose of receiving money or any other thing of monetary value;

(4) The defendant committed the offense on a judicial officer, former judicial officer, prosecutor, or former prosecutor while such prosecutor, former prosecutor, judicial officer, or former judicial officer was engaged in the performance of such person's official duties or where a major part of the motivation for the offense came from the official actions of such judicial officer, former judicial officer, prosecutor, or former prosecutor;

(5) The defendant caused or directed another to commit murder or committed murder as an agent or employee of another person;

(6) The offense was outrageously or wantonly vile, horrible, or inhuman in that it involved torture, depravity of mind, or an aggravated battery to the victim. Any murder is wantonly vile, horrible, and inhuman if the victim is less than thirteen years of age;

(7) The offense was committed against a law enforcement officer, employee of a corrections institution, or firefighter while engaged in the performance of such person's official duties;

(8) The offense was committed by a person in, or who has escaped from, the lawful custody of a law enforcement officer or place of lawful confinement;

(9) The offense was committed for the purpose of avoiding, interfering with, or preventing a lawful arrest or custody in a place of lawful confinement, of the defendant or another; or

(10) The offense was committed in the course of manufacturing, distributing, or dispensing [narcotics].

Mitigating circumstances. South Dakota does not provide by statute any mitigating circumstances to the imposition of the death penalty. Even though the state does not provide statutory mitigating circumstances, the United States Supreme Court has ruled that all relevant mitigating evidence must be allowed at the penalty phase.

Persons who may attend an execution. South Dakota law limits the number of persons who may be present at an execution. The following is provided by South Dakota Code § 23A-27A-34:

> The warden of the penitentiary shall request, by at least two days' previous notice, the presence of the attorney general, the trial judge before whom the conviction was had or the judge's successor in office, the state's attorney and sheriff of the county where the crime was committed, representatives of the victim, at least one member of the news media, and a number of reputable adult citizens to be determined by the warden. All witnesses and persons present at an execution are subject to approval by the warden.

Tennessee

General considerations. Tennessee is a capital punishment jurisdiction. The state reenacted its death penalty law after the United States Supreme Court decision in *Furman v. Georgia*, 408 U.S. 238 (1972), on February 27, 1974. Capital murder in Tennessee is punishable by death or life imprisonment with or without parole. A capital prosecution in Tennessee is bifurcated into a guilt phase and penalty phase. It is required at the penalty phase that the jury unanimously agrees that a death sentence is appropriate before it can be imposed. If the penalty phase jury is unable to reach a verdict, the trial judge is required to impose a sentence of life imprisonment.

Under Tennessee's capital punishment statute, a sentence of death is automatically reviewed by the Tennessee Supreme Court. Tennessee uses the lethal injection to carry out death sentences. Inmates who committed a capital offense prior to January 1, 1999, may choose between lethal injection and electrocution. The state's death row facilities for men and women are in Nashville. Pursuant to the laws of Tennessee the governor has authority to grant clemency in capital cases. The governor may commute a capital felon's death sentence to life imprisonment if the Tennessee Supreme Court determines the sentence warrants commutation.

Death penalty offenses. Tennessee's capital punishment offenses are set out under Tennessee Code § 39-13-202. This statute is triggered if a person commits a homicide under the following special circumstances:

(1) A premeditated and intentional killing of another;

(2) A killing of another committed in the perpetration of or attempt to perpetrate any first degree murder, act of terrorism, arson, rape, robbery, burglary, theft, kidnapping, aggravated child abuse, aggravated child neglect, rape of a child, aggravated rape of a child or aircraft piracy; or

(3) A killing of another committed as the result of the unlawful throwing, placing or discharging of a destructive device or bomb.

Aggravating circumstances used to impose death penalty. In order to impose a death sentence upon a defendant, Tennessee Code § 39-13-204(i) requires that the prosecutor establishes the existence of at least one of the following statutory aggravating circumstances at the penalty phase:

(1) The murder was committed against a person less than twelve (12) years of age and the defendant was eighteen (18) years of age or older;

(2) The defendant was previously convicted of one (1) or more felonies, other than the present charge, whose statutory elements involve the use of violence to the person;

(3) The defendant knowingly created a great risk of death to two (2) or more persons, other than the victim murdered, during the act of murder;

(4) The defendant committed the murder for remuneration or the promise of remuneration, or employed another to commit the murder for remuneration or the promise of remuneration;

(5) The murder was especially heinous, atrocious, or cruel, in that it involved torture or serious physical abuse beyond that necessary to produce death;

(6) The murder was committed for the purpose of avoiding, interfering with, or preventing a lawful arrest or prosecution of the defendant or another;

(7) The murder was knowingly committed, solicited, directed, or aided by the defendant, while the defendant had a substantial role in committing or attempting to commit, or was fleeing after having a substantial role in committing or attempting to commit, any first degree murder, arson, rape, robbery, burglary, theft, kidnapping, aggravated child abuse, aggravated child neglect, rape of a child, aggravated rape of a child, aircraft piracy, or unlawful throwing, placing or discharging of a destructive device or bomb;

(8) The murder was committed by the defendant while the defendant was in lawful custody or in a place of lawful confinement or during the defendant's escape from lawful custody or from a place of lawful confinement;

(9) The murder was committed against any law enforcement officer, corrections official, corrections employee, probation and parole officer, emergency medical or rescue worker, emergency medical technician, paramedic or firefighter, who was engaged in the performance of official duties, and the defendant knew or reasonably should have known that the victim was a law enforcement officer, corrections official, corrections employee, probation and parole officer, emergency medical or rescue worker, emergency medical technician, paramedic or firefighter engaged in the performance of official duties;

(10) The murder was committed against any present or former judge, district attorney general or state attorney general, assistant district attorney general or assistant state attorney general, due to or because of the exercise of the victim's official duty or status and the defendant knew that the victim occupied such office;

(11) The murder was committed against a national, state, or local popularly elected official, due to or because of the official's lawful duties or status, and the defendant knew that the victim was such an official;

(12) The defendant committed "mass murder," which is defined as the murder of three (3) or more persons, whether committed during a single criminal episode or at different times within a forty-eight-month period;

(13) The defendant knowingly mutilated the body of the victim after death;

(14) The victim of the murder was seventy (70) years of age or older; or the victim of the murder was particularly vulnerable due to a significant disability, whether mental or physical, and at the time of the murder the defendant knew or reasonably should have known of such disability;

(15) The murder was committed in the course of an act of terrorism;

(16) The murder was committed against a pregnant woman, and the defendant intentionally killed the victim, knowing that she was pregnant; or

(17) The murder was committed at random and the reasons for the killing are not obvious or easily understood.

Mitigating circumstances. Although the federal Constitution will not permit jurisdictions to prevent capital felons from presenting all relevant mitigating evidence at the penalty phase, Tennessee has provided by statute, Tennessee Code § 39-13-204(j), the following statutory mitigating circumstances that permit a jury to reject imposition of the death penalty:

(1) The defendant has no significant history of prior criminal activity;

(2) The murder was committed while the defendant was under the influence of extreme mental or emotional disturbance;

(3) The victim was a participant in the defendant's conduct or consented to the act;

(4) The murder was committed under circumstances that the defendant reasonably believed to provide a moral justification for the defendant's conduct;

(5) The defendant was an accomplice in the murder committed by another person and the defendant's participation was relatively minor;

(6) The defendant acted under extreme duress or under the substantial domination of another person;

(7) The youth or advanced age of the defendant at the time of the crime;

(8) The capacity of the defendant to appreciate the wrongfulness of the defendant's conduct or to conform the defendant's conduct to the requirements of the law was substantially impaired as a result of mental disease or defect or intoxication, which was insufficient to establish a defense to the crime but which substantially affected the defendant's judgment; and

(9) Any other mitigating factor that is raised by the evidence produced by either the prosecution or defense, at either the guilt or sentencing hearing.

Persons who may attend an execution. Tennessee law limits the number of persons who may be present at an execution. The following is provided by Tennessee Code § 40-23-116:

The only witnesses entitled to be present at the carrying out of the death sentence are:

(1) The warden of the state penitentiary or the warden's duly authorized deputy;

(2) The sheriff of the county in which the crime was committed;

(3) A priest or minister of the gospel who has been preparing the condemned person for death;

(4) The prison physician;

(5) Attendants chosen and selected by the warden of the state penitentiary as may be necessary to properly carry out the execution of the death sentence;

(6) A total of seven (7) members of the print, radio and television news media selected in accordance with the rules and regulations promulgated by the department of correction. Those news media members allowed to attend any execution of a sentence of death shall make available coverage of the execution to other news media members not selected to attend;

(7) Immediate family members of the victim who are eighteen (18) years of age or older. Immediate family members shall include the spouse, child by birth or adoption, stepchild, stepparent, parent, grandparent or sibling of the victim, provided that members of the family of the condemned prisoner may be present and witness the execution;

(8) One (1) defense counsel chosen by the condemned person; and

(9) The attorney general and reporter, or the attorney general and reporter's designee.

Texas

General considerations. Texas is a capital punishment jurisdiction. The state reenacted its death penalty law after the United States Supreme Court decision in *Furman v. Georgia*, 408 U.S. 238 (1972), on January 1, 1974. Capital murder in Texas is punishable by death or life imprisonment without parole. A capital prosecution in Texas is bifurcated into a guilt phase and penalty phase. It is required at the penalty phase that the jury unanimously agrees that a death sentence is appropriate before it can be imposed. If the penalty phase jury is unable to reach a verdict, the trial judge is required to impose a sentence of life imprisonment.

Under Texas' capital punishment statute, a sentence of death is automatically reviewed by the Texas Court of Criminal Appeals. Texas uses lethal injection to carry out death sentences. The state's death row facility for men is in Huntsville, while the facility for women is in Gatesville. The Texas governor has authority to grant clemency in capital cases. The governor must obtain the consent of the state's Board of Pardons and Paroles in order to grant clemency.

Death penalty offenses. Capital punishment offenses are set out under Texas Penal Code § 19.02(b). This statute is triggered if a person commits a homicide under the following special circumstances:

(1) intentionally or knowingly causes the death of an individual;

(2) intends to cause serious bodily injury and commits an act clearly dangerous to human life that causes the death of an individual; or

(3) commits or attempts to commit a felony, other than manslaughter, and in the course of and in furtherance of the commission or attempt, or in immediate flight from the commission or attempt, he commits or attempts to commit an act clearly dangerous to human life that causes the death of an individual.

In addition, under Texas Government Code § 557.012, the crime of sabotage is a capital offense when a person dies. Sabotage is defined to mean a person who, with the intent to injure the

United States, Texas, or any facility or property used for national defense, sabotages or attempts to sabotage any property or facility used or to be used for national defense.

Capital conviction circumstances. In order to convict a defendant of capital murder, Texas Penal Code § 19.03 requires that the prosecutor establish the existence of at least one of the following statutory aggravating circumstances at the guilt phase:

(1) the person murders a peace officer or fireman who is acting in the lawful discharge of an official duty and who the person knows is a peace officer or fireman;

(2) the person intentionally commits the murder in the course of committing or attempting to commit kidnapping, burglary, robbery, aggravated sexual assault, arson, obstruction or retaliation, or terroristic threat;

(3) the person commits the murder for remuneration or the promise of remuneration or employs another to commit the murder for remuneration or the promise of remuneration;

(4) the person commits the murder while escaping or attempting to escape from a penal institution;

(5) the person, while incarcerated in a penal institution, murders another who is employed in the operation of the penal institution or with the intent to establish, maintain, or participate in a combination or in the profits of a combination;

(6) the person while incarcerated murders another;

(7) the person murders more than one person during the same criminal transaction or during different criminal transactions but the murders are committed pursuant to the same scheme or course of conduct;

(8) the person murders an individual under six years of age; or

(9) the person murders another person in retaliation for or on account of the service or status of the other person as a judge or justice of the supreme court, the court of criminal appeals, a court of appeals, a district court, a criminal district court, a constitutional county court, a statutory county court, a justice court, or a municipal court.

Aggravating circumstances used to impose death penalty. Texas does not set out separate aggravating circumstances for the penalty. Instead, Texas Criminal Procedure Code Art. 37.071 requires that the jury unanimously answer the first two following special issues affirmatively (if both are applicable) and the third special issue negatively:

(1) Whether there is a probability that the defendant would commit criminal acts of violence that would constitute a continuing threat to society; and

(2) In cases in which the jury charge at the guilt phase permitted the jury to find the defendant guilty as an accomplice, whether the defendant actually caused the death of the deceased or did not actually cause the death of the deceased but intended to kill the deceased or another or anticipated that a human life would be taken.

(3) Whether, taking into consideration all of the evidence, including the circumstances of the offense, the defendant's character and background, and the personal moral culpability of the defendant, there is a sufficient mitigating circumstance or circumstances to warrant that a sentence of life imprisonment rather than a death sentence be imposed.

Mitigating circumstances. Texas does not provide by statute any mitigating circumstances to the imposition of the death penalty. Even though the state does not provide statutory mitigating circumstances, the United States Supreme Court has ruled that all relevant mitigating evidence must be allowed at the penalty phase.

Persons who may attend an execution. Texas law limits the number of persons who may be present at an execution. The following is provided by Criminal Procedure Code Art. 43.20:

The following persons may be present at the execution: the executioner, and such persons as may be necessary to assist him in conducting the execution; the Board of Directors of the Department of Corrections, two physicians, including the prison physician, the spiritual advisor of the condemned, the chaplains of the Department of Corrections, the county judge and sheriff of the county in which the Department of Corrections is situated, and any of the relatives or friends of the condemned person that he may request, not exceeding five in number, shall be admitted. No convict shall be permitted by the prison authorities to witness the execution.

Utah

General considerations. Utah is a capital punishment jurisdiction. The state reenacted its death penalty law after the United States Supreme Court decision in *Furman v. Georgia*, 408 U.S. 238 (1972), on July 1, 1973. Capital murder in Utah is punishable by death, life imprisonment without parole or a term of years. A capital prosecution in Utah is bifurcated into a guilt phase and penalty phase. It is required at the penalty phase that the jury unanimously agrees that a death sentence is appropriate before it can be imposed. If the penalty phase jury does not find a sentence of death is appropriate, the jury may sentence the defendant to life without parole or to a term of years.

Under Utah's capital punishment statute, a sentence of death is not automatically reviewed by the Utah Supreme Court. A capital felon must initiate an appeal of a death sentence. Utah uses lethal injection to carry out the death penalty. However, inmates whose sentence was given prior to May 3, 2004, may choose the firing squad. Further, under the laws of Utah if lethal injection is found unconstitutional, then the firing squad is used. The state's death row facility for men is located in Draper. An executive panel that includes the governor has authority to grant clemency in capital cases.

Death penalty offenses. Under the laws of Utah a capital prosecution is triggered if a person commits a homicide, as defined by Utah Code § 76-5-201(1)(a), as follows:

[A] person commits criminal homicide if the person intentionally, knowingly, recklessly, with criminal negligence, or acting with a mental state otherwise specified in the statute defining the offense, causes the death of another human being, including an unborn child at any stage of its development.

Capital conviction circumstances. In order to convict a defendant of capital murder, Utah Code § 76-5-202 requires that the prosecutor establishes the existence of at least one of the following statutory aggravating circumstances at the guilt phase:

(1) Criminal homicide constitutes aggravated murder if the actor intentionally or knowingly causes the death of another under any of the following circumstances:

(a) the homicide was committed by a person who is confined in a jail or other correctional institution;

(b) the homicide was committed incident to one act, scheme, course of conduct, or criminal episode during which two or more persons were killed, or during which the actor attempted to kill one or more persons in addition to the victim who was killed;

(c) the actor knowingly created a great risk of death to a person other than the victim and the actor;

(d) the homicide was committed incident to an act, scheme, course of conduct, or criminal episode during which the actor committed or attempted to commit aggravated robbery, robbery, rape, rape of a child, object rape, object rape of a child, forcible sodomy, sodomy upon a child, forcible sexual abuse, sexual abuse of a child, aggravated sexual abuse of a child, child abuse, or aggravated sexual assault, aggravated arson, arson, aggravated burglary, burglary, aggravated kidnapping, or kidnapping, or child kidnapping;

(e) the homicide was committed incident to one act, scheme, course of conduct, or criminal episode during which the actor committed the crime of abuse or desecration of a dead human body;

(f) the homicide was committed for the purpose of avoiding or preventing an arrest of the defendant or another by a peace officer acting under color of legal authority or for the purpose of effecting the defendant's or another's escape from lawful custody;

(g) the homicide was committed for pecuniary gain;

(h) the defendant committed, or engaged or employed another person to commit the homicide pursuant to an agreement or contract for remuneration or the promise of remuneration for commission of the homicide;

(i) the actor previously committed or was convicted of: (i) aggravated murder; (ii) attempted aggravated murder; (iii) murder; (iv) attempted murder; or (v) an offense committed in another jurisdiction which if committed in this state would be a violation of a crime listed in this Subsection;

(j) the actor was previously convicted of: (i) aggravated assault; (ii) mayhem; (iii) kidnapping; (iv) child kidnapping; (v) aggravated kidnapping; (vi) rape; (vii) rape of a child; (viii) object rape; (ix) object rape of a child; (x) forcible sodomy; (xi) sodomy on a child; (xii) aggravated sexual abuse of a child; (xiii) aggravated sexual assault; (xiv) aggravated arson; (xv) aggravated burglary; (xvi) aggravated robbery; (xvii) felony discharge of a firearm; or (xviii) an offense committed in another jurisdiction which if committed in this state would be a violation of a crime listed in this Subsection;

  (k) the homicide was committed for the purpose of: (i) preventing a witness from testifying; (ii) preventing a person from providing evidence or participating in any legal proceedings or official investigation; (iii) retaliating against a person for testifying, providing evidence, or participating in any legal proceedings or official investigation; or (iv) disrupting or hindering any lawful governmental function or enforcement of laws;

  (l) the victim is or has been a local, state, or federal public official, or a candidate for public office, and the homicide is based on, is caused by, or is related to that official position, act, capacity, or candidacy;

  (m) the victim is or has been a peace officer, law enforcement officer, executive officer, prosecuting officer, jailer, prison official, firefighter, judge or other court official, juror, probation officer, or parole officer, and the victim is either on duty or the homicide is based on, is caused by, or is related to that official position, and the actor knew, or reasonably should have known, that the victim holds or has held that official position;

  (n) the homicide was committed: (i) by means of a destructive device, bomb, explosive, incendiary device, or similar device which was planted, hidden, or concealed in any place, area, dwelling, building, or structure, or was mailed or delivered; or (ii) by means of any weapon of mass destruction;

  (o) the homicide was committed during the act of unlawfully assuming control of any aircraft, train, or other public conveyance by use of threats or force with intent to obtain any valuable consideration for the release of the public conveyance or any passenger, crew member, or any other person aboard, or to direct the route or movement of the public conveyance or otherwise exert control over the public conveyance;

  (p) the homicide was committed by means of the administration of a poison or of any lethal substance or of any substance administered in a lethal amount, dosage, or quantity;

  (q) the victim was a person held or otherwise detained as a shield, hostage, or for ransom;

  (r) the homicide was committed in an especially heinous, atrocious, cruel, or exceptionally depraved manner, any of which must be demonstrated by physical torture, serious physical abuse, or serious bodily injury of the victim before death;

  (s) the actor dismembers, mutilates, or disfigures the victim's body, whether before or after death, in a manner demonstrating the actor's depravity of mind; or

  (t) the victim, at the time of the death of the victim: (i) was younger than 14 years of age; and (ii) was not an unborn child.

  (2) Criminal homicide constitutes aggravated murder if the actor, with reckless indifference to human life, causes the death of another incident to an act, scheme, course of conduct, or criminal episode during which the actor is a major participant in the commission or attempted commission of: (a) child abuse; (b) child kidnapping; (c) rape of a child; (d) object rape of a child; (e) sodomy on a child; or (f) sexual abuse or aggravated sexual abuse of a child.

Aggravating circumstances used to impose death penalty. Utah does not provide separate statutory aggravating circumstances for the penalty phase jury to consider. The state imposes a death sentence based upon a conviction for one of the guilt phase special circumstances. During the penalty phase the prosecutor may present evidence regarding the guilt phase special circumstance and any other relevant aggravating factor.

Mitigating circumstances. Although the federal Constitution will not permit jurisdictions to prevent capital felons from presenting all relevant mitigating evidence at the penalty phase, Utah has provided by statute, Utah Code § 76-3-207(4), the following statutory mitigating circumstances that permit a jury to reject imposition of the death penalty:

  (a) the defendant has no significant history of prior criminal activity;

  (b) the homicide was committed while the defendant was under the influence of mental or emotional disturbance;

  (c) the defendant acted under duress or under the domination of another person;

  (d) at the time of the homicide, the capacity of the defendant to appreciate the wrongfulness of his conduct or to conform his conduct to the requirement of law was impaired as a result of a mental condition, intoxication, or influence of drugs;

(e) the youth of the defendant at the time of the crime;

(f) the defendant was an accomplice in the homicide committed by another person and the defendant's participation was relatively minor; and

(g) any other fact in mitigation of the penalty.

Persons who may attend execution. Under the laws of Utah a limitation is imposed upon the number of persons who may be present at an execution. The following is provided by Utah Code § 77-19-11:

[1] At the discretion of the director, the following persons may attend the execution:

(a) the prosecuting attorney, or a designated deputy, of the county in which the defendant committed the offense for which he is being executed;

(b) no more than two law enforcement officials from the county in which the defendant committed the offense for which he is being executed;

(c) the attorney general or a designee;

(d) religious representatives, friends, or relatives designated by the defendant, not exceeding a total of five persons; and

(e) unless approved by the director, no more than five close relatives of the deceased victim.

[2] The director shall permit the attendance at the execution of members of the press and broadcast news media, as named by the director in accordance with rules of the department; and with the agreement of the selected news media members that they serve as a pool for other members of the news media.

[3](a) The following persons may also attend the execution: (i) staff as determined by the director; and (ii) no more than three correctional officials from other states that are preparing for executions, but no more than two correctional officials may be from any one state, as designated by the director.

(b) A person younger than 18 years of age may not attend.

Virginia

General considerations. Virginia is a capital punishment jurisdiction. The state reenacted its death penalty law after the United States Supreme Court decision in *Furman v. Georgia*, 408 U.S. 238 (1972), on October 1, 1975. Capital murder in Virginia is punishable by death or life imprisonment without parole. A capital prosecution in Virginia is bifurcated into a guilt phase and penalty phase. It is required at the penalty phase that the jury unanimously agrees that a death sentence is appropriate before it can be imposed. If the penalty phase jury is unable to reach a verdict, the trial judge is required to impose a sentence of life imprisonment.

Under Virginia's capital punishment statute, a sentence of death is automatically reviewed by the Virginia Supreme Court. Virginia permits a capital felon to choose between death by lethal injection or electrocution. The state's death row facility for men is in Waverly. Pursuant to the laws of Virginia the governor has exclusive authority to grant clemency in capital cases.

Death penalty offenses. Virginia's capital punishment offenses are set out under Virginia Code § 18.2-31. This statute is triggered if a person commits a homicide under the following aggravating circumstances:

1. The willful, deliberate, and premeditated killing of any person in the commission of abduction, when such abduction was committed with the intent to extort money or a pecuniary benefit or with the intent to defile the victim of such abduction;

2. The willful, deliberate, and premeditated killing of any person by another for hire;

3. The willful, deliberate, and premeditated killing of any person by a prisoner confined in a state or local correctional facility, or while in the custody of an employee thereof;

4. The willful, deliberate, and premeditated killing of any person in the commission of robbery or attempted robbery;

5. The willful, deliberate, and premeditated killing of any person in the commission of, or subsequent to, rape or attempted rape, forcible sodomy or attempted forcible sodomy or object sexual penetration;

6. The willful, deliberate, and premeditated killing of a law-enforcement officer, a fire marshal or a deputy or an assistant fire marshal, an auxiliary police officer, an auxiliary deputy sheriff, or any law-enforcement officer of another state or the United States having the power to arrest for a felony under

the laws of such state or the United States, when such killing is for the purpose of interfering with the performance of his official duties;

7. The willful, deliberate, and premeditated killing of more than one person as a part of the same act or transaction;

8. The willful, deliberate, and premeditated killing of more than one person within a three-year period;

9. The willful, deliberate, and premeditated killing of any person in the commission of or attempted commission of a drug offense;

10. The willful, deliberate, and premeditated killing of any person by another pursuant to the direction or order of one who is engaged in a continuing criminal enterprise;

11. The willful, deliberate and premeditated killing of a pregnant woman by one who knows that the woman is pregnant and has the intent to cause the involuntary termination of the woman's pregnancy without a live birth;

12. The willful, deliberate and premeditated killing of a person under the age of fourteen by a person age twenty-one or older; and

13. The willful, deliberate and premeditated killing of any person by another in the commission of or attempted commission of an act of terrorism;

14. The willful, deliberate, and premeditated killing of a justice of the Supreme Court, a judge of the Court of Appeals, a judge of a circuit court or district court, a retired judge sitting by designation or under temporary recall, or a substitute judge when the killing is for the purpose of interfering with his official duties as a judge; and

15. The willful, deliberate, and premeditated killing of any witness in a criminal case after a subpoena has been issued for such witness by the court, the clerk, or an attorney, when the killing is for the purpose of interfering with the person's duties in such case.

Aggravating circumstances used to impose death penalty. Virginia does not set out separate aggravating circumstances for the penalty. Instead, in order to impose a death sentence upon a defendant, Virginia Code § 19.2-264.4(C) requires that the jury answers affirmatively one of the following special issues at the penalty phase:

[T]hat there is a probability based upon evidence of the prior history of the defendant or of the circumstances surrounding the commission of the offense of which he is accused [1] that he would commit criminal acts of violence that would constitute a continuing serious threat to society, or [2] that his conduct in committing the offense was outrageously or wantonly vile, horrible or inhuman, in that it involved torture, depravity of mind or aggravated battery to the victim.

Mitigating circumstances. Although the federal Constitution will not permit jurisdictions to prevent capital felons from presenting all relevant mitigating evidence at the penalty phase, Virginia has provided by statute, Virginia Code § 19.2-264.4(B), the following statutory mitigating circumstances that permit a jury to reject imposition of the death penalty:

(i) the defendant has no significant history of prior criminal activity, (ii) the capital felony was committed while the defendant was under the influence of extreme mental or emotional disturbance, (iii) the victim was a participant in the defendant's conduct or consented to the act, (iv) at the time of the commission of the capital felony, the capacity of the defendant to appreciate the criminality of his conduct or to conform his conduct to the requirements of law was significantly impaired, (v) the age of the defendant at the time of the commission of the capital offense, or (vi) the subaverage intellectual functioning of the defendant.

Persons who may attend an execution. Virginia law limits the number of persons who may be present at an execution. The following is provided by Virginia Code § 53.1-234:

At the execution there shall be present the director or an assistant, a physician employed by the department or his assistant, such other employees of the department as may be required by the director and, in addition thereto, at least six citizens who shall not be employees of the department. In addition, the counsel for the prisoner and a clergyman may be present.

Washington

General considerations. Washington is a capital punishment jurisdiction. The state reenacted its death penalty law after the United States Supreme Court decision in *Furman v. Georgia*,

408 U.S. 238 (1972), on November 4, 1975. Capital murder in Washington is punishable by death or life imprisonment without parole. A capital prosecution in Washington is bifurcated into a guilt phase and penalty phase. It is required at the penalty phase that the jury unanimously agrees that a death sentence is appropriate before it can be imposed. If the penalty phase jury is unable to reach a verdict, the trial judge is required to impose a sentence of life imprisonment without parole.

Under Washington's capital punishment statute, a sentence of death is automatically reviewed by the Washington Supreme Court. Washington permits a capital felon to choose between lethal injection and hanging as the method of execution. The state's death row facility for men is located in Walla Walla. The governor has exclusive authority to grant clemency in capital cases.

Death penalty offenses. Washington's capital punishment offenses are set out under Washington Code § 9A.32.030(1). This statute is triggered if a person commits a homicide under the following special circumstances:

(a) With a premeditated intent to cause the death of another person, he or she causes the death of such person or of a third person; or

(b) Under circumstances manifesting an extreme indifference to human life, he or she engages in conduct which creates a grave risk of death to any person, and thereby causes the death of a person; or

(c) He or she commits or attempts to commit the crime of either (1) robbery in the first or second degree, (2) rape in the first or second degree, (3) burglary in the first degree, (4) arson in the first or second degree, or (5) kidnapping in the first or second degree, and in the course of or in furtherance of such crime or in immediate flight therefrom, he or she, or another participant, causes the death of a person other than one of the participants.

Capital conviction circumstances. In order to convict a defendant of capital murder, Washington Code § 10.95.020 requires that the prosecutor establishes the existence of at least one of the following statutory aggravating circumstances at the guilt phase:

(1) The victim was a law enforcement officer, corrections officer, or fire fighter who was performing his or her official duties at the time of the act resulting in death and the victim was known or reasonably should have been known by the person to be such at the time of the killing;

(2) At the time of the act resulting in the death, the person was serving a term of imprisonment, had escaped, or was on authorized or unauthorized leave in or from a state facility or program for the incarceration or treatment of persons adjudicated guilty of crimes;

(3) At the time of the act resulting in death, the person was in custody in a county or county-city jail as a consequence of having been adjudicated guilty of a felony;

(4) The person committed the murder pursuant to an agreement that he or she would receive money or any other thing of value for committing the murder;

(5) The person solicited another person to commit the murder and had paid or had agreed to pay money or any other thing of value for committing the murder;

(6) The person committed the murder to obtain or maintain his or her membership or to advance his or her position in the hierarchy of an organization, association, or identifiable group;

(7) The murder was committed during the course of or as a result of a shooting where the discharge of the firearm, is either from a motor vehicle or from the immediate area of a motor vehicle that was used to transport the shooter or the firearm, or both, to the scene of the discharge;

(8) The victim was a judge; juror or former juror; prospective, current, or former witness in an adjudicative proceeding; prosecuting attorney; deputy prosecuting attorney; defense attorney; a member of the indeterminate sentence review board; or a probation or parole officer; and the murder was related to the exercise of official duties performed or to be performed by the victim;

(9) The person committed the murder to conceal the commission of a crime or to protect or conceal the identity of any person committing a crime, including, but specifically not limited to, any attempt to avoid prosecution as a persistent offender;

(10) There was more than one victim and the murders were part of a common scheme or plan or the result of a single act of the person;

(11) The murder was committed in the course of, in furtherance of, or in immediate flight from a robbery, rape, burglary, kidnapping, or arson;

(12) The victim was regularly employed or self-employed as a news reporter and the murder was committed to obstruct or hinder the investigative, research, or reporting activities of the victim;

(13) At the time the person committed the murder, there existed a court order, issued in this or any other state, which prohibited the person from either contacting the victim, molesting the victim, or disturbing the peace of the victim, and the person had knowledge of the existence of that order;

(14) At the time the person committed the murder, the person and the victim were family or household members and the person had previously engaged in a pattern or practice of three or more of the following crimes committed upon the victim within a five-year period, regardless of whether a conviction resulted: (a) harassment or (b) any criminal assault.

Aggravating circumstances used to impose death penalty. Washington does not provide separate statutory aggravating circumstances for the penalty phase jury to consider. The state imposes a death sentence based upon a conviction for one of the guilt phase special circumstances. During the penalty phase the prosecutor must persuade the jury that such proven aggravating circumstance outweighs any mitigating evidence.

Mitigating circumstances. Although the federal Constitution will not permit jurisdictions to prevent capital felons from presenting all relevant mitigating evidence at the penalty phase, Washington has provided by statute, Washington Code § 10.95.070, the following statutory mitigating circumstances that permit a jury to reject imposition of the death penalty:

(1) Whether the defendant has or does not have a significant history, either as a juvenile or an adult, of prior criminal activity;

(2) Whether the murder was committed while the defendant was under the influence of extreme mental disturbance;

(3) Whether the victim consented to the act of murder;

(4) Whether the defendant was an accomplice to a murder committed by another person where the defendant's participation in the murder was relatively minor;

(5) Whether the defendant acted under duress or domination of another person;

(6) Whether, at the time of the murder, the capacity of the defendant to appreciate the wrongfulness of his or her conduct or to conform his or her conduct to the requirements of law was substantially impaired as a result of mental disease or defect. However, a person found to have an intellectual disability may in no case be sentenced to death;

(7) Whether the age of the defendant at the time of the crime calls for leniency; and

(8) Whether there is a likelihood that the defendant will pose a danger to others in the future.

Persons who may attend an execution. Washington law limits the number of persons who may be present at an execution. The following is provided by Washington Code § 10.95.185:

(1) Not less than twenty days prior to a scheduled execution, judicial officers, law enforcement representatives, media representatives, representatives of the families of the victims, and representatives from the family of the defendant who wish to attend and witness the execution, must submit an application to the superintendent. Such application must designate the relationship and reason for wishing to attend.

(2) Not less than fifteen days prior to the scheduled execution, the superintendent shall designate the total number of individuals who will be allowed to attend and witness the planned execution. The superintendent shall determine the number of witnesses that will be allowed in each of the following categories:

(a) No less than five media representatives with consideration to be given to news organizations serving communities affected by the crimes or by the commission of the execution of the defendant.

(b) Judicial officers.

(c) Representatives of the families of the victims.

(d) Representatives from the family of the defendant.

(e) Up to two law enforcement representatives. The chief executive officer of the agency that investigated the crime shall designate the law enforcement representatives.

After the list is composed, the superintendent shall serve this list on all parties who have submitted an application pursuant to this section. The superintendent shall develop and implement procedures to determine the persons within each of the categories listed in this subsection who will be allowed to attend and witness the execution.

(3) Not less than ten days prior to the scheduled execution, the superintendent shall file the witness list with the superior court from which the conviction and death warrant was issued with a

petition asking that the court enter an order certifying this list as a final order identifying the witnesses to attend the execution. The final order of the court certifying the witness list shall not be entered less than five days after the filing of the petition.

(4) Unless a show cause petition is filed with the superior court from which the conviction and death warrant was issued within five days of the filing of the superintendent's petition, the superintendent's list, by order of the superior court, becomes final, and no other party has standing to challenge its appropriateness.

(5) In no case may the superintendent or the superior court order or allow more than seventeen individuals other than required staff to witness a planned execution.

Wyoming

General considerations. Wyoming is a capital punishment jurisdiction. The state reenacted its death penalty law after the United States Supreme Court decision in *Furman v. Georgia*, 408 U.S. 238 (1972), on February 28, 1977. Capital murder in Wyoming is punishable by death or life imprisonment with or without parole. A capital prosecution in Wyoming is bifurcated into a guilt phase and penalty phase. It is required at the penalty phase that the jury unanimously agrees that a death sentence is appropriate before it can be imposed. If the penalty phase jury is unable to reach a verdict, the trial judge is required to impose a sentence of life imprisonment.

Under Wyoming's capital punishment statute, a sentence of death is automatically reviewed by the Wyoming Supreme Court. Wyoming uses lethal injection to carry out death sentences, but lethal gas is available if lethal injection is found constitutionally invalid. The state's death row facility for men is located in Rawlings; the facility for women is in Lusk. The governor has authority to grant clemency in capital cases.

Death penalty offenses. Wyoming's capital punishment offenses are set out under Wyoming Code § 6-2-101(a). This statute is triggered if a person commits a homicide under the following special circumstances:

[Committed] purposely and with premeditated malice, or in the perpetration of, or attempt to perpetrate, any sexual assault, sexual abuse of a minor, arson, robbery, burglary, escape, resisting arrest, kidnapping or abuse of a child under the age of sixteen (16) years.

Aggravating circumstances used to impose death penalty. In order to impose a death sentence upon a defendant, Wyoming Code § 6-2-102(h) requires that the prosecutor establishes the existence of at least one of the following statutory aggravating circumstances at the penalty phase:

(i) The murder was committed by a person: (A) Confined in a jail or correctional facility; (B) On parole or on probation for a felony; (C) After escaping detention or incarceration; or (D) Released on bail pending appeal of his conviction.

(ii) The defendant was previously convicted of another murder in the first degree or a felony involving the use or threat of violence to the person;

(iii) The defendant knowingly created a great risk of death to two (2) or more persons;

(iv) The murder was committed while the defendant was engaged, or was an accomplice, in the commission of, or an attempt to commit, or flight after committing or attempting to commit, any aircraft piracy or the unlawful throwing, placing or discharging of a destructive device or bomb;

(v) The murder was committed for the purpose of avoiding or preventing a lawful arrest or effecting an escape from custody;

(vi) The murder was committed for compensation, the collection of insurance benefits or other similar pecuniary gain;

(vii) The murder was especially atrocious or cruel, being unnecessarily torturous to the victim;

(viii) The murder of a judicial officer, former judicial officer, district attorney, former district attorney, defending attorney, peace officer, juror or witness, during or because of the exercise of his official duty or because of the victim's former or present official status;

(ix) The defendant knew or reasonably should have known the victim was less than seventeen (17) years of age or older than sixty-five (65) years of age;

(x) The defendant knew or reasonably should have known the victim was especially vulnerable due to significant mental or physical disability;

(xi) The defendant poses a substantial and continuing threat of future dangerousness or is likely to commit continued acts of criminal violence;

(xii) The defendant killed another human being purposely and with premeditated malice and while engaged in, or as an accomplice in the commission of, or an attempt to commit, or flight after committing or attempting to commit, any robbery, sexual assault, arson, burglary, kidnapping or abuse of a child under the age of sixteen (16) years.

Mitigating circumstances. Although the federal Constitution will not permit jurisdictions to prevent capital felons from presenting all relevant mitigating evidence at the penalty phase, Wyoming has provided by statute, Wyoming Code § 6-2-102(j), the following statutory mitigating circumstances that permit a jury to reject imposition of the death penalty:

(i) The defendant has no significant history of prior criminal activity;

(ii) The murder was committed while the defendant was under the influence of extreme mental or emotional disturbance;

(iii) The victim was a participant in the defendant's conduct or consented to the act;

(iv) The defendant was an accomplice in a murder committed by another person and his participation in the homicidal act was relatively minor;

(v) The defendant acted under extreme duress or under the substantial domination of another person;

(vi) The capacity of the defendant to appreciate the criminality of his conduct or to conform his conduct to the requirements of law was substantially impaired;

(vii) The age of the defendant at the time of the crime;

(viii) Any other fact or circumstance of the defendant's character or prior record or matter surrounding his offense which serves to mitigate his culpability.

Persons who may attend an execution. Wyoming law limits the number of persons who may be present at an execution. The following is provided by Wyoming Code § 7-13-908:

(i) The director of the department of corrections and any persons deemed necessary to assist him in conducting the execution;

(ii) Two (2) physicians, including the prison physician;

(iii) The spiritual advisers of the prisoner;

(iv) The penitentiary chaplain;

(v) The sheriff of the county in which the prisoner was convicted; and

(vi) Not more than ten (10) relatives or friends requested by the prisoner.

Federal Government

General considerations. The federal government is a capital punishment jurisdiction. The federal government reenacted its death penalty law after the United States Supreme Court decision in *Furman v. Georgia*, 408 U.S. 238 (1972), in 1988. Capital murder under federal law is punishable by death or life imprisonment without parole. A capital prosecution by the federal government is bifurcated into a guilt phase and penalty phase. It is required at the penalty phase that the jury unanimously agrees that a death sentence is appropriate before it can be imposed. If the penalty phase jury is unable to reach a verdict, the trial judge is required to impose a sentence of life imprisonment.

Under the federal government's capital punishment statutes, a sentence of death must be appealed for review to a federal court of appeals. Pursuant to a regulation, 28 C.F.R. § 26.3, the federal government uses lethal injection to carry out death sentences. The federal death row facility is in Terre Haute, Indiana. Pursuant to federal laws the president has exclusive authority to grant clemency in capital cases.

Death penalty offenses. The federal government has numerous statutes which trigger a prosecution for capital punishment. Summaries of the offenses and their respective code citations are set out below:

1. Destruction of aircraft, motor vehicles, or related facilities resulting in death. 18 U.S.C. §§ 32, 33, 34;

2. A person who, in furtherance or to escape detection of a major drug offense and with the intent to intimidate, harass, injure, or maim, fires a weapon into a group of 2 or more persons and who, in the course of such conduct, kills any person. 18 U.S.C. § 36(b)(2);

3. A person who unlawfully and intentionally, using any device, substance, or weapon — (1) performs an act of violence against a person at an airport serving international civil aviation that causes or is likely to cause serious bodily injury or death; or (2) destroys or seriously damages the facilities of an airport serving international civil aviation or a civil aircraft not in service located thereon or disrupts the services of the airport, if such an act endangers or is likely to endanger safety at that airport, or attempts or conspires to do such an act. 18 U.S.C. § 37(a);

4. Retaliatory murder of a member of the immediate family of law enforcement officials. 18 U.S.C. § 115(b)(3) [by reference to 18 U.S.C. § 1111];

5. Civil rights offenses resulting in death. 18 U.S.C. §§ 241, 242, 245, 247;

6. Murder of a member of Congress, an important executive official, or a Supreme Court Justice. 18 U.S.C. § 351 [by reference to 18 U.S.C. § 1111];

7. Whoever, with intent or reason to believe that it is to be used to the injury of the United States or to the advantage of a foreign nation, communicates, delivers, or transmits, or attempts to communicate, deliver, or transmit, to any foreign government, or to any faction or party or military or naval force within a foreign country, whether recognized or unrecognized by the United States, or to any representative, officer, agent, employee, subject, or citizen thereof, either directly or indirectly, any document, writing, code book, signal book, sketch, photograph, photographic negative, blueprint, plan, map, model, note, instrument, appliance, or information relating to the national defense.

Whoever, in time of war, with intent that the same shall be communicated to the enemy, collects, records, publishes, or communicates, or attempts to elicit any information with respect to the movement, numbers, description, condition, or disposition of any of the armed forces, ships, aircraft, or war materials of the United States, or with respect to the plans or conduct, or supposed plans or conduct of any naval or military operations, or with respect to any works or measures undertaken for or connected with, or intended for the fortification or defense of any place, or any other information relating to the public defense, which might be useful to the enemy. 18 U.S.C. § 794;

8. Death resulting from offenses involving transportation of explosives, destruction of government property, or destruction of property related to foreign or interstate commerce. 18 U.S.C. § 844(d), (f), (i);

9. Murder committed by the use of a firearm during a crime of violence or a drug trafficking crime. 18 U.S.C. § 924(j);

10. Murder committed in a federal government facility. 18 U.S.C § 930;

11. Whoever, whether in time of peace or in time of war ... with the specific intent to destroy, in whole or in substantial part, a national, ethnic, racial, or religious group as such — kills members of that group. 18 U.S.C. § 1091(a);

12. Every murder perpetrated by poison, lying in wait, or any other kind of willful, deliberate, malicious, and premeditated killing; or committed in the perpetration of, or attempt to perpetrate, any arson, escape, murder, kidnapping, treason, espionage, sabotage, aggravated sexual abuse or sexual abuse, child abuse, burglary, or robbery; or perpetrated as part of a pattern or practice of assault or torture against a child or children; or perpetrated from a premeditated design unlawfully and maliciously to effect the death of any human being other than him who is killed. 18 U.S.C. § 1111(a);

13. Murder of a federal judge or law enforcement official. 18 U.S.C. § 1114;

14. Murder of a foreign official. 18 U.S.C. § 1116;

15. Murder by a federal prisoner. 18 U.S.C. § 1118;

16. Murder of a U.S. national in a foreign country. 18 U.S.C. § 1119;

17. Murder by an escaped federal prisoner already sentenced to life imprisonment. 18 U.S.C. § 1120;

18. Murder of a state or local law enforcement official or other person aiding in a federal investigation; murder of a state correctional officer. 18 U.S.C. § 1121;

19. Murder during a kidnapping. 18 U.S.C. § 1201;

20. Murder during a hostage taking. 18 U.S.C. § 1203;

21. Murder of a court officer or juror. 18 U.S.C. § 1503;

22. Murder with the intent of preventing testimony by a witness, victim, or informant. 18 U.S.C. § 1512;

23. Retaliatory murder of a witness, victim or informant. 18 U.S.C. § 1513;

24. Mailing of injurious articles with intent to kill or resulting in death. 18 U.S.C. § 1716;

25. Assassination or kidnapping resulting in the death of the president or vice president. 18 U.S.C. § 1751 [by reference to 18 U.S.C. § 1111];

26. Murder for hire. 18 U.S.C. § 1958;

27. Murder involved in a racketeering offense. 18 U.S.C. § 1959;

28. Willful wrecking of a train resulting in death. 18 U.S.C. § 1992;

29. Bank-robbery-related murder or kidnapping. 18 U.S.C. § 2113;

30. Murder related to a carjacking. 18 U.S.C. § 2119;

31. Death resulting from aggravated sexual abuse, sexual abuse, sexual abuse of a minor or ward, or abusive sexual conduct. 18 USC §§ 2241, 2242, 2243, 2244, 2245;

32. Murder related to sexual exploitation of children. 18 U.S.C. § 2251;

33. Murder committed during an offense against maritime navigation. 18 U.S.C. § 2280;

34. Murder committed during an offense against a maritime fixed platform. 18 U.S.C. § 2281;

35. Terrorist murder of a U.S. national in another country. 18 U.S.C. § 2332;

36. Use of a weapon of mass destruction resulting in death. 18 U.S.C. § 2332a;

37. Crimes against persons in the United States resulting in death, committed by a person engaged in conduct transcending national boundaries. 18 USC § 2332b;

38. Use of chemical weapons resulting in death. 18 USC § 2332c;

39. Murder involving torture. 18 U.S.C. §§ 2340, 2340A;

40. Treason. 18 U.S.C. § 2381;

41. Murder related to a continuing criminal enterprise or drug trafficking offense, or drug-related murder of a federal, state, or local law enforcement officer. 21 U.S.C. § 848(e);

42. Death resulting from aircraft piracy. 49 U.S.C. § 46502.

Aggravating circumstances used to impose death penalty. The federal government provides specific statutory aggravating circumstances for capital murder committed under its statutes for (1) espionage or treason, (2) homicide or (3) drug offense. In order to impose a death sentence upon a defendant under federal law, it is required that the prosecutor establish the existence of at least one of the following statutory aggravating circumstances at the penalty phase, premised upon a conviction for (1) espionage or treason, (2) homicide or (3) drug offense:

18 U.S.C. § 3592(b) Aggravating Circumstances for Espionage and Treason

(1) The defendant has previously been convicted of another offense involving espionage or treason for which a sentence of either life imprisonment or death was authorized by law.

(2) In the commission of the offense the defendant knowingly created a grave risk of substantial danger to the national security.

(3) In the commission of the offense the defendant knowingly created a grave risk of death to another person.

18 U.S.C. § 3592(c) Aggravating Circumstances for Homicide

(1) The death, or injury resulting in death, occurred during the commission or attempted commission of, or during the immediate flight from the commission of the destruction of aircraft or aircraft facilities, destruction of motor vehicles or motor vehicle facilities, violence at international airports, violence against members of congress, cabinet officers, or Supreme Court justices, an offense involving prisoners in custody of institution or officer, gathering or delivering defense information to aid foreign government, transportation of explosives in interstate commerce for certain purposes, destruction of government property by explosives, prisoners serving life term, kidnapping, destruction of property affecting interstate commerce by explosives, killing or attempted killing of diplomats, hostage taking, wrecking trains, offenses resulting in death, maritime violence, maritime platform violence, terrorist acts abroad against United States nationals, use of weapons of mass destruction, treason, or aircraft piracy.

(2) The defendant has previously been convicted of a federal or state offense punishable by a term of imprisonment of more than 1 year, involving the use or attempted or threatened use of a firearm against another person.

(3) The defendant has previously been convicted of another federal or state offense resulting in the death of a person, for which a sentence of life imprisonment or a sentence of death was authorized by statute.

(4) The defendant has previously been convicted of 2 or more federal or state offenses, punishable by a term of imprisonment of more than 1 year, committed on different occasions, involving the infliction of, or attempted infliction of, serious bodily injury or death upon another person.

(5) The defendant, in the commission of the offense, or in escaping apprehension for the violation of the offense, knowingly created a grave risk of death to 1 or more persons in addition to the victim of the offense.

(6) The defendant committed the offense in an especially heinous, cruel, or depraved manner in that it involved torture or serious physical abuse to the victim.

(7) The defendant procured the commission of the offense by payment, or promise of payment, of anything of pecuniary value.

(8) The defendant committed the offense as consideration for the receipt, or in the expectation of the receipt, of anything of pecuniary value.

(9) The defendant committed the offense after substantial planning and premeditation to cause the death of a person or commit an act of terrorism.

(10) The defendant has previously been convicted of 2 or more state or federal offenses punishable by a term of imprisonment of more than one year, committed on different occasions, involving the distribution of a controlled substance.

(11) The victim was particularly vulnerable due to old age, youth, or infirmity.

(12) The defendant had previously been convicted of a drug offense for which a sentence of 5 or more years may be imposed or had previously been convicted of engaging in a continuing criminal enterprise.

(13) The defendant committed the offense in the course of engaging in a continuing criminal enterprise that involved the distribution of drugs to persons under the age of 21.

(14) The defendant committed the offense against:

(A) the president of the United States, the president-elect, the vice president, the vice president-elect, the vice president-designate, or, if there is no vice president, the officer next in order of succession to the office of the president of the United States, or any person who is acting as president under the Constitution and laws of the United States;

(B) a chief of state, head of government, or the political equivalent, of a foreign nation;

(C) a foreign official if the official is in the United States on official business; or

(D) a federal public servant who is a judge, a law enforcement officer, or an employee of a United States penal or correctional institution.

(15) The defendant had a prior conviction of sexual assault or child molestation.

(16) The defendant intentionally killed or attempted to kill more than one person in a single criminal episode.

18 U.S.C. § 3592(d) Aggravating Circumstances for Drug Offense

(1) The defendant has previously been convicted of another federal or state offense resulting in the death of a person, for which a sentence of life imprisonment or death was authorized by statute.

(2) The defendant has previously been convicted of two or more federal or state offenses, each punishable by a term of imprisonment of more than one year, committed on different occasions, involving the importation, manufacture, or distribution of a controlled substance or the infliction of, or attempted infliction of, serious bodily injury or death upon another person.

(3) The defendant has previously been convicted of another federal or state offense involving the manufacture, distribution, importation, or possession of a controlled substance for which a sentence of five or more years of imprisonment was authorized by statute.

(4) In committing the offense, or in furtherance of a continuing criminal enterprise of which the offense was a part, the defendant used a firearm or knowingly directed, advised, authorized, or assisted another to use a firearm to threaten, intimidate, assault, or injure a person.

(5) The offense, or a continuing criminal enterprise of which the offense was a part, involved distribution to a person under 21 which was committed directly by the defendant.

(6) The offense, or a continuing criminal enterprise of which the offense was a part, involved distribution near a school which was committed directly by the defendant.

(7) The offense, or a continuing criminal enterprise of which the offense was a part, involved using minors which was committed directly by the defendant.

(8) The offense involved the importation, manufacture, or distribution of a controlled substance, mixed with a potentially lethal adulterant, and the defendant was aware of the presence of the adulterant.

Mitigating circumstances. Although the federal Constitution will not permit jurisdictions to prevent capital felons from presenting all relevant mitigating evidence at the penalty phase, the federal government has provided by statute, 18 U.S.C. § 3592(a), the following statutory mitigating circumstances that permit a jury to reject imposition of the death penalty:

(1) The defendant's capacity to appreciate the wrongfulness of the defendant's conduct or to conform conduct to the requirements of law was significantly impaired, regardless of whether the capacity was so impaired as to constitute a defense to the charge.

(2) The defendant was under unusual and substantial duress, regardless of whether the duress was of such a degree as to constitute a defense to the charge.

(3) The defendant is punishable as a principal in the offense, which was committed by another, but the defendant's participation was relatively minor, regardless of whether the participation was so minor as to constitute a defense to the charge.

(4) Another defendant or defendants, equally culpable in the crime, will not be punished by death.

(5) The defendant did not have a significant prior history of other criminal conduct.

(6) The defendant committed the offense under severe mental or emotional disturbance.

(7) The victim consented to the criminal conduct that resulted in the victim's death.

(8) Other factors in the defendant's background, record, or character or any other circumstance of the offense that mitigate against imposition of the death sentence.

Persons who may attend an execution. Under the laws of the federal government a limitation is imposed upon the number of persons who may be present at an execution. The following is provided by 28 C.F.R. § 26.4(c):

In addition to the marshal and warden, the following persons shall be present at the execution:

(1) Necessary personnel selected by the marshal and warden;

(2) Those attorneys of the Department of Justice whom the deputy attorney general determines are necessary;

(3) Not more than the following numbers of person selected by the prisoner: (i) One spiritual adviser; (ii) Two defense attorneys; and (iii) Three adult friends or relatives; and

(4) Not more than the following numbers of persons selected by the warden: (i) Eight citizens; and (ii) Ten representatives of the press.

Glossary of Legal Terms

acquittal A verdict made by a judge or jury that a defendant is not guilty of a charged offense.

advisory jury A jury whose verdict recommendation is not binding on a court.

affirm To agree that a conviction or sentence is correct.

affirmative defense A justification or excuse offered by a defendant for which the defendant has the burden of proof.

aggravating circumstance A factor which, if created by statute, will permit the death penalty to be imposed in a capital prosecution.

allocution Personal statement by a defendant to a judge or jury during the sentencing proceeding.

appeal The process of having an appellate court examine possible errors in a criminal judgment.

appellant The person who brings a case to an appellate court for examination of alleged errors committed in the proceeding.

appellate court A court whose jurisdiction is limited to examining the record of a case for possible errors.

appellate review Examination of a sentence by an appellate court.

appellee The person in a case who has not taken the case to an appellate court, but must defend against an adverse action to the case by the appellate court.

arbitrary A decision reached without a legally recognized rationalization.

arraignment A stage in a criminal prosecution where a defendant is formally charged with an offense and enters a plea of not guilty or guilty.

assignment of error Specifically alleged mistakes during a criminal prosecution.

bench trial A criminal trial that is presided over by the court as the factfinder.

burden *see* **burden of proof.**

burden of proof Having the obligation of persuading a factfinder of the truth of an issue.

capital crime A criminal offense that is punishable with death.

capital felon A defendant charged with, convicted of or sentenced for a capital crime.

capital felony *see* **capital crime.**

capital murder *see* **capital crime.**

capital offense *see* **capital crime.**

capital punishment jurisdiction The federal government and states that impose the death penalty for capital crimes.

capital sentence *see* **death sentence.**

certiorari *see* **writ of certiorari.**

charge An allegation that a person has committed a specific offense; also instructions given by a court to a jury.

clemency An act by an executive branch of government (governor or president) that permits permanent or temporary relief from punishment.

co-defendant An accomplice to a crime.

co-felon *see* **co-defendant**.

commutation Reducing a punishment to a lesser sanction.

concurring opinion A written decision by an appellate court judge who agrees with the outcome of a case decided by the appellate court, but disagrees with the reason given by other members of the appellate court for the outcome.

consolidation Combining an appeal of a conviction and review of a sentence by an appellate court.

constitutional Any conduct or decision that is permitted by the constitution.

constitutionally valid *see* **constitutional**.

conviction A determination that a defendant is guilty of a charged offense.

coram nobis *see* **writ of coram nobis**.

corpse A dead body.

court of general jurisdiction A judicial forum that has authority to preside over most criminal and civil cases.

crime An act or conduct that is prohibited by a statute or regulation.

cruel and unusual punishment The guarantee by the Eighth Amendment that a criminal sanction must be reasonable in the manner in which it is imposed or executed.

death-eligible offense *see* **capital crime**.

death penalty A criminal sanction that calls for the life of a defendant to be taken.

death-qualified jury Persons selected as jurors in a capital prosecution who are not predisposed to or against the death penalty.

death sentence A determination that a defendant will be legally killed for an offense he or she was convicted of committing.

defendant A person who has been formally accused of committing an offense.

dicta Language in a judicial opinion that is not necessary for the decision reached in a case and is not binding authority that must be followed.

direct appeal Appellate court examination of possible nonconstitutional errors in a criminal judgment.

dismissal The rejection of a charge against a defendant by a court that prohibits the prosecutor from proceeding further on the matter.

due process A right, guaranteed by the Fifth and Fourteenth Amendments, to have fair legal proceedings before an adverse action can be imposed upon a person.

element A factor that is part of an offense or principle of law.

equal protection A right, expressly guaranteed by the Fourteenth Amendment and inferred in the Fifth Amendment, not to be arbitrarily or capriciously treated differently from those similarly situated.

error A mistake or alleged mistake in a criminal prosecution.

evidence Anything that is accepted by a court as tending to prove or disprove a matter in dispute.

exclude To keep out.

execute To carry out a punishment.

execution *see* **execute**.

factfinder A jury or judge who hears evidence and must make a determination of what the evidence means.

felon A person prosecuted for committing a felony offense.

felony A crime that is generally punishable by more than a year of incarceration.

final appellate court The highest court in a judicial system.

finding A determination made by a court or jury.

freedom of association A guarantee by the First Amendment that a person may, without governmental interference, associate with whomever he or she desires.

frivolous Having no merit.

furlough The temporary release of an inmate from confinement due to good conduct while confined.

grand jury A group of persons (usually 16) selected according to law to investigate criminal allegations brought against a person and to determine whether the person should be prosecuted.

guilt phase The trial stage of a criminal prosecution.

habeas corpus *see* **writ of habeas corpus**.

harmless error A mistake made during a criminal prosecution that did not affect the outcome of the case.

hearsay Any statement made outside of a criminal proceeding that is being offered as substantively truthful in a criminal proceeding.

homicide Causing the death of another person without legal justification or excuse.

hung jury A jury that cannot decide an issue unanimously or under a lesser legally permitted vote.

incarceration Confinement in a jail or prison.

inchoate crime Conduct that is an offense, but which falls short of completion of the intended offense.

indictment An instrument used by a grand jury to formally accuse a person of a crime.

information An instrument drawn up by a prosecutor to formally accuse a person of a crime.

instruction Statements by a court to a jury.

intermediate appellate court The second tier court in a three-tier system.

introduce *see* **proffer**.

irrelevant Any factor which does not bear on the truth or nontruth of an issue in dispute.

issue A matter that is in dispute.

judgment A final determination by a court.

judicial stay *see* **stay**.

jurisdiction The territory over which a court has authority, or the subject matter or person over which a court has authority.

jury deadlock *see* **hung jury**.

jury instruction *see* **instruction**.

jury override A decision by a court to impose a penalty different from that recommended by a jury.

mandamus *see* **writ of mandamus**.

misdemeanor A crime that is generally punishable by not more than one year incarceration.

mitigating circumstance A factor which may cause less than the maximum penalty to be imposed.

nolle prosequi A determination by a prosecutor that he or she will not pursue a charge against a defendant.

nolo contendere A defendant not admitting guilt to a crime, but accepting the punishment.

non-weighing process Examining aggravating and mitigating circumstances to determine which are sufficient to affect the type of punishment a defendant will receive.

not true bill A determination by a grand jury that an allegation against a person is false.

notice Informing a party in a criminal proceeding of the intent to do, or refrain from doing, something prior to when it should be done.

nullify To render meaningless or unenforceable.

offense *see* **crime.**

outweigh *see* **weighing process.**

override *see* **jury override.**

panel of judges A group of three or more judicial officers who are chosen to hear and decide an issue in a case.

pardon Absolves a defendant of all consequences of an offense or a conviction and sentence.

pass constitutional muster *see* **constitutional.**

penalty phase The sentencing stage of a criminal prosecution.

per curiam opinion A written decision of an appellate court that does not reveal the name of the appellate judge who wrote the decision.

petit jury The jury presiding over a criminal trial.

petition A request made to a court asking it to do something or prohibit an occurrence.

petitioner A person who institutes a proceeding in court.

plea bargaining The process wherein the prosecutor and defendant (through counsel) attempt to negotiate an adverse plea by the defendant, in exchange for some benefit from the prosecutor.

preclude *see* **exclude.**

prejudicial error A mistake made during a criminal prosecution that influenced the outcome of the case.

preliminary hearing A stage in a prosecution wherein a court (usually magistrate) determines whether a case should be turned over to a grand jury.

privilege The ability to do something because the law permits it, though the law can prohibit it.

proffer Something that is offered as proof on an issue.

prohibition *see* **writ of prohibition.**

prosecute To formally bring charges against a person and seek to convict and sentence the person so charged.

prosecutor An attorney legally authorized to bring criminal charges against a person and to pursue a judicial conviction and sentence of the person.

prosecutorial discretion A prosecutor's ability to determine such things as whether to charge a person with a crime, the type of charges to bring or whether — in a capital crime — the death penalty should be sought.

relevant Any factor which tends to establish the truth or nontruth of an issue in dispute.

remand To send a case back to a lower court for further action.

reprieve Temporary halt to enforcement of a sentence until some requested matter is examined.

respondent A person who is named in a judicial proceeding and must answer allegations made in the proceeding.

reverse To set aside a judgment.

reversible error A mistake caused during a criminal prosecution that requires a conviction or sentence to be vacated.

review *see* **appellate review.**

right against self-incrimination The guarantee by the Fifth Amendment that a person may not be compelled by a government entity to say anything that he or she may be later criminally prosecuted for.

right to allocution *see* **allocution.**

sentence The punishment imposed on a defendant.

special circumstances Factors which cause murder to become a death-eligible offense.

standard of proof The level of evidence that must be presented in order to prevail on an issue.

stay A temporary postponement of execution of a sentence or other matter.

sua sponte Action by a court without prompting by the parties in the litigation.

sufficiency determination *see* **non-weighing process.**

three-tier system A judicial structure that has a court of general jurisdiction, intermediate appellate court and final appellate court.

trial court The court which determines in the first instance a defendant's guilt or innocence.

true bill A determination by a grand jury that an allegation against a person is valid for prosecution.

two-tier system A judicial structure that has a court of general jurisdiction and appellate court.

unconstitutional Something that is prohibited by the constitution.

vacate *see* **reverse.**

vagueness challenge An allegation that a law or element in a law has no clear meaning.

verdict The decision of a jury or judge in a nonjury proceeding.

victim A person who has had a crime perpetrated against him.

victim identity A specific characteristic of a person that is legally recognized as a basis for imposing the death penalty when such person is murdered because of the characteristic.

victim impact evidence Information given to a factfinder that involves a murder victim's identity, personal characteristics and the hardship of the victim's death on his family.

waive Give up some right through silence or inaction, or voluntarily.

weighing process Comparing aggravating and mitigating circumstances to determine which is more persuasive in affecting the type of punishment a defendant will receive.

work-release Allowing an inmate to leave confinement for the purpose of engaging in private employment, but returning to confinement at the end of the work day.

writ of certiorari A document issued by an appellate court ordering a lower court to produce the record of its proceeding in a case.

writ of coram nobis A document issued by a court to correct a judgment based upon an error that did not appear on the record of a case.

writ of habeas corpus A document directing a person holding a defendant to produce the defendant to the court, so the court may determine the lawfulness of the defendant's confinement.

writ of mandamus A document directing a government entity to perform some act it has a legal duty to perform.

writ of prohibition A document forbidding a government entity from performing some act.

Chapter Notes

Chapter 1

1. "The unambiguous meaning of 'capital punishment' is the death penalty[.]" *State v. Holmes*, 269 S0.2d 207 (La. 1972) (Tate, J., dissenting).

2. This point was noted in *Gilman v. Choi*, 185 W.Va. 177, 406 S.E.2d 200 (1990), overruled on other grounds *Mayhorn v. Logan Medical Foundation*, 193 W.Va. 42, 454 S.E.2d 87 (1994), where the court said that "[t]he term 'common law' came into use in England during the reign of Edward I (1272–1307)[.]"

3. William the Conqueror is credited with separating the ecclesiastical from the temporal courts of England. See Alison Reppy, "The Ordinance of William the Conqueror (1072)—Its Implications in the Modern Law of Succession," 42 Ky. L.J. 523 (1953).

4. *Gilman v. Choi*, 185 W.Va. 177, 406 S.E.2d 200 (1990), overruled on other grounds *Mayhorn v. Logan Medical Foundation*, 193 W.Va. 42, 454 S.E.2d 87 (1994).

5. See William Holdsworth, *A History of English Law*, Vol. 11, pp. 556–557 (1966). It will be pointed out that use of the pillory could be dangerous and even fatal. In Holdsworth's commentary he described how several prisoners were killed due to people in the community hurling stones at them while they were confined to the pillory.

6. W.F. Finalason, *Reeves' History of the English Law*, Vol. 1, p. 235 (1880).

7. W.F. Finalason, *Reeves' History of the English Law*, Vol. 1, p. 192 n.(a) (1880).

8. See Marshall D. Ewell, *Ewell's Essentials of the Law—Blackstone*, Vol. 1, p. 785 (1915).

9. See William Holdsworth, *A History of English Law*, Vol. 13, pp. 283–285 (1971).

10. William Holdsworth, *A History of English Law*, Vol. 11, p. 560 (1966).

11. W.F. Finalason, *Reeves' History of the English Law*, Vol. 3, p. 69 (1879).

12. William Holdsworth, *A History of English Law*, Vol. 11, p. 561 (1966).

13. William Holdsworth, *A History of English Law*, Vol. 11, p. 556 (1966).

14. See Louis J. Palmer, Jr., *Encyclopedia of Capital Punishment in the United States* (2d ed. 2008).

15. See Kathryn Preyer, "Penal Measures in the American Colonies: An Overview," 26 Am. J. Legal Hist. 326 (1982).

16. See Kathryn Preyer, "Penal Measures in the American Colonies: An Overview," 26 Am. J. Legal Hist. 326 (1982); William B. Stoebuck, "Reception of English Common Law in the American Colonies," 10 Wm. and Mary L. Rev. 393 (1969); Erwin C. Surrency, "The Courts in the American Colonies," 11 Am. J. Legal Hist. 347 (1967).

17. See Kathryn Preyer, "Penal Measures in the American Colonies: An Overview," 26 Am. J. Legal Hist. 326 (1982).

18. See Patrick E. Higginbotham, "Juries and the Death Penalty," 41 Case W. Res. L. Rev. 1047 (1991).

19. See Edwin R. Keedy, "History of the Pennsylvania Statute Creating Degrees of Murder," 97 U. Pa. L. Rev. 759 (1949).

20. See Thomas J. Walsh, "On the Abolition of Man: A Discussion of the Moral and Legal Issues Surrounding the Death Penalty," 44 Clev. St. L. Rev. 23 (1996).

21. See Thomas J. Walsh, "On the Abolition of Man: A Discussion of the Moral and Legal Issues Surrounding the Death Penalty," 44 Clev. St. L. Rev. 23 (1996).

22. See Thomas J. Walsh, "On the Abolition of Man: A Discussion of the Moral and Legal Issues Surrounding the Death Penalty," 44 Clev. St. L. Rev. 23 (1996).

Chapter 2

1. For a discussion of the historical development of the first 10 amendments to the constitution see R. Rutland, *The Birth of the Bill of Rights 1776–1791* (1955).

2. For a general discussion of this clause see Anthony F. Granucci, "Nor Cruel and Unusual Punishments Inflicted: The Original Meaning," 57 Cal. L. Rev. 839 (1969).

3. *Furman v. Georgia*, 408 U.S. 238 (1972).

4. *Furman v. Georgia*, 408 U.S. 238 (1972). Other clauses adopted by members of the original thirteen colonies included Delaware's Declaration of Rights (1776), Maryland's Declaration of Rights (1776), Massachusetts' Declaration of Rights (1780), and New Hampshire's Bill of Rights (1783).

5. See Anthony F. Granucci, "Nor Cruel and Unusual Punishments Inflicted: The Original Meaning," 57 Cal. L. Rev. 839 (1969).

6. This principle seeks to determine if the punishment involves the infliction of physical or mental suffering.

7. This principle seeks to determine if the punishment is uniformly imposed on everyone subject to the punishment.

8. This principle seeks to determine if society finds a particular punishment acceptable.

9. This principle seeks to determine whether a punishment is proportionately consistent with the crime. A proportionality test was developed in *Solem v. Helm*, 463 U.S. 277 (1983), which examines (1) the gravity of the

offense and the harshness of the penalty, (2) the sentences imposed on other criminals in the same jurisdiction, and (3) the sentences imposed for commission of the crime in other jurisdictions. However, the continued validity of the *Solem* test has been put in doubt. See, *Harmelin v. Michigan*, 501 U.S. 957 (1991).

10. See also *Proffitt v. Florida*, 428 U.S. 242 (1976) and *Jurek v. Texas*, 428 U.S. 262 (1976).

11. The defendant was also charged with and convicted of armed robbery.

12. For a general discussion of mandatory sentencing see Orrin G. Hatch, "The Role of Congress in Sentencing: The United States Sentencing Commission, Mandatory Minimum Sentences and the Search for a Certain and Effective Sentencing System," 28 Wake Forest L. Rev. 185 (1993).

13. Both defendants were also convicted of armed robbery. Additionally, one of the defendants was convicted of assault with a deadly weapon.

14. See J.W. Poulos, "Supreme Court, Capital Punishment and the Substantive Criminal Law: The Rise and Fall of Mandatory Capital Punishment," 28 Ariz. L. Rev. 143 (1986).

15. *Tison v. Arizona*, 481 U.S. 137 (1987). For a discussion of the felony-murder doctrine in the context of death-eligible offenses see Richard A. Rosen, "Felony Murder and the Eighth Amendment Jurisprudence of Death," 31 B.C. L. Rev. 1103 (1990); Norman J. Finkel, "Capital Felony-Murder, Objective Indicia, and Community Sentiment," 32 Ariz. L. Rev. 819 (1990).

16. There was a third confederate in the crime but she was tried separately.

17. For a discussion of this case and its impact see Andrew H. Friedman, "Tison v. Arizona: The Death Penalty and the Non-Triggerman: The Scales of Justice Are Broken," 75 Cornell L. Rev. 123 (1989); Lynn D. Wittenbrink, "Overstepping Precedent? Tison v. Arizona Imposes the Death Penalty on Felony Murder Accomplices," 66 N.C. L. Rev. 817 (1988); James J. Holman, "Redefining a Culpable Mental State for a Non-Triggerman — Tison v. Arizona," 33 Vill. L. Rev. 367 (1988); Stephen Taylor, "Cruel and Unusual Punishment — Imposition of the Death Penalty on a Non-Triggerman — Tison v. Arizona," 13 T. Marshall L. Rev. 211 (1987); Karen M. Quinn, "A Reckless Indifference to Human Life Is Sufficient Evidence to Prove Culpability in a Felony-Murder Case and Therefore Imposition of the Death Penalty Is Not a Violation of the Eighth Amendment — Tison v. Arizona," 37 Drake L. Rev. 767 (1988).

18. See *Furman v. Georgia*, 408 U.S. 238 (1972).

19. *Furman v. Georgia*, 408 U.S. 238 (1972). For an exhaustive treatment see Hugo Bedau, *The Death Penalty in America* (1967).

20. In *Graham v. Florida*, 130 S.Ct 2011 (2010), the Supreme Court held that "[t]he Constitution prohibits the imposition of a life without parole sentence on a juvenile offender who did not commit homicide."

Chapter 3

1. See Marlyn E. Lugar, "Criminal Law, Double Jeopardy and Res Judicata," 39 Iowa L. Rev. 317 (1954).

2. See Jay A. Sigler, "A History of Double Jeopardy," 7 Am. J. Legal Hist. 285 (1963).

3. See Jay A. Sigler, "A History of Double Jeopardy," 7 Am. J. Legal Hist. 285 (1963).

4. See Jay A. Sigler, "A History of Double Jeopardy," 7 Am. J. Legal Hist. 285 (1963).

5. See Walter T. Fisher, "Double Jeopardy, Two Sov-

ereignties and the Intruding Constitution," 28 U. Chi. L. Rev. 591 (1961).

6. For a general discussion of concurrent jurisdiction prosecution, see Michael A. Dawson, "Popular Sovereignty, Double Jeopardy, and the Dual Sovereignty Doctrine," 102 Yale L.J. 281 (1992).

7. See Jennifer L. Czernecki, "The Double Jeopardy Clause of the Pennsylvania Constitution Does Not Bar the Death Penalty Upon Retrial After the Trial Judge Grants a Life Sentence on Behalf of a Hung Jury: Commonwealth v. Sattazahn," 40 Duq. L. Rev. 127 (2002).

8. See William Winslow Crosskey, "The True Meaning of the Constitutional Prohibition of Ex-Post-Facto Laws," 14 U. Chi. L. Rev. 539 (1947).

9. See Notes, "Beyond Process: A Substantive Rationale for the Bill of Attainder Clause," 70 Va. L. Rev. 475 (1984).

10. See Neil P. Cohen, "Can They Kill Me If I'm Gone: Trial in Absentia in Capital Cases," 36 U. Fla. L. Rev. 273 (1984).

11. See Commonwealth v. Pantano, 836 A.2d 948 (Pa.Super. 2003).

Chapter 4

1. See Felix Rackow, "The Right to Counsel: English and American Precedents," 11 Wm. and Mary Q. 3 (1954).

2. See generally, William M. Beaney, "The Right to Counsel: Past, Present, and Future," 49 Va. L. Rev. 1150 (1963).

3. *Powell v. Alabama*, 287 U.S. 45 (1932).

4. See *Pennsylvania v. Finley*, 481 U.S. 551 (1987); *Douglas v. California*, 372 U.S. 353 (1963). See also, Alexander Holtzoff, "The Right of Counsel Under the Sixth Amendment," 20 N.Y.U. L. Q. Rev. 1 (1944).

5. See James C. Beck and Robert Shumsky, "A Comparison of Retained and Appointed Counsel in Cases of Capital Murder," 21 L. Hum. Behav. 525 (1997).

6. In a Georgia study it was shown that the odds of a capital defendant with court appointed counsel receiving a death sentence were 2.6 times higher than a capital defendant with retained counsel. See Stephen B. Bright, "Counsel for the Poor: The Death Sentence Not for the Worst Crime but for the Worst Lawyer," 103 Yale L.J. 1835 (1993).

7. Examples of inexperienced legal counsel for capital defendants include the following. The attorney appointed for Larry Heath, by the state of Alabama, filed a six page brief in the appeal before the Alabama Court of Criminal Appeal, and a one page brief in the appeal to the Alabama Supreme Court. The attorney also failed to show up for oral argument at the Alabama Supreme Court. Heath was eventually executed on March 20, 1992. During the Texas capital trial of Jesus Romero, his court appointed attorney did not call any witnesses at the penalty phase of the trial. Romero was executed on May 20, 1992. In the case of John Young, who was executed by Georgia on March 10, 1985, it was learned that his court appointed counsel was on illegal drugs during his trial (the attorney was subsequently disbarred).

8. See American Bar Association, *Guidelines for the Appointment and Performance of Defense Counsel in Death Penalty Cases* (2003).

9. See Richard L. Gabriel, "The Strickland Standard for Claims of Ineffective Assistance of Counsel: Emasculating the Sixth Amendment in the Guise of Due Process," 134 U.Penn. L. Rev. 1259 (1986).

10. See David A. Perez, "Deal or No Deal? Remedying Ineffective Assistance of Counsel During Plea Bargaining," 120 Yale L.J. 1532 (2011).

11. See Eric Rieder, "The Right of Self-Representation in the Capital Case," 85 Colum. L. Rev. 130 (1985).

12. See Marie Higgins Williams, "Pro Se Criminal Defendant, Standby Counsel, and the Judge: A Proposal for Better-Defined Roles," 71 U. Colo. L. Rev. 789 (2000).

13. See David S. Romantz, "You Have the Right to Remain Silent: A Case for the Use of Silence as Substantive Proof of the Criminal Defendant's Guilt," 38 Ind. L. Rev. 1 (2005).

14. See Albert W. Alschuler, "A Peculiar Privilege in Historical Perspective: The Right to Remain Silent," 94 Mich. L. Rev. 2625 (1996).

15. R.D. Miller, G.J. Maier, and M. Kaye, "Right to Remain Silent During Psychiatric Examination in Civil and Criminal Cases: A National Survey and an Analysis," 9 Intern'l J. Law Psych. 77 (1986).

Chapter 5

1. See American Bar Association, *Guidelines for the Appointment and Performance of Defense Counsel in Death Penalty Cases* (2003).

2. See *State v. Dellinger*, 79 S.W.2d 458 (Tenn. 2002).

3. *Riley v. Taylor*, 277 F.3d 261 (3d Cir. 2001). See *Arrington v. State*, 687 S.E.2d 438 (Ga. 2009) ("[T]here is no per se constitutional right to the appointment of two attorneys in a capital case[.]"); *Robitaille v. State*, 971 S0.2d 43 (Ala.Crim.App. 2005) ("While we recognize that in some cases there may be a need to appoint two attorneys, Alabama has no statute requiring that two attorneys be appointed to a capital defendant."). The right to appointment of two attorneys in federal capital cases is a well established one. Congress first created such a right in 1790, and, in 1948, Congress codified the two attorney requirement in 18 U.S.C. § 3005. *United States v. Waggoner*, 339 F.3d 915 (9th Cir. 2003).

4. See American Bar Association, *Guidelines for the Appointment and Performance of Defense Counsel in Death Penalty Cases* (2003).

5. See The Criminal Defense Investigation Training Council, http://www.defenseinvestigator.com/index.html.

6. See American Bar Association, *Guidelines for the Appointment and Performance of Defense Counsel in Death Penalty Cases* (2003). In *Caldwell v. Mississippi*, 472 U.S. 320, 105 S.Ct. 2633, 86 L.Ed.2d 231 (1985), the Supreme Court made it clear that there is no constitutional right to the appointment of an investigator where the defendant offers "little more than undeveloped assertions that the requested assistance would be beneficial."

7. See Jill Miller, "The Defense Team in Capital Cases," 31 Hofstra L. Rev. 1117 (2003).

8. See American Bar Association, *Guidelines for the Appointment and Performance of Defense Counsel in Death Penalty Cases* (2003).

9. See Pamela Blume Leonard, "A New Profession for an Old Need: Why a Mitigation Specialist Must Be Included on the Capital Defense Team," 31 Hofstra L. Rev. 1143 (2003); Jonathan P. Tomes, "Damned If You Do, Damned If You Don't: The Use of Mitigation Experts in Death Penalty Litigation," 24 Am. J. Crim. L. 359 (1997).

10. *Criminal Specialist Investigations, Inc. v. State*, 58 S0.3d 883 (Fla.App. 2011).

11. Mary M. Foreman, "Military Capital Litigation: Meeting the Heightened Standards of United States v. Curtis," 174 Mil. L. Rev. 1 (2002).

12. See *United States v. Brown*, 441 F.3d 1330 (11th Cir. 2006) ("[W]hile some mitigation specialists could testify as experts, it is a common practice for mitigation specialists to work as investigators in support of the work of

forensic social workers as well as other mental health professionals such as psychologists and psychiatrists.").

13. See Emily Hughes, "Mitigating Death," 18 Cornell J.L. & Pub. Pol'y 337 (2009); Daniel L. Payne, "Building the Case for Life: A Mitigation Specialist as a Necessity and a Matter of Right," 16 Cap. Def. J. 43 (2004).

14. *Kayer v. Ryan*, 2009 WL 3352188 (D.Ariz. 2009).

15. In *Kenley v. Armontrout*, 937 F.2d 1298 (8th Cir. 1991) the court reversed the death penalty imposed on the defendant, because of defense counsel's failure to present evidence at the penalty phase regarding the defendant's psychological history. Similarly, in *Antwine v. Delo*, 54 F.3d 1357 (8th Cir. 1995) the court held that the defense counsel had rendered ineffective assistance at the penalty phase of the case in failing to present evidence of the defendant's mental condition.

16. See Meghan Shapiro, "An Overdose of Dangerousness: How Future Dangerousness Catches the Least Culpable Capital Defendants and Undermines the Rationale for the Executions It Supports," 35 Am. J. Crim. L. 145 (2008).

17. See Brian Sites, "The Dangers of Future Dangerousness in Death Penalty Use," 34 Fla. St. U. L. Rev. 959 (2007).

18. See *United States v. Brown*, 441 F.3d 1330 (2006).

19. See John H. Blume, Sheri Lynn Johnson, and A. Brian Threlkeld, "Probing 'Life Qualification' Through Expanded Voir Dire," 29 Hofstra L. Rev. 1209 (20010; Shari Seidman Diamond, "Scientific Jury Selection: What Social Scientists Know and Do Not Know," 73 Judicature 178 (1990).

20. See Steven C. Serio, "A Process Right Due: Examining Whether a Capital Defendant Has a Due Process Right to a Jury Selection Expert," 53 Am. U.L. Rev. 1143 (2004).

21. In *State v. Dellinger*, 79 S.W.2d 458 (Tenn. 2002), it was held that "the appointment of a jury selection expert is not necessary when the record fails to show that the expert would have materially assisted the defense or that the defendant was deprived of a fair trial." See *Grayson v. State*, 806 S0.2d 241 (Miss. 2001).

Chapter 6

1. The non-ecclesiastic courts were the Crown's courts. Judges were appointed by the Crown. All monies paid to the court belonged to the Crown. I Frederick Pollock and Frederic Maitland, *The History of English Law*, 153–162 (1968).

2. The ordinary citizen was required to assist in the arrest of felons and misdemeanants. During the thirteenth century, communities were fined if they failed to apprehend a homicide suspect. III William Holdsworth, *A History of English Law*, 598–607 (1973).

3. VII William Holdsworth, *A History of English Law*, 4 (1973).

4. VI William Holdsworth, *A History of English Law*, 466–481 (1971).

5. *Skinner v. Dostert*, 278 S.E.2d 624 (W.Va. 1981).

6. *Skinner v. Dostert*, 278 S.E.2d 624 (W.Va. 1981).

7. *Skinner v. Dostert*, 278 S.E.2d 624 (W.Va. 1981).

8. IX William Holdsworth, *A History of English Law*, 236–244 (1966).

9. II William Holdsworth, *A History of English Law*, 357–369 (1971).

10. England did not utilize a public prosecutor until 1879, when it created the Director of Public Prosecutions office. See W. Scott Van Alstyne, Jr., "The District Attorney — A Historical Puzzle," 1952 Wis. L. Rev. 125 (1952).

11. 3 Sanford H. Kadish, *Encyclopedia of Crime and Justice*, 1286 (1983).

12. 3 Sanford H. Kadish, *Encyclopedia of Crime and Justice*, 1286 (1983).

13. 3 Sanford H. Kadish, *Encyclopedia of Crime and Justice*, 1286 (1983).

14. W. Scott Van Alstyne, Jr., "The District Attorney—A Historical Puzzle," 1952 Wis. L. Rev. 125 (1952).

15. W. Scott Van Alstyne, Jr., "The District Attorney—A Historical Puzzle," 1952 Wis. L. Rev. 125 (1952).

16. W. Scott Van Alstyne, Jr., "The District Attorney—A Historical Puzzle," 1952 Wis. L. Rev. 125 (1952).

17. W. Scott Van Alstyne, Jr., "The District Attorney—A Historical Puzzle," 1952 Wis. L. Rev. 125 (1952). England conquered New Netherland in 1664.

18. Connecticut (criminal justice commission appoints prosecutors); Delaware (attorney general appoints prosecutors); Florida (attorney general appoints prosecutors); New Jersey (governor appoints prosecutors); Rhode Island (attorney general appoints prosecutors); federal system (president appoints prosecutors).

19. See Wayne Logan, "A Proposed Check on the Charging Discretion of Wisconsin Prosecutors," 1990 Wis. L. Rev. 1695 (1990); Russell Leblang, "Controlling Prosecutorial Discretion Under State Rico," 24 Suffolk U.L. Rev. 79 (1990); Gregory Zafiris, "Limiting Prosecutorial Discretion Under the Oregon Environmental Crimes Act: A New Solution to an Old Problem," 24 Envtl. L. 1673 (1994); Douglas Noll, "Controlling a Prosecutor's Screening Discretion Through Fuller Enforcement," 29 Syracuse L. Rev. 697 (1978); Charles Bubany and Frank Skillern, "Taming the Dragon: An Administrative Law for Prosecutorial Decisionmaking," 13 Am. Cr. L. Rev. 473 (1976); James Vorenberg, "Narrowing the Discretion of Criminal Justice Officials," 1976 Duke L. J. 651 (1976); Kenneth Melilli, "Prosecutorial Discretion in an Adversary System," 1992 B.Y.U.L. Rev. 669 (1992).

20. Some jurisdictions provide for binding punishment recommendations that judges must follow, if accepted by the court. E.g., Rule 11(1)(e)(C) of the Federal Rules of Criminal Procedure. "Type C" agreements, as they are called, are rare because they do in fact invade the province of the judiciary in determining the sentence.

21. *People ex rel. Carey v. Cousins*, 397 N.E.2d 809 (Ill. 1979).

22. *State v. Koedatich*, 548 A.2d 939 (N.J. 1988).

23. *Gregg v. Georgia*, 428 U.S. 153 (1976). See *United States v. Walker*, 910 F.Supp. 837 (N.D.N.Y. 1995) (holding that mere assertion, without more, by a defendant that he or she was arbitrarily singled out by the prosecutor for death penalty prosecution will not suffice to dismiss death penalty charging instrument, so long as there is probable cause to believe the defendant committed the charged capital offense).

Chapter 7

1. I Frederick Pollock and Frederic Maitland, *The History of English Law*, 137–153 (1968).

2. I Frederick Pollock and Frederic Maitland, *The History of English Law*, 137–153 (1968).

3. There are currently only 19 jurisdictions that require felony prosecutions be initiated by grand jury indictment, in absence of a valid waiver by the defendant.

4. *Sanghetti v. State*, 618 S.W.2d 383 (Tex.Cr.App. 1981).

5. *State v. Height*, 649 N.E.2d 294 (Ohio App. 10 Dist. 1994). See also, *Morris v. State*, 892 S.W.2d 205 (Tex.App.-Texarkana 1994).

6. *Pachecano v. State*, 881 S.W.2d 537 (Tex.App.–Fort Worth 1994).

7. *People v. Diaz*, 834 P.2d 1171 (Cal. 1992). See also, *Ross v. State*, 519 A.2d 735 (Md. 1987).

8. *People v. Nitz*, 610 N.E.2d 1289 (Ill.App. 5 Dist. 1993).

9. *Johnson v. State*, 584 S0.2d 881 (Ala.Cr.App. 1991).

10. *People v. Weber*, 636 N.E.2d 902 (Ill.App. 1 Dist. 1994). See also, *State v. Just*, 675 P.2d 1353 (Ariz.App. 1983).

11. *People v. Jackson*, 599 S.E.2d 1192 (Ill.App. 1 Dist. 1992).

12. *Frazier v. State*, 362 S.E.2d 351 (Ga. 1987).

13. *Huff v. State*, 596 S0.2d 16 (Ala.Cr.App. 1991).

14. *Moreno v. State*, 721 S.W.2d 295 (Tex.App. 1986). In accord, *Nethery v. State*, 692 S.W.2d 686 (Tex.Cr.App. 1985); *Aranda v. State*, 640 S.W.2d 766 (Tex.App. 4 Dist. 1982).

15. *Yokey v. State*, 801 S.W.2d 232 (Tex.App.–San Antonio 1990).

16. *Phillips v. State*, 367 S.E.2d 805 (Ga. 1988).

17. *Ramirez v. State*, 815 S.W.2d 636 (Tex.Cr.App. 1991).

18. *Rivera v. State*, 808 S.W.2d 80 (Tex.Cr.App. 1991).

19. *Willie v. State*, 585 S0.2d 660 (Miss. 1991).

20. *Acres v. State*, 548 S0.2d 459 (Ala.Cr.App. 1987).

21. *State v. King*, 733 P.2d 472 (Or.App. 1987). See also, *Lundy v. State*, 539 S0.2d 324 (Ala.Cr.App. 1988).

22. *Beck v. State*, 485 S0.2d 1203 (Ala.Cr.App. 1984).

23. *Livingston v. State*, 542 S.W.2d 655 (Tex.Cr.App. 1976). In accord, *Ex Parte Davis*, 542 S.W.2d 192 (Tex.Cr.App. 1976).

24. *Garrison v. State*, 521 S0.2d 997 (Ala.Cr.App. 1986).

25. *Garrett v. State*, 682 S.W.2d 301 (Tex.Cr.App. 1984). See also, *Boggs v. Commonwealth*, 331 S.E.2d 407 (Va. 1985).

26. *State v. Isa*, 850 S.W.2d 876 (Mo. 1993).

27. *State v. Holmes*, 609 S.W.2d 132 (Mo. 1980).

28. *Brown v. State*, 410 A.2d 17 (Md.App. 1979).

29. *Smith v. State*, 398 A.2d 426 (Md.App. 1979).

30. *Young v. State*, 579 S0.2d 721 (Fla. 1991).

31. *Askew v. State*, 439 N.E.2d 1350 (Ind. 1982).

32. *State v. Harden*, 384 S0.2d 52 (Fla.App. 1980). See also, *Boles v. State*, 598 S.W.2d 274 (Tex.Cr.App. 1980).

33. *Vaughn v. State*, 607 S.W.2d 914 (Tex.Cr.App. 1980).

34. *Nelson v. State*, 573 S.W.2d 9 (Tex.Cr.App. 1978).

35. *State v. Woods*, 297 S.E.2d 574 (N.C. 1982).

36. *State v. Frazier*, 574 N.E.2d 483 (Ohio 1991).

37. *Kearse v. State*, 662 S0.2d 677 (Fla. 1995).

38. *State v. Rice*, 757 P.2d 889 (Wash. 1988).

39. *Myers v. State*, 510 N.E.2d 1360 (Ind. 1987).

40. *Lambert v. State*, 888 P.2d 494 (Okl.Cr. 1994).

41. *State v. Hartz*, 828 P.2d 618 (Wash.App. 1992).

42. *Alford v. State*, 906 P.2d 714 (Nev. 1995).

43. *People v. Hickman*, 684 P.2d 228 (Colo. 1984).

44. *People v. Johnson*, 284 Cal.Rptr. 579 (1991).

45. *Alford v. State*, 906 P.2d 714 (Nev. 1995).

46. *Matter of St. Pierre*, 823 P.2d 492 (Wash. 1992).

47. *Richie v. State*, 908 P.2d 268 (Okl.Cr. 1995). In accord, *Allen v. State*, 874 P.2d 60 (Okl.Cr. 1994).

48. *State v. Wilson*, 731 P.2d 306 (Kan. 1987).

49. *Givens v. Housewright*, 786 F.3d 1378 (9th Cir. 1986).

50. *Morris v. State*, 603 P.2d 1157 (Okl.Cr. 1979).

51. *People v. Diaz*, 834 P.2d 1171 (Cal. 1992). See also, *People v. Maxwell*, 592 N.E.2d 960 (Ill. 1992).

52. *State v. King*, 634 P.2d 755 (Okl.Cr. 1981).

53. *Calderon v. Prunty*, 59 F.3d 1005 (9th Cir. 1995).
54. *Burris v. Farley*, 51 F.3d 655 (7th Cir. 1995).
55. *Averhart v. State*, 470 N.E.2d 666 (Ind. 1984). See also, *State v. Reese*, 687 S.W.2d 635 (Mo.App. 1985).
56. *Tapia v. Tansy*, 926 F.2d 1554 (10th Cir. 1991).
57. *Short v. State*, 634 P.2d 755 (Okl.Cr. 1981).
58. *Clemens v. State*, 610 N.E.2d 236 (Ind. 1993).
59. *State v. Garcia*, 763 P.2d 585 (Kan. 1988).
60. *State v. Lane*, 629 S.W.2d 343 (Mo. 1982).
61. *State v. Harley*, 543 S.W.2d 288 (Mo.App. 1976).

Chapter 8

1. Kansas, New Hampshire, South Carolina, Tennessee, Washington, and the Federal System.
2. For a discussion of pretrial notice of the death penalty see, Daniel S. Reinberg, "The Constitutionality of the Illinois Death Penalty Statute: The Right to Pretrial Notice of the State's Intention to Seek the Death Penalty," 85 Nw. U. L. Rev. 272 (1990).
3. For a discussion of this case see, Christopher M. Wilson, "Criminal Procedure — Death Penalty — A Convicted Criminal Must Be Adequately Notified That the Death Penalty May Be Imposed as a Sentence — Lankford v. Idaho," 22 Seton Hall L. Rev. 974 (1992).
4. California, Georgia, Kentucky, New Hampshire, Ohio, Oklahoma, Pennsylvania, Tennessee, and the Federal System.
5. For a discussion of California's approach to pretrial disclosure generally. see Michael Alden Miller, "The Reciprocal Pretrial Discovery Provisions of Proposition 115 Apply to Both Guilt Phase and Penalty Phase Evidence — Nevertheless the Courts May Exercise Discretion Under Appropriate Circumstances and Postpone Disclosure of the Defendant's Penalty Phase Evidence Until the Guilt Phase Has Concluded," 21 Pepp. L. Rev. 1016 (1994).
6. See *Cargle v. State*, 909 P.2d 806 (Okl.Cr. 1995); *Richie v. State*, 908 P.2d 268 (Okl.Cr. 1995).
7. Delaware, Indiana, and Nevada.

Chapter 9

1. *Givens v. State*, 749 S.W.2d 954 (Tex.App.–Fort Worth 1988). See *State v. Holmes*, 388 S0.2d 722 (La. 1980) (holding that to sustain a prosecution for murder of a nontriggerman it is necessary to show defendant actively desired the death of the victim or great bodily harm thereto); *Shelton v. State*, 699 S.W.2d 728 (Ark. 1985) (holding that it is not necessary that a defendant take an active part in a homicide to be prosecuted, if he or she accompanies another who actually commits the murder and assists in some manner).
2. *State v. McAllister*, 366 S0.2d 1340 (La. 1978). See also *Coxwell v. State*, 397 S0.2d 355 (Fla.App. 1981); *People v. Steele*, 563 P.3d 6 (Colo. 1977); *State v. Wilder*, 608 P.2d 270 (Wash.App. 1980); *Daugherty v. State*, 640 P.2d 558 (Okl.Cr. 1982).
3. *Bryant v. State*, 412 S0.2d 347 (Fla. 1982).
4. *Walsh v. State*, 658 S.W.2d 285 (Tex.App. 2 Dist. 1983).
5. *State v. Lindsey*, 543 S0.2d 886 (La. 1989).
6. *Spears v. State*, 900 P.2d 431 (Okl.Cr. 1995).
7. *State v. Smith*, 563 A.2d 671 (Conn. 1989).
8. *State v. DePriest*, 907 P.2d 868 (Kan. 1995). See also, *United States v. Wilson*, 665 F.2d 825 (8th Cir. 1981); *State v. Sonnier*, 402 S0.2d 650 (La. 1981); *State v. White*, 622 S.W.2d 939 (Mo. 1981); *Ned v. State*, 654 S.W.2d 732 (Tex.App. 14 Dist. 1983); *Spears v. State*, 900 P.2d 431 (Okl.Cr. 1995). But see *Strickler v. Commonwealth*,

404 S.E.2d 227 (Va. 1991) (holding that a defendant who is present and aids and abets actual killing, but does not perform the killing may not be prosecuted for capital murder).
9. *People v. Hammond*, 226 Cal.Rptr. 475 (1986).
10. *Lockett v. Ohio*, 438 U.S. 586 (1978).
11. *State v. Ryan*, 534 N.W.2d 766 (Neb. 1995).
12. *United States v. Van Scoy*, 654 F.2d 257 (3rd Cir. 1981).
13. *Apostoledes v. State*, 593 A.2d 1117 (Md. 1991).
14. *State v. Willis*, 420 S.E.2d 158 (N.C. 1992).
15. *Fratello v. State*, 496 S0.2d 903 (Fla.App. 4 Dist. 1986). See also, *Nelson v. State*, 528 N.E.2d 453 (Ind. 1988).
16. *Contreras v. State*, 745 S.W.2d 59 (Tex.App.–San Antonio 1987). See also, *State v. Davison*, 601 S.W.2d 623 (Mo. 1979).
17. *Berkeley v. Commonwealth*, 451 S.E.2d 41 (Va.App. 1994).
18. *People v. Esquivel*, 34 Cal.Rptr.2d 324 (1994).
19. *State v. Williamson*, 382 A.2d 588 (Md. 1978). But see *Cheng v. Commonwealth*, 393 S.E.2d 599 (Va. 1990) (holding that an accessory before the fact may not be prosecuted for capital murder).
20. *State v. Johnson*, 455 S.E.2d 644 (N.C. 1995). See also, *State v. Smith*, 447 S.E.2d 175 (S.C. 1993); *State v. Suites*, 427 S.E.2d 318 (N.C.App. 1993).
21. *State v. Malone*, 671 A.2d 1321 (Conn.App. 1996).
22. *State v. Marr*, 440 S.E.2d 275 (N.C.App. 1994).
23. *State v. Lattimore*, 456 S.E.2d 789 (N.C. 1995).
24. *United States v. Reavis*, 48 F.3d 763 (4th Cir. 1995). See also, *People v. Priest*, 672 P.2d 539 (Colo.App. 1983); *State v. Toomey*, 690 P.2d 1175 (Wash.App. 1984).
25. *State v. Furr*, 235 S.E.2d 193 (N.C. 1977).
26. *State v. Barnes*, 447 S.E.2d 478 (N.C.App. 1994).
27. *Butler v. State*, 643 A. 2d 389 (Md. 1994).
28. *Thomas v. State*, 847 S.W.2d 695 (Ark. 1993).
29. *People v. Gil*, 608 N.E.2d 197 (Ill.App. 1 Dist. 1992). But see, *Commonwealth v. Gaynor*, 612 A.2d 1010 (Pa.Super. 1992) (holding that specific intent to kill is required for both principal and accomplice); *Lawton v. State*, 913 S.W.2d 542 (Tex.Cr.App. 1995) (to hold a defendant liable for capital murder premised on accomplice liability, it must be shown that the defendant had the specific intent to promote or assist in the commission of murder).
30. *State v. Apodaca*, 887 P.2d 756 (N. M. 1994).
31. *State v. Dulany*, 781 S.W.2d 52 (Mo. 1989).
32. *Commonwealth v. Bachert*, 453 A.2d 931 (Pa. 1982).
33. *State v. Hunter*, 782 S.W.2d 95 (Mo.App. 1989).
34. See also *State v. DePriest*, 907 P.2d 868 (Kan. 1995) (holding that when a solicited person murders a victim, the solicitor may be prosecuted for murder). But see *Bowie v. State*, 816 P.2d 1143 (Okl. Cr. 1991) (holding that mere knowledge that defendant offered money to anyone who would kill victim would not make a person an accomplice to the actual murder).
35. *People v. Calvillo*, 524 N.E.2d 1054 (Ill.App. 1 Dist. 1988).
36. *People v. Rodriquez*, 627 N.E.2d 209 (Ill.App. 1 Dist. 1993).
37. *People v. Smith*, 368 N.E.2d 561 (Ill.App. 1977).
38. *People v. Chavez*, 592 N.E.2d 69 (Ill.App. 1 Dist. 1992).
39. *People v. Stanciel*, 589 N.E.2d 557 (Ill.App. 1 Dist. 1991).
40. *People v. McClain*, 645 N.E.2d 585 (Ill.App. 4 Dist. 1995).

41. *Richardson v. State*, 879 S.W.2d 874 (Tex.Cr.App. 1993).

42. *People v. Montes*, 549 N.E.2d 700 (Ill.App. 1 Dist. 1989).

43. *People v. Taylor*, 557 N.E.2d 917 (Ill.App. 4 Dist. 1990).

44. *Bryant v. State*, 412 S0.2d 347 (Fla. 1982).

45. *Andrews v. State*, 744 S.W.2d 40 (Tex.Cr.App. 1987).

46. *State v. Martin*, 308 S.E.2d 277 (N.C. 1983). See also, *People v. Luparelle*, 231 Cal.Rptr. 832 (1986).

47. *People v. Bustos*, 29 Cal.Rptr.2d 112 (1994).

48. *State v. Nguyen*, 833 P.2d 937 (Kan. 1992). See also *Sands v. State*, 418 S.E.2d 55 (Ga. 1992). However, in *Kuenzl v. State*, 577 S0.2d 474 (Ala.Cr.App. 1990), it was said that a capital felony-murder conviction will stand against a confederate only if the defendant was an accomplice in the intentional killing of the victim, not merely an accomplice to the underlying felony. Further, in *State v. Reese*, 353 S.E.2d 352 (N.C. 1987), it was said that in a felony-murder prosecution of a defendant, the premeditation and deliberation of a co-felon who actually inflicted a victim's fatal injury could not be imputed to the defendant by reason of his or her participation in the underlying felony. It was also determined in *Hite v. State*, 364 S0.2d 771 (Ala.App. 1978), that a defendant who is not present at the scene of a felony he or she participated in planning, which results in a victim being killed, may not be prosecuted for capital felony-murder.

49. *Rivers v. Commonwealth*, 464 S.E.2d 549 (Va.App. 1995).

50. But see *People v. Hoard*, 618 N.E.2d 808 (Ill.App. 1 Dist. 1993) (holding that pursuant to the common design rule, an accomplice may be held liable for murder without a showing of intent to kill).

51. *People v. Novy*, 597 N.E.2d 273 (Ill.App. 5 Dist. 1992).

52. *Commonwealth v. Chipman*, 635 N.E.2d 1204 (Mass. 1994).

53. *Commonwealth v. Young*, 621 N.E.2d 1180 (Mass. App. 1993).

54. *Richard v. Commonwealth*, 415 N.E.2d 201 (Mass. 1981).

55. *Commonwealth v. Gilliard*, 629 N.E.2d 349 (Mass. App. 1994).

56. *Commonwealth v. Cook*, 644 N.E.2d 203 (Mass. 1994). See also *Commonwealth v. White*, 663 N.E.2d 834 (Mass. 1996) (holding that under felony-murder joint venture theory, the prosecutor must show that the defendant was present at crime scene with knowledge that principal intended to commit a crime, and by agreement was willing and available to help the principal if necessary).

57. *Commonwealth v. Semedo*, 665 N.E.2d 638 (Mass. 1996). See also *Stewart v. Coalter*, 855 F.Supp. 464 (D.Mass. 1994) (holding that as an aider or abettor, a joint venturer to murder must intend that the victim be killed or know that there is a substantial likelihood of the victim being killed).

58. *Commonwealth v. Green*, 652 N.E.2d 572 (Mass. 1995).

59. *Commonwealth v. Nichypor*, 643 N.E.2d 452 (Mass. 1994). In *Commonwealth v. Claudio*, 634 N.E.2d 902 (Mass. 1994) it was said that a defendant will not escape liability for murder under the joint venture theory, where the defendant planned the murder with another, but did not actually kill the victim.

Chapter 10

1. See *Federal Republic of Germany v. United States*, 526 U.S. 111 (1999) (refusing to halt the execution of German national Walter LaGrand by the state of Arizona); *Republic of Paraguay v. Allen*, 134 F.3d 622 (4th Cir. 1998) (refusing Paraguay's efforts to have the death sentence of foreign national Angel Breard set aside).

2. See Sarah M. Ray, "Domesticating International Obligations: How to Ensure U.S. Compliance with the Vienna Convention on Consular Relations," 91 Cal. L. Rev. 1729 (2003).

3. As a general matter, federal and local officials have been extremely relaxed in notifying consular officers of the arrest of nationals, and of informing foreign nationals of their right to consult with consular officers. See *Darling v. State*, 808 S0.2d 145 (Fla. 2002) ("It is unclear that the Vienna Convention creates individual rights enforceable in judicial proceedings.... However, we need not reach that issue where, as here, Darling has failed to show that he was prejudiced by the claimed violation."); *United States v. Chanthadara*, 230 F.3d 1237 (10th Cir. 2000) ("Even presuming the Vienna Convention creates individually enforceable rights, Mr. Chanthadara has not demonstrated that denial of such rights caused him prejudice."); *Rocha v. State*, 16 S.W.3d 1 (Tex.Crim.App. 2000) (holding that no remedy exists for a violation of Vienna Convention); *Murphy v. Netherland*, 116 F.3d 97 (4th Cir. 1997) ("Murphy has also failed to establish prejudice from the alleged violation of the Vienna Convention because he is unable to explain how contacting the Mexican consulate would have changed either his guilty plea or his [death] sentence."); *Faulder v. Johnson*, 81 F.3d 515 (5th Cir. 1996) (no prejudice shown from failure to notify Canadian consulate).

4. However, "[t]he United States gave notice of its withdrawal from the Optional Protocol on March 7, 2005." *Sanchez-Llamas v. Oregon*, 548 U.S. 331 (2006).

5. See *Breard v. Greene*, 523 U.S. 371 (1998).

6. See Susan L. Karamanian, "Briefly Resuscitating the Great Writ: The International Court of Justice and the U.S. Death Penalty," 69 Alb. L. Rev. 745 (2006).

Chapter 11

1. *Jurek v. Texas*, 428 U.S. 262 (1976).

2. For a discussion along these lines, see Steven F. Shatz, "The Eighth Amendment, the Death Penalty, and Ordinary Robbery-Burglary Murderers: A California Case Study," 59 Fla. L. Rev. 719 (2007); Franklin E. Zimring and Gordon Hawkins, "A Punishment in Search of a Crime: Standards for Capital Punishment in the Law of Criminal Homicide," 46 Md. L. Rev. 115 (1986).

3. For a general discussion see, John W. Poulos, "The Lucas Court and Capital Punishment: The Original Understanding of the Special Circumstances," 30 Santa Clara L. Rev. 333 (1990).

4. Arizona, California, Colorado, Delaware, Florida, Georgia, Idaho, Indiana, Kentucky, Missouri, Montana, Nebraska, Nevada, North Carolina, Ohio, Oklahoma, Pennsylvania, South Carolina, South Dakota, Tennessee, Texas, Wyoming, and the Federal System.

5. Arizona, California, Colorado, Delaware, Florida, Missouri, Nebraska, Nevada, North Carolina, Oklahoma, Pennsylvania, South Dakota, Tennessee, Wyoming, and the Federal System.

6. Georgia, Idaho, Indiana, Kentucky, South Carolina, and Texas.

7. Montana.

8. Ohio.

9. *State v. Keel*, 423 S.E.2d 458 (N.C. 1992).

10. *People v. Oaks*, 662 N.E.2d 1328 (Ill. 1996).

11. *Epperly v. Booker*, 997 F.2d 1 (4th Cir. 1993).

12. *People v. Mitchell*, 183 Cal.Rptr. 166 (1982).

13. *Clay v. State*, 440 N.E.2d 466 (Ind. 1982).

14. *State v. Cook*, 509 N.W.2d 200 (Neb. 1993).

15. *State v. Dixon*, 655 S.W.2d 547 (Mo.App. 1983).

16. *People v. Phillips*, 711 P.2d 423 (Cal. 1985).

17. *Hernandez v. State*, 819 S.W.2d 806 (Tex.Cr.App. 1991).

18. *Hounshell v. State*, 486 A.2d 789 (Md.App. 1985).

19. *State v. Raines*, 606 A.2d 265 (Md. 1992).

20. *State v. Marks*, 537 N.W.2d 339 (Neb. 1995).

21. *State v. Gallden*, 340 S.E.2d 673 (N.C. 1986).

22. *State v. West*, 844 S.W.2d 144 (Tenn. 1992).

23. *People v. Van Ronk*, 217 Cal.Rptr. 581 (1985).

24. *People v. Cisneros*, 720 P.2d 982 (Colo.App. 1986).

25. *State v. Craig*, 642 S.W.2d 98 (Mo. 1982). See also, *State v. Prevette*, 345 S.E.2d 159 (N.C. 1986).

26. *State v. Abeyta*, 901 P.2d 164 (N.M. 1995).

27. *State v. Solomon*, 456 S.E.2d 778 (N.C. 1995).

28. *Hounshell v. State*, 486 A.2d 789 (Md. App. 1985). See *Holt v. State*, 365 N.E.2d 1209 (Ind. 1977) (holding that premeditation may occur instantaneously); in accord, *Cigainero v. State*, 838 S.W.2d 361 (Ark. 1992); *Boyd v. State*, 839 P.2d 1363 (Okl. Cr. 1992); *State v. Spears*, 908 P.2d 1062 (Ariz. 1996); *State v. Clark*, 913 S.W.2d 399 (Mo. App. 1996).

29. See also *State v. Bolder*, 635 S.W.2d 673 (Mo. 1982); *State v. Olin*, 648 P.2d 203 (Idaho 1982); *Johnson v. State*, 486 S0.2d 657 (Fla.App. 4 Dist. 1986); *State v. Hunter*, 664 P.2d 195 (Ariz. 1983). But see *State v. Brown*, 836 S.W.2d 530 (Tenn. 1992) (holding that premeditation by its very nature is not instantaneous and requires some time interval for formation — more than a split second is required to form a premeditated intent to kill).

30. In accord, *State v. Drinkwalter*, 493 N.W.2d 319 (Neb. 1992).

31. *Dino v. State*, 405 S0.2d 213 (Fla.App. 1981).

32. *Archie v. Commonwealth*, 420 S.E.2d 718 (Va.App. 1992).

33. *State v. Helmer*, 545 N.W.2d (S.D. 1996). See *State v. Pirtle*, 904 P.2d 245 (Wash. 1995) (holding that factors which are relevant in determining premeditation include motive, procurement of weapon, stealth and method of killing).

34. *Hardnett v. State*, 564 S.W.2d 852 (Mo. 1978). But see, *State v. Enno*, 807 P.2d 610 (Idaho 1991) (holding that there is no legal distinction between malice and malice aforethought).

35. *State v. Proctor*, 564 S.E.2d 544 (Mo.App. 1977).

36. *State v. Love*, 250 S.E.2d 220 (N.C. 1978).

37. *State v. Marshall*, 264 N.W.2d 911 (S.D. 1978). But see *Commonwealth v. Weinstein*, 451 A.2d 1344 (Pa. 1982) (holding that malice aforethought was a general prerequisite to finding murder-without-more, and that it distinguishes this offense from any other type of homicide and includes cruelty, recklessness of consequences and social duty).

38. *State v. Chaney*, 497 A.2d 152 (Md. 1985).

39. *People v. Evans*, 416 N.E.2d 377 (Ill.App. 1981).

40. *Keys v. State*, 766 P.2d 270 (Nev. 1988).

41. *People v. Brown*, 42 Cal.Rptr.2d 155 (1995). See also, *United States v. Sheffey*, 57 F.3d 1419 (6th Cir. 1995).

42. *State v. Lacquey*, 571 P.2d 1027 (Ariz. 1977). See also, *Tucker v. State*, 263 S.E.2d 109 (Ga. 1980).

43. *Rivers v. Commonwealth*, 464 S.E.2d 549 (Va.App. 1995).

44. *People v. Nieto-Benitez*, 840 P.2d 969 (Cal. 1992).

45. *State v. Irby*, 439 S.E.2d 226 (N.C. App. 1994).

46. *Commonwealth v. Seguin*, 656 N.E.2d 1229 (Mass. 1995).

47. *Dixon v. State*, 252 S.E.2d 431 (Ga. 1979).

48. *Wright v. State*, 335 S.E.2d 857 (Ga. 1985).

49. *State v. McBride*, 425 S.E.2d 731 (N.C.App. 1993).

50. *Commonwealth v. Johnson*, 663 N.E.2d 559 (Mass. 1996).

51. *State v. Pierce*, 414 N.E.2d 1038 (Ohio 1980).

52. *State v. Jenkins*, 355 N.E.2d 825 (Ohio App. 1976).

53. *State v. Richardson*, 658 N.E.2d 321 (Ohio App. 1 Dist. 1995).

54. Alabama, Arizona, Arkansas, California, Colorado, Delaware, Florida, Georgia, Idaho, Indiana, Kansas, Kentucky, Louisiana, Mississippi, Montana, Nebraska, Nevada, New Hampshire, North Carolina, Ohio, Oklahoma, South Dakota, Tennessee, Texas, Utah, Virginia, Washington, Wyoming, and the Federal System.

55. *Watkins v. Callahan*, 724 F.2d 1038 (1st Cir. 1984).

56. Alabama, Arkansas, California, Delaware, Idaho, Kansas, Louisiana, Mississippi, New Hampshire, Oregon, Texas, Utah, Virginia, Washington, and the Federal System.

57. See 18 U.S.C. § 1751.

58. See 18 U.S.C. § 351.

59. Alabama, Arkansas, California, Kansas, Louisiana, Mississippi, New Hampshire, Oklahoma, Oregon, Texas, Utah, Virginia, Washington, and the Federal System.

60. See Michael R. Pahl, "Wanted: Criminal Justice — Colombia's Adoption of a Prosecutorial System of Criminal Procedure," 16 Fordham Int. L. J. 608 (1993). John Gotti died while in prison on June 10, 2002.

61. See *United States v. Locasio*, 6 F.3d 924 (2nd Cir. 1993); Jason Sabot, "Expert Testimony on Organized Crime Under the Federal Rules of Evidence: United States v. Frank Locasio and John Gotti," 22 Hofstra L. Rev. 177 (1993).

62. For a discussion of drugs and athletes see Kerrie S. Covell and Annette Gibbs, "Drug Testing and the College Athlete," 23 Creighton L. Rev. 1 (1990).

63. See Michael D. Paley, "Prosecuting Failed Attempts to Fix Prices as Violations of the Mail and Wire Fraud Statutes: Elliot Ness Is Back," 78 Wash. U. L.Q. 333 (1995).

64. See Paul J. Arougheti, "Imposing Homicide Liability on Gun Battle Participants for the Deaths of Innocent Bystanders," 27 Colum. J. L. and Soc. Probs. 467 (1994).

65. Alabama, Arizona, Arkansas, California, Louisiana, Washington, and the Federal System.

66. Alabama, California, Delaware, Florida, Idaho, Mississippi, Nebraska, Nevada, North Carolina, Oregon, South Carolina, South Dakota, Tennessee, Utah, and the Federal System.

67. *Vincent v. State*, 418 S.E.2d 138 (Ga. 1992).

68. For further discussion see P.K. Menon, "The International Personality of Individuals in International Law: A Broadening of the Traditional Doctrine," 1 J. Transnat. L. and Pol. 151 (1992).

69. Alabama, California, Kansas, Louisiana, Oregon, Texas, Utah, Virginia, and Washington.

70. See U.S. Department of Justice, Federal Bureau of Investigation, Uniform Crime Reports, Homicide, Table 12 (2010).

71. For a discussion of death-eligible offenses for drug related murder see Peggy M. Tobolowsky, "Drugs and Death: Congress Authorizes the Death Penalty for Certain Drug-Related Murders," 18 J. Contemp. L. 47 (1992);

Sandra R. Acosta, "Imposing the Death Penalty Upon Drug Kingpins," 27 Harv. J. on Legis. 596 (1990).

72. Arizona, Arkansas, Florida, Indiana, Louisiana, New Hampshire, and Oklahoma.

73. See Cythia F. Zebrowitz, "Offenses Against Public Administration: Increase the Possible Sentences for Prison Escape," 11 Ga. St. U. L. Rev. 122 (1994); Padraic P. Lyndon, "Escape: A Deadly Proposition? Prisoners and Pretrial Detainees," 21 New Eng. J. on Crim. and Civ. Conf. 203 (1995).

74. Arizona, Arkansas, California, Colorado, Delaware, Florida, Idaho, Nevada, Ohio, Oklahoma, Oregon, Texas, and Utah.

75. California, Colorado, and Utah.

76. *State v. Crowder*, 123 S.E.2d 42 (W.Va. 1961). In some jurisdictions no distinction is made in the nature of the proceeding, i.e., felony or misdemeanor. Jurisdictions that require the false testimony to affect a felony utilize the offense of false swearing if the false testimony affects a misdemeanor.

77. *People v. Sesi*, 300 N.W. 2d 535 (Mich. 1981).

78. Colorado and Nebraska.

79. Alabama, Arkansas, California, Idaho, Kansas, Mississippi, New Hampshire, Oregon, Texas, Utah, Washington, and the Federal System.

80. See *State v. Hines*, 919 S.W.2d 573 (Tenn. 1996).

81. See *State v. Cook*, 913 P.2d 97 (Kan. 1996).

82. California, Idaho, Nevada, North Carolina, Oregon, Utah, and the Federal System.

83. California, Idaho, Nevada, North Carolina, and the Federal System.

84. Louisiana, Oklahoma, Texas, Utah, Virginia, and Wyoming.

Chapter 12

1. See James B. Thayer, "The Burden of Proof," 4 Harv. L. Rev. 45 (1890).

2. See Lawrence M. Solan, "Refocusing the Burden of Proof in Criminal Cases: Some Doubt About Resaonable Doubt," 78 Tex. L. Rev. 105 (2000).

3. See William F. Fox, Jr., "The Presumption of Innocence as Constitutional Doctrine," 28 Cath. U. L. Rev. 253 (1979).

4. See Elisabeth Stoffelmayr and Shari Seidman Diamond, "The Conflict Between Precision and Flexibility in Explaining 'Beyond a Reasonable Doubt,'" 6 Psych. Pub. Pol'y. L. 769 (2000).

5. See John Calvin Jeffries, Jr., and Paul B. Stephan III, "Defenses, Presumptions, and Burden of Proof in the Criminal Law," 88 Yale L.J. 1325 (1979).

6. See Stephen J. Schulhofer, "Is Plea Bargaining Inevitable?" 97 Harv. L. Rev. 1037 (1984).

7. In addition to the right against self-incrimination and the right to trial by jury, a capital offender also has a constitutional right to confront his or her accusers and the right to compulsory process for obtaining witnesses in his or her favor. See *Boykin v. Alabama*, 395 U.S. 238 (1969); *Brady v. United States*, 397 P.2d 742 (1970).

8. See Joseph L. Hoffman, Marcy L. Kahn, and Steven W. Fisher, "Plea Bargaining in the Shadow of Death," 69 Fordham L. Rev. 2313 (2001).

9. See Thomas C. Hayden, Jr., "The Plea of Nolo Contendere," 25 Md. L. Rev. 227 (1965).

10. Delaware, Florida, Idaho, Ohio, Oklahoma, and Oregon.

11. See Kevin C. McMunigal, "Disclosure and Accuracy in the Guilty Plea Process," 40 Hastings L. J. 957 (1989).

12. See Iiyana Kuziemko, "Does the Threat of the Death Penalty Affect Plea Bargaining in Murder Cases? Evidence from New York's 1995 Reinstatement of Capital Punishment," 8 Am. Law Econ. Rev. 116 (2006).

13. Alabama, Arizona, Arkansas, California, Colorado, Delaware, Florida, Georgia, Idaho, Indiana, Louisiana, Mississippi, Montana, Nebraska, Nevada, New Hampshire, North Carolina, Ohio, Oklahoma, Oregon, Pennsylvania, South Carolina, South Dakota, Utah, Washington, Wyoming, and the Federal System.

14. See Susan Ehrhard, "Plea Bargaining and the Death Penalty: An Exploratory Study," 29 Just. Sys. J. 313 (2008).

15. See Curtis J. Shipley, "The Alford Plea: A Necessary but Unpredictable Tool for the Criminal Defendant," 72 Iowa L. Rev. 1063 (1987).

16. A bench trial is deemed a privilege because there is no constitutional right to trial by the court. See *Singer v. United States*, 380 U.S. 24 (1965).

17. *Duncan v. Louisiana*, 391 U.S. 145 (1968). For a general discussion of a capital felon's right to trial by jury, see Welsh S. White, "Fact-Finding and the Death Penalty: The Scope of a Capital Defendant's Right to Jury Trial," 65 Notre Dame L. Rev. 1 (1989).

18. See Welsh S. White, "Fact-Finding and the Death Penalty: The Scope of a Capital Defendant's Right to Jury Trial," 65 Notre Dame L. Rev. 1 (1990).

19. See Jere W. Morehead, "When a Peremptory Challenge Is No Longer Peremptory: Batson's Unfortunate Failure to Eradicate Invidious Discrimination from Jury Selection," 43 DePaul L. Rev. 625 (1994).

20. For a general discussion of death-qualified juries, see Barbara J. Whisler, "Sixth Amendment — Death Qualification of the Jury: Process Is Permissible Where Defendant Does Not Face Death Penalty," 78 J. Crim. L. and Criminology 954 (1988); John A. Wasleff, "Lockhart v. McCree: Death Qualification as a Determinant of the Impartiality and Representativeness of a Jury in Death Penalty Cases," 72 Cornell L. Rev. 1075 (1987); William S. Geimer and Jonathan Amsterdam, "Why Jurors Vote Life or Death: Operative Factors in Ten Florida Death Penalty Cases," 15 Am. J. Crim. L. 1 (1988); Patrick J. Callans, "Sixth Amendment — Assembling a Jury Willing to Impose the Death Penalty: A New Disregard for a Capital Defendant's Rights," 76 J. Crim. L. and Criminology 1027 (1985); Jaye Mendros, "Criminal Procedure: Morgan v. Illinois Takes a Step Toward Eliminating Hanging Juries in Capital Cases," 46 Okla. L. Rev. 729 (1993).

21. For a discussion of capital juries see, Patrick E. Higginbotham, "Juries and the Death Penalty," 41 Case W. Res. L. Rev. 1047 (1991).

22. See *United States v. Walker*, 910 F.Supp. 837 (N.D.N.Y. 1995) (holding that a capital felon is not entitled to have a nondeath-qualified jury for the guilt phase and a separate death-qualified jury for the penalty phase).

23. See Samuel R. Gross, "Determining the Neutrality of Death-Qualified Juries," 8 L. Hum. Behav. 7 (1984).

24. See Jane Byrne, "Lockhart v. McCree: Conviction-Proneness and the Constitutionality of Death-Qualified Juries," 36 Cath. U. L. Rev. 287 (1986).

25. See William J. Bowers, Benjamin D. Steiner, and Marla Sandys, "Death Sentencing in Black and White: An Empirical Analysis of the Role of Jurors' Race and Jury Racial Composition," 3 U. Pa. Const. L. 171 (2001).

26. See Theodore Eisenberg and Martin T. Wells, "Deadly Confusion: Juror Instructions in Capital Cases," 79 Cornell L. Rev. 1 (1994).

27. See Richard L. Wiener, Christine C. Pritchard, and Minda Weston, "Comprehensibility of Approved Jury

Instructions in Capital Murder Cases," 80 J. Appl. Psych. 455 (1995).

28. See Peter Arenella, "Reflections on Current Proposals to Abolish or Reform the Insanity Defense," 8 Am. J.L. and Med. 271 (1983).

29. See Bradley D. McGraw, Daina Farthing-Capowich, and Ingo Keilitz, "The Guilty but Mentally Ill Plea and Verdict: Current State of the Knowledge," 30 Vill. L. Rev. 117 (1985).

30. See Anne S. Emanuel, "Guilty but Mentally Ill Verdicts and the Death Penalty: An Eighth Amendment Analysis," 68 N.C. L. Rev. 37 (1990).

31. See Masha Bach, "The Not Guilty by Reason of Insanity Verdict: Should Juries Be Informed of Its Consequences," 16 Whittier L. Rev. 645 (1995).

32. See Joseph D. Tydings, "A Federal Verdict of Not Guilty by Reason of Insanity and a Subsequent Commitment Procedure," 27 Md. L. Rev. 131 (1967).

Chapter 13

1. It will be noted that about five months prior to the *Furman* decision, the court in *People v. Anderson*, 493 P.2d 880 (Cal. 1972) held that the death penalty violated the constitution of the state of California.

2. For a discussion of issues involved with carrying out the death penalty, see Stephen R. Mcallister, "The Problem of Implementing a Constitutional System of Capital Punishment," 43 U. Kan. L. Rev. 1039 (1995).

3. For discussion of leniency in capital sentencing, see Paul Whitlock Cobb, Jr., "Reviving Mercy in the Structure of Capital Punishment," 99 Yale L.J. 389 (1989).

4. Justices who voted in favor of the *Furman* decision were Justice Douglas, Justice Brennan, Justice Stewart, Justice White, and Justice Marshall. The dissenting justices were Chief Justice Burger, Justice Blackmun, Justice Powell, and Justice Rehnquist.

5. For a discussion of non-judicial views on the death penalty, see William J. Bowers, Margaret Vandiver and Patricia H. Dugan, "A New Look at Public Opinion on Capital Punishment: What Citizens and Legislators Prefer," 22 Am. J. Crim. L. 77 (1994). See also Samuel Cameron, "The Demand for Capital Punishment," 13 Int'l Rev. L. and Econ. 47 (1993).

6. Georgia's penalty phase scheme was patterned along the lines of a proposal created by the American Bar Association.

7. For a discussion of the period between the guilt phase and penalty phase, see Robin E. Abrams, "A Capital Defendant's Right to a Continuance Between the Two Phases of a Death Penalty Trial," 64 N.Y.U. L. Rev. 579 (1989).

8. A few jurisdictions permit the capital felon to give the opening statement first.

9. A few jurisdictions permit the capital felon to present his or her case-in-chief first.

10. *People v. Avena*, 916 P.2d 1000 (Cal. 1996). The defendant's case-in-chief encompasses rebuttal evidence. In the event that the prosecutor brings out a matter during its rebuttal that was not addressed during the defendant's case-in-chief, the trial court has discretion to allow surrebuttal by the defendant.

11. *State v. Sepulvado*, 672 S0.2d 158 (La. 1996).

12. See *Commonwealth v. Wharton*, 665 A.2d 458 (Pa. 1995).

13. New Hampshire, North Carolina, Pennsylvania, and South Carolina.

14. For further discussion of penalty phase juries, see

Marla Sandys, "Cross-Overs — Capital Jurors Who Change Their Minds About the Punishment: A Litmus Test for Sentencing Guidelines," 70 Ind. L.J. 1183 (1995); Christopher Slobogin, "Should Juries and the Death Penalty Mix? A Prediction About the Supreme Court's Answer," 70 Ind. L.J. 1249 (1995).

15. Alabama, Arkansas, California, Colorado, Delaware, Florida, Georgia, Indiana, Kansas, Kentucky, Louisiana, Mississippi, Missouri, Nevada, New Hampshire, North Carolina, Ohio, Oklahoma, Oregon, Pennsylvania, South Carolina, South Dakota, Tennessee, Texas, Utah, Virginia, Washington, Wyoming, and the Federal System.

16. See *State v. Weaver*, 912 S.W.2d 499 (Mo. 1995).

17. Arkansas, California, Colorado, Delaware, Georgia, Indiana, Kansas, Kentucky, Louisiana, Mississippi, Missouri, Nevada, New Hampshire, North Carolina, Ohio, Oklahoma, Oregon, Pennsylvania, South Carolina, South Dakota, Tennessee, Texas, Utah, Virginia, Washington, Wyoming, and the Federal System.

18. Arkansas, California, Colorado, Delaware, Florida, Georgia, Illinois, Kansas, Kentucky, Louisiana, Mississippi, Missouri, New Hampshire, North Carolina, Ohio, Oklahoma, Oregon, Pennsylvania, South Carolina, South Dakota, Tennessee, Texas, Utah, Virginia, Washington, Wyoming, and the Federal System.

19. William J. Bowers, Ph.D., is principal investigator for the CJP. He is principal research scientist in the School of Criminal Justice, University at Albany. See William J. Bowers, "The Capital Jury Project: Rationale, Design, and Preview of Early Findings," 70 Indiana L. J. 1043 (1995). See also, The Capital Jury Project, http://www.albany.edu/scj/13192.php.

20. See William J. Bowers, Wanda D. Foglia, Susan Ehrhard-Dietzel, and Christopher E. Kelly, "Jurors' Failure to Understand or Comport with Constitutional Standards in Capital Sentencing: Strength of the Evidence," 46 Crim. L. Bull. Art. 2 (2010).

21. For a general discussion of a capital felon's right to have effective assistance of counsel, see Ronald J. Tabak, "Report: Ineffective Assistance of Counsel and Lack of Due Process in Death Penalty Cases," 22 Hum. Rts. 36 (Wtr. 1995); Gary Goodpaster, "The Trial for Life: Effective Assistance of Counsel in Death Penalty Cases," 58 N.Y.U. L. Rev. 299 (1983).

22. This discretionary authority is exercised in the first instance during the guilt phase and continues through the penalty phase.

23. See *Bell v. Watkins*, 692 F.2d 999 (5th Cir. 1982); *Riley v. Snyder*, 840 F.Supp. 1012 (D.Del. 1993): *State v. Burke*, 463 S.E.2d 212 (N.C. 1995); *People v. Padilla*, 906 P.2d 388 (Cal. 1995).

24. *People v. Simms*, 659 N.E.2d 922 (Ill. 1995).

25. For a general discussion, see Robert Alan Kelly, "Applicability of the Rules of Evidence to the Capital Sentencing Proceeding: Theoretical and Practical Support for Open Admissibility of Mitigating Evidence," 60 UMKC L. Rev. 411 (1992).

26. California, Colorado, Delaware, Georgia, Idaho, Indiana, Kentucky, Montana, Nebraska, New Hampshire, North Carolina, Ohio, Pennsylvania, South Dakota, Utah, Washington, Wyoming, and the Federal System.

27. Arizona, Arkansas, and Virginia.

28. Louisiana and Missouri.

29. Alabama, Florida, Kansas, Mississippi, Nevada, Oklahoma, Oregon, South Carolina, Tennessee, and Texas.

30. But see, *Commonwealth v. Wharton*, 665 A.2d 458 (Pa. 1995) (holding that photograph of victims before they were murdered was admissible).

31. See *People v. Simms*, 659 N.E.2d 922 (Ill. 1995) (holding that hearsay evidence of other crimes by defendant is admissible if it is relevant and reliable — even if the crime was never prosecuted).

32. See *State v. McLaughlin*, 462 S.E.2d 1 (N.C. 1995) (holding that tape recorded testimony of co-defendant given at guilt phase was properly admitted during defendant's penalty phase hearing).

Chapter 14

1. It will be noted that Congress has delegated authority to the president to create aggravating circumstances for military death penalty offenses. See *Loving v. United States*, 116 S.Ct. 1737 (1996) (where the Supreme Court approved of delegation of such authority to the president). For a general discussion see, Annamary Sullivan, "The President's Power to Promulgate Death Penalty Standards," 125 Mil. L. Rev. 143 (1989).

2. For a discussion of *Tuilaepa's* impact, see David Hesseltine, "The Evolution of the Capital Punishment Jurisprudence of the United States Supreme Court and the Impact of Tuilaepa v. California on That Evolution," 32 San Diego L. Rev. 593 (1995).

3. For a discussion in this area, see Kathleen D. Weron, "Rethinking Utah's Death Penalty Statute: A Constitutional Requirement for the Substantive Narrowing of Aggravating Circumstances," 1994 Utah L. Rev. 1107 (1994).

4. For a discussion in this area, see Kenneth S. Gallant, "Ex Post Facto Judicial Clarification of a Vague Aggravating Circumstance in a Capital Punishment Statute," 59 UMKC L. Rev. 125 (1990).

5. California, Louisiana, and Virginia.

6. Oregon, Texas, Utah, and Washington.

7. Alabama, California, Colorado, Delaware, Florida, Idaho, Indiana, Kentucky, Louisiana, Mississippi, Missouri, Montana, Nevada, North Carolina, Ohio, Pennsylvania (its statute provides that all felony offenses are statutory aggravators), South Carolina, Tennessee, Texas, Utah, Virginia, Washington, and Wyoming.

8. Alabama, California, Colorado, Delaware, Florida, Idaho, Indiana, Kentucky, Louisiana, Mississippi, Missouri, Nevada, North Carolina, Ohio, Pennsylvania (its statute provides that all felony offenses are statutory aggravators), South Carolina, Tennessee, Texas, Utah, Virginia, Washington, and Wyoming.

9. Alabama, California, Colorado, Delaware, Florida, Georgia, Idaho, Indiana, Kentucky, Louisiana, Mississippi, Montana, Nevada, North Carolina, Ohio, Pennsylvania (its statute provides that all felony offenses are statutory aggravators), South Carolina, Tennessee, Texas, Utah, Washington, and Wyoming.

10. Alabama, California, Colorado, Delaware, Florida, Georgia, Idaho, Indiana, Louisiana, Mississippi, Missouri, Montana, Nevada, North Carolina, Ohio, Pennsylvania (its statute provides that all felony offenses are statutory aggravators), South Carolina, Tennessee, Texas, Utah, Virginia, Washington, Wyoming, and the Federal System.

11. California, Colorado, Delaware, Florida, Georgia, Idaho, Indiana, Kentucky, Louisiana, Mississippi, Nevada, North Carolina, Ohio, Pennsylvania (its statute provides that all felony offenses are statutory aggravators), Tennessee, Texas, Utah, Washington, and Wyoming.

12. Alabama, Arkansas, California, Colorado, Delaware, Florida, Georgia, Louisiana, Mississippi, Montana, Nevada, New Hampshire, North Carolina, Oklahoma, Oregon, Pennsylvania (its statute provides that all felony offenses are statutory aggravators), South Dakota, Tennessee, Texas, Utah, Washington, and Wyoming.

13. California and the Federal System.

14. California and Indiana.

15. Florida, Mississippi, Missouri, North Carolina, Pennsylvania, Tennessee, Utah, Wyoming, and the Federal System.

16. Missouri and Utah.

17. Georgia and Virginia.

18. Missouri.

19. Missouri.

20. Florida, Indiana, Louisiana, Pennsylvania, South Carolina, South Dakota, Virginia, and the Federal System.

21. Delaware, Georgia, Indiana, Kentucky, Louisiana, Missouri, Nebraska, Nevada, North Carolina, Ohio, Oklahoma, Oregon, South Carolina, South Dakota, Tennessee, Texas, Utah, Washington, and the Federal System.

22. Arizona, California, Colorado, Delaware, Florida, Georgia, Idaho, Indiana, Kentucky, Louisiana, Missouri, Montana, Nebraska, Nevada, North Carolina, Ohio, Oklahoma, Oregon, Pennsylvania, South Carolina, South Dakota, Tennessee, Texas, Utah, Virginia, Washington, Wyoming, and the Federal System.

23. California, Colorado, Delaware, Georgia, Indiana, Louisiana, Missouri, Nevada, North Carolina, Pennsylvania, South Carolina, South Dakota, Tennessee, Texas, Utah, and Washington.

24. Arizona, California, Colorado, Delaware, Idaho, Indiana, Kansas, Louisiana, Missouri, North Carolina, Ohio, Oregon, Pennsylvania, South Carolina, Utah, Washington, and Wyoming.

25. California, Delaware, Georgia, Idaho, Louisiana, Missouri, North Carolina, Pennsylvania, South Carolina, South Dakota, Tennessee, Utah, Washington, and Wyoming.

26. California, Colorado, Delaware, Georgia, Idaho, Indiana, Louisiana, Missouri, North Carolina, Oregon, Pennsylvania, South Carolina, South Dakota, Tennessee, Utah, Washington, Wyoming, and the Federal System.

27. A few jurisdictions use the terms "old age" and "youth" without any specific age. Those jurisdictions have not been represented in Table 14.4.

28. Texas.

29. Colorado, Florida, Indiana, Louisiana, Pennsylvania, South Carolina, and Tennessee.

30. Arizona and Delaware.

31. Wyoming.

32. Delaware.

33. Louisiana.

34. Wyoming.

35. Arizona.

36. Indiana, Louisiana, Oregon, Utah, and Washington.

37. Colorado, Delaware, Indiana, Pennsylvania, and Virginia.

38. California, North Carolina, Oregon, Washington, and Wyoming.

39. Arizona, Delaware and Pennsylvania.

40. California, Colorado, Florida, Kentucky, Missouri, Ohio, Pennsylvania, Tennessee, Utah, and the Federal System.

41. The victim of this incident was named Leon Klinghoffer. The family of Mr. Klinghoffer eventually brought a civil suit against those allegedly responsible for his death. See *Klinghoffer v. S.N.C. Achille Lauro*, 739 F.Supp. 854 (S.D.N.Y.), aff'd, 921 F.2d 21 (2d Cir. 1990). For a discussion of the murder see, Gerald P. McGinley, "The

Achille Lauro Affair — Implications for International Law," 52 Tenn. L. Rev. 691 (1985); George R. Constantinople, "Towards a New Definition of Piracy: The Achille Lauro Incident," 26 Va. J Int'l. L. 723 (1986); Gregory V. Gooding, "Fighting Terrorism in the 1980s: The Interception of the Achille Lauro Hijackers," 21 Yale J. Int'l. L. 158 (1987).

42. Arkansas, Delaware, New Hampshire, Tennessee, Wyoming, and the Federal System.

43. California, Colorado, Delaware, and Nevada.

44. *Zant v. Stephens*, 462 U.S. 862 (1983).

45. Alabama, Arizona, Arkansas, California, Colorado, Florida, Idaho, Kansas, Louisiana, Mississippi, Nebraska, New Hampshire, North Carolina, Oklahoma, Tennessee, Utah, Wyoming, and the Federal System.

46. Alabama, Colorado, Delaware, Idaho, Kentucky, Louisiana, Nebraska, Nevada, North Carolina, Oregon, South Carolina, Tennessee, Utah, Virginia, Washington, and the Federal System.

47. Alabama, Arizona, Colorado, Florida, Georgia, Idaho, Kansas, Kentucky, Louisiana, Mississippi, Missouri, Nebraska, Nevada, New Hampshire, North Carolina, Oklahoma, Pennsylvania, South Carolina, South Dakota, Tennessee, Utah, Wyoming, and the Federal System.

48. Alabama, Arizona, Arkansas, Colorado, Delaware, Florida, Indiana, Kansas, Kentucky, Louisiana, Mississippi, Montana, Nevada, North Carolina, Ohio, Oklahoma, Oregon, South Dakota, Tennessee, Utah, Virginia, Washington, and Wyoming.

49. Alabama, Arizona, Arkansas, California, Colorado, Delaware, Florida, Georgia, Idaho, Indiana, Kansas, Kentucky, Louisiana, Mississippi, Missouri, Nebraska, Nevada, New Hampshire, North Carolina, Ohio, Oklahoma, Oregon, Pennsylvania, South Carolina, South Dakota, Tennessee, Utah, Wyoming, and the Federal System.

50. Arkansas, California, Colorado, Florida, Indiana, Mississippi, North Carolina, Oregon, Tennessee, Utah, Wyoming, and the Federal System.

51. California, Georgia, Indiana, Missouri, Montana, Nevada, Oregon, Pennsylvania, South Carolina, South Dakota, Tennessee, Utah, and Virginia.

52. Alabama, Arkansas, Florida, Mississippi, Nebraska, North Carolina, and Utah.

53. This distinction has been blurred somewhat because of the sentencing trend involving "split-sentencing." Under split-sentencing a defendant is actually incarcerated for a brief period, usually not longer than six months, and released to probation after serving the confinement.

54. Arizona, Florida, Indiana and Wyoming.

55. Arizona, Indiana, Washington, and Wyoming.

56. Arizona, Arkansas, and Washington.

57. California, Indiana, Louisiana, and Washington.

58. Arizona, Delaware, Florida, Georgia, Kansas, Missouri, South Carolina, South Dakota, and Virginia.

59. California, Colorado, Indiana, and Montana.

Chapter 15

1. For a general discussion see, Gary Joseph Vyneman, "Irreconcilable Differences: The Role of Mitigating Circumstances in Capital Punishment Sentencing Schemes," 13 Whittier L. Rev. 763 (1992); Mark Andrew Stafford, "State v. Barts: North Carolina Relaxes Foundation Requirements for Mitigating Evidence in Capital Sentencing Hearings," 66 N.C. L. Rev. 1221 (1988).

2. A defendant is not precluded from presenting aggravating circumstance evidence. However, in most instances defendants do not present such evidence. There are rare occasions when a defendant wants to be executed. It is during such rare occasions that aggravating circumstance evidence may be presented by a defendant.

3. For a discussion of *Lockett* and its meaning, see Louis D. Bilionis, "Moral Appropriateness, Capital Punishment, and the Lockett Doctrine," 82 J. Crim. L. and Criminology 283 (1991).

4. See *Martin v. Wainwright*, 770 F.2d 918 (11th Cir. 1985), modified en banc on other grounds, 781 F.2d 185 (11th Cir. 1985) (upholding exclusion of testimony on the deterrent effect of capital punishment on mentally ill defendants).

5. For a discussion see Christopher Grafflin Browning, Jr., "State v. Huffstetler: Denying Mitigating Instructions in Capital Cases on Grounds of Relevancy," 63 N.C. L. Rev. 1122 (1985).

6. For further discussion see David W. Doyle, "Life or Death in Florida: What Mitigating Evidence Will the Judge Consider in Capital Cases?" 4 Cooley L. Rev. 693 (1987); Joshua N. Sondheimer, "A Continuing Source of Aggravation: The Improper Consideration of Mitigating Factors in Death Penalty Sentencing," 41 Hastings L.J. 409 (1990).

7. For further discussion of *Delo* see Wm. Scott Sims, "Eighth and Fourteenth Amendment Capital Sentencing Jurisprudence — Jury Instruction Regarding a Mitigating Factor Upon Which a Criminal Defendant Has Presented No Evidence — Delo v. Lashley," 61 Tenn. L. Rev. 1029 (1994).

8. The mitigating circumstance evidence in *Penry*, which had a two-edged sword effect, was the evidence involving the defendant's mental problem. This evidence had the potential of diminishing the defendant's responsibility for his crime, but it also had the potential for being interpreted as revealing his future dangerousness, which was a special statutory issue.

9. See Ellen Fels Berkman, "Mental Illness as an Aggravating Circumstance in Capital Sentencing," 89 Colum. L. Rev. 291 (1989).

10. For a discussion of the impact of *Penry*, see Peggy M. Tobolowsky, "What Hath Penry Wrought? Mitigating Circumstances and the Texas Death Penalty," 19 Am. J. Crim. L. 345 (1992).

11. Capital punishment jurisdictions without statutory mitigating circumstances are Delaware, Georgia, Idaho, Oklahoma, South Dakota, and Texas.

12. Alabama, Arkansas, California, Colorado, Florida, Indiana, Kansas, Kentucky, Louisiana, Mississippi, Missouri, Montana, Nebraska, Nevada, New Hampshire, North Carolina, Ohio, Oregon, Pennsylvania, South Carolina, Tennessee, Utah, Virginia, Washington, Wyoming, and the Federal System.

13. For a discussion of the use of a prior criminal record at the penalty phase, see Max J. Burbach, "Prior Criminal Activity and Death Sentencing: State v. Reeves," 24 Creighton L. Rev. 547 (1991).

14. Alabama, Arkansas, California, Florida, Indiana, Kansas, Kentucky, Louisiana, Mississippi, Missouri, Montana, Nebraska, Nevada, New Hampshire, North Carolina, Oregon, Pennsylvania, South Carolina, Tennessee, Utah, Virginia, Washington, Wyoming, and the Federal System.

15. A few jurisdictions specifically provide that the mental or emotional disturbance cannot rise to the level of a defense to prosecution.

16. Alabama, California, Florida, Indiana, Kansas, Kentucky, Mississippi, Missouri, Montana, Nebraska, Nevada, New Hampshire, North Carolina, Ohio, Penn-

sylvania, South Carolina, Tennessee, Virginia, Washington, Wyoming, and the Federal System.

17. Alabama, Arizona, Arkansas, California, Colorado, Florida, Indiana, Kansas, Kentucky, Louisiana, Mississippi, Missouri, Montana, Nebraska, Nevada, New Hampshire, North Carolina, Ohio, Pennsylvania, South Carolina, Tennessee, Utah, Washington, Wyoming, and the Federal System.

18. Alabama, Arizona, Arkansas, California, Colorado, Florida, Indiana, Kansas, Kentucky, Louisiana, Mississippi, Missouri, Montana, Nebraska, Nevada, New Hampshire, North Carolina, Ohio, Pennsylvania, South Carolina, Tennessee, Utah, Washington, Wyoming, and the Federal System.

19. Alabama, Arizona, Arkansas, California, Colorado, Florida, Indiana, Kansas, Kentucky, Louisiana, Mississippi, Missouri, Montana, Nebraska, New Hampshire, North Carolina, Ohio, Pennsylvania, South Carolina, Tennessee, Utah, Virginia, Washington, Wyoming, and the Federal System.

20. Alabama, Arizona, Arkansas, California, Colorado, Florida, Indiana, Kansas, Kentucky, Louisiana, Mississippi, Missouri, Montana, Nebraska, Nevada, New Hampshire, North Carolina, Ohio, Oregon, Pennsylvania, South Carolina, Tennessee, Utah, Virginia, Washington, and Wyoming.

21. Indiana, Montana, and South Carolina.

22. It was alluded to in *State v. Ramseur*, 524 A.2d 188 (N.J. 1987), that age should be a mitigating circumstance only when the capital felon is relatively young or relatively old.

23. Arizona and Colorado.

24. California, Colorado, Kentucky, Louisiana, and Tennessee.

25. Colorado and North Carolina.

26. *State v. Compton*, 726 P.2d 837 (N.M. 1986). See also, *State v. Guzman*, 676 P.2d 1321 (N.M. 1984).

27. Colorado, Kansas, and Washington.

28. For a discussion of this statutory mitigating circumstance, see Debra D. Burke and Mary Anne Nixon, "Post-Traumatic Stress Disorder and the Death Penalty," 38 How. L.J. 183 (1994).

29. Kansas.

30. New Hampshire and the Federal System.

Chapter 16

1. Some special circumstances are duplicated as statutory aggravating circumstances. When this duplication occurs the statutory aggravating circumstance is actually proven to exist at the guilt phase as a special circumstance. The Supreme Court held in *Lowenfield v. Phelps*, 484 U.S. 231 (1988), that the constitution does not require proving the existence of a statutory aggravating circumstance at the penalty phase, when its existence has been proven at the guilt phase as a special circumstance. See also, *Jurek v. Texas*, 428 U.S. 262 (1976).

2. Alabama, Arizona, Arkansas, Colorado, Delaware, Florida, Georgia, Idaho, Indiana, Kansas, Kentucky, Louisiana, Mississippi, Missouri, Montana, Nebraska, Nevada, New Hampshire, North Carolina, Ohio, Oklahoma, Pennsylvania, South Carolina, South Dakota, Tennessee, Wyoming, and the Federal System.

3. See *Mills v. Maryland*, 486 U.S. 367 (1988), and *McKoy v. North Carolina*, 494 U.S. 433 (1990).

4. In both *Mills* and *McKoy* death penalty statutes required penalty phase juries to unanimously agree that a proffered mitigating circumstance was shown to exist.

5. See Miranda B. Strassmann, "Mills v. Maryland: The Supreme Court Guarantees the Consideration of Mitigating Circumstances Pursuant to Lockett v. Ohio," 38 Cath. U. L. Rev. 907 (1989).

6. However, there is precedent by the Supreme Court which holds that a defendant may be required to prove insanity beyond a reasonable doubt. See *Leland v. Oregon*, 343 U.S. 790 (1952). In *Leland* the Supreme Court approved of Oregon's requirement that defendants prove the affirmative defense of insanity beyond a reasonable doubt. The *Leland* precedent does not sit well for capital felons in an era of "get tough on crime." At present, however, no capital punishment jurisdiction requires capital felons prove the existence of mitigating circumstances beyond a reasonable doubt. As precedent, *Leland* would permit such a standard.

7. Arizona, Florida, New Hampshire, Pennsylvania, Wyoming, and the Federal System. At least four jurisdictions provide the same standard of proof based upon judicial decisions: Delaware, Indiana, North Carolina, and Ohio.

8. Arkansas, California, Georgia, Idaho, Kansas, Kentucky, Louisiana, Mississippi, Missouri, Montana, Nebraska, Nevada, Oklahoma, Oregon, South Carolina, South Dakota, Tennessee, Texas, Utah, Virginia, Washington, Wyoming, and the Federal System.

9. Colorado.

10. For a critique of the weighing process, see Marcia A. Widder, "Hanging Life in the Balance: The Supreme Court and the Metaphor of Weighing in the Penalty Phase of the Capital Trial," 68 Tul. L. Rev. 1341 (1994).

11. For a discussion of *Harris* and its implications, see Abe Muallem, "Harris v. Alabama: Is the Death Penalty in America Entering a Fourth Phase?" 22 J. Legis. 85 (1996).

12. Alabama, California, Indiana, Louisiana, Montana, Nebraska, New Hampshire, Pennsylvania, and the Federal System.

13. Arizona, Colorado, Florida, Idaho, Kansas, Kentucky, Mississippi, Nevada, North Carolina, and Oklahoma.

14. Delaware.

15. Arkansas, Ohio, Tennessee, and Utah.

16. For further discussion of the distinction between weighing and non-weighing, see Srikanth Srinivasan, "Capital Sentencing Doctrine and the Weighing-Non-weighing Distinction," 47 Stan. L. Rev. 1347 (1995).

17. Georgia, Montana, Oregon, South Carolina, South Dakota, Virginia, Washington, and Wyoming.

18. There was a third non-weighing process used by the state of Connecticut. That process is no longer used because that state abolished the death penalty in 2012.

19. Georgia, Missouri, Oregon, South Carolina, South Dakota, Virginia, and Wyoming.

20. Washington.

21. A weighing or sufficiency determination that is favorable to the defendant means that the death penalty will not be imposed.

22. Alabama, Arizona, California, Delaware, Idaho, Indiana, Kansas, Ohio, Oklahoma, Pennsylvania, Tennessee, Texas, and Wyoming.

23. Oregon and Washington.

24. Colorado, Florida, Kentucky, Louisiana, Mississippi, Missouri, Montana, Nebraska, Nevada, New Hampshire, North Carolina, and the Federal System.

25. Arkansas and Utah.

26. Georgia, South Carolina, South Dakota, and Virginia.

Chapter 17

1. For a general discussion in this area see, Joseph M. Giarratano, "To the Best of Our Knowledge We Have Never Been Wrong: Fallibility vs. Finality in Capital Punishment," 100 Yale L.J. 1005 (1991).

2. For a discussion of "harmless" error analysis in death penalty cases, see C. Elliot Kessler, "Death and Harmlessness: Application of the Harmless Error Rule by the Bird and Lucas Courts in Death Penalty Cases — A Comparison and Critique," 26 U.S.F. L. Rev. 41 (1991); Linda E. Carter, "Harmless Error in the Penalty Phase of a Capital Case: A Doctrine Misunderstood and Misapplied," 28 Ga. L. Rev. 125 (1993).

3. See also, *Franz v. State,* 754 S.W.2d 839 (Ark. 1988).

4. For a general discussion of appellate review see, Ira P. Robbins, "Toward a More Just and Effective System of Review in State Death Penalty Cases," 40 Am. U. L. Rev. 1 (1990).

5. Utah requires a defendant initiate an appeal.

6. For a discussion of the waiver issue, see Tim Kaine, "Capital Punishment and the Waiver of Sentence Review," 18 Harv. C.R.C.L. L. Rev. 483 (1983).

7. Georgia, Idaho, Missouri, Nevada, Oklahoma, South Carolina, South Dakota, Virginia, Washington, and the Federal System.

8. California, Florida, Indiana, Oregon, and Texas.

9. Alabama, Arizona, Arkansas, Kansas, Montana, Washington, and Wyoming.

10. Alabama, Arizona, Colorado, Delaware, Georgia, Idaho, Kansas, Kentucky, Louisiana, Mississippi, Missouri, Montana, Nevada, New Hampshire, North Carolina, Oklahoma, Pennsylvania, South Carolina, South Dakota, Tennessee, Virginia, Washington, Wyoming, and the Federal System.

11. Additionally, in *People v. McLain,* 757 P.2d 564 (Cal. 1988), and *State v. Eaton,* 524 S0.2d 1194 (La. 1988), both appellate courts held that a death sentence is not necessarily disproportionate merely because a defendant in a factually similar case received a life sentence. For a discussion of comparative sentencing see, Gregory Michael Stein, "Distinguishing Among Murders When Assessing the Proportionality of the Death Penalty," 85 Colum. L. Rev. 1786 (1985).

12. Alabama, Arizona, Delaware, Georgia, Idaho, Kentucky, Louisiana, Mississippi, Missouri, Montana, Nebraska, Nevada, New Hampshire, North Carolina, Ohio, Pennsylvania, South Carolina, South Dakota, Tennessee, Virginia, and Washington.

13. For a discussion of comparative review of death penalty cases see, W. Ward Morrison, Jr., "Washington's Comparative Proportionality Review: Toward Effective Appellate Review of Death Penalty Cases Under the Washington State Constitution," 60 Wash. L. Rev. 111 (1989).

14. Alabama, Arizona, Ohio, and Tennessee.

15. Alabama, Arizona, Delaware, Georgia, Idaho, Kentucky, Mississippi, Missouri, Nevada, New Hampshire, North Carolina, Oklahoma, Oregon, Pennsylvania, South Carolina, South Dakota, Utah, Virginia, Wyoming, and the Federal System.

16. Alabama and Pennsylvania.

17. Alabama, Arizona, Missouri, Nevada, Tennessee, Virginia, and Wyoming.

Chapter 18

1. *Carlisle v. United States,* 517 U.S. 416 (1996).

2. See Ira P. Robbins and James E. Sanders, "Judicial

Integrity, the Appearance of Justice, and the Great Writ of Habeas Corpus: How to Kill Two Thirds (or More) with One Stone," 15 Am. Crim. L. Rev. 63 (1978).

3. That suspension was ultimately nullified by the United States Supreme Court in *Ex Parte Milligan,* 71 U.S. 2 (1866).

4. See *Williams v. Taylor,* 529 U.S. 362 (2000).

5. The requirement of exhausting direct review before resorting to habeas relief is the basis for the legal term "collateral attack" of judgment; which is simply another way of referring to a habeas proceeding.

6. See Kenneth Williams, "The Antiterrorism and Effective Death Penalty Act: What's Wrong with It and How to Fix It," 33 Conn. L. Rev. 919 (2001).

7. Quoted in Deborah L. Stahlkopf, "A Dark Day for Habeas Corpus: Successive Petitions Under the Antiterrorism and Effective Death Penalty Act of 1996," 40 Ariz. L. Rev. 1115 (1998).

8. This chapter is embodied under 28 U.S.C. § 2261 et seq.

9. *Calderon v. Ashmus,* 523 U.S. 740 (1998).

10. See Burke W. Kappler, "Small Favors: Chapter 154 of the Antiterrorism and Effective Death Penalty Act, the States, and the Right to Counsel," 90 J. Crim. L. and Criminology 469 (2000).

11. *Calderon v. Ashmus,* 523 U.S. 740 (1998). See Eric M. Freedman, "Fewer Risks, More Benefits: What Governments Gain by Acknowledging the Right to Competent Counsel on State Post-Conviction Review in Capital Cases, 4 Ohio St. J. Crim. L. 183 (2007).

12. *Bennett v. Angelone,* 92 F.3d 1336 (4th Cir. 1996).

13. See *Pennsylvania v. Finley,* 481 U.S. 551 (1987).

14. See *Douglas v. California,* 372 U.S. 353 (1963).

15. See Benjamin R. Orye III, "The Failure of Words: Habeas Corpus Reform, the Antiterrorism and Effective Death Penalty Act, and When a Judgment of Conviction Becomes Final for the Purposes of 28 U.S.C. 2255(1)," 44 Wm. and Mary L. Rev. 441 (2003).

16. *Williams v. Taylor,* 529 U.S. 362 (2000). See *Miller-El v. Cockrell,* 537 U.S. 322 (2003).

17. See Muhammad Usman Faridi, " Streamlining Habeas Corpus While Undermining Judicial Review: How 28 U.S.C. § 2254(d)(1) Violates the Constitution," 19 St. Thomas L. Rev. 361 (2007); Allan Ides, "Habeas Standards of Review Under 28 U.S.C. § 2254(d)(1): A Commentary on Statutory Text and Supreme Court Precedent," 60 Wash. & Lee L. Rev. 677 (2003).

18. See *State v. Mixon,* 983 S.W.2d 661 (Tenn. 1999).

19. *People v. Kim,* 45 Cal.4th 1078 (2009).

20. See *State v. Mixon,* 983 S.W.2d 661 (Tenn. 1999).

21. See *State v. Mixon,* 983 S.W.2d 661 (Tenn. 1999).

22. See Steven J. Mulroy, "The Safety Net: Applying Coram Nobis Law to Prevent the Execution of the Innocent," 11 Va. J. Soc. Pol'y and L. 1 (2004).

23. The appellate court in the capital case of *Workman v. State,* 41 S.W.3d 100 (Tenn. 2001) reversed a trial court's dismissal of the defendant's coram nobis petition as untimely filed.

24. *Hyman v. United States,* 444 Fed.Appx. 579 (3d Cir. 2011).

25. *United States v. Blue,* 326 Fed.Appx. 564 (11th Cir. 2009).

26. See *Dellinger v. State,* 279 S.W.3d 282 (Tenn. 2009).

27. See *Wright v. State,* 593 S0.2d 111 (Ala.Cr.App. 1991) ("The failure to raise an issue which could have been raised at the original trial and on direct appeal bars the remedy of coram nobis review.").

28. *Bowling v. Commonwealth,* 163 S.W.3d 361 (Ky. 2005).

29. See Eric Despotes, "Evidentiary Watershed: Recognizing a Post-Conviction Constitutional Right to Access DNA Evidence Under 42 U.S.C. § 1983," 49 Santa Clara L. Rev. 821 (2009).

Chapter 19

1. See Marvin Zalman, Brad Smith, and Angie Kiger, "Officials' Estimates of the Incidence of Actual Innocence Convictions," 25 Justice Quarterly 72 (2008).

2. According to the Death Penalty Information Center, it is believed that at least 10 people executed since 1976 may have been innocent. See Death Penalty Information Center, http://www.deathpenaltyinfo.org/executed-possibly-innocent.

3. Some of these defendants already had their death sentences commuted to life as a result of the temporary abolishment of capital punishment by the decision in *Furman v. Georgia*, 408 U.S. 238 (1972).

4. See The Innocence Project, http://www.innocenceproject.org/Content/The_Innocent_and_the_Death_Penalty.php.

5. Under 42 U.S.C. § 14136e of the act, it is provided that the attorney general shall establish the Kirk Bloodsworth Post-Conviction DNA Testing Grant Program to award grants to states to help defray the costs of post-conviction DNA testing. The statute authorized the appropriation of $5,000,000 for each of fiscal years 2005 through 2009 to carry out grant program.

6. See Michael E. Kleinert, "Improving the Quality of Justice: The Innocence Protection Act 2004 Ensures Post-Conviction DNA Testing, Better Legal Representation, and Increased Compensation for the Wrongfully Imprisoned," 44 Brandeis L.J. 491 (2006).

7. See Louis J. Palmer, Jr., *Encyclopedia of DNA and the United States Criminal Justice System* (2004).

8. See Louis J. Palmer, Jr., *Encyclopedia of DNA and the United States Criminal Justice System* (2004).

9. See E.S. Lander, "Research on DNA Typing Catching Up with Courtroom Application," 48 Am. J. Hum. Genet. 819 (1991).

10. See Micah A. Luftig and Stephen Richey, "DNA and Forensic Science," 35 New Eng. L. Rev. 609 (2001).

11. See Peter M. Schneider, "Basic Issues in Forensic DNA Typing," 88 Forensic Sci. International 17 (1997).

12. See Tania Simoncelli, "Dangerous Excursions: The Case Against Expanding Forensic DNA Databases to Innocent Persons," 34 J. Law Med. and Ethics 390 (2006).

13. See J.E. McEwen, "Forensic DNA Data Banking by State Crime Laboratories," 56 Am. J. Hum. Genet. 1487 (1995); Forensic DNA Databases: Linking Criminals to Crimes, http://www.dna.gov/dna-databases/.

14. See *United States v. Pitera*, 675 F.3d 122 (2d Cir. 2012) (discussing 18 U.S.C. § 3600); *United States v. Fasano*, 577 F.3d 572 (5th Cir. 2009) (ordering DNA testing). See also, Sophia S. Chang, "Protecting the Innocent: Post-Conviction DNA Exoneration," 36 Hastings Const. L.Q. 285 (2009).

15. See David A. Schumacher, "Post-Conviction Access to DNA Testing: The Federal Government Does Not Offer an Adequate Solution, Leaving the States to Remedy the Situation," 57 Cath. U.L. Rev. 1245 (2008). See also, Ala. Code § 15-18-200; Ariz. Rev. Stat. Ann. § 13-4240; Ark. Code Ann. §§ 16-112-201 to 202, 208; Cal. Penal Code § 1405; Colo. Rev. Stat. Ann. §§ 18-1-411 to 416; Del. Code Ann. tit. 11, § 4504; Fla. Stat. Ann. §§ 925.11-.12; Ga. Code Ann. § 5-5-41; Idaho Code Ann. §§ 19-4901 to 4911; Ind. Code Ann. §§ 35-38-7-1 to 38-7-19; Kan. Stat. Ann. § 21-2512; Ky. Rev. Stat. Ann. §§

422.285, 287; La. Code Crim. Proc. Ann. art. 926.1; Miss. Code Ann. § 99-39-5; Mo. Ann. Stat. §§ 547.035, 037; Mont. Code Ann. § 46-21-110; Neb. Rev. Stat. §§ 29-4116 to 4125; Nev. Rev. Stat. Ann. §§ 176.0918-0919; N.H. Rev. Stat. Ann. §§ 651-D:1 to 5; N.C. Gen. Stat. §§ 15A-269 to 270.1; Ohio Rev. Code Ann. §§ 2953.71-84; Or. Rev. Stat. §§ 138.690-698; 42 Pa. Cons. Stat. Ann. §9543.1; S.C. Code Ann. §§ 17-28-10 to 28-120; S.D. Codified Laws §§ 23-5B-1 to 17; Tenn. Code Ann. §§ 40-30-301 to 313; Tex. Code Crim. Proc. Ann. art. 64.01-05; Utah Code. Ann. §§ 78B-9-300 to 304; Va. Code Ann. § 19.2-327.1; Wash. Rev. Code Ann. § 10.73. 170; Wyo. Stat. Ann. §§ 7-12-302 to 12-315.

16. See *Slaughter v. State*, 105 P.3d 832 (Okla.Crim. App. 2005).

17. The Civil Rights Act, 42 U.S.C. § 1983, provides: "Every person who, under color of any statute, ordinance, regulation, custom, or usage, of any State or Territory, subjects, or causes to be subjected, any citizen ... or other person ... to the deprivation of any rights, privileges, or immunities secured by the Constitution and laws, shall be liable to the party injured in an action at law, suit in equity, or other proper proceeding for redress." See Eric Despotes, "Evidentiary Watershed: Recognizing a Post-Conviction Constitutional Right to Access DNA Evidence Under 42 U.S.C. § 1983," 49 Santa Clara L. Rev. 821 (2009).

18. See *Savory v. Lyons*, 469 F.3d 667 (7th Cir. 2006); *Grayson v. King*, 460 F.3d 1328 (11th Cir. 2006); *Bradley v. Pryor*, 305 F.3d 1287 (11th Cir. 2002).

19. See *District Attorney's Office v. Osborne*, 557 U.S. 52 (2009) (rejecting a request of DNA testing under § 1983).

20. The Act similarly provides aid to state and local prosecutors in litigating capital punishment cases.

21. See Benjamin H. Barton and Stephanos Bibas, "Triaging Appointed-Counsel Funding and Pro Se Access to Justice," 160 U. Penn. L. Rev. 967 (2012).

22. See Jessica R. Lonergan, "Protecting the Innocent: A Model for Comprehensive, Individualized Compensation of the Exonerated," 11 N.Y.U. J. Legis. and Pub. Pol'y 405 (2008). The Act also provides a lesser amount of compensation for those wrongfully convicted of noncapital offenses.

23. *Lyons v. United States*, 99 Fed.Cl. 552 (Fed.Cl. 2011) (discussing 28 U.S.C. § 2513).

24. See *Spencer v. United States*, 98 Fed.Cl. 34 (Fed.Cl. 2011) ("Plaintiff's conviction has neither been reversed nor set aside, and plaintiff has not presented any certificate of innocence or pardon from the District Court of Alaska."); *Reid v. United States*, 95 Fed.Cl. 43 (Fed.Cl. 2010) ("Mr. Reid has not alleged either of the requirements set forth in 28 U.S.C. § 2513(a), nor has Mr. Reid provided the court with a certificate of the court or pardon."). United States v. Graham, 608 F.3d 164 (4th Cir. 2010) (finding former prisoner neglectfully brought about his own prosecution and was thus ineligible).

25. Alabama, California, Florida, Louisiana, Mississippi, Missouri, Montana, Nebraska, New Hampshire, North Carolina, Ohio, Oklahoma, Tennessee, Texas, Utah, Virginia.

26. See Erin Tyler Brewster, "When Have They Paid Enough? The Taxability of Compensation Payments Made to Wrongfully Incarcerated Individuals," 64 SMU L. Rev. 1405 (2011).

Chapter 20

1. See David Baldus, "Comparative Review of Death

Sentences: An Empirical Study of the Georgia Experience," 74 J. Crim. L. and Criminology 661 (1983).

2. See David C. Baldus, George Woodworth and Charles A. Pulaski, Jr., "Reflections on the Inevitability of Racial Discrimination in Capital Sentencing and the Impossibility of Its Prevention, Detection, and Correction," 51 Wash. and Lee L. Rev. 359 (1994).

3. See Erwin Chemerinsky, "Eliminating Discrimination in Administering the Death Penalty: The Need for the Racial Justice Act," 35 Santa Clara L. Rev. 519 (1995).

4. See Bryan A. Stevenson and Ruth E. Friedman, "Deliberate Indifference: Judicial Tolerance of Racial Bias in Criminal Justice," 51 Wash. and Lee L. Rev. 509 (1994).

5. See Gennaro F. Vito, "The Racial Justice Act in Kentucky," 37 N. Ky. L. Rev. 273 (2010).

6. See Seth Kotch and Robert P. Mosteller, "The Racial Justice Act and the Long Struggle with Race and the Death Penalty in North Carolina," 88 N.C. L. Rev. 2031 (2010).

7. The case citation is *North Carolina v. Robinson*, No. 91 CRS 23143.

8. See generally Alex Lesman, "State Responses to the Specter of Racial Discrimination in Capital Proceedings: The Kentucky Racial Justice Act and the New Jersey Supreme Court's Proportionality Review Project," 13 J.L. and Pol'y 359 (2005).

Chapter 21

1. See Sherri Jackson, "Too Young to Die — Juveniles and the Death Penalty — A Better Alternative to Killing Our Children: Youth Empowerment," 22 New Eng. J. on Crim. and Civ. Confinement 391 (1996).

2. Gary Knell, "Capital Punishment: Its Administration in Relation to Juvenile Offenders in the Nineteenth Century and its Possible Administration in the Eighteenth," 5 Brit. J. Crim. 198 (1965).

3. Victor Streib, "Death Penalty for Children: The American Experience with Capital Punishment for Crimes Committed While Under Age Eighteen," 36 Okl. L. Rev. 613 (1983).

4. For a discussion of capital punishment and youth see, Cele Hancock, "The Incompatibility of the Juvenile Death Penalty and the United Nation's Convention on the Rights of the Child: Domestic and International Concerns," 12 Ariz. J Int'l and Comp. L. 699 (1995); Norman J. Finkel, "Prestidigitation, Statistical Magic, and Supreme Court Numerology in Juvenile Death Penalty Cases," 1 Psychol. Pub. Pol'y and L. 612 (1995); Suzanne D. Strater, "The Juvenile Death Penalty: In the Best Interests of the Child?" 26 Loy. U. Chi. L.J. 147 (1995); Bruce L. Brown, "The Juvenile Death Penalty in Washington: A State Constitutional Analysis," 15 U. Puget Sound L. Rev. 361 (1992).

5. For a specific discussion of imposing the death penalty on female youth see, Victor L. Streib and Lynn Sametz, "Executing Female Juveniles," 22 Conn. L. Rev. 3 (1989).

6. For a discussion of this case see, T. Shawn Lanier, "Juvenile Offenders and the Death Penalty: An Analysis of Stanford v. Kentucky," 45 Mercer L. Rev. 1097 (1994); Etta J. Mullin, "At What Age Should They Die? The United States Supreme Court Decision with Respect to Juvenile Offenders and the Death Penalty Stanford v. Kentucky and Wilkins v. Missouri," 16 T. Marshall L. Rev. 161 (1990).

7. U.S. Department of Justice, Bureau of Justice Statistics, Corrections, Prisoners in 2010, Table 1 (2011).

8. U.S. Department of Justice, Bureau of Justice Statistics, Corrections, Capital Punishment (2011).

9. For a general discussion of capital punishment and female capital felons, see Elizabeth Rapaport, "Some Questions About Gender and the Death Penalty," 20 Golden Gate U. L. Rev. 501 (1990); Victor Streib, "Death Penalty for Female Offenders," 58 U. Cin. L. Rev. 845 (1990).

10. Alabama, Arizona, California, Florida, Georgia, Idaho, Indiana, Kansas, Kentucky, Louisiana, Mississippi, Missouri, Montana, Nebraska, Nevada, New Hampshire, Ohio, Oklahoma, South Dakota, Utah, Wyoming, and the Federal System.

11. For a general discussion of insanity and capital felons, see Jonathan L. Entin, "Psychiatry, Insanity, and the Death Penalty: A Note on Implementing Supreme Court Decisions," 79 Crim. L. and Criminology 218 (1988).

12. Alabama, Arizona, Arkansas, California, Florida, Georgia, Kansas, Kentucky, Mississippi, Missouri, Montana, Nebraska, Nevada, Ohio, Oklahoma, South Dakota, Utah, Wyoming, and the Federal System.

13. For a general discussion of the death penalty and mental disabilities see, Michael L. Perlin, "The Sanist Lives of Jurors in Death Penalty Cases: The Puzzling Role of Mitigating Mental Disability Evidence," 8 Notre Dame J.L. Ethics and Pub. Pol'y 239 (1994); Van W. Ellis, "Guilty but Mentally Ill and the Death Penalty: Punishment Full of Sound and Fury, Signifying Nothing," 43 Duke L.J. 87 (1993).

14. For a discussion of *Penry* and its impact see, Robert L. Hayman, "Beyond Penry: The Remedial Use of the Mentally Retarded Label in Death Penalty Sentencing," 59 UMKC L. Rev. 17 (1990); J. Dwight Carmichael, "Penry v. Lynaugh: Texas Death Penalty Procedure Unconstitutionally Precludes Jury Consideration of Mitigating Evidence," 42 Baylor L. Rev. 347 (1990).

15. U.S. Department of Justice, Bureau of Justice Statistics, Corrections, Capital Punishment, Table 15 and 8 (2011).

16. For further discussion see, Gerald Kirven, "Capital Crime and Punishment: Shortening the Time Between Them," 42 Fed. Law. 20 (1995).

17. Alabama, Arizona, California, Colorado, Florida, Georgia, Indiana, Louisiana, Missouri, North Carolina, Ohio, Oklahoma, Oregon, Pennsylvania, Tennessee, Texas, Washington, and the Federal System.

18. The defendant could remain in the state system by starting state habeas corpus proceedings.

19. The defendant can begin by filing a federal habeas corpus petition in a federal district court.

20. For a critical discussion of habeas corpus see, Alan W. Clarke, "Procedural Labyrinths and the Injustice of Death: A Critique of Death Penalty Habeas Corpus," 30 U. Rich. L. Rev. 303 (1996).

21. As pointed out, the defendant can appeal to the Supreme Court the denial of habeas corpus relief by the state's highest court.

22. For a discussion of federal habeas corpus issues see, Joseph L. Hoffman, "Is Innocent Sufficient? An Essay on the U.S. Supreme Court's Continuing Problems with Federal Habeas Corpus and the Death Penalty," 68 Ind. L.J. 817 (1993); Stephanie O. Joy, "A Claim of Newly Discovered Evidence of Actual Innocence Does Not Entitle Death Penalty Claimant to Federal Habeas Corpus Relief," 4 Seton Hall Const. L.J. 361 (1993).

23. One of the Supreme Court decisions limiting habeas corpus petitions in federal court is *McCleskey v. Zant*, 111 S.Ct. 1454 (1991). For a discussion of this case and its impact, see Cheryl R. Sweeney, "McCleskey v. Zant: The Cause and Prejudice Standard in Capital

Punishment Cases," 24 U. Tol. L. Rev. 231 (1992); Martha Hallisey, "To Habe or Not to Habe: Curtailing the Writ of Habeas Corpus in McCleskey v. Zant," 19 New Eng. J. on Crim. and Civ. Confinement 397 (1993).

24. U.S. Department of Justice, Bureau of Justice Statistics, Corrections, Capital Punishment, Table 14 (2011).

25. For a discussion of executive clemency, see Daniel Lim, "State Due Process Guarantees for Meaningful Death Penalty Clemency Proceedings," 28 Colum. J.L. and Soc. Probs. 47 (1994); Bruce Ledewitz and Scott Staples, "The Role of Executive Clemency in Modern Death Penalty Cases," 27 U. Rich. L. Rev. 227 (1993).

26. For discussion of commutation see, Victoria J. Palacios, "Faith in Fantasy: The Supreme Court's Reliance on Commutation to Ensure Justice in Death Penalty Cases," 49 V. and L. Rev. 311 (1996); Daniel T. Kobil, "Due Process in Death Penalty Commutations: Life, Liberty, and the Pursuit of Clemency," 27 U. Rich. L. Rev. 201 (1993).

Chapter 22

1. See Mark D. Cunningham and Mark P. Vigen, "Death Row Inmate Characteristics, Adjustment, and Confinement: A Critical Review of the Literature," 20 Behav. Sci. Law 191 (2002).

2. See U.S. Department of Justice, Bureau of Justice Statistics, Capital Punishment, Table 4 (2009).

3. See U.S. Department of Justice, Bureau of Justice Statistics, Capital Punishment, Table 6 (2009).

4. See U.S. Department of Justice, Bureau of Justice Statistics, Capital Punishment, Table 4 (2009).

5. See U.S. Department of Justice, Bureau of Justice Statistics, Capital Punishment, Table 5 (2009).

6. See U.S. Department of Justice, Bureau of Justice Statistics, Capital Punishment, Table 5 (2009).

7. See U.S. Department of Justice, Bureau of Justice Statistics, Capital Punishment, Table 10 (2009).

8. See Louis J. Palmer, Jr., *Encyclopedia of Capital Punishment in the United States* (2d ed. 2008).

9. See Louis J. Palmer, Jr., *Encyclopedia of Capital Punishment in the United States* (2d ed. 2008).

10. See Louis J. Palmer, Jr., *Encyclopedia of Capital Punishment in the United States* (2d ed. 2008).

11. See Florida Department of Corrections, The Daily Routine of Death Row Inmates, http://www.dc.state.fl.us/oth/deathrow/index.html#Routine.

12. See Arizona Department of Corrections, Death Row Information, http://www.azcorrections.gov/dr_faq.aspx.

13. See North Carolina Department of Public Safety, Death Row and Death Watch, http://www.doc.state.nc.us/dop/deathpenalty/deathwat.htm.

14. See Louis J. Palmer, Jr., *Encyclopedia of Capital Punishment in the United States* (2d ed. 2008).

15. See North Carolina Department of Public Safety, Death Row and Death Watch, http://www.doc.state.nc.us/dop/deathpenalty/deathwat.htm.

16. Brewer's last meal request included two chicken-fried steaks with gravy and sliced onions; a triple-patty bacon cheeseburger; a cheese omelet with ground beef, tomatoes, onions, bell peppers and jalapeños; a bowl of fried okra with ketchup; one pound of barbecued meat with half a loaf of white bread; three fajitas; a meat-lover's pizza; one pint of Blue Bell Ice Cream; a slab of peanut-butter fudge with crushed peanuts; and three root beers.

Chapter 23

1. See generally Hugo Adam Bedeau, *The Death Penalty in America*, (3d ed. 1982).

2. See Michael Madow, "Forbidden Spectacle: Executions, the Public and the Press in Nineteenth Century New York," 43 Buffalo L. Rev. 461 (1995); Steven A. Blum, "Public Executions: Understanding the Cruel and Unusual Punishments Clause," 19 Hastings Con. L. Q. 413 (1992).

3. Reported in David Sternbach, "Hanging Pictures: Photographic Theory and the Framing of Images of Execution," 70 N.Y.U. L. Rev. 1100 (1995).

4. Reported in David Sternbach, "Hanging Pictures: Photographic Theory and the Framing of Images of Execution," 70 N.Y.U. L. Rev. 1100 (1995).

5. The following jurisdictions have not set out any statutory guidelines for conducting executions: Arkansas, Idaho, and the Federal System. The state of Delaware lists only two factors.

6. Delaware and Louisiana.

7. Ohio.

8. Washington.

9. See Michael Lawrence Goodwin, "An Eyeful for an Eye: An Argument Against Allowing the Families of Murder Victims to View Executions," 36 Brandeis J. Fam. L. 585 (1998).

10. Indiana and Wyoming.

11. Alabama, Arizona, California, Missouri, Oklahoma, Oregon, South Dakota, Texas, and Utah.

12. Kansas, Kentucky, Nebraska, and Ohio.

13. Mississippi.

14. Georgia, New Hampshire, North Carolina, Tennessee, and Washington.

15. Alabama.

16. Mississippi.

17. Kentucky, Mississippi, South Carolina, and Tennessee.

18. Arizona, California, Colorado, Delaware, Florida, Georgia, Kansas, Louisiana, New Hampshire, North Carolina, Pennsylvania, South Carolina, South Dakota, and Virginia.

19. Delaware authorizes the presiding trial judge to determine who shall attend the execution as witnesses.

20. Alabama, Missouri, Ohio, and Texas.

21. Indiana, Kentucky, and Wyoming.

22. Alabama and Texas.

23. Indiana, Kansas, Kentucky, Louisiana, Nebraska, Pennsylvania, South Carolina, Tennessee, Texas, and Virginia.

24. Arizona, California, Mississippi, Missouri, Oklahoma, Oregon, and South Dakota.

25. Alabama, Florida, Georgia, New Hampshire, North Carolina, Ohio, Utah, and Wyoming.

26. For a brief review of a book critical of physician participation in executions, see John Kaisersatt, "Capital Punishment: Physicians Executioners?" 22 Am. J. Crim. L. 317 (1994).

27. For a general discussion of the role of physicians in capital punishment cases see, David J. Rothman, "Physicians and the Death Penalty," 4 J.L. and Pol'y 151 (1995).

28. Arizona, Colorado, Florida, Kentucky, Nevada, New Hampshire, North Carolina, Oklahoma, Pennsylvania, Tennessee, Utah, and Virginia.

29. Alabama, California, Georgia, Indiana, Louisiana, Mississippi, Texas, and Wyoming.

30. Kansas.

31. Ohio and Oregon.

32. Arizona, California, Louisiana, South Dakota, and Utah.

33. Missouri and Nevada.

34. Florida, Georgia, North Carolina, South Carolina, Virginia, and Washington.

35. Arizona, California, Missouri, New Hampshire, Oregon, South Dakota, and Utah.

36. Oklahoma, South Dakota, Utah, and Washington.

37. South Dakota, Texas, and Washington.

Chapter 24

1. Alabama, California, Florida, Missouri, South Carolina, Virginia, and Washington.

2. Arkansas (if unconstitutional), Delaware (if unconstitutional), New Hampshire (for any reason), Oklahoma (if unconstitutional), Utah (if unconstitutional), and Wyoming (if unconstitutional).

3. Arizona, Kentucky and Utah.

4. Tennessee.

5. See Norman Mailer, *The Executioner's Song* (3rd ed. 1979).

6. Subsequent to Gilmore's execution, Utah's death penalty statute was found constitutional by a federal court of appeals in the case of *Andrew v. Shulsen*, 802 F.2d 1256 (10th Cir. 1986).

7. For a general discussion on the humaneness of execution methods, see Brian Hill, "Judicial Response to Changing Societal Values on the Death Penalty: Must the Method Chosen Be the Most Humane," 7 St. Thomas L. Rev. 409 (1995).

8. See V.A.C. Gatrell, *The Hanging Tree: Execution and the English People 1770–1868* (1994).

9. See also, *Rupe v. Wood*, 93 F.3d 1434 (9th Cir. 1996).

10. For a critical discussion of hanging and lethal gas, see Allen Huang, "Hanging, Cyanide Gas, and the Evolving Standards of Decency: The Ninth Circuit's Misapplication of the Cruel and Unusual Clause of the Eighth Amendment," 74 Or. L. Rev. 995 (1995).

11. See Robert J. Sech, "Hang 'Em High: A Proposal for Thoroughly Evaluating the Constitutionality of Execution Methods," 30 Val. U. L. Rev. 381 (1996).

12. Ryk James and Rachel Nasmyth-Jones, "The Occurrence of Cervical Fractures in Victims of Judicial Hanging," 54 Foren. Sci. Intern'l 81 (1992).

13. See Deborah W. Denno, "The Lethal Injection Quandary: How Medicine Has Dismantled the Death Penalty," 76 Fordham L. Rev. 49 (2007).

14. See James R. Wong, "Lethal Injection Protocols: The Failure of Litigation to Stop Suffering and the Case for Legislative Reform," 25 Temp. J. Sci. Tech. and Envtl. L. 263 (2006).

15. It was reported that in a 1985 execution in Texas, it took a total of 23 attempts, covering a span of 40 minutes, to inject the needle in a capital felon. It has also been argued that the drugs used do not always induce a quick and painless death.

16. See *State v. Moen*, 786 P.2d 111 (Or. 1990) (holding lethal injection not cruel and unusual); *Hopkinson v. State*, 798 P.2d 1186 (Wyo. 1990) (holding lethal injection constitutional; *People v. Stewart*, 520 N.E.2d 348 (Ill. 1988) (lethal injection not unconstitutional).

17. See Craig Brandon, *The Electric Chair: An Unnatural History* (1999).

18. See Lonny J. Hoffman, "The Madness of the Method: The Use of Electrocution and the Death Penalty," 70 Tex. L. Rev. 1039 (1992).

19. See Deborah W. Denno, "Is Electrocution an Unconstitutional Method of Execution? The Engineering of Death Over the Century," 35 Wm. and Mary L. Rev. 551 (1994).

20. See Philip R. Nugent, "Pulling the Plug on the Electric Chair: The Unconstitutionality of Electrocution," 2 Wm. and Mary Bill Rts. J. 185 (1993).

21. See Rebecca Brannan, "Sentence and Punishment: Change Method of Executing Individuals Convicted of Capital Crimes from Electrocution to Lethal Injection," 17 Ga. St. U.L. Rev. 116 (2000).

22. P.J.Zisch, "Lethal Gas as a Means of Asphyxiating Capital Offenders," 48 Medico-Legal J. 25 (1931).

23. See Raymond Hartmann, "The Use of Lethal Gas in Nevada Executions," 8 St. Louis L. Rev. 164 (1923).

24. See also, *Duisen v. State*, 441 S.W.2d 688 (Mo. 1969) (holding lethal gas not cruel and unusual punishment); *Calhoun v. State*, 468 A.2d 45 (Md. 1983) (holding lethal gas not cruel and unusual punishment); *State v. Boyd*, 473 N.E.2d 327 (N.C. 1996) (holding lethal gas not cruel and unusual punishment).

25. It should be kept in mind that the dispositions brought out here are limited to what is contained in the death penalty statutes of jurisdictions that addressed the issue in their death penalty statutes.

26. Alabama, Georgia, Kentucky, Mississippi, North Carolina, Ohio, Pennsylvania, South Carolina, South Dakota, Texas, Virginia, and Wyoming.

27. Alabama, Georgia, Kentucky, Ohio, and South Carolina.

28. Alabama, Georgia, Kentucky, Mississippi, North Carolina, Ohio, Texas, and Wyoming.

29. Alabama and Kansas.

30. Mississippi, Pennsylvania, and Texas.

31. Alabama, Georgia, Kentucky, Mississippi, North Carolina, Ohio, Pennsylvania, South Carolina, South Dakota, Texas, and Wyoming.

Chapter 25

1. See Dwight H. Sullivan, "The Last Line of Defense: Federal Habeas Review of Military Death Penalty Cases," 144 Mil. L. Rev. 1 (1994).

2. See John F. O'Connor, "Don't Know Much About History: The Constitution, Historical Practice, and the Death Penalty Jurisdiction of Courts-Martial," 52 U. Miami L. Rev. 177 (1998).

3. See John F. O'Connor, "Don't Know Much About History: The Constitution, Historical Practice, and the Death Penalty Jurisdiction of Courts-Martial," 52 U. Miami L. Rev. 177 (1998).

4. The decision in *Furman* invalidated the death penalty in civil courts.

5. See Annamary Sullivan, "The President's Power to Promulgate Death Penalty Standards," 125 Mil. L. Rev. 143 (1989).

6. See Gregory F. Intoccia, "Constitutionality of the Death Penalty Under the Uniform Code of Military Justice," 32 A.F. L. Rev. 395 (1990).

7. See Christine Daniels, "Capital Punishment and the Courts-Martial: Questions Surface Following Loving v. United States," 55 Wash. and Lee L. Rev. 577 (1998).

8. See David A. Anderson, "Spying in Violation of Article 106, UCMJ: The Offense and the Constitutionality of Its Mandatory Death Penalty," 127 Mil. L. Rev. 1 (1990).

9. See Dwight H. Sullivan, "Playing the Numbers: Court-Martial Panel Size and the Military Death Penalty," 158 Mil. L. Rev. 1 (1999).

10. See Jonathan Choa, "Civilians, Service-Members, and the Death Penalty: The Failure of Article 25A to Require Twelve-Member Panels in Capital Trials for Non-Military Crimes," 70 Fordham L. Rev. 2065 (2002).

11. See David D. Velloney, "Balancing the Scales of Justice: Expanding Access to Mitigation Specialists in Military Death Penalty Cases," 170 Mil. L. Rev. 1 (2001).

12. The Court of Appeals for the Armed Forces is a five-member court. Its judges are civilians appointed by the president with the advice and consent of the Senate to serve 15 year terms.

13. See Death Penalty Information Center, "The U.S. Military Death Penalty," http://www.deathpenaltyinfo.org/us-military-death-penalty.

14. See Alan Tauber, "Ninety Miles from Freedom: The Constitutional Rights of the Guantanamo Bay Detainees," 18 St. Thomas L. Rev. 77 (2006).

15. See Ray Murphy, "Prisoner of War Status and the Question of the Guantanamo Bay Detainees," Hum. Rts. L. Rev. 257 (2003).

16. See Richard H. Fallon, Jr., and Daniel J. Meltzer, "Habeas Corpus Jurisdiction, Substantive Rights, and the War on Terror," 120 Harv. L. Rev. 2029 (2007).

17. See *Boumediene v. Bush*, 128 S.Ct. 2229 (2008) (holding that Guantanamo Bay prisoners have right to apply for habeas corpus relief); *Rasul v. Bush*, 542 U.S. 466 (2004) (holding federal courts have jurisdiction to consider challenges to the legality of the detention of foreign nationals held at the Guantanamo Bay); *Hamdi v. Rumsfeld*, 542 U.S. 507 (2004) (holding that due process demands that a citizen held in the United States as an enemy combatant be given a meaningful opportunity to contest the factual basis for that detention before a neutral decision maker); *Rumsfeld v. Padilla*, 542 U.S. 426 (2004) (holding that Guantanamo Bay prisoner could not file habeas petition in New York federal court, but, instead had to file in a South Carolina federal court).

18. See Tung Yin, "Ending the War on Terrorism One Terrorist at a Time: A Noncriminal Detention Model for Holding and Releasing Guantanamo Bay Detainees," 29 Harv. J.L. and Pub. Pol'y 149 (2006).

Chapter 26

1. See *United States v. Jacobs*, 638 F.3d 567 (8th Cir. 2011).

2. F. Cohen, Handbook of Federal Indian Law 122 (1945).

3. See *Cabazon Band of Mission Indians v. Smith*, 34 F.Supp.2d 1195 (C.D.Cal. 1998).

4. See 25 U.S.C. § 1301.

5. See *United States v. Long*, 324 F.3d 475 (7th Cir. 2003).

6. See *United States v. Bruce*, 394 F.3d 1215 (9th Cir. 2005).

7. Tim Vollmann, "Criminal Jurisdiction in Indian Country: Tribal Sovereignty and Defendants' Rights in Conflict," 22 U. Kan. L. Rev. 387 (1974).

8. In 2000 Native American tribes operated 171 law enforcement agencies. These agencies employed a total of 2,303 full-time sworn officers. In 2007 Native American tribes and the Bureau of Indian Affairs, U.S. Department of Interior, operated 83 jails in tribal areas. In 2007 these correctional facilities had a rated capacity to house about 2,900 adult and juvenile inmates. See U.S. Department of Justice, Bureau of Justice Statistics, "American Indians and Crime 1999–2002," (2004); U.S. Department of Justice, Bureau of Justice Statistics, "Jails in Indian Country," Table 4 (2007).

9. See Department of Justice and Department of Interior, "Tribal Law and Order Act: Long Term Plan to Build and Enhance Tribal Justice Systems" (2011).

10. The rules governing criminal jurisdiction in Native American lands was summarized in *United States v. Bruce*, 394 F.3d 1215 (9th Cir. 2005) as follows:

(i). Crimes in which both the perpetrator and victim are Native American are subject to (a) federal jurisdiction under § 1153 if the crime charged is one of the fifteen enumerated crimes, or if the federal statute is one of general applicability; (b) state jurisdiction where authorized by Congress; and (c) tribal jurisdiction, perhaps running concurrent with either federal or state jurisdiction, although punishment is limited to no more than one year and $5,000.

(ii). Crimes in which the perpetrator, but not the victim, is Native American are subject to (a) federal jurisdiction under § 1152, § 1153, or pursuant to federal criminal laws of general applicability; (b) state jurisdiction where authorized by Congress; and (c) tribal jurisdiction, perhaps running concurrently with either federal or state jurisdiction, although punishment is limited to no more than one year and $5,000.

(iii). Crimes in which the victim, but not the perpetrator, is Native American are subject to (a) federal jurisdiction under § 1152, as well as pursuant to federal criminal laws of general applicability, and (b) state jurisdiction where authorized by Congress.

(iv). Crimes in which both the perpetrator and victim are non–Native American are subject to state jurisdiction or federal criminal laws of general applicability.

11. See *United States v. Graham*, 572 F.3d 954 (8th Cir. 2009) (affirming dismissal of indictment for failing to indicate defendant was a Native American).

12. See *United States v. LaBuff*, 658 F.3d 873 (9th Cir. 2011).

13. See *United States v. LaBuff*, 658 F.3d 873 (9th Cir. 2011).

14. See *United States v. Antelope*, 430 U.S. 641 (1977).

15. See *Means v. Navajo Nation*, 432 F.3d 924 (9th Cir. 2005).

16. The full text of the General Crimes Act reads as follows: "Except as otherwise expressly provided by law, the general laws of the United States as to the punishment of offenses committed in any place within the sole and exclusive jurisdiction of the United States, except the District of Columbia, shall extend to the [Native American] country. This section shall not extend to offenses committed by one [Native American] against the person or property of another [Native American], nor to any [Native American] committing any offense in the [Native American] country who has been punished by the local law of the tribe, or to any case where, by treaty stipulations, the exclusive jurisdiction over such offenses is or may be secured to the Indian tribes respectively."

17. *United States v. Cowboy*, 694 F.2d 1228 (10th Cir. 1982).

18. *United States v. Diaz*, 679 F.3d 1183 (10th Cir. 2012).

19. *United States v. Maggi*, 598 F.3d 1073 (9th Cir. 2010).

20. See *United States v. Young*, 936 F.2d 1050 (9th Cir. 1991) (assault on federal officer and firearms); *United States v. Blue*, 722 F.2d 383 (8th Cir. 1983) (narcotics).

21. See *United States v. Antelope*, 430 U.S. 641 (1977); *United States v. Bruce*, 394 F.3d 1215 (9th Cir. 2005).

22. See *United States v. Cowboy*, 694 F.2d 1228 (10th Cir. 1982).

23. See *United States v. Markiewicz*, 978 F.2d 786 (2d Cir. 1991).

24. See *United States v. Torres*, 733 F.2d 449 (7th Cir. 1984).

25. See Sidney L. Harring, "Crow Dog's Case: A Chapter in the Legal History of Tribal Sovereignty," 14 Am. Ind. L. Rev. 191 (1989); F. Browning Pipestem, "The Journey from Ex Parte Crow Dog to Littlechief: A Survey of Tribal Civil and Criminal Jurisdiction in Western Oklahoma," 6 Am. Ind. L. Rev. 1 (1978).

26. See *United States v. Gallaher*, 624 F.3d 934 (2010).

27. See *United States v. Other Medicine*, 596 F.3d 677 (9th Cir. 2010).

28. The Major Crimes Act provides the following: "(a) Any [Native American] who commits against the person or property of another Indian or other person any of the following offenses, namely, murder, manslaughter, kidnapping, maiming, a felony under chapter 109A, incest, assault with intent to commit murder, assault with a dangerous weapon, assault resulting in serious bodily injury (as defined in section 1365 of this title), an assault against an individual who has not attained the age of 16 years, felony child abuse or neglect, arson, burglary, robbery, and a felony under section 661 of this title within the [Native American] country, shall be subject to the same law and penalties as all other persons committing any of the above offenses, within the exclusive jurisdiction of the United States. (b) Any offense referred to in subsection (a) of this section that is not defined and punished by federal law in force within the exclusive jurisdiction of the United States shall be defined and punished in accordance with the laws of the state in which such offense was committed as are in force at the time of such offense."

29. See *Ex Parte Gon-Shay-Ee*, 130 U.S. 343 (1889).

30. See *United States v. Broncheau*, 597 F.2d 1260 (1979).

31. See *Oliphant v. Suquamish Indian Tribe*, 435 U.S. 191 (1978) (superseded by statute).

32. See *United States v. Jones*, 440 F.3d 927 (8th Cir. 2006).

33. See *United States v. Sands*, 968 F.2d 1058 (10th Cir. 1992) ("The State of Oklahoma does not have jurisdiction over a criminal offense committed by one Creek ... against another in [tribal] country.").

34. For example, The Kansas Act of 1940, 18 U.S.C. § 3243 confers jurisdiction on the state of Kansas jurisdiction to prosecute Native Americans for crimes against Native Americans on tribal lands. See *Negonsott v. Samuels*, 507 U.S. 99 (1993). In 1984 Congress enacted Public Law 98-290, which gave the state of Colorado express criminal and civil jurisdiction within the boundaries of the town of Ignacio, Colorado, and any other municipality which may be incorporated under the laws of Colorado within the Southern Ute Native American country. See *United States v. Burch*, 169 F.3d 666 (10th Cir. 1999).

35. See Vanessa J. Jimenez and Soo C. Song, "Concurrent Tribal and State Jurisdiction Under Public Law 280," 47 Am. U.L. Rev. 1627 (1998).

36. The following is set out under Public Law 280, 18 U.S.C. § 1162(a): "(a) Each of the states or territories listed in the following table shall have jurisdiction over offenses committed by or against [Native Americans] in the areas of [Native American] country listed opposite the name of the state or territory to the same extent that such state or territory has jurisdiction over offenses committed elsewhere within the state or territory, and the criminal laws of such state or territory shall have the same force and effect within such [Native American] country as they have elsewhere within the state or territory":

State or Territory of	[Native American] Country Affected
Alaska	All [Native American] country within the state, except that on Annette Islands, the Metlakatla [Native American] community may exercise jurisdiction over offenses committed by [Native Americans] in the same manner in which such jurisdiction may be exercised by [Native American] tribes in Indian country over which state jurisdiction has not been extended
California	All [Native American] country within the state
Minnesota	All [Native American] country within the state, except the Red Lake Reservation
Nebraska	All [Native American] country within the state
Oregon	All [Native American] country within the state, except the Warm Springs Reservation
Wisconsin	All [Native American] country within the state

37. It is provided under Public Law 280, 18 U.S.C. § 1162(d), that affected tribes may request and the United States attorney general may consent to allowing the General Crimes Act and Major Crimes Act be made applicable to the lands of a requesting tribe.

38. See *Hopland Band of Pomo Indians v. Norton*, 324 F.Supp.2d 1067 (N.D.Cal. 2004).

39. *United States v. Pemberton*, 121 F.3d 1157 (8th Cir. 1997).

40. See *United States v. Burch*, 169 F.3d 666 (10th Cir. 1999).

41. See *United States v. Person*, 427 F.Supp.2d 894 (D.Minn. 2006). The following is set out under 25 U.S.C. § 1321(a)(1): "The consent of the United States is hereby given to any state not having jurisdiction over criminal offenses committed by or against Indians in the areas of Indian country situated within such state to assume, with the consent of the Indian tribe occupying the particular Indian country or part thereof which could be affected by such assumption, such measure of jurisdiction over any or all of such offenses committed within such Indian country or any part thereof as may be determined by such state to the same extent that such state has jurisdiction over any such offense committed elsewhere within the state, and the criminal laws of such state shall have the same force and effect within such Indian country or part thereof as they have elsewhere within that state."

42. *State v. Pena*, 873 P.2d 274 (N.M.App. 1994). See *State v. McCormack*, 793 P.2d 682 (Idaho 1990).

43. See *United States v. High Elk*, 902 F.2d 660 (8th Cir. 1990).

44. See *Duro v. Reina*, 495 U.S. 676 (1990) (superseded by statute).

45. The Assimilative Crimes Act, 18 U.S.C. § 13(a) provides as follows: "(a) Whoever within or upon any of the places now existing or hereafter reserved or acquired as provided in section 7 of this title, or on, above, or below any portion of the territorial sea of the United States not within the jurisdiction of any State, Commonwealth, territory, possession, or district is guilty of any act or omission which, although not made punishable by any enactment of Congress, would be punishable if committed or omitted within the jurisdiction of the state, territory, possession, or district in which such place is situated, by the laws thereof in force at the time of such act or omission, shall be guilty of a like offense and subject to a like punishment."

46. See *United States v. Ashley*, 255 F.3d 907 (8th Cir. 2001); *Iowa Tribe of Indians of Kansas and Nebraska v. State of Kan.*, 787 F.2d 1434 (10th Cir. 1986).

47. *United States v. Thunder Hawk*, 127 F.3d 705 (8th Cir. 1997).

48. See Alvin J. Ziontz, "In Defense of Tribal Sovereignty: An Analysis of Judicial Error in Construction of the Indian Civil Rights Act," 20 S.D. L. Rev. 1 (1975).

49. See Joseph de Raismes, "The Indian Civil Rights Act of 1968 and the Pursuit of Responsible Tribal Self-Government," 20 S.D. L.Rev. 59 (1975).

50. See Donald L. Burnett, Jr., "An Historical Analysis of the 1968 Indian Civil Rights' Act," 9 Harv. J. on Legis. 557 (1971); Robert Laurence, "Martinez, Oliphant and Federal Court Review of Tribal Activity Under the Indian Civil Rights Act," 10 Campbell L. Rev. 411 (1983).

51. See *Miranda v. Anchondo*, 684 F.3d 844 (9th Cir. 2012). The following is provided by the Native American Civil Rights Act, 25 U.S.C. § 1302:

(a) In general

No [Native American] tribe in exercising powers of self-government shall —

(1) make or enforce any law prohibiting the free exercise of religion, or abridging the freedom of speech, or of the press, or the right of the people peaceably to assemble and to petition for a redress of grievances;

(2) violate the right of the people to be secure in their persons, houses, papers, and effects against unreasonable search and seizures, nor issue warrants, but upon probable cause, supported by oath or affirmation, and particularly describing the place to be searched and the person or thing to be seized;

(3) subject any person for the same offense to be twice put in jeopardy;

(4) compel any person in any criminal case to be a witness against himself;

(5) take any private property for a public use without just compensation;

(6) deny to any person in a criminal proceeding the right to a speedy and public trial, to be informed of the nature and cause of the accusation, to be confronted with the witnesses against him, to have compulsory process for obtaining witnesses in his favor, and at his own expense to have the assistance of counsel for his defense (except as provided in subsection [b]);

(7)(A) require excessive bail, impose excessive fines, or inflict cruel and unusual punishments;

(B) except as provided in subparagraph (C), impose for conviction of any 1 offense any penalty or punishment greater than imprisonment for a term of 1 year or a fine of $5,000, or both;

(C) subject to subsection (b), impose for conviction of any 1 offense any penalty or punishment greater than imprisonment for a term of 3 years or a fine of $15,000, or both; or

(D) impose on a person in a criminal proceeding a total penalty or punishment greater than imprisonment for a term of 9 years;

(8) deny to any person within its jurisdiction the equal protection of its laws or deprive any person of liberty or property without due process of law;

(9) pass any bill of attainder or ex post facto law; or

(10) deny to any person accused of an offense punishable by imprisonment the right, upon request, to a trial by jury of not less than six persons.

(b) Offenses subject to greater than 1-year imprisonment or a fine greater than $5,000

A tribal court may subject a defendant to a term of imprisonment greater than 1 year but not to exceed 3 years for any 1 offense, or a fine greater than $5,000 but not to exceed $15,000, or both, if the defendant is a person accused of a criminal offense who —

(1) has been previously convicted of the same or a comparable offense by any jurisdiction in the United States; or

(2) is being prosecuted for an offense comparable to an offense that would be punishable by more than 1 year

of imprisonment if prosecuted by the United States or any of the States.

(c) Rights of defendants

In a criminal proceeding in which a[] [Native American] tribe, in exercising powers of self-government, imposes a total term of imprisonment of more than 1 year on a defendant, the Indian tribe shall —

(1) provide to the defendant the right to effective assistance of counsel at least equal to that guaranteed by the United States Constitution; and

(2) at the expense of the tribal government, provide an indigent defendant the assistance of a defense attorney licensed to practice law by any jurisdiction in the United States that applies appropriate professional licensing standards and effectively ensures the competence and professional responsibility of its licensed attorneys;

(3) require that the judge presiding over the criminal proceeding —

(A) has sufficient legal training to preside over criminal proceedings; and

(B) is licensed to practice law by any jurisdiction in the United States;

(4) prior to charging the defendant, make publicly available the criminal laws (including regulations and interpretative documents), rules of evidence, and rules of criminal procedure (including rules governing the recusal of judges in appropriate circumstances) of the tribal government; and

(5) maintain a record of the criminal proceeding, including an audio or other recording of the trial proceeding.

52. See *United States v. Cavanaugh*, 643 F.3d 592 (8th Cir. 2011).

53. See *Means v. Navajo Nation*, 432 F.3d 924 (9th Cir. 2005); *United States v. Male Juvenile*, 280 F.3d 1008 (9th Cir. 2002).

54. See *United States v. Gallaher*, 624 F.3d 934 (2010).

55. The following is provided under 18 U.S.C. § 3598: "Notwithstanding sections 1152 and 1153, no person subject to the criminal jurisdiction of an [Native American] tribal government shall be subject to a capital sentence under this chapter for any offense the Federal jurisdiction for which is predicated solely on [Native American] country (as defined in section 1151 of this title) and which has occurred within the boundaries of [Native American] country, unless the governing body of the tribe has elected that this chapter have effect over land and persons subject to its criminal jurisdiction."

56. See *United States v. Waupoose*, 627 F.Supp.2d 930 (E.D.Wis. 2008) ("A death sentence was never a possibility for Waupoose, however, since the Menominee Tribe has not elected to have the death penalty available for crimes committed on its Reservation pursuant to 18 U.S.C. § 3598.").

57. See *United States v. Bruce*, 394 F.3d 1215 (9th Cir. 2005).

58. See *United States v. Anderson*, 391 F.3d 1083 (9th Cir. 2004).

59. See *United States v. Banks*, 372 Fed.Appx. 237 (3d Cir. 2010); *United States v. Markiewicz*, 978 F.2d 786 (2d Cir. 1992).

60. See Deborah Fins, "Death Row U.S.A.," Criminal Justice Project, NAACP Legal Defense and Educational Fund (2012), http://www.naacpldf.org/files/publications/DRUSA_Winter_2012.pdf.

Chapter 27

1. See Abbott Lawrence Lowell, "The Status of Our New Possessions: A Third View," 13 Harv.L.Rev. 155 (1899).

2. Joycelyn Hewlett, The Virgin Islands: Grand Jury Denied," 35 How. L.J. 263 (1992).

3. See Joel Colón-Ríos and Martín Hevia, "The Legal Status of Puerto Rico and the Institutional Requirements of Republicanism," 17 Tex. Hisp. J.L. and Pol'y 1 (2011).

4. *United States v. Quinones*, 758 F.2d 40 (1st Cir. 1985).

5. See *Consejo de Salud Playa de Ponce v. Rullan*, 586 F.Supp.2d 22 (D.Puerto Rico 2008).

6. The following is set out under 48 U.S.C. § 734: "The statutory laws of the United States not locally inapplicable, except as hereinbefore or hereinafter otherwise provided, shall have the same force and effect in Puerto Rico as in the United States, except the internal revenue laws other than those contained in the Philippine Trade Act of 1946 or the Philippine Trade Agreement Revision Act of 1955: *Provided, however*, that after May 1, 1946, all taxes collected under the internal revenue laws of the United States on articles produced in Puerto Rico and transported to the United States, or consumed in the island shall be covered into the Treasury of Puerto Rico."

7. See generally, Charles E. Clark and William D. Rogers, "The New Judiciary Act of Puerto Rico: A Definitive Court Reorganization," 61 Yale Law Journal 1147 (1952).

8. See *Morales Feliciano v. Romero Barcelo*, 672 F.Supp. 591 (D.Puerto Rico 1986) ("The Constitution of Puerto Rico forbids capital punishment in absolute terms: 'The death penalty shall not exist.'").

9. See Ricardo Alfonso, "The Imposition of the Death Penalty in Puerto Rico: A Human Rights Crisis in the Path Towards Self-Determination," 76 Rev. Jur. U.P.R. 1077 (2007); Elizabeth Vicens, "Application of the Federal Death Penalty Act to Puerto Rico: A New Test for the Locally Inapplicable Standard," 80 N.Y.U. L. Rev. 350 (2005).

10. See *United States v. Ayala-Lopez*, 2012 WL 3217132 (1st Cir. 2012) (defendant prosecuted for capital murder in Puerto Rico but jury recommended life imprisonment); *United States v. Catalan-Roman*, 585 F.3d 453 (1st Cir. 2009) (same); *United States v. Lopez-Matias*, 522 F.3d 150 (1st Cir. 2008) (allowing prosecutor to seek death penalty in Puerto Rico); *In re Sterling-Suarez*, 323 F.3d 1 (1st Cir. 2003) (forcing lawyer to represent defendant in capital murder prosecution in Puerto Rico, even though lawyer argued that he was not qualified to handle death penalty case).

11. See William W. Boyer, America's Virgin Islands: A History of Human Rights and Wrongs (1983).

12. The following is the full text of 48 U.S.C. § 1405q: The laws of the United States applicable to the Virgin Islands on June 22, 1936, and all local laws and ordinances in force on such date in the Virgin Islands, not inconsistent with this subchapter, shall continue in force and effect: *Provided*, that the Municipal Council of Saint Croix and the Municipal Council of Saint Thomas and Saint John, and the legislative assembly, shall have power, when not inconsistent with this subchapter and within their respective jurisdictions, to amend, alter, modify, or repeal any law of the United States of local application only, or any ordinance, public or private, civil or criminal, continued in force and effect by this subchapter, except as herein otherwise provided, and to enact new laws and ordinances not inconsistent with this subchapter and not inconsistent with the laws of the United States hereafter made applicable to the Virgin Islands or any part thereof, subject to the power of the Congress to annul the same. The laws of the United States relating to patents, trade marks, and copyrights, and to the enforcement of rights arising thereunder, shall have the same force and effect in the Virgin Islands as in the continental United States, and the District Court of the Virgin Islands shall have the same jurisdiction in causes arising under such laws as is exercised by United States district courts.

13. See generally, Diane Russell, "Some Ethical Considerations of Judicial Vacancies: A Case Study of the Federal Court System in the United States Virgin Islands," 5 Geo. J. Legal Ethics 697 (1992).

14. See Virgin Island Code tit. 14, ch. 45 § 923(b); *Browne v. People of Virgin Islands*, 2008 WL 4132233 (V.I. 2008).

15. See *United States ex rel. Richards v. De Leon Guerrero*, 4 F.3d 749 (9th Cir. 1993) ("After World War II, the United Nations established the Trust Territory of the Pacific Islands encompassing most of the islands of Micronesia, among them the Northern Mariana Islands, to be administered by the United States pursuant to a Trusteeship Agreement with the United Nations Security Council.").

16. Joseph E. Horey, "The Right of Self-Government in the Commonwealth of the Northern Mariana Islands," 4 Asian-Pac. L. and Pol'y J. 180 (2003).

17. See Marybeth Herald, "The Northern Mariana Islands: A Change in Course Under Its Covenant with the United States," 71 Or. L. Rev. 127 (1992); Lizabeth A. McKibben, "The Political Relationship Between the United States and Pacific Islands Entities: The Path to Self-Government in the Northern Mariana Islands, Palau, and Guam," 31 Harv. Int'l. L. J. 257 (1990).

18. *Hillblom v. United States*, 896 F.2d 426 (9th Cir. 1990).

19. See *Guerrero v. United States*, 691 F.Supp. 260 (D.N.Mariana Islands 1988).

20. See 48 U.S.C. § 1821.

21. See 48 U.S.C. § 1822.

22. In *Wabol v. Villacrusis*, 958 F.2d 1450 (9th Cir. 1990) the Ninth Circuit held that the government of the islands did not have authority to divest the federal court of the right to hear an appeal from an island federal district court. In *Northern Mariana Islands v. Atalig*, 723 F.2d 682 (9th Cir. 1984), it was held that the trial by jury guarantee of the Sixth Amendment was not applicable to criminal prosecutions in local island courts.

23. See Jon M. Van Dyke, Carmen Di Amore-Siah, and Gerald W. Berkley-Coats, "Self-Determination for Nonself-Governing Peoples and for Indigenous Peoples: The Cases of Guam and Hawai'i," 18 U. Haw. L. Rev. 623 (1996).

24. See Paul Lansing and Peter Hipolito, "Guam's Quest for Commonwealth Status," 5 UCLA Asian Pac. Am. L.J. 1 (1998).

25. See Hannah M.T. Gutierrez, "Guam's Future Political Status: An Argument for Free Association with U.S. Citizenship," 4 Asian-Pac. L. and Pol'y J. 122 (2003).

26. *United States v. Drake*, 543 F.3d 1080 (9th Cir. 2008). See 48 U.S.C. § 1421b. See also, Lizabeth A. McKibben, "The Political Relationship Between the United States and Pacific Islands Entities: The Path to Self-Government in the Northern Mariana Islands, Palau, and Guam," 31 Harv. Int'l. L. J. 257 (1990).

27. *Haeuser v. Department of Law, Government of Guam*, 97 F.3d 1152 (9th Cir. 1996).

28. See Guam Code Ann. tit. 9, § 16.30(b) (life imprisonment for aggravated murder).

29. See Daniel E. Hall, "Curfews, Culture, and Custom in American Samoa: An Analytical Map For Applying the U.S. Constitution to U.S. Territories," 2 Asian-Pac. L. and Pol'y J. 3 (2001).

30. See *United States v. Standard Oil Co. of Cal.*, 404 U.S. 558 (1972).

31. See *United States v. Sierra-Ledesma*, 645 F.3d 1213 (10th Cir. 2011).

32. See Uilisone Falemanu Tua, "A Native's Call for Justice: The Call for the Establishment of a Federal District Court in American Samoa," 11 Asian-Pac. L. and Pol'y J. 246 (2010).

33. See Uilisone Falemanu Tua, "A Native's Call for Justice: The Call for the Establishment of a Federal District Court in American Samoa," 11 Asian-Pac. L. and Pol'y J. 246 (2010).

34. See *United States v. Lee*, 472 F.3d 638 (9th Cir. 2006) (Hawaii prosecution); *United States v. Gurr*, 471 F.3d 144 (D.C. Cir. 2006) (allowing prosecution in Washington, D.C. even though crime occurred in American Samoa).

Chapter 28

1. See Gary Strauss, "Gallup Poll: 35% Oppose Death Penalty," http://www.usatoday.com/news/washington/judicial/story/2011-10-12/gallup-poll-death-penalty/50747430/1.

2. See Amnesty International, "Death Penalty Trends," http://www.amnestyusa.org/our-work/issues/death-penalty/us-death-penalty-facts/death-penalty-trends.

3. See Death Penalty Information Center, "Death Penalty Related Web Sites," http://www.deathpenaltyinfo.org/death-penalty-related-web-sites.

4. The statement may be found at: http://old.usccb.org/sdwp/national/penaltyofdeath.pdf.

5. See United States Conference of Catholic Bishops, http://old.usccb.org/deathpenalty/.

6. See Hugo Adam Bedau, "The Case Against the Death Penalty," http://users.rcn.com/mwood/deathpen.html.

7. See Campaign to End the Death Penalty, "Five Reasons to Oppose the Death Penalty," http://www.nodeathpenalty.org/get-the-facts/five-reasons-oppose-death-penalty.

8. This statement was attributed to former Attorney General Ramsey Clark.

9. See Louis J. Palmer, Jr., *Encyclopedia of Capital Punishment in the United States* (2008).

10. See Louis J. Palmer, Jr., *Encyclopedia of Capital Punishment in the United States* (2008).

11. See Death Penalty Information Center, http://www.deathpenaltyinfo.org/executed-possibly-innocent.

12. See Amnesty International, "Death Penalty and Innocence," http://www.amnestyusa.org/our-work/issues/death-penalty/us-death-penalty-facts/death-penalty-and-innocence.

13. See Amnesty International, "Death Penalty Trends," http://www.amnestyusa.org/our-work/issues/death-penalty/us-death-penalty-facts/death-penalty-trends.

14. See IACHR, "The Death Penalty in the Inter-American Human Rights System: From Restrictions to Abolition," http://www.oas.org/en/iachr/docs/pdf/death penalty.pdf.

Chapter 29

1. See Robert L. Spangenberg and Elizabeth R. Walsh, "Capital Punishment or Life Imprisonment? Some Cost Considerations," 23 Loyola L.A.L. Rev. 45 (1989).

2. See Ashley Rupp, "Death Penalty Prosecutorial Charging Decisions and County Budgetary Restrictions: Is the Death Penalty Arbitrarily Applied Based on County Funding?" 71 Fordham L. Rev. 2735 (2003).

3. Arthur L. Alarcon and Paula M. Mitchell, "Executing the Will of the Voters? A Roadmap to Mend or End the California Legislature's Multi-Billion-Dollar Death Penalty Debacle," 44 Loyola L.A. L. Rev. 41 (2011).

4. New Jersey has abolished the death penalty.

5. In the Okanogan County case the prosecutor sought the death penalty for a defendant accused of killing an Omak police officer. The prosecutor ultimately withdrew the death penalty request as a result of mental health issues with the defendant. By the time the prosecutor withdrew the death penalty notice the case had already cost the county almost $1 million, or 9 percent of the county's entire budget. The costs forced the county to cut public health employees, freeze employee pay, and defer purchases of police vehicles. See Barbara A. Serrano, "A Cop-Killing Trial — At All Costs — Million-Dollar Prosecution Could Bring Okanogan County to Its Knees Financially," *Seattle Times*, March 31, 1999, http://community.seattletimes.nwsource.com/archive/?date=19990331&slug=2952597.

6. See Terance D. Miethe, "Estimates of Time Spent in Capital and Non-Capital Murder Cases: A Statistical Analysis of Survey Data from Clark County Defense Attorneys," (2012), http://claimyourinnocence.wordpress.com/2012/04/16/estimates-of-time-spent-in-capital-and-non-capital-murder-cases/.

Bibliography

Articles

Alschuler, Albert W., "Plea Bargaining and the Death Penalty," 58 DePaul L. Rev. 671 (2009).

Babcock, Sandra, "The Limits of International Law: Efforts to Enforce Rulings of the International Court of Justice in U.S. Death Penalty Cases," 62 Syracuse L. Rev. 183 (2012).

Bachmann, Aaron M., "Kennedy v. Louisiana and the Abolition of the Death Penalty for Child Rape: Euthanizing Evolving Standards of Decency," 45 Wake Forest L. Rev. 231 (2010).

Baldus, David C., Catherine M. Grosso, George Woodworth and Richard Newell, "Racial Discrimination in the Administration of the Death Penalty: The Experience of the United States Armed Forces (1984–2005)," 101 J. Crim. L. and Criminology 1227 (2011).

Bandes, Susan A., "Repellent Crimes and Rational Deliberation: Emotion and the Death Penalty," 33 Vt. L. Rev. 489 (2009).

Batey, Robert, "Categorical Bars to Execution: Civilizing the Death Penalty," 45 Hous. L. Rev. 1493 (2009).

Bedau, Hugo Adam, "Racism, Wrongful Convictions, and the Death Penalty," 76 Tenn. L. Rev. 615 (2009).

Bernstein, Tyler Z., "Let's Make It a True Daily Double (Jeopardy): How James Harrison Was Acquitted of the Death Penalty Only to Face It Again," 53 B.C. L. Rev. E-Supplement 147 (2012).

Berwanger, Michael J., "Death Is Different: Actual Innocence and Categorical Exclusion Claims Under the Antiterrorism and Effective Death Penalty Act," 38 New Eng. J. on Crim. and Civ. Confinement 307 (2012).

Bright, Stephen B., "The Right to Counsel in Death Penalty and Other Criminal Cases: Neglect of the Most Fundamental Right and What We Should Do About It," 11 J. L. Society 1 (2010).

Bryant, Bethany C., "Expanding Atkins and Roper: A Diagnostic Approach to Excluding the Death Penalty as Punishment for Schizophrenic Offenders," 78 Miss. L.J. 905 (2009).

Cable, Sarah Frances, "An Unanswered Question in Kennedy v. Louisiana: How Should the Supreme Court Determine the Constitutionality of the Death Penalty for Espionage?" 70 La. L. Rev. 995 (2010).

Cantero, Raoul G., and Robert M. Kline, "Death Is Different: The Need for Jury Unanimity in Death Penalty Cases," 22 St. Thomas L. Rev. 4 (2009).

Caucci, Lisa, "Evaluating the Constitutionality of Proposals to Allow Non-Unanimous Juries to Impose the Death Penalty in Georgia," 26 Ga. St. U. L. Rev. 1003 (2010).

Cheng, David Gan-Wing, "The McCleskey Court, Jury Discretion, and the Death Penalty: What Is a Black Life Worth?" 6 S. Region Black L. Students Ass'n L.J. 109 (2012).

Connor, Eileen M., "The Undermining Influence of the Federal Death Penalty on Capital Policymaking and Criminal Justice Administration in the States," 100 J. Crim. L. and Criminology 149 (2010).

Crawford, Melanie L., "A Losing Battle with the 'Machinery of Death': The Flaws of Virginia's Death Penalty Laws and Clemency Process Highlighted by the Fate of Teresa Lewis," 18 Widener L. Rev. 71 (2012).

Dean, Michael D., "State Legislation and the Evolving Standards of Decency: Flaws in the Constitutional Review of Death Penalty Statutes," 35 U. Dayton L. Rev. 379 (2010).

Eftink, James Gerard, "Mental Retardation as a Bar to the Death Penalty: Who Bears the Burden of Proof?" 75 Mo. L. Rev. 537 (2010).

Entzeroth, Lyn, "The Challenge and Dilemma of Charting a Course to Constitutionally Protect the Severely Mentally Ill Capital Defendant from the Death Penalty," 44 Akron L. Rev. 529 (2011).

Entzeroth, Lyn Suzanne, "The End of the Beginning: The Politics of Death and the American Death Penalty Regime in the Twenty-First Century," 90 Or. L. Rev. 797 (2012).

Flickinger, Benjamin J., "Kennedy v. Louisiana: The United States Supreme Court Erroneously Finds a National Consensus Against the Use of the Death Penalty for the Crime of Child Rape," 42 Creighton L. Rev. 655 (2009).

Gee, Harvey, "Eighth Amendment Challenges After Baze v. Rees: Lethal Injection, Civil Rights Lawsuits, and the Death Penalty," 31 B.C. Third World L.J. 217 (2011).

Goodman, Chris Chambers, H. Mitchell Caldwell, and Carol A. Chase, "Unpredictable Doom and Lethal Injustice: An Argument for Greater Transparency in Death Penalty Decisions," 82 Temp. L. Rev. 997 (2009).

Grosso, Catherine M., and Barbara O'Brien, "A Stubborn Legacy: The Overwhelming Importance of Race in Jury Selection in Post-Batson North Carolina Capital Trials," 97 Iowa L. Rev. 1531 (2012).

Grosso, Catherine M., David C. Baldus, and George Woodworth, "The Impact of Civilian Aggravating Factors on the Military Death Penalty: Another Chapter in the Resistance of the Armed Forces to the Civilianization of Military Justice," 43 U. Mich. J.L. Reform 569 (2010).

Joyner, Jennifer Knepper, "The United States Supreme Court Holds That the Eighth Amendment Prohibits the Death Penalty for the Rape of a Child Where the Crime Did Not Intend or Result in the Death of the Victim," 31 U. Ark. Little Rock L. Rev. 649 (2009).

Kotch, Seth, and Robert P. Mosteller, "The Racial Justice Act and the Long Struggle with Race and the Death Penalty in North Carolina," 88 N.C. L. Rev. 2031 (2010).

Mazzochi, Sarah, "The Two Percent: The Practical Application of International Law on the Death Penalty in the United States," 38 Syracuse J. Int'l. L. and Com. 31 (2010).

Merritt, Gilbert Stroud, Jr., "Prosecutorial Error in Death Penalty Cases," 76 Tenn. L. Rev. 677 (2009).

Millemann, Michael, "Limiting Death: Maryland's New Death Penalty Law," 70 Md. L. Rev. 272 (2010).

Minsker, Natasha, "Prosecutorial Misconduct in Death Penalty Cases," 45 Cal. W. L. Rev. 373 (2009).

Moore, Krystal M., "Is Saving an Innocent Man a Fool's Errand? The Limitations of the Antiterrorism and Effective Death Penalty Act on an Original Writ of Habeas Corpus Petition," 36 U. Dayton L. Rev. 197 (2011).

Murphy, Russell G., "Executing the Death Penalty: International Law Influences on United States Supreme Court Decision-Making in Capital Punishment Cases," 32 Suffolk Transnat'l L. Rev. 599 (2009).

Mysliwiec, Paul, "The Federal Death Penalty as a Safety Valve," 17 Va. J. Soc. Pol'y and L. 257 (2010).

Nugent, Kristen, "Proportionality and Prosecutorial Discretion: Challenges to the Constitutionality of Georgia's Death Penalty Laws and Procedures Amidst the Deficiencies of the State's Mandatory Appellate Review Structure," 64 U. Miami L. Rev. 175 (2009).

Radelet, Michael L., and Traci L. Lacock, "Do Executions Lower Homicide Rates? The Views of Leading Criminologists," 99 J. Crim. L. and Criminology 489 (2009).

Roko, Ellyde, "Finality, Habeas, Innocence, and the Death Penalty: Can Justice Be Done?" 85 Wash. L. Rev. 107 (2010).

Rupp, Kathleen, "Capital Hypocrisy: Does Compelling Jurors to Impose the Death Penalty Without Spiritual Guidance Violate Jurors' First Amendment Rights?" 48 Am. Crim. L. Rev. 217 (2011).

Shatz, Steven F., and Naomi R. Shatz, "Chivalry Is Not Dead: Murder, Gender, and the Death Penalty," 27 Berkeley J. Gender L. and Just. 64 (2012).

Solomon, Shandrea P., "National Consensus, Retributive Theory, and Foundations of Justice and Morality in Eighth Amendment Jurisprudence: A Response to Advocates of the Child Rape Death Penalty Statute in Kennedy v. Louisiana," 13 SCHOLAR 583 (2011).

Thomas, Colleen, "Working with a Blank Check: The Cost of Defense or the Death Penalty Industry?" 17 Pub. Int. L. Rep. 45 (2011).

Tirschwell, Eric A., and Theodore Hertzberg, "Politics and Prosecution: A Historical Perspective on Shifting Federal Standards for Pursuing the Death Penalty in Non-Death Penalty States," 12 U. Pa. J. Const. L. 57 (2009).

Traxler, Thomas W., Jr., "Reconciling the South Carolina Death Penalty Statute with the Sixth Amendment," 60 S.C. L. Rev. 1031 (2009).

Uelmen, Gerald F., "Death Penalty Appeals and Habeas Proceedings: The California Experience," 93 Marq. L. Rev. 495 (2009).

Unah, Isaac, "Choosing Those Who Will Die: The Effect of Race, Gender, and Law in Prosecutorial Decision to Seek the Death Penalty in Durham County, North Carolina," 15 Mich. J. Race and L. 135 (2009).

von Wilpert, Marni, Holland v. Florida: "A Prisoner's Last Chance, Attorney Error, and the Antiterrorism and Effective Death Penalty Act's One-Year Statute of Limitations Period for Federal Habeas Corpus Review," 79 Fordham L. Rev. 1429 (2010).

Walker, Laura, "Victim Impact Evidence in Death Penalty Sentencing Proceedings: Advocating for a Higher Relevancy Standard," 22 Geo. Mason U. Civ. Rts. L.J. 89 (2011).

Zerylnick, Jenna, "Eighth Amendment Challenges to Death Penalty Protocols: How Baze v. Rees Will Engender Future Collateral Attacks on the Death Penalty," 10 Fla. Coastal L. Rev. 349 (2009).

Books

Abbott, Geoffrey, *The Book of Execution: An Encyclopedia of Methods of Judicial Execution*, Hodder Headline, 1995.

Acker, James R., and David R. Karp, *Wounds That Do Not Bind: Victim-Based Perspectives on the Death Penalty*, Carolina Academic Press, 2006.

Aguirre, Adalberto, and David V. Baker, Bernstein Bernstein, *Race, Racism, and the Death Penalty in the United States*, Vande Vere, 1991.

Allen, Howard W., and Jerome M. Clubb, *Race, Class, and the Death Penalty: Capital Punishment in American History*, State University of New York Press, 2009.

Arriens, Jan, *Welcome to Hell: Letters and Writings from Death Row*, Northeastern University Press, 1997.

Attridge, Harold W., *The Bible and the Death Penalty*, Yale University Press, 2007.

Baird, Robert M., and Stuart E. Rosenbaum, *Death Penalty: Debating the Moral, Legal, and Political Issues*, Prometheus Books, 2010.

Baldus, David C., Charles A. Pulaski, and George Woodworth, *Equal Justice and the Death Penalty: A Legal and Empirical Analysis*, Northeastern University Press, 1990.

Banner, Stuart, *The Death Penalty: An American History*, Harvard University Press, 2003.

Baumgartner, Frank R., Suzanna L. De Boef, and Amber E. Boydstun, *The Decline of the Death Penalty and the Discovery of Innocence*, Cambridge University Press, 2008.

Bedau, Hugo Adam, and Paul G. Cassell, *Debating the Death Penalty*, Oxford University Press, 2005.

Bedau, Hugo Adam, *The Death Penalty in America: Current Controversies*, Oxford University Press, 1998.

Berns, Walter, *For Capital Punishment: Crime and the Morality of the Death Penalty*, University Press of America, 1991.

Bessler, John D., *Cruel and Unusual: The American Death Penalty and the Founders' Eighth Amendment*, Northeastern University Press, 2012.

Block, Eugene B., *When Men Play God: The Fallacy of Capital Punishment*, Cragmont, 1983.

Bohm, Robert M., *Deathquest: An Introduction to the Theory and Practice of Capital Punishment in the United States*, Anderson, 2011.

Bosco, Antoinette, *Choosing Mercy: A Mother of Murder Victims Pleads to End the Death Penalty*, Orbis Books, 2001.

Bovee, Marvin H., *Christ and the Gallows: Or, Reasons for the Abolition of Capital Punishment*, AMS Press, 1983.

Brandon, Craig, *The Electric Chair: An Unnatural American History*, McFarland, 1999.

Brenner, Samual, *The Death Penalty*, Greenhaven, 2006.

Burkhead, Michael Dow, *A Life for a Life: The American Debate Over the Death Penalty*, McFarland, 2009.

Burnett, Cathleen, *Justice Denied: Clemency Appeals in Death Penalty Cases*, Northeastern University Press, 2002.

Cabana, Donald A., *Death at Midnight: The Confession of an Executioner*, Northeastern University Press, 1998.

Cairns Kathleen A., *The Enigma Woman: The Death Sentence of Nellie May Madison*, University of Nebraska Press, 2007.

Carter, Linda E., Ellen Kreitzber, and Scott Howe, *Understanding Capital Punishment*, LexisNexis, 2012.

Clarke, Alan W., and Laurelyn Whitt, *The Bitter Fruit of American Justice: International and Domestic Resistance to the Death Penalty*, Northeastern University Press, 2007.

Costanzo, Mark, *Just Revenge: Costs and Consequences of the Death Penalty*, St. Martin's, 1997.

Coyne, Randall, and Lyn Entzeroth, *Capital Punishment and the Judicial Process*, Carolina Academic Press, 2006.

Crawford, Bill, *Texas Death Row: Executions in the Modern Era*, Plume, 2008.

Culbert, Jennifer L., *Dead Certainty: The Death Penalty and the Problem of Judgment*, Stanford University Press, 2007.

DeMatteo, David, Daniel C. Murrie, Natalie M. Anumba and Michael E. Keesler, *Forensic Mental Health Assessments in Death Penalty Cases*, Oxford University Press, 2011.

Diaz, Joseph D., *The Execution of a Serial Killer: One Man's Experience Witnessing the Death Penalty*, BookSurge, 2007.

Dicks, Shirley, *Young Blood: Juvenile Justice and the Death Penalty*, Prometheus Books, 1995.

Dow, David, *Machinery of Death: The Reality of America's Death Penalty Regime*, Routledge, 2002.

Dudley, William, *The Death Penalty*, Greenhaven, 2005.

Eisenberg, James R., *Law, Psychology, and Death Penalty Litigation*, Professional Resource Exchange, 2004.

Elster, Jean Alicia, *The Death Penalty*, Greenhaven, 2004.

Fleury-Steiner, Benjamin, *Jurors' Stories of Death: How America's Death Penalty Invests in Inequality*, University of Michigan Press, 2004.

Foley, Michael A., *Arbitrary and Capricious: The Supreme Court, the Constitution, and the Death Penalty*, Praeger, 2003.

Franck, Hans Goran, Klas Nyman and William Schabas, *The Barbaric Punishment: Abolishing the Death Penalty*, Martinus Nijhoff, 2003.

Friedman, Lauri S., *The Death Penalty*, Greenhaven Press, 2010.

Garland, David, *Peculiar Institution: America's Death Penalty in an Age of Abolition*, Belknap Press of Harvard University Press, 2012.

Garland, David, Randall McGowen, and Michael Meranze, *America's Death Penalty: Between Past and Present*, NYU Press, 2011.

Garvey, Stephen P., *Beyond Repair? America's Death Penalty*, Duke University Press, 2002.

Gatrell, V. A., *The Hanging Tree: Execution and the English People, 1770–1868*, Oxford University Press, 1996.

Gershman, Gary P., *Death Penalty on Trial: A Handbook with Cases, Laws, and Documents*, ABC-CLIO, 2005.

Gillespie, Kay, *The Unforgiven: Utah's Executed Men*, Signature Books, 1997.

Gleason, Ron, *The Death Penalty on Trial: Taking of a Life for a Life Taken*, Nordskog, 2009.

Golston, Syd, *Death Penalty*, Lucent, 2009.

Gottfried, Ted, *Capital Punishment: The Death Penalty Debate*, Enslow, 1997.

Grabowski, John F., *The Death Penalty*, Lucent Books, 1998.

Gross, Bob, *Death Penalty: A Guide for Christians*, Books on Demand, 1991.

Guernsey, JoAnn Bren, *Death Penalty: Fair Solution or Moral Failure?*, Twenty-First Century Books, 2009.

Haas, Kenneth C., and James A. Inciardi, *Challenging Capital Punishment: Legal and Social Science Approaches*, Books on Demand, 1988.

Haines, Herbert H., *Against Capital Punishment: The Anti-Death Penalty Movement in America, 1972–1994*, Oxford University Press, 1999.

Haney, Craig, *Death by Design: Capital Punishment as a Social Psychological System*, Oxford University Press, 2005.

Hanks, Gardner C., *Against the Death Penalty*, Herald Press, 1997.

Heilbrun, Alfred B., *The Death Penalty: Beyond the Smoke and Mirrors*, University Press of America, 2006.

Herda, D. J., *Furman v. Georgia: The Death Penalty Case*, Enslow, 1994.

Hood, Roger, *The Death Penalty: A Worldwide Perspective*, Oxford University Press, 2003.

Hopcke, Robert H., *Catholics and the Death Penalty: Six Things Catholics Can Do to End Capital Punishment*, Saint Anthony Messenger Press and Franciscan, 2004.

Jackson, Bruce, and Diane Christian, *Death Row*, Transaction, 1980.

Jackson, Jesse L., Jesse L. Jackson, Jr., and Bruce Shapiro, *Legal Lynching: The Death Penalty and America's Future*, Anchor, 2003.

Jones, Sandra J., *Coalition Building in the Anti-Death Penalty Movement: Privileged Morality, Race Realities*, Lexington Books, 2010.

Kay, Judith W., *Murdering Myths: The Story Behind the Death Penalty*, Rowman and Littlefield, 2005.

Koch, Larry W., Colin Wark, and John F. Galliher, *The Death of the American Death Penalty: States Still Leading the Way*, Northeastern University Press, 2012.

King, Rachel, *Don't Kill in Our Names: Families of Murder Victims Speak Out Against the Death Penalty*, Rutgers University Press, 2003.

King, William M., *Going to Meet a Man: Denver's Last Legal Public Execution, 27 July 1886*, University Press of Colorado, 1990.

Koosed, Margery B., *Capital Punishment: The Philosophical, Moral and Penological Debate Over Capital Punishment*, Garland, 1996.

Kudlac, Christopher S., *Public Executions: The Death Penalty and the Media*, Praeger, 2007.

Kukathas, Uma, *Death Penalty*, Greenhaven, 2007.

Kurtis, Bill, *Death Penalty on Trial: Crisis in American Justice*, Public Affairs, 2007.

Lane, Charles, *Stay of Execution: Saving the Death Penalty from Itself*, Rowman and Littlefield, 2010.

Lanier, Charles S., William J. Bowers, and James R. Acker, *The Future of America's Death Penalty: An Agenda for the Next Generation of Capital Punishment Research*, Carolina Academic Press, 2008.

Latzer, Barry, *Death Penalty Cases: Leading U.S. Supreme Court Cases on Capital Punishment*, Butterworth-Heinemann, 1997.

Mandery, Evan J., *Capital Punishment in America: A Balanced Examination*, Jones and Bartlett Learning, 2011.

Marquart, James W., Sheldon Olson, and Jonathan R. Sorenson, *The Rope, the Chair, and the Needle: Capital Punishment in Texas, 1923–1990*, University of Texas Press, 1998.

Martin, Robert P., *The Death Penalty: God's Will or Man's Folly*, Simpson, 1992.

McCafferty, James A., *Capital Punishment*, Aldine Transaction, 2009.

Megivern, James J., *The Death Penalty: An Historical and Theological Survey*, Paulist Press, 1997.

Mello, Michael A., *Dead Wrong: A Death Row Lawyer Speaks Out Against Capital Punishment*, University of Wisconsin Press, 1999.

Miller, Arthur S., and Jeffrey H. Bowman, *Death by Installments: The Ordeal of Willie Francis*, Greenwood, 1988.

Miller, Karen S., *Wrongful Capital Convictions and the Legitimacy of the Death Penalty*, LFB, 2006.

Mitchell, Greg, *Dead Reckoning: Executions in America*, Sinclair Books, 2011.

Murphy, Russell G., *Voices of the Death Penalty Debate: A Citizen's Guide to Capital Punishment*, Vandeplas, 2010.

Nakell, Barry, and Kenneth A. Hardy, *The Arbitrari-

ness of the Death Penalty, Temple University Press, 1987.

Nelson, Lane, and Burk Foster, *Death Watch: A Death Penalty Anthology*, Prentice Hall, 2000.

O'Shea, Kathleen A., *Women and the Death Penalty in the United States, 1900–1998*, Greenwood, 1999.

Oshinsky, David M., *Capital Punishment on Trial: Furman v. Georgia and the Death Penalty in Modern America*, University Press of Kansas, 2010.

O'Sullivan, Carol, *Death Penalty: Identifying Propaganda Techniques*, Greenhaven, 1990.

Owens, Erik C., John D. Carlson, Eric P. Elshtain, and J. Budziszewski, *Religion and the Death Penalty: A Call for Reckoning*, Wm. B. Eerdmans, 2004.

Parks, Peggy J., *Does the Death Penalty Deter Crime?*, Referencepoint Press, 2009.

Paternoster, Raymond, Robert Brame, and Sarah Bacon, *The Death Penalty: America's Experience with Capital Punishment*. Oxford University Press, 2007.

Pojman, Louis P., and Jeffrey Reiman, *The Death Penalty: For and Against*, Rowman and Littlefield, 1997.

Prejean, Helen, *Dead Man Walking: An Eyewitness Account of the Death Penalty in the United States*, Random House, 1994.

Radelet, Michael L., *Facing the Death Penalty*, Temple University Press, 1990.

Randa, Laura E., *Society's Final Solution: A History and Discussion of the Death Penalty*, University Press of America, 1997.

Recinella, Dale S., *The Biblical Truth About America's Death Penalty*, Northeastern University Press, 2004.

Reed, Emily F., *The Penry Penalty: Capital Punishment and Offenders with Mental Retardation*, University Press of America, 1993.

Russell, Gregory D., *The Death Penalty and Racial Bias: Overturning Supreme Court Assumptions*, Greenwood, 1993.

Sarat, Austin, *The Killing State: Capital Punishment in Law, Politics, and Culture*, Oxford University Press, 1998.

Schabas, William S., *The Abolition of the Death Penalty in International Law*, Cambridge University Press, 2002.

Schonebaum, Steve, *Does Capital Punishment Deter Crime?*, Greenhaven Press, 1998.

Schwed, Roger E., *Abolition and Capital Punishment: The United States' Judicial, Political, and Moral Barometer*, AMS Press, 1983.

Sheleff, Leon S., *Ultimate Penalties: Capital Punishment, Life Imprisonment, Physical Torture*, Ohio State University Press, 1987.

Sinclair, Billy Wayne, and Jodie Sinclair, *Capital Punishment: An Indictment by a Death Row Survivor*, Arcade, 2011.

Stearman, Kaye, *The Death Penalty*, Hodder Wayland, 2007.

Steelwater, Eliza, *The Hangman's Knot: Lynching, Legal Execution, and America's Struggle with the Death Penalty*, Westview Press, 2003.

Steffen, Lloyd H., *Executing Justice: The Moral Meaning of the Death Penalty*, Pilgrim Press/United Church Press, 1998.

Streib, Victor L., *A Capital Punishment Anthology*, Anderson, 1997.

Sundby, Scott E., *A Life and Death Decision: A Jury Weighs the Death Penalty*, Palgrave Macmillan, 2005.

Turow, Scott, *Ultimate Punishment: A Lawyer's Reflections on Dealing with the Death Penalty*, Picador, 2004.

Vila, Bryan, and Cynthia Morris, *Capital Punishment in the United States: A Documentary History*, Greenwood, 1997.

Vollum, Scott, *Last Words and the Death Penalty: Voices of the Condemned and Their Co-Victims*, LFB, 2010.

Walker, Ida, *The Death Penalty*, Abdo, 2008.

Weinglass, Leonard, *Race for Justice: Mumia Abu-Jamal's Fight Against the Death Penalty*, Common Courage Press, 1995.

White, Welsh S., *The Death Penalty in the Nineties: An Examination of the Modern System of Capital Punishment*, University of Michigan Press, 1994.

Williams, Bill, *Tit for Tat: The Conspiracy to Abolish the Death Penalty*, BADM Books, 1997.

Williams, Kenneth, *Most Deserving of Death? An Analysis of the Supreme Court's Death Penalty Jurisprudence*, Ashgate, 2012.

Winters, Paul A., *The Death Penalty: Opposing Viewpoints*, Greenhaven, 1997.

Yorke, Jon, *Against the Death Penalty*, Ashgate, 2008.

Zimring, Franklin E., and Gordon J. Hawkins, *Capital Punishment and the American Agenda*, Cambridge University Press, 1990.

Index

Index